are women human?

and other international dialogues

CATHARINE A. MacKINNON

are women human?

and other international dialogues

THE BELKNAP PRESS OF HARVARD UNIVERSITY PRESS

Cambridge, Massachusetts, and London, England ••• 2006

Library of Congress Cataloging-in-Publication Data

MacKinnon, Catharine A.
  Are women human? : and other international dialogues / Catharine A. MacKinnon.
     p. cm.
  Includes index.
  ISBN 0–674–02187–8 (alk. paper)
  1. Women's rights. 2. Women—Legal status, laws, etc. 3. Women—Violence
against. I. Title.
  HQ1236.M337 2006
  341.4'858—dc22   2005044747

for
Asja Armanda
and
Jessica Neuwirth

Preface

In the mid-1980s, as the new Charter of Rights and Freedoms came into force, I began working for legal equality in Canada, largely with the Women's Legal Education and Action Fund (LEAF). The results diverged strikingly from those in the United States, stimulating comparative thoughts. In late 1991, right after Vukovar fell, Bosnian and Croatian women's request to work with them took my work international, as it has remained. The present volume—originally part of *Women's Lives, Men's Laws* (Harvard, 2005), now its transnational companion—collects selected comparative and international writings and speeches from this period.

The pieces, arranged in approximate chronological order within themes, appear here essentially as they were when originally spoken or written. The ideas develop over time, particularly in the Bosnian case. Most of these writings were first given as speeches, self-contained and free-standing, with the consequence that certain locutions or source texts recur, if in somewhat different form, throughout the collection. Footnotes alert the reader to situations that are now dramatically different from the way they are represented in the text. This happens fairly regularly, as these dialogues were often part of making changes in the world with which they are engaged.

Since 1990, the University of Michigan Law School, notably its unsurpassed Law Library, has given me the support and freedom to pursue my own path. As one place to follow it, the Center for Advanced Study in the Behavioral Sciences (CASBS) at Stanford, California, has been idyllic. These institutions put their resources where their principles are. Kent Harvey and Nancy Ruth have been there throughout. Charlotte Croson, John Stoltenberg, Lori Watson, Anna Baldwin, Emma Cheuse, and Shiri Regev, with a last minute assist from Shannon MacKinnon, shouldered with skill and humor, even heroism, the technical tasks that make a pile of manuscripts, transcripts, and offprints into a book. I am grateful to them all.

Special thanks go to Peter Nelson Rowe, my first international teacher;

always to Robert Dahl, who never stops inspiring; to the late Andrea Dworkin, who insisted from the beginning that we ground our work against pornography in international law; to Christine Chinkin for the learning of joint teaching; to the Federation of Women Teachers Associations of Ontario (FWTAO) for its vision of women's genius and model of women's solidarity; to all the women of Equality Now, especially Jessica Neuwirth, for our years of work together; and to Natalie Nenadic and Asja Armanda and to my clients and colleagues from Bosnia-Herzegovina and Croatia, who gave me the world.

Catharine A. MacKinnon
Stanford, California

Contents

part three ▪ through the bosnian lens

part four ▪ on the cutting edge

are women human?

and other international dialogues

Introduction
Women's Status, Men's States

They had been, if not social equals, homemakers and mothers with families and homes to care for, farmers with land and livestock, lawyers and judges in a legal system, workers with jobs in factories and businesses, schoolgirls whose mothers were alive and whole. These Bosnian Muslim, Bosnian Croat, and Croatian women and children survived the atrocities of Serbian extremist forces in Bosnia-Herzegovina and Croatia from 1991 to 1994 determined to stop the genocide, to hold the perpetrators accountable, and to change the way sexual violations are seen in society and treated in law.[1] Converging with other developments, their responses to their experience of violent sexual and ethnic inequality combined have contributed to making women's resistance to their status and treatment the cutting edge of change in international human rights around the turn of the twenty-first century.[2]

Women's refusal to accept the double-edged denial of their humanity—the denial that sex-specific violations are commonly committed and that they are inhuman—has long been slowly shifting the form and content of the transnational human rights paradigm. Women, largely excluded from governments, have organized their own international nongovernmental organizations (NGOs) that have increasingly made grassroots civil society a factor to be reckoned with in international relations. Recognition that states

Earlier versions of some of the ideas in this introduction were published in the University of Michigan Law School's *Law Quadrangle Notes*, Fall–Winter 1999, 3. They benefited from being presented to the European Court of Justice at a meeting held by the University of Michigan Law School at the Hay-Adams Hotel, Washington, D.C. (Apr. 19, 2000), and delivered as the Contemporary Civilization Coursewide Lecture at Columbia University titled "Women's Worlds, Men's States" (Apr. 29, 2004) and from the discussions that followed. Comments from Jessica Neuwirth, Lisa Cardyn, José Alvarez, and Tom Bender made it better. Exceptional technical assistance under pressure was provided by Anna Baldwin and Emma Cheuse and the University of Michigan Law Library. The University of Michigan Law School and a fellowship at the Center for Advanced Study in the Behavioral Sciences (CASBS) at Stanford supported its writing.

1

per se are often not the most immediate violators of women's humanity (although they often collaborate in it) has required recognition, in turn, that other-than-state actors regularly perpetrate serious human rights violations.[3] And since states too often do not represent women, whether by acts or failures to act within the sphere of their power and authority, women facing unresponsive official mechanisms, doctrines, and authorities have reached, often through their own NGOs, to hold the law in their own hands, seeking perpetrator accountability directly to them through civil legal means. Women's assertion of their human rights can thus be seen, on one level, at once not only as an attempt to make states adhere to human rights but as an attempt to separate states from the human rights they guarantee and violate, including by ignoring them. In supplementing or even at times supplanting the state as international law's historically nearly exclusive unit, women have pushed for the formal changes they need to secure their substantive rights, moving human beings—violators and violated alike—to the center of the human rights process.[4]

In the mid-1990s in particular, Bosnian women, while their communities were still being attacked by Serbian forces, spoke out about being raped en masse as an instrumentality of a genocide that was being conducted in part through war. The assault and their resistance to it challenged the lines between genocide and war and, ultimately, between war and peace.[5] Although inequality in peace and genocide through war are not equivalent, rape both in and outside zones of recognized conflict was clarified as more a collective than an individual crime.[6] To be adequate to these women's violations, human rights law needed to come further to terms with the fact that group identifications make up much of the content of the human, making group-based injuries central to the denial of humanity, with sex- and ethnically-based harms at the core of, rather than peripheral to, human rights. To enhance the accountability of international processes to such survivors, civil proceedings have been favored,[7] as have civil remedies— not because perpetrators should not be incarcerated, but because social change and reparation are more effective relief and deterrence than is punishment alone.[8] Steps toward establishing these features of what might be termed the women's model of human rights—not because it is exclusive to one sex but because it is predicated on women's distinctive experiences of violation and of denial of that violation—are beginning to make human rights an honest term.

Becoming human in both the legal and lived senses is a social, legal, and political process.[9] It requires prohibiting or otherwise delegitimating all acts by which human beings as such are violated, guaranteeing people what they need for a fully human existence, and then officially upholding those standards and delivering on those entitlements.[10] But, in circular epistemic fashion, seeing what subordinated groups are distinctively deprived of, subjected to, and delegitimated by, requires first that they be real to power: that they first be seen as human.

Put another way, human rights can be observed to be a response to atrocity denied. Before atrocities are recognized as such, they are authoritatively regarded as either too extraordinary to be believable or too ordinary to be atrocious. If the events are socially considered unusual, the fact that they happened is denied in specific instances; if they are regarded as usual, the fact that they are violating is denied: if it's happening, it's not so bad, and if it's really bad, it isn't happening. The given status of certain people is seen as tautologous with, even justified by, the deprivations of their human rights. Law often collaborates by making an unusual or extreme form of a common violation illegal, so that what is illegal almost never happens, yet the law appears to stand against the violation. Victims are thereby ideologically rendered appropriate to their treatment, the unequal treatment serving to confirm their ontological status as lesser humans. When nothing is done, the treatment, and social status accordingly, confirm and create who one is. Legally, one is less than human when one's violations do not violate the human rights that are recognized. Acts common in human experience, such as rape in war and rape in peace, have been beneath serious notice because they are so familiar, while acts that are uncommon, like the Nazis' industrial murder and the Serbs' industrial rape, have been beyond belief. While disbelief and associated impunity reign, the violated are—systemically and effectively speaking—rendered not fully human legally or socially. When and where this denial is overcome and rights against the extreme and the normal are recognized, the treatment is defined as inhuman and the victims human. Women are in the midst of this process.

Meantime, the status and treatment of men still tacitly but authoritatively define the human universal, eliding the particularity of being a man. The state, an apex form in which the power of men is organized both among men and over women while purporting to institutionalize peace and justice, has been revealed as an institution of male dominance,[11] its behavior and norms partial and gendered. Masculinity observably marks what men want and have and touch and make and do in social space, political institutions included. If the state is a male institution not only demographically but socially and politically—its structures and actions driven by an ideology predicated on an epistemic angle of vision with concomitant values, attitudes, and behaviors based on the status location of the male sex in society, members of which (with variations) occupy a superior position in gender hierarchy, resulting in a sexual politics[12]—is the international system a counterbalance? Or is it metamale?

If the state has a gender (as well as usually a sex), so that the state through its distinctive instrument, law, sees and treats women the way men in society see and treat women,[13] does international law challenge this, or does it reproduce it at a yet higher level? Seen in its gendered dimensions, does the move from national to international essentially simply magnify the scale and diversity of law's masculinity, or does it at the same time offer distinct dynamics, opportunities, and challenges? Even as international law and institutions could challenge or limit the power of individual states, do they build and depend upon and support the power of states as such at the same time? As the state appears outmoded to some, superseded by institutions and forces with bases of power independent of states, such as globalization, multinational corporations, organized criminality, and religion, has the masculinity of international laws, norms, and institutions withered away, or is male dominance equally present in and transmuting into transnational forms? Is gender a transnational force—both from the top down, ensuring male dominance, and, with women's emergence as a global force, from the bottom up, challenging that dominance—that has long been largely overlooked?

These international questions can be asked through four dimensions along which national behavior through law has been analyzed in gendered terms. State behavior that promotes and institutionalizes male dominance has been found to distinguish public from private, naturalize dominance as difference, hide coercion behind consent, and obscure sexual politics behind morality.[14] Does the order that states have created among states behave in similar gendered ways?

At least since the critique of the distinction between that torture that violates international law because states do it and that torture that does not because nonstate actors do it,[15] the international structure has emerged as a set of internesting boxes defined by layers upon layers of distinctions between public and private.[16] The public is formally supreme over the private, the private a space inside which power is left alone by public authorities. Women have historically been relegated to and identified with the private, excluded from and, when present, subordinated in public. The supreme, validated, hierarchically superior side of the line, the locale of legitimated force, is the ideologically male side, defined by distinction from the subordinate, lesser, no-force-permitted female side.[17] Power may be held accountable, if at all, for its abuse outside the border's threshold that delineates where the public begins.

The hierarchy of the state over civil society provides one transnational example. The state has power over civil society, a feminized realm within which male dominance is permitted free rein, simultaneously masculinizing the state. War and peace offer another international distinction with classic sex-stereotyped dimensions. Men violently dominating other men for control of states is called war; men violently dominating women within states is relegated to peace.[18] Parallel legal categories distinguish combatants, widely thought of in male terms (permitted to engage in force) from civilians, construed in female terms (unarmed and putatively to be protected).[19] Apart from the relatively constant fact that men organize themselves to compete and conflict with other men, contemporary conflicts among men have increasingly become more group-to-group than state-to-state, resembling women's treatment by men more than they resemble classic armed conflict. International politics has much to learn from understanding women's treatment by men.

Public/private lines also discernibly distinguish the conventionally so-called generations of human rights.[20] The first generation is considered to be political and civil rights, amounting to what empowered men feel they need against other empowered men. These rights define where public ordering is considered axiomatic. Economic and social rights, those rights of which women as such are largely deprived along with many men, are usually regarded as second generation, even though they are in the Universal Declaration of Human Rights and recognized as interdependent with the so-called first generation throughout the covenants themselves. Their terrain is considered more private: social, not political, and often not readily enforceable or implementable in the usual form rights take. Public intervention here is often contested. Group or collective rights are called the third generation. These are regarded as definitively social, quintessentially private; these rights are least guaranteed, sometimes not considered properly rights at all in the enforceable sense. This hierarchical ordering among generations, controversial in itself, ranks systemic regard. From women's standpoint, it might well be reversed. Women are men's unequals as groups. Real equality rights are collective in the sense of being group-based in their essential nature. Individuals may suffer discrimination one at a time, but the basis for the injury is group membership. Lacking effective guarantees of economic and social rights, women have found political and civil rights, however crucial, to be largely inaccessible and superficial. The generational distinctions and their rankings, questionable for men as well, are clearly premised on gendered assumptions, perceptions, and priorities.

But it is in jurisdiction—the doctrine governing who has power to decide what and where—that the public/private distinction finds its natural home. Jurisdiction delineates turf. Internationally, jurisdiction revolves around sovereignty. A sovereign has exclusive dominion within a sphere, a concept that is spatial conceptually as well as often concretely, accountable, if at all, only to equal sovereigns (and often not voluntarily). A state is sovereign. This means that it is defined by a public/private line at its border, which is principally territorial, such that what happens within is private, meaning that it is the exclusive domain of the patriarchal order called government. This line that includes by excluding creates the same unit that is incarnated in international law as at once the guarantor and violator of women's human rights. Dynamically described, male power quintessentially sets itself up as exclusive within, justifying its hegemony as protection, then violates the protected with relative impunity or permits their violation by those it empowers by ignoring them (appearing to some not to be acting when it does nothing about this violation). Think marital rape, incest. With the globe divided spatially into nation-states, male dominance over women begins at home, within and beneath states, internal to jurisdictions including the family. Male structural privacy is the principle that animates the geography of both male power and international justice. It rules the world.

Because jurisdiction gives men power over a sphere, encompassing women within it, the international jurisdiction, which could make these men accountable to other men, is jealously guarded and carefully constrained. On the international level, the fact that state boundaries define the line where men divide power among themselves, within which they seek to exercise exclusive dominion, including over women, explains why the Convention on the Elimination of All Forms of Discrimination Against Women (CEDAW) is so widely reserved.[21] Similarly, among the most reserved international provisions in all treaties are those jurisdictional provisions that designate the authority to resolve disputes.[22] Tellingly, CEDAW, along with the Convention on the Rights of the Child, has no state-to-state procedure, while the Convention on Torture, the International Covenant on Civil and Political Rights (ICCPR), and the Convention on the Elimination of All Forms of Racial Discrimination (CERD) all do.[23] This is what a real hierarchy of rights looks like. Of course, interstate claims are rare even where available. Interpreted in gendered terms, men respect other men's control over their own domains in the hope and expectation of reciprocity: the male bond.

States resist having nonstate acts adjudicated by anyone other than themselves, the usual perpetrator group, without their express consent or at all, and domestically often insist on sovereign immunities for official acts and acts of states.[24] The result is to insulate states from accountability to anyone. A systemic structural bias militates against holding perpetrators of injuries to women as such responsible to public authority, meaning any authority beyond the men who rule the private realm in which a woman's violation occurs and is typically effectively permitted.[25] Even the Rome Statute of the International Criminal Court does not claim universal jurisdiction but sets preconditions for its exercise over international crimes, relying on a state committing the crime or adopting the statute.[26] The particular combination of requiring state acts for many international violations with layers of immunity for official acts and acts of state, added to rules favoring local resolution and disallowing extraterritorial jurisdiction and to the lack of interstate claims, shuts women out.

If men have guarded against partiality, classically thought to be based on identification with people-like-me, by replacing government of men with rule of law, women continue to be governed by the rule of men's laws. Their best hope has been to appeal up the jurisdictional hierarchy to men and laws more jurisdictionally (meaning spatially) distant from, thus hopefully less controlled by and identified with, the men/laws that violate them, exactly those sites where they have been least likely to be granted access to rights and where implementation and enforcement are least assured and least concrete. In this context, the ruling in the United States in Kadic v. Karadžić, which permitted sexually violated Bosnian women to seek remedies under international law for rape as genocide in another country against the self-declared leader of a rogue regime at home,[27] is a signal victory on the jurisdictional frontier.

In the face of these deeply gendered legal arrangements and the recognition that inequality with men is women's global condition, the spread and effectiveness of international equality rights provide sensitive and striking indicators of women's progress in becoming human in the legal sense. Considerable strides have been made in the courts of some countries, notably Canada and South Africa,[28] beyond the formal equality approach of sameness with a dominant (male) standard and toward substantive equality, measuring laws and policies against realities of subordination and gender hierarchy.[29] India's constitutional equality thinking has a chance to reach an equal future from an unequal present.[30] Sweden has notably moved effectively against prostitution through a de facto sex equality approach.[31] Although historically women have not found strength in numbers, where facing facts and respecting principle and living up to commitments and shaming fail, and effective external enforcement remains unavailable and corruption rules, perhaps democracy will lead states to promote sex equality in reality instead of merely in form—maybe even to see it as in their interest.

As in most states, sex equality rights in the major human rights instruments have tended to employ the purportedly neutral sameness/difference model.[32] Showing more vision, the UN Human Rights Committee, interpreting the ICCPR, has taken a substantive and subtle approach to the sex equality questions in its sphere.[33] So, to some extent, has CEDAW,[34] which guarantees women *as a group* the right not to be discriminated against, focusing on the concrete situation of a substantive group of people instead of abstract spheres called civil, political, economic, and social as the primary units of analysis. By its language, CEDAW also reaches private acts,[35] although it can do so only through states, the parties to it. Most of CEDAW's active provisions admittedly grant women equality of rights in gender-neutral terms. This approach, producing some advances, limits women to what men need, resulting in difficulty in dealing, for example, with pregnancy (which CEDAW covers) and sex-specific and sexual violence. Seeming to realize that violence against women is not just one issue on a list of important problems but goes to the core of women's status and the relation of states to it, CEDAW has been interpreted to prohibit violence against women as sex discrimination.[36] No state has yet proven capable of this recognition.[37] The CEDAW Committee may be coming to recognize male dominance as the real name of the problem of discrimination against women.[38]

Two of the finest illustrations of a substantive equality approach internationally are regional: the Inter-American Convention on the Prevention, Punishment and Eradication of Violence Against Women (Convention of Belém do Pará)[39] and the African Protocol on the Rights of Women,[40] to which women from cultures across the regions contributed. The Convention of Belém do Pará recognizes violence against women, "a manifestation of the historically unequal power relations between women and men," as a distinctive human rights violation "based on gender, which causes death or physical, sexual or psychological harm or suffering to women, whether in the public or private sphere."[41] The Convention squarely grants "every woman . . . the right to be free from violence in both the public and private spheres," backed by "the right to simple and prompt recourse to a competent court for protection against acts that violate her rights."[42] The right to freedom from violence notably includes "the right of women to be valued and educated free of stereotyped patterns of behavior and social and cultural practices based on concepts of inferiority or subordination," implemented by "progressively specific measures" to modify and counteract such prejudices and practices that "legitimize or exacerbate violence against women."[43] This is what a substantive equality approach with the necessary substance looks like.

The African Protocol embeds its sex equality and antiviolence guarantees in a broadly conceived substantive vision. Its positive equality recognizes rights for women "to live in a positive cultural context" and to peace and sustainable development.[44] Leaving formalistic negative equality—content to reflect unequal social arrangements, declaring equality in law when people are legally sorted into existing social orderings—in the dust,[45] the African Protocol explicitly and in diverse concrete settings prohibits violence against women, not recognized as sex discrimination but defined to include "all acts perpetrated against women which cause or could cause them physical, sexual, psychological, and economic harm."[46] The Protocol guarantees appropriate and effective measures to enact and enforce laws against "unwanted or forced sex whether . . . in private or public,"[47] covers "verbal violence,"[48] and rejects violence against women in "private or public life in peacetime and during situations of armed conflicts or of war."[49]

Far from being paralyzed by cultural differences or intimidated by cultural relativism,[50] the African Protocol at once guarantees rights to women in polygamous unions and prefers monogamy.[51] It moves to eliminate "harmful practices which negatively affect the human rights of women and which are contrary to recognized international standards," including "female genital mutilation."[52] Its economic and social rights run to "the informal sector" and "work of women in the home"[53] as well as covering the public workplace. The Protocol not only guarantees women's right to control their fertility and to decide whether and when to have children[54] but also, uniquely in a multilateral treaty, requires states to authorize "medical abortion" in certain circumstances.[55] It puts Africa on a par with Latin America on the question of violence against women and in the lead on women's equality in world law.[56]

As more and more of the substantive reality of women's deprivation of humanity has been reflected in law, recognition of sex equality as a peremptory international norm has advanced.[57] Sex equality, although subject to varying interpretations, is nearly universally embraced as an international norm.[58] International human rights law, including the United Nations Charter, pervasively guarantees the right to equality before the law without discrimination on the basis of sex.[59] Many, even most, countries recognize sex equality as a value in their legal systems, widely guaranteeing legal equality based on sex in constitutions and other foundational statements— this despite the fact that sex discriminatory laws continue in force around the world[60] in settings of pervasive social inequality of the sexes in reality. The fact that a norm is not lived up to or delivered upon with consistency does not mean that it is not a norm. Much like racial discrimination, which is widely recognized to violate customary international law, the rejection of sex discrimination is normatively vigorous if feebly implemented, displaying strong belief in legal obligation but weak state practice. Virtually no one says they support sex discrimination.

Even more unanimous than the rejection of discrimination against women by law is the rejection of the idea of the biological inferiority of women to men[61] and the condemnation of the subordination of women by men, particularly when it is violent. If discrimination by law is widely rejected on principle if not in practice, ideologies of sex-based inferiority by nature and violent sexual subordination in society are broadly condemned, at least ostensibly. Rape, a form of sex inequality widely practiced and permitted, is nonetheless universally abhorred officially and virtually uniformly made criminal. The ad hoc criminal tribunals are moving the international order toward an understanding of sexual violence against women as a crime of violent inequality.[62] Perhaps the pervasive presence of women pressuring male states to recognize their humanity in principle as well as in practice is shifting professed custom.[63] By these measures, particularly for gross or systematic acts, sex equality is moving toward recognition as a peremptory norm at the highest level of international principle.[64]

Despite this level of acceptance of sex equality as a principle, women's actual second-class status continues to be concealed, therefore maintained, by pervasive practices, among which is the tendency of law to present functioning divisions of power as a discourse in ideas of right and wrong, garbing politics as morality. If the equality of the sexes is recognized to be a fact, equalizing socially unequal groups is merely a problem to be solved. But if sex equality is seen as a value, it can be accepted or rejected as one side in a normative discussion. In policy, a fact is either reflected or distorted; a value can be debated endlessly. Its recognition ebbs and flows with time and place, majorities and hegemonies.

This distinction in logical status and some of its implications can be illustrated by comparing two passages in the preambular language of

CEDAW with that of CERD. CERD's ratifiers are "[c]onvinced that any doctrine of superiority based on racial differentiation is scientifically false, morally condemnable, socially unjust and dangerous, and that there is no justification for racial discrimination, in theory or in practice, anywhere."[65] Racial equality is a fact. Doctrines of racial supremacy are based on the lie of the superiority of some races over others. At bottom, racism is inaccurate.

Nothing in the preamble to CEDAW approximates this level of rejection of sexism. The closest it comes is "Recalling that discrimination against women violates the principles of equality of rights and respect for human dignity, is an obstacle to the participation of women, on equal terms with men, in the political, social, economic and cultural life of their countries, hampers the growth of the prosperity of society and the family and makes more difficult the full development of the potentialities of women in the service of their countries and of humanity."[66] Sex discrimination violates other abstract ideas; that discrimination violates equality principles is a tautology. The strongest reality-based argument against discrimination against women here is consequentialist: it interferes with the ability of families and societies and countries to use women to grow and prosper.

CERD's formulation does not just turn up the rhetorical heat. It grounds a politics of equality in the world of reality. The only reason not to reject racism is left exposed as the interest of one racial group seeking to dominate another. Racism is naked: the ideology of the self-interest of bigots. The CEDAW preamble, by distinction, rejects sexism principally not as false and inherently without basis but as a barrier to the exercise of other rights, hence derivative, and an inefficient use of human resources. Sex equality inhabits the realm of the good idea, the right view, a guide to proper thought and action, rather than being the only position consistent with the evidence. The operational language of CEDAW squarely addresses many concrete problems this preambular language leaves in question, including the traditional roles of the sexes, traditional cultural and religious practices, prostitution, and reproduction.[67] But on the level of express principle, CEDAW never says that sexism is a lie. It does not say that there is no justification for the inferiority of women in theory or practice anywhere. Nowhere does it state that the doctrine of male supremacy based on sexual differentiation can never justify the subordination of women. As significant an advance for women as CEDAW is, opposition to discrimination based on sex is, on this preambular level of principle, framed as a moral judgment of value. Sexism remains clothed, sexual politics ungrounded.

International law often gets further in addressing the realities of sex inequality when it uses other legal frameworks. International trafficking prohibitions, for instance, show more awareness of the dynamics of sex-based inequality that women and girls face in a sex-unequal world than does anything in sex equality law per se.[68] Similarly, the International Criminal Tribunal for Rwanda transcended the moral approach typical of national laws regulating hate speech[69] in holding three media leaders guilty of genocide and persecution (a crime against humanity) for broadcasts and publications that impelled the killing of Tutsi and moderate Hutu civilians in the Rwandan genocide of 1994.[70] The point of the ruling was not to decry the negative and hateful statements but to find and prohibit what was done to people as a result of them. Fear-mongering, making aggression into self-defense, circulating hit lists and targeting individuals' movements and locations, and spreading a climate of ethnic animosity and terror so that one spark could ignite the prairie fire in which 800,000 people were massacred inside of three months were found to be genocidal and an international delict.[71] The issue was not defamation but the power of media to kill. Cartoons that sexualized hate and fear of Tutsi women were linked to their mass rape.[72] The approach to causality taken by this case, called the *Media Case*, offers powerful guidance for the regulation of pornography, including racist pornography, a practice of inequality connected to violence against women outside as well as within zones of recognized conflict.[73]

Observably gendered against women's interests, the international system has nonetheless produced gains for women unavailable elsewhere. In challenging men's rule to produce these gains, women as such have emerged as not only a group in itself—a transnational group created through treatment that is not limited by national boundaries—but also as a group for itself, self-consciously realized through organizing.[74] That the international is the authentic locale for the fight for women's rights explains the explosive productivity of the series of international conferences of the past three decades.[75] Consciousness of sex-based subordination and the possibilities for change went global through these conferences, mobilizing women worldwide and producing influential forward-looking (despite some crucial shortcomings)[76] drafts of legislation and policy, blueprints for where women's world could move. These documents have led international opinion and focused national efforts under an international umbrella. In this process, the legitimacy of the NGOs that have spoken for women whom states have long ignored has been repeatedly questioned, even as the legitimacy of states in representing their countries' women—half the population excluded from the public order for centuries and remaining outside public power even in most democracies today—is left unquestioned.

Women are a global group in the sense that the distinctive social definition, treatment, and status of women as a sex relative to men is recognizable in diverse forms all over the world.[77] Both women's subordination and their resistance to it have been global all along, predating what is now called globalization—a moment of perception catching up to women's longtime reality (similar to the phrase "the feminization of poverty"). Gender inequality is a global system. National particularities give some of its forms the exemption of culture, casting the rest as natural, rendering every form of oppression known to woman either culturally universal (so we "can't" do anything about it) or culturally specific (so we "shouldn't" do anything about it). Nowhere is sexuality not central to keeping women down. Nowhere are the universal and the culturally particular, in their versions of "sameness" to and "difference" from men, not vaunted as reasons why that lesser place is woman's rightful place and as reasons to do nothing about it.[78] Even as such features unite the many forms of subordination into one system, solutions need to be diversely tailored with care to many local forms of that system.

Women's world—both status and struggle to change it—is the globe, in inherent tension with subsumption of women and their rights to states. The international arena thus presents at once a specific problem of organized male dominance and a world-scale opportunity for the solutions to fit the scale of the problem. In this light, work within nations, however essential, amounts to seeking equality for women in one country, a task ultimately incapable of achievement by itself. As women in one country achieve more equality, men seek out women with fewer options elsewhere—a pattern observable sexually in sex trafficking, sex tourism, and mail-order brides and economically in labor trafficking, international outsourcing to sweatshops, and relocation of production in dominant countries to sources of cheap female labor in countries whose gross domestic product is less than that of some of the multinational corporations that locate there.[79] No more than clean air can women's equality be successfully achieved in one country. No woman will be free until all women are equal.

As the mountain of women moves, the state in its male form is arguably becoming anachronistic, even obsolete. Increasingly a shell of force, if with considerable remaining clout, the state never has monopolized the means of violence within its borders, unless male violence against women is seen as encompassed within it. Its illegitimacy more naked by the day, the state may be increasingly irrelevant to women, who have never had men's stake in it anyway.[80] In the absence of states' tools of implementation, international law—like women largely lacking access to legitimate force to compel adherence to its will—has had to develop a wider range of means to be effective. Not to valorize lack of enforcement, but force is not all there is to effectiveness or even to power. Many women comply with the dictates and limits of male dominance even when not individually forced to do so. Most decisions of the International Court of Justice are complied with even though it commands no military forces.[81] For years, the Berlin Wall was feared and unassailable concrete and wire with armed guards, but what held it up did not change the day it came down. People dismantled the Berlin Wall with their bare hands the day the world stopped believing in it. On August 13, 2004, hundreds of women in Nagpur, India, stabbed their rapist to death with kitchen knives on the white marble floor of a courthouse. He was about to be released to terrorize them again after years of official complaints resulting in no action, as when the police laughed at one irate victim the perpetrator called a prostitute and threatened to rape again.[82] Rape is socially felt to be inevitable to the extent the inhumanity of women is believed. These women refused to accept that their intimate violation with their state's ratification of it was inevitable one more day. That day, they took back their humanity.

Sexual violation may be law's ultimate challenge. Rationalized as consensual, it is coerced. Considered private, its shared and public role and reality demand public redress. Attributed to sexual difference, it enacts sexual dominance. Endlessly moralized, it is political, sexually political. Ignored, it is condoned. Sexual violation is a crime of inequality of status, to which those who are low in status and its power are subjected and to which those who are subjected are lowered. Its centrality to women's inequality to men (and some men's inequality to other men) plays out through culture, honor, religion, family, dignity, identity, intimacy, integrity, and respect. It dehumanizes. No material recompense or punishment can fully restore its intangible, invisible harm. Official force alone, although essential, is not enough. Beyond incarceration, punishment, and other retribution; beyond damages and other reparations; beyond truth and reconciliation and symbolism; beyond restitution for the irreparable loss of family members; beyond the return of farms, homes, jobs, and legal systems, human rights can give back the humanity the rapist takes away. Global consciousness of women's right to human status, beginning with intimate inviolability, is exploding across the potent artifice of states' barriers, erupting through the fissures of state subordination, and rising from the ashes of states' collapse.

part one

theory and reality

On Torture

Torture is widely recognized as a fundamental violation of human rights.[1] Inequality on the basis of sex is also widely condemned, and sex equality affirmed as a basic human rights value and legal guarantee in many nations and internationally.[2] So why is torture on the basis of sex—for example, in the form of rape, battering, and pornography—not seen as a violation of human rights?[3] When women are abused, human rights are violated; anything less implicitly assumes women are not human. When torture is sex-based, human rights standards should be recognized as violated, just as much as when the torture is based on anything else.

Internationally, torture has a recognized profile.[4] It usually begins with abduction, detention, imprisonment, and enforced isolation, progresses through extreme physical and mental abuse, and may end in death. The torturer has absolute power, which torture victims believe in absolutely and utterly. Life and death turn on his whim. Victims are beaten, raped, shocked with electricity, nearly drowned, tied, hung, burned, deprived of sleep, food, and human contact. The atrocities are limited only by the torturer's taste and imagination and any value the victim may be seen to have alive or unmarked. Verbal abuse and humiliation, making the victim feel worthless and hopeless, are integral to the torture having its intended effect. Often torture victims are selected and tortured in particular ways because they are members of a social group, for example, Jews in 1977 Argentina.[5] Torturers also exploit human relationships to inflict mental suffering; a man will be forced to watch his wife being raped, for example. Victims are forced to drink their own urine, to eat their own excrement.

This speech was given at an international conference on human rights on November 10, 1990, in Banff, Alberta, Canada. It was originally published as "On Torture: A Feminist Perspective on Human Rights," in *Human Rights in the Twenty-first Century: A Global Challenge* 21 (Kathleen E. Mahoney and Paul Mahoney, eds., 1993).

Sometimes drugs are forcibly administered that alter personalities and make bodily or mental control or even self-recognition impossible. Torture is often designed as a slow process toward an excruciating death. Even when one survives, events move and escalate toward death, which is sometimes wished for to escape the agony. One is aware that one could be killed at any point. Many are.

What torture does to a human being is internationally recognized. Its purpose is to break people. People change under such extreme pressure, studied under the rubrics of brainwashing, post-traumatic stress, and the Stockholm syndrome. Long-term consequences include dissociation, which promotes survival but can be hard to reverse. What one learns being tortured, and what is necessary to survive it, can make living later unbearable, producing suicide even after many years. The generally recognized purpose of torture is to control, intimidate, or eliminate those who insult or challenge or are seen to undermine the powers that be, typically a regime or a cadre seeking to become a regime. Torture is thus seen as political, although it often seems that its political overlay is a facilitating pretext for the pure exercise of sadism, a politics of itself.

When these things happen, human rights are deemed violated. It is acknowledged that atrocities are committed.[6] While there is no ultimate answer to the question "Why do they do it?" and in the context of torture little agonizing over the question, nothing stops the practice from being identified and universally opposed as a crime jus cogens.

With this framework in mind, consider the following accounts:

> "Linda Lovelace" was the name I bore during the two and one half year period of imprisonment beginning in 1971. Linda "Lovelace" was coerced through physical, mental and sexual torture and abuse, often at gunpoint and through threats on her life to perform sex acts, including forced fellatio and bestiality so that pornographic films could be made of her.[7]

Ms. "Lovelace" then describes encountering Chuck Traynor, a pimp, as follows:

> [W]hen in response to his suggestions I let him know I would not become involved in prostitution in any way and told him I intended to leave he beat me up physically and the constant mental abuse began. I literally became a prisoner, I was not allowed out of his sight, not even to use the bathroom, where he watched me through a hole in the door. He slept on top of me at night, he listened in on my telephone calls with a .45 automatic eight shot pointed at me. I was beaten physically and suffered

mental abuse each and every day thereafter. He undermined my ties with other people and forced me to marry him on advice from his lawyer. My initiation into prostitution was a gang rape by five men, arranged by Mr. Traynor. It was the turning point in my life. He threatened to shoot me with the pistol if I didn't go through with it. I had never experienced anal sex before and it ripped me apart. They treated me like an inflatable plastic doll, picking me up and moving me here and there. They spread my legs this way and that, shoving their things at me and into me, they were playing musical chairs with parts of my body. I have never been so frightened and disgraced and humiliated in my life. I felt like garbage. I engaged in sex acts for pornography against my will to avoid being killed. Mr. Traynor coerced me into pornography by threatening my life first with a .45 automatic eight shot and later with an M 16 semi-automatic machine gun which became his favorite toy. I was brutally beaten whenever I showed any signs of resistance or lack of enthusiasm for the freaky sex he required me to act like I enjoyed. The lives of my family were threatened. Each day I was raped, beaten, kicked, punched, smacked, choked, degraded or yelled at by Mr. Traynor. Sometimes all of these. He consistently belittled and humiliated me. I believed Mr. Traynor would have killed me and others if I did not do what he demanded of me. I didn't doubt he would shoot me. I made myself go numb as if my body belonged to someone else . . . Simple survival took everything I had. I managed to escape on three separate occasions. The first and second time I was caught and suffered a brutal beating and an awful sexual abuse as punishment. The third time I was at my parents' home and Mr. Traynor threatened to kill my parents and my nephew if I did not leave immediately with him. The physical effects of this are still with me. During my imprisonment my breasts were injected with silicone which has since broken up and has been dangerous and painful. All of the surface veins of my right leg were destroyed because I used it to protect myself from the beatings. My doctor told me that because of the abuse, it was unsafe for me to have another child so I had an abortion when I wanted to have the child. It took a long time to even begin to deal with the mental effects. A person can't be held prisoner for two and one half years and the next day trust society, trust the people who have put me there and just go on with the life that you once thought was yours.[8]

Now consider this account:

My name is Jayne Stamen. At one time I thought there was no one who could help me to get away from my husband. There wasn't a day that went by I didn't think was my last as he totally lost control. He slept with a gun beside him every night as he promised he would kill me and then shoot himself if I didn't submit to his obsession of slavery and bondage and beatings during sex. I was raped 11 times between March '84 and November '86. I had four broken hands during my marriage, caused by my husband. I was put into the hospital in traction for two weeks due to a beating by him. I walked with a walker several months after that. When I was raped by Jerry, I was always tied to my bed. Tied where my legs were spread apart. He tied me with nylon cords and extension cords. I even got tied up while I was sleeping at times. He would then penetrate me with objects such as his rifle or a long necked wine decanter or twelve inch artificial rubber penises. He would shave all of the hair off my private area as he said he wanted to "screw a baby's cunt." He would slap me while I was tied, call me all sorts of horrible names. I broke my arm on two occasions trying to get away from him. When he would watch porno movies on our VCR, he would tell me to do exactly what the women in the movies had done to the men. I would tell him to forget it and then he would continue to slap me around until he'd get so angry that I was afraid he'd beat me so hard he'd kill me. At times he'd grab a large knife he kept in the drawer beside our bed and he'd hold it to my face or breasts and tell me to do as he said or he'd cut me up. If I didn't act like I was enjoying pleasing him he'd threaten me again and then replay the scene he wanted acted out from the movies. I had no place to run as I never had any money of my own. He cut off the phone which was my only contact with the outside world. He would make me visit him when he finished his mailman routine and give him a blow job on the public street while people were passing by. I really wanted to die.[9]

Now consider this composite account of the systematic violation of a woman named Burnham by a man named Beglin, her husband: Beglin was watching an X-rated movie on cable television in the family room. He entered the bedroom, threw her on the bed, and bound her. He ripped off her clothing and began taking photos of her. He then sexually assaulted her. Crisis center workers and an emergency room doctor testified that her wrists and ankles were marked from being tied to the bed by ropes. He forced her sixty-eight different times to have sex with neighbors and strangers while he took photographs. She was forced through assault and holding their child hostage to stand on the corner and invite men in for sex and to have sex with the dog. He beat her so that she was nearly killed.

She testified to episodes of torture with a battery-charged cattle prod and an electric eggbeater. She was asked about photographs in an album showing her smiling during the sexual encounters. She said that her husband threatened her with violence if she didn't smile while these photographs were taken.[10]

In the accounts by these women, all the same things happen that happen in Amnesty International reports and accounts of torture—except they happen in homes in Nebraska or in pornography studios in Los Angeles rather than prison cells in Chile or detention centers in Turkey. But the social and legal responses to the experiences are not the same at all. Torture is not considered personal. Torture is not attributed to one sick individual at a time and dismissed as exceptional, or if it is, that maneuver is dismissed as a cover-up by the human rights community. Torture victims are not generally asked how many were there with them, as if it is not important if it happened only to you or you and a few others like you. With torture, an increase is not dismissed as just an increase in reporting, as if a constant level of such abuse is acceptable. Billions of dollars are not made selling as entertainment pictures of what is regarded as torture, nor is torture as such generally regarded as sexual entertainment. Never is a victim of torture asked, didn't you really want it?

A simple double standard is at work here. What fundamentally distinguishes torture, understood in human rights terms, from the events these women have described is that torture is done to men as well as to women. Or, more precisely, when what usually happens to women as these women have described it happens to men, which it sometimes does, women's experience is the template for it, so those men, too, are ignored as women are. When the abuse is sexual or intimate, especially when it is sexual and inflicted by an intimate, it is gendered, hence not considered a human rights violation. Torture is regarded as politically motivated; states are generally required to be involved in it. What needs asking is why the torture of women by men is not seen as torture, specifically why it is not seen as political, and just what the involvement of the state in it is.

Women are half the human race. To put the individual accounts in context, all around the world, women are battered, raped, sexually abused as children, prostituted, and increasingly live pornographic lives in contexts saturated more or less with pornography.[11] Women do two-thirds of the world's work, earn one-tenth of the world's income, and own less than one-hundredth of the world's property.[12] Women are more likely to *be* property than to own any. Women have not even been allowed to vote until very recently and still are not in some countries. Women's reproductive capacities are systematically exploited. While the rate and intensity of these atrocities and violations vary across cultures, they are never equal or substantially reversed on the basis of sex. All this is done to women as women by men as men.

Data contextualizes this, and a few selected examples show it with more texture. In the United States, 44 percent of all women at one time or another are victims of rape or attempted rape; for women of color, the rates are higher.[13] In 1988, 31 percent of murdered women were killed by husbands or boyfriends.[14] In egalitarian Sweden, one woman is battered to death every week to ten days.[15] Dramatic increases in the rate of reported rape are debated there; the debate is over whether the increases are "real" or "merely" reflect an increase in reporting. Where women are chattel or have only recently even legally emerged from the condition of being chattel, as is the situation in Japan, what can rape mean? If a woman exists to be sexually used, to what sexual use of her is the right man not entitled? Sweden, the United States, and Japan are all saturated with pornography. In the United States, women disappear on a daily basis—from their homes, from supermarket parking lots. Sometimes they are found in ditches or floating down rivers. Sometimes we dig up their bones along with those of ten or fifteen other women ten or fifteen years later. Serial rapists and serial murderers, who are almost always men, target women almost exclusively.

Why isn't this political? The abuse is neither random nor individual. The fact that you may know your assailant does not mean that your membership in a group chosen for violation is irrelevant to your abuse. It is still systematic and group-based. It defines the quality of community life and is defined by the distribution of power in society. It would seem that something is not considered political if it is done to women by men, especially if it is considered to be sex. Then it is not considered political because what is political is when men control and hurt and use other men, meaning persons who are deserving of dignity and power, on some basis men have decided is deserving of dignity and a measure of power, like conventional political ideology, because that is a basis on which they have been deprived of dignity and power. So their suffering has the dignity of politics and is called torture.[16] Women as such are not seen as deserving of dignity or power, nor does the sexuality that defines us have dignitary standards, nor is women's belief in our own dignity given the dignity or power of being regarded as a political ideology. The definition of the political here is an unequal one, determined on the basis of sex such that atrocities to women are denied as atrocities by being deprived of political meaning.

Often the reason given for not considering atrocities to women to be torture is that they do not involve acts by states. They happen between nonstate actors in civil society hence are seen as not only unofficial but unconscious and unorganized and unsystematic and undirected and unplanned. They do not happen, it is thought, by state policy. They just happen. And traditionally, international instruments (as well as national constitutions) govern state action.

First of all, the state is not all there is to power. To act as if it is produces an exceptionally inadequate definition for human rights when so much of the second-class status of women, from sexual objectification to murder, is done by men to women without express or immediate or overt state involvement. If "the political" is to be defined in terms of men's experiences of being subjected to power, it makes some (but only some) sense to center its definition on the state.[17] But if one is including the unjust power involved in the subjection of half the human race by the other half—male dominance—it makes no sense to define power exclusively in terms of what the state does when it is defined as acting. The state is only one instrumentality of sex inequality. To fail to see this is pure gender bias. Often this bias flies under the flag of privacy, so that those areas that are defined as inappropriate for state involvement, where the discourse of human rights is made irrelevant, are those "areas in which the majority of the world's women live out their days."[18] Moreover, the fact that there is no single state or organized group expressly dedicated to this pursuit does not mean that all states are not more or less dedicated to it on an operative level or that it is not a deep structure of social, political, and legal organization. Why human rights, including the international law against torture, should be limited by it is the question.

Second, the state actually is typically deeply and actively complicit in the abuses mentioned, collaborating in and condoning them. Linda "Lovelace" describes her escape from Mr. Traynor: "I called the Beverly Hills police department and told them my husband was looking for me with an M 16. They told me they couldn't be involved with domestic affairs. When I told them his weapons were illegal, they told me to call back when he was in the room."[19] She testified before a grand jury in an obscenity case involving one of the films made of her. The grand jury looked at the films and asked her how she could have ever done that. She said because a gun was at her head. It did nothing.[20] As Linda Marchiano, she later tried to have an ordinance passed that would have made it possible for her to bring a civil action against the pornographers for damages for everything they did to her and to remove the pornography of her from distribution.[21] This ordinance, a sex equality law, was invalidated by the United States courts as a violation of freedom of expression, even though the court of appeals that invalidated it recognized all of the harms pornography did to women and agreed that it actually did those harms. This court held that pornography must be protected as speech in spite of its harm to sex equality—indeed, *because* of these harms, inasmuch as the value of the speech for purposes of protection was measured by the harm it did to women and to their equality.[22] When this result was summarily affirmed by the U.S. Supreme Court, the U.S. government legalized an express and admitted human rights violation on the view that the harm that pornography causes is more important than the people it hurts.[23] This is certainly state ratification of her abuse. It also raises the question, if someone took pictures of what happens in prison cells in Turkey, would they be sold as protected expression and sexual entertainment on the open market, with the state seen as uninvolved? The pornography of Linda continues to proliferate worldwide.

Jayne Stamen wrote her account from the Nassau County Correctional Facility in New York, where she was imprisoned. She was convicted of manslaughter in Jerry's killing by three men she supposedly solicited. Evidence of "battered women's syndrome" was excluded from her trial, to the reported accompaniment of judicial remarks such as "I'm not going to give any woman in Nassau County a license to kill her husband" and "Jerry Stamen is not on trial here but Jayne Stamen is."[24] Prosecution and jailing are state acts. Can you imagine a murder prosecution by a state against a torture victim who killed a torturer while escaping? If you can, can you imagine Amnesty International ignoring it?[25]

In the *Burnham* case, the conviction for marital rape that the wife won at trial was overturned on appeal because of the failure of the judge below *sua sponte* to instruct the jury that the husband might have believed that Ms. Burnham *consented.*[26] There was no standard beyond which it was regarded as obvious that a human being was violated hence true consent was inconceivable. No recognition that people break under torture. No realization that anyone will say anything to a torturer to try to make it stop. When women break under torture, we are said to have consented, or the torturer could have thought we did. Pictures of our "confessions" in the form of pornography follow us around for the rest of our lives. Few say, that isn't who she really is, everybody breaks under torture. Many do say, he could have believed it; besides, some women like it.

This is the *law* of pornography, the *law* of battered women's self-defense, the *law* of rape. Why isn't this state involvement? Formally, its configuration is very close to the recent case Velásquez-Rodríguez v. Honduras,[27] in which a man was violently detained, tortured, and accused of political crimes by a group that was allegedly official but was actually a more or less unofficial but officially-winked-at death squad. He has never been found. What was done to him was legally imputed to Honduras as a state under international law mostly because the abuse was systematically tolerated by the government. The abuse of the women described was not official in the narrow sense at the time it happened, but its cover-up, legitimization, and legalization after the fact were openly so. The lack of effective remedy was entirely official. The abuse was done, at the very least, with official impunity and legalized disregard. The abuse is systematic and known, the disregard is official and organized, and the effective governmental tolerance is a matter of law and policy.

Legally, the pattern is one of national and international guarantees of sex equality coexisting with massive rates of rape and battering and traffic in women through pornography effectively condoned by law. Some progressive international human rights bodies are beginning to inquire into some dimensions of these issues under equality rubrics—none into pornography, some into rape and battering.[28] Rape is now more likely to look like a potential human rights violation when it happens in official custody.[29] A woman's human rights are more likely to be deemed violated when the state can be seen as an instrumentality of the rape. Yet the regular laws and their regular everyday administration are not seen as official state involvement in legalized sex inequality.[30] The fact that rape happens is regarded by some far-thinking groups and agencies as a violation of a *norm* of sex equality. But the fact that the *law* of rape protects rapists and is written from their point of view to guarantee impunity for most rapes is officially regarded as a violation of the *law* of sex equality, national or international, by virtually nobody.

High on my list of state atrocities of this sort is rape law's defense of mistaken belief in consent. This permits the accused to be exonerated if he thinks the woman consented, no matter how much force he used. This is the law in Canada, New Zealand, and the United Kingdom, as well as some parts of the United States, including California, where the *Burnham* case was adjudicated. Another example is abortion's unconstitutionality, as in Ireland. A further example is the affirmative protection of pornography in the United States, including under the case in which Linda "Lovelace" participated.[31] Of course, the United States, an international outlaw of major proportions, is not bound by most of the relevant international agreements, not having ratified them. But other countries where the pornography of her, and others like her, is trafficked are. I would also include in this list of state atrocities the decriminalization of pornography, first in Denmark, then in Sweden. Those were official state acts, however beside the point of the harm to women their prior pornography laws were. No pornography laws at all is open season on women with official blessing. So is the across-the-board legalization of all participants in prostitution.

Why are there no human rights standards for tortures of women as a sex? Why are these atrocities not seen as sex equality violations? The problem can be explained in part in terms of the received notion of equality, which has served as a fairly subtle cross-cultural template for the legal face of misogyny. The traditional concept is the Aristotelian one of treating likes alike and unlikes unalike—mostly likes alike. In practice, this means that to be an equal, you must be the same as whoever sets the dominant standard. The unlikes unalike part has always been an uncomfortable part of equality law, really an internal exception to it, so that affirmative action, for example, is regarded as theoretically disreputable and logically problematic, even contradictory. The Aristotelian approach to equality, which dominates worldwide, never confronts several problems that the condition of women exposes. One is, why don't men, particularly white upper-class men, have to be the same as anyone in order to get equal treatment? Another is, men are as different from women as women are from men: equally different. Why aren't they punished for their differences like women are? Another is, why is equality as well satisfied by equalizing down as up? In other words, if equality is treating likes alike and unlikes unlike, if you get somebody down in the hole that the unlikes are in, in theory that is just as equal as elevating the denigrated to the level of the dominant standard set by the privileged.

The upshot of this approach is what is called in American law the "similarly situated" test, a concept that is used in one form or another around the world wherever law requires equality.[32] As applied to women, it means if men don't need it, women don't get it. Men as such do not need effective laws against rape, battering, prostitution, and pornography (although some of them do), so not having such laws for women is not an inequality; it is just a difference. Thus are these abuses rendered part of the sex difference, the permitted treating of unalikes unalike. Because there are relatively few similarly raped, battered, or prostituted men around to compare with (or they are comparatively invisible and gendered female), such abuses to women are not subjected to equality law at all. Where the lack of similarity of women's condition to men is extreme because of sex inequality, the result is that the law of sex equality does not properly apply.

Sex inequality, in this view, is not simply a distinction to be made properly or improperly, as in the Aristotelian approach. It is fundamentally a hierarchy, here initially a two-tiered hierarchy. Inequality produces systematic subordination, as in the situations of the women discussed.[33] The Canadian Supreme Court in its *Andrews* decision and cases following has come closer than any other court in the world to beginning to recognize this fundamental nature of inequality, leading the world on the subject.[34] To be consistent with equality guarantees in this approach is to move to end sex inequality. Wherever the law reinforces gender hierarchy, it violates legal equality guarantees, in national constitutions and in international covenants as well.

Understanding inequality as hierarchy makes the torture of women because of sex an obvious human rights issue, obscure only because of its pervasiveness. In this light, laws that prohibit what women need for equality, such as restrictions on abortion, and unenforced laws, such as the law against battering, which can make violence women's only survival option, need to be rethought. They violate human rights. Laws that don't fit the violation, such as the law of self-defense, rape, and obscenity in most places, violate human rights. All are affirmative state acts or positive omissions that discriminate on the basis of sex and deny relief for sex equality violations. The lack of laws against the harms women experience in society because we are women, such as most of the harms of pornography, also violates human rights. Women are human there, too.

If, when women are tortured because we are women, the law recognized that a human being had her human rights violated, the term "rights" would begin to have something of the content to which we might aspire, and the term "woman" would, in Richard Rorty's phrase, begin to become "a name for a way of being human."[35]

2

Human Rights and Global Violence
Against Women

You know those bones that archaeologists dig up from ancient civiliza-
tions? Did you ever wonder about women the kinds of questions that can
be asked of bones: How old was she when she had her first period? Did
she get that old? Did she eat last? Do her ligament attachments show she
dug and lifted too much for her frame? Did she bear a child? Was she
still a child then? Were women's skulls, backs, and legs cracked and
broken by blows when they were still alive? Bones leave the kind of trace
that softer tissues—vaginas, mouths, anuses—do not. We will never know
if these women were ripped open or cut into. Her brain leaves no trace
either and often no record of its contents. We will never know if her mind
was fractured, her self splintered, her spirit shattered. What we have left
of her is silent here. We will never hear the words she spoke. No ancient
tablet will likely tell us what she said or whether she learned to write.

What I want to know the most about women of the past is: How did
she die? Did she burn accidentally from volcanic ash or on purpose from
lit kerosene? Did she make light like Buddhist monks or go into darkness
like most of us? Did she die bleeding in childbirth and from other wounds
considered domestic? Was she one of the pampered few we hear so much
about, bathed in milk and paraded about—meaning, I sometimes think,
used by only one man at a time, her clitoris sliced out long since, perhaps
dying quietly of some "woman's disease" we like to think today is obsolete?
Did she die trying to come between men in their bonding conflicts and
get run through like the Sabine women in some man's immortal painting?
Did she die for a point—but whose point?—like the women at Masada?[1]
Was she exposed at birth because she was not a boy and the selective
technology for aborting her and only her had not yet been developed?

This is from a transcript of a talk that was presented to the conference "Global Strategies for
Achieving Fairness in the Courts: Domestic Violence," United Nations, Geneva, Switzerland,
February 5, 1992.

Was she a human sacrifice in a religion that has in our time gone secular or underground? Was she essentially fucked to death, her insides torn out, the rest of her disposed of when these parts were not useful in this way anymore? Did she die by her own hand, dignified and powerful, yet the greatest capitulation in a world that wants women dead?

Most of the time, it is hardly worth asking whether the way she died, including when violent, was effectively permitted. Now a truly other-worldly question: Her government, did it know she existed, then ceased to exist? Was her existence and passing ever even counted? Did she register enough to become a statistic? For the women who are around us now, beginning slowly in 1970, gaining momentum after 1980, answers to questions like these began to be known. What has been learned since as a result about violence against women globally changes everything—or should—about how women's lives and deaths are understood. Once such facts can be seen to be part of a system, the way human rights are understood, particularly the meaning of equality, also changes, or should.

By violence against women, I mean aggression against and exploitation of women because we are women, systemically and systematically. Systemic, meaning socially patterned, including sexual harassment, rape, battering of women by intimates, sexual abuse of children, and woman-killing in the context of poverty, imperialism, colonialism, and racism. Systematic, meaning intentionally organized, including prostitution, pornography, sex tours, ritual torture, and official custodial torture in which women are exploited and violated for sex, politics, and profit in a context of, and in intricate collaboration with, poverty, imperialism, colonialism, and racism.

Research on these realities around the world presents a picture of aggression that is physical, verbal, and emotional; acts that are unconscious and reckless as well as intentional, threatened as well as delivered. This system is society-wide, private as well as public, directed against children as well as adults. Its official impunity is granted by omission as well as commission, by what it fails to do as well as by what it does. When the social systematization and legal institutionalization of this abuse becomes visible, connections emerge between marriage and the family, and prostitution and sexual harassment. Both require sexual delivery for material survival. The man—husband, employer, pimp, john—is in the social position to exploit, dominate, and use. In such systems, what is called violence when it is noticed as such is endemic, not exceptional, as well as epidemic and pervasive. In societies characterized by such arrangements, and most are, women are objects for sexual use, owned as property for possession and exchange, to be violated and abused at will.

Worldwide research on violence against women documents an over-

whelming amount of it, always underestimated and considered to be un-
dercounted. Overwhelmingly, men do it to women. It takes culturally specific forms but is seemingly never not there. Government does next to
nothing effective about it anywhere. Violence against women tends not to
be organized into discrete campaigns, like the Middle Passage or the Holocaust. With variations, it has been a relative cultural constant. It may be
slowly globally escalating, but even the past or present known amounts
that exist are enough for an emergency.

Cross-cultural studies of violence against women in intimate settings,
drawn mostly but not exclusively from the West, present illuminating data
on wife abuse. Cross-cultural studies show that rates of husband-to-wife
violence are about equal in the United States, Japan, and India.[2] One study
of India finds that "[d]omestic hooliganism and violence against married
women . . . occur all over the world on a significant and disturbing scale."[3]
The study concludes that in male dominant societies (most are), aggression
by husbands against wives is socially effectively allowed. A study of Papua
New Guinea finds up to 67 percent of women battered by male intimates.[4]
In Kuwait, a study finds the same for 51 of 153 women surveyed.[5] In Kenya
and Thailand, studies of newspapers report significant amounts of domestic
violence against women.[6] In Nigeria and Uganda, small informal studies
confirm the same.[7] One study of various societies in East and Central
Africa shows that "[t]he wife is the most often victimized and most often
killed person within the immediate domestic group."[8] A study of Scotland
concludes that "it is in the marital setting that women are most likely to
be involved in violence, and usually as victims."[9] In Canada, from 1961 to
1974, 60 percent of women homicide victims were killed in their families,
most often by their husbands.[10] In the United States, official estimates are
that one-fourth to one-third of women are battered in their homes, many
seriously.[11] It is possible that the U.S. rates are not the highest in the
world—a truly horrible thought.[12]

A 1989 UN report summarizes these findings as follows: "The risk of
violence and violation within the household is one thing women, irrespective of their social position, creed, colour or culture, share in common."[13]
It might have added that social hierarchical factors such as social position,
race, and culture can increase women's vulnerability to this risk of abuse.
The same study also stated, "[V]iolence is part of the dynamics of many
family situations. In developing and developed societies, industrial and not,
women are being murdered, assaulted, sexually abused, threatened, and
humiliated within their own homes by men to whom they have committed
themselves. This does not seem to be considered unusual, or uncommon

behavior."[14] The report continues to observe, with regard to battery in particular, that "it has gone largely unpunished, unremarked and has even been tacitly, if not explicitly, condoned."[15] Although there is little controversy on the existence of this problem anywhere, it seems that most places need to do their own study to convince them that yes, it happens here too.[16]

Explaining battering is more controversial than documenting its existence. In the literature, battery of women is attributed to, among other things, alcohol, drugs, stress, underdevelopment, mental illness, and a cycle of violence. These explanations fail to explain why not all men who are so afflicted batter, and why some of those men who are not so afflicted— those developed, sober, sane men—do. Perhaps this is where stress comes in, but it would have to be the stress of privilege. Nothing explains, or attempts to explain, why women—who are poorer than men, lack development resources too, are more stressed, have been brutalized for generations, sometimes drink and take drugs to deal with it, and are often driven crazy by it—do not batter men more.

Seeing violence against women as a form of the social inequality of the sexes is the analysis that has come out of the shelters where the beaten women go. It is the analysis and explanation the grassroots women's movement worldwide has produced, increasingly explored empirically in work like that of the Dobashes.[17] The grassroots women's movement is also responsible for governmental attention to the problem. Before the women's movement documented its existence, governments did not deign to notice it, far less keep track of it.[18] Moreover, even scholarship that notices that inequality between women and men explains violence against women tends not to discuss what that inequality of the sexes is itself about. If sex inequality explains violence against women, what, in turn, explains sex inequality? What is the violence that is part of gender inequality about? In particular, why does sex inequality, which is society-wide, so markedly produce battering of women in intimate contexts?

Consider that battering of women may be about sex in the combined sexual and gender senses: the power of men getting what they want and feel socially entitled to; the thrill of dominance that is both literal and ejaculatory; the desire for domination that is codified as masculine identity and experienced as affirmation and pleasure; violence as an act of power over another that is sexual dominance's ultimate turn-on and final expression. This might make some sense of the way battering is romanticized, eroticized, exonerated, and encouraged, hence effectively permitted, in many of our cultures. It makes sense of the embedding in law of roles of masculinity and femininity, parallel to the dynamics of battering's dominance and submission, action and passivity. It makes sense of the rhythms and cycles of battering,[19] which track those of sadomasochism. It makes sense of the tacit and effective legal acceptability of battering, including murder, under rubrics of crimes of honor and passion,[20] configured as expressions of the male role and the intensity of heterosexual love and the honor of the family.

Seeing sex as an eroticization of hatred is problematic for many people, but I think that misogyny is the name of the system we are confronting here, and part of the difficulty of explaining that system, so persistent and tenacious, lies with leaving sex out. In this connection, note that the UN definition of domestic violence includes battering, rape, incest, and emotional abuse,[21] yet most of the data collected elsewhere under the rubric of domestic violence do not include its sexual forms at all, even rape. Predictably, the more women are sexualized in a society, the higher the actual (not reported) rate of battering would be. This would make sense of the escalation in battering that women report from developing countries with the influx of pornography, which sexualizes inequality on a mass scale, although less public means of sexualizing women can also be effective.

Hopefully, women of the future will know more about us than our ossified remains can tell. But now that we have a better idea of what is happening to the bones of the women around us, what to do? When violence against women becomes a perspective, it changes what you see, or should: the family that breeds it, the customs that justify it, the cultural specificity that hides it, the religion that excuses or sanctifies it, the wars that make its organized quality official, the legal notions like torture that exclude it, the institutions of law enforcement that essentially legalize it. Human rights have ignored it almost completely.

Existing legal approaches to battering revolve around whether the criminal law-and-order approach or the mediation-conciliation therapy-and-education approach is better. Neither appears to really work. The criminal solution does not work in part because the state is not on side. The mediation-conciliation approach sometimes reduces recidivism but does not seem to have made much of a dent in the incidence rates. Batterers keep on being produced. Since solutions should fit problems, if battering is a social problem of sex inequality, its legal solution should lie through sex equality law. Although you wouldn't know it, equality law exists in some form nearly everywhere, but nowhere does it seem to mean that government must give women freedom from male dominance, that is, end sex inequality in all its forms, including gender-based violent ones. Instead, criminal laws treat violence against women unequally, with no constitutional controls, while civil legislation gives individuals actions for sex discrimination in many areas of social life—except when they are hurt through male violence.

Instead of empowering the state, as criminal law does, law could put more power in the hands of women both to confront the state, where necessary, including through international and national forums, and to directly confront men in society who harm them. The recognition that women are violated, a form of unequal treatment, because we are women needs legal teeth. The connections need to be made between the structure of marriage, sexual harassment, and prostitution, hence between rape, battering, and sexual humiliation and abuse at home, in brothels, at work, on the streets, and in pornography. At the same time, connect women's poverty with men's wealth, exposing the link between the presence of a white industrialized military and women and children becoming a cash crop in countries of color, showing prostitution, as a 1985 UN report revealed, to be a movement of poor women toward rich men and sex tourism to be a movement of rich men toward poor women.[22] We can start anywhere because all these issues are interconnected. But we need to start, institutionalizing and internationalizing sex equality rights in women's hands to de-institutionalize, and finally to end, the governmental pattern, national and international, of collaboration in the violent sexualized subordination of women.

3

Theory Is Not a Luxury

Audre Lorde showed that poetry is not a luxury of the privileged but a necessity for the disempowered.[1] Her militant reclamation of what had been considered an elite male project inspired these remarks.

"Theory" is often used as a club to invalidate criticism of established ways of looking at things. It is said that the critics lack theoretical rigor, or, if they have a theory, they have just a theory. As Moira McConnell put it, "the designation 'theory' [is] a political statement as to the existence of some non-theory position"; the "non-theory position" is the one "imagined by the men who have dominated the world's power structures."[2] We have a theory; they have reality. While sympathetic with the resulting impulse to jettison theory, I hope to persuade you not to give it to men. That would mean accepting reality as the most powerful men see and define it, which ultimately means accepting reality as they make and live it. Women can no more afford this in the international legal order than anywhere else. New theories help make new realities. Interpreted in this light, Moira McConnell's statement can be claimed *as* theory.

Theory appropriates reality in a certain way—its way is method—to make the world accessible to understanding and change. It is a way of getting a grip on things. To help move toward new theory, I identify common themes in the papers delivered on this panel and then consider, in light of them, the international legal structure's response to a current example of women's unequal treatment.

Common themes easily emerge from these papers.[3] The hand of men as such is seen moving behind the international legal order, with conse-

This talk was given on a panel for the Women in International Law Interest Group at the American Society of International Law's 87th Annual Meeting, April 3, 1993, in Washington, D.C. It was first published in *Reconceiving Reality: Women in International Law* 83 (Studies in Transnational Legal Policy No. 25, *American Journal of International Law*)(Dorinda G. Dallmeyer, ed., 1993).

quences for the status and treatment of women as such. Women's position under international law is identified as much like women's position in domestic legal regimes: marginalized, excluded, subordinated. It is quite a trick to keep a people, particularly when they are the majority, on the edge, out, and down at the same time, but men have figured out how to do it to women. Each paper treats this question of location by seeking to situate women in the international legal order. Barbara Stark sees women at the center; Moira McConnell shows women marginalized. The papers also understand the need to change more than perception to change women's position in this order. Another discernible theme, explicit in some, subtext in others, is the "there is no common theme" theme: the diversity of women's experience leading to the disruption of categories, the complexity and instability of concepts and world. Here, women's situation defies ordered generalization, reduction to rule, and codification. This notion can resist imposed forms of thinking and being, but it can also deny reality's rigidities and imposed patterns. It is almost as if there is no such thing as the status and treatment of women. You will find me in tension with this latter view. A final theme, both obvious and incapable of being repeated too often, is the need for change. This animates Hilary Charlesworth's call to "change the heartland,"[4] Barbara Stark's urging of a "bottom-up" transformation and distancing from women's subordination,[5] and Moira McConnell's "break[ing] [of] the molds."[6]

Hilary Charlesworth provides a masterful summary of emerging feminist literature on international law (indeed, she co-wrote some of the best of it). This literature recognizes the state as patriarchal, militarized, and hierarchical on the basis of sex. She argues that, more fundamentally, it is sovereign. The example I will discuss with you takes up this analysis, illustrating how sovereignty as a definition of the state as such, within an international order defined as an order of sovereign states, has worked to deny the human rights of women. States bond with each other internationally to permit men to violate women across state borders, just as men bond with each other for this end within states.[7] In Barbara Stark's terms, this example chooses process over abstract theory. In my terms, it makes theory out of practice. This analysis aspires to build a piece of theory of the kind we need rather than to talk about how theory is or should be done.

In October 1992, a piece of reality arrived over my fax machine. It eventually resulted in my being retained pro bono by what are now five women's groups, three in Croatia and two in Bosnia-Herzegovina, to seek international legal justice for mass sexual atrocities. It stated:

Serbian forces have exterminated over 200,000 Croatians and Muslims thus far in an operation they've coined "ethnic cleansing." In this genocide, in Bosnia-Herzegovina alone, over 30,000 Muslim and Croatian girls and women are pregnant from mass rape. Of the hundred Serbian-run concentration camps, about twenty are solely rape/death camps for Muslim and Croatian women and children. There are news reports and pictures here of Serbian tanks plastered with pornography and reports that those who catch the eye of the men looking at the pornography are killed. Some massacres in villages as well as rapes and executions in camps are being videotaped as they're happening. One Croatian woman described being tortured by electric shocks and gang-raped in a camp by Serbian men dressed in Croatian uniforms who filmed the rapes and forced her to "confess" on film that Croatians raped her. In the streets of Zagreb, UN troops often ask local women how much they cost. There are reports of refugee women being forced to sexually service the UN troops to receive aid. Tomorrow I talk to two survivors of mass rape— thirty men per day for over three months. We've heard the UN passed a resolution to collect evidence as the first step for a war crimes trial, but it is said here that there is no precedent for trying sexual atrocities.

The events are familiar, illegal or not, in every country in the world every day, as well as in war: rape, forced motherhood, prostitution, pornography, sexual murder, all on the basis of sex and ethnicity combined. The international legal order is not predicated on the need to address them, but many are formally prohibited under international law, all of them in armed conflicts. Whether they are formally prohibited or not, these practices are nonetheless widely permitted as the liberties of their perpetrators, excess of passion, spoils of victory, or by-products of war. Virtually nothing is done about them, within or among nations. They tend to be legally and socially rationalized, officially winked at, or in some instances formally condoned. Most of all, they are overlooked.

The particular conflict described in the fax exemplifies how existing human rights institutions, as criticized by these papers, can work to cover up and confuse who is doing what to whom and thus effectively condone atrocities. The parties to this conflict and the atrocities in it are covered by international humanitarian law and the laws of war.[8] Yet nothing so far has been invoked to stop the abuses or to hold the perpetrators accountable. The fact of Serbian aggression is beyond question, just as the fact of male aggression against women, both in this war and every day, is beyond question. "Ethnic cleansing" is a Serbian policy of extermination of non-Serbs with the goal of creating a "Greater Serbia." It is a euphemism for genocide. Yet this aggression has repeatedly been construed as bilateral, as a civil war or an ethnic conflict, to the accompaniment of much international wonderment that people cannot get along and pious clucking at ancient hatreds and the bad behavior of "all sides." It is reminiscent of blaming women for getting ourselves raped by men we know and then chastising us for not liking them very well afterwards.

These rapes are not grasped as a strategy in genocide or as a practice of misogyny, far less as what they are, which is both at once. What is happening to Bosnian Muslim and Croatian women at the hands of Serbian forces in this genocide is continuous both with an ethnic war of aggression in the region and the gendered war of aggression of everyday life. This war is to rape every day what the Holocaust was to anti-Semitism every day: without the everyday, the conflagration could not exist, but do not mistake one for the other.[9]

In this onslaught, Muslim and Croatian women and girls are raped, then murdered; sometimes their corpses are raped as well. When this is noticed, it is called *either* genocide *or* rape, rather than rape as a practice of genocide directed specifically against certain women. It is seen as either part of a campaign of Serbia against non-Serbia, or a war by combatants against civilians, or an attack by men against women. Sometimes it is seen as just another instance of aggression by all men against all women all the time, especially in all wars, rather than what it actually is, which is rape by some men against certain women in this genocide, which is being carried on in part through war.

The point of much of the theorizing that has gone on around this conflict appears to be to obscure by any means available exactly who is doing what to whom and why and to define the problem so that no one can or need do anything about it. When the women survive, the rapes tend to be regarded as an inevitability of armed conflict—the war of all against all—or as a mere continuation of the hostilities of civil life, of all men against all women. So why intervene, and on what side? Rape does occur in war among and between all sides. Rape is also a daily act by men against women and is always an act of domination by men over women. But the fact that *these* rapes are part of an ethnic war of aggression being misrepresented as a civil war among equal aggressors means that Muslim and Croatian women are facing twice as many rapists with twice as many excuses—two layers of men on top of them rather than one, one layer attempting to exterminate the other layer, with two layers of impunity serving to justify the rapes, the "just war" level and the "just life" level. And nothing is being done about either of them.

Like all rapes, these rapes are particular as well as generic; the particularity does matter. This is ethnic rape by official policy. It is not only by pattern of male pleasure and male power unleashed, not only by intent to defile, torture, humiliate, degrade, and demoralize the other side, and not only in an attempt to gain advantage and ground over other men. What this is—this invokes the international legal context specifically—is rape under orders. It is not rape out of control. It is rape under control. It is also rape unto death, rape as massacre, rape to kill and to make victims wish they were dead. It is rape as an instrument of forced exile, to make you leave your home and never want to come back. It is also rape to be seen and heard by others: rape as spectacle. It is the rape of misogyny liberated by xenophobia and unleashed by official command. It is rape to shatter a people, to drive a wedge through a community to destroy it. It is rape as genocide.

If this were racial rape, in the American sense, it would be rape as pollution. The children would be regarded as "dirty" and "contaminated," that is, their mothers' babies, Black babies, as in the American South under slavery. But in this particular ethnic rape, which has no racial markers, the children are regarded as magically clean and purified, as their fathers' babies, Serbian babies—or, as clean as anyone with a woman's blood on them and in them can be. The Serbian idea seems to be to create a fifth column within Croatian and Muslim society, children—who the Serbian forces seem to imagine will all be sons—who will rise up and join their fathers. Much of this Serbian ideology and practice simply takes a page from the Nazi book. But in the Serbian abuse of women's reproductive capacity, an ultimate racialization of society has been achieved: the view that culture is genetic. The spectacle of the UN troops violating the people they are there to protect adds a touch of perversity. And the openness of the use of pornography, the conscious making of pornography of the atrocities, and its use as Serbian war propaganda make this perhaps the first truly modern war.

Now return to Hilary Charlesworth's discussion of why the international human rights of women are more fragile than other rights. International instruments dealing with women, she notes, have weaker implementation obligations and procedures. The institutions designed to monitor them are under-resourced, their roles often circumscribed compared with other human rights bodies. The widespread practice of making reservations to fundamental provisions is tolerated, as is the failure of states to fulfill their obligations under the instruments.

Searching for international justice for Bosnian and Croatian women, I have learned that these observations are accurate. To say that the international system is gendered is no exaggeration, and its gendered dynamics do revolve around state sovereignty. These women are not a state; they do not control a state; no state represented them until Bosnia sued Serbia for genocide in the International Court of Justice.[10] With a few exceptions (exceptions that either do not apply here or have no teeth), human rights instruments empower states to act against states, not individuals or groups to act on their own behalf, whether against states or individuals. Given that mainly only state violations of human rights are recognized as violations, this is particularly odd—especially after 1945, when it might have been learned that states can violate the human rights of those who are not states and who have no state to act for them. Under international law, states remain the dominant unit. They are imagined the primary violators of human rights as well as being the ones empowered to redress those violations. How convenient.

Not only does this statist structure of international human rights leave out men's so-called private acts against women, it also means that no state has an incentive to break ranks with states as such by moving to set a human rights standard for women's status and treatment that no state yet meets within itself or (seems to) want to be held to internationally. Why, otherwise, has no state—those with the power to do something about these atrocities—stepped up to act on behalf of these women under the human rights instruments available only to states? Perhaps because it is a standard by which its own behavior has failed, since no state effectively guarantees women's human rights within its borders. So, internationally, men's states protect each other from women's rights the way men protect each other from women's rights within states. Sovereignty is the name of the principle in the name of which men respect this. At least this is one explanation, consistent with the papers and this experience, for the failure of the international system in this instance so far. Which state is in a position to challenge another on the human rights of women? Which state will?

As to men's so-called private acts against women, wartime is something of a legal exception. More of what men do to women is formally covered in war than in peace. Atrocities by soldiers against civilians, so long as they are in the scope of armed conflict, are always seen as essentially state acts. But men do in war what they do in peace. When it comes to women as civilian casualties, the complacency that surrounds peacetime extends to war, however the laws read. Barbara Stark showed that certain rights get treated the way women get treated. The more a conflict can be framed as within a state, as a civil war, as social, as domestic, the less human rights are recognized to be violated. The closer a fight comes to home, the more feminized the rights and the victims (no matter their sex) become, and the less likely international human rights will be found to be violated, no matter what was done.

How "indeterminate" is this reality? It is not characterized by "ephemerality," "discontinuity," or "fragmentation."[11] How much "radical rethinking"[12] does the fact of a genocide need? Do we want "chaotic"[13] war crimes trials? The theory developed here has not had the luxury of withholding commitment or refusing to be pinned down, nor can it rest on the margin unless it plans to give up women's lives. Are there some "easy categories"[14] here we need to resist? Here, as usual, women's particularity is not in conflict with our commonalities; the deeper the particulars go, the more commonality we find.

That is to say, some of the disavowal of the project of theorizing the reality of women's lives in these papers is disturbing. Against this disavowal, this analysis is offered in the engaged spirit that otherwise animates the papers: as bottom-up theorizing directed toward a change in the still cold heartland of international law and its institutions, where genocidal rape remains condoned.[15]

4

Are Women Human?

The Universal Declaration of Human Rights defines what a human being is.[1] In 1948, it told the world what a person, as a person, is entitled to. It has been fifty years. Are women human yet?

If women were human, would we be a cash crop shipped from Thailand in containers into New York's brothels?[2] Would we be sexual and reproductive slaves? Would we be bred, worked without pay our whole lives, burned when our dowry money wasn't enough or when men tired of us, starved as widows when our husbands died (if we survived his funeral pyre), sold for sex because we are not valued for anything else? Would we be sold into marriage to priests to atone for our family's sins or to improve our family's earthly prospects? Would we, when allowed to work for pay, be made to work at the most menial jobs and exploited at barely starvation level? Would our genitals be sliced out to "cleanse" us (our body parts are dirt?), to control us, to mark us and define our cultures? Would we be trafficked as things for sexual use and entertainment worldwide in whatever form current technology makes possible?[3] Would we be kept from learning to read and write?[4]

If women were human, would we have so little voice in public deliberations and in government in the countries where we live?[5] Would we be hidden behind veils and imprisoned in houses and stoned and shot for refusing? Would we be beaten nearly to death, and to death, by men with whom we are close? Would we be sexually molested in our families? Would we be raped in genocide to terrorize and eject and destroy our ethnic communities, and raped again in that undeclared war that goes on every day in every country in the world in what is called peacetime?[6] If women were human, would our violation be *enjoyed* by our violators? And,

This analysis was originally published in *Reflections on the Universal Declaration of Human Rights* 171 (Barend van der Heijden and Bahia Tahzib-Lie, eds., 1999).

if we were human, when these things happened, would virtually nothing be done about it?

It takes a lot of imagination—and a determinedly blinkered focus on exceptions at the privileged margins—to see a real woman in the Universal Declaration's majestic guarantees of what "everyone is entitled to." After over half a century, just what part of "everyone" doesn't mean us?

The ringing language in Article 1 encourages us to "act towards one another in a spirit of brotherhood." Must we be men before its spirit includes us? Lest this be seen as too literal, if we were all enjoined to "act towards one another in a spirit of sisterhood," would men know it meant them, too? Article 23 encouragingly provides for just pay to "[e]veryone who works." It goes on to say that this ensures a life of human dignity for "himself and his family." Are women nowhere paid for the work we do in our own families because we are not "everyone," or because what we do there is not "work," or just because we are not "him"? Don't women have families, or is what women have not a family without a "himself"? If the someone who is not paid at all, far less the "just and favorable remuneration" guaranteed, is also the same someone who in real life is often responsible for her family's sustenance, when she is deprived of providing for her family "an existence worthy of human dignity," is she not human? And now that "everyone" has had a right "to take part in the government of his country" since the Universal Declaration was promulgated, why are most governments still run mostly by men? Are women silent in the halls of state because we do not have a human voice?

A document that could provide specifically for the formation of trade unions and "periodic holiday with pay" might have mustered the specificity to mention women sometime, other than through "motherhood," which is more bowed to than provided for. If women were human in this document, would domestic violence, sexual violation from birth to death, including in prostitution and pornography, and systematic sexual objectification and denigration of women and girls simply be left out of the explicit language?

Granted, sex discrimination is prohibited. But how can it have been prohibited for all this time, even aspirationally, and the end of all these conditions still not be concretely imagined as part of what a human being, as human, is entitled to? Why is women's entitlement to an end of these conditions still openly debated based on cultural rights, speech rights, religious rights, sexual freedom, free markets—as if women are social signifiers, pimps' speech, sacred or sexual fetishes, natural resources, chattel, everything but human beings?

The omissions in the Universal Declaration are not merely semantic.

Being a woman is "not yet a name for a way of being human,"[7] not even in this most visionary of human rights documents. If we measure the reality of women's situation in all its variety against the guarantees of the Universal Declaration, not only do women not have the rights it guarantees—most of the world's men don't either—but it is hard to see, in its vision of humanity, a woman's face.

Women need full human status in social reality. For this, the Universal Declaration of Human Rights must see the ways women distinctively are deprived of human rights as a deprivation of humanity. For the glorious dream of the Universal Declaration to come true, for human rights to be universal, both the reality it challenges and the standard it sets need to change.

When will women be human? When?

5

Postmodernism and Human Rights

For an American feminist . . . reading *The Newly Born Woman* is like going to sleep in one world and waking in another—going to sleep in a realm of facts, which one must labor to theorize, and waking in a domain of theory, which one must strive to (f)actualize.

—Sandra M. Gilbert[1]

It has been over a quarter of a century since, according to Mary Joe Frug, "MacKinnon . . . launched feminism into social theory orbit."[2] In the context of the women's movement practice at the time, my thought in taking up method was that women's situation lacked and needed a full-dress theory of its own, and that the experience of women had a distinctive contribution to make to political theory, including on the epistemic level. Back then, my view was that the relation between knowledge and power was the central issue that women's situation and formal theory posed for each other, and that sexuality was where this issue was crucially played out.[3] Almost thirty years later, the discussion launched then is far from finished.

I

Feminism's development as theory is impelled by the realities of women's situation. Women's lives, the women's movement has found, have contours with content. Centrally, women's lives were found to have been lived mainly in silence, of which existing theories were ignorant. Almost totally

These thoughts were originally a talk given in Valencia, Spain, to the seminar on Feminism and Politics for the International University Menendez y Pelayo (UIMP), University of Valencia, on July 4, 1996. They were first published as "Points Against Postmodernism," 75 *Chicago-Kent Law Review* 687 (2000).

silenced has been women's sexual violation by men. Beginning in the early 1970s, direct engagement with this social reality—not reality in the abstract, *this* reality in the broken-down immediate socially lived-out concrete—exposed the regularities and widespread extent and trauma of sexual abuse in childhood, the pervasiveness of rape and other sexual assault, the torture and shame of battering, the routine existence of sexual harassment at work, in school, and on the street, and the endemic abuse constituted by pornography and prostitution. The extent and nature of these practices and their place in sexual politics, hence politics, were uncovered and examined. Once this genealogy and its continuity with sexuality more generally were established, nothing from the state to interest groups to culture to intimate relations looked as it had. One implication was that both knowing and the known had to be remade to contend with the role of male power in constructing them.

This practical confrontation with the specific realities of sexual and physical violation created feminist theory, including so-called high theory, in form and content. That these realities were gendered was not assumed, posited, invented, or imagined. Gender was not created in our minds after reading philosophy books other people wrote; it was not a Truth that we set out to establish to end academic debates or to create a field or niche so we could get jobs. It was what was found there, by women, in women's lives. Piece by bloody piece, in articulating direct experiences, in resisting the disclosed particulars, in trying to make women's status *be* different than it was, a theory of the status of women was forged, and with it a theory of the method that could be adequate to it: *how* we had to know in order to know *this*.

This particular theory, so built, was a theory of sex inequality and more broadly of sexual politics. In and from the experience of woman after woman emerged a systematic, systemic, organized, structured, newly coherent picture of the relations between women and men that discernibly extended from intimacy throughout the social order and the state. Our minds could know it was real because our bodies, collectively, lived through it. It therefore socially existed. Nor did its diversity undermine its reality; it constituted it. We said: this happens. The movement quickly became global as women everywhere identified sex inequality in their own experience and its place in denying them whole lives.[4] This particular cohered reality was not an example of what a new way of thinking about knowing or a new angle of vision produced by way of data; it was a specific reality that, collectively conscious, called for a new way of thinking about knowing.

Everything about this theory was, to repeat, particular. It was not general. It was concrete. It was not abstract. It was specific and grounded. It was not a uniform homogeneous unity. It was a complex whole. The point of the discussion of method in *Toward a Feminist Theory of the State* was to articulate the consequences of this new knowledge and the way it was apprehended for theory—specifically for the kind of philosophy that thought that a thought had to be general and abstract, meaning free of particularity of position or substantive social content, not experienced—in order to be validly theoretical. And to connect this new information on what took place in women's lives, silenced by prior theory, to law: law as a state practice, one that has also claimed its validity in putting generality and abstraction into a particular lived form backed by power and authority. The point was to take women's experience seriously enough—both the how and the what of it—to end the inequality. The process was to get to the bottom of the theoretical constructs that had covered it up and defined its reality as theoretically invalid and empirically nonexistent or at most marginal, and had institutionalized that theory and its products as governing norms in law.

"Women" was not an abstract category. "Women" in feminist theory, in contours and content, was thus, as a theoretical matter, formally largely new. Its content was the substantive experience that women in all their particularities and variations had. Not because the theory corresponded to this reality, but because it *was constituted by it.* This was not a general theory of particulars, it was a theory built of these particulars: a particular theory. It was built on, and accountable to, women's experiences of abuse and violation. Its grounded construction and engaged accountability were not a posture it adopted or a flag it flew. They were what it was made of, what it did. It did not purport to be the one true account of how everything really is. It claimed to be accurate and accountable to the social world that constituted it. It related to the reality it theorized in this new way.

Feminism did call for rethinking everything. For one simple instance, the distinction drawn since the Enlightenment between the universal and the particular was revealed to be false, because what had been called universal was the particular from the point of view of power. For another, the subjective/objective division was revealed to be false, because the objective standpoint—or so I argued in *Toward a Feminist Theory of the State*—was specifically the view from the male position of power. That is, those who occupy what is called the objective standpoint socially, who also engage in the practice from that standpoint called objectification—the practice of making people into things to make them knowable—their standpoint and this practice are an expression of the social position of dominance that is occupied by men. This standpoint is not positionless or point-of-viewless, as it purports to be; it does not simply own accuracy and fairness, as many believe; it embodies and asserts a specific form of power, one that had been invisible to politics and theory but, by feminism, lay exposed as underlying them.

This theory was not an affirmation of the feminine particularity as opposed to the masculine universal. It was not a claim to female subjectivity or a search for it. It saw that these concepts, and the purported divide between them, are products of male power that cannot see themselves or much else. Until exposed, these concepts looked general, empty of content, universally available to all, valid, mere tools, against which all else fell short. Feminism exposed how prior theory was tautologous to its own terms of validation and could hardly be universal because it had left out at least half the universe.

Neither did feminism precisely lay claim to the territory that women had been assigned under this system. More, it was its claim to us that we sought to *disclaim.* We were not looking for a plusher cell or a more dignified stereotype. We were not looking to elaborate the feminine particularity as if it was ours; we had been living inside its walls for centuries. We were not looking to claim the subjectivity or subject position to which we had been relegated any more than we sought to oppress others by gaining access to the power to objectify and dominate that we had revealed as such. All this would have left what we were trying to challenge squarely in place; by comparison with our agenda, it was playing with, or within, blocks. Identity as such was not our issue. Inside, we knew who we were to a considerable extent. Gender identity—the term introduced by Robert Stoller in 1964 to refer to the mental representation of the self as masculine or feminine—situates women's problem in the wrong place.[5] Our priority was gaining access to the reality of our collective experience in order to understand and change it for all of us in our own lifetimes.

My own work provides just one illustration of how this philosophical approach of theory from the ground up has been productive in practice. This theory, applied, produced the claim for sexual harassment as a legal claim for sex discrimination.[6] So now, when a woman is sexually harassed and she speaks of it, that is not simply a woman speaking in a different voice or narrating her subject experience of her situation. She is saying what happened to her. And what happened to her, when it happens, is now authoritatively recognized in law as inequality on the basis of sex, that is, as a violation of women's human rights. The civil remedy under the

Violence Against Women Act used the same logic to recognize that rape and battering can be practices of sex discrimination.[7] Similarly, Andrea Dworkin's and my proposed law that pornography be recognized as a practice of sex discrimination is based on the realities of the experience of women violated through the making and use of pornography. Under it, women's testimony about their abuse through pornography would be recognized as evidence, so that pornography is legally seen to do the injuries that it does in reality.[8] The same approach produced the argument, adopted by the Second Circuit, that when rape is an act of genocide in fact, it is an act of genocide in law. That is, sexually violating women because they are women of a particular ethnic or religious community aims to destroy that community.[9]

Just these few examples of the practice of this theory show a two-pronged transformation taking place. By including what violates women under civil and human rights law, the meaning of "citizen" and "human" begins to have a woman's face. As women's actual conditions are recognized as inhuman, those conditions are being changed by requiring that they meet a standard of citizenship and humanity that previously did not apply because they were women. In other words, women both change the standard as we come under it and change the reality it governs by having it applied to us. This democratic process describes not only the common law when it works but also a cardinal tenet of feminist analysis: women are entitled to access to things as they are and also to change them into something worth our having.

Thus women are transforming the definition of equality not by making ourselves the same as men, entitled to violate and silence, or by reifying women's so-called differences, but by insisting that equal citizenship must encompass what women need to be human, including a right not to be sexually violated and silenced. This was done in the Bosnian case by recognizing ethnic particularity, not by denying it. Adapting the words of the philosopher Richard Rorty, we are making the word "woman" a "name of a way of being human."[10] We are challenging and changing the process of knowing and the practice of power at the same time. In other words, it works.

Feminism made a bold claim in Western philosophy: women can access our own reality because we live it; slightly more broadly, living a subordinated status can give one access to its reality. Not reality with a capital R—this particular social reality. Since women were not playing power games or trying to win academic debates, we did not claim privilege. We simply claimed the reality of women's experience as a ground to stand on and move from, as a basis for conscious political action. As it turned out, once rescued from flagrant invisibility, women's realities could often be documented in other ways, and nearly anyone proved able to understand them with a little sympathetic application. Women turned the realities of powerlessness into a form of power: credibility. And reality supported us. What we said was credible because it was real. Few people claimed that women were not violated in the ways we had found or did not occupy a second-class status in society. Not many openly disputed that what we had uncovered did, in fact, exist. What was said instead was that in society, nothing really exists.

II

During the same twenty-five-year period that this theory and practice have been ongoing, a trend in theory called postmodernism has been working on undoing it. Its main target is, precisely, reality. Postmodernism, I will argue—or more narrowly, the central epistemic tendency in it that I am focusing on—derealizes social reality by ignoring it, by refusing to be accountable to it, and, in a somewhat new move, by openly repudiating any connection with an "it" by claiming "it" is not there.

Postmodernism is a flag flown by a diverse congeries, motley because lack of unity is their credo and they feel no need to be consistent. Part of the problem in coming to grips with postmodernism is that, pretending to be profound while being merely obscure (many are fooled), slathering subjects with words, its self-proclaimed practitioners fairly often don't say much of anything.[11] Another part of the problem is that some commentators credit postmodernism with ideas that serious critical traditions originated and have long practiced. For example: "Balkin has been one of the few legal writers willing to explore postmodern issues such as the social construction of reality, the role of ideology, and the problem of social critique."[12] Jack Balkin does explore these themes, calling that work postmodern, but legal feminists have been exploring them in depth for about thirty years, as have Marxists and some legal realists, beginning long before, to name only some. A further part of the problem is that postmodernism steals from feminism—claiming, for example, that the critique of objectivity is a postmodern insight—and covers its larceny by subsuming feminism as a subprovince of postmodernism.[13]

In any event, the appellation "postmodernism" does cohere a constellation of recent tendencies and sentiments in theory. To trace my particular theme, I analyze three issues that are central to women, politics, and theory to see what postmodernism has made of feminism's methodological break-through just described. These three issues roughly parallel Jane Flax's discussion of postmodernism as revolving around the death of man, the death of metaphysics, and the death of history.[14] I do not criticize all that is called postmodern or defend everything said by its detractors; in particular, the American mutation I focus upon is distinguishable from some European poststructuralists whom the Americans appropriate for a patina of authority. Far from attempting to tar them all with this brush, I invite anyone to disidentify with what I describe and to stop doing it any time.

A. "Women"

Postmodernism's rejection of universals has been described by Lyotard, defining postmodernism, as "incredulity toward metanarratives."[15] In its feminist guise, this theme runs under the criticism of "the grand narratives" of feminist theory,[16] questioning in the name of "differences" whether "women" exist and can be spoken of or died with "man." As Mary Joe Frug articulated this point: "I am in favor of localized disruptions. I am against totalizing theory."[17] Antiessentialism is one facet of this objection: the view that there is no such thing as "women" because there are always other aspects to women's identities and bases other than sex for their oppressions. The defense of multiculturalism is another facet of it: there is no such thing as women in the singular; there are only women in the plural, many different particularized, localized, socially constructed, culturally modified women, hence no "women" in what postmodernists imagine is the feminist sense.

If anyone does "grand narratives," I suppose I do, so I think that I'm entitled to say that I don't know what they're talking about. As to "totality"—a bloated, overfed, but also oddly empty term—what is one against when one is "against totalizing theory"? Why doesn't anyone say what is meant by the term? Why aren't there footnotes to the charge?[18] One imagines that it is a reference to Marx and Freud. It is apparently a synonym for "universal," but, just to begin with, no analysis that is predicated on a gender division can be a universal one in the usual sense.

Feminism has also never, to my knowledge, had what is called a "monocausal" narrative;[19] at least I haven't. We do not say that gender is all there is. We have never said that it explains everything. We have said that gender is big and pervasive, never not there, that it has a shape and regularities and laws of motion, and that it explains a lot—much otherwise missed, unexplained. It is a feature of most everything, pervasively denied. That does not mean that everything reduces to gender, that it is the only regularity or the only explanation, the single cause of everything, or the only thing there. It is also worth repeating that sexual politics, in feminism, is not an overarching preexisting general theory that is appealed to in order to understand or explain, but a constantly provisional analysis in the process of being made and remade by the social realities that pro-duce(d) it.

The postmodern critique of feminism seems to assume that the "women" of feminist theory are all the same, homogeneous, a uniform unit. I do not know where they got this idea either. Not from me. They don't say. This notion that everyone must be the same to have access to the label "women" is not an idea that operates in feminist theory to my knowledge. That uniformity is a standard theoretical property of a category does not mean that it is feminism's concept of women. Women, in feminist theory, are concrete; they are not abstract. They are not sex or gender, they are marked and defined and controlled by it. Gender, in feminist analysis, is also ob-served to be powerfully binary in society, but not exclusively so; power divisions are observed to exist within sex-defined groups as well as between them, so also in the feminist theory of gender.

Feminism in one sense started the critique of universality as currently practiced by showing how women are left out of the human episteme. We took the critique of society as socially constructed to a new depth by showing how even something often thought by others to be biological— sexuality—is social and draws power lines. Feminism does not "assume,"[20] but rather builds, its "women" from women who socially exist. When feminism makes its "women" from the ground up, out of particularities, from practice, rather than from the top down, out of abstractions and prior theory, the so-called essentialism problem cannot occur.[21] The claim that feminism is essentialist also serves to obscure the formative role of women of color and lesbians, among others, in every part of the feminist theory discussed. They as much as any, and more than most, created the women's movement's, and feminism's, "women."

Postmodernism natters on about how feminism privileges gender,[22] but seldom says what that means either. If to privilege gender means that feminism arranges gender at the top of some hierarchy of oppressions, the allegation is false, at least as to me. I don't do hierarchy. If these critics mean that feminists think gender matters a lot, and often read situations in terms of dynamics of gender hierarchy, and refuse to shut up about gender as a form of domination, they're right. They should say why, in each instance, we are wrong to do so, why its place in our analysis is unearned. Male supremacy "privileges" gender; we criticize it.

A related argument is that feminism "essentializes" gender. One concept of antiessentialism (there are many) is defined by Tracy Higgins as "the rejection . . . of the idea that particular characteristics can be identified with women over time and across cultures."[23] It seems to me that this presents an empirical rather than a conceptual question. Do characteristics exist that can be identified with—meaning found in the reality of—the status of women across time and place, including by those women themselves? Women report the existence of such regularities: sex inequality, for one. It is either there or it is not. One does not oppose the observation that it is there in the name of an idea that rejects thinking that it is there. Once it has been found to exist, to say it isn't there, show it isn't there—show, for example, that female genital mutilation is a collective delusion or harmless or a practice of equality. Women worldwide say that society after society contains practices that treat them unequally to men. To contest this, find a society where they are equal, where unequal practices do not exist. To contest the documentation of common characteristics of women's status across time and place, show they are not there. Of course, social reality has to exist to pursue this. What the postmodernists seem to be saying here is that they don't like the idea that women are unequal everywhere. Well, we don't like it either.

Much of what has animated the critique of the so-called essentialism of feminist theory is the criticism that feminism is racist—that the image of "the feminine" in feminism, according to this critique, has a white woman's face. This criticism applies to the racism of the academy that calls itself feminist but refuses to credential women of color as theorists or appropriates their work as part of its pluralism while itself doing nothing any differently than it did before. It also applies to the racism of the media that presents itself as sympathetic but does not, for example, show how women of color formed feminism since its beginning and continue to do so today. It best criticizes the feminist face of liberal elitism that passes for feminism in some quarters, including in the women's movement. But unlike "essentialism," which sounds like you're talking theory, racism is an ugly, academically nonpresentable, and risky political word that pisses off white people. So instead of saying that something or someone is racist, which they often are, we get the obscure philosophical swear word "essentialist," or we hear that feminists do not take "difference" into account.[24]

Nice neutral word, difference, and it has all that French credibility. Never mind that differences can simply be fragmented universals. It doesn't improve one's ability to analyze hierarchy as socially constructed to add more pieces called differences if the differences are seen as biologically determined to begin with. You can have a biological theory of race just like you can have a biological theory of gender, and you've gotten equally nowhere in terms of dismantling social hierarchy. Put another way, if women don't exist, because there are only particular women, maybe Black people don't exist either, because they are divided by sex. Probably lesbians can't exist either, because they are divided by race and class; if women don't exist, woman-identified women surely don't exist, except in their heads. We are reduced to individuals, which, of all coincidences, is where liberalism places us. With its affirmation of women's commonalities in all their diversity, it is feminism that rejects the view that "woman" is a presocial, that is, biologically determined, category and the notion that all women are the same. Feminism and essentialism cannot occupy the same space.

The postmodern attack on universality also proves a bit too much. Inconveniently, the fact of death *is* a universal—approaching 100 percent. Whatever it means, however it is related to culturally and spiritually, whatever happens after it, it happens. Much to the embarrassment of the antiessentialists, who prefer flights of fancy to gritty realities, life and death is even basically a binary distinction—and not a very nuanced one either, especially from the dead side of the line, at least when seen from the standpoint of the living, that is, as far as we know. And it is even biological at some point. So the idea that there is nothing essential, in the sense that there are no human universals, is dogma. Ask most anyone who is going to be shot at dawn.

Multiculturalism is a politically normative version of the anthropological notion of cultural relativism premised on the view "that all cultures are equally valid."[25] The postmodern version of the multiculturalist critique assumes that the speaker takes their own culture and its values to be valid and criticizes other cultures from the standpoint of their own. Feminism, however, questions the cultural validity of subordinating women to men anywhere. Feminism does not assume that "other" cultures[26] are to be measured against the validity of their own, because feminism does not assume that anyone's culture, including their own, is valid. How could we? Defenses of local differences, as they are called,[27] are often simply a defense of male power in its local guise. Male power virtually always appears in local guises; one might hazard that there *are nothing but* local guises for male power. The fact that they are local does not improve them.

Two criminal cases in which a multicultural so-called cultural defense was employed show this multiculturalism's dynamic, particularly its erasure of indigenous women, in operation. In *Chen,*[28] a Chinese immigrant man who beat his wife to death with a claw hammer was defended on the grounds that his rage and violence at the imagined infidelity of his wife were normal in his culture of origin. In another, *Rhines*,[29] an African American man was accused of rape through physical force and verbal abuse of an African American woman. His defense was that he mistakenly believed that she consented to the rape because Black people are routinely violent and yell at each other.[30] Presumably the racism of these assumptions is apparent, although the defenses were made in the name of opposing the racism of white culture in punishing these men for raping women of color and beating them to death. The African American woman in the rape case was very clear that she was raped. If African Americans yell at each other, she might be the first to know what it meant and not be silenced by it into acting as if she wanted to have sex, or so he could think.

I would also like to know in what culture some men *don't* kill their wives for perceived infidelity (or just because . . .), and in what culture men are *not* supported in culturally specific ways in believing that force is part of sex. (Let's move there.) What postmodernism gives us instead is a multicultural defense for male violence—a defense for it wherever it is, which in effect is a pretty universal defense. Pornography also provides an excellent cultural defense to rape in most Western cultures: the more pornography is consumed, the more difficult it is for men to know that they are using force when they force women into sex—so they *will* culturally believe that women consent to sex no matter how much force is used.[31] Why are we coming up with a multicultural defense for *each* culture in which men specifically and particularly are permitted to believe rape is sex, instead of looking at the assumption that rape happens in a man's mind rather than in a woman's body in all of them? None of this would be possible if the dissenting women of each culture—the women who say, I was raped—were credited with knowing the reality of what was done to them.

B. Method

Postmodernism as practiced often comes across as style—petulant, joy-riding, more posture than position. But it has a method, making metaphysics far from dead. Its approach and its position, its posture toward the world and its view of what is real, is that it's all mental. Postmodernism imagines that society happens in your head. Back in the modern period, this position was called idealism. In its continuity with this method, to offer a few examples, postmodernism has made the penis into "the phallus," and it is mostly observed to signify.[32] Women have become "an ongoing discursive practice"[33] or, ubiquitously, "the female body,"[34] which is written on and signified but seldom, if ever, raped, beaten, or otherwise violated. Racism and homophobia are elided "differences" in disguise.

Abuse has become "agency"—or rather challenges to sexual abuse have been replaced by invocations of "agency," women's violation become the sneering wound of a "victim" pinned in arch quotation marks.[35] Instead of facing what was done to women when we were violated, we are told how much freedom we had at the time. (For this we need feminism?) Agency in the postmodern lexicon is a stand-in for the powerless exercising power; sometimes it means freedom, sometimes self-action, sometimes resistance, sometimes desire. We are not told which of these is meant, precisely, or how any or all of these things are possible under the circumstances. It would be good to know. Oddly missing in this usage is what an agent legally is: someone who acts for someone else, the principal, who is pulling their strings.

Domination, postmodernists know exists, but they don't tell us how or where or why. It is something that no one does or has done to them but somehow winds up in "gendered lopsidedness."[36] What we used to call "what happened to her" has become, at its most credible, "narrative." But real harm has ceased to exist.

So whole chapters of books with "pornography" in their titles can be written without ever once talking about what the pornography industry concretely does, who pornographers are, or what is done to whom in and with the materials.[37] There is no discussion of how pornography exploits and mass-produces sexual abuse. There is not even an extension of the early work on the scopic drive by Foucault, Lacan, and Irigaray (who are even French)—an analysis that is readily extendable to describe the aggressive appropriation and trafficking of women in pornography.[38] Nor have I noticed the multiculturalists out there opposing the spread of pornography from Scandinavia, Germany, and the United States on grounds of cultural imperialism, and it's taking over the world. The point of postmodernism is to get as far away from anything real as possible.

Postmodern feminists seldom build on or refer to the real lives of real women directly; mostly, they build on the work of French men, if selectively and often not very well.[39] Foucault, for instance, studied some real practices, though he mostly missed gender, which from the standpoint of feminism is a rather big thing to miss. Foucault's elision of gender, feminist postmodernists try endlessly to fix, but his actual engagement with reality—"I'm an empiricist"[40]—they have totally abandoned. Feminist postmodernism is far, far away from the realities of the subordination of women. All women should be so fortunate.

C. Reality

It is my view that it is the *relation* of theory to reality that feminism changed, and it is in part a reversion to a prefeminist relation of theory to reality that postmodernism is reimposing. This is not about truth. Truth is a generality, an abstraction of a certain shape and quality. Social realities are something else again. Postmodernism has decided that because truth died with God, there are no social facts. The fact that reality is a social construction does not mean that it is not there; it means that it is there, in society, where we live.

According to postmodernism, there are no facts; everything is a reading, so there can be no lies. Apparently it cannot be known whether the Holocaust is a hoax, whether women love to be raped, whether Black people are genetically intellectually inferior to white people, whether homosexuals are child molesters. To postmodernists, these factish things are indeterminate, contingent, in play, all a matter of interpretation. Similarly, whether or not acts of incest happened or are traumatic to children become fogged over in "epistemological quandaries" as beyond thinking, beyond narrative, beyond intelligibility, as "this event that is no event"—as if survivors have not often reported, in intelligible narratives, that such events did happen and did harm them.[41] That violation often damages speech and memory does not mean that one was not violated—on the contrary. Recall when Bill Clinton, asked about his sexual relationship with a young woman intern, said that it all depended on what "is" means. The country jeered his epistemic dodge as a transparent and slimy subterfuge to evade accountability: get real. The postmodernists were strangely silent. But you can't commit perjury if there are no facts. Where are these people when you need them?

What postmodernists want, I have come to think, apart from to live in their heads instead of in the world (that old dodge), is to vault themselves out of power methodologically. They want to beat dominance at its own game, which is usually called dominating. They want to win every argument in advance. Also, if everything is interpretation, you can never be wrong. Feminism has faced that you know what is real not by getting outside your determinants (which you can't do anyway) but by getting deep inside them with a lot of other people with the same foot (or feet) on their necks. Abdicating this, feminism's source of power, postmodernism has swallowed the objective standpoint while claiming to be off on a whole new methodological departure. Then postmodernists sigh and admit that they might have to concede partiality,[42] meaning admitting only knowing part. What, again, was the alternative? Totality? What's wrong with partiality— except from the objective standpoint, which thinks it means you can't be right? Who said there is either the whole or a part? Postmodernism keeps becoming what it claims to supersede.[43]

If feminism is modernist—which is highly problematic, because it is as much a critique of modernism[44]—and postmodernists want to be postfeminist, they have to take feminism with them and go further. They often claim to. To be postmodern in this sense, the insights of modernism and its critics into the inequalities of sex, race, and class must, it seems to me, be taken on board before they can be gone beyond.[45] Instead of superseding these insights, postmodernists routinely elaborately deny them, ignore them, act as if they are not there. This is premodern, as if feminism never existed. On the question of continuity, whether postmodernism has much if anything to say that modernism didn't is also worth asking. The great modern Gertrude Stein wrote in 1946: "[T]here aint any answer, there aint going to be any answer, there never has been an answer, that's the answer."[46] How is postmodernism post that?

What I mean to say on the question of reality in theory is this: When something happens to women, it happens in social reality. The perspective from women's point of view does not mean that women's reality can only be seen from there, hence is inaccessible to anyone else and can't be talked about and does not exist. Rather, what can be seen from the point of view of the subordination of women has been there all along—too long. We wish it didn't exist, but it can't be wished out of existence. Anyone can see it. It can be found. It can be ascertained. It can even be measured sometimes. It can be discussed. Before us, it has been missed, overlooked, made invisible.

In other words, the harm of second-class human status does not pose an abstract reality question. In social life, there is little that is subtle about most rapes; there is nothing complex about a fist in your face; there is nothing nuanced about genocide—although many nuanced questions no doubt can be raised about them. These social realities, central to feminism, do not raise difficult first-order reality questions, not any more.

It is the *denial* of their social reality that is complicated and raises difficult philosophical questions. Understand that the denial of the reality of such events has been a philosophical position about reality itself. Unless and until it is effectively challenged, only what power wants to see as real is granted reality status. Reality is a social *status*. Power's reality does not have to establish itself as real in order to exist, because it has the status as real that power gives it; only the reality of the powerless has to establish itself as real. Power can also establish unreality—like the harmlessness of pornography or smoking—as reality. That doesn't make it harmless. But until power is effectively challenged on these lies—and they are lies—only those harmed (and those harming them, who have every incentive to conceal) have access to knowing that that is what they are. So it has taken us all this time, and a movement that has challenged male power, to figure out that women's reality is also a philosophical position: that women's reality exists, including women's denied violation, therefore social reality exists separate from its constitution by male power or its validation by male knowledge.

This analysis raises some questions about postmodernism that are not simply a report on my current mental state: Can postmodernism stop the rape of children when everyone has their story, and everyone is presumably exercising sexual agency all the time? Can postmodernism identify fascism if power only exists in microcenters and never in systematic, fixed, and determinate hierarchical arrangements? How can you oppose something that is always only in play? How do you organize against something that isn't even really there except when you are thinking about it? Can postmodernism hold the perpetrators of genocide accountable? If the subject is dead, and we are dealing with deeds without doers,[47] how do we hold perpetrators accountable for what they perpetrate? Can the Serbian cultural defense for the extermination of Croats, Bosnian Muslims, and Kosovar Albanians be far behind? If we can have a multicultural defense for the current genocide, because that's how the Serbs see it, why not a German cultural defense for the earlier one? Anti-Semitism *was* part of German culture. Finally, for another old question, if you only exist in opposition, if you are only full in opposition to the modern,[48] it has determined you. Don't you need an account of how you are not merely reiterating your determinations? From postmodernists, one is not yet forthcoming. The postmodernist reality corrosion thus makes it not only incoherent and useless—the pragmatists' valid criticism[49]—but also regressive, disempowering, and collaborationist.

There *is* reality to many of the postmodernists' favorite concepts, although they seldom talk about it. Take their "fragmented self."[50] In the material world they largely refuse to engage or countenance, the fragmented self is a multiple personality. Multiplicity is created through extreme, usually sexual, torture at a very young age.[51] Postmodernists ought to have to confront the human pain of the ideas they think are so much fun.[52] Take being nomadic. My Bosnian women clients are refugees. Will Rosi Braidotti's *Nomadic Subjects* help them get through the day?[53] Being a real nomad can include being forced to flee your own country for your own survival as your family is exterminated in front of you. Postmodernism celebrates interculturality as a liberating head trip for its cultural rootlessness and multiple possibilities. The actual experience can be something else again. But then, Rosi did say homelessness got fun only after she got tenure.[54]

One final example puts together these points about postmodernism on women, method, multiculturalism, and therefore social reality. It centers on a question, large in Western philosophy, of whether the world exists independently of our ideas of it. This has been a big male problem. An introduction to the postmodern collection *Dominating Knowledge* by Stephen Marglin addresses it by stating that the material world has objective reality but the social world does not.[55] His example is that although he knows the earth is round (he doesn't say how), people used to think it was flat; in human society, according to him, there is no reality, hence no knowing, like that.[56] The idea is, if you believe the social equivalent of the world is flat—like, say, that women are inferior to men—it is. In society, there is no reality; there is only what is thought to be real.

To illustrate this, he discusses the subject of "human sacrifice" in a society that believes in its necessity:

> Imagine the priestess called upon to explain the consequences of a failure to sacrifice the requisite virgins in the requisite manner. She might well say, "Society will fall apart. Our women and our land will become barren because our men will become impotent as lovers and ineffective as cultivators." *And she will be right.* Believing themselves to be impotent in the hammock and inefficient in the field, the men will be unable to perform in either context. The birth rate will decline, and the harvest will fail. Society *will* fall apart. . . . [B]eliefs bring about the very conditions that will make these beliefs come true.[57]

What we have here is a multicultural sexual and economic rationalization for the murder of little girls. We also have a situation in which men's erections can be dependent on killing female children. Male impotence occupies the status of a fact; erections, I guess, exist. What I want to say about this sort of thing is that no one is asking the girls. The description of "the way things are" is from the position of a man who is about to kill a child. Of course, in this example, it's put in the mouth of a woman. Women often serve male power and do have power over children, but postmodernists have to portray women actually having power that men largely have in order to confuse people about power. (That they want to avoid being called sexist in the process, we have accomplished.)

My point is this: what happens to the virgin being sacrificed is independent of what she thinks about it. *She* may think that the crops will grow just as well if she is alive tomorrow as if she is killed today. She may even think her human rights are being violated. It makes no difference to the reality of her getting killed today. No matter what she thinks about it, she will be—*be*—dead. This seems to me very simple: the reality of people who don't have power exists independently of what they think. The social constructs that control their lives very often are not their constructs. What women think doesn't tend to make things be the way we think because we don't have the social power to do them or to stop them. Any woman who doesn't know this, in my opinion, has not pushed very hard on the walls around her and other women or has been, so far, very privileged and very lucky.

The reason that it doesn't appear to men (especially men of the theory class) that the world exists independently of their minds is because they largely do have the power to do whatever happens in their minds. If they want, in their minds, to kill her, they can do that in the world. If they want it to give them erections, it will. So they naturally don't know what comes first, it or them. What this means is that women are the ones who know something about social reality as such, which is the extent of its independence of mind. If social reality is independent of *our* minds, it's independent of mind, and men just think it isn't because of their social location.

Women are in a position to know this to the extent that reality does not respond to us. What we know is that the power to make reality be real is a product of social power to act, not just to imagine. We know that reality is about power because we can imagine change all day long and nothing is any different. This is a criticism; it is not an inevitability. We can collectively intervene in social life, but not if we deny that it is there or what makes it be there. We can even imagine, long enough to organize to stop these men, what could happen if some such girls got away with their lives and the crops kept right on growing. Stephen Marglin is not asking this girl if society will fall apart if she lives. We are. We are, if you will, an improbable movement of the escapees and survivors of such sacrifice.

Yes, society is largely made of people's consciousness of social relations. That doesn't mean that everyone's consciousness constitutes social reality equally. As long as social reality is a product of inequality, and postmodernists refuse to contend with social inequality methodologically, postmodernism will go on adopting the methodological position of male power, and the politics of the women's movement of the 1970s will be dead, in theory. Meantime, women in the world will go on fighting to change the unequal social realities of women's lives as if postmodernism did not exist.

III

If it is to contribute to feminism's future, postmodernism has, I think, some questions to answer. What is its account of itself? How convenient to repudiate account-giving when it seems to have none, at least no presentable one. What are its grounds? Now this is an aggressive question. Thinking grounds matter, they repudiate as "foundationalism." But what are the sexual and material preconditions for this theory? David Harvey traces the economic and cultural forces of late-twentieth-century capitalism that, in his analysis, have produced, read determined, postmodernism.[58] What does this suggest about their ability to promote change? What is postmodernism's project? How linear, how teleological, how serious. To whom and what is it accountable? I say it is accountable to academic hierarchy. Who else can afford this theory?

Postmodernism appropriates its methodological pretensions and gestures from feminism, but it doesn't practice them. Its reality position is closer to the premodern, certainly the prefeminist, a throwback to before the feminism initially described. So it's forward to the past: to yet another set of abstractions with no accountability to subordinated peoples' reality and an implicit but total accountability to power, with familiar if fancier reasons for doing nothing—radical-sounding, but with the same origins, a dislocated elite, and the same consequences, a disengaged theory, that corrodes material resistance to power.

Postmodernism's analysis of the social construction of reality is stolen from feminism and the left but gutted of substantive content—producing Marxism without the working class, feminism without women. It's an abstract critique of abstract subjects. The hall of mirrors (that's plural) that much of postmodernism substitutes for any attempt to grasp a real social world is an ultimate collapse into liberalism's relativism regresses. As mildly put by Alan Sokal and Jean Bricmont, "relativism is an extremely weak foundation on which to build a criticism of the existing social order."[59] Once postmodernism's various acts of theft and sellout are exposed, what is left is a pose, an empty gesture of theatrical anarchism (to which Marx's critique applies), a Hegelian negation of the status quo (and just as determined by it), liberalism's terrible child (many liberals look plenty grounded

and engaged by comparison), a precious politics of abdication, complacency, and passivism.

I do know this: we cannot have this postmodernism and still have a
meaningful practice of women's human rights, far less a women's movement. Ironically, and how postmodernism loves an irony, just as women
have begun to become human, even as we have begun to transform the
human so it is something more worth having and might apply to us, we
are told by high theory that the human is inherently authoritarian, not
worth having, untransformable, and may not even exist—and how hopelessly nineteenth-century of us to want it.[60] (That few of the feminist postmodernists, had it not been for the theory of humanity they criticize, would
have been permitted to learn to read and write—this is perhaps a small
point.)

The reason postmodernism undermines a practice of human rights is not
because it corrodes universality. Human rights in the real world are
proving far less attached to their Enlightenment baggage than are the intellectuals who guard its theory. The reason is, the reality of violation is
the only ground the violated have to stand on to end it. Power and its
pretenders think they can dispense with ground because they are in no
danger of losing theirs or the power that goes with it. Postmodernism
vitiates human rights to the extent it erects itself on its *lack* of relation to
the realities of the subordinated because it is only in social reality that
human violation takes place, can be known, and can be stopped.

This analysis in turn raises a question feminism has not had to answer
before, as critically as we do now, because we never had a theory class
before: what is the place of the academy in the movement? Postmodernism,
empty as much of it is, is taking up a lot of feminist theoretical energy in
this one world that we all go to sleep in and wake up in. Postmodernism
is an academic theory, originating in academia with an academic elite, not
in the world of women and men, where feminist theory is rooted. In the
early 1970s, I (for one) had imagined that feminists doing theory would
retheorize life in the concrete rather than spend the next three decades on
metatheory, talking *about* theory, rehashing over and over in this discon-
nected way how theory should be done, leaving women's lives twisting in
the wind. Too, theorizing about little except other theories of theories
provides little experience on how to do it.

My feeling is, if the postmodernists took responsibility for changing even
one real thing, they would learn more about theory than everything they
have written to date put together. Instead, as practiced by postmodernists,
the job of theory, as the blood sport of the academic cutting edge, is to

observe and pass on and play with these big questions, out of touch with and unaccountable to the lives of the unequal. Their critically minded students are taught that nothing is real, that disengagement is smart (not to mention career-promoting), that politics is pantomime and ventriloquism, that reality is a text (reading is safer than acting any day), that creative misreading is resistance (you feel so radical and comfortably marginal), that nothing can be changed (you can only amuse yourself). With power left standing, the feminism of this theory cannot be proven by any living woman. It is time to ask these people: what are you *doing?*

6

The Promise of CEDAW's Optional Protocol

The Optional Protocol to the Convention on the Elimination of All Forms of Discrimination Against Women,[1] which came into force on December 22, 2000, put a new legal tool into the hands of women, empowering them to claim their internationally protected equality rights.[2]

If justice inheres in procedures, it has been long in coming under the Convention on the Elimination of All Forms of Discrimination Against Women (CEDAW or "the Convention").[3] For twenty years, CEDAW's substantive guarantees have been marginalized and disregarded, hampered by multiple reservations[4] and enforcement limited to reporting.[5] Lack of procedural mechanisms for direct victims to claim violations has constrained the Convention's effectiveness against official acts and failures to act, and against those interactions of state with nonstate action that so powerfully enforce women's subordinate status and treatment.[6] Laws that discriminate against women remain in effect in ratifying countries around the world.[7] CEDAW's mandates to promote women's equality in political, economic, social, and cultural life[8] are widely ignored. The Convention's efficacy as a force for change—from transforming social and legal norms to initiating domestic legislative and policy reform to strengthening forces for equality in civil society—has been seriously undermined.

If women take it up, the Optional Protocol could end that. It encompasses all provisions in the Convention, not just those expressly stated in terms of rights.[9] Direct complaint may be made against ratifying countries to the Committee on Discrimination Against Women ("the Committee"), the treaty body of elected experts that interprets the Convention.[10] Two mechanisms are available: individuals and groups can initiate communications,[11] and the Committee itself can undertake inquiries based on information submitted to it containing evidence of "grave or systematic vi-

This article originally appeared in 14:4 *Interights Bulletin* 141 (2004).

olation."[12] States can opt out of the inquiry procedure, but, uniquely among comparable instruments, the Optional Protocol permits no reservations.[13]

Standing to initiate a communication for "victims"[14] is confined to individuals or groups of individuals who claim actual injury due to CEDAW violations. Others can act on their behalf[15] with their consent, or if good reasons exist that their consent should not be required.[16] The scope of permitted representation of victims will be determined by the Committee as its jurisprudence develops, as will the requisites of consent to complain on behalf of another and the reasons their consent may not be required. No doubt these determinations will be influenced by the practices of other treaty bodies with complaint mechanisms, although enabling women to claim their rights as women may call for independent solutions. Anonymous complaints are not allowed,[17] but an unprecedented prohibition on retaliatory "ill-treatment or intimidation" of complainants, representatives, or witnesses provides some promise of security.[18] Together, these provisions give nongovernmental organizations (NGOs) a legitimated role in the complaint process, expanding the practical possibility of bringing claims while at the same time ensuring that complaints are grounded in, and hopefully accountable to, real people who have suffered real human rights violations. The compromises behind these provisions balance legitimacy with practicality and realism.

Admissibility criteria under the Optional Protocol leave latitude for Committee interpretation as well. "All available domestic remedies" must be exhausted unless they are "unreasonably prolonged or unlikely to bring effective relief."[19] Domestic laws against CEDAW violations often exist but are not effectively enforced, such as those against domestic violence; some are largely ineffectual by their design, such as laws against pornography. When CEDAW violations are pervasively tolerated, can formal laws against them be construed as "unlikely to bring effective relief"? What about groups of women challenging partial remedies, such as laws that produce more women in public office but do not solve their dramatic underrepresentation, or quotas of less than 50 percent? What might a complainant be required to do to exhaust domestic remedies to complain about lack of legal remedies for sex discrimination in civil society in light of Article 2(e)'s requirement that states parties take all appropriate measures against discrimination "by any person, organization or enterprise"? Only domestic remedies need be exhausted, not international ones. Indeed, the Optional Protocol's communication procedure (not the inquiry procedure) is exclusive.[20] But will European procedures, embedded in the laws of each country, have to be exhausted, or will they be regarded as conflicting? Perhaps if a remedy is incorporated in domestic law, it is required by, but not preclusive of, the Optional Protocol. Exhausting remedies without exhausting women may prove challenging or unproblematic.

Communications are examined in "closed meetings,"[21] with the Committee's views transmitted to the parties.[22] Inquiries "shall be conducted confidentially," with much dependant upon the level of cooperation of the state party, to whom the Committee's views are communicated.[23] Nothing makes the fact of a decision to hold an inquiry necessarily secret, however, just as nothing formal restricts disclosures by states parties subject to inquiries or by others involved in the process, such as those submitting information requesting that an inquiry be initiated. Because confidentiality of inquiries exists for the benefit of the state party, presumably the state could waive it, enhancing the visibility and transparency, and with it the effectiveness, of the proceedings. It is envisioned that decisions in communications will be made public by the Committee, with the state undertaking to facilitate access to them.[24]

Uniquely among comparable instruments, the Optional Protocol requires states to provide a written response to communications within six months.[25] Interim measures are available "to avoid possible irreparable damage."[26] As usual with human rights treaties, the Optional Protocol provides no enforcement power as such. All outcomes are effectuated by voluntary compliance.[27] The visibility and legitimacy of the process become particularly crucial when enforcement depends on little more than the mobilization of shame, which relies mainly on public pressure. Apart from the educational function of the proceedings themselves, Optional Protocol cases can help bring attention to issues in the national context, encouraging domestic change against systemic discrimination in particular and supporting civil society initiatives as well as official ones.[28] The procedure's publicity requirements[29] are designed to sustain these functions. Hopefully they will not be ignored.

Untried procedures are doubtless daunting, and women encounter specific barriers for accessing their human rights. To date four communications have been registered; the Committee has also begun work on an inquiry into the decadelong and ongoing disappearances and murders, many of them sexual, of women in Ciudad Juárez, Mexico, with virtual official impunity.[30] More communications and inquiries may be expected as word spreads that the Committee is open for business. Inviting initial complaints include the many discriminatory laws, policies, and practices that blatantly violate CEDAW's substantive provisions, such as citizenship, nationality, inheritance, and property laws that give women lesser rights, domestic violence cases where national law has not provided an adequate remedy, and labor laws that exclude categories of labor commonly undertaken by women such as domestic work. More innovative uses may also emerge as the jurisprudence develops. Victims of discrimination need not be nationals of the country they complain against, so a survivor of trafficking (for example) might complain against a ratifying destination country if she was under its jurisdiction when the violation occurred. Eventually, broad reservations that undermine the Convention's universality might be challenged in appropriate cases for incompatibility with CEDAW's object and purpose.

Human rights cannot depend exclusively for their implementation on the same state entities that violate, and permit violations of, those rights. The new compliance mechanism offered by the Optional Protocol encourages action on the international level by women whom discrimination has harmed—whose numbers are legion—supported by NGOs in exposing governmental failures and social patterns of abuse, and by lawyers independent of their governments' control and unafraid of their displeasure. As the process brings international credibility to equality seekers, women will bring credibility and vitality, imagination and energy, to the Convention, illuminating CEDAW's applicability to their lives in diverse cultural settings. By handing women themselves the power to complain against discrimination directly, the Optional Protocol holds out at once the possibility of reinvigorating the international human rights framework and hope for equality to women.

part two

struggles within states

7

Making Sex Equality Real

This moment, at the dawn of Canada's new Charter of Rights and Freedoms, is full of possibilities for all Canadians. It is also a good time for fundamental reconsideration of equality theory.

Most countries do not even have one equal rights amendment to Canada's two. Section 15 is the more abstractly framed provision but contains the crucial substantive element of disadvantage.[1] Section 28, speaking of male and female persons concretely, is even more substantively framed.[2] In my view, theoretical approaches to legal equality need to be reanalyzed in light of the gender inequality that socially exists. Canada's Charter provisions call for an analysis of the social inequality of the sexes that opens onto a legal equality theory that enables sex inequality to be identified where sex equality is legally mandated. Interpreted as proposed here, the Charter would draw a line and set a tone as well as cast a shadow that becomes a standard, giving equality concrete meaning in women's lives, making sex equality real.

Historically, equality law and philosophy have been created in a vacuum of critical attention to sex as an inequality. Sex has more typically been a counterexample to equality arguments proper or their reductio ad absurdum.[3] As a result, equality theories have not adequately addressed the inequality of women relative to men, making them inadequate and incomplete as theories of equality per se. To anticipate the conclusion: if Canada interprets equality as usual—including the way most U.S. courts and mainstream commentators in the Anglo-American jurisprudential tradition do— it will maintain the inequality of the sexes. Women will remain a perpetual economic, social, and political underclass. Women's inferiority, powerlessness, relative negligibility will continue, both through positive acts of gov-

This talk was first published in *Righting the Balance: Canada's New Equality Rights* 37 (Lynn Smith et al., eds., 1985).

ernment and neglecting, hence permitting, social practices like marital rape and the pornography industry, acts and institutions so socially systematic that positive law has seldom been needed to enforce them.[4]

Equality theory can be read as an answer to a question it does not pose directly: "What is an equality question a question of?" The standard answer in law and philosophy has been that an equality question is a question of sameness and difference, to be resolved by treating likes alike and unlikes unalike. The word "equal" means "same." It is code for sameness. Its normative thrust as a principle flows from an empirical determination of similarity or dissimilarity. Hence American judicial equality methodology's fixation on categorization, that categories fit empirical reality. When it is said that they must be rational, it means they must fit the world as it is. "Fit"[5] means the empirical term and the normative purpose must correspond—the classification must, say, fit a valid state purpose for which it is drawn. Categories, to fit, must, in the somewhat carnivorous language of two American commentators, carve the social world at a natural joint.[6] What makes a joint seem natural, or whether punishing some peoples' nature and privileging other peoples' is what equality means, is often ignored.

This mainstream approach gives women two alternative routes to equality. One, be the same as men. This is the leading rule, termed "gender neutrality" or "the single standard." The alternative is to ask for recognition of our differences, termed the "special benefit rule" or the "double standard." The sameness standard gets women, when they are like men, access to what men already have; the differences rule seeks to cushion the impact of women's distinctiveness or value women as they are under existing conditions. Stella Bliss, unable to work because she was pregnant, met both standards so got the benefit of neither.[7]

The sameness standard is the legally and theoretically preferred principle in existing law and theory, including in Charter deliberations and among most Canadians. Usually it is simply called "the equality rule." Women who wish to be equal to men must show themselves to be the same as men. This is an equality argument. Most proposed interpretations of Section 15 revolve around this standard. It shows how substance becomes form in law that this is regarded as "formal equality." This approach prioritizes as equality issues those in which women's social options and conditions are already most like men's. It also prioritizes the claims of those women whose social conditions are already most like men's, the most privileged women. And it defines women's goals in terms of (some) men's actualities.

As this rule has worked out concretely in American law, it has mainly gotten men the benefit of those few things women have historically had. In family law, it has transformed custody and divorce by giving men an equal chance at custody of children and at alimony.[8] It has gotten men access to women's schools,[9] women's jobs,[10] and mothers' benefits.[11] It mobilizes the idea that the way to get things for women is to get them for men. It has also gotten for women—those who can show that we are the same as men—some things to which men have previously had almost exclusive access. Employment and education, the public pursuits, have been prioritized. Women have received some access to academic and professional advancement, blue-collar work, the military, and more than nominal access to athletics. This approach has not allowed women to question the phallocentricity of knowledge, competition as the point of sports and careers, domination as the model and means of power, or war as a peculiarly ejaculatory means of conflict resolution.

This doctrine has broken down when faced with real sex differences, for instance, pregnancy. Patently, there are problems with an equality principle that does not know how to handle distinctions that advantage one group at another's systematic expense.[12] Such problems include socially situated differences such as the de facto sex segregation of the labor force resulting in lack of equal pay for work of comparable worth, so that women on average make much less income than men. Equality law in its mainstream form cannot address the most systematic social disadvantages, the most sex-differential abuses of women. Included in these abuses are not only segregation into less valued jobs, but also the range of issues of violence against women that have been systematically tolerated by virtually every government in the world, despite cultural differences or similar formal equality guarantees. These abuses include the massive amount of rape and attempted rape about which virtually nothing is done; the sexual assault of children endemic to the patriarchal family; the battery of women that is systematic in homes; prostitution, women's fundamental economic option; and pornography, which makes inequality sexy to the tune of billions of dollars in profit every year.

These issues are silenced out of the sameness definition of equality largely because they happen almost exclusively to women. Understand: for this reason, they are considered *not* to raise equality issues. They belong, if at all, on the criminal side of the law. I think the major reason these abuses are not regarded as raising equality issues is that the treatment they involve is regarded as expressing "the sex difference." Implicit in the notion that equality is a question of sameness and difference is the setting of a substantively male standard for women's treatment under equality law, calling that sameness, and precluding from being addressed those problems that predominantly women have, calling them differences. It excludes from attack such treatment as is systematically, almost uniquely, done to women by assimilating those abuses to "the sex difference." In this framework, rape, battery, prostitution express "the sex difference." Certainly, the practices that enforce women's particular subordination are "different." The whole point of women's social relegation to inferiority is that these things are seldom done to men. But that does not make them essentially female; it only makes them pervasively imposed upon women.

Observe that men are as different from women as women are from men. The sexes are *equally* different. Men, however, are not paid half of what women are paid for doing the same things on the basis of their equal difference. Everything they touch does not turn valueless because they touched it. When they are hit, a person has been assaulted. When they are sexually violated, especially if they are straight and white and adult, it is not generally disbelieved or simply tolerated or found entertaining or defended as the necessary structure of the family or the price of civilization.

The question "What is an equality question a question of?" needs a new answer, a realistic one in the context of actual inequality. An equality question is a question of dominance and subordination. Inequality is a question of hierarchy. The fundamental issue of equality is not whether one is the same or different; it is not the gender difference; it is the difference gender makes. In this perspective, equality is not exclusively or even primarily an issue of differentiation that is rational or not. To be on the bottom of a hierarchy is certainly different from being on the top of one, but it is not simply difference that most distinguishes the two. It is, in fact, the lesser access to resources, privileges, credibility, legitimacy, authority, pay, bodily integrity, security, and power that makes the two unequal. The issue here is not entirely how to make access to those things nonarbitrary, because the situation we are confronting is anything but simply arbitrary. It does have an inner logic. The issue is systematic male supremacy and how to end it. Confronting this problem requires a less abstract and more substantive approach to equality. Under it, to be equal is not to be subordinated on a group ground. If systematic relegation to inferiority is what is wrong with inequality, the task of equality law is to end that status, not to focus on conditions under which it can be justified. Equality in this sense is not voided by difference and is satisfied only by real parity.

If inequality is subordination, to mandate equality on the basis of sex legally means that a decision has been made: the proposition that women can be treated as subhuman is no longer debatable. The only question is whether or not a practice or distinction is equal or unequal, subordinating or not. Whether laws or practices reflect existing social relations or are a morally good idea is not relevant. Antisubordination could be the distinctive guiding interpretive principle of Section 28 in particular and could also be built into Section 15. Under Section 28, equality between women and men is guaranteed "notwithstanding anything else in this Charter" and is also not subject to legislative override.

Section 28 was fought for by women to mean something more than the traditional meaning of "nondiscrimination on the basis of sex," and it does. Nonsubordination, opposition to disadvantage, is a substantive principle. I think that if you expose, as Section 15 could and Section 28 particularly could, the substance beneath the gloss of gender neutrality, a substantive approach to inequality issues could emerge. When women are raped, for example, and the state effectively condones it, women's equality rights would be violated. Certain traditional evidentiary standards, eroded to some degree but still cautioning that victims of sexual assault are especially not to be believed,[13] would be facially invalid. They assume that women lie. Some subordination of women to men partially but ineffectually pursued by the state—for example, its regulation of the pornography industry—might also be challenged. Comparable worth for public employees should be achievable, as should pregnancy leave. Such an approach will begin to reveal and dismantle the complicity of law in the sex-unequal structure of Anglo-American society, which operates as an affirmative action plan for white men.

Because sex inequality is pervasive and potent in this structure, expressly legalizing it has often not been necessary. Women have had virtually no voice in the design of existing law or society to date, having been kept out and down. For this reason, to realize sex equality will require more affirmative governmental action than the simple negation of existing law. To the extent the Canadian Charter is interpreted as a negative document, its assumptions about society will not apply to the situation of women—for example, if it assumes that speech is free, and, therefore, the principal threat to freedom of speech is government intervention,[14] or that society is equal, and the principal threat to equality is laws that impose inequalities. Its equality provisions do not have to be interpreted in this way. Resist this. It is not true that women's speech is free and its restriction comes only or even primarily from government. It is not the case that society is equal and the problem of inequality is only or even primarily expressly legislatively imposed.

To women who work with the law in your hands, what is the meaning of your presence as lawyers and judges in a system that keeps women out and down? Compared with most women, we are in and up. I believe we are let into this system on the condition that we abide by its norms, one of which is to keep women out and down, while our presence conveys that that is not the system at all. If we do abide by its norms, most women's lives will remain what they have always been: a cycle of dependence, poverty, forced labor, forced sexual access, forced reproduction, and for many an untimely death. The position that some of us have moved up and out of will be filled by another woman. Women will be used until we are used up. Women will be born, degraded, and die.

I think that Sections 15 and 28 are a popular and principled mandate for a change in this. To make their promise come true, women who are now in power in the existing system must not accept anything less than real social equality for all women. We must not allow ourselves to be used to show we made it, all women can. As it is, all women can't. If the combination of the principles of Sections 15 and 28 is kept in mind—if the substantive mandate of Section 28 is observed together with the more formal mandate of Section 15, together with its substantive antidisadvantaging norm—if we do not forget that Section 15's "sex" discrimination prohibition is really about what Section 28's substantive guarantees to "women and men" are about—Susan B. Anthony's goal will come to pass sooner in Canada than in the United States: "men, their rights and nothing more; women, their rights and nothing less."[15]

8

Nationbuilding in Canada

After successful agitation, Canadian women secured in Canada's new constitution, the Charter of Rights and Freedoms, sex equality guarantees with more potential to produce actual sex equality than yet exists in any other constitutional language. These equality provisions, which came into effect in April 1985, prohibit discrimination on the basis of sex through law[1] and also expressly guarantee all Charter rights equally to "male and female persons."[2] The first decision under the broad equality rights provision, Andrews v. Law Society of British Columbia[3] begins to deliver upon the promise of the Charter's language. It openly rejects the usual "similarly situated" approach, under which equality means treating likes alike and unlikes unalike, and takes a purposive and substantive approach, aiming to equalize the disadvantage of historically subordinated groups.

A defect in the 1982 compact that created the Charter was its lack of approval by Quebec. A long-term tension has existed in Canadian society between its English and French heritage, culture, language, and peoples. Francophones are in the minority except in Quebec; Anglophones dominate throughout Canada but are a numerical minority in Quebec. The cultural dignity and particularity of the French are felt to be insufficiently respected by much of Anglo Canada, producing a wariness of the Charter as a possible device for imposing Anglo-Canadian values, culture, legal traditions, and language. At the same time, the nonacceptance of the Charter by Quebec leaves for many a legal and political gap, a sense in which the nation is not whole.

Eleven men—ten premiers and the Prime Minister—met in 1987 to

This testimony was delivered to the Legislative Assembly of Ontario, Select Committee on Constitutional Reform, on March 31, 1988. See 1987 Constitutional Accord, Hansard Official Report of Debate, 34th Parl., 1st Sess., C-1162–C-1172 (Mar. 31, 1988). It was first published in 25 *Tulsa Law Journal* 735 (1990).

attempt to devise terms for confederation acceptable to all. The Meech Lake Accord was the result. It provides for the recognition of Quebec as "a distinct society" within Canada[4] and also reiterates the recognition of multicultural and aboriginal rights, thought to be in jeopardy without re-affirmation.[5]

Women, including some in Quebec, reacted immediately to the lack of recognition of sex equality rights in the Accord. At the same time, any criticism of the Meech Lake Accord has often been taken as, and has often been, anti-French. As the debate has progressed, concerns with the Accord that nonetheless respect the French "distinct society" have been virtually drowned out by often vicious (and sometimes subtle but equally invidious) anti-French sentiment. It has become almost impossible to be heard as anything other than anti-Quebec when expressing reservations about the Accord.

Under rules that seem to require unanimity, by the deadline for ratification by the provinces, June 23, 1990, two refused to ratify and one talked of rescinding. The opposition of one Manitoba legislator, a Native man, prevented its ratification. Alternatives being actively discussed after this failure of ratification include further negotiation of terms, possible companion resolutions, continued limbo, or the partial or complete separation of Quebec.[6]

When the Ontario legislature approved Meech Lake, women sang songs of protest in the gallery.[7] Perhaps the testimony here, given at the request of the Ontario legislature at hearings on the Accord and slightly revised, will resonate elsewhere, such as in Eastern Europe. Its argument is that national unification should not be accomplished at women's expense.

Testimony Before the Legislative Assembly of Ontario:

As an American constitutional lawyer and political scientist working internationally in the area of sex equality, I will offer for your consideration a comparative perspective on the potential impact of the Meech Lake Accord on women's equality in Canada.

When women ask about the impact the Accord may have on their legal rights, they are reassured that the issues are not legal, but political, hence nonbinding and negotiable. When they ask about the impact of the Accord on their political status, they are reassured that the issues are legal and will be dealt with by the courts. This supports a cross-cultural suspicion women have about the relation between law and politics, which is that the politics of men are the law for women, at the same time that the laws of men determine women's standing in the political order. To avoid this in Canada, we need a grasp of both.

Comparatively viewed, the Canadian Charter of Rights and Freedoms is advanced beyond any comparable instrument in the world today in promising full citizenship to women. Its combination of equal protection of the laws with specific nondiscrimination guarantees, together with its substantive recognition of disadvantage and support for affirmative relief on a constitutional level, singles it out in laying a legal foundation for some of the most significant advances in sex equality ever to be made for women under law.

The Canadian commitment to diversity, with the political mobilization of the women's community that the Charter has occasioned, has produced an equipoise among the various bases for nondiscrimination under Section 15, and also an equipoise between equality rights and other rights throughout the Charter. This means, for one thing, that women's interests are not divided between those based on sex and those rooted in language, culture, nation, religion, ethnicity, and race. A unified approach to social inequality is possible under the Charter. The Meech Lake Accord disturbs this structural equality among equality rights and threatens to qualify, limit, and undermine both the Charter's distinctive legal contributions in this area and the climate of political will so crucial to a realistic delivery on their promise.

For purposes of comparison, the experience of the United States with sex equality rights—more accurately, the lack of them—may be instructive as a negative object lesson. Sex equality in the United States has constitutional dimension only by analogy. The Equal Protection Clause of the Fourteenth Amendment was passed to respond to a perceived emergency to the unity of the nation, specifically to white America's imposition of chattel slavery, social segregation, and disenfranchisement on Black Americans. The Equal Protection Clause was, in current parlance, part of a national reconciliation, the need for which had been created by these institutions of racial bigotry.

The Equal Protection Clause is gender-neutral on its face, except that the part on voting is confined to male citizens.[8] The rest does not mention sex, but then again, neither does it mention race. Attempts to add express sex equality guarantees to the U.S. Constitution, which would remove the question of the U.S. government's commitment to sex equality from the vicissitudes of political winds and the contingencies of shifting majorities, have failed. So the constitutional text is not in equipoise. In 1971, the

Equal Protection Clause was first applied to gender[9] and has increasingly been used since, moving forward largely through an uneven and often inadequate process of analogizing sex to race. The experience of the difficulties of attempting to achieve sex equality, not on its own terms—as is possible under the Canadian Charter—but through analogical method, highlights the dangers for all women, including women of color, of structurally elevating some bases for prohibited discrimination over others.

Section 2 of the Meech Lake Accord enters the field of rights selectively, potentially elevating some cultural rights over equality rights. Section 16 does as well. By combination, the "distinct society" clause, with the guarantees and recognitions of aboriginal and multicultural rights, is structural to Canadian federalism, and equality rights are not. Some rights are more important than others, and some equality rights are more equal, in George Orwell's phrase, than others.[10]

This poses concerns for the effective pursuit of a sex equality that is relegated to a nonstructural constitutional plane. It poses concerns for the vitality of Section 15's protections from discrimination on the many bases Section 15 covers, all of which are crucial for the advancement of women. It poses concerns for the coherent and predictable development, even the development at all, of Section 15 jurisprudence. It also presents concerns about balances to be struck in cases of potential conflicts of rights, both under Section 1[11] and otherwise, because some constitutional rights are given more weight than others.

Examples have proven treacherous in this area; no one wants it implied that he or she would discriminate. It speaks well for Canada that the value of equality is so widely held that no one wishes to be considered as even a hypothetical perpetrator of sex discrimination. But it is a fact that, across cultures, sex inequality is more rule than exception. Most cultures and groups discriminate on the basis of sex, often without intending or meaning to. Sex discrimination is typically regarded as not sex discrimination, being valued as culture, religion, privacy, or expression.

There are two sides to every sex inequality claim; the issues between them are often decided by interpretation. It is when there is doubt, and with legal actions there usually is at least some, that a structural weighting can be dispositive. It is also a bit hard to be required to give examples of what might happen under a projected legal state of affairs, only to be told that because these things have not yet happened under a legal regime that is as yet untested and uncertain, the examples are merely hypothetical.

To hazard an example: Were a significant advance to be made in an area covered by the Accord, analogies to the areas the Accord does not mention might not be available as they otherwise would, with the rights in equipoise as they are in the Charter without the Accord. Suppose that a significant advance were made in, say, the recognition of some group's cultural rights, and an analogy were sought to support a parallel initiative for women's rights—women at once having a culture and having been denied a culture through inequality, but both women and the other cultural group being threatened by the dominant culture. The Accord would militate against full application of such an analogy as precedent in a sex equality case. Similarly, could hate literature laws be upheld over an expressive rights challenge as applied to, for example, Jews, with the support of Meech Lake, but not, were such laws amended to cover sex, as applied to all women, without the Accord's support?

Suppose after Meech Lake, Native women chose to challenge a sex inequality within their nations, and the rule they challenged as discriminatory was defended as a necessary and integral part of aboriginal culture and aboriginal rights. Postcontact tribal rules could be argued as not culturally authentic. But if Native women chose to try to use the Charter, the question the Accord raises is whether they would meet a deck stacked against them as women. Meech Lake could well structure the Charter against their claim, just as many features of Anglo culture are premised on sex inequality and could be defended under multicultural rights. You may find this farfetched, but consider if a provision restricting pornography were passed to further women's equality rights. It could be attacked not only as a restriction on Subsection 2(b) expressive rights, but also potentially as a restriction on cultural rights, rights that, under Meech Lake, could outweigh sex equality rights. For American pornographers, at any rate, nothing is farfetched. Note that none of these examples is limited or particular to Quebec's women, whose rights under the Accord are probably in no more jeopardy and—given Quebec's laws and political culture—possibly less than those women of elsewhere in Canada.[12]

The point is, sex equality litigation and legislation can already be opposed under existing Charter provisions. The Meech Lake Accord would give more support to some of those other Charter provisions. Equality rights would find themselves unequally situated in the Charter in a way that they are not now without the Accord. To ask whether the Accord overrides the Charter is thus not precisely the issue, or the only issue. There will be conflicts of rights within the Charter. The Accord takes sides in some of those disputes in advance in ways that can harm women and their equality.

There has been something of a double standard in the discourse on whether equality rights should be added to the Meech Lake Accord. This committee has been told, for example, that Sections 2 and 16 of the Accord are hortatory and largely symbolic, not strictly legal. Yet one searches your transcripts in vain for concrete examples of how the "distinct society" clause, which is clearly essential to the fair deal that Quebec was promised, is concretely contemplated to change legal outcomes in particular cases. Yet it was included because someone thought it would make a difference. The difference has been explained in these terms: (1) It was important to bring Quebec into the confederation; they required it and they count. (2) It grants legitimacy and recognition to the distinct society. Then the rationale for Section 16 is provided on a similar level. It provides (3) reassurance that the rights of cultural groups and aboriginal peoples will be respected. Section 2 may not be adequate for the rights of French people outside Quebec, and Section 16 may not be adequate for the rights of many cultural groups or for aboriginal peoples, but the voice of women was regarded as so negligible in this process that it was seen as something that could afford to be ignored entirely. When women ask, in essence, politely but firmly (as one does in Canada), "Is it not important to bring women into the confederation?" they are treated as if their consent to this structure of government can be assumed. No one seems very worried that they might be alienated from the state or that they might regard their implied consent as coerced—as they clearly do, for example, in the marital rape context.

Do women not require national reconciliation? When women ask for legitimacy and recognition for women's equal place in the state, they are told that it is so obvious as to be redundant. If it is redundant for women, why is it not also redundant for aboriginal groups and multicultural interests? If it is merely redundant, what harm is there in stating it? Why the resistance to it? Apparently, stating it would add something that someone who counts does not want added. The only other argument I have heard is that if women are granted equality rights under the Meech Lake Accord, many other issues will have to be reopened—the perennial slippery-slope question. Women are over half the population and half of virtually every other group involved in this process. They are not like any other group, their interests just any interests. Or, perhaps those other issues should be reopened as well.

When women seek reassurance that the pact the Charter made with them is not being impliedly abrogated, they are told that it is only a matter of interpretation. As Mary Eberts put it, they are told, "Trust us." Real guarantees were considered appropriate to reassure other groups—other groups that matter, other groups that one cannot help noting include men, as well as being half women. The Accord apparently gave a satisfactory answer to the question "What does Quebec want?" It did not answer the question "What do women want?" because, as has so often been the case worldwide, it was not asked.

In your hearings, you have been told that the insult of women's exclusion from the Meech Lake Accord has no practical significance because the Accord is merely interpretive, while other sections of the Charter are rights-granting. With respect, this is a false distinction in legal practice. For example, which was the *Morgentaler* case?[13] Section 7 by its language does not grant women a right to abortion.[14] But, by interpretation, Section 7 was strong enough to invalidate the procedures for access to it as impermissibly restrictive.

Few constitutional rights are entirely self-executing. Those that are rarely wind up in court. Most of women's rights are not in that category. Most women's rights are contested; we get them in application and by interpretation or not at all. To observe that the Meech Lake Accord is only a matter of weight is therefore not reassuring either. In law, interpretation is everything, and, in interpretation, emphasis can be all. After being told that it is all just interpretive, making women's disquiet seem overblown, a most basic canon of statutory interpretation is left out: *exclusio unius,* that which is not mentioned is excluded.

Consider, in light of the unequal situation of women, what the Charter of Rights and Freedoms, as it is beginning to be interpreted now, can offer. Women have historically been second-class citizens in Canada as elsewhere, with indices of disadvantage including unequal pay, allocation to disrespected work, and demeaned physical characteristics. Women have been targeted for rape, domestic battery, sexual abuse as children, and systematic sexual harassment. Women have been depersonalized, used in denigrating entertainment, and forced into prostitution. These abuses have occurred in a historical context characterized by disenfranchisement, exclusion from public life, preclusion from property ownership, sex-based poverty, forced maternity, definition as sexual objects, deprivation of reproductive control, and devaluation of women's contributions in all spheres of social life—a situation that continues to the present day.

Constitutions are both statements of belief and vehicles for actualizing those beliefs. They are aspirational and admonitory as well as declarative and prohibitory. In the face of the social reality of sex inequality, and in light of the Charter's initial interpretation, its equality guarantees are positioned to be goal-oriented as well as aspirational. It becomes a matter of interpretation whether the Charter will treat equality as a positive goal needing to be affirmed, extended, and realized, supporting and even requiring positive legislation, including over conflicting claims of right. It can be applied in areas where equality is urgently needed, such as rape and battering. Or equality can be interpreted in negative terms and considered achieved so long as the state does not itself discriminate actively, keeping government out of the social sphere, leaving most sex inequality in place.

Perhaps the deepest cause for concern is the effect that the Accord in its present form would have on the social process of constitution-building as the Charter's political culture begins to deliver promised rights. Equality guarantees do not change societies only when they are strictly applied in courts. In addition to being a species of law, the Accord would work in civil society. It would set priorities and agendas and values and affect resource allocations. As constitutional law, the Accord is also a political act of national self-definition. It enters into the atmosphere that defines the level of commitment to equality rights on a day-to-day basis. There, a constitution becomes meaningful or dies as a piece of paper.

On this level, whether or not it is implemented concretely or can be invoked technically, a constitution affects perceptions, actions, and outcomes from family court and rape trials to human rights adjudications. It shapes women's fortunes in the boardroom and at the bargaining table, in the home and on the street, where it is raised and when it is never mentioned alike. A political act like the Meech Lake Accord either supports or detracts from this climate of concern, affecting outcomes in particular cases even when it does not technically apply, shifting the ground beneath legal arguments, determining what is persuasive and what has to be taken seriously, what has to be proven and what can be taken for granted. It becomes part of what gives life to law.

On this level, constitutional process begins as politics, becomes law, and goes on as social life. This is what Quebec wanted and why it wanted it, and what it got in the Accord. If what it got was only redundant or just interpretive, why bother? It is on this level also that multicultural groups and aboriginal peoples were regarded as needing reassurance—they got it, appropriately so. This is also the level on which the equality rights of women are a valid concern. They were neglected. The place of sex equality as a fundamental commitment is as much constituted by documents like this as it is reflected in them. Make no mistake, leaving it out does say something, and it does do something. In choosing to reaffirm some rights and interests and not to include equality, some rights are made structural to Canadian federalism. Equality, including sex equality, is not one of them.

The U.S. Constitution's record on women's equality makes all too clear that neglecting to mention women's rights at constitutive moments like this one is predictably not gender-neutral in its effects, particularly under conditions, like women's situation, that require active change in the status quo in order for equality to be created. If leaving gender out of the Accord is considered gender-neutral, it should be noted that facial gender neutrality in a non-gender-neutral world does not even guarantee gender neutrality, far less actual sex equality.

The damage done to women's rights in Canada at this point, of concern to all women worldwide, will be especially acute if no remedial action is taken, given that the issue has been so directly raised. Meech Lake fulfills the promise made in 1982 to Quebec to accommodate its aspirations within the Charter of Rights. Failing to include reference to Sections 15 and 28 of the Charter in it, or neglecting to make clear that nothing in the Charter is abrogated by the Accord, squarely poses the question whether sex equality is basic to the Canadian polity. As things stand, it seriously undermines the compact that the Charter made between women and the Canadian state.

9

Misogyny's Cold Heart

Fighting pornography in the United States, feminists have found that women live in a world the pornographers have made. We already knew what seemed like a lot about sex inequality, sexual objectification, the sexualization of male dominance and female subordination, and sexual abuse, especially rape, sexual abuse of children, prostitution, sexual harassment, and battery of women. But finding pornography was like coming upon a sacred, secret codebook that had both obscured and determined our lives. There laid bare was the cold heart of misogyny: sexual violation enjoyed, power and powerlessness as sex. Pornography linked sexual use and abuse with gender inequality by equating them.

Women in pornography are bound, battered, tortured, harassed, raped, and sometimes killed. Or, in the glossy men's entertainment magazines, they are merely humiliated, molested, objectified, and used. In all pornography, they are prostituted. This is done because it means sexual pleasure to pornography's consumers and profits to its providers. But to the women and children who are exploited through its making or use, it means being bound, battered, tortured, harassed, raped, and sometimes killed or merely humiliated, molested, objectified, and used because someone who has more power than they do, someone who matters, someone with rights, a full human being and a full citizen, gets pleasure from seeing it, or doing it, or seeing it as a form of doing it.

Specifically, in the hundreds and hundreds of magazines and pictures and films and videocassettes and so-called books that constitute the pornography industry, women's legs are splayed in postures of sexual submission, display, and access. We are named after men's insults to parts of our bodies and mated with animals. We are hung like meat. Children are presented as adult women; adult women are presented as children, fusing

This article was originally published in German as "Das kalte Herz," in *Emma* (October 1987).

the vulnerability of a child with the sluttish eagerness for sex said to be natural to the female of every age. Racial hatred is sexualized by making every racial stereotype into a sexual fetish. Asian women are presented so passive they cannot be said to be alive, bound so they are not recognizably human, hanging from trees and light fixtures and clothes pegs in closets. Black women are presented as animalistic bitches, bruised and bleeding, struggling against their bonds. Jewish women orgasm in reenactments of death camp tortures. In so-called lesbian pornography, women do what men imagine women do when men are not around, so men can watch. Pregnant women and nursing mothers, amputees and other disabled or ill women and retarded girls are used as deemed sexually exciting. In some pornography called "snuff," women or children are tortured to death, murdered, to make a sex film. Goebbels's film documenting the slow torture-murder by hanging from piano wire of the generals who plotted to kill Hitler may have been a forerunner. The pornographers today have learned something, though, because audiences do not run vomiting from the theatres as Germans did then. They stay and they masturbate. Andrea Dworkin once said to me that if Hitler had discovered what the pornographers know about sex, there would not be a Jew alive in Europe. For women, living in the world the pornographers have made means living with the implications of that.

On the basis of this critique, Andrea Dworkin and I wrote a law to place the power to oppose these practices where it belongs: in the hands of the victims. And we directed it against those who should answer to them: their victimizers. Our law makes the women being raped more important than the pleasure of the men who like to watch them. It says that buying and selling women is inconsistent with any serious mandate of sex equality. In doing this, we took on organized crime, which runs the pornography industry, buying with terror any support it cannot buy with money; the left and the intellectuals that defend pornography as sexual liberation and, with the liberal press, as freedom of speech; the right that cooperates by pushing useless moralism and worse-than-useless legal approaches; the consumers and the courts who do not see women as human beings; and the collaborators, the women (mostly liberal lawyers and academics) who defend the pimps. Not surprisingly, the courts held that the U.S. Constitution protects pornography as "speech" because–granted that it does all the harm we proved it does–it also expresses a "point of view." Our fight continues as you read this.

Because the pleasure pornography gives is sexual, it has been considered exempt from scrutiny, repressive to question. We have been called fascists for refusing to accept its authority and unscientific for believing women's testimony about its impact on their lives. Yes, pornography is propaganda; yes, it is an expression of male ideology; yes, it is hate literature; yes, it is the documentation of a crime; yes, it is an argument for sexual fascism; yes, it is a symbol, a representation, an artifact, a symptom of male dominance; yes, it conveys ideas like any systematic social practice does. It is also often immoral, tasteless, ugly, and boring. But none of this is what pornography distinctively is, how it works, what is particularly wrong with it, or why we have to stop it. Was the evil of the Holocaust what it *said* about Jews? Was ending it a form of thought control? If Auschwitz had been required to make anti-Semitic propaganda, should it have been protected speech? Pornography is a systematic act against women on every level of its social existence. It takes acts against women to make it; selling it is a series of acts (transactions) that provide the incentive to make it and mass-produce the abuse; consuming it is an act against women and spawns more acts that make many more women's actual lives dangerous, meaningless, and unequal. It is therefore an act against women to protect and defend it.

Through its production, pornography is a traffic in female sexual slavery. Through its consumption, pornography further institutionalizes a subhuman, victimized, second-class status for women by conditioning orgasm to sex inequality. When they use pornography, men experience in their bodies that unilateral sex—sex between a person and a thing—is sex, that sexual use is sex, sexual abuse is sex, sexual domination is sex. This is the sexuality they then demand, practice, and purchase. Pornography makes sexism sexy. It is a major way that gender hierarchy is enjoyed and practiced. The problem with pornography is not what it says but what it does: violate women's human rights.

In our hearings in Minneapolis, where our law was first introduced, the harm of pornography was extensively documented in proceedings one observer likened to the Nuremberg trials. Researchers and clinicians documented what women know from life: pornography increases attitudes and behaviors of aggression and other discrimination by men against women. Women testified that pornography was used to break their self-esteem, to train them to sexual submission, to season them to forced sex, to intimidate them out of job opportunities, to blackmail them into prostitution and keep them there, to terrorize and humiliate them into sexual compliance, and to silence their dissent. They told how it takes coercion to make pornography, how pornography is forced on women and children in ways that give them no choice about viewing the pornography or performing the sex. They told how pornography stimulates and condones rape, battery, sexual harassment, sexual abuse of children, and forced prostitution. We learned that the more pornography men see, the more abusive and violent they want it to be; the more abusive and violent it becomes, the more they enjoy it, the more abusive and violent they become, and the less harm they see in it. In other words, pornography's consumers become unable to see its harm because they are enjoying it sexually. Men often think that they use pornography but do not do these things. But pornography makes it impossible for them to tell when sex is forced, that women are human, and that rape is rape. Pornography makes men hostile and aggressive toward women, and it makes women silent. Anyone who does not believe this should speak out against pornography in public some time.

In our human rights law, which permits victims to seek civil damages and stop the pornographers when they can prove harm, pornography is defined as the sexually explicit subordination of women through pictures or words that also includes women presented dehumanized as sexual objects who enjoy pain, humiliation, or rape; women bound, mutilated, dismembered, or tortured; women in postures of servility or submission or display, being penetrated by objects or animals. Men, children, or transsexuals, all of whom are sometimes violated like women are through and in pornography, can sue for similar treatment. Subordination is an active practice of placing someone in an unequal position or in a position of loss of power. To be a subordinate is the opposite of being an equal. Prisoner/guard, teacher/student, boss/worker define subordinate relations. Our idea is that man/woman not be such a relation. Many people apparently cannot imagine sex without this.

Our definition of pornography simply lists what has to be in it for it to work, sexually. Part of the male definition of pornography has been its undefinability. No man dares define it because some other man might include what his penis responds to. Our definition is the pornographer's definition. Pornography is created by formula. It does not vary. No pornographer has any trouble knowing what to make. No "adult" bookstore has any trouble knowing what to stock. No customer has any trouble knowing what to buy. We only described what they already know.

Under American law, speech interests are outweighed to some degree when pictures and words are found false, obscene, indecent, racist, coercive, threatening, intrusive, inconvenient, or inaesthetic. Using a child to make sex pictures, or distributing or receiving such pictures, is a crime. Yet we are told that because pornography expresses a viewpoint about women, it does not matter if it is also coerced, assaultive, or discriminatory. The courts have so far decided that an entire class of women will be treated in these ways so that others can have what they call freedom of speech:

freedom meaning free access to women's bodies, free use of women's lives, speech meaning women's bodies as a medium for those others' expression. As Black slaves were once white men's property under the U.S. Constitution, women are now men's "speech." It seems that our pain, humiliation, torture, and use is something they want to say.

Pornography cannot exist as it does now without harming its victims, who will remain victims until something effective can be done. So long as the pornography exists as it does now, women and children will be used and abused to make it, as they are now, and it will be used to abuse them, as it is now. The question for women everywhere is whether we will wait for each act of victimization to occur that we know will occur, confining ourselves to cleaning up after the pornographers one body, one spirit, one devastated life at a time—never noticing the gender of the bodies, never noticing that the victimization is centrally actualized through pictures and words, and never noticing that we encounter the pornography in the laws, in the courts, every time we try to prove that a woman has been hurt.

Women, it is said, should be loyal to pornography because our freedom and equality depend on protecting it. This is because pornography is freedom and equality, so doing anything about it is repression, fascism, and censorship. In practice, this means that whatever the pornographers do is "speech," and whatever those who oppose them do is censorship. Women screaming in pain in a pornography film is "speech"; women screaming in the audiences to express their pain and dissent is breach of the peace and interferes with speech. "Snuff" is "speech," but demonstrators who use strong language to protest it are arrested for obscenity. When *Penthouse* hangs Asian women from trees, it is "speech"; when antipornography activist Nikki Craft leaflets with the same photographs in protest, she is arrested for obscenity. When pornographers make pornography of Andrea Dworkin, that is "speech"; when publishers refuse to publish her work, saying that publishing Andrea Dworkin is bad for freedom of speech because of her opposition to pornography, that is the way freedom of speech is supposed to work. Nor could she get an article published discussing these examples. When the Attorney General's Commission on Pornography wrote a letter to solicit information on pornography sales, it was sued by pornographers saying that these words were intimidating, and a court enjoined publication of the results. So now the pornographers censor the government in the name of freedom of speech, and Andrea Dworkin and I are publicly likened to Hitler for refusing to stop speaking about women's rights against them. It is beginning to seem that the sexuality of pornography is the fascism of contemporary America, exported worldwide, and we are in the last days of Weimar.

10

On Sex and Violence

Introducing the Antipornography Civil Rights Law in Sweden

Sweden is famously for sex and against violence. The two are defined by distinction: what is sex cannot be violence, and what is violence cannot be sex. Regrettably, this distinction does not hold in the pornography setting.

In Sweden, as elsewhere, pornography is largely understood as a matter of morality, of good and bad. The right's morality on the subject revolves around sex, the left's around violence. The right's morality views pornography as obscene, meaning sex that is bad or wrong to see: sex is filthy, women's bodies are dirty, homosexuality is perverse. The materials are smut. The left's morality sees a problem with pornography, if at all, when it shows violence. Seeing violence in pornography is helpful. But neither approach solves the real problem pornography poses for women. Ideas of good and bad in what is said and seen do not reach the harm that is being done. Neither left nor right addresses the realities of who pornography hurts, how, why, and how they get away with it.

Everything in pornography is sex for someone, or it would not be there. This includes any amount of violence, such as sadomasochism's torture or someone being killed or dismembered, tortured to death, to make a snuff film. If some consumer did not experience all this as sex, there would be no pornography made of it, yet it is violence by any standard. Pornography sexualizes violence. The violence doesn't cancel the sex; it *is* the sex. The reality is closer to the sex canceling the violence: the consumer's sexual response to the violence makes him not see that what is being done is violent.

Sex is imagined to be inherently consensual; violence, inherently coer-

This is an edited transcript of a speech given in Stockholm, Sweden, November 2, 1990. Andrea Dworkin and I were deeply honored to have been asked to address a Swedish parliamentary committee and work with Swedish women against pornography in Sweden.

cive. This could mean that anything violent is understood as nonconsensual. But in pornography, it means that force can be used so long as someone—the consumer, usually a man—experiences it as sexual, which then means it is felt by him to be consensual, including for the person being forced. The upshot is because the user is sexually enjoying watching, no matter how much force is inflicted, no matter how much the woman is being violated, he experiences the materials as presenting a consenting woman. In other words, once the materials produce an erection, they are sex, so the consumer feels that the woman wants it, no matter what is being done to her. To support this perception, it is common for women in pornography to be smiling. Often she is forced to smile. The consumer is often not shown the force that coerces her to smile, so the perception of the user is that she is consenting because she is smiling, not that she is smiling because she is being forced to.

Even more deceptively, often the violence is off-screen, outside the frame of what you see. The lesser pimp who abducted or entrapped the woman and sold her to the bigger pimp—the pornographer—uses force that you do not see in the film. Sometimes you can see the woman's bruises, as you could see them on Linda "Lovelace" in the pornography film *Deep Throat,* bruises from the beating she got from her pimp, of whom she was a captive, during the shooting.[1] But you have to look for them; they are not the sex in this particular film. *Deep Throat* shows no explicit violence, yet it took violence to make. Whatever people mean by violence, the force that got Linda into *Deep Throat* is not visible in it. What you see is an actor portraying an ecstatic smiling woman who loves to take a penis to the bottom of her throat being sexually fulfilled by doing so. Here is a woman who was violently coerced into pornography, doing fellatio she had to be hypnotized to suppress the natural gag response to accomplish,[2] yet the pornography shows no violence. It is all off-stage.

Materials like *Deep Throat* and what is known around the world as Swedish erotica are the materials rapists favor. Studies of convicted rapists show that those are the materials—not the so-called violent materials— that they most often use to get them aroused for their rapes and to help them select whom they want to rape.[3] Some rapists do use violent pornography, but rapists more typically want to see women waiting and wanting to have done to them what these men want to do and enjoying being raped, at least by the end. Rapists also use pornography to decide which "type of" woman to attack, women their bodies then come to believe desire to be raped. It is a dry run. This includes materials that are not themselves violent in the usual sense of showing violent acts but promote violence against women in the world. So-called "positive-outcome rape" pornography, in which women initially resist but eventually ecstatically submit to a sexual attack, is documented to be the most potent pornography made in terms of arousal and effects.[4] Is it sex or violence? Who decides? When pornography that does not show violence is made with violence and produces violence, when sexual materials that do show violence are not experienced as violent to the extent the consumer is sexually aroused by the violence, when acts are presented as violent but are shown to be experienced by the target of the violence as sexually arousing and satisfying, which is the sex and which is the violence?

Other than the negative value judgment the word "violence" conveys, it is very slippery and seldom, if ever, defined. I have observed it being used to describe what men do as men to hurt other men. It is masculine to use guns on men; men cut men with knives. So the hope in calling pornography violence is that if men use guns on women and cut women with knives, that will be seen to be violence, hence not allowed because men know they do not want it and do not like it. Well, dream on. While men sometimes do rape men, usually they rape women. At any rate, rape is an act in which the perpetrator is gendered male and the victim is gendered female, socially. So it is unlikely to be seen as violent whoever the victim is, because the act defines the victim rather than the other way around. But more directly to the present point, even when the same things men do to men to hurt them are done to women, they often are not seen as being the same. When a man is cut, he screams, he bleeds, he hurts, he is in pain. The blood is real. The hope in addressing pornography as violence, not sex, is that when women are cut and we scream, maybe it will be believed that our pain is real and that the blood is human blood. That it is violence, so the left thinks it is wrong. The problem, though, is that is exactly what pornography destroys: the ability to see that violence against women is violence and that women are human. Pornography turns the violence into sex. Her screams become screams of pleasure; her violation becomes her fulfillment; her resistance becomes her affirmation. Her violation is sex, so that blood, her blood, is not human blood.

After twenty years of saturation of society with pornography, as has happened here in Sweden, it is not surprising that the law prohibiting spreading depictions of sexual violence[5] is ineffectual and interpreted to apply to almost nothing. Once pornography has conditioned a population, violence done to a woman in media, no matter how much, is widely perceived as sex, as consensual, as not violence at all. After pornography has socially existed unrestrained, passing a law against sexual violence is easy, both because some people will be upset about it and because such a law is unlikely to stop very much. Those who have been consuming the pornography—usually including those who write and enforce and interpret the laws and have power in society—do not imagine that such a law applies to many materials that are actually there. The term "violence" means negative, exceptional, extreme, not everyday, not positive. The pleasure of sexual arousal is a powerful positive reinforcer. Pornography comes to stand for the positive value judgment that goes with sex, no matter how much violence it shows. Once violence is sexualized, it is less likely to be seen as violence. It will be mentally switched into a fantasy realm that makes the violence unreal so the sex of it can be experienced as pleasure. The desensitization that pornography consumption accomplishes thus works to protect it, even under a law that on the surface would seem, with a little critical distance, to make much of it illegal.

Addressing the reality of this problem, Andrea Dworkin and I have created a law against pornography that, although it covers violent materials, captures the real violations pornography does, which extend beyond what is called violent. Our approach addresses violations of women that existing laws miss. It is a human rights law, an equality law. Its basic idea is to hold the pornographers accountable for the sexual abuse they commit and cause, to make them pay the cost of the damage they do, and, in this way, eventually to stop them from doing it.

This law is based on the recognition that pornography is a practice of sex inequality. It addresses the concrete practices of this inequality, not ideas about what is seen and said about sex. This law is not predicated on what we do not enjoy seeing or are offended by seeing. It addresses what hurts real people in real ways that can be proven. We have the victims to show for it. All we need is a chance to prove the connection with the pornography that harmed them.

This law is based on the recognition that coercion, in a society of sex inequality, will sometimes appear in a form recognized as violence but will more often appear in more systemic, institutionalized, and internalized forms. Inequality as a form of force may not look like violence is thought to look. It looks like age: being a little child. It looks like disability: dependence on a caretaker. It looks like the authority of the police over people being arrested or incarcerated. It looks like the authority that comes with marriage, with sexual access being routinized and assumed, in most countries' context of the wife's economic dependency. It looks like being a non-Scandinavian immigrant in Scandinavia, dependent on another to stay in the country and facing danger if forced to return elsewhere. The examples that are not gender-based are widely recognized as ways social inequality is organized: between guards and prisoners, employers and employees, teachers and students, citizens and aliens, police and citizens, adults and children, caretakers and wards. All arrange unequal power widely seen as hierarchies in society. The realization that they are real comes largely, I think, from the fact that men are typically as on the bottom of them as on the top. Being on the bottom produces an understanding that you are beneath someone who is on top of you. Being on the top seems to obscure that position. It has been difficult to establish the hierarchy that is sex because mostly men are not on the bottom of this one (and those who are tend to be socially feminized thereby) and the arrangement is sexual. Gender is no less real a hierarchy, however.

We define pornography as sexually explicit materials that subordinate women through pictures or words, when the materials also include women being dehumanized as objects or things or commodities, being penetrated by objects or animals, presented in scenarios of torture or degradation or filth, being bruised, beaten, humiliated, raped, or enjoying incest and rape, and other particulars.[6] The list of particulars describes what is in the materials produced by the pornography industry. The definition of pornography centers on abuse of women because it is primarily women who are hurt by and through pornography on the basis of their sex. But the definition also covers men whenever the same things are done to them because they are men, or members of particular groups of men, and sometimes they are. It covers both boys and girls, to whom the same things are commonly done, including here in Sweden, still. It includes transsexuals, who tend to be regarded by equality law as neither women nor men, thus need specific mention. They are used in pornography in all the same ways as well.

The term "subordination" means social practices that keep people down, enforce hierarchy, keep it in place.[7] Subordination refers to the concrete dynamic and material acts of social inequality between the sexes, which must actually be *done* to be covered by this law. The materials must also be sexually explicit, meaning explicitly show sex. The definition encompasses the full range of pornography from *Playboy* to snuff. Pornography is animated by a logic of the sexuality of death that begins with the most primitive of hierarchies: person over thing, live over dead. Pornography is a thing. The woman in *Playboy* is, in it, made into an object, an unalive image she typically disassociates from her own identity to make, through which (usually) a man experiences his sexuality. He is a person. He buys her in this thingified form. He has access to her, he can use her in whatever way he wishes. He does. Her so-called consent is to universal use for masturbation by millions of men she has never met. The sexuality his body learns is a one-sided sexuality between a person and a thing being accessed and used. It is no surprise if one feels like a thing when one has sex with a man who has learned his sexuality from pornography. He has been having sex with things: dead, flat women delivered to him by media technology open for use. Real intimacy is not possible under these conditions.

These effects come from what are commonly referred to as "only" the *Playboy*-type materials. The logic holds and escalates as the aggression that is implicit in hierarchy becomes explicit. It escalates through sadomasochism and eventuates in snuff, in which a person becomes a thing literally: a living woman becomes her corpse, her final thing. This is pornography's inner logic, where it all is headed. Killing, murder really, is the ultimate sex act in pornography. It is the ultimate act of eroticism required by pornography's inner logic, by this hierarchy of person over thing, this inequality in which man is person and woman or child is thing. We begin reduced to a dead object, flat on a page, to be masturbated over, and end literally killed to make a sex movie. As to the murder, when cornered, the pornographers and their defenders insist it is all simulated; some of it doubtless is. But the consumer sexually believes it is real, and there is evidence that some of it is.[8]

Our law recognizes concrete harms. Sweden's obscenity laws prohibit the display, sale, or distribution of certain materials.[9] Our law, by contrast, stands against the real harms being *done.* Under it, survivors could sue for being coerced into pornography. A person ought to be able to stop the pornography of her and receive damages from everyone who hurt her and benefited from her coercion. When a woman is hauled off the street or lured into a lingerie modeling ad and suddenly finds herself in pornography, tied up with a man with a gun at her head saying, "Smile or I'll kill you. I can get a lot of money for women who smile when they're tied up like you,"[10] that woman would be able to stop the pornography made of her as well as receive money damages for the acts of aggression it took to make them. This law, in other words, is not exclusively about what is depicted. It is about what had to be done to the woman's life to make the pornographers' so-called depictions and what will be done because it is so-called depicted.

Women could also sue whoever forces them to consume pornography against their will, as happens in marriages, in homes, in schools. Little girls are forced to see the atrocities being committed on their mothers all night as they hear them scream through the wall. Showing her the pornography, father says to daughter, in essence, "If you tell, this is what I'll do to you."[11] Women are forced to consume pornography in doctors' offices.[12] Some women have been forced to read *The Story of O* and to act out its scenarios in their daily life as part of their therapy.[13] Some women have pornography forced on them in their employment as a form of sexual harassment.[14] A woman's spread legs look at them from the platen of their typewriter. Or they open their locker to pornography stuffed inside it.[15] Or in cold weather on construction jobs, they go to a rest shack for lunch and there is the pornography. The only warm place on their worksite is papered with the open vaginas of other women.[16] Pornography is a form of workplace segregation and sexual harassment,[17] as well as terrorism, including in the home. Women who are hurt when it is used against them in these ways should be able to get a court order to stop it—and damages.

Women are also assaulted because of particular pornography. Prostituted women are told, as the trick gets more and more violent, "I know you love it, I saw it in...," and they mention specific pornography.[18] A young boy brings pornography with his friends and they jump his little sister, hold her down, hold up the pornography, tell her to put your arms like this, your legs like that, now smile like she is in the picture, now say this. They gang-rape the girl, turn the page, turn the girl, gang-rape her again for hours.[19] The pornography is not separate from these acts. It is *there*. It is an instrument of the assault. It is a script, a direction book; it says here how to tie the knots.[20] When pornography can be proven to cause assaults directly, pornographers ought to be able to be stopped from selling it. If pornography is proven to directly cause an assault of one woman, it will cause assaults of more women. It should be stopped.

Pornography also defames women. Particularly feminists who oppose pornography have been used in pornography in this way, including Gloria Steinem, Andrea Dworkin, and Susan Brownmiller.[21] With Susan Brownmiller, the point was to say she really wanted to be raped, that's why she wrote this book against rape.[22] This false and defamatory lie in this pornography reported a putative date: I had a date with Susan Brownmiller, we were about to have hot sex, she was very aroused, all of a sudden she started screaming about rape. You're not going to rape me, are you? You're not, are you, oh really? I hope you're not going to rape me! In sexually explicit terms, page after page after page.[23] Susan Brownmiller is in pornography as a woman who wants to be violated, whose no means yes. Consumers of this pornography have a sexual experience of Susan Brownmiller to invalidate her opposition to rape. If Susan Brownmiller, a leading feminist opponent of and authority on rape, secretly wants to be raped, what woman doesn't? Our law would end these lies by making it possible to sue for defamation through pornography that, because it is sexual, has a special credibility that other speech does not have and other speech cannot counter, one that destroys women in ways that existing law on public women in most countries does not reach.

Finally, trafficking in the production, sale, exhibition, or distribution of pornography as defined should end. Pornography is a slave trade produced by the coercion of poverty as well as by physical force, drug addiction, and homelessness (where states do not provide homes) and by employment discrimination based on sex and race. So long as women are discriminated against in the paid workforce and kept poor as women, as they are in most places—women of color and foreign-born and noncitizen women in particular—women will be in pornography and prostitution, pornographized and prostituted. As long as some countries are impoverished while other countries are rich, women from poorer countries will be sexually preyed upon by men in richer countries. Pornography is an arm of prostitution. Typically, sexual abuse of young women in their families makes the street look like an improvement. The sexual torture and abuse with impunity in the family produce an entire population of young girls who leave home thinking that nothing could be worse and end up, in their own country or half a world away, in this slave trade in women, this trafficking in women and children that is the pornography industry.

All the harms that pornography produces in society as a whole through its consumers, including through the sexualized bigotry against women that it engenders, would be addressed through the trafficking provision. The degradation of women in pornography, this sexualized lowering and dehumanization of women, reflects and reinforces and reproduces and reifies the lower status of women throughout society. The women who are in those materials, who become women in general, are not the people who become authorities: powerful, legitimate, respected. In pornography, women become cunts. Would you want one operating on your brain or heading your government? Pornography creates bigotry, hostility, and contempt toward women, as well as aggression. It engenders that sense you cannot seem to break through that you are not real to the men around you, no matter what you say or do. It engenders resentment of your presence when your voice registers in the larger society, the sense that you do not belong, a sense made visceral hence felt as natural when sexualized through pornography. Whether or not any of its other violations hit individual women, these larger attitudinal and ideological dynamics affect all women to varying degrees in a society as saturated by pornography as Sweden is.

Several additional features of our human rights law contrast with existing Swedish law on pornography. First, our proposed law has a definition of pornography. Having one makes the materials identifiable to people and gives less room for discretion by authorities to fail to apply it or to misapply it. A concrete definition like ours makes it difficult for the pornographers and their friends to say that it is impossible to know what is and is not pornography. This is a stupid thing to say in any event. The pornographers know what pornography is. They know how to make it and what to put in it. The people who order it for the stores know what to order, and the people who go out to buy it know what they are looking for and what to buy. All these people know how to distinguish pornography from other materials. All we have done is write a definition that captures what all these people already know: everything that is pornography and nothing that is not. Politically and legally, the definition says what pornography is by describing what it does, which is subject to evidence, rather than employing vague moral or sentimental judgments like obscenity or violence. It describes only those materials that do the harm of sex inequality to women in the way that only pornography does it.

Legally, our law locates the injury of pornography in the right place: in the law of equality. Here in Sweden, you are surrounded by a rhetoric of equality, as we are in the United States, with less basis in reality. The traditional concept of equality that you use, and is commonly used internationally, may be difficult to imagine fitting with the harms described. The received notion of equality in Sweden is, to the extent one is the same, one is entitled to equal treatment. If women are like men, they can be treated as well as men. This traditional notion of equality does not ask why men do not have to be the same as anybody except one another to be treated as equals or why women are regarded as the ones who are different from men. Men are just as different from women—equally different. It does not ask why the consequences of that equal difference are not the same, and are worse for women than for men.

Standard equality law is most at home at work, where the contribution of the sexes is most likely to be seen as the same and valued according to a gender-neutral work product. Labor is also a place where men experience inequality, so inequality on various arbitrary grounds is more likely to be prohibited there, if anywhere, because men understand it there, if anywhere. But the idea of equality remains the male standard: if men don't need it, women don't get it. The Swedish Constitution has improved on this notion to some extent: "No law may imply the discrimination of any citizen on account of his sex unless the relevant provision forms part of efforts to bring about equality between men and women."[24] Some steps to bring about equality where women need it and men do not are allowed, but as exceptions to a rule against discrimination. When you are promoting equality, you may discriminate on the basis of sex. This does not consider that redressing sex-based subordination in which women are distinctively damaged in ways that overwhelmingly men are not might not be discrimination at all, but rather its opposite.

If laws equalizing the sexes would be considered sex discrimination unless an exception were made for it, the question is raised what discrimination generally means and how equality is generally promoted. If giving the unequal what they need to end inequality is the exception, what is the main rule? The main concept appears to be what it usually is: to address inequality best when, in fact, it exists the least. Promoting equality in society in the sense of ending sex-based subordination, transforming the sex-based hierarchy, requires addressing inequality in substance, when it is there the most.

More grounded clues to Swedish equality thinking pertinent to the subject of pornography emerge from the well-known 1981 report on prostitution. This report criticized asking only how and why women could prostitute themselves instead of asking how and why men demand that they do so, quoting Johansson, a critical member of the governmental committee on the regulation of prostitution, who argued back in 1910 that if all customers—for instance, because they were concerned for society's general well-being—suspended their relations with prostituted women, the social institution of prostitution would cease to exist.[25] This report noticed that prostitution—of which pornography is a form—is supplied because it is demanded. All is not equal out there. The traffic is pulled by men, the demand, not pushed by women, the supply. Reality has been recognized: men's demand creates prostitution. If men did not buy prostitutes, there would be no prostitution, and if there was no prostitution, there would be no pornography. Women have to sell sex because men want to buy it. Because this is not a symmetrical world, it does not call for a symmetrical legal solution. It is an unequal world and calls for a law against the men using the women, not against the women being used.

While the report makes vividly visible men's violence against women in prostitution[26]—the substance of gendered inequality, men's pornography as played out in women's world—it misses that prostitution is a matter of sex inequality for precisely this reason. Having faced the vicious reality of the situation, and that it cannot be addressed by looking at the women alone, the report goes off the rails by not seeing beyond the conventional equality model. For example, it regards criminalizing only the customers as a practical and ethical problem, a double standard reminiscent in reverse of the moralistic Swedish state regulations of 1847–1918 that disproportionately burdened the women in prostitution.[27] Conventional abstract equality theory has symmetry problems like this. In that model, similarly, equalizing down—men prostituting, or arresting men for prostitution as often as women—would be just as sex-equal as women not prostituting or as not arresting women for prostitution would be. By the same logic, sex equality in pornography would be achieved by women sexually consuming and violating men, or by people consuming and violating people of the same sex to the same extent that existing pornography does the opposite. But just as the false symmetry in the current law of prostitution needs to be changed to face the far-from-symmetrical reality, the traditional legal conception of equality that does not recognize the sex inequality in prostitution needs to be changed as well, facing its unequal reality. To do otherwise makes a mockery of women's substantive degradation, which only runs in one direction: from the top down, with women on the bottom. If the report had pursued its initial insight and the vision driving its perception of reality, it would have seen that ending prostitution by ending the demand for it is what sex equality under law would look like.[28]

Subordination cannot be ended by assuming a symmetry that does not exist. It can be ended by laws directed to ending group-based, top-down social relations, ending hierarchy on the basis of sex. No exceptions are needed to pursue this rule. Consistent with developments in international law, this concept has been adopted in Canada as the interpretation of the new Canadian Charter of Rights and Freedoms,[29] inspired in part by the Swedish model. In this approach, equality is promoted when less favorable treatment—subordination—based on sex is ended. Because pornography is a practice of gender inequality, injuring and exploiting women because they are women, ending it promotes equality. This is the notion of equality mobilized in the work of ROKS[30] (the National Organization for Women's Shelters in Sweden) and the other Swedish organizations that pursue equality for women.

This is not only a political approach but also a legal one. Imagine a woman is raped and there is a law against it, but that law does not envision the way the woman was raped. Imagine there is a law against battering, but the police do not enforce it. Imagine you have a guarantee of sex equality at work, but there is no law against being sexually harassed there, so your economic survival can still depend on being sexually available, and the law does not recognize it as sex discrimination. You do not need much imagination, do you? Women need effective legal guarantees of personal security and sexual integrity to have equality. The Swedish Constitution addresses the law. It has a requirement of sex equality. *Where is your legal equality?* Is it in your law of rape? battering? workplace discrimination? prostitution?

Is your legal equality principle alive in your law of pornography? The Swedish law of pornography, with respect, is the wrong law. It is not based on the reality it prohibits, and even the law you have is not enforced. You have a law against sexual violence in pornography, and you are surrounded by sexual violence in pornography. Nothing is done about it. It seems that the most the authorities can even consider addressing legally are the cartoons, which are bad enough, but no flesh-and-blood women are immediately abused to make them, which makes a much less real case—almost, so to speak, a cartoon case. A law against sexual harassment has been recommended and hopefully will soon exist,[31] but no law addresses the harms of pornography.

Your law against pornography does not promote sex equality. To make it possible for Swedish women to address the harms of pornography would implement the constitutional requirement of equal laws. It would further Sweden's international human rights commitments, conventions under which sex-specific abuses are beginning to be recognized as sex inequality violations. International law has yet to realize pornography's place in this, but Sweden could exercise its traditional world leadership role in this area.

Unlike your pornography law, ours is civil, not criminal. This is crucial. Your current law against spreading depictions of sexual violence is a good example of how criminal laws against pornography tend to function. Nothing happens. Those with power can act against it; they do not want to, so they don't. A civil law, women keep in our own hands. It empowers women to act with state support, as if our lives are at stake here, which they are. As if we are the ones who need to act, as we do. As if we know how to do it, and we do, and they don't. Women would go to civil court when we decide to go. Not first the police, then a prosecutor, then the ombudsman to get the police and the prosecutor to do what they were supposed to do and don't, and then the ombudsman doesn't make them do it either. We don't need their permission. Women who are coerced can use the courts to fight the pimps who coerced them; women can sue the men who forced pornography on them, the men who assaulted them because of pornography. Women can bring a legal action against the pornographers who make, and anyone who sells or exhibits or distributes, the materials that fit our definition, showing it subordinates women, and stop them. Any one of you could go to civil court and get an order to stop them. It makes each woman into a potential representative for all women, empowering each woman who can prove harm to act for women as such under law.

If you introduce this law, it is unclear what will happen. You will be told a lot of lies about how pornography does not do any harm, when in fact it does and the evidence shows that it does. But you have already probably heard these lies, and you know that it produces these harms. You will be told that pornography is speech and thus must be preserved, and that by comparison, women's lives do not matter. Swedish law is beginning to get it right on this question. In the law of Sweden, depictions of sexual violence, child pornography, group defamation, and others are listed as "offenses against freedom of speech" rather than free speech itself. In the United States, it is the laws against these practices that are commonly termed offenses against freedom of speech.[32] Laws that restrict this trafficking in sexual violation may be decried as offenses against freedom of speech.[33] But those things themselves—the pornography, the defamation—are not even imaginable there as offenses against freedom of speech. Swedish law recognizes these things for what they are. Because it silences women, pornography by our definition belongs on that list.

If you do not introduce this law, what will happen is clear. There will be no real sex equality as long as pornography saturates your society. Rape and battery will increase, and reporting of them may decrease as desensitization to sexual abuse and women's perception that they will not be responded to if they report increase. As the real rape rate rises, if it is noticed or reported at all, it will be minimized as an increase in reporting. Well, suppose there *is* "just" an increase in reporting. Now you know how much rape there has been all along. Why is a constant level of rape acceptable, cause for worry only if it increases? Then we find that the constant level is twice what it was thought to be. Why is no one worried?

Political action against all of this is crucial and must be continued. But law is politics by other means. We are told to use education, not law; change attitudes. Translation: let men continue to enjoy themselves abusing women with impunity while we try to make them think better thoughts. If you in Sweden figure out how to argue with an orgasm better than we have in the United States, please let us know. There is little as educational as knowing you will be sued, and little that educates people to the meaning of bigotry better than civil liability for discrimination.

The law, as you know, as all women know, is not ours. It is treacherous. It is slow. It also should not be let off the hook. It promises you equality. Get it. It is too powerful to be ignored. It says it is doing something about sexual violence. Its legitimacy is a form of power in itself. Anyone who wants to stop something cannot ignore law's ability to do nothing while looking like it is doing something. How do people plan to stop pornography without the force of law? Why is it that when women who are hurt demand redress from the state, everyone suddenly discovers the limits of the law? Why is it that when we ask it to do something for us, we are lectured on our individual responsibility to stop rapists and how the law really, sadly, can only do so much? Working with law is an improvement on violence, if not by much.

Maybe the law would be less limited in our hands than it has been in theirs. If one envisions turning around the entire Swedish state to stop pornography after twenty years of saturation, that poses the limits of law. But if you imagine the law in the hands of several million women acting against their own injuries on their own behalf, more is possible. The state does need to give women this law. The Swedish state, the beacon of affirmative governmental concern in the western world, hopefully does not intend to turn its back on Swedish women in this respect.

Perhaps it is time for the Swedish example to the world to bear the marks of the pain of Swedish women, and of their solidarity with women here and throughout the world, with the battered women who are those shadows walking past the windows in the Women's House, where we have only to see the pornography to imagine the electric shocks, the dogs, and the beatings that put them there. Solidarity with the woman raped in the subway while a hundred people watched, as they watch in the pornography. And solidarity with Catrine da Costa, who was prostituted and dismembered, whose life was pornography, whose death was pornography.[34] You can stand with these women. We hope you will.

11

Equality Remade

Violence Against Women

Equality guarantees are everywhere, but nowhere is there equality. Equality on the basis of sex is widely guaranteed—in Austria and other European countries, in the United States, in some regions, and internationally—but women are unequal to men in all these places both under law and in life. This disparity between principle and reality is promoted by equality's traditional logic, particularly as applied to violence against women.

Equality is *the* democratic norm for law. Formally, it is central to the rule of law as such; law's application is supposed to depend on what people do, not on who they are. In positive law worldwide—international, constitutional, and statutory—equality is also a legal doctrine. Further, it is a jurisprudence, a policy norm for law's relation to society, even when it is not doctrinally invoked. Paralleling these dimensions, this talk is divided into three parts. "Equality made" critically describes the traditional approach. "Equality remade" reframes equality with women's inequality primarily in mind. "Equality revisioned" finds sex equality beginning to emerge as a worldwide jurisprudential movement, animating social change for women at the point where law and society interact.

In what has become at once the common sense and common law of equality, Aristotle defined equality as treating likes alike and unlikes unalike. Treating those who are the same the same, first-class equality in this approach, is termed gender neutrality for sex, colorblindness for race. Its secondary rule, accompanied by an aura of inferiority, treats differently those seen as different; it is typically termed "special benefits" or "special protection." Legal equality has accordingly revolved around arguments of

This talk was delivered at the Test the West Conference sponsored by the Austrian Federal Ministry of Women's Affairs and the Federal Chancellery in Vienna, November 13–15, 1992, and originally published in *Test the West: Gender Democracy and Violence* (Vienna, 1994).

sameness and difference. Equality is basically equivalent to sameness, with difference, when undeniable, bringing up the rear. In this framework, women claiming equality have argued that we are the same as men when we can, and different from men when we can't, men's equals because we are the same, entitled to compensation when we are different.[1] That pregnancy benefits are termed "positive discrimination"[2] in Europe, for example, classifies them as discrimination but of an acceptable sort.

The goal of legal equality campaigns for women has been to secure equality on these terms. The equality concept itself has almost never been questioned. The closest to a critique has been the cultural feminist protest that women's difference should be seen as a good thing, not a bad thing. But the sameness/difference notion as fundamental to equality has remained in place.

Missing in how Aristotle's theory has developed under law over time is an account of the original distribution of goods according to particular traits, a theory of the social creation of difference, a critical awareness of the way attribution of difference can support systematically worse treatment, an understanding of the standard against which anything else is deemed different, hence less, as being a strategy for social dominance, a grasp of the resulting system as reproducing social superiority and inferiority, and any conception of the fact that those who set the dominant standard presumptively get first-class treatment without having to be the same as anyone. Principle, in this approach, has been defined as ignoring whether a given group begins or ends better or worse off, termed "neutrality."[3] Crucially as applied to sex, the worst inequalities of women as a group, such as lack of equal pay for sex-segregated work of comparable value and the failure of equal protection of the law for crimes of gendered violence, become unrecognizable as sex inequalities because they are merged with the sex difference. Treating such situations less well becomes treating unalikes unalike, hence equal.

This equality logic has descended in an unbroken line from Aristotle through the Enlightenment traditions of English and French liberalism that gave birth to human rights, to the slave laws and legalized racial segregation in the United States, to the Third Reich, to the liberatory movements of the 1960s, arriving fundamentally unchanged in the equality law of Europe[4] and the United States today. Historically, this approach has rationalized segregation in the United States on the view that Black people are "different" from white people, claiming equal but separate is equal.[5] The Third Reich adopted the same approach, treating "non-Aryans" differently from "Aryans" on the basis of their "difference."[6] One chilling emblem of this was "Jedem das Seine" emblazoned over a concentration camp: "To each what they deserve." As you are, so you are treated. The different are treated differently: exterminated. Aristotelian equality is satisfied. Of course, these results in both Europe and the United States have been repudiated, but the equality logic that sustained them has not been. This is an approach that seeks to have law mirror life: likes in life treated as likes in law, unlikes in life treated as unlikes in law. But what if social life is unequal? Legal equality then becomes a formula for reinforcing, magnifying, and rigidifying the social inequalities it purports to be equalizing and might have rectified.

Consistent with this logic and history, massive institutions of sex-based disparity like sexual violence are seldom addressed by equality law—typically only when a facial sex-based distinction is made, usually one that disadvantages men.[7] Sexual violence seems assimilated to the difference between the sexes, so a woman is not considered treated unequally when she is sexually victimized, just treated differently for her differences. Sexual assault is seen as inevitable. The fact that women are generally victimized and men generally perpetrate is not considered subject to equalization. When women are treated "differently" from men, from sexual objectification to sexual murder, the traditional equality rule is not seen as violated because the distinction made by the practice fits the empirical definition of the group. Women being defined as rapable, raping them doesn't violate them; it merely treats them as women: unlikes unalike.

Embodied in the law of the male state, this equality interpretation builds antidemocratic norms into the very doctrines that most promise democracy. At the outset, 53 percent of the population or so is largely effectively excluded from this equality, plus men unequal on the basis of their race, ethnicity, religion, and sexuality, plus class, and all children are excluded as well. Added together, equality law builds in treating "differently," including worse, maybe nine-tenths of humanity. The legal equality principle is said to be satisfied when permanent underclasses are being maintained. It is an extremely smart trick.

A worldwide movement of women moving against their determinants is remaking equality. In its practice, sexual violence is recognized as central to our inequality. The misogyny animating sexual violence is recognized as a mainspring of the inequality on the basis of sex that destroys our lives in reality. The movement against this abuse is not abstract or universal in the usual sense; it is everywhere but concrete and always socially specific within the culture with which women identify. Women's diversity is extraordinary; yet everywhere, always in socially particular ways, women are found to be below some men.[8] The equality of this movement is not premised on being the same as men, but on ending violation and abuse and second-class citizenship because one is a woman.

In this movement, African women oppose clitoridectomy and infibulation. Philippine and Thai and Japanese and Swedish women organize against the international sex trade. Women in Papua New Guinea and women who work for the United Nations resist sexual harassment. Brazilian and Italian women protest domestic battery and honor as a male excuse for killing them. Indian women protest dowry and suttee as a male excuse for killing them. Canadian women protest the use of feminism as a male excuse for killing them. American women protest domestic battery and romantic love as a male excuse for killing them. Women everywhere rise up against rape, even in cultures in which we are told it does not exist or is rare, cultures in which women until recently have been regarded as chattel or are still defined as sexual objects. Forced motherhood is opposed from Ireland to Germany to Bangladesh. Female infanticide and objectifying advertising are denounced and legislated against in India. Women in the United States, Scandinavia, the United Kingdom, and the Philippines resist pornography.[9]

This movement does notice that men are not usually treated in these ways. Men do not have gasoline thrown on them and lit and have it called a kitchen accident. Men do not have their genitals sliced up and torn apart so that HIV is even more likely and intercourse is excruciating or pleasureless. But this does not limit women to imitating men. No one demands the equal right to cover men with gasoline and light it. Put conceptually, women everywhere appreciate that difference itself does not mean being second-class. Imposed inferiority does. This movement shows a keen sense that socially organized dominance is the problem as well as criticizes its excesses. Women everywhere realize both that men have too much power and that power is based on the wrong things, organized in the wrong ways. Women want power redistributed as it is redefined—redistributed to women as it is redefined so that someone is not always above someone else, in an arrangement at once forced and sexualized, defining who can do that as a man and a superior being.

From this work has come a concept of equality as lack of hierarchy rather than sameness or difference, in a relative universality that embraces rather than eliminates or levels particularity. A refusal to settle for anything less than a single standard of human dignity and entitlement combines here with a demand that the single standards themselves be equalized. All this leaves Aristotle in the dust. The scope and depth of this uprising for social equality, spontaneous and indigenous across cultures, offers a principled basis for a positive equality. Its principles include: if men do not do it to each other, they cannot do it to us, and ending the subordination of women because we are women.

In women's experience, sexual violence is central to gender inequality, not outside it or a subdivision of gender-neutral violence that just happens to hit women. And sexual violence is sexual. The everyday sexuality of masculinity and femininity exists on a continuum with the aggression that becomes violence against women that is expressed in rape, sexual harassment, sexual abuse of children, prostitution, battering, pornography, and sexual murder around the world.

Legal equality theory is emerging from this work in one place: Canada. Equality remade in Canada interprets the constitutional equality mandate in light of historical reality. The Supreme Court of Canada assesses legislation, policy, and official practice in social context with the goal of eliminating group-based social disadvantage.[10] Equality law's active role in social change is thus part of constitutional doctrine. The Canadian approach requires that laws promote equality to be constitutional: go forward, not just sit here and reflect existing inequalities. Once social reality contextualizes the calculus, gender neutral laws may promote inequality. Further, if law either promotes inequality or equality, which is it doing in an unequal society if it is doing nothing? Once this lever is inserted, the mountain moves.

The Supreme Court of Canada has recognized that to promote equality requires promoting a society in which all are recognized as having equal human dignity, resources, and access to social power. It thus "has a large remedial component";[11] often, something has to change for a constitutional equality mandate to be correctly interpreted. Canadians do not divide affirmative action from nondiscrimination; it is all one thing. To end discrimination, promote equality in society; it is that simple. Fundamentally, this approach recognizes that social inequality exists and sets out to change it. Sometimes this takes differentiation, sometimes recognition of sameness, but who is being hurt and how is always noticed and put in historical context. The point is to eliminate the inequality of historically disadvantaged groups. Who people are and how they have been treated, who has been advantaged at whose expense—again, context—is key to the doctrine.

In work with the Canadian group Women's Legal Education and Action Fund (LEAF), which argued this approach to the Supreme Court of Canada, equality principles have been extended to sexual harassment, so that it is seen no longer as simply how men behave toward women, but as a form of sex discrimination.[12] Pregnancy benefits that were not paid under the traditional equality approach—no regular disability benefits because pregnancy was not a regular disability, and no pregnancy benefits because they differentiated on the basis of sex—are now required. To do otherwise disadvantages women because they are women.[13] LEAF also argued that criminalizing pornography because it is offensive or disgusting or immoral violates rights of freedom of expression, but stopping it because pornography harms women is constitutional on sex equality grounds. The injuries it does to women—the rapes, the sexual harassment, the battering, the sexual abuse of children, the prostitution that are required to make it and are necessary consequences of its use—make criminalizing it constitutional. The Supreme Court of Canada agreed, upholding the provision against it on an explicit sex equality rationale.[14]

In Canada, as equality is becoming a robust doctrine, it is also becoming, more broadly, a jurisprudence. Equality is being reenvisioned. LEAF argued that giving men power to veto women's abortions violates women's equality rights[15] and that "fetal rights" should be women's rights.[16] The Court agreed with the results without using sex equality logic explicitly. We argued that the statute of limitations for incest was too short because it did not recognize the realities that victims of sexual abuse face. The Court ruled that the required time for bringing that legal claim runs from the time you know that he did it to you.[17] How simple: Your rights date from the moment it is real to you that you have them. Another case recognizes the reality of battering in marriage from women's point of view, again without sex equality doctrine explicitly.[18] Another upholds a publication ban on the names of victims of sexual assault, solving a problem exposed by a critique of sex inequality but not using sex equality doctrine to address it expressly.[19] Another case takes inequality in the institution of marriage into account in allocating spousal benefits on dissolution without calling the problem a sex inequality problem or giving women sex equality rights.[20] The new equality logic also secured relief for a woman kept addicted to drugs in exchange for having sex with her doctor. The traditional common law approach held it her fault because she went along with it. The Court agreed with LEAF's analysis that the power relationship between the male doctor and the female patient had been exploited and was illegal.[21]

Gratifying as it is to win, it would be better if these victories were grounded on sex equality rights expressly, rather than treating equality as one more good idea. Good ideas allow those with power to pick and choose when they will be recognized and when not. Women's experience with this has not been good. Rights give you more entitlement to stand on. One wonders what it means that a body of law is being built that promotes sex equality in reality without calling it sex equality by name.

In any event, this legal theory of equality, the first to emerge from a subjected people, is making law into a potentially active tool for social change. It confronts male supremacy in society with the democratic demand that legal institutions work for all of us. Based on getting existing institutions to face women's reality, it also potentially redistributes power from the state to women. One example is the pornography ordinance conceived by Andrea Dworkin and me that would allow hurt women to hold pornographers accountable directly, rather than relying on the state to take action that it will not take or does not take.[22]

None of this expresses faith in law. It acts on determination to pursue law's promises and possibilities. When all the forms of violence against women in society, and impunity for it in law, are recognized as sex inequality violations, law will be made new in women's hands.

12

Pornography's Empire

When the British Empire was at its height, it was said that the sun never set on British soil. Today, the sun never rises on the pornographers' empire, which British-based laws help keep in the dark.

In a night that encircles the globe, somewhere on former imperial ground, women and children are every moment being violated to make pornography, brutalized through its consumption, bought and sold in this technologically sophisticated slave traffic. Because men enjoy pornography sexually, because most of its abuses occur in private, because its victims are regarded as socially worthless, and because pornography is not seen as an official invader and occupier, identified with another state, the pornographers' empire is largely invisible. Societies keep it in shadows; law leaves it behind a veil, heightening its desirability by periodic spasms of prohibition. Yet any man who wants it, virtually anywhere, can get it. The result is that the pornographers, largely organized crime, make off with immense profits—and the equality, freedom, and human dignity of women in the process.

British law being one of the most durable features of its empire, the closest the law of Commonwealth countries comes to addressing the problem of pornography is through its adaptations of the English common law of obscenity. This is not very close. The obscenity approach takes the view that the harm of pornography is its tendency to "deprave and corrupt those whose minds are open to such immoral influences and into whose hands a publication of this sort may fall."[1] Although exactly what this means is unclear, I think it means that obscenity stimulates men to masturbate, taking them further from God. In secular terms, the obscenity

This talk was prepared for the Ninth Annual Commonwealth Law Conference, April 16–22, 1990, Auckland, New Zealand. The research assistance of Carmela Castellano is gratefully acknowledged.

approach enforces morals. In practice, it prohibits depictions of sex that some men find offensive—that is, the public showing of sex that some men want to say they do not want other men to see. It takes the view that sex is dirty, women are dirty, and homosexuality is bad—in other words, it takes the same view of pornography that pornography takes of sex.[2] In the wake of British colonialism, its legal system colonizing the globe long after its military has left, the obscenity concept, with minor local variations, grounds the legal approach to pornography from India[3] and Australia,[4] to the United States[5] and Canada,[6] to Kenya[7] and Zambia.[8] It cares more about whether men blush than whether women bleed. It is designed to suppress, not eradicate; does nothing to hold pornographers accountable for promoting aggression, bigotry, and discrimination; and cannot empower pornography's victims. Virtue and vice are its concerns; women and children are not.

Its likelihood of actually doing anything about the industry approaches zero, although what these governments do about the presence and visibility of pornography in the name of obscenity regulation varies considerably. The variance seems to depend, among other things, upon cultural supports for its suppression, such as a sense that pornography undermines cultural specificity and traditional values;[9] upon the government's perception that its suppression is politically useful, as in South Africa;[10] upon how determined the censors are, which ebbs and flows;[11] upon women's level of resistance, which in some countries, such as India, has been substantial;[12] upon how determined the pornographers' marketing strategy is and whether they have gotten there yet.[13] The public legitimacy and visible presence of pornography are only one level of its injury, the level of acknowledged public standards for women's treatment. Addressing its public visibility, which is the most obscenity law does, does nothing about the harms of its production and consumption. To the best of my information, nowhere that pornography has once penetrated has it been effectively controlled by obscenity law.[14] Everywhere it has ever been, it thrives, either aboveground or in a black market.[15]

The inadequacy of the law of obscenity to address the harms of child pornography has increasingly been recognized by law, on the view that making sex pictures harms the child and the distribution extends that harm.[16] The total inadequacy of the obscenity approach to pornography's harms to women has virtually never been recognized by law. India enacted its Indecent Representation of Women Act, which at least notices that women are affected, defines women's indecent representation as depicting the figure or any part of the women's form or body when it has the "effect of being indecent, or derogatory to, or denigrating women, or is likely to deprave, corrupt or injure the public morality or morals."[17] What about injuring women? Canada's obscenity law has come closest to such a recognition. Portrayals of sexual violence against women can be part of what makes sexual materials deemed legally obscene.[18] Yet much violence is done to make pornography that is not shown in the materials,[19] and much violation is done as a result of the consumption of materials that do not themselves show aggression by conventional standards. Actual harm is strictly irrelevant to the standard obscenity approach, making it intrinsically unable to remedy the real harms of pornography. These harms happen not in the mind but in the world; are matters not of morality but of civil and political status and treatment; and are mainly done not to consumers, most of whom are men, but to the consumed, most of whom are women. Obscenity is about what men think of sex. Pornography is about what men do for sex.

Most pornography of adult women in the world today is produced and distributed by organized crime. Much of it comes from the United States,[20] although substantial amounts available in the Commonwealth come also from Britain and Europe.[21] Concretely, the pornography traffic is integrally connected with trafficking for international prostitution of both women and children.[22] American, British, and European pornographers also produce pornography in the countries of sale (say Australia),[23] which gives it an indigenous and local feel.[24] American pornographers gross billions of dollars a year domestically. No one even tries to estimate their international gross.[25]

Qualities characteristic of but not unique to the United States—including common and casual sexual violence and racism—are, through pornography, promoted throughout the world as sex. From American women's standpoint, the international pornography traffic means that American women are violated and tortured and exploited so that pornography can be made of them, in order that women in the rest of the world can be violated and tortured and exploited through its use. In this way misogyny American style colonizes the world on the social level as obscenity law British style, having colonized the world on the legal level, makes sure nothing is done about it.

To understand how pornography works and what it does, it is necessary to know what is in it. Women in pornography are bound, battered, tortured, harassed, raped, and sometimes killed. Or, in the glossy men's entertainment magazines, "merely" humiliated, molested, objectified, and used. In all pornography, they are prostituted. This is done because it means sexual pleasure to pornography's consumers and profits to its providers, largely organized crime. But to those who are exploited, it means being bound, battered, tortured, harassed, raped, and sometimes killed, or merely humiliated, molested, objectified, and used. It is done because someone who has more power than they do, someone who matters, someone with rights, a full human being and a full citizen, gets pleasure from seeing it, or doing it, or seeing it as a form of doing it.[26] It is done because he wants it done. In order to make what the consumer wants to see, it must first be done to someone, usually a woman, a woman with few real choices. Most women in pornography, if they are not directly abducted, are poor, desperate, addicted to drugs, sexually abused as children, or are children. If spreading your legs for a camera is a woman's autonomous choice, as the myth goes, wouldn't you think that the women with the most choices rather than the fewest, with the most preconditions for autonomy rather than the least, would be the women doing it?

In the hundreds and hundreds of magazines and pictures and films and videocassettes and so-called books that compose this slave trade, women's legs are splayed in postures of sexual submission, display, and access. We are named after men's insults to parts of our bodies and mated with animals. We are hung like meat. Children are presented as adult women; adult women are presented as children, fusing the vulnerability of a child with the sluttish eagerness to be fucked said to be natural to the female of every age. (Pornography exists of an adult man attempting to penetrate an eight-month-old girl.) Racial hatred is sexualized by making every racial stereotype into a sexual fetish. Asian women are presented so passive they cannot be said to be alive, bound so they are not recognizably human, hanging from trees and light fixtures and clothes hooks in closets. Black women are presented as animalistic bitches, bruised and bleeding, struggling against their bonds. Jewish women orgasm in reenactments of death camp tortures. The favorite racism of each locality is made into sex in pornography. In so-called lesbian pornography, women do what men imagine women do when men are not around, so men can watch. Pregnant women and nursing mothers, amputees and other disabled or ill women, and mentally retarded girls, their conditions or stumps or prostheses fetishized, are used for sexual excitement. In some pornography called "snuff," women or children are tortured to death (usually through dismemberment, suffocation, or hanging), murdered to make a sex film.

Hearings held by the city council in Minneapolis, Minnesota, in the United States in December 1983 documented the harms of pornography's making and use.[27] The studies of researchers and clinicians documented the same reality women documented from life: pornography increases attitudes and behaviors of aggression and other discrimination by men against women. Women told how pornography was used to break their self-esteem, to train them to sexual submission, to season them to forced sex, to intimidate them out of job opportunities, to blackmail them into prostitution and keep them there, to terrorize and humiliate them into sexual compliance, and to silence their dissent. They told of being used to make pornography under coercion, of the force that gave them no choice about viewing the pornography or performing the sex. They told how pornography stimulates and condones rape, battery, sexual harassment, sexual abuse of children, and forced prostitution.

In these hearings, women and men spoke in public about the devastating impact pornography had on their lives. Women spoke of being coerced into sex so that pornography could be made of it. They spoke of being raped patterned on specific pornography that was read and referred to during the rape or repeated like a mantra throughout the rape, of being turned over as the pages were turned over. They spoke of living or working in neighborhoods or job sites saturated with pornography. A young man spoke of growing up gay, learning from heterosexual pornography that to be loved by a man meant to accept his violence, and as a result accepting the destructive brutality of his first male lover. Another young man spoke of his struggle to reject the thrill of sexual dominance he learned from pornography and to find a way of loving a woman that was not part of it. A young woman spoke of her father using pornography on her mother and, to silence her protest against her mother's screams, threatening to enact the scenes on the daughter if she told anyone. Another young woman spoke of the escalating use of pornography in her marriage, unraveling her self-respect and belief in her future, destroying any possibility of intimacy, violating her physical integrity. She spoke of finding the strength to leave. Another young woman spoke of being gang-raped by hunters who looked up from their pornography at her and said, "There's a live one." Former prostitutes spoke of being made to watch pornography and then duplicate the acts exactly, usually starting as children. Many spoke of the self-revulsion, the erosion of intimacy, the unbearable indignity, the shattered self, the shame, and also the anger and anguish and outrage and despair at living in a country where their torture is enjoyed and their screams are heard only as the "speech" of their abusers. They spoke of, and out of, the silence that pornography had imposed on them.

Therapists told of battered women tied in front of video sets and forced to watch, then participate in, acts of sexual brutality. Psychologists who worked with survivors of incest spoke of the role of pornography in sexual tortures involving sex with dogs and electric shocks. One study documented more rapes in which pornography was specifically implicated than the total number of rapes reported at the time in the city where the study was done. Another study showed correlations in increases in the rate of reported rape with increases in a measure of consumption figures of major men's entertainment magazines. Laboratory experiments showed that pornography that portrays sexual aggression as pleasurable for the victim (as so much pornography does) increases the acceptance of the use of coercion in sexual relations, that acceptance of coercive sexuality appears related to sexual aggression, and that exposure to violent pornography increases men's punishing behavior toward women in the laboratory.[28] Pornography increases the perceptions of men who are not predisposed to sexual aggression that women want rape and are not injured by rape. It increases their view that women are worthless, trivial, nonhuman, objectlike, and unequal to men.

The testimony, taken as a whole, revealed that the more pornography men see, the more abusive and violent they want it to be; the more abusive and violent it becomes, the more they enjoy it and the more aroused they get, the more abusive and violent they become, and the less harm they see in what they are seeing or doing. Men often think that they use pornography but do not do these things. The evidence shows that they are poor authorities on this subject. The use of pornography makes it impossible for them to tell when sex is forced, that women are human, and that rape is rape. Pornography makes men hostile and aggressive toward women, and it makes women silent.

In this light, pornography, through its production, is a traffic in female sexual slavery. Through its consumption, pornography further institutionalizes a subhuman, victimized status for women by conditioning men's orgasm to sex inequality. When men use pornography, they experience in their bodies, not just in their minds, that one-sided sex—sex between a person (them) and a thing (it)—is sex, that sexual use is sex, sexual abuse is sex, sexual domination is sex. This is the sexuality they then demand, practice, purchase, and live out in their everyday social relations with others. Pornography works by making sexism sexy. As a primal experience of gender hierarchy, pornography is a major way that sexism is enjoyed and practiced as well as learned. Through the use of pornography, power and powerlessness are experienced as sex. The inequality between women and men is what is sexy about pornography, every social inequality exploited to heighten the pleasure, the more unequal the sexier.

On the basis of this evidence and analysis, feminist writer Andrea Dworkin and I designed a law that defines pornography as a practice of sex discrimination. We defined it as what it is, in terms of what is there and what has to be there for it to work: graphic materials that subordinate women through sexually explicit pictures and words.[29] Not "offensive depictions" or "indecent" representations, in obscenity's morality of the right, or violent pictures, in the morality of the left, but an actual practice of subordination on the basis of sex. Five practices are actionable: coercion into pornography, forcing pornography on a person, assault due to specific pornography, defamation through pornography, and trafficking in pornography.

We do not claim that no harms that happen through pornography ever happen without it. We say that sometimes it is because of pornography that they happen, and when they do, something should be able to be done about it. We do not claim that these acts are the only things that happen because of pornography. We say that no matter what else happens, these do. We also think that one of the reasons existing laws against these acts are so ineffectual is that pornography is permitted to exist, acting as an effectively protected sexual and financial incentive to perform them. In this view, pornography is not a prediction or instant replay or representation of second-class citizenship acted out elsewhere, but an active, integral part of the here-and-now experience of second-class citizenship for women. As an exceptionally potent and widespread vehicle for the sexualization of inequality, pornography plays a major role—direct and subtle—in escalating abuse and discrimination by men against women around the world. It violates human rights.

Unlike the obscenity approach, the antipornography civil rights law would work. Unlike obscenity law, it is civil, not criminal. It puts enforcement authority in the hands of victims, not the state, empowering victims, not the state. We know how well state authorities protect women and children through criminal law from their dismal record on battering, rape, sexual abuse of children, and prostitution. Unlike obscenity law, it would not create an underground. It brings the pornography into the light of day, because there is no place where pornography exists that it does not make victims. Unlike obscenity law, this approach does not make pornography more attractive through prohibition. Making pornography actionable as a form of sex discrimination undermines rather than heightens its attractiveness by defining its producers as pimps and its consumers as sex bigots. For these reasons, it is properly a civil rights law, meaning a law that empowers members of socially subordinated groups to act through law for their equality in civil society. For this to work, the law must be civil rather than criminal, it must define pornography's harms as the pornography industry inflicts them in reality, it must recognize that pornography is sex discrimination, and it must address the materials and the traffic itself as well as the individual harms.

Since the civil rights approach to pornography was created, every official commission on pornography—in the United States,[30] Canada,[31] and New Zealand[32] specifically—has recommended its consideration or adoption in some form. It testifies to the power of the pornographers and the powerlessness of pornography's victims that no country has yet even introduced the law on a federal level. The law has been passed several times in the United States,[33] but because of the legal intervention of the pornographers' fronts, it has not yet been permitted to go into effect. In the controlling case, all the harms that pornography does were conceded, but the court measured the value of the materials, hence their constitutional protection as speech, by their effectiveness in doing those harms.[34] These results are not legally final in the sense that the U.S. Supreme Court could yet find a civil rights ordinance on pornography constitutional in a proper case. Meantime the abuse continues as the sexuality of fascism, colonialism, racism, exoticism, and conquest is trafficked to the world by the imperial pornographers as the sexuality of liberation and equality.

Women in many countries are working to introduce this law, adapted to their specific concerns and legal systems. The resistance to acting against pornography ranges from denial that pornography significantly affects women's lives to elevating its value over women's value. Countries where censorship is most effective are often the most complacent because injuries are most hidden from view, but the complacency sweepstakes pornography's has many contenders. Our experience internationally is that the civil rights approach to pornography galvanizes women across cultures. It tells the truth and puts a tool in women's hands, offering, in Andrea Dworkin's words, what the pornographers have taken away: "hope rooted in real possibility."[35]

13

Sex Equality Under the Constitution of India

Problems, Prospects, and "Personal Laws"

The traditional legal approach to equality that comes from the West is predominantly used worldwide. A promising alternative that is gaining recognition can be found already implicit in the best of the Indian constitutional equality tradition, as well as in some western equality law. This alternative has real potential for furthering women's social equality through law, including for resolving the difficult political and legal questions presented by India's family law, termed "personal laws."

I

The meaning of equality in law nearly everywhere descends in a direct line from Aristotle's dictum that equality means treating alikes alike, unalikes unalike.[1] As developed through the Enlightenment, this conception revolves around sameness and difference. When people are seen to be relevantly the same but are not treated the same, their treatment is considered unreasonable and arbitrary and is prohibited by law as unequal under the "likes alike" imperative. When they are seen as different, they can be treated differently—unlikes unalike; that too is considered to be equality. This standard, termed formal equality, is traditionally regarded as fair, objective, and neutral as well as socially progressive. It is in a sense em-

In it's original form, this talk was delivered to The Second Lawyers Collective Women's Rights Initiative Colloquium on Justice for Women—"Empowerment Through Law, Gender Justice and Personal Laws: A Constitutional Perspective," New Delhi, December 14–16, 2001. In an earlier form, it was published as an essay. It is also published in *Culture, Law and the People* (Indira Jaising, ed., New Delhi: Women Unlimited, 2005) and also 4 *International Journal of Comparative Law* (I.CON)-2006. I thank Indira Jaising for her collegiality and support. Helpful comments and research assistance were provided by Lisa Cardyn, Jessica Neuwirth, Shirin Keen, Chen Chao Ju, and Swati Mehta.

pirical: law is to reflect reality. The problem it seeks to solve is misclassi-
fication. People within a classification are to be the same as one another;
people in different classifications are to be different from one another.
Equality consists in treating the same people who are accurately classified
as similar, differently people who are accurately classified as different. In
many quarters, this logic passes for rationality and common sense.

Without having been given much critical thought on the level of first
principles, this equality model has been explicitly or tacitly accepted as the
obvious content of equality in most jurisdictions that have legal equality
guarantees. It predominates under international law and European Union
law, guides the interpretation of the United States Equal Protection
Clause,[2] and has primarily defined the Supreme Court of India's application of Article 14 of the Constitution, as seen in the foundational *Royappa*
and *Dalmia* cases.[3] Certainly, this mainstream equality theory can be useful
for addressing some inequality problems, prominently including those af-
flicting elite individuals, as well as some members (often the least injured)
of subordinated groups; it may, with creativity, be helpfully deployed in
the hands of those already committed to producing social equality through
legal equality. Affirmative action, which treats unlikes alike on the basis of
their unalikeness, is entirely unAristotelian. For this reason, it has been
difficult, even agonizing, for this equality theory (and produces diversity,
a wholly unAristotelian good).[4] The subordinate status of women relative
to men is not prominent among the inequality problems the Aristotelian
model has solved. The questions are why and what to do about it.

This framework, when created, was not predicated on an understanding
that women are men's equals kept pervasively unequal by social orderings.
Confining women to the home, excluding them from voting and public office, precluding them from gainful employment, raping and prostituting
them—these were not seen as inequalities. Bluntly put, women's inequality
to men was not a problem that western equality thinking was created to
solve, because it did not see women as men's full human equals. To telescope
a long story, it imagined them as different, which translated into inferior
when measured by the tacitly male standard for the human. Women were
thought, by habit of mind, to be not fully human by virtue of their sex. One
paradox this has generated is that between the image of women being placed
on a special pedestal or especially protected for their differences when, in
reality, they are widely violated, exploited, and murdered with widespread
impunity in connection with the same settings and attributes. The result has
been the rationalization of systematic social inferiority by terming it difference, rendering most sex-based subordination not an inequality problem at

all. The fact that equality, as originally conceived in the West, was never designed to alter women's pervasively inferior social and legal status to men
goes a long way toward explaining why it has not done so.

Understanding that the most widespread social inequalities of women to
men have been imagined as women's differences from men, hence not inequalities, helps explain why equality law has traditionally not been used to
address violence against women, one of the most commonly occurring examples of unequal treatment based on sex. Rape and battering, it seems,
have tacitly been regarded as a feature of the sex difference. Looking across
cultures, we do see women abused, exploited, and violated in a range of
practices that have included rape, domestic violence, prostitution, and
sexual harassment in their culturally specific forms, with equality law there
standing on the sidelines. Most cultures simply see these practices as inevitable or criminal but not as unequal in the legal sense. Practices seen to at-
tach to differences do not give rise to claims for unequal treatment because
the sexes are seen as different rather than unequally treated in those respects.
Unlikes are, in Aristotle's terms, simply being treated unalike.[5] So, little to
nothing is done about such practices, certainly not by equality law.

Being defined as different—sex is generally socially seen as "the sex difference"—thus can, under the traditional equality model, result in being
treated worse or as less without that being regarded as unequal treatment.
For instance, when women perform different work from men, as most
women in the world do, they may be paid less for it, and that is not seen as a
problem of inequality because the work is different work. This often remains
the case even if the work is of comparable value.[6] Disadvantages are attached
to pregnancy because pregnancy is a difference between women and men,
with the result that disadvantageous treatment of the actually or potentially
pregnant is classically not seen as sex inequality.[7] When subordination tracks
lines of socially recognized difference, and it usually does, women can be
subordinated to men consistent with equality rules because the treatment is
seen as equal treatment for equal differences. Never mind that social subordination itself can create not only differences, such as less access to job qualifications among excluded groups and the view that pregnancy is a job dis-
qualification when it is not, but can also create the perception of differences,
including stereotyping and internalized oppression. Because unlikes can be
treated unalike, including worse, domination and subordination—which
form a hierarchy—can and do coexist with sex equality rules around the
world, with male dominance and female subordination seamlessly being
maintained under legal equality regimes.

In the mainstream equality theory, discrimination is treating someone who
has the same rank, status, or qualities as if they were not the same as others

of that group. But if someone is not already of that group, they are not relevantly the same as others in it and can be treated less well, and that is not seen as unreasonable or arbitrary. It is just treating them as who they are. Given that socially imposed inferiority has real consequences or it would be harmless, how arbitrary is it, ultimately, to treat someone who has been deprived of educational advantages as less educated? This equality approach thus can map itself onto existing social hierarchies, ratifying rather than challenging them. In this light, it makes perfect sense that formal equality could justify racial segregation, as it did under the Equal Protection Clause in the United States. It drew lines of difference where society drew them. All who were racially alike were treated alike—in separate railway cars.[8] It also makes sense that the policies of Germany's Third Reich could be, and were, legally justified as equal. "Non-Aryans" were treated differently from "Aryans" by being exterminated.[9] When practices of inequality are social tautologies, they can be ratified as equal with no logical defect. Although these rulings have been repudiated, the logic that produced them has not been.

So rather than being a means of ending hierarchical arrangements based on group rank, formal equality can be a way to maintain unequal status. Indeed, its success can be inconsistent with substantive equality, which may require social change. Its methodology of ascertaining reasonableness in categorization is to reflect reality as it is. If a person has managed to escape their group's hierarchically imposed status or manages to appear equal in spite of social assignment as an unequal, the model works for them. But it is not designed to work for those who have not escaped their status, which by definition most members of socially subordinated groups will not have. It will thus become reasonable, not arbitrary, to reflect their existing status—that is, the unequal status quo—in law. Equality becomes a right that those who need it most are least well situated to claim and those who need it least are most successfully positioned to assert.[10]

People who are already equal, in other words, can most readily claim injury when treated as though they are not equal. This is not to say that people who lack qualifications or merits should be treated as though they have them. It is to ask, when is the equality paradigm going to dismantle large group-based inequalities? Where does this model leave the structurally unequal, for our purposes here on the basis of sex? The result of the existing equality theory's logical application has been that the deepest and most widespread inequalities, including those of sex, those inequalities that inflict the greatest damage and have become the most socially institutionalized, including those stereotypes that have become real and those oppressions that have become internalized as well as cultural, are addressed least. Because its doctrine is structured to affirm sameness as a strategy for promoting equality, the higher up the "tiers of scrutiny" one ascends under the U.S. Equal Protection Clause, thus signaling greater concern for inequality, the greater the reality of social inequality one ignores. The observation by Justice Mukharji in 1951 that "[t]he craze for American precedents can soon become a snare"[11] applies with force here.

The point is not that it is impossible, with ingenuity and benevolent determination and smart lawyering, to make this model work for some equal ends on the margins. The point is that these are marginal, and it is just as possible if not more so to use this theory to entrench existing social inequalities, especially where the vision and will to produce equality are lacking. If an equality doctrine can go either way, depending on extrinsic inputs, is it really an equality doctrine? If it depends on goodwill and political commitment to work, its secular tendency will be to fail exactly for those people and at those times when egalitarian spirit is lacking, which is just when it is needed most. And that, in fact, is what has arguably happened. Sex equality laws exist nearly everywhere, and sex equality exists virtually nowhere.

II

Growing underneath, throughout, and next to this dominant model has been another quite distinct equality theory originated by peoples subordinated on the basis of race and sex, an alternative conception that has animated some legal work against racism in the United States and against violence against women worldwide. It takes the position that inequality is not predicated on sameness or vitiated by difference but is a practice of social subordination, of second-class status, of ranking as inferior, of historical hierarchy. In its view, the opposite of equality is not difference but hierarchy. Equality thus requires promoting equality of status for historically subordinated groups, dismantling group hierarchy. The Supreme Court of Canada, seeing that the Aristotelian paradigm as applied would not effectively produce social equality in a diverse society, embraced this alternative contextual notion as its standard for measuring the constitutional equality of legislation.[12] This alternative is influencing the jurisprudence of South Africa's Constitutional Court and increasingly animating international rulings.[13]

Sexual harassment law, which first argued that being in a subordinated sexual position was not a sex difference that justified sexual abuse but was rather a violation of sex equality rights, illustrates this alternative model.[14] That sexual harassment, by another name, is a common and culturally ingrained practice between men and women, arguably part of what is called the sex difference, was not allowed to obscure the fact that it is a practice of subordinate social status, hence an act of unequal treatment. If women's and men's sexual differences mean that men can sexually harass women—in the standard model's terms, treat them differently than they do men sexually because women and men are sexually different—either sexual harassment is not sex discrimination or a new vision of equality is needed. One can agree with the earlier courts that sexual harassment is not sex discrimination[15] or see that sexual harassment is precisely what sex discrimination looks like and imagine a new equality model: neither premised on sameness nor negated by difference, neither punishing difference nor privileging sameness, but targeting social hierarchy by making civilly actionable as sex discrimination a practice through which members of one social group have been permitted to treat others as inferiors.[16]

Thus was the Gordian knot cut that otherwise prevents equality law from remedying subordination. It did, and does, this by confronting directly the problem that members of socially subordinated groups often are not "similarly situated"—that is, the same—as members of socially dominant groups, often precisely because of their inequality. Formal equality can preclude substantive equality because in its calculus, difference—inequality can be one—may justify worse treatment, thus disabling formal equality logic from addressing social hierarchy simply because it empirically exists. The status quo distribution of entitlements and resources is thus built into the traditional western equality analysis in which dominant groups, who are just as different from subordinated groups as the reverse, have not had to be like anyone else to get and keep what they have. The alternative theory counters this deep bias by targeting directly and in substance the problem of systemic social subordination of groups that has so comfortably coexisted with the promise of equality the law has made but failed to deliver upon for so long.

To put it slightly differently, when inequality is socially institutionalized, it creates distinctions between people that can themselves serve as reasons that treating people worse not only will appear to be, but will indeed be, reasonable and not arbitrary at all. When reasonableness is established by mirroring society as it is, inequality is validated by an unequal status quo. The alternative conception begins in the context not of these abstractions of sameness and difference but of asking whether a concrete, historical, social hierarchy exists. On the assumption that no social group is inferior to any other, if its members are systematically then found socially unequally ranked or treated or situated, social inequality has occurred, and laws and policies and practices that collaborate in the social inequality of that group are illegal.

Courts are well suited to apply this approach because it is precisely concrete historical reality that comes to courts through the facts of cases that they are asked to adjudicate. Asking whether a particular group is historically disadvantaged, as the alternative conception does, is a factual inquiry that builds historical context in. It requires courts to look at the reality of social hierarchy, not away from it. It is subject to evidence. It makes the recognition of historical reality into an adjudicative principle, rather than a disreputable embarrassment to principle or a realist strategic consideration for the cynical litigator. This alternative theory requires that the law promote equality for subordinated groups by ending subordinating practices that promote group-based disadvantage. It deserves the name of substantive equality because it takes substantive inequality as its point of departure and produces equality in substance at its point of arrival.

III

India's equality jurisprudence has long exhibited inklings of formal equality's limits, undertows, intransigence, and backlash potential and displayed a vigorous sense that a more substantive notion of equality has been needed. As far back as 1963, Justice Rao's dissent in *Lakhman Dass* famously challenged classification theory as the be-all and end-all of equality.[17] He grasped the essential point: as between equality and classification, the tail has been wagging the dog. A similar perception animated the separate opinion by Justice Bhagwati, joined by Justice Iyer, in *Royappa,* where it is observed of the so-called new doctrine that equality is "a dynamic concept with many aspects and dimensions and it cannot be 'cribbed, cabined and confined' within traditional and doctrinaire limits."[18] Their antiarbitrariness standard was resisting the same equality thinking I have identified: the traditional limits of western equality thinking that have "cribbed, cabined and confined" equality law in India, requiring a new departure to be true to the essence of the principle and produce equality in reality.

Once the potential dynamism inherent in the equality concept is revealed in claims by subordinated peoples, as foregrounded in the alternate conception, a rich substantive equality tradition is revealed beneath existing equality jurisprudence in India. Along with the prominent cases on caste, perhaps its most visible exemplars,[19] some cases on women's rights, by taking the social context of sex-based disadvantage clearly into account, foreshadow and embody a substantive equality approach to sex. The jurisprudence upholding sex reservations in employment,[20] along with some asymmetrical lower court equality rulings permitting what is sometimes termed discrimination favorable to women,[21] and the sexual harassment rulings in *Vishaka*[22] and *Chopra*[23] drawing on international law, along with some decisions on equal pay[24] and comparable worth,[25] are all animated by a substantive sex equality concept. One Supreme Court case recognizes that prostitution is anathema to sex equality.[26] Some of the Supreme Court's recent progressive decisions on rape exhibit a sex equality sensibility that awaits only being doctrinally so labeled.[27]

Crucially, and fundamental to these decisions, India's constitutional text holds great potential to ameliorate the subordination of women to men. A signal beacon compared with many western equality guarantees, the textual language of Article 15 recognizes in the structure and provisions of the Constitution of India itself that sex has been made into a social disadvantage for women, in violation of the equality principle. Along with Canada's Section 15(2), India's Article 15(3) specifically suggests a substantive recognition of women's unequal social status by permitting special provisions to rectify their inequality. As a result, steps to end the hierarchy of men over women are here not violations of an equality rule that are nevertheless permitted. Because such steps promote equality, they are not exceptions to an antidiscrimination rule; they are not discrimination at all. Certainly, one could not legally promote women's *in*equality by law consistent with Article 15. Such a substantive awareness is lacking as a basis for women's equality rights in most other countries in the world, particularly in the West, far less does it take textual form. The provisions of Article 15 offer a substantive lens through which women's equality rights can be read.

In India's legal foundations and case law are thus strongly prefigured a basis and a readiness for the next "next step" in the evolution of judicial equality thinking—this time, for women. Formal equality could be confined to Article 14. Article 15, through Article 15(3) in particular, could provide the basis for a substantive equality doctrine that stands against disadvantage: the hierarchy of men over women.[28] Sex would encompass gender, its castelike socially disadvantaging form,[29] rather than being confined to biological sex "only"[30] or sex "alone" in the narrowest sense.[31] Some cases not formerly considered sex equality cases doctrinally, such as the Muthura rape case,[32] in which a sixteen-year-old tribal girl sexually assaulted by two policemen at a police station was found by the Supreme Court not to have been raped, would be understood as violations of constitutional sex equality rights. If the sex equality in substance achieved for women under other such legal doctrines were combined with developments in equality law in search of an adequate unifying rationale, supplying a theory to match the vision and text that are already there, the pieces would fall into place.

IV

India's jurisprudence having come this far for women, bearing such enormous promise, one major exception stands out. Out of step is the judicial reluctance to apply sex equality principles to the personal laws. To varying degrees, the personal laws of all of India's religions have contained facial and applied sex-based distinctions to women's disadvantage. Yet in the family area, the courts often permit them, even as the provisions are strained (sometimes to the breaking point) to provide an approximation or appearance of sex equality in result. In the employment setting, the apex Court unhesitatingly invalidated a rule that required a woman but not a man member of the Indian Foreign Service to obtain permission of the government to marry. Contemplating the facial sex discrimination there, Justice Iyer wondered "whether [Articles] 14 and 16 belong to myth or reality."[33] When legislated in the family law context proper, facially sex-unequal provisions are repeatedly permitted to stand.

One wonders where the Court's clarity on sex inequality has gone when reading its upholding in 1996 of the property partition provisions of the Hindu Succession Act. Sons of intestates were there allowed to unilaterally block division of property on sale of a dwelling house by living in it regardless of marital status, so daughters would inherit nothing until later, while daughters could live in the house only if they were unmarried.[34] Although women had fewer rights than men, the law was allowed to stand on a rationale that suggested it all came out roughly equal in the end. Githa Hariharan's case, challenging a Hindu guardianship rule providing that "after" the lifetime of the father, the mother is the child's guardian, gives rise to similar unease. "After" was interpreted to mean "in the absence of," as if this solved the sex inequality. The mother was the child's guardian only in lieu of the father, not in her own right, her guardianship one step behind, the size of his absence.[35] Until very recently, the Christian personal laws prescribed different grounds of divorce for men and women, men being permitted to divorce on a single ground, while women had to have more than one.[36] Muslim personal laws require a Muslim wife to be monogamous, while a husband can have up to four wives. They also allow husbands but not wives to divorce unilaterally without fault, institutionalize dower arrangements that arguably amount to selling women in marriage, grant male heirs twice the share of female heirs, and do not allow mothers to be guardians of minor children.[37] Myth or reality, indeed.

Even when legal decisions in the family area favor women's equality in outcome, as some have from *Shah Bano*[38] to *Latifi*,[39] courts resist predicating the results on sex equality grounds. It is not unusual in such cases for there to be no discussion of sex equality in the legal sense at all.[40] Thus the Court insisted on a statutory ground for voiding the second marriage of a former Hindu man who converted to Islam,[41] rather than holding polygamy in the absence of polyandry or mutual consent of all, a violation of sex equality guarantees. Courts appear more comfortable construing statutes to interpret personal laws within religious dictates, despite some embarrassment to canons of statutory interpretation and the risk of further criticism of the kind *Shah Bano* generated, when the Court was bitterly resented for presuming to construe religious concepts in the family area without the religious authority to do so. It appears to be more important to leave the determinations of family life to religion than to deliver on the constitutional and international sex equality rights that the Court has shown itself capable of guaranteeing in other arenas and the challenges to family laws have so amply justified. Why?

The decision in Madhu Kishwar's case in 1996 expressed the concern that invalidating existing law "would bring about a chaos in the existing state of law."[42] If existing law is unequal, requiring it to be equal will no doubt be unsettling, but surely that provides evidence of the pervasiveness of the inequality to be addressed rather than a reason that no inequality exists to be remedied. A more basic reason behind the reluctance to apply sex equality principles to personal laws is the (tired but far from toothless) charge that sex equality is a western and hegemonic idea that shows insufficient respect for cultural diversity. As the initial analysis showed, conventional equality analysis is western, and the alternative conception sketched is not particularly. Too, women are not equal to men in any western culture known. Clearly sex equality is not very western, even as sex equality is hardly unknown in nonwestern cultures. To give the West equality obscures its presence, its diversity and dynamism, as an ideal and partial reality around the world. It also distorts and insults the indigenous movements of women for equality everywhere—as if their desire for equality were not their own, as if they are not autonomous actors capable of recognizing and acting on their own interests. It also obscures their leadership in the global movement for the liberation of women. It was Hansa Mehta, not Eleanor Roosevelt, who was responsible for the traces of sex equality embodied in the Universal Declaration of Human Rights.[43] The United States still has not ratified CEDAW; India has.

The charge that sex equality is a foreign invention is a feature of men's culture in most places. It is the near-universal response by men around the world to women seeing their own value in terms men have denied them, when women oppose their denigration as all their culture has to offer. Nonwestern women need only compare their treatment not with western women's but with men *in their own cultures* to see the problem. The idea that western feminism functions to justify attack on minority religions to support the superiority of the West and to justify its intrusion has a lot of currency; it has happened in the past. But what the West has to gain in promoting equality for women in India today, an equality it does not practice or often even preach at home, is seldom specified. It is beyond irony that the principle of cultural particularity is so often invoked by westerners in defense of men of subordinated minorities subordinating women within their own cultures, and so little respected otherwise.[44]

Finally, sometimes the wrong people have the right idea, even if they express it in appalling ways. The historical example comes to mind of eleven-year-old Phulmani Bai, who died in 1891 of sexual intercourse with her husband. The parliamentary initiative to raise the age of marriage from ten to twelve was opposed even by many who favored it because the British—who were said thereby to be interfering with religious affairs and couched their objection in religious terms—were for it. Without doubt, young women's welfare became a pretext for colonialist cultural intervention.[45] But does that mean that girls who are raped to death in marriage, behavior hardly confined to India, are not being harmed by it? Does that mean nothing should be done? Defending something that hurts your own people because people who hurt you are against it seems to me a sign of a colonized mind.

The underlying, almost axiomatic reason for the reluctance to invalidate sex-biased family laws appears to be the fact that these laws involve the family. Looking more deeply in cross-cultural light at the reality of this family sphere, termed "personal," along with attention to the way women, a substantively historically disadvantaged group, are treated there, one sees that the family is a crucible of women's unequal status and subordinate treatment sexually, physically, economically, and civilly. The family, across cultures, is a site of violence against women, including sexual use, a place where women are violated with a distinct and almost indelible impunity.[46] It is a context in which, on the basis of sex, some are not permitted to be born, are not fed, or nurtured, are not even allowed to grow up to be battered, raped, and murdered. In this "personal" sphere, across cultures, women are often essentially sold to men and owned by them; women's labor is exploited with little or no remuneration; women are often, at men's pleasure, kept dependent within a relationship so long as it continues and discarded into destitution and civil exile when it ends. In interaction with the rest of society, in which women are discriminated against on the basis of sex in employment, they are impoverished. The family is also a place where women are required to take responsibility for children and are often given few resources to care for them and little voice in decisions that affect their joint lives.

States are far from uninvolved in this so-called personal sphere. They enter it, among other ways, by legislating and enforcing family law that effectively supports these practices. One kind of equality question is posed if the state never enters an area at all. But once entering, under well-established constitutional and international principles, they have to enter on a sex-equal basis. Certainly when states legislate sex discrimination, enforcing the subordinated social status of women to men on the lines just described, constitutional and international obligations are violated no less than when states act officially in any other area of society to the disadvantage of one sex.

Nonetheless, we encounter a pervasive and categorical reluctance to recognize sex equality rights in the family. This reluctance is not unique to any one culture but rather is shared by patriarchal cultures (and most are male dominant, although forms vary) around the world. The Supreme Court of the United States, for instance, so far looks at family law under equality rubrics only for facial distinctions,[47] when in reality family law in the United States operates as a dynamic engine for impoverishing women and producing and reinforcing their unequal status as a sex society-wide.[48] A majority of women in the United States marry under law, and most divorce through the judicial process. But no sex equality standards have been applied to the results or standards of either process—with the result, for example, that the marriage contract remains unscrutinized (say, for sub rosa voiding the rape law where marital rape is not recognized), and women's standard of living is permitted to plummet after divorce.[49] Because courts seem not to wish to recognize that the family is a sphere of sex inequality under law, sex inequality within it and on dissolution has been effectively exempt from legal sex equality intervention. In the result, the family is publicly regulated to women's disadvantage.

The family is well recognized as a central force in the public organization of relations between the sexes and, in all its various forms, as a crucible of the ideology and realization of male dominance worldwide. As the *Latifi* Court put it in the family context in India, "Indian society is male dominated, both economically and socially and women are assigned, invariably, a dependant role, irrespective of the class of society to which she belongs."[50] In most religious and cultural groups, if in diverse forms and with variations, the family is an institution of this male dominance. Personal laws often serve to legalize this dominance of men over women in forms particular to each religion—unilateral divorce by men in some, inadequate maintenance after divorce in another, inheritance by men only in another, sex-biased ownership and control of property and succession rules in others, multiple marriages only for men in some, custody of children to men only on dissolution in another, and so on. The common factor is male dominance—that is, sex inequality—in culturally specific and not infrequently religiously rationalized form.

The use and referent of the word "personal" in this setting is reminiscent of its place in the development of the law of sexual harassment. Sexual harassment was long regarded as personal in that when a man sexually harassed a woman, it was treated as simply between him and her, meaning personal rather than deriving from the collective respective social positions of the parties as members of their sex or other hierarchies or implicating society at large. It was especially regarded as personal by virtue of being sexual, thus inappropriate and off-limits for legal intervention. When sexual harassment was first brought to court as a claim for sex discrimination, the courts' reaction was precisely that it was personal, therefore not sex-based.[51] What they meant was, because sexual harassment is sexual, it is private, intimate, and individual, hence intrinsically unsuited to legal regulation, which is public, institutional, and categorical. In response, it was argued that the acts involved may have been intimate to the man, but the only sense in which the harassment was intimate to the woman was that she was intimately violated by it. It may have been personal to the perpetrator in the sense of involving him as a unique individual, but the personal wishes of the women who did not want it were not being taken into account. It was also not personal to the victims in the sense that they were being subjected to it because they were women, as members of their gender-based group. When the courts responded favorably to this argument and came to regard sexual harassment as actionable as sex discrimination,[52] what they were doing was recognizing that it made no sense to call this abuse personal, since it happened to women as women.

My point here is, when law and treatment are based on sex, there is nothing properly personal about them. To call law that is based on sex "personal" then becomes a way of saying that women, a group whose status is so decisively constructed in and of the arenas denominated personal, will have no recognized legal rights to equality. The injury may cut close to the person, as many aspects of group identity and life do, but when the experience is shared with other women, including other women of one's religion, it becomes sex-based. It is no coincidence that what is denominated the personal is often precisely where sex inequality of women to men is crucially enacted. The exemption from sex equality principles for the "personal" is a way of saying that women have no equality rights under law where they most matter. As the Supreme Court of India forthrightly recognized in the *Masilamani Mudaliar* case, "personal laws conferring inferior status on women is anathema to equality."[53] Once it is recognized that the family is a terrain of sex inequality, calling the law of that area personal is revealed as little more than a way of precluding women's assertion of equality there.

In this light, the phrase "personal laws" might be said to be something of an oxymoron, one the *Narasu Appa Mali* holding of 1952 in Bombay on the Hindu Bigamous Marriages Act attempted to rationalize by ruling that because personal laws do not derive their authority from legislation, they are not "laws in force" thus not laws at all for Article 13 constitutional purposes.[54] (It also held, in true formal equality form, that Article 14 was not offended because making special rules for Hindus was "based on reasonable and rational considerations."[55]) Personal laws are legislated. The state may or may not be the ultimate source of their authority, but it has made them legally and socially authoritative and has given its authority to them. Just as if family were personal in the truest sense of the word, it would not need to be governed by law, if the authoritativeness of the personal laws were other than legal, there would be no need to legislate them. Instead, the so-called personal laws are defined as off-limits to judicial intervention when challenged by those they hurt and are otherwise officially and judicially enforced like any other law.

Sex equality standards govern laws. Or, rather, whatever else they do or might do, it is laws that they govern. When they do not because the laws are called "personal," the term is revealed as code for an exemption deal men make with one another—here, that some men will allow other men to have access to women on their own terms, in exchange for those other men's allowing the others to have the same access to their women on their own terms. It is as if men agree to civil peace among one another on the condition of respecting each group's cherished mores for inequality of the sexes—in other words, at the expense of each group of women. It is this commonality among men as supreme relative to women that reaches across status and religion, and not their differences on those grounds, that can be seen to determine whether the personal laws will be governed by constitutional sex equality standards. It is, in this light, men's dominance in the family of every religion that is at stake in what is presented as religious and cultural diversity, the terms of men's power over women in the family that some men are allowing other men to set on religious grounds. If personal laws were subject to sex equality standards, the deal whereby men mutually tolerate one another's dominance over women, each group of men in their own way, would be off for all of them.

In the case of sexual harassment, until this same deal was exposed as a form of sex discrimination, sexual harassment distributed sex and money to keep control of both in men's hands and to keep women poor so that they had to deliver sexually to survive, with no legal recourse. When sex equality principles are inoperative, both sexual harassment and personal laws leave women and money in men's hands, the terms of their distribution arranged by men among one another. Unlike formal equality, which can leave this arrangement in place, substantive equality theory highlights who is doing what to whom, who benefits, and at whose expense.

Sexual harassment law has proven able to address multiple grounds of discrimination,[56] a sensitivity badly needed in the area of personal laws as well. A difficult issue for a substantive antihierarchical theory of equality arises with women subordinated within subordinated communities, when the claim is made that the subordinated community would be denied self-determination, sovereignty, or equality by intervention in its cultural forms of subordinating women. Substantive equality has a double potential for rectifying that subordination, as exemplified by the initial cases of sexual harassment that were brought by women who are African American and at the bottom of the labor market.[57] Their converged discrimination by sexual harassment, once substantively addressed, solved the problem of sexual harassment for everyone, as well as exposed the way sexual access and use was and could be simultaneously racist and sexist.

Legal equality solutions for those subordinated within subordinated communities challenge equality law but also provide an opportunity to promote equality across the board. In this perspective, the effective exemption of laws from constitutional and international scrutiny when they are denominated personal, laws that in fact are public and indeed political in the sense that they enforce the sexual politics of the relationship between women and men, is a way of institutionalizing male dominance, subordinating women by law. Not enforcing equality in the law of the family is thus an official means of keeping women second-class citizens in society. This larger dynamic is hidden behind religion when the personal laws are debated as a matter of cultural diversity alone. As applied to the personal laws, the substantive equality approach frames the question as one of disentangling male dominance from cultural survival, so that cultures can freely flourish, and women can too.

V

In cases challenging sex inequality in personal laws, Indian courts appear paralyzed by the fear of being tarred by the brush of cultural insensitivity. Insensitivity to minority women's sex equality rights, they appear able to live with. As to the family and religion, as they put it, reform has to come from within rather than be imposed from without. In this light, one possible way out of the legal and political thicket—a compromise that faces the fact that many of these laws violate sex equality standards but recognizes the judicial reluctance (however unprincipled) to invalidate them— could be to enact a uniform code of family law pursuant to Directive Principle 44 that provides for sex equality in all respects between women and men on its face and in application,[58] with its use optional at woman's discretion, including as relief for proven sex inequality in a community's personal law.

Communities could adopt the uniform code in its entirety. But for those that did not, whenever a provision of any religion's personal law was challenged and found to disadvantage women under a substantive reading of Article 15—such litigation infusing life into the interpretation of its substantive provisions at the same time—the woman would be allowed to elect the remedy of a civil code provision comparable to the religious law under which her family issue would otherwise be adjudicated. Article 15 could only be used in this way where sex is made a disadvantage. Once one woman had challenged each provision, the same election would be available to all women similarly situated without litigation. Instead of invalidating the sex-discriminatory provisions—concededly preferable on principle but apparently politically inexpedient[59]—a declaration would issue that any woman who so chose could thereafter be governed by the code provision instead of the religious one, in order to promote sex equality.

Sex equality would not be imposed on anyone. Women who wanted to be governed by the personal laws of their communities would be. But any woman, of whatever community, who wanted to choose sex equality could. Courts have found that "judicially enforcing on [each religion or culture] the principles of personal laws applicable to others, on an elitist approach or on equality principle, by judicial activism, is a difficult and mind-boggling effort."[60] This assumes that equality means uniformity when it should be understood to mean nonsubordination. Diverse standards for diverse communities are not the problem; standards that subordinate women to men are. If this equality is too difficult for courts to contemplate, women of each religion and culture can provide it for themselves with the backing of the state. The women of each religion, making the election, are *of* their cultures, so no cultural imperialism is involved.

This option for relief would be available for whole communities to adopt but also for women of any religious culture who wanted to elect it, one at a time. If, for example, Muslim women were faced with maintenance ending with *iddat*[61] and a uniform code provided longer as a remedy for sex inequality in the family and in society,[62] those who could not support themselves after divorce would not need to invalidate the Muslim law or have it overridden by the criminal law. They would simply decide for themselves which legal regime to elect, receiving maintenance longer or doing without the maintenance for religious reasons. As to whether a husband could marry an additional wife, perhaps a uniform code would provide for two-person marital units or perhaps for the agreement of the existing wife or wives in the expansion of the family, on the rationale that it is their family too. Whatever about this sphere is legitimately personal, it is just as personal to the women in it. The principle advanced here is that because of sex inequality, women would make the choice of law.

Such a solution would be consistent with India's reservation to CEDAW that family laws not be imposed on minority communities except at their initiative and not without their consent.[63] Under this proposal, a sex-equal family law would be available to all religious communities at the initiative and with the consent of the women of those communities. Women of nonadopting communities would take the initiative, and each woman would consent. No woman who did not want her marriage governed under the uniform sex-equal code would have it enforced on her. It is preferable that sex-unequal laws be changed by the affected communities (and that the CEDAW reservation be withdrawn). Other sections of CEDAW that are unreserved may compel the same result. But this compromise is consistent with India's international obligations, reserved or not.[64]

This proposal would promote change from within. Law would not be held not law. Courts would not apply facially sex discriminatory legislation as if it is consistent with constitutional and international sex equality guarantees. Tortured statutory interpretations that rationalize laws that discriminate on the basis of sex and religion combined[65] would be avoided. Secular judicial bodies would no longer offend religious communities by construing the meaning of their rules. It would also be far more difficult for courts to refuse to give the women of each culture a sex equality option for them to exercise than it has been for those same courts to refuse to strike down laws that are presented as the laws of each community, whether women have had a voice in designing them or not. This proposal is consistent with the impulse behind other innovations in the equality tradition, in which sex-unequal laws are not always struck down but are sometimes read up.[66] And it promotes equality in substance.

The downside of the proposal is, obviously, that the burden to claim and exercise the rights is on women individually; the social coercion and community costs would be hers to bear. With India's liberalized locus standi rules, the legal burdens of establishing the rights are less than they otherwise would be, though, and the burdens are also less than the laws, as they are now, impose. There is risk to each woman in electing her sex equality rights, but she would not be alone; on the assumption that many women would so elect, the results would not only be group-based in their grounding but also in their results. My experience representing Muslim women for over a decade confirms that they know well what to do with choices, even those with risks, so long as the choices are materially real. It would be up to those who work in each community to try to create the preconditions for the realistic exercise of the choice. With the men of each religious culture no longer doing all the speaking for the culture as a whole, what is cultural and what is male in each culture would quickly become visible. More women would live under equal laws than do today. No magic bullet, this half step would allow the women of all religions to vote with their feet, to walk out from under sex-biased family laws, perhaps facilitating their outright invalidation, toward the time when these laws, this compromise probably included, will look untenably unprincipled.

Building on the activism of India's women, exemplary and renowned worldwide, on the courage and principle of its progressive judiciary, and on its propitious equality foundations, India is perfectly positioned to develop substantive sex equality. It values individuals but sees group membership as constitutive of human dignity rather than in tension with it. It understands that there is no contradiction between economic and social rights such as family maintenance and political and civil rights such as equality, knowing that economic and social rights make access to rights of citizenship meaningful. It is a country that understands that equality and freedom are not opposed, but work together. By experimenting with new partnerships between legislative and judicial branches, India is well situated to exercise leadership to promote substantive equality under law between and among women and men—even if initially through less-than-ideal solutions—in the so-called personal realm as well as everywhere else.

part three

through the bosnian lens

14

Crimes of War,
Crimes of Peace

Where, after all, do universal human rights begin? In small places, close
to home.

—Eleanor Roosevelt

I

Behind all law is someone's story—someone whose blood, if you look
closely, leaks through the lines. It is not only in the common law that the
life of the law is experience.[1] The loftiest legal abstractions, however stren-
uously empty of social specificity on the surface, are born of social life:
amid the intercourse of particular groups, in the presumptive ease of the
deciding classes, through the trauma of specific atrocities, at the expense
of the silent and excluded, as a victory (usually compromised, sometimes
pyrrhic) for the powerless. Principle begins in reality. Law does not grow
by syllogistic compulsion; it is pushed by the social logic of domination
and challenge to domination, forged in the interaction of change and resistance to change. Text does not beget text; life does. The question—a
question of politics and history and therefore law—is whose experience.

Human rights principles are not based on the experience of women. It
is not that women's human rights have not been violated. When women
are violated like men who but for sex are like them—when women's arms
and legs bleed when severed, when women are shot in pits and gassed in
vans, when women's bodies are salted away at the bottom of abandoned

This lecture was given at Oxford University on February 4, 1993, and first published in *On Human
Rights: The Oxford Amnesty Lectures 1993* 83 (Stephen Shute and Susan Hurley, eds., 1993). The
help and contributions of Natalie Nenadic, Asja Armanda, Susanne Baer, Jeffrey Masson, Jessica
Neuwirth, Joan Fitzpatrick, Cass Sunstein, Andrea Dworkin, Richard Rorty, Kent Harvey, Rita
Rendell, and the wonderful staff at the University of Michigan Law Library are gratefully ac-
knowledged.

mines or dropped from planes into the ocean, when women's skulls are sent from Auschwitz to Strasbourg for experiments—this is not recorded as the history of human rights atrocities to women. They are Argentinian or Honduran or Jewish. When things happen to women that also happen to men, like being beaten and disappeared and tortured to death, the fact that they happened to women is not noted in the record books of human suffering. When no war has been declared and still women are beaten by men with whom they are close, when wives disappear from supermarket parking lots, when prostitutes float up in rivers or turn up under piles of rags in abandoned buildings, these atrocities go unmarked entirely in the record of human suffering because the victims are women and it smells of sex. What happens to women is either too particular to be universal or too universal to be particular, meaning either too human to be female or too female to be human.

Women are violated in many ways that men are not, or rarely are; many of these violations are sexual and reproductive.[2] Ranging from objectification to killing,[3] from dehumanization and defilement to mutilation and torture to sexual murder, this abuse occurs in forms and settings and legal postures that overlap every recognized human rights convention but is addressed, effectively and as such, by none. What most often happens to women escapes the human rights net. Something—jurisdictional, evidentiary, substantive, customary, or habitual—is always wrong with it. Abuses of women as women rarely seem to fit what these laws and their enforcing bodies have in mind; the more abuses there are, the more they do not fit. Whether in war or in what is called peacetime, at home or abroad, in private or in public, by our side or the other side, man's inhumanity to woman is ignored.

Women's absence shapes human rights in substance and in form, effectively defining what a human and a right are. What does it mean to recognize a principle called human rights that does not really apply to the systemic and systematic violations of the dignity and integrity and security and life of over half the human race? It means that what violates the dignity of others is dignity for them; what violates the integrity of others is integrity for them; what violates the security of others is as much security as they are going to get. Even death to a full human being is less serious for them. Half of humanity is effectively defined as nonhuman, subhuman, properly rightsless creatures, beings whose reality of violation, to the extent it is somehow female, floats beneath international legal space.

For a compressed illustration of some current realities that are at once a hair's breadth and a gendered light-year away from the atrocities that ground human rights principles and fill the factual reports of Amnesty International,[4] consider this communication from a researcher of Bosnian and Croatian descent gathering information in Croatia and Bosnia-Herzegovina:

> Serbian forces have exterminated over 200,000 Croatians and Muslims thus far in an operation they've coined "ethnic cleansing." In this geno-cide, in Bosnia-Herzegovina alone over 30,000 Muslim and Croatian girls and women are pregnant from mass rape. Of the 100 Serbian-run con-centration camps, about 20 are solely rape/death camps for Muslim and Croatian women and children. . . . [There are] news reports and pictures here of Serbian tanks plastered with pornography—[and reports that those who] catch the eye of the men looking at the pornography are killed. . . . Some massacres in villages as well as rapes and/or executions in camps are being videotaped as they're happening. One Croatian woman described being tortured by electroshocks and gang-raped in a camp by Serbian men dressed in Croatian uniforms who filmed the rapes and forced her to "confess" on film that Croatians raped her. In the streets of Zagreb, UN troops often ask local women how much they cost. . . . There are reports of refugee women being forced to sexually service them to receive aid. . . . Tomorrow I talk to two survivors of mass rape, thirty men per day for over three months. . . . The UN passed a resolution to collect evidence, a first step for a war crimes trial, but it is said there is no precedent for trying sexual atrocities.[5]

Human rights were born in a cauldron, but it was not this one. Rape, forced motherhood, prostitution, pornography, and sexual murder, on the basis of sex and ethnicity together, have not been the horrors that so "outraged the conscience"[6] of the relevant legal world as to imprint them-selves on the international legal order.

Formally illegal or not, as policy or merely as what is systematically done, practices of sexual and reproductive abuse occur not only in wartime but also on a daily basis in one form or another in every country in the world. Under domestic and international law, whether or not prohibited on their face, these practices are widely permitted as the liberties of their perpetra-tors, understood as excesses of passion or spoils of victory, legally ration-alized or officially winked at or formally condoned.[7] Even where interna-tional instruments could be interpreted to prohibit such practices, it is telling that their cultural supports are more likely to provide the basis for exempting states from their reach than the foundation for a claim of sex discrimination.[8]

The war against Croatia and Bosnia-Herzegovina exemplifies how existing approaches to human rights can work to cover up and confuse who is doing what to whom and effectively condone atrocities. All state parties are covered by the relevant international human rights guarantees, laws of war, and customary international law.[9] But nothing has yet been invoked to stop the abuses described in the communication or to hold the perpetrators accountable.[10] What is the problem? The fact of Serbian aggression is beyond question, just as the fact of male aggression against women is beyond question, here and everywhere. "Ethnic cleansing" is a Serbian policy of extermination of non-Serbs with the goal of "all Serbs in one nation," a "Greater Serbia" encompassing what was called Yugoslavia.[11] "Ethnic cleansing" is a euphemism for genocide. Yet this genocidal war of aggression has repeatedly been construed as bilateral, a civil war or an ethnic conflict, to the accompaniment of much international wonderment that people cannot get along and pious clucking at the behavior of "all sides"[12] in a manner reminiscent of blaming women for getting themselves raped by men they know. To call this a civil war is like calling the Holocaust a civil war between German Aryans and German Jews.

One result of this equalization of aggressor with aggressed-against is that these rapes are not grasped either as an instrumentality of genocide or as a practice of misogyny, far less as both at once, continuous at once with this ethnic war of aggression and the gendered war of aggression of everyday life. This war is to everyday rape what the Holocaust was to everyday anti-Semitism. Muslim and Croatian women and girls are raped, then murdered, by Serbian military men, regulars and irregulars, in their homes, in rape/death camps, on hillsides, everywhere. Their corpses are raped as well.[13] When this is noticed, it is either as genocide or as rape, or as femicide but not genocide, but not as rape as a form of genocide directed specifically at women. If it is seen either as part of a campaign of Serbs against non-Serbs or as an onslaught by combatants against civilians, it is not seen as an attack by men against women. Or, in the feminist whitewash, it becomes just another instance of aggression by all men against all women all the time, rather than what it is, which is rape by certain men against certain women. The point seems to be to obscure, by any means available, exactly who is doing what to whom and why.[14]

When the women survive, the rapes tend to be regarded as an inevitability of armed conflict, part of the war of all against all, or as a continuation of the hostilities of civil life, of all men against all women. Rape does occur in war among and between all sides; rape is a daily act by men against women and is always an act of domination by men over women.

But the fact that these rapes are part of an ethnic war of extermination being misrepresented as a civil war among equal aggressors[15] means that Muslim and Croatian women are facing twice as many rapists with twice as many excuses, two layers of men on top of them rather than one, and two layers of impunity serving to justify the rapes: just war and just life.

Like all rapes, these rapes are particular as well as generic, and the particularity matters. This is ethnic rape as an official policy of war:[16] not only a policy of the pleasure of male power unleashed; not only a policy to defile, torture, humiliate, degrade, and demoralize the other side; not only a policy of men posturing to gain advantage and ground over other men. It is rape under orders: not out of control, under control. It is rape unto death, rape as massacre, rape to kill or make the victims wish they were dead. It is rape as an instrument of forced exile, to make you leave your home and never come back. It is rape to be seen and heard by others, rape as spectacle. It is rape to shatter a people, to drive a wedge through a particular community. It is the rape of misogyny liberated by xenophobia and unleashed by official command.[17] It is rape as genocide.

It is rape made sexy for the perpetrators by the defenselessness and youth of many of the victims and the rapists' absolute power to select victims at will. It is rape made more arousing by the ethnic hostility against a designated enemy—"For Serbia"—and made to seem right by lies about the behavior of that enemy. It is rape made exciting by knowing that there are no limits on what can be done, that the women can be raped to death. Most of all, it is rape made sexually irresistible by the fact that the women are about to be sacrificed, by the ultimate power of reducing a person to a corpse, by the powerlessness of the women and children in the face of their imminent murder at the hands of their rapist. It is murder as the ultimate sexual act. Do not say it is not sex for the men. When the men are told to take the women away and not bring them back, they rape them, *then* kill them, then sometimes rape them again, cut off their breasts, and rip out their wombs.[18] One woman was allowed to live so long as she kept her Serbian captor hard all night orally, night after night after night.[19]

This is rape as torture and rape as extermination. Some women who are not killed speak of wanting to take their own lives. It is at once mass rape and serial rape indistinguishable from prostitution. It is concentration camp as brothel: women impounded to be passed around by men among men.[20] It is also rape as a policy of ethnic uniformity and ethnic conquest, annexation and expansion, acquisition by one nation of others, colonization of women's bodies as colonization of the culture they symbolize and embody as well as of the territory they occupy. It is rape because a Serb wants your apartment. It is rape for reproduction as ethnic liquidation: Croatian and Muslim women are raped to help make a Serbian state by making Serbian babies.[21]

This is ethnic rape. If this were racial rape, it would be pure pollution, the children regarded as dirty and contaminated: their mothers' babies, as in the American South under slavery, Black babies. Because it is ethnic rape, the children are regarded as clean and purified: their fathers' babies, Serbian babies, as clean as anyone with a woman's blood in them and on them can be. The idea seems to be to create a fifth column within Croatian and Muslim society, children (all sons?) who will rise up and join their fathers. Much Serbian ideology and practice takes a page from the Nazi book. Combining with it the archaic view that the sperm carries all the genetic material, the Serbs have achieved the ultimate racialization of culture, the (one hopes) final conclusion of Nazism: now culture is genetic.[22]

The spectacle of the UN troops violating the population they are supposed to protect adds a touch of the perverse. My correspondent observes that "there are . . . reports of UN troops participating in raping Muslim and Croatian women from the Serb rape/death camps. Their presence has apparently increased trafficking in women and girls through the opening of brothels, brothel-massage parlors, peep-shows, and the local production of pornographic films."[23] A former United Nations Protection Force (UNPROFOR) commander reportedly accepted offers from Serbian commanders to bring him Muslim girls from the camps for orgies.[24] This paradigmatic instance of the male bond across official lines pointedly poses, in the gender context, Juvenal's question of who shall guard the guardians—especially when the guardians are already there to guard the other guardians. The Nazis took pictures, but in its sophisticated employment of media technology, in the openness of its use of pornography, in its conscious making of pornography of its atrocities, this is perhaps the first truly modern war.[25]

Where do international human rights law and humanitarian law stand on this? In real terms, the rules that govern the law's treatment of women elsewhere pertain here as well: A human is not one who is sexually and reproductively violated. One is not human "down there." Nor is a human right something a man in society or in a state of nature takes away from you and others like you. In fact, there are no others like you, because "a man" defines what "an individual" means, and human rights are mostly "individual" rights. Men have their human rights violated; rather, when someone's human rights are recognized as violated, he is probably a man.

Men are permitted to be individuals so can be violated as individuals. If you are hurt as a member of a group, the odds that the group will be recognized as violated, considered human, are improved if it includes men. Under guarantees of international human rights, as well as in everyday life, a woman is "not yet a name for a way of being human."[26]

A right, as this legal definition is lived in reality, becomes something no woman, as a member of the group women, has to lose. A right is also something only an entity with the power of a nation can violate; it is a duty of government not to interfere with civil and political liberties as they socially exist. The role of international law has been largely, in Isaiah Berlin's sense,[27] negative. It could be so much more, but it tends to foster human rights less through mandating governmental intervention than through enforcing governmental abstinence. In other words, if your human rights are going to be violated, pray it is by someone who looks like a government, and that he already acted, and acted wrong.

In Europe, some basis exists for interpreting international law to require that governments act in situations like these; the affirmative state is more congenial to the European legal tradition in any case.[28] Sometimes international human rights law is stretched to countenance action against private violations, but this is pursued selectively. Honduras was held responsible for murders by private death squads that both acted as if they were official and were officially permitted to operate.[29] "Mainstream human rights groups have taken on the phenomenon of 'disappearances' in Argentina, murder of indigenous rubber tappers in Brazil, and racially-motivated hate crimes—all abuses perpetrated by private individuals," notes Lori Heise, "but when it comes to the beating and murder of millions of women each year, their hands are tied."[30]

The violations of the human rights of men better fit the paradigm of human rights violations because that paradigm has been based on the experiences of men. Male reality has become human rights principle, or at least the principle governing human rights practice. Men have and take liberties as a function of their social power as men. Men have often needed state force to get away with subjecting other men; slavery and segregation in the United States and Hitler's persecutions were explicitly legalized. So the model of human rights violation is based on state action. The result is when men use their liberties socially to deprive women of theirs, it does not look like a human rights violation. When men are deprived of theirs by governments, it does.

In the case of women, because male dominance is built into the social structure, social force is often enough to deprive them of human rights on a mass scale. Even so, states do collaborate elaborately, not just by abdicating social life but by intervening legally to entitle men to much of the power they socially exercise, legitimating what men can get away with in fact. But even recognizing this fairly active state involvement, most women are not directly raped, forcibly impregnated, and trafficked by state policy, at least not most of the time. Although the state in some way stands behind most of what men do to women, men typically have enough power to control and violate women without the state's explicitly intervening to allow it. As a result, women are not seen as subjected by the state as such, so their condition is regarded as prelegal, social and hence natural, and so largely outside international human rights accountability.

Now consider that most human rights instruments empower states to act against states, rather than individuals or groups to act on their own behalf. Given that only state violations of human rights are recognized, this is very odd. States are the only ones recognized as violating human rights, yet states are also the only ones empowered to redress them. It is not only the fox guarding the henhouse, it is the guardians guarding the guardians. Not only are men's so-called private acts against women left out; power to act against public acts is left exclusively in the hands of those who commit those acts. No state effectively guarantees women's human rights within its borders. No state has an incentive to break ranks by setting a human rights standard for women's status and treatment that no state yet meets. Internationally, men's states protect each other the way men protect each other from accountability for violations of women within states. At least this is one explanation for the failure of international human rights law effectively to empower individuals or groups of women to enforce their own human rights against individuals and states alike.[31] Which state is in a position to challenge another state on women's human rights? Which state ever will?

Wartime is exceptional in that atrocities by soldiers against civilians are always essentially state acts. But men do in war what they do in peace. When it comes to women, at least to civilian casualties, the complacency that surrounds peacetime extends to war, however the laws read. And the more a conflict can be framed as *within* a state, as a civil war, as social, as domestic, the less human rights are recognized as being violated.[32] In other words, the closer a fight comes to home, the more "feminized" the victims become no matter their gender, and the less likely international human rights will be found to be violated, no matter what was done.

II

The received concepts at work here have a complex history, mostly a western one, which can be read and compressed as follows. The contractarian liberals, building on Greek and Roman antecedents, opposed medieval status notions that assigned human value within a rigid hierarchy based on birth. Seeking to secure human freedom against state tyranny, they posited the radical notion that each person, qua human, had, meaning had by nature, irrevocable and equal entitlements to life, liberty, security, dignity, property, and so on. Through the American and French revolutions, this idea of inalienable human worth called individual rights was entrenched, checking organized power in the form of government. Subsequently, some transnational agreements further elevated and enshrined the same recognitions as binding among state parties.

Then the Third Reich utterly violated all such rights—inter alia by manipulating the pre-1945 system that left minority protection exclusively to states[33]—isolating and liquidating those it saw as inferior or polluting or oppositional. In particular, the official attempted extermination of the Jews as a people galvanized the notion of supranational guarantees of human rights with a survival urgency. This organized genocide by government policy indelibly marked and fundamentally shaped the content, priorities, sensitivities, and deep structure of the received law of human rights in our time. In a reading of this reality, more than any other, contemporary human rights finds its principled ground.

Largely beneath notice in this tradition has been the status of women as such, socially subordinated to men and excluded or ignored, marginalized or subjected by state policy. Women's enforced inequality has been a reality on which all these systems are materially predicated so seamlessly it has been invisible. Women were not citizens in Greek democracy; they were wives, slaves, prostitutes.[34] In this setting, Aristotle formulated his equality principle as treating likes alike and unlikes unalike—a concept fundamentally unquestioned since, including in the international human rights context. In this approach, it does not matter whether one was hurt or helped, permitted to dominate or kept subordinated; all that matters is that empirical condition, no matter how created, fits normative treatment.[35] That women were apparently so different to Aristotle as not to be treated unequally under his principle when excluded from citizenship has not been considered a drawback or an indication that something is amiss.

Building on this tradition, the original liberals formulated their social compacts in and for societies in which women could not even vote. With the exception of John Stuart Mill,[36] they did not see a problem in this, projecting their purportedly universal notions of what have come to be called human rights in ways that did not explicitly include women and effectively kept most women from access to them. Humans own property; women mostly cannot; more often they are property. Humans are equal because they can kill; women are socialized not to kill and are punished, not glorified, when they do. Humans consent to a regime or leave it; women have no voice to dissent, no place to go, and no means of leaving.[37] At the same time, guarantees women specifically need because of sex inequality in society, in order to live to a standard defined as human—like freedom from being bought and sold as sexual chattel, autonomous economic means, reproductive control, personal security from intimate invasion, a credible voice in public life, a nonderivative place in the world— were not considered at all.

What women need for equality was not only not guaranteed; much of women's inequality was guaranteed in the form of men's individual civil liberties.[38] In these theories, abuses of women were tacitly if not explicitly condoned as individual rights. What were called individual rights have become, in life, rights of men as a group over women individually and as a class. Women's rape becomes men's liberty, gang-rape their fraternity, prostitution their property, forced pregnancy their family and their privacy, pornography their speech. Put another way, whatever their rebellions accomplished for human freedom, and it was substantial, the American Revolution did not free the slaves, and the French Revolution did free the Marquis de Sade—facts connected by legitimating a traffic in human beings and the sexual abuse of women for economic gain. This is what the received concept of equality meant and largely still means.

Because women are a group whose claim to human status is tenuous and denied, the attempt to apply human rights law to women as such makes two more general problems worse. Human rights have no ground and no teeth. As to teeth, human rights are enforced internationally primarily between states, states that agree to them. Many, such as the United States, do not agree to many of them. Enforcement is mainly through reporting, meaning moral force, meaning effective nonenforcement. Signatory countries are even permitted formal excuse from compliance, a practice disproportionately used to evade sex equality provisions.[39] The covenants against trafficking women, for example, are many and venerable,[40] yet the traffic continues unabated, untouched, flourishing. Thailand even traffics in women by policy.[41] China may officially force abortions and sterilizations,[42] yet nothing is done. Enforcement of human rights against states' lack of action and against private parties may be possible in principle but is virtually absent in practice. For women, international human rights present the biggest gap between principle and practice in the known legal world.

Many existing international instruments guarantee sex equality.[43] Yet so little of women's experience of violation of human rights has been brought under them that it becomes necessary to inquire into the foundations of human rights to explain why. The primary foundation of human rights has been natural law, a secular religion that moves only those who believe in it. Its content tends to redescribe the social status quo and attribute it to nature. (Emphatic use of the existential verb to affirm loudly and often that women "are" human beings carries only the clout of its speaker's decibel level.) Positive law helps little more, since women have had little voice in its formulation in most places. Morality, an alternative ground, can be moving, but does not mean anyone has to do anything, as illustrated by the use of the phrase "moral victory" to refer to an actual defeat. All these grounds come down to social power in the end. If you have it, you can meet the tests for "human"; but power is exactly what women are socially denied, which is why their human rights can be violated and why they need them recognized.

At its philosophical foundations, the naturallaw tradition on which human rights remain primarily based has never been clear on whether women are men's natural equals. Rather, to oversimplify a complicated debate, it has been relatively clear that they are not and has provided no method for resolving different conclusions, each equally firmly said to be predicated on the law of nature. Nor has it reconciled its observation that sex is a natural difference with its view that equality is predicated on natural identity. To those who ground human rights in the opportunity to live out one's life project rationally,[44] it should be pointed out that, socially speaking, women as women have not been permitted a life project[45] and are widely considered as not possessed of rationality, or of what passes for reason among men. Others ground human rights in basic personal liberty[46] or in fundamental human dignity,[47] the problem being that you already have to have them to have a human right violated when you are denied them. So, it's back to nature.

Mortimer Adler exemplifies rather than exposes this circularity when he says, "If there are no natural rights, there are no human rights; if there are no human rights, there cannot be any crimes against humanity."[48] Women's problem has been that society and law do not agree that nature made them human, so nothing that is done to them is a crime against humanity, so to speak, because they have none. If society gives you no rights, such that a state need never deny them to keep you from having them, it may do you little good to have them formally guaranteed in international law. Free of this essentialist circularity, the task is to ground a claim to crimes against humanity clear of natural rights, which are not recognized to exist in nature unless they are recognized to exist in society. In other words, all discourse about nature is a social discourse.

Horror at the Holocaust grounds modern morality. No one knows what is good, but nearly everyone knows that the Holocaust was evil. We may not know what human is, but the Holocaust was inhuman. Jewish women were distinctively abused in ways that connect to anti-Semitic misogyny to this day and startlingly resemble the tortures of Croatian and Muslim women by Serbs. The horrific tortures and extermination of millions of Jews of both sexes because they were Jews has overshadowed everything then and since.

Considered in terms of equality theory, the Third Reich can be seen to follow an unbroken line from Aristotle through American segregation of treating "likes alike and unlikes unalike"—Jews having been rendered "unlike" Aryans.[49] Yet human rights law still uses the same equality concept, without reassessment. The dominant lesson that seems to have been learned instead was that Jews could be and were annihilated because they were "different," not that something is wrong with an equality standard that permits extermination for "differences." The Jews failed the equality test—not the equality test failed the Jews. Not that a better equality theory would have stopped Hitler. But what is one to make of an equality principle apparently logically consistent with, and undisturbed by, genocide? If equality's abstractions are receptive to Nazi substance, are they perhaps a flawed vehicle for social justice? The fact that international law pervasively guarantees sex equality, yet there is no sex equality, while mass rape and forced childbearing go on both in peacetime and in war, including in genocidal war, suddenly begins to make sense.

III

[T]he refusal to demand . . . one absolute standard of human dignity is
the greatest triumph of antifeminism over the will to liberation. . . . A universal standard of human dignity is the only principle that completely re-
pudiates sex-class exploitation and also propels all of us into a future
where the fundamental political question is the quality of life for all
human beings.

—Andrea Dworkin, *Right-Wing Women* (1983)

One approach to this problem might be to interpret existing international sex equality guarantees as grounded in the global women's movement against sex inequality, including sexual and reproductive abuses, and apply the resulting concepts in peace and in war. A right to equality, both as a right in itself and as a basis for equal access to other rights, would ground its definition of inequality, and by implication its concept of the human, in the universal—meaning worldwide and everywhere spontaneously indigenous—movement for women's rights.

The reality recognized by this movement is generating new principles: new in content, form, reach, operation, and relation to social life. In law, the principles of this movement are best approximated in North American equality law, pioneered by the Black civil rights movement in the United States in the 1960s and 1970s and the women's movement in Canada in the 1980s and 1990s. These equality rights are implemented by individuals and groups against other individuals and groups as well as by and against governments. They allow governments to proceed but do not limit to governments the ability to act against discrimination. They allow complaints for indirect and systemic inequality. To be fully realized, they call for relief against state inaction as well as action. Such devices add enforcement potential rather than let states off the hook.

In the received international human rights tradition, by contrast, equality has been more abstract than concrete, more transcendent than secular, more descended from natural law than admittedly socially based. The Universal Declaration of Human Rights grants equality "without distinction of any kind,"[50] as if distinction were the problem and lack of distinction the solution. The Convention on the Elimination of All Forms of Discrimination Against Women defines discrimination against women in largely gender-neutral and referential terms, guaranteeing enjoyment of all other rights "on a basis of equality of men and women."[51] This has mostly been interpreted nonsubstantively, has not allowed claims by individuals or groups, claims against government inaction, or claims against private parties. The committee that oversees it is coming to recognize, however, that violence against women is a form of sex discrimination and seeks to make states responsible for "private acts" if they fail to prevent, investigate, or punish discriminatory acts of violence.[52] But reporting is its primary tool for effectuation.[53]

As a basis for an expanded equality principle, women's resistance to sex inequality is ubiquitous and everywhere concrete and socially specific. It is not based on being the same as men but on resistance to violation and abuse and second-class citizenship because one is a woman. It starts close to home. African women oppose genital mutilation. Philippine, Thai, Japanese, and Swedish women organize against the sex trade. Women in Papua New Guinea and the United States and workers at the United Nations resist sexual harassment. Brazilian and Italian women protest domestic battery and "honor" as a male excuse for killing them. Indian women protest dowry and suttee as a male excuse for killing them. American women protest domestic battery and romantic love as a male excuse for killing them. Canadian women protest the use of feminism as a male excuse for killing them. Women everywhere rise up against rape, even in cultures where women have recently been regarded as chattel. Women in the United States, Scandinavia, and the Philippines resist pornography. Forced motherhood is opposed from Ireland to Germany to Bangladesh. Female infanticide and objectifying advertising are legislated against in India. Everywhere women seek access to literacy, which they have often been denied as women, and to survival based on the work they do, as well as to access to doing all kinds of work.[54]

One feature of this movement is its combination of socially specific comparison—men are not treated this way—with its refusal to be limited to imitating or emulating men. Women's diversity is extraordinary, yet everywhere, with social particularity, below some man. This produces an appreciation for the fact that difference by itself is certainly not the excuse for second-class citizenship it has become, but that imposed inferiority is everything. The movement criticizes socially organized power itself, as well as its excesses.

This movement has produced a rich concept of equality not as sameness but as lack of hierarchy. Its everywhere relative universality, its refusal to settle for anything less than a single standard of human dignity and entitlement, and its demand for elevation in that standard have left Aristotle in the dust. The scope and depth of this uprising for social equality offers a neglected ground for sex equality as a human right. The movement provides a principled basis in social reality for women's human rights, for a positive equality. Its principles include: If you do not do it to each other, you cannot do it to us, and ending the subordination of women because they are women.

"Civil rights" have been considered a subprovince of human rights, typically distinguished from political, social, economic, and cultural rights, as well as rights of personhood. A more embracing sense of equality is developing and being applied in North America, originating in the civil rights struggle of Blacks for social equality through legal equality in the United States and extending to its current pinnacle formulation in the Supreme Court of Canada's equality jurisprudence originating in the women's movement. This equality is not confined to equal access to other rights, as it is in international human rights law[55] and most domestic equality law, but is a principle in its own right. This equality looks to social context, broadly and in each particular, to eliminate imposed stratification. It envisions an active role for equality law in implementing the necessary changes.

In Canada, the approach takes the form of requiring that laws "promote equality." This "entails the promotion of a society" of equal dignity and respect. In the words of the Supreme Court of Canada, "[I]t has a large remedial component."[56] It recognizes that social inequality exists and must be changed, rather than assuming a neutral and equal social world and avoiding legal differentiation to preserve it. Its approach is based on noticing the reality of inequality in order to end it, rather than on enforcing a colorblindness and gender neutrality, which have often meant a blindness to the unequal realities of color and gender. This mandate is interpreted with particular sensitivity to, and priority upon, eliminating the inequality of groups that have traditionally been socially disadvantaged.

This equality looks to "civil society" on the level of ordinary transactions and interactions: buying and selling, work and education and accommodations, home and the street, communications and insurance, as well as voting, elections, and juries. It encompasses prohibition of racially segregated toilets and teaching racial hatred, sexual coercion by doctors, and denial of pregnancy benefits. It is rooted in everyday life, looking beyond the legal formalism of formal equality to social consequences. It understands that although inequality hurts individuals, it hurts them as members of social groups. It addresses the most systemic inequalities as well as ones that happen only to a few individuals. It practices a social, contextual, relational, antihierarchical equality jurisprudence.

As currently defined, international human rights are so abstract that people who concretely believe polar opposites can agree on them on principle and give them equally to no one. Both a Stalin and a Solzhenitsyn embrace them. That neither would likely favor civil rights as described here suggests the tension between such "civil rights" and "human rights" as currently conceived, in particular between abstract "human rights" equality and substantive "civil rights" equality. Civil rights begin at home or close to it; human rights seem to improve the further one gets from home. By a preference for direct civil remedies in the hands of the unequal, civil rights distribute power from government to people as they redistribute power among people. Human rights tend to see the state as the enemy of equality; civil rights see it as their potential promoter. Human rights locate equality in eliminating irrational differentiation; civil rights see equality as much in affirmative claims of cultural particularity, in ending oppression whether based on real differences or not, and in altering the mainstream to accommodate an uncompromised diversity.

The current political force of the mainstream human rights view takes its deep text, on my analysis, from a reading of the Nazi experience: Survival lies in blending in, in being indistinguishable from one's surroundings, in nondifferentiation. Cast in equality terms, instead of criticizing the view that killed you for being different, you fight for the right to be recognized as the same and to become the same because it will keep you alive. So many Polish Jews died, it is said, because they only spoke Yiddish. They could not "pass" as not Jews. Aryan-appearing German Jews were more likely to survive. It should follow that assimilation—sameness—guarantees an equal right to live, not to be exterminated because of who you are. This is nonarbitrary recognition for meeting the dominant standard, integration over self-determination. Do not think about whether integration is ultimately possible; do not think about those who will never be permitted to meet the standards; do not challenge the standards themselves.

An analogy could be drawn to the psychology of battered women, which is also a dimension of femininity more generally. The only reality is the power of the abuser; keeping your head low keeps you alive. This, too, acquiesces in the dominant standard and concedes the permanent powerlessness of an underclass. The shame of being who you are—as if that is validly and forever the real reason for your subordination—leads to always wanting and trying to become who you are not, which women know is a living lie until they become it. This is the victim-side adaptation to the perpetrator-defined reality. It converges with the final solution to the inequality problem: annihilation.

This is the equality of Aristotle, of the Enlightenment, of the Nazis, of the mainstream U.S. equality jurisprudence today, and of international human rights law. It seems rather late in the pursuit of equality to seek fair conditions of extermination on the basis of speaking Polish or looking German. It is like a battered woman's seeking not to be beaten by serving dinner on time and providing regular sex. Such equality does nothing about the annihilation machine itself, so long as it sorts likes from unlikes accurately. It may mean survival for some under unequal conditions, but do not call it equality. Such equality means conceding the standards under which one is measured, monitoring only their recognition without irrational distinction. One can understand trying to construct an equality principle to ensure survival under conditions of genocide; yet this is very close to conceding genocidal conditions in the construction of the equality principle, with the result that, so far as the equality principle is concerned, we will never live under any but genocidal conditions.

How equality is defined in the North American movements, by contrast, is self-respecting but not isolationist, self-determinant but not segregationist, uncompromised but not absolutist, solid at the core but forgiving at the edges. Its equality is not absolute but relative to the best society has to offer, insisting on an expanded role for the subordinated in redefining standards from the point of view of those living under them. Such a theory may appear to lack principled definition, grounded as it is in response to an unprincipled social world. But its relativism gives it substance that defines rather than undermines its principle. Perhaps if white men had been lynched, as Black men were in the American South, substantive relative rights would be more of a problem; the fact is, they were not. Given that no society systematically traffics men as men for sex, rapes men at will and with impunity, forces men to reproduce, batters men in homes, sometimes to death, on an everyday basis, pays men as a group less than women, or presents male sexuality in demeaned ways for entertainment and profit on a large scale, the comparative dimension to the standard has a lot to offer. It also helps avoid imposing foreign cultural standards in diverse social settings, since women are not seeking equality with foreign women but with men of their own cultural groups.

In legal practice in Canada, this approach has proven capable of addressing a substantial number of realities of sex inequality that have eluded prior attempts. A woman has been permitted to sue her city police force for failure to warn of a serial rapist.[57] Sexual harassment[58] and pregnancy discrimination[59] have been recognized as human rights violations. Under the tutelage if not the direct control of this approach, common law remedies for sexual abuse have recognized inequalities of power,[60] and statutes of limitations for incest have been revised based on the experience of victims.[61] Criminal laws against wife-battering have been interpreted to recognize the woman's reality,[62] and publication of the names of sexual assault victims has been prohibited.[63] After the Court's refusal to recognize women's equality rights to keep their sexual histories out of rape trials,[64] a whole new rape law was introduced.[65] Significant decisions have also been made in light of this approach in the area of reproductive rights, preventing men from gaining a veto over women's abortions[66] and recognizing women's rights in and over their fetuses.[67] Perhaps most tellingly, when the rights to freedom of expression of anti-Semites and pornographers were balanced against the equality rights of their targeted victims, equality won.[68] In Canada, some of the reality of inequality is becoming the basis for the legal equality principle.

IV

Against this backdrop, what will become of the Muslim and Croatian women violated by the Serbs? The basis in a women's movement for a meaningful equality exists, but interpreting what law? Since November 1991, feminists in Zagreb in particular have been working with refugee survivors of the sexual atrocities of genocide through war. Their account-ability to the victims has been continuous and absolute; their documen-tation and relief effort, committed and accurate.[69] If jurisdiction can be secured, and it should be able to be, laws do exist to cover many of the atrocities.[70] Rape, enforced prostitution, and indecent assault are already recognized as war crimes.[71] There is even precedent for trying them.[72] After World War II, Japanese generals were tried for sexual atrocities committed under their command: rape, imprisonment of girls in hotels and subjecting them to repeated rape, mass rape, cutting off breasts, killing women civil-ians and raping their corpses.[73] Other than the breeding aspect, this has happened in wars before, right down to tortures of fingers and feet.

There are many more examples in which nothing was done, as analyzed by Joan Fitzpatrick, "the mass rapes of women during the war for inde-pendence in Bangladesh, the systematic rape of women suspected of com-plicity in the insurgency in Kashmir, and the belated but growing scandal concerning the 'comfort women' who were abducted and forced into pros-titution by the Japanese army during the Second World War."[74] Evidence on rape was presented by the French and Soviet prosecutors at Nurem-berg.[75] Sexual forms of torture were documented,[76] but sexual assault was not charged in the indictments. One can only speculate that it was not seen to be within the tribunal's emphasis "not on individual barbarities and perversions" but only on the Nazi "Common Plan."[77] Rape has so often been treated as extracurricular, as just something men do, as a product rather than a policy of war.

Proceeding through war crimes tribunals on behalf of Muslim and Cro-atian women would create accountability, but it would not redistribute power to women in situations other than war. On the civil side of human rights, these atrocities violate every sex equality guarantee in international law, properly interpreted, and they do not fail to do so because this is wartime. Surely these are crimes against humanity, a "consistent pattern of mass violation of human rights."[78] Perhaps this would be a good occasion to use equality guarantees to address violence against women; there is no state-action problem. Such an approach could establish precedents for use by women in peacetime as well.

As a practical matter, it helps that these incidents happened in a war. Men know men hurt men in war, so maybe there is an analogy? It does not help for recognizing them now, or for creating a precedent that could affect nonwar interpretations, that similar acts are common everywhere in peacetime and are widely understood as sex. Yugoslavia's pornography market was "the freest in the world"[79] before this male population was officially mobilized to commit the atrocities they had already been sexually conditioned to enjoy. It does help that men did these acts in declared military groups, instead of one on one everywhere at once and all the time, or in small packs, murdering, raping, pimping, and breeding but not recognized as an army of occupation. Will there be command responsibility for these rapes? Will women have to identify each individual man, often numbering in the hundreds, who raped them? In legal terms, it does not help that no state raped these women and got them pregnant; it does help that a state's men did.[80]

Will these atrocities be seen as human rights abuses? If the Muslims were Jews, would the world be allowing this to happen? Must a group first survive genocide for it to be recognized next time? Will principle see reality? Will it connect with similar acts in everyday life? The murders maybe; the rapes possibly, and if so, probably because they are ethnic, hurting a group that includes men; the pregnancies, less likely (and what to do with the children?); the prostitution, for all the twenty-two treaties against it, little chance; the pornography never, meaning if ever, probably not soon.

Or will this situation and these women, here and now, be the time and place in which the word "woman," like the word "Jew," will finally come to stand, among its meanings, for a reality of abuse that cannot be forgotten, a triumph of survival against all that wanted you dead, a principle of what cannot be done to a human being? Will women, at last, get amnesty?

15

Turning Rape into Pornography

Postmodern Genocide

"Everything was dark, but the bed on which they were raping was lit up, like when they interrogate you and point the light only on you. Only that bed was lit up with a spotlight. . . . I had a feeling that they were sometimes recording or filming." In what is called peacetime, pornography is made from rape in film studios, on sets, in private bedrooms, in basements, in alleys, in prison cells, and in brothels. It should be no surprise to find it being made in a "rape theater" in a Serbian-run concentration camp for Muslims and Croatians in Bosnia-Herzegovina—as reported above by one survivor, a twenty-eight-year-old Croatian and Muslim woman. Still, it comes as a shock, a clarifying jolt. When Linda "Lovelace" reported her coercion into the pornographic film *Deep Throat*,[1] Gloria Steinem reworded the essence of the disbelief and blame Linda encountered as amounting to asking her, "What in your background led you to a concentration camp?"[2] If this was ever only an analogy, it isn't anymore.

Exploding the strategy pioneered a year earlier on Croatia, Serbian military forces in Bosnia-Herzegovina have been, as the world now knows, carrying out a campaign called "ethnic cleansing." This is a euphemism for genocide. It means removal or liquidation of all non-Serbs from the territory that was called Yugoslavia. This campaign of expansion through ethnic extermination has included rape, forcible impregnation, torture, and murder of Muslim and Croatian women, "for Serbia." A Bosnian Muslim soldier—call him "Haris" to protect his identity—who spied on Serbian

This essay was originally published in *Ms.*, 24 (July/August 1993). Asja Armanda and Natalie Nenadic contributed to its research, analysis, and theory. They, the Kareta Feminist Group, Zorica Spoljar, and the survivors with whom they work made the essay possible. All uncited quotations are from testimonies gathered in original research conducted and translated by Natalie Nenadic and Asja Armanda. For security reasons, survivors quoted are not named, although I know who they are.

forces described what he saw them do, from Vaganac in Serbian-occupied Croatia to Grabež in Serbian-occupied Bosnia: "Everything that's Muslim or Croatian, they slaughter, kill, set on fire. Nothing's supposed to remain alive, not even a chicken, cat, or bird, if they know it's Muslim or Croatian. . . . One said, 'There's a dog; it's Muslim, kill it.'" The raped women, the filmed women, the pregnant women, and probably the murdered women as well as the men suffer not only from these atrocities but also from knowing that they are intended to be the last of their people there.

This genocidal war has repeatedly been mischaracterized as a "civil war," aggressor equated with victim, "all sides" blandly blamed for their "hatred." Yet Serbian aggression against non-Serbs is as incontestable and overwhelmingly one-sided as male aggression against women in everyday life. Wars always produce atrocities, especially against women civilians. But there is no Muslim or Croatian *policy* of territorial expansion, of exterminating Serbs, of raping Serbian women. This is not a reciprocal genocide. The reluctance to say who is doing what to whom is reminiscent of the mentality that blames women for getting ourselves raped by men we know and then chides us for having a bad attitude toward them. Asja Armanda, of the Kareta Feminist Group in Zagreb, theorizes that the closer to home atrocities come, the more they are domesticated, made into love gone wrong. The more "feminized" the victims thus become, the more hesitant other men are to intervene in a family quarrel, and the more human rights can be violated and atrocities condoned.

The rapes in the Serbian war of aggression against Bosnia-Herzegovina and Croatia are to everyday rape what the Holocaust was to everyday anti-Semitism: both like it and not like it at all, both continuous with it and a whole new departure, a unique atrocity yet also a pinnacle moment in something that goes on all the time. As it does in this war, ethnic rape happens every day. As it is in this war, prostitution is forced on women every day: what is a brothel but a captive setting for organized serial rape? Forced pregnancy is familiar too, beginning in rape and proceeding through the denial of abortions; this occurred during slavery and still happens to women who cannot afford abortions—who in the United States are disproportionately African American or Latina. Also familiar is the use of media technology, including pornography, to make hatred sexy. Women are abused by men in these ways every day in every country in the world. Sex has also been used before to create, mobilize, and manipulate ethnic hatred, from the world of the Third Reich to the world of *Penthouse*. Yet the world has never seen sex used this consciously, this cynically, this elaborately, this openly, this systematically, with this degree of technological and psychological sophistication, as a means of destroying a whole people.

With this war, pornography emerges as a tool of genocide. Natalie Nenadic, an American of Croatian and Bosnian heritage, writes from Zagreb that she learned from Muslim sources that "some massacres in villages as well as rapes and/or executions in camps are being videotaped as they're happening." One woman who survived the Bučje rape/death camp in Serbian-occupied Croatia reports the making of pornography of her rapes this way: "In front of the camera, one beats you and the other—excuse me—fucks you, he puts his truncheon in you, and he films all that. . . . We even had to sing Serbian songs . . . in front of the camera." Account after account documents that Serbian forces film as they rape. As they do it, they watch, laugh, encourage each other, and spew ethnic curses and epithets. "*Ustaša* whore" is particularly commonplace. "*Ustaša*" is a derogatory political term that refers to the fascist regime in Croatia (then including Bosnia-Herzegovina) that collaborated with Hitler. Serbian soldiers use it for Muslim and Croatian women—most of whom were not even born until after World War II.

In a military trial in Sarajevo in March 1993, Borislav Herak, a Serbian soldier, testified that the rapes he committed had been ordered for "Serbian morale."[3] As an instrument for their morale building, the Croatian-Muslim survivor quoted earlier—one of whose twin sons was decapitated in her arms—reports that as they raped her, Serbian soldiers "were telling them 'Croatia needs to be crushed again. *Balijas* need to be crushed completely. You are half this and half that. You need to be crushed to the end. Because you're Croatian, you should be raped by five different men—and because you're a *Bula,* you should be raped by five more.'" *Balija* and *Bula* are derogatory terms for Muslims. Xenophobia and misogyny merge here; ethnic hatred is sexualized; bigotry becomes orgasm. Whatever this rape does for the rapist, the pornography of the rape mass-produces. The materials become a potent advertisement for a war, a perfect motivator for torturers, who then do what they are ordered to do and enjoy it. Yes, it improves their morale.

Some of the rapes that are made into pornography are clearly intended for mass consumption as war propaganda. One elderly Croatian woman who was filmed being raped was also tortured by electric shocks and gang-raped in the Bučje concentration camp by Serbian men dressed in generic camouflage uniforms. She was forced to "confess" on film that Croatians raped her. This disinformation—switching the ethnic labels—is especially easy where there are no racial markers for ethnic distinctions. It is a standard

Serbian technique. Another such incident of switched victims and murderers was dismissed as "a shameless lie" by relief officials, according to a UN spokesperson in Sarajevo.[4] One woman captured by the Serbs described how she was forced to participate in such lies by reading a scripted false "confession" about her activities as a "terrorist" for a TV Novi Sad camera. She knew that the fabrication aired because she was recognized by a Serbian guard who said that he had seen her on Belgrade TV.

Serbian propaganda moves cultural markers with postmodern alacrity, making ethnicity unreal and all too real at the same time. Signs and symbols, words, images, and identities are manipulated to mean anything and its opposite—all in the service of genocide, a single reality that means only one thing. When human beings are "represented" out of existence, playing reality as a game emerges as a strategy of fascism.

Actual rapes of Muslim and Croatian women by Serbian soldiers, filmed as they happen, have been shown on the evening news in Banja Luka, a Serb-occupied city in western Bosnia-Herzegovina. The women were presented as Serbian, and as being raped by Muslim or Croatian men. In September 1992, one woman around age fifty, entirely naked with visible bruises, was shown being raped on television. A Serbian cross hung around her neck; the rapist—using a term for Serbian fascist collaborator that has become a badge of pride among Serb forces—cursed her *chetnik* mother; someone was yelling "harder." The verbal abuse was dubbed—and unmistakably Serbian in intonation and word usage. The man's face was not visible, but the woman's was. In another televised rape a few days later, a woman near age thirty-five, with short dark hair, was shown on the ground; her hands were spread and tied to a tree, her legs were tied to her hands. Many men watched her raped in person; thousands more watched her raped on television. This time, in an apparent technical lapse, about four or five seconds of the actual sound track was aired: "Do you want sex, *Ustaša*? Do you like a Serbian stud horse?" Earlier in the war, according to Asja Armanda of the Kareta Feminist Group, a news report showed Serbian tanks rolling in to "cleanse" a village. The tanks were plastered with pornography.

How does genocide become so explicitly sexually obsessed? How do real rapes become ordinary on the evening news?

Pornography saturated Yugoslavia before the war. Its market, according to Yugoslav critic Bogdan Tirnanić, was "the freest in the world."[5] A major news magazine, *Start*, with a *Newsweek*-like format and the politics of the *Nation*, had *Playboy*-type covers and a centerfold section showing naked women in postures of sexual display and access. Select women who were privileged under the Communist regime, and who presented themselves as speaking for women, regularly published there and even occasionally served as editors. (The presentation of pornography as a model of feminism repelled many women from feminism.) When pornography is this normal, a whole population of men is primed to dehumanize women and to enjoy inflicting assault sexually. The *New York Times* reported that "piles of pornographic magazines" were found in the bedroom of Borislav Herak, the captured Serbian soldier who calmly admitted to scores of rapes and murders.[6] At his war crimes trial in Sarajevo, when asked where he learned to kill, he described being trained by killing pigs.[7] No one asked him where he learned to rape, although he testified that his first rape in this war was his first sexual experience. Pornography is the perfect preparation—motivator and instruction manual in one—for the sexual atrocities ordered in this genocide.

Pornography, known to dehumanize women for its consumers, pervades some rape/death camps, according to survivors. In one military prison, the pornography was customized to suit the guards' sexual tastes, in echoes and parallels to the acts they performed. One woman in her mid-thirties, a mother of two, recalls how some men drew little penises next to women in the pornography with whom they wanted to have sex, and wrote their names on the penises. Next to the men in the materials, some wrote "I have a longer one than you" and signed their names. One Serbian guard "draws a picture of his own dick and an arrow showing where he'd go with it." In other words, these men do to women in the materials what they do to women in the camp: ". . . the women were cut out, but the man remains whole." And speaking of personalized weaponry, survivors in the Bosnia-Herzegovina Refugee Women's Group, Žene BiH, in exile in Zagreb, report finding the name of Jovan Tintor, a *chetnik* commander, inscribed on the remains of projectiles that were aimed at, and hit, a Sarajevo maternity ward.

When pornography is this common and this accepted, the lines dividing it from news, entertainment, and the rest of life are so blurred that women may know no word for it. The woman who survived the Serbian military prison described a thick sex book that made the rounds. It showed, she said, "men with animals and women with animals, how you get AIDS." The book was "so read that it was completely falling apart." Another woman spoke of seeing "those magazines with the nude women, the sex." The women in the military prison grasped for words to describe them: "either they remain standing and are nude or . . . you have a woman lying on a woman or a woman lying on a man, all those poses that are done. I don't know what those magazines are called." Asked what was on the walls of the room where the guards slept—pictures of political leaders perhaps?—another woman answered, "I can't say I saw Milošević or Tito. These pictures were mainly naked women . . . those usual pictures from *Start* and those things. Male things."

The conditions in the camps throughout the occupied areas of Croatia and Bosnia-Herzegovina are subhuman. Some peacetime brothels have become wartime rape/death camps—a kind of surreal camouflage through blatancy. Some are outdoor pens ringed with barbed wire. Some are animal stalls. Some were arenas, factories, schools. Women are typically allotted one thin slice of bread a day. Humanity is jammed into closet-size concrete cells, begging even for boards to sleep on, waiting for the few to be selected out for systematic torture, to be taken to the rooms with the beds with the bloody sheets. "When night came," as one survivor put it, "death in life came." Those who are allowed to live often must sexually service their captors. One woman was forced to keep her Serbian captor's penis hard in her mouth from midnight to 5:00 A.M. for fourteen nights in a Serb-run concentration camp in Vojvodina. "My job was to please him, to excite him that whole time, so that he would be able to ejaculate. . . . Sometimes I began to suffocate, and when [he] began to spurt out on the cement, he would beat me up. I had to remain kneeling."

Often the atrocities are arranged to be watched by other soldiers. In televised rapes, the viewer can see other boots, standing around, walking around. The Croatian-Muslim woman quoted earlier says of her experience: "These soldiers would invite their friends to come watch the rapes. That was like in the movie theater. All sit around while others do their job. . . . Sometimes those who were watching put out cigarette butts on the bodies of the women being raped." The Serbian soldier Borislav Herak described how other soldiers watched him rape one young girl after another—all of whose names he remembered.[8] This is live pornography.

We will never know what happened to most of the women who were killed—until we uncover the mass graves or the pornography. A gang-rape observed by Haris, the Bosnian soldier, gives a rare glimpse into the sexual spectacles staged for private viewing, proceeding on orders from a superior at Ličko Petrovo Selo, a village in Serbian-occupied Croatia: The woman was tied to four stakes in the ground, "in a lying position but suspended." While they were raping her, the soldiers said "that Yugoslavia is theirs . . . that they fought for it in World War II, partisans for Yugoslavia. That they gave everything for Yugoslavia." The national politics are fused with sex. Haris reports that the men laugh and chide each other for "not satisfying her," for not being able to "force a smile out of her," because she is not showing "signs of love." They beat her and ask if it is good for her. The superior who is ordering them says, "She has to know that we are *chetniks*. She has to know this is our land. She has to know that we're commanding, that this is our Greater Serbia, that it'll be this for everyone who doesn't listen." Does it ever occur to them that the woman is a human being? "I don't know if they ever even think this is *person*," Haris says.

Is there a relationship between the pornography consumed, the sexualization of the environment of torture and predation, and the sexual acts that are performed? This is not an academic question.

One woman reported that she saw done to a woman in a pornography magazine what was also done to her. Describing materials in the camps, she says, "Those pictures with those things you hit them with . . . like you have a chain like this, and like this they hang you to a bed. He hangs her from the ceiling." Without missing a beat, she moves from describing the materials to describing what was done to her: "I know there was some kind of wooden board on the side, a woman tied to it by chains, she had a mask over her eyes and he was hitting her with some kind of thick whip-crop. I mean that whip-crop reminded me of the Begejci concentration camp, because there in Begejci, they had a thick whip, a crop made like that one—from leather—and they beat the captives in that way. I mean, I was whipped like that once in Begejci with that whip-crop, so I know that it hurts."

Many tortures in the camps are organized as sexual spectacles, ritualized acts of sadism in which inflicting extreme pain and death are sexual acts, performed and watched for sexual enjoyment. Haris, hiding in a tree, observed a small concentration camp in Serbian-occupied Croatia in April 1992. It was wholly outdoors, with "hungry, tortured people, beaten, bloody." He watched a man and a woman—who appeared to be seven or eight months pregnant—being taken to a clearing in the woods. The woman was tied vertically to a cross, legs pressed together and arms extended. They ripped her pregnant belly open with a knife. "It was alive . . . it moved." The woman took about fifteen minutes to die. The man, apparently her husband and father of the baby, was bound to a nearby tree and forced to watch. The attackers attempted to force him to eat the baby's arm. Then "they hacked him up, cut the flesh on him so that he would bleed to death." While they were doing this, "they were laughing. . . . 'We're going to slaughter all of you. This is our Serbia.'" Haris is certain it was filmed.

Change the politics or religion, and victims of ritual torture in this country report the same staged sexual atrocities ending in sacrifice. Some say these "snuff" scenes, too, are videotaped.

The Nazis were precocious with the media technology of their time. They used it to create images of events that never took place. They also took pictures of some of their horrific medical experiments and executions. They imprisoned women in brothels, forced women in camps to run naked before cameras, and paraded naked women for pictures just before their executions. They published sexually explicit anti-Semitic hate propaganda.[9] Since then, visual technology that uses human beings as live targets has become cheap, mobile, and available. Nearly half a century of deployment of pornography worldwide has escalated its explicitness, intrusiveness, and violence. With this in hand, the Serbs make the Nazis' efforts look comparatively primitive.

Rape was not charged in the post–World War II indictments of the Nazis at Nuremberg, although sexual forms of torture, including rape, were documented at the trials. Perhaps this omission was a casualty of the tribunal's emphasis "not on individual barbarities and perversions" but on the Nazi "Common Plan." Rape in war has so often been treated as extracurricular, as just something men do, as a product rather than a policy of war. Yet the propagandist Julius Streicher—editor of the anti-Semitic newspaper *Der Stürmer*, which contained pornographic anti-Semitic hate propaganda—was indicted for "crimes against humanity" for incitement to hatred of the Jews.[10] Streicher, described by prosecution documents at the Nuremberg trials as a brutal sadist who carried a leather whip attached to his wrist, was found guilty and condemned to death by hanging.[11] In the war crimes trials for the genocidal war against Bosnia-Herzegovina and Croatia, will those who incited to genocide through rape, sexual torture, and murder—the Serbian pornographers as well as high policymakers and the underlings—get what they deserve?[12]

Women hesitate to report that pornography is made of their rapes even more than they hesitate to report the rapes themselves. Disbelief from outside combines with humiliation, shame, and a sense of powerlessness inside. It is unbearable to know that even after you are dead—maybe soon, on tape—thousands will see you this way. The depth of despair at stopping the rape becomes an infinity of hopelessness at stopping the pornography of it.

Even though women in rape/death camps know that the same things are being done to other women, and sometimes are even forced to watch them, still the sense of isolation is total. Always they fear reprisals, especially for speaking out against the pornography, even when they are what is called free—meaning they and their families are not literal captives of armed men.

What do we owe them, women for whom "you were lucky if they only raped you"? What will make it possible for them to speak of what was done to them? As one survivor put it, "I have no use for telling you the rest. I have no security. I have nothing." When the films of her rape are sold as pornography—emblem of democracy and liberation in post-Communist Eastern Europe and increasingly protected as speech world-wide—she will have even less than that.

16

Rape as Nationbuilding

The conflagration in Croatia and Bosnia-Herzegovina has been going on for more than three years. The bodies of the raped continue to pile up in public view. What is going on here? Arguably, we are witnessing a formative international as well as national governance process with profound implications.

The conflict in this region is a genocide euphemized as "ethnic cleansing."[1] This campaign of extermination of non-Serbian peoples is being carried out by a phalanx of Serbian fascists in collaboration with the regime in Belgrade for political expansion and hegemony through ethnic uniformity, to achieve the "Greater Serbia" they have long planned. It is a genocide through war. It is not a war in the usual sense of armies fighting against other armies retreating and advancing over territories, or guerrilla bands from one side raiding troops and towns of another side. The sides are defined not by place or governmental allegiance or politics in the conventional sense, but by ethnicity. The objective, what is to be conquered and possessed and subdued and subjugated and ruled by force, is a land grab, but the targets are people. Ninety percent of the casualties are civilian.[2] This is a war against people.

In the standard lexicon of war, the closest term we have for this kind of war is "civil war." In Croatia and Bosnia-Herzegovina, though, it is a misnomer if it means two sides fighting each other. Or it was until after some years of describing it that way—years of treating a war of aggression against people who have no armed forces and are forbidden to arm themselves, as if this were equal and reciprocal aggression, years in which the international community trivialized the attacks and distanced itself from them as if this were a domestic dispute, years of treating it the way most

This talk was delivered to the Global Structures Convocation in Washington, D.C., on February 5, 1994. Emma Cheuse and Anna Baldwin provided research assistance of the highest quality.

states treat rape in marriage—and in large part because it was treated that way, now the international community has its civil war, or elements of one within what remains international aggression.

In the genocide that is the engine of the onslaught, all non-Serbs go, dead or alive. To this end, systematic rape has been a prominent weapon, planned and ordered from the top as well as permitted on a wide scale. Muslim and Croat women and girls are raped, sometimes killed afterward, sometimes their corpses are sexually violated by Serbian military men, regulars and irregulars in various formations, and also by neighbors, on their doorsteps, on hillsides, in camps—camps that were factories, mines, sports arenas, restaurants, animal stalls. Sometimes men are raped as well on the basis of their ethnicity. Some of the rapes are filmed and photographed as pornography and propaganda. The women are raped to death or raped and made to live with having been raped. This is rape as forced exile: to make you leave your home and never go back. It is rape as spectacle: to be seen and heard and watched and told to others. It is rape as humiliation: for certain men to take pleasure from violating certain women, or certain men, or to take pleasure watching certain men be forced to violate certain women or girls. This rape is torture; it is sex and ethnic discrimination combined. It is rape as ethnic expansion through forced pregnancy and childbearing. It is rape to establish dominance, to shatter a community. It is rape to destroy a people: rape as genocide. It is rape as nationbuilding: to create a state.

What has the world's response been? To watch, let it go on. No doubt some people are horrified. But at the same time, these rapes seem to have fallen into some deep well of understanding and empathy, into the arms of de facto world condonation. Call it history, call it geopolitics or realpolitik, call it complacency, call it isolationism and lack of a national interest, call it fear—whatever it is, a lot of other men have a lot of respect for it and give it a lot of rope. Tolerance is what emerges from the foot-dragging reluctance, the excuses, the jockeying for position, the vacillations, the evasions, the denials, the cover-ups, the slippery-sloped sovereignty arguments, the doubletalk, the procedural morasses,[3] as thousands upon thousands of rapes sink beneath public view while being carried out in plain sight. If you read what the world's leaders do rather than listen to what comes out of their mouths, what you see is that many of the men who run this world recognize something, identify with something, in this conflict. It reminds them of something. The Serbs could win. This is how states are made.

The fact is, the more the Serbs rape and kill, the more respect they get, the more dignity and seriousness the demands of these international war criminals are accorded, the closer they come to being able to get away with it all, and the clearer it becomes that this is one way communities are destroyed and states are created: by whom you can rape. The same ac- quiescence in this process underlies the much-heard palliative response these days beyond even the one that it is happening on all sides here.[4] It is: rape happens in all wars all the time. Relax. This is no different from usual, why get so exercised? Well, does one have to be surprised to be violated? Perhaps it is more unvarnished, undiluted, unashamed, undis- guised, intentional, blatant this time. This time, women refuse to be silent about it. But suppose it *is* always there. They *always* do this? Getting away with *this* creates that legitimate monopoly on force of which nation-states are said to be made? This puts might makes right in a whole new light.

In this system, violating other men's women is planting a flag; it is a way some men say to other men, "What was yours is now mine." He who gets away with this, runs things. Doing this institutionalizes the rulership of some men over other men even as it establishes the rulership of all men over all women. You cannot govern the dead. Better that those you rule live in terror, knowing you have something over them, knowing what you can do to them at any time. This makes the power of government look like a form of the power of the rapist over the raped. Is this a dynamic in how states are run internally as well, in between their international con- flicts? There, too, men define who they are in relation to other men and over all women by which women they can get away with violating. In this light, perhaps rape in peacetime, which no state does anything serious about, which is seen to violate human rights nowhere because humanity is not something women as such are thought to have, especially sexually— perhaps this is a way to keep state power at once out of the hands of women and over all women, as well as away from some men. Perhaps permitting rape of women by men, or all women by some men, is a device of internal order within states, of defining hierarchy of men over women and other men, just as it is between states.

In the male system, rape of women becomes an act by some men against other men. Women become a way men establish their power among one another. For raped women, it is always an act against women, often by certain men against certain women. In other words, it may be a sign and form of expression to men, a way men communicate with one another, but to women it is a real violation. As often happens when men plant flags, someone was already living there.

In the Bosnian situation, instead of being understood as male supremacy or xenophobia, the culprit is often said to be nationalism. When men begin behaving to some other men and women the way they have been behaving to "their own" women all along, it is not called male dominance, it is called nationalism. Serbian fascists are called Serbian nationalists, as if their victims object to their having a nation, rather than to their having a genocide in order to have one. Every nation has its fascists; the question is, are they running your government? My clients are called nationalists for describing their rapists in the terms in which the rapists describe themselves: as Serbs. Women survivors of Serbian genocide are called nationalists, the same as their torturers and killers, for thinking they should not be tortured and killed because of their ethnicity. In this discussion, if you own yourself, claim yourself and identify with your own community, and publicly resent being raped because you are a member of it, you are called a nationalist. I have never heard Native Americans called nationalists for objecting to being subjected to genocide and for wanting their own nation back.

The charge of nationalism, like calling this a "civil war," is one more way to avoid calling it what it is: a genocide. The "civil war" cover-up is the latest symmetry trap, equalizing aggressor and aggressed-against—as if a will to exterminate is the same as a will to survive extermination, as if a fascist concept of nation is the same as a multiethnic one. It is as if those who are raped and killed because of the group to which they belong should find some higher, more enlightened, less particularized ground from which to object to their rape and murder. Objecting to it on the ground on which it is happening apparently is not good enough.

If the process we are witnessing is a part of a process through which nation-states have often been created, it also raises the question whether the international order has been built, and will continue to be built, on the same basis. No nation, not even any democracy, is accountable to women. Will international law be? Auschwitz raised the question whether poetry survived it.[5] Is there international law after Bosnia? Or will these rapes and the handling of those charged with them set off a new round of more of the same on the ground, at the negotiating table—where men make deals and there are no women—and in international tribunals? Will these violations of women only intensify as authoritarian regimes fall and democracy spreads, opening opportunities for yet more men to more freely violate women along lines formerly suppressed but always there? Will all these raped and tortured and murdered women become just another bargaining chip in building a state, sucked into men doing their business as usual, with even the international adjudication of the crimes against women becoming just another move in men's politics with one another?

A principled vision to animate a new international order could begin here: not only that rape would end, but that it stops working. That men stop using violation of women to get what they want from one another because it is no longer functional or effective. Because it gets contempt rather than respect. Because the world mobilizes to get in the way of it instead of standing around and watching it and rewarding it with territory and rule. Because those who do it are cast out of the human community instead of being treated like diplomats. Violation of women should violate the real rules, not just the rules on paper, rather than being a part of the unwritten rules, so that states are built on the backs of women on their backs no more.

17

From Auschwitz to Omarska,
Nuremberg to The Hague

The biggest difference between the Nuremberg Tribunal after World War II and the International Criminal Tribunal for the Former Yugoslavia (ICTY)[1] is that the ICTY, which sits in the Hague, is in place as the genocide goes on. This gives it a chance to end the impunity of the perpetrators before the last victim dies and to be part of the peace process, a creative chance the Nuremberg Tribunal did not have. It also creates difficulties the Nuremberg Tribunal did not face, including problems with defendants coming to their trials and opportunities for intimidation of witnesses, giving rise to a corresponding need for serious and innovative security measures, since families and compatriots of victims and witnesses can still be in the control of the indicted criminals.

Although each genocide is unique, the analytical and factual parallels between the Holocaust by the Nazis and the ethnic cleansing by the Serbs are many and close. Both are genocide on ethnic grounds with a religious dimension, conducted through aggression and invasion, using war as a tool of the genocide. Both are long planned, with deep roots in perpetrator culture, cynically carried out to win and directed from the top with official state involvement. Both share an obsession with "blood," a *Volk*ish definition of nation, and a long-nursed sense of grievance and persecution from the past promoting a sense of the legitimacy, even sanctity, of their mission in the present. Both have historical excuses. Both love symbolism and have a flair for and commitment to the use of propaganda. Both lie—a lot. Bigotry and terror mark a common fascism. As a post-Communist left-wing insurgency comes to resemble a postdemocratic right-wing one, fascism emerges as neither left nor right but a politics in itself.

Although the Serbian fascists' operation is less streamlined, systematic,

---

This is an edited transcript of a talk given at a Yale Law School panel titled "From Auschwitz to Bosnia" on April 23, 1994.

and precise than the Nazis' was, it is easy to identify in survivor reports from Bosnia and Croatia facts reminiscent of the Nuremberg indictments: the transports, selections, subhuman conditions, systematic beatings, so-called interrogations, burnings (using preexisting crematoria in Brčko), gassing (CO_2 in buses, which is how the Nazis started), humiliation, degradation, starvation, and systematic terror and liquidation. The grounds are also parallel: Serbs seek destruction of non-Serbs on the basis of ethnicity and religion (Muslims as Muslim, Croatians as Catholic).

In early 1994, survivors reported torture in the region. One Croatian man described to me the bodies he was forced to dig up by his Serbian captors from a hole they had apparently been in for about a month: "We had to take off all their clothes. We covered the clothes with earth and brought the corpses to the road. There we had to wash them and put on white sheets. I saw chopped heads without eyes, chopped arms, scorched wounds, genitals tied with string and pulled out, cut throats and everything. They made photos of it."[2] Other survivors tell of symbolic use of blood for degradation: "We would find pieces of bread soaked in blood. We had to take it and eat it. They said, 'Your blood is dirty and you have to eat that dirty blood.'" Many report even more explicit symbolism, such as four Cyrillic Cs[3] cut into in a man's back by his Serbian captors with a broken bottle, a cross carved into a woman's cheek with a knife, an embroidery of a mosque in a woman's home defaced by a cross cut across it. Pogroms against Muslims and Catholics were timed for Ramadan and Bayram and Catholic holidays. Some coincided with Serbian Orthodox holidays, apparently celebrations. With adjustments for the particulars, none of this would have been out of place in the Shoah.

Striking parallels exist in the ways the onslaught developed on the ground. Reminiscent of the Nuremberg Laws, signs on stores in some parts of Bosnia-Herzegovina have said, "No Muslims or Croatians allowed" for some time. Once the more active violence started, theft of property was legalized, owners being forced to sign it over in exchange for being allowed to leave alive. Pretextual charges of atrocities are leveled against members of targeted groups. Doctors have been killed for allegedly inventing a way to sterilize Serbian women, a psychiatrist for allegedly brainwashing Serbs. Muslim and Croatian doctors fear each shift at their hospital; if a Serbian patient dies, they will be killed.

Some parallels are startlingly precise. Radovan Karadžić, head of the Bosnian Serbs, stated in Parliament that if it did not remain part of Yugoslavia, one nationality would be made to disappear.[4] This statement was understood as a threat to exterminate the Muslim nationality. Himmler,

speaking of Jewish women and children specifically, stated that "dieses
Volk von der Erde verschwinden zu lassen": these people will be made to
disappear from the earth.[5] Serbs call what they are doing "ethnic
cleansing."[6] In 1942, Himmler said: "It is with anti-Semitism as with de-
lousing. Removing lice is not a matter of world-view. It is a matter of
cleanliness."[7] Prisoners from Serbian-run death camps report a constant
demand that they sing a song with the refrain "Who says, who lies, who
says Serbia is small." It used to be called *Lebensraum.*

The Holocaust is not only precedent and parallel. Auschwitz lives on in
Bosnia. The most common epithet used against non-Serbs, including as
they are being tortured and murdered, is *ustaša*, a term that refers to the
Nazi puppet Croatian regime. (That there was also a Nazi puppet regime
in Serbia, one even more efficient in slaughtering Jews,[8] seems to have
been forgotten.) This would be like calling a French person "Vichy." One
man told me: "They said Croatians were a genocidal people and connected
with Hitler. They slit the throat of my friend because he was blond and
had freckles. The Serbs didn't like that." Another said, "I had a name, a
first and last name. Then the war broke out, and I had just one name,
'ustaša.'"

However widespread or patterned rape has been in wars and genocides
before, in Bosnia there is evidence that it is ordered as well as organized,
in and out of the rape/death camps. Rape in this conflict has a role, by
analogy, in what the Nuremberg indictments called the Common Plan.[9]
Survivors, captured soldiers, and some extrinsic evidence support the view
that it is ordered—not that it has to be ordered to happen or to be criminal, but that here, it is. The systematic and instrumental nature of these
rapes marks them. Pogroms were one thing, designing and fielding the gas
chambers was another. Rape as most women generally know it and these
rapes have a similar difference. Auschwitz was industrial murder. Omarska
has industrial rape: intended, planned, mass-produced, serially executed,
instrumentalized. It comes closest to the experiences of prostituted women,
serially raped in what is called peacetime.

Distinctively, though, some of this rape is intended to be reproductive.
One man who incarcerated his Muslim woman neighbor of seven years for
months in a shack, where she was raped nearly daily by many different
Serbian soldiers until she escaped, said the first day he raped her: "We've
been waiting for this for twenty years, for Muslim women, clean women,
to make *chetnik* children . . . you will give birth to a boy *chetnik* who will
have a cross on his brow and who will kill Muslims when he grows up."
In this war, ethnic politics are sexualized. The women are violated with

ethnic and sexual terms combined, the ubiquitous *"ustaša* whore" and *"Balija* whore," both degrading terms for ethnicities combined with a degrading term for a woman. Serbian men spout men's politics as they rape women: "Fuck you Izetbegovic." "Fuck your God. The fucking God is on our side." "Fuck you, Alija fucks you." "Fuck you, Franjo Tudjman." They scream this as they rape. The French prosecutor submitted some evidence of sexual assault at Nuremberg,[10] but nothing in this depth or detail was presented by anyone. The Bosnian genocide, with its echoes in the Nazi past, forefronts its sexual obsessions.

Reminiscent of the Nazis too is the demasculinization of men of the subordinated ethnicity. One Serbian man who tortured a Muslim woman sexually in a house for two days and nights straight said during the rape: "You Turkish women, your genitals are very good, but so far you were fucked by half a penis, now we will fuck you with a whole penis. For Serbs, it's fuck or kill." Some Croatian men from eastern Croatia heard reports that Muslim men are being raped and sexually tortured in some camps, usually former prisons, in some instances being forced to rape one another, acting out a vicious stigmatization of Muslim men's sexuality as homosexual.[11] If, instead of tracing the Auschwitz in Bosnia, we look for the Bosnia in Auschwitz, shining a light back on the Holocaust from what is known from the war against Croatia and Bosnia-Herzegovina, the role of sexual abuse stands out as distinct. Rape was not contained in the indictments of the major war criminals at Nuremberg.[12] It seems incredible that all that abuse could go on without rape; there had to have been more than reported, if only because this is virtually always true. Likely, sexual assault was minimized both quantitatively and in terms of its genocidal importance. Maybe the *Rassenschande* prohibition on intergroup sex worked, but I profoundly doubt it. Perhaps that applied only to sex, and rape was considered something else.[13]

Whatever the place of rape in the actuality of the Holocaust, its absence at Nuremberg has had a major impact on the development of international law. Nuremberg gave human rights its principled ground in our time. The fact of, and revulsion against, the Holocaust largely impelled and shaped the structure and content of international human rights as we know them. Rape was prominently included in the Tokyo trials, but those trials do not occupy this signal place. The fact that injuries to women as such were invisible at Nuremberg, the fact that gender as a feature of humanity that could be systematically violated was not recognized there, has helped keep women from being full human beings under international law.

The incipient recognition of sexual crimes of violence against women in the ICTY statute thus marks a signal distinction between Nuremberg and the ICTY. This time, crimes against the humanity of women, such as rape and enforced prostitution, are up front, at least initially. They are not entirely adequately there, but they are there. In the founding statute of the ICTY, rape and enforced prostitution are mentioned, if not expressly under genocide. In its evidentiary rules, Rule 96 provides that in sexual assaults, no corroboration is required, consent is not allowed as a defense, and no evidence of prior sexual conduct is allowed.[14] This is what a rape law might look like when a context of force is legally acknowledged. Through interpretation, the rapes may legally come to be seen as what they are in this conflict: genocidal acts, integral to the destruction of a people as such. The ICTY stands poised to develop an international jurisprudence of sexual assault as integral to the law of nations for the first time.

Will Nuremberg and the ICTY form parentheses in the human and legal history of the search for international justice through law, not war, for building states on consent, not rape? Will the ICTY be a step in women's becoming citizens of the world, or will it become a site for revisionism before there is even a history to revise? Holocaust revisionism flourishes fifty years after Nuremberg. What has made it possible to say today that the acts documented and tried there did not take place? Does that process tell us anything about the denial of the genocide in Croatia and Bosnia-Herzegovina even as is happening before our eyes? Today, a legal revisionism attempts to recast the role that anti-Semitic hate propaganda had during the Holocaust, contending that it was wrong to hold its publisher responsible for incitement to genocide, as he was at Nuremberg. The role of pornography in Bosnia shows that Nuremberg was right, Telford Taylor wrong when he later implied from a comfortable distance that publishing these materials was not an international crime.[15]

To have a revised history, you first need a history to revise. Will the history of this war be written by those real victors, the bystanders, the ones who sat it out? Will it say, as they say now to justify their inaction, that it was a "civil war" with ancient hatreds and implacable nationalisms? Will they condemn atrocities on all sides, equating the few and the many, policy and lapse of policy, official planned acts and a few extremist individuals running amok, to avoid taking sides until it is all over? Will they say rape happens in all wars, not as a fact to end starting here, but as a boys-will-be-boys denial of the specific atrocity that is here and now, a cover-up sometimes even paraded, obscenely, under feminism? If these at best half-truths, at worst genocide denials, become the official story, revisionism will look good. They pose a challenge for the ICTY: could Nuremberg have made today's real and paper Eichmanns[16] impossible?

For the survivors and those alive today who will not survive, the fact that the ICTY comes after Nuremberg, established as the genocide goes on, adds a new depth to despair. Living after Nuremberg, they once had hope. This genocide goes on as the world watches. Auschwitz was not on CNN. As the Holocaust's atrocities came out, and a stunned world looked upon what it said it had not really known, the question loomed: if the world *had* really known, would it have allowed this to happen? Fifty years later, Bosnia has given us the answer, and it is yes.

18

Rape, Genocide, and
Women's Human Rights

Human rights have not been women's rights—not in theory or in reality, not legally or socially, not domestically or internationally. Rights that human beings have by virtue of being human have not been rights to which women have had access, nor have violations of women as such been part of the definition of the violation of the human as such on which human rights law has traditionally been predicated.

This is not because women's human rights have not been violated. The eliding of women in the human rights setting happens in two ways. When women are violated like men who are otherwise like them—when women's arms and legs are cut and bleed like the arms and legs of men; when women, with men, are shot in pits and gassed in vans; when women's bodies are hidden with men's at the bottom of abandoned mines; when women's and men's skulls are sent from Auschwitz to Strasbourg for experiments—these atrocities are not marked in the history of violations of women's human rights. The women are counted as Argentinian or Honduran or Jewish—which, of course, they are. When what happens to women also happens to men, like being beaten and disappearing and being tortured to death, the fact that those it happened to are women is not registered in the record of human atrocity.

The other way violations of women are obscured is this: When no war has been declared, and life goes on in a state of everyday hostilities, women are beaten and raped by men to whom we are close. Wives disappear from supermarket parking lots. Prostitutes float up in rivers or turn up under piles of rags in abandoned buildings. These atrocities are not counted as

Earlier versions of this material were delivered at the United Nations World Conference on Human Rights, Vienna, on June 17, 1993, and at the Zagreb University Law School, Zagreb, on June 25, 1993. The intellectual and research collaboration of Natalie Nenadic and Asja Armanda, all women of the Kareta Feminist Group, and the survivors made this work possible. It was first published in 17 *Harvard Women's Law Journal* 5 (1994).

human rights violations, their victims as the *desaparecidos* of everyday life. In the record of human rights violations they are overlooked entirely because the victims are women and what was done to them smells of sex. When a woman is tortured in an Argentine prison cell, even as it is forgotten that she is a woman, it is seen that her human rights are violated because what is done to her is also done to men. Her suffering has the dignity, and her death the honor, and her legal status the recognition of a crime against humanity. But when a woman is tortured by her husband in her home, humanity is not seen to be violated. Here she is a woman—*only* a woman. Internationally, her violation outrages the conscience of few beyond her friends.

Put more schematically, in the perspective of human rights, what is done to women is either too specific to women to be seen as human or too generic to human beings to be seen as about women. Atrocities committed against women are either too female to fit the concept of human or too human to fit the idea of female. "Human" and "female" are mutually exclusive by definition; one cannot be a woman and a human being at the same time. Women's rights are, in other words, not yet human rights, nor are human rights yet women's rights.

Certainly, women are violated in many ways in which men are violated. But women are also violated in particular ways that men are not, or that are exceptional for men. Many of these sex-specific violations are sexual and reproductive. Women are routinely violated sexually and reproductively every day in every country in the world.[1] The idea that these acts violate women's human rights has been created by women, not by states or governments. National laws seldom effectively recognize that women are violated in these ways and sometimes even make them criminals for being raped (having sex outside marriage) or having abortions (resisting forced motherhood). Women across cultures have created the idea that women have human rights, refusing to believe that the reality of violation we live with is what it means for us to be human—as our governments seem largely to believe. Women have created the idea of women's human rights by refusing to abandon ourselves and one another, out of attachment to a principle of our own humanity—one defined against our context and our experiences. They have been defined not by transcending the reality of our violations but by refusing to deny them. In this project, women have learned that one day of real experience is worth volumes of all their theories. If we believed existing approaches to human rights, we would not believe we had any. Rather than looking at human rights law to see how much of women's lives can be fit into it, as we are taught to do as lawyers, look at the reality of women's lives and hold human rights law accountable to what women need and do not have.

Pursuing this reality-based approach, consider one situation of the mass violation of women's human rights now occurring in the heart of Europe. In this campaign of extermination, which began with the Serbian invasion of Croatia in 1991 and exploded in the Serbian aggression against Bosnia and Herzegovina in 1992, evidence documents that women are being sexually and reproductively violated on a mass scale, as a matter of conscious policy, in pursuit of a genocide through war. In October 1992, I received a communication from an American researcher of Croatian and Bosnian descent working with refugees and gathering information on this war. She said that Serbian forces had exterminated Croatians and Muslims in the hundreds of thousands "in an operation they've coined 'ethnic cleansing'"; that in this genocide thousands of Muslim and Croatian girls and women were raped and made forcibly pregnant in settings including Serbian-run concentration camps, of which "about twenty are solely rape/death camps for Muslim and Croatian women and children."[2] She had received reports of the making and use of pornography as part of the genocide. "One Croatian woman described being tortured by electric shocks and gang-raped in a camp by Serbian men dressed in Croatian uniforms who filmed the rapes and forced her to 'confess' on film that Croatians had raped her."[3] She also reported that some United Nations troops were targeting women: "In the streets of Zagreb, UN troops often ask local women how much they cost. There are reports of refugee women being forced to sexually service the UN troops to receive aid. Tomorrow I talk to two survivors of mass rape—thirty men per day for over three months. We've heard the UN passed a resolution to collect evidence as the first step for a war crimes trial, but it is said here that there is no precedent for trying sexual atrocities."[4]

Whether or not these practices are formally illegal—and it is easy to say with complacency that rape, prostitution, pornography, and sexual murder are illegal—they are widely permitted under both domestic and international law. They are allowed, whether understood, one man to another, as an excess of passion in peace or the spoils of victory in war, or as the liberties, civil or otherwise, of their perpetrators. They are legally rationalized, officially winked at, and in some instances formally condoned. Whether or not they are regarded as crimes, in no country are they effectively prohibited and no place are they recognized as violations of the human rights of their victims.

This genocidal war exemplifies how existing approaches to violations of women's human rights can serve to confuse who is doing what to whom and thus can cover up and work to condone atrocities. These atrocities also give an urgency, if any was needed, to the project of reenvisioning human rights so that violations of humanity are seen to encompass what happens to women.

The war against Croatia and Bosnia-Herzegovina, and their partial occupation, is being carried out by Serbian forces in collaboration with the Serbian regime in Belgrade, governing what remains of Yugoslavia. This is an international war. All the state parties have adopted relevant laws of nations that prohibit these acts; they are covered in any case by customary international law and jus cogens.[5] Yet so far nothing has been invoked to stop these abuses or to hold their perpetrators accountable. The excuses offered for this lack of action are illuminating.[6]

In this war, the fact of Serbian aggression is beyond question, just as the fact of male aggression against women is beyond question, both here and in everyday life. "Ethnic cleansing" is a euphemism for genocide. It is a policy of ethnic extermination of non-Serbs with the aim of "all Serbs in one nation," a clearly announced goal of "Greater Serbia," of territorial conquest and aggrandizement. That this is a war against non-Serbian civilians, not between advancing and retreating armies, is also beyond question. Yet this war of aggression—once admitted to exist at all—has repeatedly been construed as bilateral, as a civil war or an ethnic conflict, to the accompaniment of much international head scratching about why people cannot seem to get along and a lot of pious clucking about the human rights violations of "all sides" as if they were comparable. This three-pronged maneuver is familiar to those who work with the issue of rape: blame women for getting ourselves raped by men we know, chastise us for not liking them very well afterward, and then criticize our lack of neutrality in not considering rapes of men to be a comparable emergency. The obscuring of the ethnic specificity of rape is common outside wartime settings as well.

One result of this approach is that the rapes in this war are not grasped as either a strategy in genocide or a practice of misogyny, far less both at once. They are not understood as continuous both with this particular ethnic war of aggression and with the gendered war of aggression of everyday life. Genocide does not come from nowhere, nor does rape as a ready and convenient tool of it. Nor is a continuity an equation. These rapes are to everyday rape what the Holocaust was to everyday anti-Semitism. Without everyday anti-Semitism a Holocaust is impossible, but anyone who has lived through a pogrom knows the difference.

What is happening here, in fact, is first a genocide, in which ethnicity is a tool for political hegemony; the war is an instrument of the genocide; the rapes are an instrument of both. The Bosnian Serbs under the command of Radovan Karadžić do not control the state; their war is against the people and the democratically elected government of Bosnia-Herzegovina. If you control the state and want to commit genocide, as the Nazis did under the Third Reich, you do not need a war. You do it with the state mechanisms at hand. This is being done now, quietly, to Hungarians and Croatians in occupied eastern Croatia and in Vojvodina, formerly an autonomous region now annexed to Serbia,[7] virtually invisible to the world.

The Albanians in Kosova are in a particularly precarious situation, surrounded, within a state. When Serbia moves on them militarily, going beyond the segregation and oppression they suffer now, it may not look like a war to anyone else. It will not cross international borders, the way much international law wants to see before it feels violated. But it will be another facet of the campaign to eliminate non-Serbs from areas targeted for "cleansing," a genocide.[8] To call these campaigns to exterminate non-Serbs "civil war" is like calling the Holocaust a civil war between German Aryans and German Jews. If and when the reality in Vojvodina comes out, or Albanians are "cleansed," perhaps that too will be packaged for Western consumption as ancient ethnic hatreds, a bog like Vietnam, or some other formulation to justify doing nothing about it.

In this genocide through war, mass rape is a tool, a tactic, a policy, a plan, a strategy, and an instrumentality, as well as a practice. Muslim and Croatian women and girls are raped, then often killed, by Serbian military men, regulars and irregulars in a variety of formations, in their homes, on hillsides, in camps—camps that used to be factories, schools, farms, mines, sports arenas, post offices, restaurants, hotels, or houses of prostitution. The camps can be outdoor enclosures of barbed wire or buildings. There, people are held, beaten, and killed; women, and sometimes men, are raped. Some women are also raped after they are killed. Some of these camps are rape/death camps exclusively for women, organized like the brothels of what is called peacetime, sometimes in locations that were brothels before the war.

In the West, the sexual atrocities in this conflict have been discussed largely as rape *or* as genocide, not as what they are, which is rape as genocide, rape directed toward women because they are Muslim or Croatian. It is as if people cannot think more than one thought at once. The mass rape is part of a campaign by Serbia against non-Serbia, or an onslaught by combatants against civilians, or an attack by men against women, but never all at the same time. Or—this is the feminist version of the whitewash—these atrocities are presented as just another instance of aggression by all men against all women all the time. If this were the opening volley in a counteroffensive against rape as a war against all women all the time, it would be one thing. But the way it works here is the opposite: to make sure that no one who cares about rape takes a side in *this* war against *these* particular rapes. It does not so much galvanize opposition to rape whenever and wherever it occurs as cover up the fact that these rapes are being done by *some* men against *certain* women for specific reasons, here and now. The point seems to be to obscure, by any means available, exactly who is doing what to whom and why.

The result is that these rapes are grasped in either their ethnic or religious particularity, as attacks on a culture, or in their sex specificity, meaning as attacks on women—never both at once. Attacks on women, it seems, cannot define attacks on a people. If they are gendered attacks, they are not ethnic; if they are ethnic attacks, they are not gendered. One cancels the other. But when rape is a genocidal act, as it is here, it is an act to destroy a people. What is done to women defines that destruction. Besides, aren't women a people?

These rapes are also widely treated as an inevitable by-product of armed conflict. Every time there is a war, there is rape. Of course, rape does occur in all wars, both within and between all sides. As to rape on one's own side, aggression outside borders is customarily sustained by corresponding suppression and manipulation at home. When the army comes back, it visits on the women at home the escalated level of assault the men were taught and practiced on women in the war zone. The United States knows this well from the war in Vietnam. Men's domestic violence against women escalated—including their skill at inflicting torture without leaving visible marks. Sexual aggression against Asian women through prostitution and pornography exploded in the United States during this period. American men got a particular taste for violating them over there. This must be happening to Serbian women now.

Rape *is* a daily act by men against women; it is always an act of domination by men over women. But the role of these rapes in this genocidal war of aggression is a matter of fact, not of ideological spin or theoretical analysis. Muslim and Croatian women are facing two layers of men on top of them rather than one, one layer engaged in exterminating the other, and two layers of justification—"just war" and "just life." Add the misrepresentation of this war as a civil war among equal aggressors, and these women are facing three times the usual number of reasons for the world to do nothing about it.

All the cover-ups signally ignore the fact that this is a genocide. The "civil war" cover-up obscures the role of Belgrade in invading first Croatia, then Bosnia-Herzegovina, and in occupying parts of both. A civil war is not an invasion by another country. If this is a civil war, neither Croatia nor Bosnia-Herzegovina is a nation, but both are recognized as such. In a civil war, aggression is mutual. This is not a reciprocal genocide. Muslims and Croatians are not advancing and retreating into and out of Serbia. They are not carrying out genocide against Serbs on their own territories. There are no concentration camps for Serbs in Sarajevo or Zagreb. The term "civil war" translates, in all languages, into "not my problem." It makes it domestic, the way what men to do women everywhere everyday is domestic. In construing this situation as a civil war at bottom, the international community has defined it in terms of what it has so far been willing to do about it: nothing.

It is not that there are no elements of common culture among the parties here, at least as imposed through decades of Communist rule, meaning Serbian hegemony. It is not that there are no conflicts between or within sides, or shifting of sides in complex ways, that provide elements of civil war. It is not that the men on one side rape and the men on the other side do not. It is, rather, that none of these factors defines this emergency, none of them created it, none of them is driving it, and none of them explains it. These are smoke screens, propaganda tools, sincere or cynical, behind which Serbia continues to expand its territory by exterminating people and raping women en masse.

The feminist version of the cover-up is especially useful to the perpetrators because it seems to acknowledge the atrocities—which are hard to deny (although they do that too)—and occupy the ground on which outrage against them has been effectively aroused. But its function is to exonerate the rapists and to deflect intervention. If all men do this all the time, especially in war, how can one pick a side in this one? And since all men do this all the time, war or no war, why do anything special about this now? Such analysis is often accompanied by a blanket critique of "nationalism," as if identification with the will to exterminate can be equated with identification with the will to survive extermination; as if an ethnic concept of nation (like the Serbian fascist one) is the same as a multiethnic concept of nation (like the Bosnian one); and as if those who are being killed because of the nation they belong to should find some loftier justification for staying alive and resenting the basis on which they are being exterminated than national survival. The upshot is, this conflict becomes just a form of business as usual.[9] But genocide is not business as usual—not even for men.

Like all rape, genocidal rape is particular as well as part of the generic, and its particularity matters. This is ethnic rape as an official policy of war in a genocidal campaign for political control. That means not only a policy of the pleasure of male power unleashed, which happens all the time in so-called peace; not only a policy to defile, torture, humiliate, degrade, and demoralize the other side, which happens all the time in war; and not only a policy of men posturing to gain advantage and ground over other men. It is specifically rape under orders. This is not rape out of control. It is rape under control. It is also rape unto death, rape as massacre, rape to kill and to make the victims wish they were dead. It is rape as an instrument of forced exile, rape to make you leave your home and never want to go back. It is rape to be seen and heard and watched and told to others: rape as spectacle. It is rape to drive a wedge through a community, to shatter a society, to destroy a people. It is rape as genocide.

It is also rape made sexy for the perpetrators by the power of the rapist, which is absolute, to select the victims at will. They walk into rooms of captive women and point, "You, you, and you," and take you out. Many never return. It is rape made more arousing by the ethnic hostility against the designated "enemy," made to feel justified by the notion that it is "for Serbia," which they say as they thrust into the women and make them sing Serbian patriotic songs.[10] It is rape made to seem right by decades of lies about the supposed behavior of that enemy—years and years of propaganda campaigns, full of historical lies and falsified data, including in schools. In this effort, rapes and murders carried out by Serbs against non-Serbs are presented to the Serbian population on television as rapes and murders of Serbs by Muslims and Croats. The way in which pornography is believed in the men's bodies as well as in their minds gives this war propaganda a special potency.

This is also rape made especially exciting for the perpetrators by knowing that there are no limits on what they can do, by knowing that these women can, and in many instances will, be raped to death. Although the orders provide motivation enough, the rapes are made sexually enjoyable, irresistible even, by the fact that the women are about to be sacrificed, by the powerlessness of the women and children in the face of their imminent murder at the hands of their rapists. This is murder as the ultimate sexual act.

It will not help to say that this is violence, not sex, for the men involved. When the men are told to take the women away and not bring them back, first they rape them, then they kill them, and then sometimes rape them again and cut off their breasts and tear out their wombs.[11] One woman

was allowed to live only as long as she kept her Serbian captor hard all
night orally, night after night after night, from midnight to 5:00 A.M. What
he got was sex for him. The aggression was the sex.

This is rape as torture as well as rape as extermination. In the camps, it
is at once mass rape and serial rape in a way that is indistinguishable from
prostitution. Prostitution is that part of everyday nonwar life that is closest
to what we see done to women in this war. The daily life of prostituted
women consists of serial rape, recognized war or no war. The brothel-like
arrangement of the rape/death camps parallels the brothels of so-called
peacetime: captive women impounded to be passed from man to man in
order to be raped.

This is also rape as a policy of ethnic uniformity and ethnic conquest,
of annexation and expansion, of acquisition by one nation of other nations.
It is rape because a Serb wants your apartment. This is also rape as ethnic
expansion through forced reproduction. African American women were
forcibly impregnated through rape under slavery. The Nazis required
Eastern European women to get special permission for abortions if they
were impregnated by German men.[12] In genocide, it is more usual for the
babies on the other side to be killed. Croatian and Muslim women are
being raped, and then denied abortions, to help make a Serbian state by
making what the perpetrators imagine as Serbian babies.[13]

If this were racial rape, as Americans are familiar with it, the children
would be regarded as polluted, dirty, and contaminated, even as they are
sometimes given comparative privileges based on "white" blood. But because this is ethnic rape, lacking racial markers, the children are regarded
by the aggressors as somehow clean and purified, as "cleansed" ethnically.
The babies made with Muslim and Croatian women are regarded as Serbian babies. The idea seems to be to create a fifth column within Muslim
and Croatian society of children—all sons?—who will rise up and join
their fathers. Much Serbian fascist ideology simply adopts and adapts Nazi
views. This one is the ultimate achievement of the Nazi ideology that culture is genetic.

The spectacle of the UN troops violating those they are there to protect
adds a touch of the perverse. My correspondent added that some UN
troops are participating in raping Muslim and Croatian women taken from
Serb-run rape/death camps. She reports that "the UN presence has apparently increased the trafficking in women and girls through the opening
of brothels, brothel-massage parlors, peep shows, and the local production
of pornographic films."[14] There are also reports that a former United
Nations Protection Force (UNPROFOR) commander accepted offers from

a Serbian commander to bring him Muslim girls for sexual use.[15] All this is an example of the male bond across official lines. It pointedly poses a problem women have always had with male protection: Who is going to watch the men who are supposedly watching out for us? Each layer of male protection adds a layer to violence against women. Perhaps intervention by a force of armed women should be considered.

Now, the use of media technology is highly developed. Before, the Nazis took pictures of women in camps, forced women into brothels in camps, and took pictures of naked women running to their deaths. They also created events that did not happen through media manipulation. In this war, the aggressors have at hand the new cheap, mobile, accessible, and self-contained moving-picture technology. The saturation of what was Yugoslavia with pornography upon the dissolution of communism—pornography that was largely controlled by Serbs, who had the power—has created a population of men prepared to experience sexual pleasure in torturing and killing women. It also paved the way for the use on television of footage of actual rapes, with the ethnicity of the victims and perpetrators switched, to inflame Serbs against Muslims and Croatians.[16] In the conscious and open use of pornography, in making pornography of atrocities, in the sophisticated use of pornography as war propaganda, this is perhaps the first truly modern war.

Although these acts flagrantly violate provision after provision of international law, virtually nothing has been done about them for years. Then the international machinery seemed finally to be lumbering into action, even as more men, women, and children were liquidated daily. To explain this slow response, it is important to consider that most human rights instruments empower states to act against states, not individuals or groups to act for themselves. This is particularly odd given that international human rights law recognizes only violations of human rights by state actors. In other words, only entities like those who do the harm are empowered to act to stop them. It would have seemed clear after 1945 that states often violate the rights of those who are not states and who have no state to act for them. The existing structure of international law was substantially created in response to this, yet without for the most part empowering individuals and groups to act when their human rights were violated.[17]

This problem is particularly severe for women's human rights because women are typically raped not by governments but by what are considered individual men. The government just does nothing about it. This may be tantamount to being raped by the state, but it is legally seen as "private" therefore not as a human rights violation. In an international world order in which primarily states can violate human rights, most rape is left out. The role of the state in permitting women to be raped with impunity can be exposed, but the structural problem in addressing it remains.

The convergence here between ways of thinking about women and ways of thinking about international law and politics is this: the more a conflict can be framed as within a state—as a civil war, as domestic, as private—the less effective the human rights model becomes. The more it looks like the construction of the oppression of women, the less can structurally be done about it. The closer a fight comes to home, the more "feminized" the victims become, no matter their gender, and the less likely it is that international human rights will be found violated, no matter what was done.[18] Croatia and Bosnia-Herzegovina are being treated like women,[19] like women being gang-raped on a mass scale. This is not an analogy; far less is it a suggestion that this rape is wrong only because the women belong to a man's state. It identifies the treatment of a whole polity by the treatment of the women there.[20]

In the structure of international human rights, based as it is on the interest of states in their sovereignty as such, no state has an incentive to break ranks by going after another state for how it treats women—thus setting a standard of human rights treatment for women that no state is prepared to meet within its own borders or is willing to be held to internationally. When men sit in rooms, being states, they are largely being men. They protect each other; they identify with each other; they try not to limit each other in ways they themselves do not want to be limited. In other words, they do not represent women. There is no state we can point to and say, "This state effectively guarantees women's human rights. There we are free and equal."

In this statist structure, each state's lack of protection of women's human rights is internationally protected, and that is called protecting state sovereignty. A similar structure of insulation between women and accountability for their violations exists domestically. Raped women are compelled to go to the state; men make the laws and decide if they will enforce them. When women are discriminated against, they have to go to a human rights commission and try to get it to move. This is called protecting the community. It is the same with international human rights, only more so: only the state can hurt you, but to redress it you have to get the state to act for you. In international law there are a few exceptions to this, but in the current emergency in Bosnia-Herzegovina and Croatia they are of no use. Each state finds its reasons to do nothing, which can be read as not wanting to set a higher standard of accountability for atrocities to women than the one they are prepared to be held to themselves.

Formally, wartime is an exception to the part of this picture that exempts most rape, because atrocities by soldiers against civilians are always considered state acts. The trouble has been that men do in war what they do in peace, only more so, so when it comes to women, the complacency that surrounds peacetime extends to wartime, no matter what the law says. Every country in this world arguably had a jus cogens obligation to prevent genocide by stopping the Serbian aggressors from doing what they are doing, but until Bosnia-Herzegovina went to the International Court of Justice and sued Serbia for genocide, including rape, no one did a thing.[21] In so doing, Bosnia-Herzegovina is standing up for women in a way that no state ever has. The survivors I work with also filed their own civil suit in New York against Radovan Karadžić, leader of the Bosnian Serb fascists, for an injunction against genocide, rape, torture, forced pregnancy, forced prostitution, and other sex and ethnic discrimination and atrocities that violate women's international human rights.[22]

A war crimes tribunal to enforce accountability for mass genocidal rape is being prepared by the United Nations.[23] There are precedents in the Tokyo trials after World War II for command responsibility for mass rape. Beyond precedent, the voices of the victims have been heard in the structuring of the new tribunal. To my knowledge, no one asked Jewish survivors how the trials at Nuremberg should be conducted, nor do I think the women raped in Nanking were asked what they needed in order to be able to testify about their rapes. The issue of accountability to victims has been raised here formally for the first time: How can a war crimes tribunal be created that is accessible to victims of mass sexual atrocity? What will make it possible for victims of genocidal rape to speak about their violations?[24]

The genocidal rapes of this war present the world with a historic opportunity: That this becomes the time and place, and these the women, when the world recognizes that violence against women violates human rights. That when a woman is raped, the humanity of a human being is recognized to be violated. When the world says never again—not in war, not in peace—and this time means it.

19

Gender-Based Crimes
in Humanitarian Law

No international convention expressly prohibits gender-based crimes. No codified and ratified international criminal law includes "based on sex" as an element.[1] Crimes against humanity, which traditionally can be gender-based,[2] have not been part of treaty law.[3] Although many international crimes are based on sex in fact, such as rape in war and trafficking in women, international law tends to suppress their gendered element.[4] In the international crime of genocide, the sex-specific destruction of women as members of their religious, national, or ethnic communities is largely ignored. No international crime recognizes what Andrea Dworkin calls "gynocide"[5] or what Diana Russell and others call "femicide"[6]—the destruction of women as women, as a group or as members of the group. The pattern is presence in reality and absence in law.

There has been some conceptual progress in recognition of crimes against women in the jurisprudence of international crimes, but delivery to victims has not kept pace. The practical delivery of the law of the crime of genocide, for example, from the perspective of its victims in Croatia and Bosnia-Herzegovina in particular, has lagged far behind the commission of these crimes against them in reality. It has not come anywhere near close. A similar disproportion can be observed in responses to the Rwandan genocide. Perpetrators of humanitarian violations are way ahead of international lawyers in grasping the role of rape in genocide.

The denial of gender inequalities in the crimes humanitarian law addresses has resulted in a gap between crimes that are gender-based in fact and those that are gender-based in law. This absence has a continuous structure from domestic through international law, one exposed in high relief in

This talk was given on a panel sponsored by the Asser Institute, The Hague, July 3, 1997. It was first published in *Contemporary International Law Issues: New Forum, New Applications* 150–53 (W. P. Heere, ed., 1998).

the case of Kadic v. Karadžić,[7] in which the international law of genocide is being adjudicated in a situation of rape in genocide in a domestic U.S. court. Of the many barriers to effective recognition of gender-based crimes in humanitarian law, drawing on Kadic v. Karadžić, I want to consider the contribution of sovereignty as an element of male ideology. Implicitly or explicitly, the notion of sovereign dominion structures legal recourse in the form of doctrines of jurisdiction at every level of procedure, from the domestic through the international. It begins at home, "a man's . . . castle." He is the state in the home. Historically, women have had to leave home to get justice within it because it was *his* castle. Overcoming a systemic reluctance to intervene in what are called domestic conflicts in the private sphere that continues to this day, women got local regulations, state or provincial laws, recourse keeping us as close to home as possible, yet with a toehold in the public sphere. However, these remedies were hampered in their effectiveness for the same reason. Laws against rape and domestic violence, for example, continue to be interpreted and implemented through a familiarity exemption, meaning the closer the man is to the woman, the more he can violate her. And local law enforcement officials, who are usually local men, are likely to know and identify with the perpetrator.

So women, seeking a bigger hammer, have had to range further and further from home to get justice for gender-based acts. They have gone to men who might be less controlled by their perpetrators so may be accountable to law, thus to violated women. Continuing this motion outward, because criminal law of localities had so systematically failed women, U.S. women managed to achieve a national civil law against gender-motivated crimes of violence—the Violence Against Women Act,[8] a law constitutionally attacked on jurisdictional grounds.[9]

In *Kadic,* women survivors of Karadžić's genocidal attempt to destroy non-Serb communities by, among other means, systematic rape of non-Serb women had to go to the United States to try to get justice against him under international law. Karadžić resisted jurisdiction, contending that he should not be held accountable under international law in other men's courts for how he treats (his) women at home, in what he tellingly (and falsely) referred to as a domestic conflict. Implicit in his argument was a threat: If you can hold me accountable to you for how I treat my women in my home, other men will be able to hold you accountable to them for how you treat your women in your home. If you can do this to me, other men will be able to do this to you. Amazingly, he lost.[10]

Immunities govern and mark every level of this sovereignty scheme. Marital immunity has governed the family, including a widespread exemption for rape in marriage. Familiarity immunity still de facto governs the criminal law of acquaintance or intimate relationships. Official immunity protects state actors within states. Sovereign immunity protects them in the law of nations.[11] This is patriarchy writ large and small at once. On this reading, the reason the litigation against Karadžić has been able to proceed is that he did not win the war so never became sovereign. Had he won, he might not have been able to be sued for the genocide. In this light, the balance of terror between men through which some men respect other men's license to abuse women at home underlies the notion of "comity" in this area, as well as effective exemptions from international prohibitions on misogynistic cultural practices.[12] Under U.S. domestic law, "federalism," formerly "states' rights," works in the same way. The ad hoc International Criminal Tribunal for Crimes in the Former Yugoslavia in The Hague has not been explicitly fettered by sovereignty constraints. It has largely inherited the existing structure of humanitarian crimes in its founding statute, which minimizes women's injuries and has yet to recognize gender-based crimes in so many words. In the statute itself, rape is recognized as a crime against humanity but not as genocide.[13] The practice of the ICTY is also subject to the accretion of centuries of denial of harm to women and legally institutionalized sex inequality, as well as reflexive international institutional deference to states, which in this area are two sides of the same coin; rather, the second has become a means of achieving the first. This may be the reason that the ICTY has as yet not adequately addressed sex-specific injuries in the Yugoslav conflict, failing to name them as what they are and leaving many women without effective recourse for atrocities committed against them.

What might a gender-based crime in international law look like? Taking genocide as the model, it would preferably be explicitly reality-based, as the Genocide Convention was intended to be when it was written. It would prohibit the destruction of a group or a part of a group as such. It would include real-life concrete particulars of how the crime was carried out, including the acts of which the drafters were aware. It could require purpose. Preferably, it would not. Modeled on crimes against humanity, it would permit inference of group basis from patterns in the evidence, discerning the ground of the destruction on the basis of sex in widespread systematic practices.

Practices it would certainly include, in order as they arise in life, would be sex-selective abortions, female infanticide, and deprivation of nutrition on the basis of sex—cultural practices that guarantee that millions of girls never are even born or grow up to become second-class citizens, becoming in Amartya Sen's term "missing" women, the truly disappeared.[14] It would include sexual abuse in childhood, rape, battering, dowry burnings, suttee, being stoned to death for not wearing proper apparel, "honor" killings, and, depending on its central concept, homophobic violence. It would include destructive acts against women "in part" on ethnic grounds combined with sex, such as forced sterilizations and rape/death camps in genocidal war. Rape in genocide would be seen as genocide but also gynocide. Prostitution as female sexual slavery, in peace as well as war, and pornography as an arm of prostitution and trafficking would also be recognized as part of the intentional destruction of women as a group.

These acts, taken together, would be recognized as a complex of gender-based acts, as none of them has yet been effectively addressed, in part by virtue of not having been recognized as interconnected in a systematic way, as united by being gender-based. Recognition of such a crime could take the form of a new convention or be embodied in a new protocol to the Genocide Convention. Its concept, in the meantime, could be used as a benchmark against which existing law and practice could be measured for shortfall, developing customary international law to prohibit gender-based criminality.

20

War Crimes Remedies
at the National Level

The most particular can be the most universal. This conclusion emerges from the contrast between bringing human rights claims in a national forum and bringing the same violations of the same people under the same laws in an international forum. The people are Bosnian Muslim and Croat women survivors of the genocide carried out by Serbs in Bosnia-Herzegovina and Croatia. The violations are sexual atrocities. The laws are international prohibitions against genocide, war crimes, and crimes against humanity. The forums are the federal Southern District of New York in the United States, on the one hand, and the International Criminal Tribunal for Serious Crimes in the Former Yugoslavia (ICTY), on the other.

When a coalition of five groups of Bosnian and Croat survivors of Serbian genocidal sexual atrocities approached me in 1992 to represent them in seeking what they called "international justice," my first question was, "Where?" Their answer was, "That's your first job": find or make a forum. They wanted to be heard by a war crimes tribunal like Nuremberg, so we conceived and pressed for the establishment of what became the ICTY. But, contrary to what we asked for, the ICTY was not designed to be accountable to survivors, but to international bodies, which has meant mainly nation-states, and has remained most sensitive to international politics. This is a particular problem for women, who are largely excluded from meaningful voice within official international arenas. Because the survivors wanted a process and lawyers who would be accountable to them, we proceeded in the Southern District of New York.

Even before having a place to take these injuries, the survivors needed

This talk was delivered to the University of Michigan Law School Reunion of International Alumni, University of Michigan Law School, on a panel with Professor José Alvarez, October 18, 1997. It was originally published in 6 *Journal of the International Institute* 1 (1998). This talk, with all our work for the survivors, is possible only because of the vision, insight, and determination of Asja Armanda and Natalie Nenadic.

to be believed. Substantially through the efforts of our clients, the press eventually published (what to the rest of the world was) news of the "mass rapes" in Bosnia-Herzegovina and Croatia. Press coverage gave credibility to the fact of their rapes that women speaking about them did not and also brought international attention to the genocide as a whole. Human rights organizations that up to that point had denied or minimized the rapes then decided to believe that the rapes were real.[1]

Meantime, we canvassed avenues for legal relief in light of the clients' priorities. Their first priority was to stop the genocide. They knew this was not a war with "ethnic cleansing" as one part. It was (is) a genocide euphemized as "ethnic cleansing" conducted in part through war. They wanted it stopped. Second, the clients wanted to hold those responsible for it, from the top to the bottom of the hierarchy, accountable to them for what they had done to them. International bodies were not set up to achieve either of these goals. The applicable international law, as is not unusual, was strong in principle but weak on delivery. Domestic law in many countries had the reverse problem: short on principle by international standards but long on teeth. We concluded that if you wanted a statement of principle, go to an international forum; if you wanted delivery, go to a national court. The clients were not attracted to a confidential investigation by an international inquiry leading to a secret report in which perpetrators might be told they did something bad. The genocide was ongoing. The survivors had real and severe damages. There was no regional human rights association with jurisdiction over their claims to bridge this gap, as in some other places. The survivors needed the kind of followthrough that domestic courts best provide on the basis of principles that are best articulated under international law.

The central problem in using international law was that women are not states. In an international system that remains centrally a community of nations, no state took up these women's international injuries. Nobody who could have stepped forward to carry Bosnian or Croatian women's injuries in the International Court of Justice (ICJ), for example, did so. Bosnia-Herzegovina itself did later include sexual atrocities in its own claim for genocide against Serbia and Montenegro in the ICJ,[2] representing all its violated people.

The legal abdication of victims at that time went hand in hand with the military one. No one who could have intervened to stop the genocide on the ground did that either. They diddled for years. The international community was largely denying that the conflagration was a genocide at all. Preferring to think of it as a "civil war," they absolved themselves of taking sides or stopping it. Part of this denial came from believing Serbian propaganda. Part of it stemmed from an image of genocide that required the Holocaust to be replicated, when the legal definition of genocide is not so limited.[3] Mainly, as we saw it, this reluctance was driven by a desire to avoid admitting that this conflict was a genocide, since that would have intensified international pressure to intervene. The Serbian aggression in the region was not being called a genocide in law or in fact not because it was not one, but rather for the realpolitik reasons that no country found it convenient to take on its army, a large and well-supplied one, to stop it. Then, unexpectedly to us, Radovan Karadžić, leader of the Bosnian Serbs committing the genocide in collaboration with the Milošević regime in Belgrade, showed up in New York City one day. We served him with a civil action under the Alien Tort Claims Act[4] and the Torture Victim Protection Act[5] and now had our own forum, a national one, for our international claims.

The Alien Tort Claims Act is unusual if not unique in the world. It provides jurisdiction in United States federal district courts for non-U.S. citizens to sue for torts committed against them in violation of the law of nations. It is interpreted to give jurisdiction to a plaintiff who has both served process personally—the defendant has to be personally handed the lawsuit—and established federal subject-matter jurisdiction.[6] Precedent has established that subject-matter jurisdiction exists when customary international law or international treaties are violated.[7]

The survivors' case, Kadic v. Karadžić was filed in early March 1993[8] claiming rape as genocide, rape as a war crime, and rape as torture, as well as other injuries, including murder of family members, resulting from Karadžić's intentional destruction of non-Serbian communities and peoples. This case brought civil claims for these international crimes, seeking declaratory relief (acknowledgment that what happened to them violated these laws), an injunction against the genocide (requiring Karadžić order it to end and not recommence), and substantial damages for the human atrocities that were committed under color of his policy of genocidal aggression.

Karadžić contested most strongly our right to bring the case at all. The district court initially dismissed it for legal insufficiency, accepting Karadžić's assertions of immunities of all sorts, known and some previously unknown. The judge also incorrectly held that Karadžić was not a state actor, therefore we had no case under international law. He also implied that the issues were (or would soon become) political questions, meaning they had consequences for foreign affairs and were properly matters for the executive branch, so we should not be permitted to litigate them.[9] We appealed and won on all these grounds.[10] The U.S. Supreme Court decided to leave that decision standing by declining to accept review.[11] Then, after fighting hard for over three years, Karadžić folded. Over this time period, our case contributed to delegitimizing him and his campaign; he was not being treated as a diplomat anymore, but as an internationally hunted, indicted criminal and refugee from justice. Once we won a discovery motion ordering him to appear for a deposition in New York—our clients had some questions they wanted him to answer—he wrote the judge a letter saying he would no longer fight our claims at the trial level. He is in default. We are moving toward a default judgment and an inquest on relief.[12]

What has been accomplished, and what did our choice of forum contribute? First, we got jurisdiction over Karadžić under international law. The ICTY has yet to accomplish this. Second, we established the role of rape in genocide under international law for the first time in a court of law. Now when rape is an act of genocide in fact, it can be recognized as an act of genocide in law. The ICTY is crawling—or we hope they are at least crawling—in this direction.[13] Finally, our clients wanted to testify about their rapes in a court of law. The ICTY has presented little to none of this testimony to date. Do the formal features of a domestic civil forum, compared with those of an international criminal one, explain these differences? In part they do—we represent our clients, respond to their needs, shape the claim to what happened to them, take their security needs seriously, select and work closely with translators they trust, for example. But they do not have to. Nothing about what we have done except for seeking damages needs to be confined to domestic forums or to civil courts.

One way to evaluate a process is against its goals. Some conventional values pursued in international criminal law enforcement are punishment, deterrence, closure, reconciliation, and spread of the rule of law. Our survivors have a somewhat different list: (1) stopping the violations; (2) calling them what they are; (3) securing accountability to the violated for what was done to them; and (4) changing law, so that what is done here has meaning beyond the context of these proceedings.

Attempting to stop a genocide may seem ambitious, but we sought an injunction to end this one. The ICTY is not even set up to try, although it has at least as much power at its disposal as we do. As an analogy, civil rights injunctions, such as the structural ones racially integrating schools, have been routinely enforced within U.S. borders.[14] The United States already has a military force in Bosnia-Herzegovina carrying out peacekeeping responsibilities—although it is beyond comprehension how civilians will be protected without firing back against a military force intent on exterminating them. But enforcing a federal court injunction against one man who has ordered this genocide, if unusual, is not beyond the pale at all.

The ICTY is very sensitive to avoiding behavior for which the Nuremberg Tribunal was criticized. Failing to face the group nature of the atrocities does not seem to be among them, however. Nuremberg has been criticized for evading the anti-Semitism of the crimes it prosecuted, almost as if the Holocaust were an adjunct to the war. The ICTY is charging genocide, conventional law for fifty years now. It can fight the last war. The question is whether it can fight the current one. As ethnicity was evaded at Nuremberg, sex—in this case sex and ethnicity combined—is being systematically ignored by the ICTY. Rape is charged; genocide is charged. But rape is not being charged as an act of genocide, failing fundamentally to name the atrocities for what they are: genocidal rape. Our case named and claimed them under international law. It can be done.

A forum in which survivors choose their own lawyer, shape their own claims, and direct their own case leaves the process of justice more in their own hands. The process, by design, is accountable to them—not to the press, not to international politics, not to the bureaucratic imperatives of international organizations, not to fundraising competitions or turf battles or empire-building sweepstakes of human rights organizations, and not to criminal prosecutors enhancing their careers by claiming to represent "the law" and looking to move up or on. The ICTY is not accountable to survivors by design or in practice. Survivors have no decisive voice in it. This could change with an attitude shift in its personnel. Hopefully it will.

Woman after woman has been willing to risk standing up in public to testify about her own rape in our civil case. They have to date been unwilling to provide the same testimony to the ICTY. Why? It is certainly not because we have more money to conduct our case than the millions the ICTY has, or a better system to guarantee their security, although we do take security more seriously because we take the people involved seriously. The reason is also not really because we are more sensitive to their personal needs or to the nature of their injuries, although they say we are. The reason is that this case is *their* case. We are working for them; they are not working for us. Maybe the ICTY will figure out how to work for them as well. Whose tribunal is it, if not theirs?

As to closure: surely so long as a genocide is ongoing, it cannot be "closed." Of course, the survivors want these events behind them, but not at the cost of forgetting what happened or having it discarded. Not at the cost of a process that walks over them, colonizes them, exploits, ignores, and misrepresents them. Not at the cost of shoving what really happened under the rug and dehumanizing further those whose human rights have already been violated. Not for more accountability to an elite international legal community than to those whose families were exterminated. Not to assuage the guilt of bystanders. What is this "closure" for? Who wants it? It is the only item on the conventional list of values that purports to be specifically for the victims. Our survivors are critical of premature closure. Who wants this over with in court, especially when they are not yet willing truly to end it on the ground? Who wants it "put behind us," instead of stopped, named, remedied to the extent possible, remembered, and used to make change?

The survivors want law to work for women for a change. This desire underlies their goal of continuity, their version of the rule of law. Sexual atrocities, including sexualized ethnic ones, do not happen only in war or genocide. Our clients want to make rape law work in the daily war against women everywhere. Establishing international accountability for their violations through domestic civil litigation has been one way to pursue that goal. Its results are influencing the ICTY and other international forums as well.

Signally, this case marks the first time that women as a subordinated people were able to complain officially of systematic violations of their human rights during a war while that war was going on. In pursuing international relief for such injuries, the legal system has a lot to learn from survivors' choice of a process they shape themselves.

21

Collective Harms Under the Alien Tort Statute

A Cautionary Note on Class Actions

Class actions are representative actions: the one stands for the many. The slowly unfolding corporate catastrophes, such as illnesses from asbestos exposure, for which they are often used involve discrete torts from a single physical cause in varying etiological scenarios. The injuries are not group-based in the more usual human rights sense. That is, many people are injured because of where they were or what they did but not because of who they are. Human rights violations like genocide and crimes against humanity are not mass accidents. They involve every imaginable tort to a human being and are done because of who the victims are: based on their race, ethnicity, religion, nationality, and sex. People are also politically tortured on the basis of their politics and ethnicity, and war crimes are increasingly concerted acts against civilians defined by group membership. When war is an instrument of genocide, war crimes, too, can become group-based acts.

A still small but increasing number of class actions for mass human rights violations are being brought under the United States' federal Alien Tort Statute,[1] posing the question whether U.S. class action instruments[2] are well adapted to international human rights violations that are not only numerous but take a collective form. Focusing in particular on the *Karadžić* cases, and to a lesser extent on the *Marcos* cases and the *Holocaust Victim Assets* litigation, my concern here is with the fit between domestic class action techniques, particularly the "limited-fund class action" device,[3] and international human rights goals for group-based injuries.

Class actions are typically brought for injuries to large groups of people

This talk was given on the Panel on the Alien Tort Claims Act, International Law Society meetings, New York City, November 5, 1999. It was first published in 6 *ILSA Journal of International and Comparative Law* 567 (2000).

when common questions of fact and law are raised in situations where either the injury to each individual is de minimis but taken together is substantial, or where too many plaintiffs or defendants makes joining them impractical. Some of the devices are mandatory; in these, everyone who was hurt is deemed included.[4] Some permit people to opt out of the class, voluntarily excluding themselves; some do not.[5]

To speak very generally, class actions in the 1960s and 1970s could be called the darlings of the left. They recognized and made it possible to redress collective injuries, including to groups, on a scale that approximated the scale on which they were inflicted. Many of these class actions produced civil rights initiatives that resulted in social change through law, prominently in education, employment, housing, and prisons. The civil rights class action was assumed to be in the interest of the class it represented. Without it, most of its members would have received nothing. Dissenting class members were cast as greedy spoilers, selfish outliers, individualistic troublemakers. Individuals who sought to opt out of these actions, actions assumed to be in the interest of every member of the group as a group including them, were considered self-seeking contrarians, free-riders who were denying their own actual group membership and obstructing the group's welfare, something like scabs in a union drive. They were also a huge pain in the neck for litigators, who imagined themselves pursuing the greatest good for the group, doing justice.

To again draw a bit of a caricature, in the 1980s and 1990s, class action devices became the darlings of the right. Corporations, even whole industries, found that class actions were made in heaven for controlling their legal exposure to victims of the widespread harms they did. Class actions became perceived as useful for limiting the liability of mass tort-feasors. Some corporations, it was alleged, and some industry groups, or so plaintiffs asserted, went so far as to initiate their own collusive class actions against themselves, bringing together all the possible victims in one case that they controlled in order to settle low and exclude some injured parties from relief altogether. With mandatory classes, the result was that everyone's liability was limited to whatever those who represented the plaintiffs—who could be real plaintiffs or not—settled for. The class representatives were permitted to settle everyone's claims in a way that bound class members whether they consented to be bound or not, then or later—with res judicata effect. In massive and unpredictable cases like the asbestos litigation (in some jurisdictions, around a fifth of all civil cases were asbestos cases),[6] mandatory class actions proceeded with the grateful acquiescence of courts ever in pursuit of docket control.

The tension between these two images of the class action—the earlier presumption that class plaintiffs had the interest of the class at heart and the later suspicion that something else may be afoot—came to a head in the case of Ortiz v. Fibreboard Corp. The U.S. Supreme Court decision[7] in that case revealed the legal-cultural shift from assuming that it is best to get something as opposed to nothing for everyone to questioning whether it is valid to bind all to a group resolution whether they wanted it or not. The older view saw only some relief as opposed to none for a group of disenfranchised people whom no one would otherwise represent. The newer view saw an overly hasty, presumptuous, even overreaching, potentially collusive (whether in fact or in intent) resolution of varied claims that cuts off the possibility of better relief later in a form susceptible to agendas far removed from relief or justice for the victims. Such agendas can include, to mention a few, politics, media attention and public-speaking opportunities, career and turf-building, development of expertise or its appearance, credentialing and training, fundraising, and attorneys' fees. When the interests of hurt people are not entirely driving the litigation, class actions can become more in the interest of perpetrators and vehicles for others' advancement than engines of vindication and reparations for survivors.

The class action chameleon of particular concern in Ortiz was the "limited fund class." The classical limited fund class action arises, for instance, when an insured ship sinks. The fund for everyone's recovery of injuries is limited because the ship is insured for only so much. A fixed number of people have a stake in the ship, and the policy limits total recovery, producing a zero-sum situation, so the thought is that all claims should be litigated together. Such classes are mandatory in the sense that no opting-out is permitted except very rarely by judicial discretion. No notice is required to limited-fund classes.[8] Affected people can wind up bound by the adjudication without ever having heard that it happened. The results bind all class members whether or not they took part in the litigation or even knew about it.

The Court in Ortiz, which concerned a settlement class in asbestos litigation, held that certification of a mandatory settlement class required a showing that the fund is limited independent of the agreement of the parties. In other words, the lawyers for the class cannot simply get together with the lawyers for the companies, agree to stipulate that "this is all there is," and divide up the pie. This invites abuse, such as exchanging the avoidance of bankruptcy for the companies for large attorneys' fees to the class lawyers. So, the Court held, the fund had to be shown to be limited in an external way, interclass conflicts had to be addressed, and class members had to be equitably treated.

How do these concerns and safeguards map onto human rights concerns? How, in particular, do they square with large victim and survivor classes who have injuries that are collective in nature, such as those increasingly occurring on the international stage? Given a specific plaintiff class action, how do you know whether it is beneficial and progressive, on the one hand, or complicitous and exploitive, on the other?

Most Alien Tort cases have not been class cases. They have been brought on behalf of harmed individuals whose human rights were violated, sometimes on or implicating group grounds, sometimes not. In the spring of 1993, two separate civil actions were brought against Radovan Karadžić, the leader of a group of Bosnian Serb fascists who carried out a genocide through war to exterminate and eliminate non-Serbs in Bosnia-Herzegovina. The two *Karadžić* cases were brought under the Alien Tort Statute and the Torture Victim Protection Act for genocide, torture, and war crimes in the Southern District of New York by Bosnian Muslim and Croat survivors, seeking relief for torts of ethnic cleansing committed against them. One case, Kadic v. Karadžić,[9] emphasized claims for rape as genocide, rape as torture, and rape as a war crime. We sought relief specifically for injuries of genocidal sexual atrocities perpetrated as a result of Karadžić's policy of ethnic cleansing in collaboration with Slobodan Milošević's administration in Belgrade, Serbia. Damages were sought for the named individuals and groups, with an injunction that Karadžić order the genocide to stop. This was a representative action in the sense that the injuries had a group basis and the injunctive relief would have a group impact. If you stop a genocide, you stop it for everyone, but the moving parties claimed to represent only those who brought the case. The plaintiffs were one rather large survivor group, a smaller group, and the named individuals. The second case, Doe v. Karadžić, seeking damages, was brought by the Center for Constitutional Rights on behalf of two unnamed young girls claiming to represent a class of "all people who suffered injury as a result of rape, genocide, summary execution, arbitrary detention, disappearance, torture or other cruel, inhuman or degrading treatment inflicted by Bosnian-Serb Forces under the command and control of defendant between April 1992 and the present."[10]

By court practice, these two cases proceeded in tandem under a single caption. Jurisdiction was established over Karadžić by beating immunity claims; a civil claim was held permitted under the Alien Tort Statute for rape as an act of genocide.[11] Then the *Doe* lawyers moved to certify the class,[12] which would have subsumed the *Kadic* plaintiffs' case. After some months, this motion was amended to seek, in the alternative, limited fund class certification, because Karadžić's assets were claimed to be limited. This claim was based on a letter Karadžić had sent to the judge contending, inter alia, that he did "not have the financial resources to bring witnesses for my defense to the United States for either depositions, or trial."[13] The *Kadic* plaintiffs sought to opt out of the class. The judge, however, certified the class on the limited-fund theory and denied the *Kadic* motion to opt out[14] over not only the support of the class but over lack of opposition from the defendant as well. The *Kadic* plaintiffs then moved to decertify the class. The issues under domestic law were to be resolved as procedural and due process matters under *Ortiz* and prior precedents.

Two other recent cases have raised similar issues, or potentially so. *Marcos* was a limited-fund case for torture that received a verdict of $2 billion at trial.[15] The *Holocaust Victim Assets* cases were brought beginning in 1997 for claims under the Alien Tort Statute for human rights violations, as well as violations of contract, conversion, breach of fiduciary duty, and other rights. One case claimed a class of all those persecuted and targeted for persecution by the Nazis in three subclasses: those deprived of their assets by banks, those subjected to slave labor, and those forced to become refugees.[16] The settlement proposal would permit opting out, even though a fixed amount of total recovery is agreed to between certain Swiss bank defendants and the plaintiffs.[17]

This small cluster of crucial cases raises two related issues for class actions: adequacy of relief and adequacy of representation. The issue of adequacy of relief is illustrated in both the *Marcos* and *Karadžić* cases. To the *Kadic* plaintiffs, limiting the relief of all the survivors of the Bosnian genocide because Karadžić said he could not afford to come to New York and send witnesses seemed both wrong and small—and dangerous. In the *Marcos* case, a Philippine court disapproved a proposed settlement that would have reduced the $2 billion verdict to $1.5 million based on a Marcos Swiss bank account, noting that a quarter of this amount was slated to go to the lawyers.[18] That court also pointedly noted that it was principally in the interest of the Marcos estate, not the victims, to reduce the very large amount they had won to the much smaller amount of the settlement proposal, "consequences which are extremely beneficial to the Marcoses and of minimal benefits for the human rights victims."[19]

The plaintiffs would have received something rather than nothing, but that may be all they could ever get for the atrocities of the Marcos regime, according to this court, in a suit against anyone. The Philippine court, noting that Philippine procedural law is heavily based on U.S. law and citing U.S. authorities on class suits, took the view that the settlement it disapproved would likely preclude future additional relief: "Whether [the plaintiffs] will initiate a new action against new defendants over the same cause is open to question. Whether they can even legally do so at this time is speculative. . . . Whether human rights victims for the period 1972 to 1986 can still initiate separate suit *against anyone else anywhere else* is . . . doubtful."[20] The court also noted that the Hawai'ian decision in *Marcos* was "binding under res judicata principles upon all members of the class, whether or not they were before the court."[21] The res judicata effect of discrimination class actions has also precluded class members from suing subordinate tort-feasors for the discrimination.[22] While such a result should be resisted, it threatened to preclude future relief, for example, for individuals who run into their individual rapists on the streets of the United States in the future, because Karadžić's liability to the class in *Doe* was predicated on all the acts of all the people who carried out his orders and policies. The complaint attributed all of it to him; the class definition seeks relief for all of it from him. If relief from him is then limited by the limited fund, but his responsibility for the genocide is total, a vast amount of injury was just reduced, on the defendant's say-so, to less than the price of a few tickets to New York. And seeking future relief for the survivors' injuries, in this or any other proceeding, is thus, if not undone, rendered speculative to nil.[23]

Inadequacy of representation is also a real danger. A class could be asserted in human rights litigation when the members have, and can have, no real contact with their purported representatives. The survivors are far away and speak another language; they may number in the thousands or, as in the Bosnian situation, in the hundreds of thousands. In ongoing policy development, one claims to represent huge numbers of people with whom one has no contact, speaking for them in public or policy settings, taking positions on issues that deeply and directly affect their lives, on which they have diverse and nuanced opinions. The structure of the limited fund class claims in particular seems actually to discourage contact, even to discourage telling members of the class that one is representing them. Their involvement would make things cumbersome and complex, create cross-currents, become time-consuming, require resources. Actually representing badly hurt people takes a lot of work. As some of the affiants in the *Kadic* motion supporting the decertification motion noted, the *Doe* class usurps many of the functions of elected representatives, which is undemocratic.[24] It could even be termed colonizing.

Unsought and unwanted representation in a class also raises the possibility that some of the intangible and expressive gains from human rights litigation, especially for group-based injuries like rape in genocide, may be undermined. Human rights litigation offers people their humanity back. What is stolen from them when they are violated can be partially or potentially returned to them through a process that does not reduce them to the ciphers of group membership that their perpetrators did. It treats them as more than the sum of the injuries done to them. It gives them back a voice in their fate and the dignity of a place at the table. For this to work, the process must be accountable, personal, and responsive. Being forcibly lumped into a group-based class, especially if deprived thereby of direct or actual representation, being represented in name (or no name) only, survivors of group-based atrocities can experience the process as furthering the deprivation of the very humanity that human rights law promises to restore.

On March 27, 2000, the *Kadic* plaintiffs won their motion to decertify the *Doe* class under *Ortiz*. Judge Peter K. Leisure cited, among other grounds, the *Kadic* plaintiffs' insistence that those who spoke for the *Doe* plaintiffs "have been unresponsive to their attempts to secure adequate representation" and "perhaps their most serious accusation . . . the Doe plaintiffs' willingness to accept defendant's 'profession of poverty' in order to obtain mandatory class treatment."[25] On August 10, 2000, a New York jury awarded the *Kadic* plaintiffs a total of $745 million in compensatory and punitive damages and a permanent injunction.[26]

22

Genocide's Sexuality

[N]or do those who commit genocide forget that to destroy a people, one must destroy the women.

    —Andrea Dworkin[1]

I do not fear the shells and bombs that may fall on my house. They do not ask for my name. I fear the foot soldiers who come into my house and kill and wound in a very personal way and commit atrocities in front of my children.

    —Bosnian Muslim woman[2]

To destroy a people, mass slaughter should be enough. Actual genocides testify to the contrary. Extermination destroys peoples, but peoples are also destroyed by certain acts short of killing. Sexual atrocities in particular first became highly visible as genocidal in Croatia and Bosnia-Herzegovina from 1991 to 1994. There, along with mass slaughter, Serbs aiming to eject and destroy non-Serbs as peoples sexually attacked women and some men on a mass scale.[3] Looking back from this pivotal Bosnian moment to the Holocaust of World War II and then forward to Rwanda, where Hutu committed mass sexual atrocities against Tutsi in the 1994 genocide, focuses the question: What is the sex *doing* in the genocide? Sexuality in various forms can express, mobilize, and deploy destructive group animus

This essay was originally delivered on April 11, 2002, as the 2002 Otto Mainzer Lecture at New York University. It was published in *Political Exclusion and Domination* 313 (Melissa S. Williams and Stephen Macedo, eds., 2005). The generous sponsors of the Otto Mainzer Lecture, were memorable models of support, response, graciousness, and stimulation. The helpful comments of Kent Harvey, Melissa Williams, Lisa Cardyn, Daniel Rothenberg, Jose Alvarez, Ryan Goodman, and Jessica Neuwirth and the research and technical assistance of Ron Levy, Hillary Cameron, Lisa Cardyn, Leila Masson, John Stoltenberg, and the University of Michigan Law Library are gratefully acknowledged. Translations are mine.

with particular potency, observation of its role in these three genocidal situations suggests. But what makes sexual forms of abuse available for specifically genocidal ends? What genocidal functions does it serve? In other words, why can sexuality become an instrumentality of genocide, and how does it work to destroy a people as a people?

It is assumed here that when an attack is sexual, that fact is relevant information, on the view that social behavior is not random and that its regularities are evidence. By illustration, when batterers rape rather than beat, a specific tool of domination is selected, a distinctive message and meaning conveyed, a particular social pattern reinforced, a specific form of power drawn upon, a distinctive group dynamic expressed and enacted. When men rape and do not kill, or rape then kill, or kill then rape, the same is true in genocide. Presumably as well, tools of domination that impose social hierarchies are selected in part for their efficacy: if they did not work or were not thought to work, they would not be used. Under precepts of diagnostic economy, the specific weapon selected may even do something that cannot be done in any other way.

To be genocidal under law, specified acts must be undertaken with intent to destroy a racial, ethnic, religious, or national group "as such."[4] For purposes of social analysis, however, individual perpetrators down the chain of command need not necessarily know why sexual means of destruction are deployed and are destructive (although often they do) in order for them to inflict such attacks and for the attacks to promote genocidal ends. The purpose of this essay is not to establish situations as genocidal through showing that certain acts for specific motives took place. It does not suggest that some sexual assaults are more serious or worse than others. It investigates and analyzes sexual atrocities that have been largely ignored within known genocidal settings. On these assumptions and observations, and for this purpose, the recurrent use of specifically sexual atrocities to destroy peoples has sources, meanings, and implications. This essay looks at them through the Bosnian lens.

I

Sexual atrocities exploded in the Bosnian genocide; certainly awareness of them did. In the spring of 1992, Serbian men who had lived next door to Muslim women for years put on flak jackets and raped their neighbors in the name of Greater Serbia, the neo-equivalent of *Lebensraum*. When Serbian military forces, regular and irregular, massed and took over town after town, Muslim and Croat women were first raped and then slaughtered the way animals are slaughtered, their throats slit with knives, on hillsides, in yards, in their own fields. Adolescent girls torn from their families, young Muslim wives abducted with their children, were locked into former cafés or roadside hotels or shacks for animals that were recast as brothels and violated serially by soldiers for months until they escaped or died. As non-Serbian peoples were murdered or impounded or ejected, non-Serbian women were rounded up by Serbian forces and interned in houses or former public buildings to be called out, night after night, and raped. Violently anti-Muslim and anti-Catholic epithets, slurs, and insults routinely accompanied these rapes.

Some women were held captive and repeatedly used for sex in concentration camps that were mainly for men, where the women also cooked and cleaned up after the torture of male captives. Some were impregnated, held for several months, refused abortions, and released in prisoner exchanges after abortion was unsafe. In some of the rape/death camps, men were also sexually tortured in lynchinglike atrocities, including through public attacks on their genitals. Serbian forces raped ethnic Muslim and Croat women, they said, to create what they imagined would be Serbian babies, using sex reproductively on an ethnic basis with the aim of producing a dominant ethnicity. Integral to the Serbian policy of "ethnic cleansing" (these perpetrators' euphemism for this genocide),[5] these coordinated sexual assaults were mounted for the purpose of destroying peoples of non-Serbian ethnicity in order to create an ethnically homogeneous Serbian state.[6] Hundreds of thousands of people were killed, and tens of thousands of women and girls were raped.[7]

Rape and other forms of sexual assault were also employed as genocidal spectacle in the Bosnian conflagration. Public rape served as ritual degradation of Muslim women. Serbian guards forced men to sexually assault family members and forced other family members to watch, for example.[8] Serbs filmed non-Serbian women being raped by Serbian soldiers; these films are out there, somewhere.[9] Sexuality was also enlisted to serve a more conventional propaganda function. Before the outbreak of violent hostilities, pornography sexualized abuse of non-Serbs, eroticizing ethnicity to denigrate the targets, desensitizing users to violence against them, priming the perpetrator group sexually for the enactment of sexual violence.[10]

In an unprecedented development, women sexually violated on the combined sex and ethnic/religious/national basis spoke out in public about what was being done to women while the genocide was still going on. In Bosnia, sexual atrocities were exposed after a historical period in which rape had been publicly reframed as a political outrage to women, supporting disclosure. One could say that the world came to comprehend that the Serbian campaign was genocidal (as opposed to a civil war) through understanding that the rapes in it were real and were being systematically directed against non-Serbian women. Most distinctively, in the Bosnian onslaught, sexuality, including forced sex and forced pregnancy, became conscious, organized weapons of a genocidal policy.[11] Or at least, observers distinctively became aware that it was serving this purpose, and thus collected and connected the evidence.

Unlike in the Bosnian setting, sexual atrocities have not been prominently visible in the Holocaust, the paradigmatic genocide. When the Genocide Convention, written soon after, listed as part of the definition of genocide what the Nazis specifically did to try to destroy the Jews as a people, sexual atrocities were not explicitly listed. This was not, however, because no sexual atrocities had occurred, and it was not because the Holocaust had no salient sexual dimensions.[12] Rather, with survivors reticent and the rest of the world content to be relatively oblivious and complacent, sexual attacks could be minimized both in numbers and significance, the integral function of sexual violation in genocidal destruction overlooked.[13] Looking back at the Holocaust after Bosnia can reconfigure aspects of its history that had previously formed no clear pattern.

As Dagmar Herzog notes, "The Nazis . . . used sexuality to consolidate their appeal."[14] Hostility to Jews was sexualized in Nazi hate propaganda, a record that survives in the material itself. Julius Streicher's well-known propaganda engine, *Der Stürmer,* presents eroticized pictures and words of intense hostility toward Jews. The sexualized drawings and text convey, among other things, that the Jews should be destroyed because Jewish men take over "Aryan" women when they have sex with them. Described as "often lewd and disgusting" by the Nuremberg court,[15] *Der Stürmer,* if barely sexually explicit by today's desensitized standards, is virulently anti-Semitic. Its sexualized denigration of its Jewish stereotype harnessed sexual excitement in the service of genocidal animus.[16] Yet the Third Reich is widely portrayed as antisex, George Mosse going so far as to assert that Nazism is hostile to "all printed material that . . . could produce an erotic effect."[17] Hardly. Precisely that was deployed by the Nazis for genocidal purposes.

The Nazis used law to control sexual activity, both wanted and unwanted, of women and men, along the lines of their genocide. Under the Third Reich, heterosexual intercourse between the group the genocide principally sought to destroy, Jews, and those it sought to establish as racially supreme, so-called Aryans, was prohibited by the Law for the Protection of German Blood and Honor, enacted in 1935.[18] Its crime of so-called *Rassenschande*,[19] or racial defilement, literally race-shaming or race-rape, was directed primarily against wanted intergroup sexual intercourse on an antimiscegenation rationale. Just as antimiscegenation laws in the United States were written to protect only so-called white people from marrying people of African descent, doing nothing for Black women who were raped by white men (which was routine and routinely permitted), *Rassenschande* was not made a crime to protect Jewish women from being raped by German men. A huge banner at a Nazi mass rally, "Women and girls! The Jews are your seducers!"[20] patently referred to German "Aryan" women and girls. Its point was to keep German "Aryan" women for German "Aryan" men, to create a pretext for prosecuting Jewish men, and to stigmatize the sexuality of Jewish women and men to further dehumanize the group. The blood-and-honor law was variously enforced and ignored, making Jewish people vulnerable to capricious denunciations while successfully stigmatizing Jewish women and men sexually.[21]

Ensuring the triumph of the master race called not only for preventing "blood"-mixing with "undesirables" but for supporting the propagation of racially desirable children. Sexuality was thus impressed into affirmative reproductive service under the Third Reich. The aim of Himmler's *Lebensborn* project was for German "Aryan" men to reproduce with women of "Aryan" racial stock.[22] About 20,000 children were estimated to have been born in *Lebensborn* homes in Germany and Nazi-occupied Norway; there were more in France, Belgium, and Luxembourg.[23] Whether the *Lebensborn* program initiated pregnancies or only welcomed already pregnant women is disputed. Indeed, whether women voluntarily had sex with Nazis and were then warmly received or lucked onto or were dragooned into the *Lebensborn* maternity homes after illegitimate conception; whether the women were impregnated consensually or forcibly, abducted or romanced; the degree to which even physically unforced participation (including that of German "Aryan" women) was manipulated or pressured under the official program; and whether the resulting children were stolen or abandoned or exterminated by the Germans—all this remains fairly murky. Some evidence exists for each description.[24] *Lebensborn* clearly intended to stimulate and support propagation of a master race through reproductive means. Whether or not the program encompassed sexual intercourse per se, that had to happen for it to proceed. But neither the Nuremberg prosecutors, who investigated the project quite extensively, nor contemporary historians, concerned to avoid the titillating,[25] have investigated the sexual conditions of the impregnations involved.

Lebensborn baby-catching certainly converged with large-scale impregnation of non-German women by German soldiers. Thousands of French women conceived with German military occupiers, attracting the racial scrutiny of the Nazis, who impounded the women and the children if deemed desirable or exterminated them if not.[26] Yet whether any of these women were raped seems not to have been asked then or since. Nordic women who conceived with German soldiers were often brutally stigmatized as traitors in their own communities, the resulting children spirited away to foster parents in Germany or exterminated—again depending on Nazi judgments of their racial value. Although it is widely conceded that the German occupation of Nordic countries relied on terror and violent repression of the population, and some claims are being brought at long last on behalf of the forsaken *Lebensborn* children,[27] no actual information has yet emerged on whether the sexual relations the Nordic and other women had with German soldiers leading to these births were forced or free. Most sources coyly assume the latter.[28]

The Nuremberg prosecutors' accounts of Nazi eugenic practices that amounted to forced abortions of non-German women who worked as slaves, by contrast, are factually detailed, straightforward, and conceptually fairly subtle on the same questions:

> The Nazis paid lip service to the idea that all abortions were voluntary but this was obviously not the case. These unfortunate women working as slaves under terrible conditions in a hostile country found themselves subjected to all manner of pressure, both direct and indirect. They lived and labored under conditions which would not permit them to take care of their children. Moreover, every pregnancy had to be reported to the dreaded Gestapo. The suggestions of an abortion by that organization did not invite argument from Polish and Russian women. . . . [Abortion] was nothing more than another technique in furtherance of the basic crime of genocide and Germanization.[29]

Women under occupation also lived under conditions of severe constraint—conditions under which they are widely supposed to have been having a fling.

To this day, the absence of interest in the sexual conditions under which women conceived with German soldiers during military occupation is matched by a lack of inquiry into how the enslaved women who had the forced abortions became pregnant. It is not known whether they were pregnant only with men of their own nationalities or whether the sex preceding the unwanted pregnancy was wanted. One recent study based on contemporaneous documents and interviews with witnesses and survivors substantiates the fact of forced abortions and killings of newborns of Polish forced laborers in Germany, but as to the sex that produced the pregnancies, this is all that is said: "Many of the children had been fathered by local men who took sexual advantage of these young foreign girls who had neither rights nor advocates."[30] When it comes to having sex, though, the "terrible conditions in a hostile country" under which the enslaved women were "subjected to all manner of pressure, both direct and indirect," are not even mentioned. If women could not care for any children they might conceive and had to report their pregnancies to the dreaded Gestapo, can the meaningfulness of their initiative or control over the sexual interactions in which they became pregnant, even with men of their own group, be presumed? What of those pregnancies caused by German men? If abortion under these circumstances was Germanization, and "nothing more than another technique in furtherance of the basic crime of genocide," what was the sex that preceded it?

Moreover, to assume that there was no forced sex between Jewish women and German men because all sex between them was illegal, a prohibition doubtless a deterrent in some instances, is not only to misunderstand the primary point of the *Rassenschande* law, which was to prohibit mutually desired sexual contact between Jewish people and "Aryans." It is also to conflate wanted and unwanted sex, to minimize the extent to which sexuality was harnessed for genocide by the Third Reich, and to substitute presumption for evidence. Reports of Jewish women being raped by German men during the Holocaust are scant; analysts who stress their exceptionality are plentiful. For Jews who survived and for their successor communities, identification of facts *of* sexual assault—even if their shame rightly belongs to the perpetrators—seems to entail identification *with* those facts, making their relative obscurity unsurprising. Underreporting of sexual assault even under better circumstances, together with the utter absence of responsive authorities to whom to report, combined with overwhelming starvation and mass murder demanding priority, suggests that such evidence as does exist and could be found may be the tip of an iceberg.

Sexual contact across the group lines that marked the Shoah was a crime when wanted but appears likely to have been officially ignored when forced by members of the dominating group, particularly by its military men, on members of the subordinated one. Actually, reports of forced sex during the Holocaust seem more prominent in accounts at the time than since. One book published in 1943, with supporting first-person affidavits from

Warsaw in 1940, stated simply: "The racist principles of the Nuremberg Laws were not always strictly applied by the Germans to the Jews of Poland. This was especially true of the primary racist tenet which forbids the mixing of Aryan with Jewish blood. Nazis forced their way into Jewish houses and raped Jewish women, and even young girls. Their brutality in such cases reached extreme proportions."[31] Single girls and young women were reported raped prior to being murdered in *Einsatzgruppen* actions.[32] A well-documented early report recounts that a Warsaw ghetto *Judenrat* was ordered by the Nazi health department to set up a brothel of fifty Jewish women for the use of German soldiers: "Don't let the race-laws bother you," a Nazi official reportedly said. "War is war, and in such a situation all theories die out."[33] In 1942, the *New York Times* printed extracts of a translated letter from a Jewish schoolgirl from Kraków describing the intended suicide by poison of herself and ninety-two of her fellow students rather than submit to the prostitution imminently to be forced upon them by German soldiers.[34] Raul Hilberg notes an archival document of 1943 reporting that "German private army managers kept Jewish women as sexual slaves" in the Galician area of Poland.[35] Without being able to know for certain in hindsight if the acts were freely willed or forced, Birgit Beck interprets wartime documents to estimate that between 50 and 80 percent of the SS and police forces stationed in Eastern Europe fell afoul of the standards of the racial laws through acts in which coerced intercourse played a role.[36] Some Jewish women said they were raped by Gentiles when in hiding,[37] but "the Anne Franks who survived rape don't write their stories."[38]

Concentration camp settings provide further accounts. One survivor reported her uncle said he witnessed mass raping of Jewish girls who were then buried alive in mass graves they had been forced to dig.[39] One survivor was told by a mother that, in a forced labor camp, "she was forced to undress her daughter and to look on while the girl was violated by dogs whom the Nazis had specially trained for this sport" and that "[t]hat happened to other girls."[40] One survivor, after describing Jewish girls taken out of her block to be raped, said: "Rape of Jewish girls was allowed. That was no *Rassenschande*."[41] And the direct: "I was raped in Auschwitz."[42] One consequence of these actions' being legally forbidden appears to have been that the women were frequently killed afterward.[43] Since so many of these women were killed anyway, their sexual injuries were submerged in the tide of murder.

Historians who pronounce rape rare under the Third Reich plainly are not thinking of the brothels in these terms.[44] Under the Nazis after 1939, prostitution was legal, institutionalized, and officially run throughout the Reich.[45] The Nazis seem to have thought that using women sexually served to motivate men to fight and work harder.[46] State- and police-run brothels were organized in communities for civilians, military brothels were set up for the *Wehrmacht*, foreign women were impressed into brothels for the foreign slave laborers, and prisoners were used in brothels in the concentration and extermination camps by the captives and staff of those camps. These brothels were organized along genocidal lines in two ways. People at the bottom of the Nazi social hierarchy, who could only use and be used by their own group in the brothels, were sexually constrained by the racial laws. The SS elite ignored those laws (as did the *Wehrmacht* generally, at least until 1942),[47] making the brothels just one more way that Jewish women could be destroyed.

At Himmler's determined instigation, there were at least nine brothels in the concentration camp system by the end of the war, Christa Paul estimates.[48] Many women imprisoned in Ravensbrück were forced or recruited into them, as well as into the army and the SS brothels.[49] Before the Nazis embraced prostitution, tens of thousands of prostituted women had been sent to concentration camps as "asocial"; some of them, along with women impounded for *Rassenschande,* were then forced to work in the brothels, sexually exploited twice over.[50] Women who "volunteered" were told they would be fed, would not have to work, and would be released after six months of "service to clients."[51] "SS men were known to occasionally 'try out' a volunteer before rendering a decision on her qualifications."[52] Some of the brothel women were German, Polish, Chechen, Russian, and Hungarian; women in the brothels for foreign workers were of the same nationalities as the slave laborers. However, ten women recruits arriving at Flossenburg for the brothel were described by one surviving prisoner as "almost all Jews and Gypsies."[53] In the slave labor camps, where brothel visits were rewards for exceptional productivity at work, records were kept of visits, and payment was made through labor coupons.[54] For food to stay alive, to keep better jobs, and for protection from other sexual aggression, many young men in the concentration camps became "dolly-boys" of Kapos and other privileged inmates, who used them sexually nightly.[55] The men who used the camp brothel women were mainly Jewish,[56] but block seniors and Kapos (far fewer in number and often not Jewish) used them as well.

Jewish women were imprisoned in special brothels in some places for use by the elite SS guards.[57] One report from a woman survivor who was used in this way recounts that attractive women at the first selection at

Auschwitz were "ordered out of the line" and subsequently "used for the most licentious purposes, kept alive solely to satisfy the base instincts of several sadistic and bestial Nazis."[58] A document at the time confirms that the women for the brothels "would be selected by the doctor and the commander [sic], went on the transport, the best for the SS and officers, the worse quality for the prisoners."[59] One survivor recalls, "Despite the Nazi theories on racial pollution, we heard that a number of attractive internees were drafted for these brothels."[60] Christa Paul concludes, "No doubt remains that, despite the prohibition on intercourse with Jews, Jewish women were taken away to military brothels. . . . The women had to sexually serve the soldiers under threat of death."[61] Thus did the Nazis institutionalize the violation of their own sexual racial laws. The women in the camp and army brothels were forced to exchange sex for survival and freedom;[62] as often happens in prostitution, the exchange largely failed them. Most were exterminated. This did not prevent the later insinuation that any woman survivor had whored.[63] Although the realities varied by time and place, these brothels, where serial rape was organized in the form of prostitution, functioned integrally to the genocide.

Survivor chronicles of the period provide a wider context in which everyday life for the women of the genocidally targeted group both in and outside camps contains features of prostitution. The extreme vulnerability of Jews under genocidal conditions, starving and desperate, facing death at every turn, meant that sex could be, and therefore often was, exacted to make life possible. Survivor accounts of the time, in and outside camps, provide windows into lives lived on prostitution's terms: rape for survival. "Women were prepared to sell their bodies for food."[64] With starvation, "food was the coin that paid for sexual privileges."[65] Perhaps better: sex was the coin that paid for the privilege of staying alive. One woman raised orthodox in Chelm described being taken aback when her mother told her to "do anything anybody asks you to do, just so you save your life." Months later, she remembered this when she was "faced with a situation in which I had to make a snap decision about bestowing a sexual favor in exchange for a temporary rescue from the German authorities."[66] In such a situation, intimate access becomes at once a currency of exchange and a tool for dehumanization. Any glimmer of humanity involved looms larger in fiction than in recorded historical reality; presumably, where humanity was found, survival did not come at a sexual price. In the Holocaust, a corrupted sexual economy of force targeted Jewish women for prostitution in all its forms, integrally to the genocidal destruction of the Jewish people.

Sexual aggression in the concentration camp setting that took advantage of genocidal vulnerabilities and furthered genocidal aims was hardly limited to heterosexual intercourse. On admission to the camps, women were made to strip and stand genitally exposed on two stools where they were internally searched and genitally shaved while being sexually ridiculed. In one account, women were reported forced to lie on their sides naked while being poked in their private parts as SS officers gawked and jeered.[67] A member of the Sonderkommando reported that one SS officer "had the custom of standing at the doorway . . . and feeling the private parts of the young women entering the gas bunker. There were also instances of SS men of all ranks pushing their fingers into the sexual organs of pretty young women."[68] After Jewish women were gassed, they were then "also searched to see if they had not hidden jewelry in the intimate parts of their bodies."[69] As Myrna Goldenberg observed, "[N]ot only were they violated in life, but they were violated in death as well."[70]

Jews were live pornography for Nazis when the SS leader at Auschwitz "had holes drilled in the brothel rooms for himself and his SS underlings, so that they would get a good look at the 'love life' of their prisoners,"[71] and when Jewish men nearly dead in the freezing experiments were put into bed with naked women to see if "animal heat" would revive them.[72] The sexual use of Jewish women in camps was organized as public sexual spectacle when they were made to exercise naked so German guards could watch, or, just before being killed in gas chambers, to run naked to be filmed by guards. The films remain.[73] How they were used at the time is not yet publicly known. The dehumanization and humiliation of these Jewish women was clearly sexual, its link with their murders at once enhancing the sexual potency of the films and underlining their place in the genocide. Finally, the most explicit instances of sexual sadism were not *Rassenschande;* the torture that was also sex was allowed and sexual precisely because it was inflicted by Germans as supposed superiors on Jews as supposed inferiors.

If a pattern of the use of sex to destroy a people can be discerned in hindsight under the Third Reich, it takes no reconstruction to see it in the Rwandan genocide of April to July 1994.[74] There, integral to the organized slaughter of half a million to a million people in less than four months, Hutu raped and otherwise sexually violated Tutsi women en masse as part of the attempted destruction of that ethnic group as such.[75] In some cases, the leaders, such as Laurent Semanza, ordered these killings. A credible witness claims that Semanza said the following: "Are you sure you're not killing Tutsi women and girls before sleeping with them. . . . You should do that and even if they have some illness, you should do it with sticks."[76] Interahamwe men went through Tutsi women like scythes through wheat fields. Some observers say that not a single Tutsi woman or girl who remains alive from the conflagration was not sexually assaulted.[77] "[R]ape was the rule and its absence the exception."[78] Vicious sexualization and denigrating sexual stereotyping of Tutsi women was a staple on the radio and in newspapers preceding and throughout the atrocities.[79] Many sexual attacks as public spectacle were also reported.[80] Anti-Tutsi slogans made their genocidal animus and objective vivid.[81] Rape and other sexual violence were often accompanied by "humiliating utterances, which clearly indicated that the intention underlying each specific act was to destroy the tutsi group as a whole . . . [for example,] 'The pride of the Tutsis will end today.'"[82] Each genocide is unique, but perhaps Bosnia provided or exposed a new model of the mass instrumentalization of sexuality for genocidal purposes. It certainly advanced awareness of sexual atrocities in genocides by outsiders.

II

What accounts for the presence of sexual atrocities in genocide? The ubiquity of rape and other sexual abuse in social life does not fully explain its particular escalation and chosen deployment for specifically genocidal ends. Nor does the violence of genocides or violence in general fully explain the specifically sexual forms that violence takes, when it does. Given the ubiquity of male dominance and the place of rape in it, no doubt men rape in part because and when they can, so that anything that increases opportunity, access, and impunity increases sexual assaults. But neither chaos hypotheses nor opportunism completely accounts for the decision and policy and planned campaign of sexual forms of abuse—including rape both executed under orders and pervasively permitted, live sexual spectacles, and pornography—for the purpose of destroying groups on a racial, ethnic, national, or religious basis that is in evidence in genocidal settings. Perhaps the reasons sexual abuse is functional are specific to each genocide. But the increasingly prominent, perhaps increasing, role of mass sexual atrocities in the genocides that marked the late twentieth century frames the more general question: How and why do sexual attacks destroy a people?

While the genocidal utility of rape seems obvious to those who do it, its genocidal role has been long denied or elided, continuing to elude some observers who enter after the fact.[83] As legal interpretation (approached here as statutory construction), the conceptual fit of sexual assault in genocide is not difficult, however. Under the Genocide Convention (1949), genocide occurs when any of a list of acts is "committed with intent to destroy, in whole or in part, a national, ethnical, racial or religious group, as such."[84] The covered acts include killing group members, causing them serious bodily or mental harm, deliberately inflicting on them conditions of life calculated to physically destroy the group, and imposing measures intended to prevent births within the group. As a matter of usage, the term genocide is not considered legally applicable unless large numbers of people are so treated, and many are killed on purpose.

In this framework, once intent and group ground are established, obviously many acts short of extermination contribute to the destruction of peoples as such, hence are genocidal.[85] Although it has always been a legal (as well as real) fact that not only killing is genocidal, the recognition of this has grown in part because of the visibility of rape in genocides since the Bosnian one.[86] Sexual atrocities readily fit into the definition's subcategories. Some victims are raped to death or otherwise lethally assaulted sexually (such as by being vaginally penetrated with machetes and other objects). Rape necessarily inflicts serious bodily and mental harm.[87] Systematic rape over time, imposed as a condition of life, is physically destructive. Perhaps the least numerically significant of sexuality's roles in genocide seems most easily grasped by many: every woman pregnant with the child of an attacking group is prevented from conceiving a child of other biological heritage. Each act of sexual abuse committed with intent to destroy the (usually) women of a group defined by its nationality, ethnicity, religion, and/or race is therefore legally an act of genocide. Rapes undertaken as part of a genocide in fact are thus genocidal in law,[88] as the Rwanda Tribunal recognized in *Akayesu*.[89]

On many levels, rape is rape. Yet genocidal rape can be distinguished, for example, from rape in war in a number of respects. Even though many civilians are often killed in wars because of who they are, and genocides can be carried out in part through war, war is not always genocidal. Rape is pervasive in wars and often has an ethnic component, as in the "Rape of Nanking" during which Japanese military forces mass-raped Chinese women,[90] or the rape of German women by the invading Russian forces at the end of World War II. In neither situation were the rapes genocidal, because neither situation was a genocide: there was no intent to destroy the peoples as such on the proscribed grounds. Similarly, rape on an ethnic or national basis can be officially organized in war, as with the so-called comfort women—the Japanese government's organized use of women of various ethnicities (prominently Korean) as sexual slaves to service Japanese military men during World War II. This forced prostitution was officially organized ethnic rape, but if it lacked intent to destroy their ethnic groups as such, it was not genocidal. As a weapon or tool of war, rape in war aims to further the war effort, whether that is taking over land, government, or people, or pacifying and motivating soldiers. As a by-product of war, rape in war also merges with male violence in war and generally. Rape in war is a war crime. It is not genocidal until it is part of an aim to destroy a people as such on one of the listed grounds. The rapes of Jewish women during World War II are commonly misinterpreted as a side effect of the war, although they were as genocidal as the Holocaust to which they were integral.

Genocide is a war against peoples, which legally speaking is not a war at all.[91] The line between genocide and war is not always a fine one in practice, as conflicts like that in Guatemala, with its combined political war and genocidal attacks on Mayan peasants that included sexual atrocities, illustrate. But the line is there. Armed conflict by definition takes place between combatants, whether regulars or irregulars, usually for territory or state rule. The target of genocides is groups in civil society; the goal is their destruction as such, not simply their rule. Genocides are often carried out with only one side armed, as under the Third Reich and in Bosnia-Herzegovina, with victims having no army of their own. War has combatants on at least two sides; rape in war is also typically bilateral in being inflicted on women on both sides of the conflict. Genocide is relentlessly one-sided. So is rape in genocide, even when the genocide is carried out in part through war, and some war-related rape occurs on both sides, as it usually does (and did in Germany and in Bosnia-Herzegovina). If the targets of a genocide eventually manage to fight back, its victims do not simply become the civilian casualties of war, making the question of the role of rape in genocide one version of its role in war. The victims of some war rapes do not even know which soldiers or side raped them.[92] Genocidal rapes do not happen this way. In genocides, the perpetrators and the victims know who they are in terms of group identification. None of the participants are under any illusions: their social group membership is why the rape is happening.

Descriptively, rape in war (the role of which is also doubtless incompletely understood) aims to terrorize and degrade, hence demoralize, the vanquished, to symbolically and sexually reward and revenge the victors, and/or to interrupt reproductive continuity.[93] It has been used as a ritual of degradation of the other side, a way of instilling terror, a tactic of demoralization, a plundering of booty, and a humiliation rite for the men on the other side who cannot (in masculinity's terms) protect "their" women. Many of these acts make women's bodies into a medium of men's expression, the means through which one group of men says what it wants to say to another. Apart from affirming manhood, which rape always does, rape in war thus serves as specific psychological warfare and a method of communication, providing symbolic as well as actual reward and symbolic as well as actual revenge. It means supremacy: we are better than you. And possession: we own you. Rapes in genocide often have the same or similar effects and often work in the same or similar ways. But only when the purpose, the victory, is the destruction of the peoples of which the raped are members, only when the message as well as the means is the destruction of peoples as such, is the rape genocidal. For that, it need not take place in a war.

What further marks rape in war, which generally happens through cadre initiative, is its mostly out-of-control quality. It is what armed men do in groups when there is nothing to stop them. Rape in genocide is anything but rape out of control. It is rape under control. Men do it in groups usually because they are told or encouraged or systematically permitted or ordered to, knowing they are doing it as members of their race, ethnicity, religion, or nationality. It happens on purpose, not just with the function of harming people, or of having sex, or of planting a flag, but to destroy peoples as such on the designated group bases. The destruction of peoples on the group basis is not a by-product of the rape. It is its point.

Genocide goes beyond war. It can, and does, take place in civil society and among noncombatants, outside any armed conflict proper. Its specific purpose to end the existence of a people marks the sexual atrocities that take place in it. Genocide is actually more continuous with discrimination than with war: it is a violent practice of discrimination. It is extreme inequality, effectuated through systematic violence—violence that is sometimes spearheaded through a state and sometimes more loosely deployed through cadres or unofficial military forces. Even if sexual atrocities do in genocides some things that they do in wars, and even if genocides are carried out in part through wars, genocides, and the genocidal work performed in them by sexual assault, remain distinct phenomena.[94]

III

Genocide, both in reality and by conventional definition, is defined by the intent to destroy "groups as such." If all members of a group are killed, the group is presumably destroyed as such. But genocide is defined by aim, not success, and acts that aim at destroying a group as such "in part" are also genocidal. Destruction, in other words, is more than killing. The core of what makes acts genocidal is the meaning of "as" in relation to the groups whose grounds are prohibited as a basis for destruction. What does it mean to be killed or raped *as* a member of one's group—as a Jewish woman or as a Tutsi woman—and how is that combined group dimension to be known, evidenced, identified? The same question arises in discrimination law—for example, in asking whether a sexually harassed woman is harassed because she is a woman, that is, whether her sexual abuse is "based on sex," or is harassed "based on race and sex."

In the law of genocide, the term "group as such," although key to distinguishing genocides from other mass atrocities, has to date been given little clear meaning on its own. Most crimes, including international ones, are traditionally conceived as acts of individuals against individuals. This seems to make the collective quality of some crimes—those not merely mass in numbers but inherently group-based in nature—difficult for law to grasp and articulate. Authorities accordingly tend to collapse the "group as such" element into the *mens rea* of "willful destruction" or to treat it as an appendage to the numerical calculus of "in whole or in part."[95] In *Eichmann,* the term was part of the scale or overarchingness of the crime— "the all-embracing total form which this crime is liable to take."[96] Clarifying language often tends to restate what is to be clarified, even when it is not wrong, as when the Ad Hoc Committee on Genocide (1948) said that "as such" means "qua group,"[97] or when the International Criminal Tribunal for the Former Yugoslavia (ICTY) said that "the significance of the phrase 'as such'" is that the evidence must establish that "the group had been targeted, and not merely specific individuals within that group."[98] Although arguably crucial in distinguishing genocide from other crimes, the "as such" element has often functioned as a makeweight, adding little or nothing unique. But it is more than a highlighter or backstop for other terms.

Coming close to the heart of the matter, the International Law Commission explained that under the Genocide Convention, "the intention must be to destroy the group 'as such,' meaning as a separate and distinct entity, and not merely some individuals because of their membership in a particular group."[99] Homing in more precisely, the Commission of Experts on war crimes in the former Yugoslavia explained that "as such" indicated that "the crimes against a number of individuals must be directed against them in their collectivity or at them in their collective character or capacity."[100] The Rwanda Tribunal in its *Akayesu* opinion advanced furthest:

"The victim of the act is therefore a member of a group, chosen as such, which, hence, means that the victim of the crime of genocide is the group itself and not only the individual."[101] As this insight was later formulated in *Rutuganda,* "as such" means "the victim of the crime of genocide is the group itself and not the individual alone."[102] To attempt to destroy a group "as such" is thus to attack, through attacking group members because they are group members, that aspect of the group whole that is more than the sum of its individual parts, that quality of collectivity and identifications that make up the substance and glue of community that lives on when individual members die. In some real sense, to destroy a group, especially to end it forever, is to destroy the idea and meaning of it within and between those whose relationships compose it.

Now notice that what is done in genocides to destroy women of racially, ethnically, nationally, or religiously designated groups is routinely done to women everywhere every day on the basis of their sex. All the sexual atrocities that become genocidal in genocides are inflicted on women every day under conditions of sex inequality. Arguably, they are inflicted on them as women.[103] Rape, prostitution, forced pregnancy, forced and precluded abortion, violating sexual spectacles, pornography—all of these are inflicted on women not only within wars and genocides but outside them, because they are women, often because they are women of a specific race, ethnicity, religion, nationality. In this light, examination of genocidal sexual atrocities, as one potent form of group destruction short of physical extermination, may illuminate the crucial but shadowy legal element of destruction "as such."[104] Why sexuality can be made to work genocidal destruction and what the term "as such" means may thus have simultaneous answers close at hand.

Consider that sexual atrocities, acts in which men dominate women on the basis of sex, destroy women as such, both as individuals and as a group.[105] Sexual atrocities on this analysis are inherently collective crimes, directed against the group through violating its members, meaningless without the social meaning of being a woman that they destroy (and, in destroying, in part create). This well-traveled road then becomes one avenue to destruction of groups on the basis of ethnicity, race, religion, and nationality, when the women of those groups are destroyed in that same way. Every day, the existence of the group—women—is not sought to be ended in the precisely genocidal sense of extermination, but it is precluded as human. Many women are killed for misogynistic reasons;[106] sexual atrocities might be said to seek the destruction of the group women as such in the sense of debasing their human status or creating them in the image of a socially destroyed self. Just as an ethnic group can be destroyed without killing all its members, perhaps the group women illustrates how a group can be destroyed while leaving its members alive and seemingly intact, subordinated as lesser humans, with sexual atrocities distinctively performing this function. If this is right, rape in genocide—gender combined with ethnicity, nationality, or religion in genocidal rape—does to women and men on a combined sex and racial, ethnic, national, and religious basis what rape does to women outside genocides on a sex and gender basis every day.

Suppose further that this same behavior of sexual subordination, outside war and genocide, also contributes to creating women as a subordinated group under conditions of sex inequality by defining them as a group, hence individually, on the basis of their social availability for sexual use and abuse.[107] Perhaps women are destroyed as a people as such by this—so destroyed as such as never to have been thought of as a "people" at all. Women are thus created as a destroyed group in part through sexual abuse. In this light, sexual assault destroys women as women, including their capacity to cohere as such, just as genocidal rape destroys or seeks to destroy Muslims and Croats and Tutsis and Jews, defining, and in so doing in part constituting, the groups as subordinated peoples. Pioneered and practiced on women as such with stunning effectiveness on a daily basis, rape can just as effectively destroy peoples as such on racial, ethnic, national, and religious grounds. Thus men do to women (and some men) through sexual abuse outside of genocides what some men do in genocides when they sexually abuse women (and some men, especially sexually defined groups of men such as gay men) on the basis of their ethnicity, religion, nationality, or race.

Much sexual attack outside genocides is ethnically and racially inflected and grounded much of the time, of course, even as much racist violence is sexual.[108] This confluence points up the continuity between rape in and out of genocide without making each instance of ethnic rape genocidal, the relation between discrimination and genocide being one of degree.[109] Enslaved women of African descent in the United States, for example, were raped as chattel for both sexual and reproductive purposes, including to increase the slave labor force. Since slavery, African American women have been raped by white men to subordinate them based on their ethnicity and sex combined, fusing racism with sexism. This process, needless to say, has been extremely destructive of African peoples in America even in the absence of an intent to literally destroy them as such in the sense of the legal definition of genocide.[110] In a reality that highlights the artificiality of the intent requirement in the genocide definition, these rapes in particular, however destructive they were to the women and the communities, were arguably not for the purpose of destroying a people but for enslaving a people, and to use, denigrate, and subordinate African American women as women.

But *why* does sexual assault destroy groups? In genocidal rape, ethnic or racial or religious identity, combined with sex, is the basis for intimate violation. Socially, sexuality means intimacy; forced sex violates a person in a way that, as intimate, is seen and experienced as especially violating. Because sex is relational, sexual atrocities destroy relationships. Perhaps in part because it is seen and felt to destroy one's humanity and relational place in community indelibly and irreparably, in a way the victim never lives without, rape is sometimes termed "worse than death."[111] A Rwandan witness testified that a woman "who was left for dead by those who raped her, had indeed been killed in a way."[112] People identify closely with their sexual selves; sexuality is socially central to gender identity, both to oneself and to others. When that is seen as having been violated, one's self is often experienced as spoiled, stolen, ruined. Sexuality socially means possession; forced sex means that the raped belongs to the rapist, instead of to herself or to the people with whom she identifies herself and to whom she gives herself intimately. It is the identity and identification that are destroyed when this particular form that humanity takes when embodied in group identity is violated, destroyed. This may go some way to explain why rape destroys women as such: it violates the female-identified part of a woman, a deeply and closely held aspect of self-conception that intrinsically involves identification with, and identification by others with,[113] one's group. It is an inherently relational and collective element of social, hence personal, identity. When women are raped because they are Muslim women or Jewish women or Tutsi women, it works on the combined grounds in the same way.

Genocidal rape parallels rape outside genocidal contexts in its combination of systematicity and randomness. Women every day are raped, systematically, as women, and are randomly selected as individuals within that group, sometimes systematically on an ethnic or other group basis. The way genocide works is similar: people are selected systematically for domination as peoples by randomly, within the group, picking out certain ones for certain atrocities, sometimes systematically on the basis of sex or other group ground. The atrocities against each individual function to destroy the solidarity of—terrorize and control and subject, that is, work the destruction of—the group. Genocidal rape is thus doubly effective. Being relatively random within the group while systematic to the group as such, rape in male dominance generally works the same way that genocidal rape works in genocide: it creates dominance of the men of one group over the men and women of another by destroying the target group's definition as one of dignity, security, and self-determination and replacing it with fear, self-revulsion, and a degraded identity.

Functionally, what sexual assault does on the basis of race, ethnicity, religion, and nationality is what it does on the basis of sex: create a cowed, submissive, controllable, terrorized, dissociated group of people who know this could be done to them at any time, who feel shame at being who they are, who want to leave the place where it happened and never come back, who may hate themselves and despise others who are identified with them by their common ability to be subjected to this form of abuse at any time, who are often socially regarded as a lower form of life because this is something that can be and has been done to them, who may identify with and even idealize their violators even as and often because, they fear them. People who are seen as, and see themselves as, stained and stigmatized by having been used and being usable sexually will do a lot to avoid being a person who is treated this way. If and when these effects do not happen, it is because resistance has succeeded. But just because the Holocaust did not succeed in destroying the Jews as such does not mean it was not genocidal.

Attempting to avoid rape, meaning, under these circumstances, avoiding being much of who one is, to oneself and others, can be a form of resistance but can also create a captive, compliant population with an urgent desire to please its captors and to display its compliance. For lack of a better descriptive vocabulary, all the signs of mass post-traumatic stress, including denial, fear, disidentification, and sometimes identification with the aggressor,[114] characterize large numbers of women. They also describe members of classically dispossessed survivor groups subjected to genocidal attacks, at least for a time. Literal disassociation may operate on an interpersonal and social level as powerfully as it does on an individual psychological one. Perhaps the public displays of sexual atrocities make surviving women loyal to the aggressors, the only ones who can protect them from it. (Or perhaps the perpetrators think this.) Rape is thus an excellent means of social control and domination, as the evidence of the group women—many of whom have been raped at least once by conventional definition,[115] many of whom have been sexually assaulted many times over—eloquently testifies. It should be no surprise that sexual abuse works in controlling and dominating ethnically, racially, and religiously-defined populations as well.

In other words, if what effectively destroys women as such (with or without intent to do so) is done to an ethnic group as part of a genocide, not only will the women of that group be destroyed on the basis of their sex and ethnicity combined; the acts in so doing will work to destroy the ethnic group as such. Women are a subordinated group throughout the world; sexuality is used both to create the sex women as such and to destroy them as such; sexual assault both subordinates them as women one at a time and keeps them a subordinated group. What creates and defines women as a subordinated group—vulnerability to and subjection to sexual assault—engenders disidentification with women as a people, destroying women as a people. Identification with the identity sought to be appropriated and defiled can reclaim and restore part of what the rape destroyed: the particularity of one's humanity and the particular meaning of collective identity. This partly explains why understanding that one was raped as a woman, not as an individual—identification with women in that sense—can be experienced as affirming and healing. It can go some distance toward restoring the specific part of one's humanity that sexual violation took away.

Sexual atrocities thus give a distinctive content to the term "as such" in genocide's definition. Just as women very often want to leave where they were raped and never return, making rape a useful weapon for forcing deportation, sexual atrocities can reasonably produce revulsion to the identity that marked the person for the intimate violation, making the raped want to abandon who they are forever. When the shared identity for which one is raped is ruined, shattered in oneself and relationally between oneself and others, the group quality of the group so defined is destroyed. In this respect, as in others, rape functions much as other torture can when inflicted on a group basis. When Jewish women were sexually used in brothels in concentration camps during the Holocaust, they were used as Jewish women "as such," no matter who else was used with them.[116]

Sexual atrocities shatter community, the ability to relate and cohere through a common identification, to identify with one another. As in life outside genocide, this result can be aggravated or mitigated depending on whether the men and women of the targeted communities reject or support those who are sexually violated. It is common for victims to be rejected. As one survivor of genocidal rape in Rwanda put it, "[A]fter rape, you don't have value in the community."[117] Whatever the response, the destructive power of sexual assault—robust across cultures, if with variations—seems to lie in what rape means: the (usually) women have been intimately violated, subjugated, claimed for the other, used, defiled, ruined, lowered.

Just as women often do not want to identify with one another, members of communities subjected to genocidal attack through sexual atrocities often disidentify as well. Rape is human code for domination, for being made less, for subjugation per se; it means violation itself, inferiority as such. Even if members are left alive, their cohesion, their identification with one another, the identification of others with them, can be destroyed. In this light, what rape does in genocide is what it does the rest of the time: ruins identity, marks who you are as less, as damaged, hence devastates community, the glue of group. It destroys the willingness to identify with the group designation on the basis of which the rape took place, hence works to destroy the group as such. Who wants to be one of them?

The term "symbolic" is sometimes used to describe this function. However intangible, the consequences are highly material: it is what makes a group be a group that is destroyed even as its members remain alive. To destroy a group "as such" is to attack the groupness of the group, its meaning to its members and others. Sexual atrocities despoil and rupture the meaning of the group identity through making it an object of violation, ultimately (as is the case for women) through making the group name mean violation itself. To be sexually attacked on the basis of being a woman or a Muslim woman or a Tutsi woman, to be raped by men who "ask for my name,"[118] thereafter indelibly stains the group name as it becomes part of defining what being a member of that group means.

Women not being considered a people, there is as yet no international law against destroying the group women as such. "Sex" is not on the list of legal grounds on the basis of which destruction of peoples as such is prohibited. For women as such, there is no legal equivalent to genocide—the destruction of women as such that Andrea Dworkin proposed calling gynocide[119]—presumably because it is commonplace, built into the relative status of the sexes in everyday life. That the destruction of the group women may often not be intentional in the way the conventional definition of genocide requires serves to underscore the fact that no law has been shaped to the realities of the destruction of the group women, as it has for some destruction of some groups defined on some other grounds. Because much sexual force is built into existing social standards for how sexuality is supposed to work, the destructive functions of sexual atrocities are more visible when directed against groups on the basis of ethnicity, race, nationality, or religion as well as sex than when they are directed on the basis of sex alone. Andrea Dworkin observed, "It has been easiest to see rape as hostile and hating when the rape is nationalistic or racist or colonial."[120]

On the same group grounds, it has been easier to see rape as destructive to groups as such.

One judicial opinion identified specific evidence going to "group as such" that could also describe the role of sexual atrocities in genocides. In *Krstic,* a prosecution for the mass murders of Bosnian Muslims at Srebrenica, the ICTY said: "[T]here is a strong indication of the intent to destroy the group as such in the concealment of the bodies in mass graves, which were later dug up, the bodies mutilated and reburied in other mass graves located in even more remote areas, thereby preventing any decent burial in accord with religious and ethnic customs and causing terrible distress to the mourning survivors, many of whom have been unable to come to a closure until the death of their men is finally verified."[121] Defilement, desecration, distress at indignity of violation give concrete meaning to the intent to destroy a group "as such." If digging up and moving dead bodies does so does rape, not to mention rape of dead bodies, which produces similar effects on members of groups who share with the violated the identification on which the atrocities were based. Such survivors are "unable to come to a closure" because in a sense the injury never ends. When children are conceived in such rapes, this becomes even more true. Destroying a people in these ways short of killing them all gives new dimension to the old view that rape is a fate worse than death.

Public sexual spectacles are particularly effective for purposes of destruction. In the Rwandan genocide, a Tutsi woman was vaginally penetrated with a sharp pointed stick after she was dead, her corpse left with the stick protruding by a public road for three days.[122] In Gujarat, much as in the Holocaust, "groups of [Muslim] women were stripped naked and then made to run for miles, before being gang-raped and burnt alive. In some cases religious symbols were carved onto their bodies."[123] Sexually destroying the women of these groups in these ways destroys the group. When the women are murdered in such instances, the genocidal point lies less in what such acts do to the violated women who are sacrificed to make it and more in what the atrocities say and do to the surviving group members. In such spectacles, sexual abuse performs, and in so doing enacts, the destruction of the target peoples. It performs genocide.

Bosnian Muslim and Croat women subjected to sexual atrocities often said that in that genocide, Bosnia-Herzegovina was being feminized. In light of the analysis proposed here, this was not metaphor. The destruction of women through sexual assault, common outside genocidal settings, was enlisted there against both women and men by the Serbian fascists on an ethnic, religious, and national basis. Men dominated men and women of non-Serbian ethnic groups the way men dominate women under male dominance. Male dominance was thus made to serve genocidal ends. Genocidal rape did to race, ethnicity, religion, and nationality what rape outside genocides does to sex. When and to the degree that it works, rape destroys national and ethnic groups in genocides as it destroys women as a group under sex inequality.

In actualizing and expressing dominion, sexual abuse does in genocide what it does in misogyny; indeed, it deploys misogyny against ethnic groups. Whatever group it is leveled against, the fact that this particular act means violation and subjugation constitutes its distinctive injury to the group. As expressive action, what it does and what it says are inseparable. That men occupy the status over women of being the people who can do this and are therefore socially supreme is widely taken for granted, making rape on the basis of sex both common and widely regarded as inevitable. When an ethnic, racial, religious, or national group—a group that includes men—loses its sovereignty this way, the group and ground may make the atrocities noticed. That sexual atrocities would first be seen as destructively group-based in international law in situations in which they are used for racial, ethnic, or religious domination is thus far from coincidence.[124]

In the Holocaust, in particular, the genocidal role of sexual atrocities has been largely denied, the women as such being as relatively invisible as their sexual abuse has been. Holocaust survivors understandably do not want to be pornography. Although it is not simple, sexual atrocities can be exposed and analyzed without fueling them. Certainly, the fact that atrocities are sexual does not mean they should not be investigated and studied. Suppressing sexual abuse fuels it more than criticizing it openly does. Arguably, covering up the realities of sexual abuse in genocide has enhanced its eroticization, partly by supporting the illusion that Holocaust pornography is fantasy, not fascism. Plausibly, public exposure of sexual abuse as integral to mass extermination could go some distance toward countering its present mass exploitation in pornography and allure in other fiction.

Once the sexual abuse in genocide is brought more fully into the open, its function faced, the legal definition of genocide—including its group grounds (should sex be added?), its subparts (should sexual atrocities be made express?), its intent element (should it be there at all? should it reflect how misogyny actually works?)—as well as the advisability of a separate gynocide protocol or convention can be revisited in a more realistic factual and theoretical context. Elizabeth Heineman urges analyzing "the ways that sex enables people to commit genocide."[125] For those who come after, this has been a missing piece of the genocidal paradigm. Sexual abuse, in reality, is a perfect genocidal tool. It does to ethnic, racial, religious, and national groups as such what has been done to women as such from time immemorial in one of the most effective systems of domination-to-destruction in history. The perpetrators have not failed to notice.

part four

on the cutting edge

23

Defining Rape Internationally

A Comment on *Akayesu*

Each time a rape law is created or applied, or a rape case is tried, communities rethink what rape is. Buried contextual and experiential presumptions about the forms and prevalence of force in sexual interactions, and the pertinence and modes of expression of desire, shape determinations of law and fact and public consciousness. The degree to which the actualities of raping and being raped are embodied in law tilt ease of proof to one side or the other and contribute to determining outcomes, which in turn affect the landscape of expectations, emotions, and rituals in sexual relations, both everyday and in situations of recognized group conflict.

Illegal rape is commonly defined to revolve around force and unwantedness in sexual intercourse.[1] Many jurisdictions—by statute, interpretation, or in application—tend to emphasize either compulsion or lack of agreement. Some weight one to the relative exclusion of the other; some permit one or the other alternately or simultaneously.[2] Many require proof of both.[3] In life, the realities of compulsion and lack of accord in sexual interactions overlap and converge. Force abrogates autonomy just as denial of self-determination is coercive. Although the determinants of desire and techniques of compulsion (and the mutual interactions of the two) are far from simple, anyone who has sex without wanting to was compelled by something, just as someone who had sex they wanted was not forced in the conventional sense. Yet conceptually speaking, emphasis on nonconsent as definitive of rape sees the crime fundamentally as a deprivation of

These remarks in their original form were delivered at a workshop at the International Criminal Tribunal for Rwanda, Arusha, Tanzania, on November 15, 2003. Jessica Neuwirth, Judge Navenathem Pillay, Kent Harvey, Steve Schulhofer, William Schabas, and Renifa Madenga are owed special thanks for their work and their support, as are Michele Ehlerman and the University of Michigan Law Library for their excellent research assistance. This analysis is also published in *44 Columbia Journal of Transnational Law* (2005).

sexual freedom, a denial of individual self-acting.[4] Emphasis on coercion as definitive, on the other hand, sees rape fundamentally as a crime of inequality, whether of physical or other force, status, or relation.[5]

Where coercion definitions of rape see power—domination and violence—nonconsent definitions envision love or passion gone wrong. Consent definitions accordingly turn proof of rape on victim and perpetrator mental state: who wanted what, who knew what when. This crime basically occurs in individual psychic space. Coercion definitions, by distinction, turn on proof of physical acts, surrounding context, or exploitation of relative position: who did what to whom and, often, in some sense, why. This crime basically takes place on the material plane. Accordingly, while consent definitions tend to frame the same events as individuals engaged in atomistic one-at-a-time interactions, coercion definitions are the more expressly social, contextual, and collective in the sense of being group-based.

The statutes of the ad hoc criminal tribunals for Yugoslavia and Rwanda,[6] conflicts in the 1990s where sexual atrocities were deployed for ethnic destruction,[7] were established to adjudicate international violations of the laws of war and humanitarian law. Rape under these statutes is thus not a free-standing crime but must be charged as an act of war, genocide, or crime against humanity.[8] Expressly defining rape under international law for the first time in 1998, the *Akayesu* decision of Trial Chamber I of the International Criminal Tribunal for Rwanda (ICTR) held that rape, there charged as a crime against humanity, is "a physical invasion of a sexual nature committed on a person under circumstances which are coercive."[9] As with torture,[10] to which it was analogized, rape's purpose to the perpetrators[11] in context, together with its specific nature as sexual, defined it. *Akayesu* defined rape as an act of coercion not reducible to narrow bodily description: "The Chamber considers that rape is a form of aggression and that the central elements of rape cannot be captured in a mechanical description of objects and body parts."[12] Crucially, "[c]oercive circumstances need not be evidenced by a show of physical force" but "can be inherent in circumstances like armed conflict or military presence of threatening forces on an ethnic basis."[13]

Interpreted in light of the distinction between force-centered definitions, on the one hand, and consent-centered definitions, on the other, to be sexually invaded under coercive circumstances, as *Akayesu* terms it, is clearly to be subjected to an unwelcome act, but that did not make nonconsent a matter of proof for the prosecution. Under the conditions of overwhelming force present in a "widespread or systematic attack against any civilian population on national, political, ethnic, racial or religious grounds"[14] that constitutes a context of crimes against humanity, in acts found part of this campaign, inquiry into individual consent was not even worth discussion. Mr. Akayesu was found individually criminally responsible for crimes against humanity for ordering, instigating, aiding, and abetting the sexual violence under his aegis that took place as part of such a widespread and systematic attack on civilians.[15] And, arguably for the first time, rape was defined in law as what it is in life.

In *Akayesu*, acts of rape and other sexual violence were also charged as genocide for "causing serious bodily or mental harm" when committed as part of an intentional campaign to destroy a people as such on an ethnic basis.[16] Because facts of sexual violence were indicted under this existing legal definition of genocide, rape was not defined in this connection; the kind of sexual violence that constitutes genocide is defined by whatever causes serious bodily or mental harm. As was first judicially found in Kadic v. Karadžić[17] addressing the Bosnian conflict in the United States, the ICTR trial chamber stressed that rapes under the *Akayesu* factual circumstances were acts of genocide[18] "in the same way as any other act, as long as they were committed with the specific intent to destroy, in whole or in part, a particular group, targeted as such."[19] Mr. Akayesu was found individually criminally responsible for genocide for abetting the infliction of serious bodily and mental harm on Tutsi women for the purpose of destroying the Tutsi group as such.[20] Again, rape was recognized in law as what it was in life: an act that inflicted serious harm with intent to destroy an ethnic group as such.

In the line of cases that followed, the International Criminal Tribunal for the Former Yugoslavia (ICTY) led in tipping the definition of rape for both tribunals away from the *Akayesu* breakthrough resolution and, step by step, back in the direction of nonconsent. Although the ICTY trial chamber's *Delalic* decision initially embraced *Akayesu*'s definition,[21] in a reversion first publicly visible[22] late in 1998, the ICTY's *Furundzija*[23] trial decision, acknowledging that rape was a forcible act,[24] mentioned the *Akayesu* definition only to ignore it. In nothing other than the "body parts" definition *Akayesu* had expressly rejected as mechanical and missing the whole point three months earlier,[25] the *Furundzija* tribunal required a showing of vaginal or anal penetration by a penis or object, or oral penetration by a penis.[26] "[W]ithout the consent of the victim"[27] crept back in at the same time. By five years later, this regression culminated in the ICTR's *Semanza*[28] and *Kajelijeli*[29] trial decisions turning rape on nonconsent.

The *Furundzija* trial chamber predicated these developments on a lengthy recital of national laws, the purpose for which was a claimed need for "specificity" and "accura[cy]" in definition.[30] This rationale was supported by the implication (in Latin) that without such specification, the defendants—guards of concentration camps charged with sexual assault on prisoners in their custody—might not have known with sufficient precision that what they were accused of doing was a crime.[31] Although the tribunal purported to avoid mechanically drawing on "common denominators"[32] among national rape laws in writing its international definition, it failed to note the fundamental tacit presumption they shared: that coerced sex was not a routine phenomenon instrumentalized as a tool of group coercion in their jurisdictions.

Even before *Furundzija*, the ICTY's rape prosecutions were marked by missteps and missed opportunities. In the first case to be resolved at trial, *Tadic*, brought against a guard at the Omarska camp notorious for systematic rape of a group of women captives,[33] the one count for rape of a woman victim had to be withdrawn, leaving a sexual attack on a man the only sexual assault adjudicated in the case.[34] Particularly, women survivors of captivity in Omarska found this to be an insulting, even traumatic misrepresentation, a public mockery of their experiences. Making matters worse, the ICTY's Rule 96, which had originally provided that "consent shall not be allowed as a defense"[35] to charges of rape under the tribunal's jurisdiction, giving the tribunal considerable credibility with survivors, was changed by the tribunal so that it no longer ruled out consent entirely.[36] That the tribunal could imagine that rapes that were part of war, genocide, or a campaign of crimes against humanity could be consensual outraged many women survivors of that conflict and badly damaged the tribunal's credibility with that community.[37]

A further and connected problem has been the long-term reluctance of the ICTY to charge rape as an act of genocide. Many perpetrators have been indicted for rape and other sexual violence under other rubrics, and others for genocide for other acts,[38] but despite *Akayesu* showing the way, only ten ICTY cases have indicted rape as genocide, prominently culminating in the Milošević indictment in 2001,[39] compared with almost four times as many by the ICTR.[40] Since survivors of rape in the Serb-led genocide against Bosnia-Herzegovina and Croatia typically understood that they had been raped precisely to destroy their ethnic and religious communities, in acts of sexual violence against women because they were not Serbian,[41] the ICTY's seeming reluctance to grasp the entire point of their victimization made survivors unwilling to put themselves in its hands, damaging trust and opportunities for cooperation. The limited access to witnesses that ensued no doubt had a circular effect on charging practices, supporting the stubborn misperception that "ethnic cleansing" in the "former Yugoslavia"[42] was something other than a euphemism for genocide. How mass rapes could fail to be genocidal when they were committed as part of the same campaign, by and against the same peoples, attendant to and simultaneous with, indeed sometimes as acts of, the same mass murders that are recognized as genocidal, remains a mystery.

The soft-pedaling of the genocidal conditions faced by non-Serbian women in the region, realities to which the rapes were integral, became judicial minimization of the organized collective realities of coercion, a vacuum filled in rape cases by inquiry into the comparatively individual factors of body parts and consent. A perfect vehicle for this process, the *Furundzija* case first reflected and then exacerbated it. That Mr. Furundzija is Croatian[43] placed his case far from the Serbian genocidal core of the conflict; that he was not indicted for his own sex acts but for those he witnessed being performed by his subordinates distanced him somewhat from the acts themselves; and that the sexual aggression in question prominently included forced fellatio[44] seemed to some (those who continue to see rape as confined to a penis penetrating a vagina) to call for legal exertions to render it recognizably rape. In contrast, the Rwanda Tribunal's general clarity that it was facing a genocide[45] to which rape and other sexual atrocities were integral components encouraged a conception of the acts focused not on the absence of individual consent but on the presence of group force.[46] Where extremist Hutu exterminated and raped and otherwise sexually violated Tutsi by the hundreds of thousands, as in Rwanda, the decontextualized interaction of discrete body parts and one-at-a-time mental states was simply irrelevant, otherworldly. Simply put, the ICTR grasped that inquiring into individual consent to sex in a clear context of mass sexual coercion made no sense at all.

In its first major successful prosecution of rape, the ICTY's 2001 trial chamber decision in *Kunarac* found the rapes of a group of women in a brothel-like setting in Foča to be a form of enslavement. If not genocide, at least enslavement was a collective concept with an ethnic resonance, although little was made of ethnicity in the case. Reviewing the definitional issue again, the *Kunarac* trial chamber took the view that "the basic underlying principle common to the legal systems surveyed in *Furundzija*" was that "sexual penetration will constitute rape if it is not truly voluntary or consensual on the part of the victim" and that "the true common denominator which unifies the various systems may be a wider or basic principle of penalising violations of sexual *autonomy*."[47] This was observed to be particularly the case in common-law systems. Rather than nonconsent being a presumed corollary of the presence of force, evidence of force became reduced to evidence of nonconsent.[48]

Casting a critical eye on this decision, the ICTY appellate decision in *Kunarac* noted that the trial chamber "appeared to depart from the Tribunal's prior definitions of rape" in "focus[ing] on the absence of consent as the condition sine qua non of rape."[49] The Appeals Chamber leaned to "the need to presume non-consent here,"[50] given that the defendants were convicted of raping women in de facto custody where they "were considered the legitimate sexual prey of their captors."[51] It concluded that "[s]uch detentions amount to circumstances that were so coercive as to negate any possibility of consent."[52] Note the use of the *Akayesu* terms: "circumstances that were . . . coercive." Consent was held "impossible"[53] on such facts. This holding, while strongly militating against a nonconsent definition of rape and constituting a precedent for similar cases, did not yet squarely hold against the nonconsent definition per se. Instead, it found that the coercive circumstances in the Foča captivities *in fact* precluded the legal possibility of proof of nonconsent. By ruling thus on the facts, the *Kunarac* appellate chamber, while siding with a coercion-based definition, stopped short of finding consent legally irrelevant on principle in cases where the rapes have a nexus to war, crimes against humanity, or genocide.

Back at the ICTR, which endorsed the *Akayesu* definition in *Musema*[54] and *Niyitegeka*,[55] one trial chamber, following the lead of the ICTY, reverted to the consent-based rape definition that *Akayesu* had already superseded. The *Semanza* ruling in 2003, termed the *Akayesu* definition "broad"; the ICTY's definition—"the non-consensual penetration, however slight, of the vagina or anus of the victim by the penis of the perpetrator or by any other object used by the perpetrator, or of the mouth of the victim by the penis of the perpetrator"—was termed "narrower."[56] It is unclear what these two terms mean except that they imply that some acts included in the *Akayesu* definition are not actually rapes. In any case, many rapes clearly encompassed by the *Akayesu* definition become difficult or impossible to prove under the *Semanza* definition, which makes the forest indiscernible for the trees. Centering its definition of rape on nonconsent, the *Semanza* trial chamber held that "the mental element for rape as a crime against humanity is the intention to effect the prohibited sexual penetration with the knowledge that it occurs without the consent of the victim."[57] At least consent was to be "assessed within the context of the surrounding circumstances."[58]

Nothing in the *Semanza* record called for the conflicting reversion to the consent-based rape definition. There was no implication that the women who were sexually violated before they were murdered might have consented. Testimony showed that Semanza said to those under his command, "Are you sure you're not killing Tutsi women and girls before sleeping with them. . . . You should do that, and even if they have some illness, you should do it with sticks."[59] Why such facts called for regression to a consent standard is unclear. As rape under law effectively went from being a physical act inflicted on the body of a victim to a psychic act committed in the mind of a perpetrator, the circumstances of war, crimes against humanity, and genocide in which the rapes legally and materially participated receded into the background. Indeed, Semanza was not charged with genocide for these sexual atrocities.

Instead of foregrounding the larger (and statutory) context of reality in which the acts took place, proof was now to focus on mechanical interactions of specified body parts of individuals and what individual perpetrators were thinking about what their victims were thinking—almost as if the *Interahamwe* might have been going on a date with the Tutsi women they hunted down and slaughtered with machetes. In defining rape exclusively by nonconsent, *Semanza* completed the full turn backward to the English common law. No other crime against humanity has ever, once the other standards are met, been required to be proven nonconsensual. With sex, it seems, women can consent to what would otherwise be a crime against their humanity, making it not one.

Continuing the *Semanza* trajectory, the ICTR trial chamber decision in *Kajelijeli* in late 2003[60] further combined body part interactions (called "more detailed")[61] with nonconsent, incorrectly citing the *Kunarac* appellate decision as authority.[62] Again, nothing in the facts or issues of the case conduced to such a definition. *Kajelijeli* was not about whether women were raped or whether the defendant raped them but about whether Mr. Kajelijeli, the rapists' superior, could be held responsible for the rapes that had in fact been perpetrated by his subordinates.[63] In the relatively rare acquittal, the trial chamber majority found Mr. Kajelijeli innocent of rapes proven to have been committed by forces under his command, both rapes he allegedly ordered and those he allegedly knew or should have known about.[64] Nor was Mr. Kajelijeli indicted for genocide for these rapes.

It is hard to believe that the individual decontextualized focus on the one-at-a-time image of rape had nothing to do with the tribunal's unwillingness to hold the superior responsible for these rapes. The less rapes are framed as mass atrocities, and the more they are framed as potentially wanted individual sexual interactions, the less courts may be willing to hold others responsible for them. The assertion that the majority decision in *Kajelijeli* was based on inconsistencies and inadequacies in the testimonial evidence was challenged (arguably demolished) by the powerful dissent of Judge Arlette Ramaroson, who in effect exposed the majority's double standard for evaluating facts going to superior accountability for killings on the one hand and rapes on the other.[65] While not expressly said, the point that superiors are more readily found responsible for murders than for rapes, acts said by the same witnesses to have been committed at virtually the same time, emerges starkly.

Charting the beginning of its recovery from the *Semanza* detour, the *Muhimana* trial decision in 2005 marked the ICTR's return to the course *Akayesu* began. In an accurate synthesis of prior rulings with the facts of the cases both tribunals confront, *Muhimana* applied *Akayesu* toward resolving the definitional debate. It held that "coercion is an element that may obviate the relevance of consent as an evidentiary factor in the crime of rape"[66] and that most international crimes "will be almost universally coercive, thus vitiating true consent."[67] It pointed out that *Akayesu* and *Kunarac* are neither "incompatible [n]or substantially different in their application."[68] Judicially tactful and substantially valid, this latter point evaded the fact that *Akayesu*, having satisfied the mens rea for genocide and crimes against humanity of which the rapes were shown to be a part, required no additional mens rea for rape—the function of nonconsent that *Furundzija* and *Semanza* thought was needed, and that *Kunarac* on appeal incompletely rejected as a matter of law. To the degree daylight was discernible between *Akayesu* and *Kunarac* in this respect, however, *Muhimana* tended to side with *Akayesu*.

Extending the present definitional analysis of rape to legal and factual settings beyond those of the ad hoc tribunals requires beginning with the true context of rape, coercive inequality of the sexes,[69] and the true common denominator of rape laws: they do not work. Most rapes are unreported because most women know they will not get justice; state rape is a more appropriate description of their experiences, with rapes ineffectually addressed to a discriminatory degree.[70] In most legal settings outside recognized zones of conflict, a woman charging rape is still effectively presumed to have wanted the act, an assumption for which consent is a proxy, no matter how much force was involved, turning the acts back into sex based on specific body part interactions, presumptive consent that she must rebut, often with little more than her word. *Akayesu* in effect reversed this presumption for rapes proven inflicted as part of war, genocide, or crimes against humanity, defining rape in terms of its function in collective crimes. Appropriate to such contexts, its definition shifted the focus of proof from individual interactions to collective realities, from proof of defendant subjective psychological state to proof of objective facts inflicted on the complainant with others similarly located. No longer burdened by presumptive consent, *Akayesu* built into its rape definition the context of violent inequality common to the crimes the ad hoc tribunals are statutorily authorized to prosecute. Once a context of coercion was shown, from a crime notoriously stacked against victims, rape became an act provable by prosecutors with relative ease by usual legal means. The question becomes, what distinguishes other settings in which rape occurs?

To make a transition to settings where no collective conflict is recognized to exist, for example, to global sex inequality with its attendant violence against women,[71] requires bringing into focus the extent of force that exists as a background condition for specific rapes in these other settings. The *Akayesu* approach and the pattern of outcomes in cases since support the suggestion that rape laws fail because they do not recognize the context of inequality in which they operate, focusing as they so often do on isolated proof of nonconsent against a false background presumption of consent in an unreal context of equality of power. Consent often operates as a flag of freedom flown under the illusion that, if it is instituted as a legal standard, whatever sex women want will be allowed and whatever sex women do not want will be criminal. Legal consent standards do not conform to this fantasy anywhere, wholly apart from the complexities that inequality introduces to what members of powerless groups can want or reject. But an unnoticed slippage in the discussion of the term between social myths of and desires for freedom, on the one hand, and legal discussions of actual rules that tacitly reflect and impose inequalities, on the other, gives the term an appeal it does not earn.

Put another way, body parts and consent fit together in rape definitions in being utterly decontextualized. If rape is fundamentally an interaction of body parts, it is essentially sex unless something else is wrong with it, which is where nonconsent is supposed to come in. Even if social customs deeply define consent, conceptually it is inherently individual in the sense of taking place within an individual's psyche. By contrast, although overwhelming force is a physical reality, coercion is largely social in the sense that the hierarchies and pressures it deploys are inherently contextual. In the context of international humanitarian law, to look to coercion to define rape is to look to the surrounding collective realities of group membership and political forces, alignments, and clashes. If sex was being engaged in simply for sexual gratification, for instance, it would predictably not be one-sidedly imposed on one ethnic group by another, as it was when inflicted on Muslim and Croat women in Bosnia-Herzegovina and Croatia and on Tutsi women in Rwanda. Such collective realities of group-based destruction expose the instrumentalization for acts that are part of it through which victim consent is rendered practically, hence properly legally, irrelevant.

The *Akayesu* definition is clearly well suited to addressing rapes that are part of mass group-based atrocities. Its focus on real world external rather than subjective realities also makes it more susceptible to standard forms of legal proof. For the same reasons, it is adaptable to situations of inequality outside conventionally recognized conflicts. *Akayesu* has legs, having already been incorporated into legislation in two states in the United States.[72] Since rape can be a crime against humanity under the International Criminal Court's (ICC) Rome Statute,[73] targeted on the basis of sex, might the highest rape rate in the world, that in South Africa,[74] qualify? That rape becomes banal does not disqualify it as a crime against humanity—to the contrary. In light of the realism and administrability of the *Akayesu* definition, it is regrettable that the ICC codified rape for its international purposes in the chronological middle of the tribunals' process described here, taking one page from *Akayesu*'s invasion of a sexual nature under coercive circumstances and one from *Furundzija*'s body parts without consent,[75] straddling the definitional difference rather than resolving it. Although the ICC's elements lean toward force and coercion in defining sexual assault crimes, the door that *Akayesu* shut so decisively and appropriately was left once more ajar by its evidentiary code,[76] through which rapists might walk away following rapes in international conflicts that show no sign of stopping.[77]

24

Pornography as Trafficking

In material reality, pornography is one way women and children are trafficked for sex. To make visual pornography, the bulk of the industry's products,[1] real women and children, and some men, are rented out for use in commercial sex acts. In the resulting materials, these people are then conveyed and sold for a buyer's sexual use. Obscenity laws, the traditional legal approach to the problem, do not care about these realities at all. The morality of what is said and shown remains their focus and concern. The injuries inflicted on real people to make the materials, or because they are used,[2] are irrelevant to what is illegal about obscenity.[3] Accordingly, the trafficking constituted by the exhibition, distribution, sale, and purchase of materials that do these harms is ignored. Laws against sex trafficking, international and domestic, criminal and human rights laws—specifically their concept of commercial sexual exploitation, around which international consensus is growing[4]—recognize the realities of the global sex industry increasingly well. These provisions are more promising for addressing pornography than has been recognized.

Realities and Concepts

Pimps are typically paid for the sexual use of the real people who are bought and sold to engage in the sex acts for money that are what most pornography is made of. The pornographers then are paid to repimp these people in the pornography itself, producing sexual pleasure for the con-

This talk was given at the conference "Pornography: Driving the Demand in International Sex Trafficking," cosponsored by Captive Daughters and the International Human Rights Law Institute of Depaul University, Chicago, Illinois, on March 14, 2005. It was originally published at 26 *Michigan Journal of International Law* 993 (2005). Valerie Hletko, Emma Cheuse, and Anna Baldwin provided superb research assistance when it was needed most. This work is dedicated with love to the memory of Andrea Dworkin.

sumers and immense profits for the pornographers, which both seek to repeat. From the standpoint of the person used to make the materials, the image of the person is still that person. And the sexual use of the person in the materials by the consumer is a real, actual, sexual act for the user. When Linda Boreman said, "every time someone watches that film, they are watching me being raped,"[5] she did not say they are watching the rape of "an image of me" or "a representation of me" being raped. If these were anything but sex pictures, the rights of the people in them over the materials made by their use would be legally recognized.[6] Defamatory lies about them in pornography, for example, destroying their reputations, would be actionable.[7] Knowing the pornography of you is always out there is a particular kind of trauma.[8]

Although legitimate corporations increasingly traffic the materials, the pornography industry, like other means of human trafficking, remains at base an organized crime industry built on force, some physical, some not.[9] As with all prostitution, the women and children in pornography are, in the main, not there by choice but because of a lack of choices. They usually "consent" to the acts only in the degraded and demented sense of the word (common also to the law of rape) in which a person who despairs at stopping what is happening, sees no escape, has no real alternative, was often sexually abused before as a child, may be addicted to drugs, is homeless, hopeless, is often trying to avoid being beaten or killed, and is almost always economically desperate, acquiesces in being sexually abused for payment even if in most instances it is payment to someone else. Many are children; most enter the industry as children.[10] Most pornography is, in pure John Millerese, "made by slaves."[11]

Need it be said (it still seems to), the individuals so used say they usually feel nothing sexually.[12] Most of the time, the sex they are shown having is with someone they have no sexual interest in, doing things that do nothing for them sexually. The pleasure is routinely faked. They certainly never meaningfully consent to be intimately accessible to the thousands or millions of men they are then sold to, for money to others, over years and miles, as and for sex. Consent to sex is intimate, not transitive. Yet every step in the making and use of these materials is what is defended as sexual freedom, referring to the people in it. Women must be the only group, and sex the only means, in which a form of oppression is openly defended, not to mention sold as pleasure and even accepted by some of the oppressed, as a means of their liberation.

The force it took to make the pornography is shown or not, depending on the taste of the consumer. *Deep Throat* and *Playboy*[13] do not show it,

Extreme Productions does.[14] Whether the material itself shows less aggression or more, from the vulnerability of sexual body parts in the glossy men's entertainment magazines through the sexual servicing in the "fuck and suck" genre to the torture of sadomasochism and the murder of snuff, just as throwing money at victims of sexual abuse does not make it a job, taking pictures of it does not make it freely chosen or desired.[15] It makes it pictures of paid rape—rape in the real, if regrettably seldom in the legal, sense.[16]

No amount of fancy footwork built into one phony distinction after another in the law and public discourse on this subject can alter these realities of the pornography industry. But these distinctions do seem to confuse many people who cling to bright-line binaries that lack correlates in life. To distinguish pornography from prostitution, for example, California courts notwithstanding,[17] is to deny the obvious: when you make pornography of a woman, you make a prostitute out of her. In the immortal words of one trick, "Yes, the woman in pornography is a prostitute. They're prostituting right before the cameras. They're getting money from a film company rather than individuals."[18] It is also to deny the plain fact that pornographers are pimps, third-party sex profiteers, buying and selling human beings to johns, who are consuming them as and for sex. In some instances, women are directed to perform sex acts by a john from a computer terminal in real time.[19] So what is it, prostitution or pornography? That the sexually used are transported on paper or celluloid or digitally may make the transaction seem more distanced, but it is no less real a commercial act of sex in which sex from one person is exchanged for money from another for any of the people involved. As a report of the UN Secretary-General on victims of crime, discussing exploitation of prostitution and trafficking in women, put it in 1985, "It is hard to make distinctions (if any should be made) between prostitution and other sexual services, including those of the pornographic media."[20] Sex from one person is exchanged for money from another, the media being the go-between, the trafficker.

Although the degree of force applied varies from one situation to the next, the distinction between forced prostitution and "voluntary" prostitution[21] has similar dimensions of unreality. The point of the distinction is to hive off a narrow definition of force in order to define as voluntary the conditions of sex inequality, abuse, and destitution that put most women in the sex industry and keep them there. By the same token, to analyze so-called voluntary prostitution as "work" and trafficking/forced prostitution as "crime"[22] is, among other things, to decide that there is a class of women to whom human rights laws against sexual harassment at work—and other laws inconsistent with the realities of force inherent in being prostituted[23]—will not apply. If this is work, what can it mean to prohibit sexual harassment at work when the sexual harassment is the work? This is a form of sex/violence distinction, two things that industry of sexual violation makes into one thing.[24]

To distinguish between children and adults—on the assumption or with the effect of suggesting that child pornography is a serious problem while pornography of adult women is not or is less so—lacks foundation in the real world as well. The majority of adults enter the industry as children and are exploited in ways that do not disappear when they reach the age of majority, including through materials in which children are used as women and women infantilized as children. To purport to address child sexual exploitation while doing nothing effective for adult women is to suppose that an age line is enforceable on, or respected by, an industry that is organized to exploit the powerless, and to accept the false notion that women become equal at age eighteen. For example, a law that invents scienter requirements[25] to regulate an industry that traffics fake IDs along with its children blinkers the fact that in this world, children and women are not two distinct groups of people. They are the same people at two increasingly indistinguishable points in time. Requiring that a john *know* that the person he uses is a child in order to be convicted also effectively drops the age of consent for use in pornography to puberty. Children will never be protected until adult women have rights that are respected.

Finally, building on these distinctions, to distinguish trafficking from prostitution, as if trafficking by definition is forced and prostitution by definition is free, is to obscure that both use money to compel sexual use, that the whole point of sex trafficking is to deliver women and children into prostitution, and that not crossing a jurisdictional line does not make the unequal equal or the forced free. Jurisdictional lines are drawn according to men's politics with other men. Being taken far away can make exit from a condition of prostitution more difficult, but being used for sex is being used for sex. Trafficked or local, the buyers of prostituted women do not much care, making this distinction irrelevant from a demand standpoint except for the exotics market. It is also irrelevant from the supply standpoint. Women can be enslaved without ever leaving home.

Thus the pornography industry, in production, creates demand for prostitution, hence for trafficking, because it is itself a form of prostitution and trafficking. As a form of prostitution, pornography creates demand for women and children to be supplied for sexual use to make it, many of whom are trafficked to fill that demand. The pornographers, then traffic these same people, in turn in various mediated forms.

Pornography then further creates demand for prostitution, hence for trafficking, through its consumption. Consuming pornography is an experience of bought sex, of sexually using a woman or a girl or a boy as an object who has been purchased. As such, it stimulates demand for buying women and girls and boys as sexual objects in the flesh in the same way it stimulates the viewer to act out on other live women and girls and boys the specific acts that are sexualized and consumed in the pornography. Social science evidence, converging with testimonial evidence of real people, has long shown the latter.[26] As observed by T. S. in the hearings on the antipornography civil rights ordinance that Andrea Dworkin and I organized for the Minneapolis City Council at their request: "Men witness the abuse of women in pornography constantly, and if they can't engage in that behavior with their wives, girlfriends, or children, they force a whore to do it."[27] On the basis of the experiences of a group of women survivors of prostitution and pornography, she told how pornography was used to train and season young girls in prostitution and how men would bring photographs of women in pornography being abused, say, in effect, "I want you to do this," and demand that the acts being inflicted on the women in the materials be specifically duplicated.[28] Research by Mimi Silbert and Ayala Pines on prostituted women in San Francisco also reported that the women spontaneously mentioned being raped by johns who said, essentially, "I [have] seen it in all the movies . . . You know you love it," referring to a specific pornography "flick."[29] Melissa Farley and her colleagues found that 47 percent of prostituted women in nine countries were upset by someone asking them to perform a sex act that had been seen in pornography.[30] Forty-nine percent reported that pornography was made of them in prostitution.[31] Mary Sullivan's research in Victoria, Australia, where prostitution has been legalized for a decade, reports women describing pornography videos running constantly in brothels—to set the tone and mood, apparently—making safe sex more difficult.[32] Pornography is documented to create demand for specific acts, including dangerous and demeaning ones inflicted on prostituted people, as well as for bought sex in general. If this is right—and Melissa Farley's preliminary results show that it is—the more men use pornography, the more they use prostitutes.[33]

Most denials of the role of pornography in these dynamics come down to some version of a mind-body distinction—as though people, especially people who can get away with it, don't do what they want to do, and as though sexuality is neither body nor mind when it is both. This denial runs under the rubric of "fantasy."[34] It plays out in distinctions especially ubiquitous in the United States between pictures and words, thoughts, attitudes, and speech, on the one hand, and acts, practices, policies, and crimes, on the other. None of what I have described here is limited to the mind of the consumer. It takes acts to make the pictures and words; the so-called thoughts in pornography are predicated on practices and reproduce those practices through its consumers; the attitudes the pornography generates are lived out on women, including by being institutionalized in laws and policies; and the so-called speech, the materials themselves, is actually a product of crimes against women and children, produces crimes against women and children, and is in itself one way that sex-based discrimination is socially practiced.

One distinction in these dynamics does make some sense. Pornography, I think, is supply-driven. Men do not want it until they see it. The more they use it, the more they want to use it. The desensitization and addiction so well documented in its users[35] puts their sexuality under the control of pimps. (One waits for them to resent this. It severely limits their autonomy even if it builds their power.) Using pornography is like drinking salt water. It looks like the real thing but isn't; the more you drink, the thirstier you become. Pornography creates demand for itself and for prostitution (of which it is one form). In a real sense, men don't use it because they want it, they want it because they use it; the more it is there, the more of it they get, the more of it they want. This makes pornographers pushers.

Prostitution, on the other hand, I think is meaningfully demand-driven. Women are in prostitution because men want to use them that way, pure, in this part of the sexual economy in which women and men are already otherwise socially organized. If men want pornography because it is there, prostitution is there because men want it. Pornography helps create that desire. So the relation between the two is ultimately circular: pornography supplies the objectified sexuality of male dominance, both creating and filling the demand for the trafficking that is prostitution, providing a pleasure motive for johns and a profit motive for pimps for paid rape.

Pornography Under Criminal Antitrafficking Laws

Under existing law, these realities are better reflected in antitrafficking laws, and in some human rights laws, than elsewhere. The 1949 Convention (which the United States has not ratified),[36] binds states parties to punish "any person who, to gratify the passions of another . . . (2) exploits the prostitution of another person, even with consent of that person."[37] To make and sell pornography is virtually always to exploit the prostitution of another person. Pornographers are almost all third-party sellers of the prostitution of other people; few sell pornography of themselves. Under the 1949 law, "consent," usually being paid or someone else being paid (query again if either is what consent to sex means in real human language),[38] expressly does not mean that the person is not being exploited.

The 1949 Convention was intended to cover the gap in existing law on "the traffic in women of full age," as remarks by the Secretary-General put it at the time, "with their consent, even if the victims were not taken abroad."[39] No mystification about age, consent, or jurisdictional lines here. This treaty came into force before pornography was as overwhelmingly the traffic in persons that it is today, with the ascendancy of visual technologies, requiring new women and children daily, dominating cognitively and culturally as well as sexually and economically. Yet even then UNESCO glimpsed pornography's role in trafficking in persons. The travaux préparatoires show UNESCO's regret at pornography's omission from the Convention. Using the language of the time, UNESCO proposed restricting, for purposes of prevention, "the circulation of obscene publications or the public display of obscene works through the medium, more particularly, of the cinema, the radio or television."[40] In the context of prevention, UNESCO grasped the pornographer's role in creating demand for prostitution: "Suppress the demand, and you suppress the supply and the part played in that supply by the intermediary, who is a corrupted corrupter."[41]

The abolitionist rather than prohibitionist framework of the 1949 Convention provides a highly congenial approach to the elimination of pornography understood as a form of sexual exploitation. Prohibition criminalizes everyone involved. Abolitionists saw that this could be counterproductive as well as unjust, even discriminatory against the victims.[42] The travaux of the 1949 Act disclose a telling decades-long dispute over whether the term "for gain" should be included in the definition of trafficking. Those opposed to including this term opposed prosecuting the victims, the prostituted people, and sought instead to reach the entire range of their exploiters.[43] With "for gain" not being included, a space for criminalizing demand—both that of pornography pimps, who demand women and children from lesser pimps, and the ultimate demand by the johns who consume women and children in pornography, providing the profit motive for their sexual exploitation—was opened under international law.

Advances in the international laws against trafficking have built on this foundation.[44] Most important is the Palermo Protocol's 2000 definition of trafficking in persons:

> "Trafficking in persons" shall mean the recruitment, transportation, transfer, harbouring or receipt of persons, by means of the threat or use of force or other forms of coercion, of abduction, of fraud, of deception, of the abuse of power or of a position of vulnerability or of the giving or receiving of payments or benefits to achieve the consent of a person having control over another person, for the purpose of exploitation. Exploitation shall include . . . the exploitation of the prostitution of others or other forms of sexual exploitation . . . [45]

Pornography is clearly covered as sex trafficking under this definition. For pornography, women and children are recruited, transported, provided and obtained for sex acts on account of which, typically, money is given to pornography pimps and received by lesser pimps. Then, each time the pornography is commercially exchanged, the trafficking continues as the women and children in it are transported and provided for sex, sold and bought again. Doing all these things for the purpose of exploiting the prostitution of others—which pornography intrinsically does—makes it trafficking in persons.

Along similar lines, the U.S. Protect Act 2000 defines sex trafficking simply as "the recruitment, harboring, transportation, provision or obtaining of a person for the purpose of a commercial sex act."[46] Pornographers participate in the commercial flow of these acts to make pornography. Often they do them directly themselves, then again when they sell the products. A "commercial sex act" is defined simply as "any sex act, on account of which anything of value is given to or received by any person."[47] That is, it is prostitution, through which commercial pornography is customarily made. When a john buys pornography, it is for sex.

The U.S. Department of State's model law includes a definition of trafficking for purposes of exploitation that defines exploitation to include "commercial exploitation, including but not limited to pimping, pandering, procuring, profiting from prostitution, maintaining a brothel, [and] child pornography."[48] It does not explain why only child pornography, but it is only an "including," so adult pornography is not precluded. It does include the Palermo Protocol's definition of sex trafficking, encompassing not only force, coercion, abduction, fraud, and deception, but "abuse of power or of a position of vulnerability, or by the giving and receiving of payments or benefits to achieve the consent of a person having control over another person."[49] The latter is not limited to children, nor is pornography made by these means limited to children. This law squarely describes how most pornography is made, defining pornography as a form of sex trafficking. The U.S. Presidential Directive on the subject mentions pornography explicitly, saying that "trafficking in persons refers to actions, often including use of force, fraud or coercion, to compel someone into a situation in which he or she will be exploited for sexual purposes, which could include prostitution or pornography."[50]

Pornography is most expressly recognized as a form of sexual exploitation in the trafficking context by the European Union. Pursuant to the Palermo Protocol and other developments, the European Council Framework Decision of July 2002 on combating trafficking in human beings enacted a definition covering recruitment, transport, transfer, harboring, including exchange or transfer of control over the person where coercion, force, threat, deceit, or fraud is used, or authority or position of vulnerability is abused, "such that the person has no real and acceptable alternative but to submit to the abuse involved."[51] The Framework Decision also covers payments made to one person to get consent by another "for the purpose of the exploitation of the prostitution of others or other forms of sexual exploitation *including in pornography.*"[52] Laws of members of the EU are to conform to this decision.

Pornography Under Human Rights Laws Against Trafficking

The UN's Recommended Principles and Guidelines on Human Rights and Human Trafficking (2002) direct that "strategies aimed at preventing trafficking shall address demand as a root cause of trafficking."[53] Since pornography both creates and fills demand for trafficked persons, it should be a part of these demand-focused strategies. The flow of sex for money (supply side) and money for sex (demand side) is a mass market in human flesh, one technological level of mediation removed from skin-on-skin or, with the Internet, two. But it is a form of sexual trafficking in human beings nonetheless. The UN High Commission for Human Rights Sub-Commission on Human Rights Resolution 2002/51 effectively recognized this when it "[u]rge[d] Governments to take appropriate measures to address the root factors . . . that encourage trafficking in women and children, in particular girls, for prostitution and other forms of commercialized sex."[54]

In its interpretation and application of the Convention on the Elimination of All Forms of Discrimination Against Women, the CEDAW Committee is increasingly moving in the direction of this recognition as well,

as are some countries that report to it. Article 6 of CEDAW directly prohibits "all forms of traffic in women and exploitation of the prostitution
of others" as a form of discrimination against women, which states must
"take all appropriate measures, including legislation, to suppress."[55] Exploitation of prostitution, of course, is not "prostitution." But the distinction is the same as that between prohibition and abolition in the 1949
Convention: the exploited, the prostituted women, are victims of crime
and sex discrimination, not criminals or sex discriminators. Who is exploiting the poverty and discrimination and sexual abuse in childhood that
put women in prostitution if not the buyers who use them, whose demand
for their use is the reason the industry exists? What greater inducement
or incitement to prostitution is there than being paid for sex when no one
will pay you for anything else? In other words, criminalizing the buyers of
prostitutes promotes sex equality: voilà, the Swedish model. Sweden's law
criminalizing buying people in prostitution has, in fact, been reported by
Sweden to CEDAW as evidence of its compliance with its article 6 obligations.[56] The CEDAW Committee itself has read article 6 consistent with
this interpretation from the beginning, asking question after question about
"clients," "customers," "sex tourists," and "men" (now that we say "demand," we do not need to say "men"), and many about "eradicating"
prostitution per se.[57] The CEDAW Committee has taken the view that the
demand for prostitution is covered by the Convention against discrimination against women.

The demand for pornography, as a form of the exploitation of prostitution, is encompassed under the same principles. Pornography is occasionally mentioned in CEDAW reporting under article 6[58] and sometimes
under article 5, where it is referred to as a "harmful relic and custom" of
the (one wishes) past. Neither prostitution nor pornography is treated as
an institution of sex equality just waiting to be legalized for its discriminatory harm to women to be eliminated. CEDAW's General Recommendation 19, recognizing violence against women as a violation of CEDAW's
prohibition on discrimination against women, expressly sees pornography
as a product of sex inequality. It also observes that gender-based violence
is produced by pornography, in part because it promotes subordinate roles
and constricted options for women, which in turn "contribute to the propagation of pornography and the depiction and other commercial exploitation of women as sexual objects, rather than as individuals."[59] The circular causality of reality registers here. When it undertook to adapt the
commands of CEDAW and other world standards for the treatment of
women, the African Union's protocol on women's rights required states

parties to "take effective legislative and administrative measures to prevent the exploitation and abuse of women in advertising and pornography."[60]

Long before, the Beijing Platform for Action (1995), setting standards that countries agreed to achieve, recognized that "the use of women and girls as sex objects, including pornography,"[61] is a "factor[] contributing to the continued prevalence of violence" against women.[62] The Beijing platform directs governments to "take appropriate measures to address the root factors . . . that encourage trafficking in women and girls for prostitution and other forms of commercialized sex" and to protect their rights through both criminal and civil measures.[63] A strategic objective on violence against women finds pornography "incompatible with the dignity and worth of the human person" along with racism, xenophobia, ethnic cleansing, and terrorism.[64] At Beijing, states committed themselves to "take effective measures including appropriate legislation against pornography" and to "establish, consistent with freedom of expression, professional guidelines and codes of conduct that address violent, degrading or pornographic materials concerning women in the media."[65] Like most everything else to which governments committed themselves in the Beijing Platform for Action, this has yet to be done.[66]

One of the most insightful developments in the international system on the subject of pornography can be found in the Human Rights Committee's General Comment 28 on Equality of Rights Between Men and Women under the International Covenant on Civil and Political Rights (which the United States has ratified).[67] Article 19 guarantees freedom of expression; the Human Rights Committee took the view that all states should inform it of laws or other factors that impede women in exercising these rights: "As the publication and dissemination of obscene and pornographic material which portrays women and girls as objects of violence or degrading or inhuman treatment is likely to promote these kinds of treatment of women and girls, States Parties should provide information about legal measures to restrict the publication or dissemination of such material."[68] Dissemination, precisely trafficking, is recognized here to silence women's speech! The United States did not reserve to article 19, only to article 20, which provides that advocacy of national, racial, or religious hatred that constitutes incitement to discrimination shall be prohibited.[69] That reservation seeks to reduce the ICCPR's obligations to the size of existing U.S. First Amendment law. If article 20 does not mention sex-based or sexual hatred that constitutes incitement to sex discrimination, as pornography arguably does, neither does the U.S. reservation on the point. Sometimes invisibility works to your advantage. The point is, there is no "speech" barrier in international law of human rights to proceeding against pornography. On the contrary, there is more like an invitation to address it, based on the realization that pornography silences speech.[70]

The one legal provision that squarely recognizes pornography as trafficking is the trafficking provision of the civil rights antipornography ordinances conceived and drafted by Andrea Dworkin and me. Trafficking is defined there as the production, sale, exhibition, or distribution of pornography, which is defined in turn as graphic sexually explicit subordination of women through pictures and words that also include a list of specific presentations.[71] American Booksellers Association v. Hudnut found this ordinance unconstitutional by holding that while pornography is sex discrimination, its effectiveness in doing the harm it does makes it constitutionally protectable.[72] This holding was summarily affirmed by the U.S. Supreme Court.[73] Although the Committee's interpretation is permissive, the United States is clearly out of step with its understanding of the meaning of the ICCPR's guarantee of freedom of speech. Accession to the ICCPR could become one of several intervening developments in the reassessment of the constitutionality of the antipornography ordinance in the United States. Passage of the ordinance, federally authorized under the commerce power—pornography being nothing if not commerce, its trafficking taking place in national as well as global markets—would put the United States back in conformity with the direction of international law.

The United States could also ratify the 1949 Convention, although it has no obligatory cause of action. Both the 1949 Convention and the Swedish model, for all their crucial advances against demand, leave out the people in the materials: the trafficked. These approaches get the criminal law off their backs but give them no positive rights against their abusers or the materials produced through their abuse. Empowering the industry's first victims is the most direct and effective route to its abolition; it cannot survive paying the cost of operation if it has to pay its victims for what it does to them. This the antipornography civil rights ordinance would do, simultaneously addressing pornography's contribution to demand for prostitution and its role in and as trafficking, upon an awareness of which international law is increasingly converging.

25

Women's September 11th

Rethinking the International Law of Conflict

The configuration of acts and actors of September 11, 2001 is not one that international law, centered on states, has been primarily structured to address.[1] Neither was most of men's violence against women in view when the laws of war, international humanitarian law,[2] and international human rights guarantees were framed.[3] The formal and substantive parallels between the two—prominently their horizontal legal architecture, large victim numbers, and masculine ideology[4]—make both patterns of violence resemble dispersed armed conflict, but the world's response to them has been inconsistent.

Since September 11th, the international order has been newly willing to

These thoughts benefited greatly from exchanges surrounding their delivery in prior forms at the Northwestern University Law School (April 17, 2002); the Law and Terrorism Conference, Hofstra Law School, Nice, France (July 17, 2002); the Barbara Aronstein Black Lecture, Columbia University Law School (September 17, 2002); Hofstra Law School (December 5, 2002); the Mellon Lecture, University of Pittsburgh Law School (April 14, 2003); the Ralph Spielman Lecture, Bucknell University (September 25, 2003); Kalamazoo College (October 4, 2004); the Dewey Lecture, University of Chicago Law School (October 9, 2003); University of Denver Sturm College of Law (March 10, 2005); Stanford Law School (April 14, 2005); the University of Paris X (Nanterre) (Golden Gate Law School) (June 29, 2005); the New Scholarship in International Law Workshop, Harvard Law School (October 6, 2005); the University of San Francisco (November 3, 2005); and memorably, Hebrew University (January 11, 2006). I thank all these audiences for their engagement. Some parts appeared in "State of Emergency: Who Will Declare War on Terrorism against Women?" 19/6 *Women's Review of Books* 7–8 (2002). José Alvarez, Tal Becker, Tom Bender, Karima Bennoune, Christine Chinkin, George Fletcher, Linda Gardner, Jack Goldsmith, Ryan Goodman, Jack Greenberg, Kent Harvey, Laura Beth Nielsen, Jessica Neuwirth, Michael Reisman, Diane Rosenfeld, Abe Sofaer, Eric Stein, and Mary Ellen O'Connell generously contended with, and made suggestions on, prior drafts. Comments from three anonymous reviewers were also exceptionally useful. The University of Michigan Law Library, Melanie Markowitz, and especially Ron Levy provided research assistance. Emma Cheuse and Anna Baldwin contributed superb technical help. I am deeply grateful for all of their support. The Center for Advanced Study in the Behavioral Sciences (CASBS) provided a supportive setting for its final revision, which was first published in 47 Harvard Journal of International Law (forthcoming, 2006).

treat nonstate actors like states as a source of violence invoking the law of armed conflict. Much of the international community has mobilized forcefully against terrorism.[5] This same international community that turned on a dime after September 11th has, despite important initiatives,[6] yet even to undertake a comprehensive review of international laws and institutions toward an effective strategic response to violence against women[7] with all levels of response on the table, even as the "responsibility to protect" from gross and systematic violence is increasingly emerging internationally as an affirmative duty.[8] The post-September 11th paradigm shift, permitting potent response to massive nonstate violence against civilians in some instances, exemplifies if not a model for emulation, a supple adaptation to a parallel challenge. It shows what they can do when they want to. If, in tension with the existing framework, the one problem can be confronted internationally, why not the other?

I

Viewed through a gendered lens, September 11th was markedly sex-neutral on the victims' side. Women, along with men—if, one supposes because of sex discrimination in employment, not equal numbers of them—were people that day.[9] At the World Trade Center, women and men together rushed up and up to help, crawled down and down being helped, jumped unbearably, ran covered with fear and ash, became ash. Then, day after day, month after month, there they all were, one at a time on the special memorial pages of the *New York Times*,[10] often smiling, before. In remembrance, they were individuals, did everything, had every prospect. Then on one crushing day, they were vaporized without regard to sex.

On the perpetrators' side, the atrocities were hardly sex- or gender-neutral. Animated by a male-dominant ethos, this one in the guise of religion—a particular fundamentalist extremism that has silenced women, subordinated them in private, and excluded them from public life—these men bound for glory and pleasure, some for virgins in a martyr's paradise,[11] exterminated people by the thousands to make a point. The rest of the world is still trying to figure out exactly what that point was. But this aggression, these atrocities, this propaganda by deed, made September 11th an exemplary day of male violence. Every other day, as well as this one, men as well as women are victimized by men's violence. But it is striking that the number of *people* who died at these men's hands on September 11th, from 2800 to 3000, is almost identical to the number of *women* who die at the hands of men every year in just one country, the same one in which September 11th happened.[12] Women murdered by male intimates alone could have filled one whole World Trade Tower of September 11's dead.[13] This part of a war on women in only one country, variously waged in all countries,[14] is far from sex-equal on either side.

To call violence against women "a war," especially in a legal context, is usually dismissed as metaphorical, hyperbolic, and/or rhetorical. Since the UN Charter, when war ceased being the definitive legal term, international law speaks of "armed conflict" or "armed attack." This body of law primarily regulates the use of force between or within states or for control of states.[15] If one side is armed and the other side is not, or if states are not the units or focus of the fighting, the conflict may not qualify. Whether the fighting has reached the point where peacetime law and institutions have broken down is a prime criterion. Violence against women has not looked like a war in this system in part because states are not seen to wage it, nor does it present armies contending within or across or against or for control or for definition of states. It is not about state power in the usual way. Nor do the sexes look like combatant groups are thought to look. Neither sex is considered to be in uniform. The regularities of their social behavior are not seen as organized, so their conflict looks more chaotic than ordered. Women are usually unarmed, many weapons used against women are not regarded as arms, and women do not typically fight back. Even attacks on women by men that employ conventional weapons are not considered "armed attacks" or a "use or threat of force" in the international legal sense.[16] The battle of the sexes simply does not look the way a war is supposed to look.

So, no Geneva Conventions set limits. There are no rules of engagement, no rules of combat, unless domestic criminal laws count—laws so underenforced it can almost seem as if they are not there.[17] Women get no quarter; surrender means more force. Because so much violence against women takes place in what is called peacetime, its atrocities do not count as war crimes unless a war among men is going on at the same time. Instead of being regarded as war crimes—as beyond the pale, if to some degree inevitable in exceptional contexts—acts of violence against women are regarded not as exceptional but inevitable, even banal, in an unexceptional context, hence beyond no pale. In this "war," no one is a noncombatant with protected civilian status. These "combatants" cannot be distinguished from civilians who are off-limits to attack, either by their lack of command structure or by their clothing; no dress code here, just socially prescribed attire that targets women by screaming "female" and makes it hard to run. Nor does aggression against women count as crimes against the peace, as aggression against states is called, women not being a state. All this makes "All's fair in love and war" only half true; in war, all is not fair.

Acts of violence against women are legally considered to be everyday crimes, of course, left to national and other local systems. For this reason, and because the actors under the UN Charter are states, not people,[18] responsive force by people, including women, has not been considered authorized under the Charter as self-defense.[19] Women's countermeasures are not usually found justified as self-defense under most national and state systems either.[20] Parallel norms of immediacy and proportionality,[21] created with conflicts between men in mind,[22] are enforced against women defendants claiming self-defense in most states in the United States, as if women have the power that states have.[23] Self-defense standards are seldom effectively enforced on nations; their sovereignty is defended by force with relative legal impunity through acts that are sometimes proportionate and sometimes not, and little to nothing is done.[24] But women who defend themselves from male violence with lethal force are likely to wind up convicted of murder and on death row.[25] In no case—except, for example, de facto through jury nullification or, at a stretch, when pardoned—are they treated anything like protected combatants.[26]

This is not to suggest that men's capturing and killing of women should be legal, as it would be if the war on women were legally considered a war. Yet even if it was, rape would still be a war crime. However ignored in practice, rape has long been considered unfair in men's wars[27] and is being adjudicated internationally under increasingly serious rules that recognize a context of force[28] that no domestic rape law yet does. It is to observe that while daily life goes on almost as if violence against women is legal, daily life lacks the legal benefits to noncombatants that a recognized state of war confers. If women in everyday life are not formally considered combatants, with combatants' rights, neither do they effectively receive the benefits the law of war confers on civilians during combat. Even as the alleged September 11th perpetrators (and those lumped together with them) are inconsistently considered soldiers and criminals under U.S. law, while consistently receiving the benefits of neither the war model nor the crime model,[29] most men who commit violence against women are legally considered neither soldiers nor criminals, yet often receive the effective impunity that is the practical benefit of both.

If violence against women were considered a war inside one country, an armed conflict "not of an international character," much of what happens to women every day all over the world would be crisply prohibited by the clear language of Common Article 3 of the Geneva Conventions.[30] Its protections for civilians during conflicts that are not among nations are thought to be the least that must be available for acts with a nexus to armed conflict. It prohibits violence to life and the person, especially murder, mutilation, cruel treatment, and torture, and outrages on personal dignity, especially humiliating and degrading treatment.[31] Imagine women's everyday lives without all that. Common Article III even guarantees that people not taking part in hostilities are to be treated without discrimination on the basis of sex. The absence, for women around the world outside what are termed zones of conflict, of such guarantees for noncombatants in war puts women in the practical position of being combatants in daily hostilities, while at the same time generally being unarmed and considered criminals if they fight back. Realized in what is called peacetime, Common Article 3 would transform the lives of women everywhere. But you need a war for it to apply.

<h2 style="text-align:center">II</h2>

The threshold legal barrier to addressing male violence against women internationally has been that both the perpetrators and the victims are private persons, termed nonstate actors. But Osama bin Laden and his Al Qaeda network—assuming they are behind the 9/11 attacks[32]—are also private citizens. Allegations have been made of varying levels of state involvement, linkage, and backup to their plot, but, so far as is known, Al Qaeda was not working for any state. If anything, Osama bin Laden may have hijacked Afghanistan, its illegitimate regime potentially working for him rather than the other way around. An Al Qaeda connection with Saddam Hussein's regime has been officially floated in the United States and is widely believed, but no direct evidence for it has yet surfaced.[33] Under the laws of war, conduct of private persons or entities has required some degree of state control or adoption to be attributable to states.[34] As to September 11th, state action has not only not been proven; it has so far barely been credibly alleged.

On the victim side, the Pentagon would have been a military target in a war (although it cannot legally be hit with civilian aircraft), but the World Trade towers, which Mr. bin Laden apparently regarded as some sort of official target, were private buildings full of mostly private citizens working for private corporations. The twin towers certainly were *in* the United States, symbolized the nation to some, and were a cultural icon of sorts, but for legal purposes, they were not the United States. They were not a military target, for which, in a war, a military response is legal. In a war, they would be a civilian target, a war crime to attack, to be pursued judicially. And before, on, and since September 11th, Al Qaeda's victims have transcended national boundaries, as do the victims of the war on women.

So, on September 11th, nonstate actors committed violence against mostly nonstate (nongovernmental and civilian) actors. It has been basically inconceivable within the Westphalian system that such an act could be so damaging or provide the predicate for the level of response it has occasioned.[35] Yet from that moment forth, in a usage that slides between the legal and the ordinary, the concrete and the rhetorical, the United States has told the world, "We are at war."[36] With no state yet in view behind the aggression, U.N. Security Council resolutions concerning September 11th implied that the events of that dreadful day were an "armed attack."[37] NATO invoked collective defense for the first time in its history.[38] So this becomes a war—complete with war crimes, military tribunals, potentially justified acts of self-defense, and prisoners of war.[39] The fact that the existing structure of international law does not have a conflict like this primarily in mind has not stopped the wartime scale response, complete with military mobilization, finance, ordnance, rhetoric, and alliances. Few have called the time since September 11th peacetime.

This international effort, the "war on terrorism," calls the acts of September 11th "terror," a term that has a far less settled international definition than armed conflict has.[40] Yet UN Security Council resolutions have used it repeatedly in reference to the events of September 11th without definition,[41] over little protest. Clearly, the acts of that day fall within a widely understood meaning of the term. Common elements include premeditation rather than spontaneity, ideological and political rather than criminal motive, civilian targets (sometimes termed "innocents"), and subnational group agents.[42] What about violence against women fails to qualify? Much of it is planned, including many gang rapes and serial murders, much stalking and sexual harassment, a lot of pornography production, and most sex trafficking. Are women somehow not "innocent," qua women existentially at fault? If the language of war reveals women as de facto conscripts, always non-civilians yet never combatants, the language of terrorism shows that women are seldom innocent enough. And just what about women's status relative to men is not "political"? If sex is one way power is socially organized, forming a sexual politics, sexual violence is a practice of that politics, misogyny its ideology.[43]

Some definitions of terrorism also require that the violence target a third party (say, civilians) in order to coerce a principal target (for example, a government or an international intergovernmental organization).[44] Despite scant proof of what the United States was supposed to be coerced into doing by the attacks of September 11th[45] (apart from giving up its way of life), the label "terrorism" has not been said *not* to apply to those attacks for this reason. This definitional element serves to further underline that, as with what makes a war, official entities tend to be what count. When this element is adopted, attacks on people matter only when they are a means of coercing states, something that does matter. And violence against women, except in wars, is usually not engaged in for the purpose of coercing states.

Although in some respects violence against women is much like terrorism, the acts of which can also be acts of armed conflict, it is not as such regarded as an act of war in the *jus ad bellum* sense nor necessarily a war crime.[46] But the attempt to control terrorism, despite not yet being defined by the Rome Statute[47] of the International Criminal Court (ICC), has produced decades of international debate and scores of international conventions.[48] With respect to male violence against women, by contrast, there have not been any special ad hoc tribunals or truth and reconciliation commissions even proposed, much less created, to get out the truth, heal this social division, and restore justice—places where men would come and confess everything they had ever done to a woman, where those women, should there be rooms big enough to hold them, could decide whether to give their abusers amnesty.[49]

The acts of September 11th surely are crimes against humanity under international humanitarian law, as is much violence against women, making both internationally illegal anytime, at least in theory, not only in war (and not as such an act of war).[50] Yet crimes against humanity have been widely legally unimplemented. The ICC, which was not in force on September 11, 2001, might become a place to seek justice for (heaven forbid) any such future atrocities, even potentially for non-ratifying states (like the United States).[51] For violence against women, not even the ICC, an improvement in so many ways,[52] fully solves the problem. Apart from crimes against humanity, the acts of September 11th most closely fit a legal category that is interestingly almost never invoked for them: genocide, "the intentional killing of members of a national group . . . in part, with intent to destroy the group as such."[53] One evocative definition of terrorism is "bit by bit genocide."[54] If women were seen to be a group, capable of destruction as such, the term genocide would be apt for violence against women as well.[55] But that is a big if.

In light of this analysis, it is the "war on terror" that is the metaphor—legally a mixed one at that—although its pursuit has been anything but, and violence against women that qualifies as a *casus belli* and a form of terrorism every bit as much as the events of September 11th do.

III

Those who contend that men's daily violence against women ought to be a recognized violation of international law—as some of us who work on these issues have been arguing under various rubrics for years[56]—have long been told, in essence, that we do not know what we are talking about. International law, including human rights law, it is said, is designed mainly to control official acts; hence, it applies primarily to official entities, either state-to-state or individual-to-state. Exceptions are mainly for genocide and crimes against humanity, which are widely thought to have to occur on a scale that usually requires some official backing or at least official condonation. The international law of war may address internal armed conflicts—that is, conflicts internal to states, as in civil wars, contest by guerrilla forces of state power, or wars of national liberation—but not what are routinely termed individual acts of violence by some people in civil society against other people, acts seen to be sporadic and isolated, called "private." Even when violence against women takes place in armed conflicts of men against other men such that the laws of war apply, it has taken years of work to begin to get a serious legal response. Although rape in war has long been illegal, sexual atrocities were ignored at Nuremberg, were raised only in part in the Tokyo Trials,[57] are beginning to be addressed by the Yugoslav Tribunal,[58] are being addressed by the Rwanda Tribunal,[59] and have been codified in war by the statute of the ICC.[60]

But even with this progress, international law still fails to grasp the reality that members of one half of society are dominating members of the other half in often violent ways all of the time, in a constant civil war within each civil society on a global scale—a real world war going on for millennia. It little imagines a war, or crimes of war, or crimes against the peace taking place in which states as such are neither the source nor the name of the power being violently exercised, nor the object sought, nor the violated party. It does not envision conflicts in which it is not the boundaries of nations or the sovereignty of states that are attacked or defended, but the boundaries of the person as a member of a group that are transgressed, and the sovereignty of members of a group of people to live life every single day that is infringed—all the while being regarded as life as normal. Nothing imagines a conflagration with one side armed and trained, the other side taught to lie down and enjoy it, cry, and not wield kitchen knives. Why international law cannot address gender conflict is not specified. It is said that it cannot for historical reasons—meaning it cannot because it has not.

Women have no state, are no state, seek no state—this being the Virginia Woolf–meets–September 11th moment in this discussion.[61] Since this history never seems to get around to including us, and genocide does not cover women on the basis of sex,[62] and crimes against humanity were implemented nowhere until the ICC (which still prioritizes state enforcement), what are women violated by men to do? Internationally, what we *have* done is labor to get states on the hook by meeting, expanding, or weakening the legal requirements for official action, essentially the same move under international law as state action requirements under U.S. constitutional law.[63] The effort is to triangulate the connection between the so–called individual man, the woman, and the state in order to secure state accountability for what he does to her.

But states that do what exactly? What precisely do they do to make men's impunity for violence against women so close to total? Sometimes state actors commit the crimes in their official capacities; sometimes they affirmatively cover them up. But this is a drop in the ocean quantitatively. How to address so many laws seemingly useless by design, full of traps for the violated called "doctrine," entrenched before women were even allowed to vote, now enshrined as precedent? How to make that kind of connection into the affirmative, hopefully conscious and intentional, preferably facial even conspiratorial link that the law (which women also did not write) wants to see before anything can be done (and one is also called paranoid for claiming)? How to get at the endless doing of nothing that enables something—a pattern we are frequently told is inaction, not action? Letting die can be killing, bystanders to international atrocities half a world away are said to be complicit, but letting men abuse women at home is seldom acknowledged as abusing women, and watching them do it, as in pornography, is a constitutional right in some countries and simply allowed in most.[64] How to capture the larger reality of men getting away with violence against women and knowing they can—a force that operates between the sexes like gravity? How to include the pervasive support for men being men (grown up boys being boys) in countless guises that we are endlessly told is social and cultural, not political much less criminal, hence a form of freedom (men's), not coercion (women's)? When men are violated, particularly certain men, eventually it will be seen to form a politics, on the way to having human rights. When women are violated, it is still called culture, the latest cover for standing by.

Then, late on September 11th, out of the mouth of President Bush came an answer of sorts: "We will make no distinction between the terrorists who committed these acts, and those who harbor them."[65] The state harbors them. This notion of harboring has not had quite this prominence until now in this area of law, although human rights conventions often by their terms hold states accountable for violations on their territory that they do not stop,[66] and regional jurisdictions have been expanding the net of official responsibility for human rights violations in this direction for some time.[67] Since September 11th, though, the international motion in this direction in the security arena has been precipitous. On the level of institutional practice, the UN Security Council rushed to embrace the formerly radical notions that nonstate acts can be attributed to states that harbor terrorists, and that self–defense and a threat to the peace under the UN Charter can be triggered by harboring and even by the mere continuing threat of terrorist acts.[68] The Security Council in 2004 used its Chapter VII powers to require states to adopt and enforce effective laws against "any nonstate actor" proliferating and delivering nuclear, chemical, and biological weapons "in particular for terrorist purposes."[69] This, they can manage. On the level of state practice, had the Taliban not existed, the United States would almost have had to invent Afghanistan's relation to Al Qaeda in order to have a state to bomb and invade, to turn what would otherwise be crimes against humanity responding to crimes against humanity, state terrorism retaliating for nonstate terrorism, male violence against male violence, into this thing called war. Having demolished one state sanctuary (and parts of already–damaged Afghanistan with it), the United States has moved to pursue Al Qaeda worldwide, a network of potential harboring so far said to extend to up to sixty countries.[70]

The fact that Al Qaeda is not organized into a nation with armies and territory did not stop this international response before it started. No one argued that the bigger Al Qaeda is, the less can be done about it. Yet the fact that male dominance is not organized as a state, but like Al Qaeda is literally transnational and pervades the world, is used to keep male violence against women largely unopposed in the international system. That men are not a state (never mind that they run most every state) even seems to get them treated as if they have no power over women at all. Whether any state entity is as central to Al Qaeda's terrorist network as it is to giving a target the look and feel and thus potential justification of a war remains to be seen. And whether violent men whose targets are women, who operate with essential impunity worldwide, will be seen as "harbored" by the states that effectively permit, hence condone and support, their acts, or whether male violence against women will ever be regarded as urgent enough to ignore—or preferably restructure—international law to address it, remains to be seen as well.

Compare the response to September 11th with excuses for doing nothing about violence against women. As the roots of September 11th are uncovered deep in social and economic life around the world, in belief and identity, its acts as expressive as they are masculine, will the war on terror grind to a halt? Will it be said that some individuals are just violent, so nothing can be done? Will terrorism be seen as cultural, hence protected? Will the United States throw up its hands when it learns that Al Qaeda, like some pornographers and other sex–traffickers (sex their religion as well as their business) is organized in (what for men are) unconventional ways? Violence against women is imagined to be nonstate, culturally specific, expressive acts of bad apple individuals all over the world that is so hard to stop. Terrorism, which is all of these, is said to be so serious that there is no choice but to stop it, while seriously addressing threats to women's security is apparently nothing but a choice, since it has barely begun.

Here is the question: What will it take for violence against women, this daily war, this terrorism against women as women that goes on every day worldwide, this everyday, group–based, systematic threat to and crime against the peace, to receive a response in the structure and practice of international law anything approximate to the level of focus and determination inspired by the September 11th attacks? Assuming that women are a group, a collectivity though not a state, to ask this is not simply to contend that because violence against women is systemic and systematic (although it is), it should be addressed at this level of urgency. A lot of socially built–in death and mayhem is legally ignored. This parallel is closer than, for example, that with the systemic death of the thousands of children who die from preventable diseases daily.[71] And the point is not a moral one: that this is bad and should be stopped. It is legal: both September 11th and most violence against women are acts by formally nonstate actors against nonstate targets. It is analytical: both are gender–based violence. And it is empirical: the body count is comparable in just one country in just one year.[72]

This is not to argue that the only effective response to a war is a war.

It is to ask, when will the international order stop regarding this very condition as peace and move all at once, with will, to do whatever is necessary to stop it, shaping the imperatives of the response to the imperatives of the problem? It is to ask why one matters, the other not. Why does the international order mobilize into a concerted force to face down the one, while to address the other squarely and urgently seems unthinkable? That the configuration of parties on September 11th failed to fit the prior structure and assumptions of the international legal order did not deter the response one whit. That actions like those taken since September 11th produce the structure and assumptions that become international law—customary international law in the making[73]—is, for better and worse, closer to the truth. At this point, it is hard to avoid noticing that terrorism threatens the power of states, while male violence against women does not; state power might be said to be one organized form of it.

Asked another way: Why did the condition of Afghan women, imprisoned in their clothes and homes for years, whipped if an ankle emerged, prohibited education or employment or political office or medical care on the basis of sex,[74] and subjected to who yet knows what other male violence, not rank with terrorism or rise on the international agenda to the level of a threatening conflict? Why were those who sounded the alarm about their treatment ignored? Why, with all the violations of international law and repeated Security Council resolutions, was their treatment alone not an act of war or a reason to intervene (including, yes, militarily) on any day up to September 10, 2001? To the suggestion that Afghan women should instead complain through international mechanisms, imagine the reaction to the suggestion that the United States, instead of responding with force to the acts of September 11th, should remove its reservation to Article 41 of the International Covenant on Civil and Political Rights (ICCPR) and enter a declaration against Afghanistan.[75]

Except to pacifists, some things justify armed intervention. How governments treat their own people, including women, has traditionally not been one of them. In the approach taken throughout the 1930s, for example, so long as Hitler confined his extermination of Jews to Germany, only Germany was generally regarded as properly concerned. It was after other *countries* were attacked that the rest of the world became involved. Is the approach to women's treatment still stuck back then, so that men inside each country are allowed to do to women what men cannot do to women of other countries? The record supports something close to that as an operative rule.

Women are incinerated in dowry killings in India or living in fear that they could be any day.[76] They are stoned to death for sex outside marriage in some parts of South Asia and Africa. They are dead of botched abortions in some parts of Latin America and of genital mutilations in many parts of the world. Girls killed at birth or starved at an early age, or aborted as fetuses because they are female, are documented to number in the millions across Asia.[77] If foreign men did all this inside one country, would that create a state of war? (Come to think of it, what does that make sex tourism in Thailand?)[78] The nationality of the perpetrators has little to do with the injury to the women. While some of this is finally beginning to be seen as a violation of human rights, at least in theory,[79] none of it is thought to constitute a use of force in the legal sense. On its own, it has yet to create what is perceived as a humanitarian emergency or to justify military intervention. Peacetime laws and institutions, for their part, far from breaking down and failing to operate from time to time in this context as the law of armed conflict envisions, simply never have worked for women on a large scale anywhere. But instead of these unredressed atrocities being recognized as armed conflict for this reason, because the events happen with relative impunity all the time instead of just sometimes, or perhaps because they do not happen in front of television cameras all on one day, they raise little international concern.

What does being done by domestic men inside each country make these acts in international terms? What do we call the conservatively counted one in four women raped, one in three sexually abused in childhood, one in four battered in their homes (including being crushed and burned), the uncounted prostituted women, systematically raped and thrown away, women of color and indigenous women the most victimized and the least responded to: the record of women living in non–metaphorical terror in the United States who have no effective relief at home?[80] Although it has been documented and analyzed by survivors and social scientists since 1970,[81] chronicled by international observers in the United States and elsewhere,[82] women's pervasive fear of violence has not even been noticed in the literature on terrorism,[83] far less produced an organized uprising by the international community or spurred rethinking of the structure, content, and priorities of international organizations brought to a crossroads, as September 11th has.[84] Comprehensive international strategies for world peace and security have never included sustained inquiry into violence itself as a gendered phenomenon.[85]

Acts of violence against women are mass atrocities, mass human rights violations, widespread and systematic attacks on the basis of sex, crimes against humanity pervasively unaddressed. But are they not also violent, organized conflict? Do these women not count as casualties in some war? Will the Marines never land for them? A kind of war is being fought unrecognized in a conflict that one suspects would be seen as such if men were not the aggressors and women the victims.[86] Why does no international model—not war, not criminal law, not yet even human rights—intervene effectively in this anywhere? Why does finding effective modes of intervention raise no international sense of urgency? In the American war against the Taliban, for a brief moment women had a foreign policy, or briefly became part of a pretext for one.[87] But when men subordinate women within one country (and where do they not?), that apparently makes it non-international, no one else's business, more off-limits to international intervention than even civil wars have been, including in places where women have no effective recourse at home (and where do they?). If nothing else, September 11th showed that the bounded view of sovereignty is an illusion that failed to protect people across national lines. It does not protect women within them either.

The war in Iraq has taken these questions to a whole new level. Apart from enforcement of UN Security Council resolutions,[88] the primary U.S. rationale for invasion was preemptive self-defense, meaning because we are scared of you, we can kill you. Apart from not being firmly established as a legal ground of self-defense,[89] and factually yet to be supported in this instance, imagine what the principle of fear justifying aggression in advance would permit women to do to men, with centuries of facts behind it. Moreover, the United States did not invade Iraq to stop what Saddam Hussein's regime did to the Kurds in 1988, or to the Shiites after 1991, or to the Marsh Arabs throughout—all genocidal atrocities analytically similar to the domestic treatment of women worldwide, and also not recognized as justifying resort to force under the UN Charter absent Security Council authorization. The United States and Britain did institute no-fly zones in part on such a rationale, and the Security Council let it happen,[90] a level and intensity of response never made for women anywhere. As the invasion of Iraq progressed, and weapons of mass destruction were not found, and the U.S. government made more of Saddam Hussein's atrocities to his own people (if little of their legal description), self-defense was trumpeted and twisted less, the liberation of the Iraqi people (who certainly needed it) more.[91] This shift occurred against the backdrop of the UN Charter, which on conventional reading allows use of force only in self-defense in response to armed attack,[92] although "perfect charity" has been a potential justification for war at least since Grotius[93] and, under the rubric of humanitarian intervention's defense of others, has been growing as a rationale for forceful response to mass attacks.[94] But never yet for women as such.

The point here is that the invasion of Iraq was not sought to be legally justified by past and continuing acts of genocide and crimes against humanity, no doubt in part because those violations have not, absent Security Council authorization, yet made armed intervention legal.[95] Should the UN Charter be revised so that what have been humanitarian crimes of *jus in bello* or human rights violations can also be *jus ad bellum* triggers? If this question is being increasingly asked, it is so far never suggested that brutal systematic violence against women, even with official impunity or participation, could legally justify resort to force unless it occurs as part of a conflagration in which men are also attacking other men.

The larger connection between men's treatment of women and men's treatment of other men is lost on the international system. When the photographs of American soldiers sexually humiliating Iraqi detainees at Abu Ghraib prison surfaced,[96] the fact that identical acts are routinely committed against women (and some men) in pornography was typically mentioned, if at all, to excuse the crimes, not to indict the pornography.[97] The connection was not lost on one Iraqi man who was abused by Americans in prison. "They wanted us to feel as though we were women," he said, "the way women feel, and this is the worst insult, to feel like a woman."[98] The photos, mild by pornography's standards, were routinely referred to as pictures of torture,[99] yet calling pornography pictures of torture is usually derided as an extremism comparable to calling violence against women a war. Even when an American newspaper was duped into publishing pornography as wartime atrocities,[100] the public penny did not drop. People were upset by what they saw—concerned about the woman shown being raped in the picture—*until* they found out that it was pornography. Then the hoodwinked newspaper apologized for poor journalism in not investigating how the pictures were made.[101] As the world recoiled and realigned in response to the photographs of Arab men sexually abused by Americans, as heads roll and trials proliferate, pornographers continue to traffic women being sexually violated, tortured, and humiliated worldwide in plain sight. Inquiry into the making of that pornography is on no public agenda—journalistic or legislative, domestic or international.[102]

IV

All this makes one want to look again at the smiling faces of the women on the special pages of the *New York Times* after September 11th and wonder: Who hurt her before? If she had died from male violence on some other day, at the hands of men close to her at home, would the *Times* have noticed? Would her dying have had the dignity of politics? Would her nation have responded? Or was she more equal on the basis of sex on that day than on any day in her life? If she had lived, would she have been as full a citizen of the United States as she has been dead? Indeed, with her death benefits computed on male income tables,[103] is she more economically equal dead than she ever would have been alive? Given the record of law enforcement on violence against women in the United States, what would have been her tribunal?

Particularly hard to take is the systematic slaughter built into everyday life in quiet, ignored crises of normality that are effectively permitted by most authorities, national and transnational, while crises *from* normality—the exceptional counter-hierarchical acts like September 11th—mobilize much of the world with outrage and determination to walk straight through legal walls. In this, the situation of women is far from alone.[104] As Walter Benjamin once put it, "The tradition of the oppressed teaches us that the 'state of emergency' in which we live is not the exception but the rule."[105]

In this view, neither September 11th nor violence against women are "tragedies," like dying from an erupting volcano or a lightning strike, nor blank supernatural "evil," the term favored by those more comfortable condemning events than explaining them. Both phenomena are more social and political in origin, more under human control, more contingent— hence changeable—than either term evokes. The connection between the treatment of women by men and the events of September 11th is not ultimately the moralistic one: the way women are treated tells us how civilized we all are. Nor is it quite the opportunistic, if also accurate, one: ignoring how these men treated women endangered everyone. It is this: what these men do to women every day is what they did to both women and men on that day. Men's behavior in their roles and status as men is the real context of September 11th. Metaphysically put, who they are to women is who they are. It is hard to avoid the impression that what is called war is what men make against each other, and what they do to women is called everyday life. So wars are fratricidally fought, and then are fraternally over, while everyday life never ends.

That day, being a man was no protection, hence the world's response. The losses of September 11th were real to power in a way women's losses never have been. Playing out the same dynamic on the domestic level in the United States, equal protection of the laws suddenly became real to power when some men's access to something real to them—the presidency—was at stake. It was not real to the same people just a few months earlier when women's equal access to justice for men's violence against them was at issue. Just as international legal barriers to action suddenly dissolved on September 11th, the federalism (i.e., states' rights) that was found to preclude women's access to equal protection of state criminal laws against rape and battering—found in *United States v. Morrison* to require the invalidation of the civil sex equality remedy in the federal Violence Against Women Act[106]—simply dissolved when some men's access to equal protection of state election laws was at stake, and the U.S. Supreme Court's decision in *Bush v. Gore* put President Bush into office.[107]

By the same token, policing the world, multilateralism, regime change, nation-building, new federal departments, federalization of formerly private labor forces, and sweeping executive authority—all formerly opposed, ridiculed, by their current American proponents—became no problem, necessary, urgent, even legal, after September 11th. On that day, for some, "everything changed," eventuating so far in an invasion and occupation of Iraq that legally is at worst aggression, at best preemptive self-defense combined with unauthorized enforcement of Security Council resolutions under unprecedented circumstances.[108] On the domestic side, U.S. law enforcement in national security areas now focuses on prevention, an approach to domestic security that American women have been urging for thirty years. During this time, countless women have instead received endless variations of what Linda "Lovelace" was told by police when she phoned them from a hotel room after escaping her violent pimp: "You say he's coming after you with an AK47? Lady, call us back when he's in the room."[109] This is not to argue that the war on terror is the right model for opposing violence against women. It is rather to expose, against the template of one reality of what men getting serious looks like, the commonalities between the problems they address and those they ignore, as well as what unites the solutions they implement and the problems they continue to fail to solve.

For whom did everything change on September 11th 2001?[110] Once men, many of them white middle-class nationals of the United States, in the midst of their daily lives, became victims along with women and men of all colors and nations and classes, on a respected target ground, the fact that the violence was nonstate—the same issue under international law as U.S. constitutional equality law—was not seen to reduce September 11th to mass murder, merely a local crime. Nor did it produce an international police action leading to criminal trials of foreign men under national auspices, like the Eichmann trial, or in a third country, as the Lockerbie bombings did.[111] The U.S. government did not instruct citizens to wait to call law enforcement from our cell phones when we saw a terrorist on an airplane and to collect data in the meantime. In the rush and determination to respond as quickly and effectively as conceivable, the unofficial status of the parties was barely noticed. What changed was this: the danger was real because certain men were afraid. They knew they were targeted because of who they are. As further evidence of its realness, no one has yet made September 11th into sex. No one speaks of its victims and injuries in scare quotes. (Where have those postmodernists gone?) There is no talk yet of closure. Where people count, any means thought necessary are energetically pursued, no matter if against nonstate actors attacking unofficial targets, unimpeded by law and institutional constraints.[112] The structure of international institutions is reshaped to create an approach that fits the shape and scale of the problem.[113] The legal framework is urgently interrogated in light of the reality, not the other way around.

By converging civil human rights law with criminal humanitarian law, consideration of the treatment and status of women could be injected into all levels of discussion of humanitarian intervention, including UN Charter revision. A new humanitarian protocol to the Geneva Conventions to address the gaps on violence against women could be purposed, defining some widespread and grave forms of it as violent conflict under the law of war. Discussion of the subject of gender based violence could become part of debates and diplomacy on definitions of terrorism. The Security Council could consider resolutions under Chapter VII against violence against women with impunity by the worst state offenders as threats to international peace and security, perhaps beginning with situations that are international in the more conventional sense. An international restructuring effort might move toward an international convention on violence against women that recognizes its transnational existence, complete with implementation and an affirmative duty to protect from sexual violence with clear standards, which, when breached, could ultimately trigger corrective intervention by transnational forces.[114] Once the issue is reframed, other deeper restructuring possibilities will doubtless emerge.

In the process, real difficulties will have to be faced. That prostitution and sex trafficking increase with international policing and military involvement, while being common in domestic policing and military forces, reveal the police and the military to be a site of this problem as well as a potential part of its solution. Maybe all the blue helmets on such missions should be women. Post-conflict micro-policing and law enforcement against domestic violence are avoided for some of the same reasons: the dangers of house-to-house engagement accompanied by a sense of futility. But the fact that anyone with a choice prefers pitched armed combat on an official battlefield to intervening in the places where women and children live out their days hardly recommends the status quo. Stopping thousands of actors is concededly more complex than bringing down a big leader or a symbolic entity, but so is counterinsurgency. Maybe, on some level, men have organized their conflicts the way they have in order to keep them simple and to confine the contenders to those who already wield their comfortable forms of power. Perhaps September 11th is emblematic of other men having broken that code and that agreement. In any case, the fact that male violence against women makes conventional war look safe and simple and easy and doable by comparison does not support abandoning women to their attackers.

Those who oppose international policing in this context might be asked whether they also oppose domestic policing. Those who question, apart from ineffectual domestic mechanisms, why violence against women should be addressed internationally might ask why the events of September 11th are being addressed internationally. The attackers were foreign, but they did not cross international boundaries to do the deed that day, and it was not seen as an attack by Saudi Arabia, the country of which most of the attackers were nationals. Both forms of violence transcend national borders; state boundaries are irrelevant to both, if differently so.[115] And if states' hegemony is threatened by terrorists, but male states have an investment in male dominance, the argument for independent international intervention may be stronger for violence against women than it is for terrorism, even as domestic police forces need to be involved and transformed to address either effectively. Presumably, once they knew intervention was a real possibility, states would take steps to avoid it by moving to correct the problem. Protectionism, well understood by women around the world, would have to be confronted to keep intervention from becoming yet another way the violated are violated more. The point is to stop the abuse in a way that empowers the unequal rather than adds to the power of the already powerful.

In the absence of such initiatives, as the unfolding aftermath of September 11th flexibly reconfigures international rules, norms, and structures for response to force, including with force, women remain unreal and expendable to the systems we live under. And the male dominance common to both problems, and to the norms and institutional structures of the existing systems for responding to them, continues to be ignored. Among the best of existing responses, the so-called post-conflict peace-building strategies[116] presume an operative model of peace that is the other side of the masculine coin of armed conflict. If conflict is an episodic eruption of men fighting other men, something that begins and ends, then peace becomes periods in which this is not happening. Male violence against women is tolerated in both, perhaps more in the latter than in the former. How will male violence ever end when the very idea of peace presumes and permits it? Opposing violence against women teaches that peace-building is an active social process, not a mere lack of overt fighting, far less a document-signing ritual of contract or an arm-twisting exercise to get the parties in bed together in the silence of power having prevailed.

Resort to arms inflicts disproportionate casualties on women and children,[117] but so does the present peace. Who is counting its risks? After a century of increasing convergence in status and numbers between the civilian casualties of wars and the noncombatant casualties of peace,[118] it is time to ask: what will be done for the women all over the world whose own September 11th can come any day?

Notes

Introduction: Women's Status, Men's States

1. Their desire for justice led to our federal lawsuit in New York under the Alien Tort Claims Act, 28 U.S.C. § 1350, Kadic v. Karadžić, 70 F.3d 232 (2d Cir. 1995), *reh'g denied*, 74 F.3d 377 (2d Cir. 1996), *cert. denied*, 518 U.S. 1005 (1996), by named individuals and groups against the leader of the Bosnian Serbs, Radovan Karadžić, for atrocities under his command and control in Bosnia-Herzegovina and some parts of Croatia.

2. Part III of this volume reflects my developing thoughts over more than a decade of representing these women.

3. This theme is discussed in "On Torture," below at No. 1, and most extensively in "Women's September 11th: Rethinking the International Law of Conflict," below at No. 25.

4. For a brief, lucid discussion of how "the challenge of human rights is inextricably bound up with the history of the modern state," see Christian Tomuschat, *Human Rights: Between Idealism and Realism* 7, 6–23 (2003).

5. See "Crimes of War, Crimes of Peace," below at No. 14; "Women's September 11th: Rethinking the International Law of Conflict," below at No. 25.

6. "Genocide's Sexuality," below at No. 22, and "Defining Rape Internationally: A Commentary on *Akayesu*," below at No. 23, discuss these themes.

7. See, e.g., "The Promise of CEDAW's Optional Protocol," below at No. 6.

8. Of course, this idea is not entirely new. Civil remedies have been included, for example, in the nonbinding rulings of the United Nations Human Rights Committee since it began finding that states parties that violate the International Covenant on Civil and Political Rights (ICCPR), 999 U.N.T.S. 171, have an obligation to repair and compensate the victim for damage. U.N. Hum. Rts. Comm., Views on Uruguay Communication No. 8/1977, *submitted by* Beatriz Weisman et al., CCPR/C/9/D/8/1977 (adopted on Apr. 3, 1980), *reprinted in Selected Decisions Under the Optional Protocol*, U.N. Doc. CCPR/C/OP/1 at 45, 49, ¶ 17 (1985). They can also be found in the European Convention for the Protection of Human Rights and Fundamental Freedoms art. 41, Nov. 4, 1950, 213 U.N.T.S. 222 [hereinafter European Convention] ("just satisfaction"); American Convention on Human Rights art. 63, adopted Nov. 22, 1969,

O.A.S.T.S. No. 36, 1144 U.N.T.S. 123 [hereinafter American Convention] ("fair compensation"); and the Convention Against Torture and Other Forms of Cruel, Inhuman and Degrading Treatment or Punishment art. 14(1), Dec. 10, 1984, 1465 U.N.T.S. 85 [hereinafter Torture Convention]. The International Criminal Tribunal for the Former Yugoslavia (ICTY) refers victims to national courts for this purpose, ICTY *Rules of Procedure and Evidence* 106, U.N. Doc. IT/32 (1994), *reprinted in* 33 *International Legal Materials* 484; the Rome Statute of the International Criminal Court arts. 77 and 79, July 17, 1998, U.N. Doc. A/CONF.183/9, 37 *International Legal Materials* 999 [hereinafter Rome Statute] permits a Victim Trust.

9. For an inspired tracing of this international legal process, see Arvonne Fraser, "Becoming Human: The Origins and Development of Women's Human Rights," 21 *Human Rights Quarterly* 853 (1999).

10. The ways in which women have been failed by international human rights in both senses is the topic of "Are Women Human?" below at No. 4.

11. This was first argued in Catharine A. MacKinnon, *Toward a Feminist Theory of the State* (1989), and further elaborated regarding the United States throughout Catharine A. MacKinnon, *Women's Lives, Men's Laws* (2005).

12. Again, MacKinnon, *Toward a Feminist Theory of the State*, makes this argument at length.

13. This, too, is argued in MacKinnon, *Toward a Feminist Theory of the State*.

14. Id.

15. See, e.g., "On Torture," below at No. 1.

16. The foundational discussion of this theme is Hilary Charlesworth, Christine Chinkin, and Shelley Wright, "Feminist Approaches to International Law," 85 *American Journal of International Law* 613, 625–630 (1991).

17. See the abortion discussion in MacKinnon, *Toward a Feminist Theory of the State*, above note 11, at 184.

18. This point is discussed more fully in "Women's September 11th: Rethinking the International Law of Conflict," below at No. 25.

19. Id.

20. Karel Vasak, "A 30-Year Struggle," *UNESCO Courier*, 29 (Nov. 1977), apparently first used this term. See Hilary Charlesworth and Christine Chinkin, *The Boundaries of International Law: A Feminist Analysis* 203–207 (2000) [hereinafter Charlesworth and Chinkin, *Boundaries*], for further discussion in feminist terms.

21. See Rebecca J. Cook, "Reservations to the Convention on the Elimination of All Forms of Discrimination Against Women," 30 *Virginia Journal of International Law* 643 (1990); Charlesworth and Chinkin, *Boundaries*, above note 20, at 102–113. See generally *Human Rights as General Norms and a State's Right to Opt Out: Reservations and Objections to Human Rights Conventions* (J. P. Gardner, ed., 1997).

22. See Cook, "Reservations," above note 21, at 713; Rebecca J. Cook, "State Responsibility for Violations of Human Rights," 7 *Harvard Human Rights Journal* 125, 172–173 and 173 n.257 (1994); Louis Henkin, "U.S. Ratification of Human Rights

Conventions: The Ghost of Senator Bricker," 89 *American Journal of International Law* 341, 345 (1995).

23. Torture Convention art. 21; ICCPR art. 41; International Convention on the Elimination of All Forms of Racial Discrimination art. 11, Jan. 4, 1969, 660 U.N.T.S. 195 [hereinafter CERD]; International Convention on the Protection of the Rights of All Migrant Workers and Members of Their Families art. 76, Dec. 18, 1990, 30 *International Legal Materials* 1317 (entered into force July 1, 2003).

24. The law of the United States illustrates the basic concepts as they often exist in national law in Argentine Republic v. Amerada Hess Shipping Corp., 488 U.S. 428 (1989); Princz v. Federal Republic of Germany, 26 F.3d 1166 (D.C. Cir. 1994); Foreign Sovereign Immunities Act of 1976 § 1604, 90 Stat. 2891 (codified as amended at 28 U.S.C. § 1330, 1602–1611 (2000) ("a foreign state shall be immune from the jurisdiction" of U.S. courts except as provided in §§ 1605–1607)).

25. This analysis is discussed further in "Disputing Male Sovereignty," in MacKinnon, *Women's Lives, Men's Laws*, above note 11, at 206.

26. Rome Statute arts. 12 and 13.

27. The writings and speeches in Part III below discuss this case, Kadic v. Karadžić, 70 F.3d 232 (2d Cir. 1995).

28. See "On Torture," below at No. 1, "Nationbuilding in Canada," below at No. 10, and "Equality Remade: Violence Against Women," below at No. 11. The South African Constitution built on Canadian developments. See, e.g., S. v. Baloyi, 2000 (2) SA 425 (CC) para. 11 (S. Afr.) (finding that the Prevention of Family Violence Act had to be construed with the Constitution and thus "understood as obliging the State directly to protect the right of everyone to be free from private or domestic violence"); Carmichele v. Minister of Safety and Security, 2001 (4) SA 938 (CC) para. 44 (S. Afr.) (deciding that law enforcement officials owed a woman who had been raped a legal duty to protect her under the circumstances and that they had negligently and unlawfully failed to do so, such that they were legally liable to her, since "[i]n some circumstances there would also be a positive component which obliges the State and its organs to provide appropriate protection to everyone through laws and structures designed to afford such protection"). *Carmichele* at para. 45 distinguished its view that the South African Constitution requires the state to protect individuals from the view of the same question taken by the U.S. Supreme Court that it has no such responsibility, as stated in DeShaney v. Winnebago County Department of Social Services, 489 U.S. 189 (1989). For background, see generally Mark S. Kende, "Stereotypes in South African and American Constitutional Law: Achieving Gender Equality and Transformation," 10 *Southern California Review of Law and Women's Studies* 3 (2000) (arguing that South African constitutionalism reflects the antidominance gender equality model adopted in Canada). For discussion of the equality approach taken in Canada, see "Making Sex Equality Real," below at No. 7, "Nationbuilding in Canada," below at No. 10, and "Equality Remade: Violence Against Women," below at No. 11.

29. Catharine A. MacKinnon, *Sex Equality* (2001), examines this distinction in detail conceptually and comparatively.

30. See "Sex Equality Under the Constitution of India: Problems, Prospects, and 'Personal Laws,'" below at No. 13.

31. See "On Sex and Violence: Introducing the Antipornography Ordinance in Sweden," below at No. 9.

32. This analysis is developed in MacKinnon, "Toward a New Theory of Equality," in *Women's Lives, Men's Laws*, above note 11, at 44, and explored throughout MacKinnon, *Sex Equality*, above note 29.

33. See U.N. Hum. Rts. Comm., *General Comment 18: Non-discrimination*, ¶ 7, 37th Sess. (1989), U.N. Doc. HRI/GEN/1/Rev.1 at 26 (1994), *reprinted in* U.N. High Comm'r for Hum. Rts., *Compilation of General Comments and General Recommendations Adopted by Human Rights Treaty Bodies*, at 147, U.N. Doc. HRI/GEN/1/Rev.7 (2004).

34. See Convention on the Elimination of All Forms of Discrimination Against Women, Dec. 18, 1979, 1249 U.N.T.S. 13 (entered into force Sept. 3, 1981) [hereinafter CEDAW].

35. CEDAW states that "'discrimination against women' shall mean any distinction, exclusion or restriction made on the basis of sex which has the effect or purpose of impairing or nullifying the recognition, enjoyment or exercise by women . . . on a basis of equality of men and women . . . of human rights and fundamental freedoms," not just such distinctions made by state actors. CEDAW art. 1. CEDAW goes on to condemn sex discrimination "in all its forms" and to call for legislation creating "sanctions where appropriate," presumably against private actors who discriminate against women. Id. arts. II and II(b). Crucially, CEDAW explicitly calls on states parties "[t]o take all appropriate measures to eliminate discrimination against women by any person, organization or enterprise." Id. art. II(e). It also addresses the need "[t]o modify the social and cultural patterns of conduct of men and women," areas clearly involving private acts and customs. Id. art. V(a). By condemning "all forms of traffic in women and exploitation of prostitution by women," CEDAW obviously refers to the mainly private commercial sex trade. Id. art. VI. CEDAW requires the protection of women's rights among the obviously private "non-governmental organizations and associations." Id. art. VII(c). Finally, the various provisions dealing with women's rights protection in education, employment, health care, rural areas, marriage, and family relations necessarily reach the so-called private sector, as far as states parties are involved in these areas, which involvement tends to be substantial. Id. arts. X–XVI.

36. CEDAW Committee, *General Recommendation No. 19: Violence Against Women* (11th Sess. 1992), U.N. Doc. A/47/38 at 1 (1993).

37. The U.S. Congress achieved this recognition in passing the Violence Against Women Act, but the U.S. Supreme Court in United States v. Morrison, 529 U.S. 598 (2000), later struck down this provision as exceeding the federal legislative power. For analysis, see MacKinnon, "Disputing Male Sovereignty," in *Women's Lives, Men's Laws,* above note 11, at 206.

38. See, e.g., the CEDAW Committee's finding that "to overcome centuries of male domination of the public sphere, women . . . require the encouragement and support

of all sectors of society." U.N. Comm. on the Elimination of Discrimination Against Women (CEDAW Committee), *General Recommendation No. 23: Political and Public Life* ¶ 15 (16th Sess. 1997), U.N. Doc. A/52/38/Rev.1 Part II at 61 (1997) (on CEDAW art. 7); see also CEDAW Comm., *General Recommendation No. 21: Equality in Marriage and Family Relations* ¶ 12 (13th Sess. 1992), U.N. Doc. A/49/38 at 1 (1994) ("Even where de jure equality exists, all societies assign different roles, which are regarded as inferior, to women."). Verging further on this awareness is the 2005 report on its inquiry into the abduction, rape, and murder of hundreds of women in Ciudad Juárez, Mexico, with impunity, in which the CEDAW Committee described the importance of a full "realization of the extent of the problem, as a phenomenon that goes beyond isolated cases in a structurally violent society." CEDAW Comm., *Report on Mexico Produced by the Committee on the Elimination of Discrimination Against Women Under Article 8 of the Optional Protocol to the Convention, and Reply from the Government of Mexico* ¶ 34, U.N. Doc. CEDAW/C/2005/OP.8/MEXICO (Jan. 27, 2005). The CEDAW Committee required focus on "resolving the underlying sociocultural problem. Along with combating crime, resolving the individual cases of murders and disappearances, finding and punishing those who are guilty, and providing support to the victims' families, *the root causes of gender violence in its structural dimension and in all its forms*—whether domestic and intra-family violence or sexual violence and abuse, murders, kidnappings, and disappearances must be combated, specific policies on gender equality adopted and a gender perspective integrated into all public policies." Id. (emphasis added).

39. Basic Documents Pertaining to Human Rights in the Inter-American System 101, Organization of American States, Inter-American Commission on Human Rights, Inter-American Court of Human Rights, Inter-American Convention on the Prevention, Punishment and Eradication of Violence Against Women (Convention of Belém do Pará), OEA/Ser.L/V/I.4 rev. 8, 22 May 2001, 33 *International Legal Materials* 1534 (entered into force Mar. 5, 1995) [hereinafter, Convention of Belém do Pará].

40. Protocol to the African Charter on Human and Peoples' Rights on the Rights of Women in Africa, *opened for signature* July 11, 2003, O.A.U. Doc. CAB/LEG/66.6 (1999), *available at* http://www.achpr.org [hereinafter African Protocol].

41. Convention of Belém do Pará, preamble; art. 1.

42. Id. arts. 2, 3, 3(g).

43. Id. art. 6, art. 8.

44. African Protocol, art. 17(1) ("Women shall have the right to live in a positive cultural context and to participate at all levels in the determination of cultural policies."); id. art. 10(1) ("Women have the right to a peaceful existence and the right to participate in the promotion and maintenance of peace."); id. art. 19 ("Women shall have the right to fully enjoy their right to sustainable development.").

45. For further discussion, see MacKinnon, "Toward a New Theory of Equality," in *Women's Lives, Men's Laws,* above note 11, at 44; "Sex Equality Under the Constitution of India: Problems, Prospects, and 'Personal Laws,'" below at No. 13; "On

Sex and Violence: Introducing the Antipornography Ordinance in Sweden," below at No. 9; "Nationbuilding in Canada," below at No. 10.

46. African Protocol art. 1(j).

47. Id. art. 4(2)(a).

48. Id. art. 3(4).

49. Id.

50. A range of views on the subject can be found in Radhika Coomaraswamy, "'To Bellow like a Cow': Women, Ethnicity, and the Discourse of Rights," in *Human Rights of Women: National and International Perspectives* 39 (Rebecca J. Cook, ed., 1994); Abdullahi A. An-Na'im, "State Responsibility Under International Human Rights Law to Change Religious and Customary Laws," in *Human Rights of Women*; Isabelle R. Gunning, "Arrogant Perception, World-Travelling, and Multicultural Feminism: The Case of Female Genital Surgeries," 23 *Columbia Human Rights Law Review* 198 (1992).

51. African Protocol art. 6(c) (states parties are to enact legislation to guarantee that "monogamy is encouraged as the preferred form of marriage and that the rights of women in marriage and family, including in polygamous marital relationships are promoted and protected").

52. Id. art. 5 chapeau and 5(b) ("States Parties shall take all necessary legislative and other measures to eliminate such [harmful] practices, including . . . prohibition, through legislative measures backed by sanctions, of all forms of female genital mutilation, scarification, medicalisation and para-medicalisation of female genital mutilation and all other practices in order to eradicate them.").

53. Id. art. 13(e) and (h).

54. Id. art. 14(1)(a) and (1)(b).

55. The circumstances are "sexual assault, rape, incest, and where the continued pregnancy endangers the mental and physical health of the mother or the life of the mother or the foetus." Id. art. 14(1)(c).

56. Ratified by the requisite 15 states, the African Protocol came into force November 25, 2005.

57. On this point, the Inter-American Court of Human Rights has stated that "this Court considers that the principle of equality before the law, equal protection before the law and non-discrimination belongs to jus cogens, because the whole legal structure of national and international public order rests on it and it is a fundamental principle that permeates all laws. Nowadays, no legal act that is in conflict with this fundamental principle is acceptable, and discriminatory treatment of any person, owing to gender . . . is unacceptable." Juridical Condition and Rights of the Undocumented Migrants, Advisory Opinion OC-18, 2003 (requested by Mexico), Inter-Am. Ct. H.R. (Ser. A) No. 18/03, at 101 (Sept. 17, 2003).

58. Beijing Declaration and Platform for Action, Fourth World Conference on Women, Sept. 15, 1995, A/CONF. 177/20 (1995) and A/CONF. 177/20/Add. 1 (1995), *endorsed by* G.A. Res. 50/203, U.N. Doc. A/RES/50/203 (Dec. 22, 1995) [hereinafter Beijing Declaration]; Declaration on the Elimination of Violence Against

Women, G.A. Res. 48/104, at 217, U.N. GAOR Supp. (No. 49), U.N. Doc. A/48/49 (1993); Declaration on the Elimination of Discrimination Against Women art. 3, G.A. Res. 2263 (XXII), U.N. Doc. A/6880 (Nov. 7, 1967).

59. See, e.g., U.N. Charter art. 1, para. 3; Universal Declaration of Human Rights art. 2, G.A. Res. 217A, at 71, U.N. GAOR, 3d Sess., 1st plen. mtg., 71, U.N. Doc. A/810 (Dec. 10, 1948); ICCPR arts. 3 and 26 (entered into force Mar. 23, 1976); International Covenant on Economic, Social and Cultural Rights, art. 3, *opened for signature* Dec. 16, 1966, 993 U.N.T.S. 3 (entered into force Jan. 3, 1976); American Convention arts. 1 and 27 (entered into force July 18, 1978); European Convention art. 14 (entered into force Sept. 3, 1953); African (Banjul) Charter on Human and Peoples' Rights preamble, arts. 2 and 18, *adopted* June 27, 1981, 21 *International Legal Materials* 58 (entered into force Oct. 21, 1986). Sex discrimination is even prohibited in armed conflict by Common Article 3 of the Geneva Conventions. See, e.g., Geneva Convention Relative to the Treatment of Prisoners of War art. 3, Aug. 12, 1949, 6 U.S.T. 3316, 75 U.N.T.S. 135 (requiring protection for civilians "without any adverse distinction founded on . . . sex . . .").

60. See Equality Now, *Words and Deeds: Holding Governments Accountable in the Beijing + 10 Review Process* (Mar. 2004, updated May 2005 *available at* www .equalitynow.org.); Jessica Neuwirth, "Inequality Before the Law: Holding States Accountable for Sex Discriminatory Laws Under the Convention on the Elimination of All Forms of Discrimination Against Women and Through the Beijing Platform for Action," 18 *Harvard Human Rights Journal* 19 (2005).

61. The General Assembly's Declaration on the Elimination of Discrimination Against Women, Article 3, went further, mandating taking all appropriate measures to eradicate "practices which are based on the idea of the inferiority of women." Declaration on the Elimination of Discrimination Against Women art. 3, G.A. Res. 2263 (XXII), U.N. Doc. A/6880 (Nov. 7, 1967).

62. See, e.g., rape as a crime against humanity in the Statute of the International Criminal Tribunal for the Prosecution of Persons Responsible for Genocide and Other Serious Violations of International Humanitarian Law Committed in the Territory of Rwanda and Rwandan Citizens Responsible for Genocide and Other Such Violations Committed in the Territory of Neighboring States, S.C. Res. 955, U.N. SCOR, 3453 mtg. at 3, U.N. Doc. S/RES/955, Annex (1994), art. 3(g), reprinted in 33 *International Legal Materials* 1598, 1602 [hereinafter ICTR Statute]; see also "Defining Rape Internationally: A Commentary on *Akayesu*," below at No. 23.

63. For a discussion of the tension between normative and empirical in determinations of customary international law, see Anthea Elizabeth Roberts, "Traditional and Modern Approaches to Customary International Law: A Reconciliation," 95 *American Journal of International Law* 757 (2001).

64. On standards for customary international law, see Statute of the International Court of Justice art. 38(1)(b), June 26, 1945, 59 Stat. 1055, T.S. No. 993 (custom being "evidence of a general practice accepted as law"); North Sea Continental Shelf (Federal Republic of Germany v. Denmark; Federal Republic of Germany v. Netherlands), 1969

I.C.J. 3, 43–44 (Feb. 20); Military and Paramilitary Activities (Nicaragua v. United States), 1986 I.C.J. 14, 98 ¶ 186 (June 27). For a range of views on the process, see Theodor Meron, *Human Rights and Humanitarian Norms as Customary Law* (1989); Anthony A. D'Amato, *The Concept of Custom in International Law* (1971); Bruno Simma and Philip Alston, "The Sources of Human Rights Law: Custom, Jus Cogens, and General Principles," 1988–1989 *Australian Yearbook of International Law* 82; W. Michael Reisman, "The Cult of Custom in the Late 20th Century," 17 *California Western International Law Journal* 133 (1987). For an authoritative overview, see International Law Association, "Statement of Principles Applicable to the Formation of General Customary International Law," London Conference (2000). For a focused discussion of gender discrimination in the context of the scope of customary human rights law, as well as under jus cogens and standards for obligations erga omnes, see Oscar Schachter, *International Law in Theory and Practice* 340–345 (1991).

65. CERD preamble.

66. CEDAW preamble.

67. To combat the discrimination inherent in traditional roles, CEDAW directs states parties to "take all appropriate measures . . . (a) [t]o modify the social and cultural patterns of conduct of men and women, with a view to achieving the elimination of prejudices and customary and all other practices which are based on the idea of the inferiority or the superiority of either of the sexes or on stereotyped roles for men and women," and "(b) [t]o ensure that family education includes a proper understanding of maternity as a social function and the recognition of the common responsibility of men and women in the upbringing and development of their children." Id. art. 5; see also id. art. 10(c) (dealing with "elimination of any stereotyped concept of the roles of men and women at all levels and in all forms of education"). In addition, CEDAW speaks specifically to culture in other areas. See id. arts. 1, 3 and 13(c); see also id. art. 2(f) (directing states parties "[t]o take all appropriate measures, including legislation, to modify or abolish existing laws, regulations, customs and practices which constitute discrimination against women"). CEDAW deals directly with prostitution by calling on states parties "to suppress all forms of traffic in women and exploitation of prostitution of women." Id. art. 6. On reproduction, CEDAW requires, inter alia, states parties "eliminate discrimination against women in the field of employment in order to ensure . . . [t]he right to protection of health and to safety in working conditions, including the safeguarding of the function of reproduction." Id. art. 11(f).

68. This is true from the Protocol to Amend the International Agreement for the Suppression of the White Slave Traffic, signed at Paris on May 18, 1904, and the International Convention for the Suppression of the White Slave Traffic, signed at Paris on May 4, 1910, May 4, 1949, 2 U.S.T. 1997, 98 U.N.T.S. 103, to the 1949 Convention, Convention for the Suppression of the Traffic in Persons and of the Exploitation of the Prostitution of Others, Mar. 21, 1950, 96 U.N.T.S. 271, to the breakthrough language of the Palermo Protocol, see Protocol to Prevent, Suppress and Punish Trafficking in Persons, Especially Women and Children, Supplementing the United Nations Convention Against Transnational Organized Crime, *opened for signature*

Dec. 12, 2000, 40 *International Legal Materials* 335 (entered into force Sept. 9, 2003). For further discussion and documentation, see "Pornography as Trafficking," below at No. 24.

69. Canada is an exception, see Regina v. Keegstra, [1990] 3 S.C.R. 697.

70. Prosecutor v. Nahimana, Barayagwiza, and Ngeze, Case No. ICTR 99-52-T, Judgment and Sentence (Dec. 3, 2003) (appeals pending) [hereinafter *Nahimana*]. See Catharine A. MacKinnon, "International Decision: Prosecutor v. Nahimana, Barayagwiza, and Ngeze," 98 *American Journal of International Law* 325 (2004).

71. The radio broadcasts, the massacres, and the cause and effect between the two are vividly chronicled from firsthand observation by Roméo Dallaire, head of UNAMIR, along with his disgust with those distant authorities who insisted on preserving the freedom of speech of the broadcasters while people were slaughtered as a result of them. See Roméo Dallaire, *Shake Hands with the Devil* 123, 133, 227, 230, 261, 272, 277, 375 (2003).

72. *Nahimana*, ¶¶ 139, 152, 188, 245, 1079. The media figures were charged with murder as well as its incitement, but they were inexplicably not prosecuted for rape, even though rapes were often committed at the same time by the same people in similar relation to the publications as the killings.

73. Id. See "Pornography's Empire," below at No. 12; "Pornography as Trafficking," below at No. 24; Part II, Section B of MacKinnon, *Women's Lives, Men's Laws*, above note 11, at 297.

74. On the latter, for one investigation, see Margaret E. Keck and Kathryn Sikkink, *Activists Beyond Borders: Advocacy Networks in International Politics* 165–198 (1998). On the distinction between groups in themselves and for themselves, see Jean-Paul Sartre, *Being and Nothingness* (Hazel E. Barnes, trans., 1956).

75. See, e.g., Beijing Declaration, above note 58; Implementation of the Nairobi Forward-Looking Strategies for the Advancement of Women, G.A. Res. 161, U.N. GAOR, 49th Sess., Agenda Item 97, U.N. Doc. A/Res/49/161 (1995) (the Nairobi document itself dates from 1985); Programme of Action of the International Conference on Population and Development, U.N. Doc. A/CONF. 171/13 (1994) (Cairo); United Nations World Conference on Human Rights: Vienna Declaration and Program of Action, 32 *International Legal Materials* 1661 (1993) (registering the substantial input of the parallel mobilization of women in its "women's rights are human rights" breakthrough); Forward-Looking Strategies for the Advancement of Women, Nairobi, July 15–26, 1985, *Report of the World Conference to Review and Appraise Achievements of the United Nations Decade for Women: Equality, Development and Peace*, U.N. Doc. A/Conf.116/28/Rev.1(1986); *Report of the World Conference of the International Women's Year, Mexico City*, U.N. Doc. E/CONF.66/34 (1976).

76. See, for a prominent instance, Diane Otto, "Lesbians? Not in My Country: Sexual Orientation and the Beijing World Conference on Women," 20 *Alternative Law Journal* 288 (1995).

77. See "Sex Equality Under the Constitution of India: Problems, Prospects, and 'Personal Laws,'" below at No. 13; "On Sex and Violence: Introducing the Antipor-

nography Ordinance in Sweden," below at No. 9; "Nationbuilding in Canada," below at No. 10.

78. For more extensive discussion of some of the issues raised here, see "Postmodernism and Human Rights," below at No. 5.

79. See, e.g., Shu-Ju Ada Cheng, "Labor Migration and International Sexual Division of Labor: A Feminist Perspective," in *Gender and Immigration* 43 (Debra L. DeLaet and Gregory Kelson, eds., 1999); Dan Gatmaytan, "Death and the Maid: Work, Violence, and the Filipina in the International Labor Market," 20 *Harvard Women's Law Journal* 229 (1997); Nicole L. Grimm, "The North American Agreement on Labor Cooperation and Its Effect on Women Working in Mexican Maquiladoras," 48 *American University Law Review* 179 (1998); Suzanne H. Jackson, "To Honor and Obey: Trafficking in 'Mail-Order Brides,'" 70 *George Washington Law Review* 475 (2002).

80. This is no more a moral argument that some peoples should not have their own states than that women should not have or control them.

81. See Colter Paulson, "Compliance with Final Judgments of the International Court of Justice Since 1987," 98 *American Journal of International Law* 434 (2004) (reviewing empirical studies of countries' compliance with the Court's decisions throughout its history and finding that compliance levels are, and have always been, quite high).

82. See Raekha Prasad, "Arrest Us All," *Guardian* (Sept. 16, 2005). According to this report, based on interviews with the women involved, the perpetrator, Akku Yadav, had terrorized the 300 families of Kasturba Nagar, a mainly dalit area, with his gang for over a decade, barging into homes and demanding money. "He violated women to control men," the article reported. Police he bribed protected him and told the women they were loose or having an affair with him. Dozens of times, the rapes were reported, but police told the perpetrator who had reported the rapes, whom he would then come after. Charges were routinely dropped by courts. At least three neighbors were reported murdered by Yadav. Five women were accused of murder in his killing but were released pending trial after a demonstration. "Now every woman living in the slum has claimed responsibility for the murder [telling] the police to arrest them all." Id.

1. On Torture

1. See Convention Against Torture and Other Cruel, Inhuman or Degrading Treatment or Punishment, U.N. Doc. A/RES/39/46 (Dec. 10, 1984).

2. See, e.g., Universal Declaration of Human Rights, General Assembly Resolution 217A(111) (Dec. 10, 1948), arts. 2 and 7; International Covenant on Civil and Political Rights, G.A. Res. 2200A (XXI), 21 U.N. GAOR Supp. (No. 16) at 52, U.N. Doc. A/6316 (1966), 999 U.N.T.S. 171, *entered into force* Mar. 23, 1976, art. 2(1). The Convention for the Elimination of All Forms of Discrimination Against Women, U.N. Doc. A/RES/34/180 (1979). Many nations have explicit sex equality provisions in their constitutions. For examples, see *Constitutions of the Countries of the World* (Gisbert H. Flanz and Albert P. Blaustein, eds., 1971–1994).

3. Since this speech was given and published, some jurisdictions have recognized that rape, at least in official custody or by potentially official forces or when ignored by official instrumentalities, can be torture. See, e.g., Aydin v. Turkey, [1998] 25 E.H.R.R. 251; Mejia v. Peru, Case No. 10.970, Inter-American Committee on Human Rights, Report No. 5/96, OEA/Ser.L./V/II.91 Doc. 7 rev. (1996), available at www .cidh.org/annualrep/95eng/Peru10970.htm. See also M. C. v. Bulgaria, [2003] E.C.H.R. 646 (Dec. 4, 2003).

4. See Amnesty International, *Torture in the 80's* 18–26 (1984).

5. For an account, see Jacobo Timerman, *Prisoner Without a Name, Cell Without a Number* (Toby Talbot, trans., 1981).

6. Much of this analysis was inspired by Andrea Dworkin's essay "Pornography: The New Terrorism," in *Letters from a War Zone: Writings, 1976–1989* 199–200 (1989).

7. Declaration of Defendant-Intervenor Linda Marchiano, Village Books et al. v. City of Bellingham (Marchiano Affidavit), para. 2, No. 88–14701 (unpublished) (W. D. Wash., Feb. 9, 1989). The original publisher asked me to explain the language used here. This is her language. Rarely are the voices of victims of sexual abuse heard unmediated, raw, and direct. Only comparatively unspeakable language exists for women's violations. Academic euphemisms cover them up. To make these accounts pretty through less direct language is a kind of lie. The realities are not pretty, and nobody makes them less direct for the women who live through them. A distanced discourse removes the reader from what happened, perhaps producing comfort but also making action less likely. These accounts *should* be hard to take. Living through them was unbearable.

8. Id., ¶¶ 7–11, 15, 22–23.

9. Jayne Stamen statement, February 14, 1988 (on file with author).

10. This account is drawn from the following sources: *Los Angeles Times* (May 19, 1981); *Costa Mesa Daily Pilot* (May 29, 1981); *Los Angeles Herald Examiner,* A-1 (May 30, 1981); *Sun-Star* (Merced, Cal.) (May 29, 1981); *Sun-Star* (Merced, Cal.) (May 27, 1981); *Times-Delta* (Tulare County, Cal.) (June 6, 1981); *Sun-Star* (Merced, Cal.) (May 28, 1981); *Sun-Star* (Merced, Cal.) (June 5, 1981); People v. Burnham, 222 Cal. Rptr. 630 (Ct. App. 1986), *rev. denied* (May 22, 1986).

11. See International League for Human Rights, *Human Rights Abuses Against Women: A Worldwide Survey* (May, 1990) for excerpts from the U.S. State Department's 1990 Country Reports on Human Rights (1990); Lori Heise, "The Global War Against Women," *Utne Reader,* 45 (Nov./Dec. 1989). No data are kept on the prevalence of pornography.

12. United Nations, *The State of the World's Women 1979,* quoted in Burns H. Weston, Richard A. Falk, and Anthony A. D'Amato, *International Law and World Order* 578–580 (1980). See also Marilyn Waring, *Counting for Nothing: What Men Value and What Women Are Worth* (1988).

13. Diana E. H. Russell, *Sexual Exploitation* 35 (1984); Gail E. Wyatt, "The Sexual Abuse of Afro-American and White American Women in Childhood," 9 *Child Abuse and Neglect* 507 (1985). See also Senate Judiciary Committee Majority Staff Report,

"Violence Against Women: The Increase of Rape in America 1990," 102d Cong., 1st Sess. (Mar. 21, 1991).

14. U.S. Department of Justice, *Crime in the United States* (Uniform Crime Reports) 13 (Aug. 6, 1989).

15. *Yearbook of Juridical Statistics,* Statistics Sweden, 1989, as cited in R. A. Elman and M. Eduards, "Unprotected by the Swedish Welfare State: A Survey of Battered Women and the Assistance They Received" (unpublished paper) (1990), at p. 1.

16. Exceptions include, for instance, gay men, who can be seen to be feminized by this process, and so are not exceptions to the degree their abuse as gay is not seen as political either.

17. Even among men it is inadequate. Such a definition also excludes racist atrocities often committed against men of color, such as lynching, unless proven done under color of law, and racism generally, and class-based oppression, which harms both men and women.

18. Noreen Burrows, "International Law and Human Rights: The Case of Women's Rights," in *Human Rights: From Rhetoric to Reality* 82 (Tom Campbell et al., eds., 1986). See Eschel M. Rhoodie, *Discrimination Against Women: A Global Survey* 92 (1989) ("This [public/private] dichotomy is deeply engrained in the laws of some countries and thus the law plays a critical role in maintaining gender stratification."). The Convention on the Elimination of All Forms of Discrimination Against Women covers both the conventionally public and private in its guarantees.

19. See Declaration of Defendant-Intervenor Linda Marchiano, above note 7, at ¶ 17, p. 7.

20. Id. at ¶ 21, p. 8.

21. *Public Hearings on Ordinances to Add Pornography as Discrimination Against Women,* Minneapolis, Minn., Dec. 12, 1983, pp. 45–57, published in *In Harm's Way: The Pornography Civil Rights Hearings* 60–68 (Catharine A. MacKinnon and Andrea Dworkin, eds., 1997).

22. American Booksellers Ass'n v. Hudnut, 771 F.2d 323, 329 (7th Cir. 1985) ("Depictions of subordination tend to perpetuate subordination. The subordinate status of women in turn leads to affront and lower pay at work, insult and injury at home, battery and rape on the streets. In the language of the legislature, '[p]ornography is central in creating and maintaining sex as a basis of discrimination. Pornography is a systematic practice of exploitation and subordination based on sex which differentially harms women. The bigotry and contempt it produces, with the acts of aggression it fosters, harm women's opportunities for equality and rights [of all kinds].' Indianapolis Code § 16–1(a)(2). Yet this simply demonstrates the power of pornography as speech.").

23. Hudnut v. American Booksellers Ass'n, Inc., 475 U.S. 1001 (1986) (summary affirmance).

24. Personal correspondence from Jayne Stamen to the author, March 11, 1988.

25. The New York State Department of Correctional Services Web site lists Jayne Stamen as released on parole on July 17, 2003, after over fifteen years in prison.

26. People v. Burnham, above note 10.

27. Inter-American Court of Human Rights, Velásquez-Rodríguez v. Honduras Series C, No. 4, (Judgment of July 29, 1988) (1989), 28 *International Legal Materials* 291.

28. See, e.g., Directorate of Human Rights, Council of Europe, Information Sheet No. 24 (Nov. 1988–July 1989), Appendix XXXII, Declaration on Equality of Women and Men (Nov. 16, 1988). General Recommendation No. 12, Report of the Committee on the Elimination of Discrimination Against Women on Its 8th Session, U.N. Doc. A/44/38 (1989) 81 (considering that Articles 2, 5, 11, 12, and 16 of the Convention require states parties to act to protect women against violence of any kind occurring within the family, at the workplace, or in any other area of social life, effectively reading in an obligation to take steps to address violence against women). On efforts to eradicate violence against women within society and the family, see *Report by the Secretary-General,* U.N. Doc. E/CN.6/1988/6 (1987). Regarding pornography, see Directorate of Human Rights, Council of Europe, Information Sheet No. 24 (Nov. 1988–July 1989), Recommendation No. R (89) 7 (principles on distribution of violent, brutal, or pornographic videos). After this speech was given, the CEDAW Committee promulgated its General Recommendation 19, see CEDAW, General Recommendation 19 (11th Sess. 1992), Report of the Committee on the Elimination of Discrimination Against Women on Its 11th Session, U.N. Doc. A/47/38 (1992), interpreting CEDAW's anti-discrimination provision to encompass violence against women and its official condonation. The CEDAW Committee has also recognized pornography's role in violence against women in its General Comment 12: "These attitudes also contribute to the propagation of pornography and the depiction and other commercial exploitation of women as sexual objects, rather than as individuals. This in turn contributes to gender-based violence." Id. at Comment 12. The Human Rights Committee's General Comment 28 on sex equality under the International Covenant on Civil and Political Rights finds that pornography is likely to promote violence or degrading and inhuman treatment. Human Rights Committee, General Comment 28, Equality of Rights Between Men and Women (Article 3), U.N. Doc. CCPR/C/21/Rev.1/Add.10 (2000), para. 22.

29. See, e.g., Prepared Statement of Amnesty International USA, Hearings on Human Rights Abuses Against Women, Hearing Before the Subcommittee on Human Rights and International Organizations, Committee on Foreign Affairs, U.S. House of Representatives, March 21, 1990 ("[S]ome governments do not consider rape, sexual assault and sexual abuse as serious a crime as other types of physical assaults. This is particularly alarming when the perpetrators of the rape are government officials charged with the protection of the public" Id. at 6.). Amnesty International has, since this speech was published, increasingly taken on sexual torture in official custody as part of its mandate.

30. But see U.S. State Dept. Cable, "In recent legislative report language, the Senate Foreign Relations Committee observed that government tolerance of violence and abuse against women appears to be widely practiced and tacitly condoned in many parts of the world. Noting that such abuse is a violation of human rights as defined in existing legislation, the Committee called on the Department to pay special attention to these

abuses in the cruelty reports." International League for Human Rights, *Human Rights Abuses Against Women: A Worldwide Survey* (May 1990). See above note 11, at Appendix 2.

31. Hudnut, above note 23.

32. In some places, there are various ingenious methods for cushioning the impact or qualifying the irrationality of the "similarly situated" test, usually by recognizing "differences" in some form, but it remains the main rule.

33. This critique is discussed more fully in Catharine A. MacKinnon, "Reflections on Sex Equality Under Law," 100 *Yale Law Journal* 1281 (1991), reprinted in *Women's Lives, Men's Laws* 116 (2005).

34. See Andrews v. Law Society of British Columbia, [1989] 1 S. C. R. 143; Regina v. Turpin, [1989] 1 S. C. R. 1296; Regina v. Lavallée, [1990] 1 S. C. R. 852; but compare Regina v. Hess, [1990] 2 S. C. R. 906.

35. See Richard Rorty, "Feminism and Pragmatism," 30 *Michigan Quarterly Review* 231, 234 (Spring 1991).

2. Human Rights and Global Violence Against Women

1. For a powerful exploration of this question in fiction, see Andrea Dworkin, *Mercy* 273–307 (1990).

2. See, e.g., Fumie Kamagai and Murray A. Straus, "Conflict Resolution Tactics in Japan, India, and the USA," 14 *Journal of Comparative Family Studies* 377, 382–383 (1983).

3. Nidhi Gupta, "Success of Feminist Jurisprudence in India: A Critical Analysis from the Point of View of Implementation" 64 (1998–1999) (unpublished LL.M. paper, European Academy of Legal Theory, Brussels).

4. Susan Toft, ed., "Law Reform Commission of Papua New Guinea, Domestic Violence in Urban Papua New Guinea," Occasional Paper No. 19, at 21–23 (1986).

5. B. A. Al-Awadi, Kuwaiti case study (Safat, University of Kuwait), as cited in United Nations Centre for Social Development and Humanitarian Affairs, *Violence Against Women in the Family* 20 (1989) (hereinafter *UN Center Study 1989*).

6. B. N. Wamalwa, Nairobi, Public Law Institute (1987) (Kenya); S. Skrobanek (Bangkok: Women's Information Centre, 1987) (Thailand), as cited in *UN Center Study 1989* 20 (citing studies), above note 5.

7. Id.

8. Tibamanya Mwene Mushanga, "Wife Victimization in East and Central Africa," 2 *Victimology* 479 (1978).

9. Rebecca Emerson Dobash and Russell P. Dobash, "Wives: The 'Appropriate' Victims of Marital Violence," 2 *Victimology* 435–437 (1978). See also Rebecca Emerson Dobash and Russell Dobash, *Violence Against Wives: A Case Against the Patriarchy* 20 (1979) ("The home is a dangerous place for women (and children) and markedly less dangerous for men. This is the crucial point.").

10. Linda MacLeod with Andrée Cadieux, for the Canadian Advisory Council on the Status of Women, *Wife Battering in Canada: The Vicious Circle* 10 (Jan. 1980).

11. Dobash and Dobash, *Violence Against Wives,* above note 9, at 14–20 (1979); Roger Langley and Richard Levy, *Wife Beating* (1979); Harold R. Lentzner and Marshall M. DeBerry, Bureau of Justice Statistics, U.S. Department of Justice, *Intimate Victims: A Study of Violence Among Friends and Relatives* (1980); Evan Stark, Anne Flitcraft, and William Frazier, "Medicine and Patriarchal Violence: The Social Construction of a Private Event," 9 *International Journal of Health Services* 461–493 (1979); Lenore Walker, *The Battered Woman* 19–20 (1979).

12. This possibility was confirmed as real in 2000, when the percentage of adult women physically assaulted by an intimate partner at one point in their relationship was found to be 58 percent in Turkey, 47 percent in Bangladesh, 45 percent in Ethiopia, 40 percent in India, 34 percent in Egypt, and 31 percent in Nigeria in a study that found 22 percent in the United States, likely an undercount. The questions were not identical across countries. Center for Health and Gender Equity, *Population Reports,* Series L, No. 11, Table 1 (2000).

13. *UN Centre Study 1989* 12, above note 5.

14. Id. at 20.

15. Id. at 11.

16. Since this talk was given, the United Nations has done extensive analysis of violence against women worldwide. See Radhika Coomaraswamy, *Report of the Special Rapporteur on Violence Against Women, Its Causes and Consequences,* U.N. ESCOR Hum. Rts. Comm'n, 52d Sess., Prov. Agenda Item 9(a), U.N. Doc. E/CN.4/1996/53 (1996); Radhika Coomaraswamy, *Report,* U.N. ESCOR Hum. Rts. Comm'n, 53d Sess., Prov. Agenda Item 9(a), U.N. Doc. E/CN.4/1997/47 (1997); and Radhika Coomaraswamy, *Report Submitted by the Special Rapporteur on Violence Against Women, Its Causes and Consequences,* Commission on Human Rights, 50th Sess., Agenda Item 11(a), U.N. Doc. E/CN.4/1995/42 (1995).

17. Dobash and Dobash, *Violence Against Wives,* above note 9.

18. Since this talk was given, the CEDAW Committee has squarely recognized that violence against women is a form of sex discrimination. CEDAW, General Recommendation 19 (11th Sess. 1992), Report of the Committee on the Elimination of Discrimination Against Women on Its 11th Session, U.N. Doc. A/47/38 (1992).

19. Walker, *The Battered Woman,* above note 11; Lenore Walker, *The Battered Woman Syndrome* (1984).

20. Compare, e.g., Texas Penal Code, V.T.C.A., § 19.02(a)(2): "'Sudden passion' means passion directly caused by and arising out of provocation by the individual killed or another acting with the person killed which passion arises at the time of the offense and is not solely the result of former provocation," and § 19.02(d): "At the punishment stage of a trial, the defendant may raise the issue as to whether he caused the death under the immediate influence of sudden passion arising from an adequate cause. If the defendant proves the issue in the affirmative by a preponderance of the evidence, the offense is a felony of the second degree." Ex Parte Watkins, 73 S.W.3d 264, 269 (Tex. Crim. App. 2002) ("In this case, the jury was given a special issue at the punishment phase which specifically asked whether Jimmy Dean Watkins acted in the heat of sudden passion when he murdered his wife. The jury answered yes. Thus, the jury

necessarily found that appellant acted in the heat of sudden passion when he murdered his wife."), with Jordanian Penal Code No. 16, Art. 340 (1960): "1. He who discovers his wife, or one of his female relatives, committing adultery with somebody and kills, wounds, or injures one or both of them, shall be exempt from any penalty. 2. He who catches his wife, or one of his female ascendants or descendants or sisters with another in an unlawful bed, and he kills, wounds or injures one or both of them, benefits from a reduction in penalty." As of this writing, Article 340 has been repealed, but Article 98 remains in effect: "He who commits a crime in a fit of fury resulting from a wrongful and dangerous act on the part of the victim shall benefit from a reduced penalty." Jordanian Penal Code No. 16, Art. 98. Thus the law may have been gender-neutralized on its face without gender-neutralizing its reality. For discussion, see Ferris K. Nesheiwat, "Honor Crimes in Jordan: Their Treatment Under Islamic and Jordanian Criminal Laws," 23 *Penn State International Law Review* 251 (2004). For discussion of the honor crimes defense in Brazil, which the Supreme Court of Brazil repudiated, see Melissa Spatz, "A 'Lesser' Crime: A Comparative Study of Legal Defenses for Men Who Kill Their Wives," 24 *Columbia Journal of Law and Social Problems* 597, 617 (1991) ("The 'legitimate defense of honor' was created by the Brazilian judiciary, with no statutory basis. Pursuant to this defense, a man who killed his wife because she had offended his honor would receive little or no punishment. The Supreme Court's rejection of this defense is clearly a major accomplishment for the women's movement. Yet a review of the defense as it was used raises some questions as to how successful the decision will be in protecting women."). Haiti, Morocco, and Syria, as examples, also have honor crimes laws, all predicated on sexual ownership of women. In Haiti, "[M]urder by a husband of his wife and/or partner immediately upon discovering them in flagrante delicto in the conjugal abode is to be pardoned." Haitian Penal Code Art. 269. In Morocco, "murder, injury and beating are excusable if they are committed by a husband on his wife as well as the accomplice at the moment in which he surprises them in the act of adultery." Penal Code of Morocco Art. 418. In Syria, "[h]e who catches his wife or one of his ascendants, descendants or sister committing adultery or illegitimate sexual acts with another and kills or injures one or both of them benefits from an exemption of penalty." Syrian Penal Code Art. 548. Information from Equality Now, *Words and Deeds: Holding Governments Accountable in the Beijing + 10 Review Process,* Women's Action 16.5, Update March 2004, at 25–26, *available at* www .equalitynow.org.

21. See Declaration on the Elimination of Violence Against Women, G.A. Res. A/ RES/48/104 (Feb. 23, 1994), art. 1 (defining violence against women as "any act of gender-based violence that results in, or is likely to result in, physical, sexual or psychological harm or suffering to women, including threats of such acts, coercion or arbitrary deprivation of liberty, whether occurring in public or in private life"). See also Recommendations and Conclusions Arising from the First Review and Appraisal of the Implementation of the Nairobi Forward-Looking Strategies for the Advancement of Women to the Year 2000, U.N. Econ. & Soc. Council [ECOSOC] Res. 1990/15, U.N. ECOSOC, 1st Sess., 13th plen. mtg. (May 24, 1990), U.N. Doc. E/1990/INF/6

(July 16, 1990) ¶ 23; Violence Against Women in All Its Forms, U.N. Econ. & Soc. Council [ECOSOC] Res. 1991/18, U.N. ECOSOC, 1st Sess., 12th plen. mtg. May 30, 1991), U.N. Doc. E/1991/INF/5 (July 5, 1991) ¶ 23. Fortunately, as a formal matter, this is less the case in 2005 than it was in 1992. See above notes 16 and 18.

22. Report of the Secretary-General, *Victims of Crime: The Situation of Women as Victims of Crime,* A/CONF.121/16 (May 17, 1985), Seventh United Nations Congress on the Prevention of Crime and the Treatment of Offenders (Milan, Italy, August 26 to September 6, 1985), paras. 50–67.

3. Theory Is Not a Luxury

1. Audre Lorde, "Poetry Is Not a Luxury," in *Sister Outsider* 36 (1984).

2. Moira McConnell, "Feminist Theory as the Embodiment of Marginalization," in *Reconceiving Reality: Women in International Law* 61, 63 (Dorinda G. Dallmeyer, ed., 1993) (Studies in Transnational Legal Policy No. 25, *American Journal of International Law*) [hereinafter *Reconceiving*].

3. These papers are collected in *Reconceiving,* above note 2.

4. Hilary Charlesworth, "Alienating Oscar? Feminist Analysis of International Law," in *Reconceiving,* above note 2, at 1, 15.

5. Barbara Stark, "The 'Other' Half of the International Bill of Rights as a Post-modern Feminist Text," in *Reconceiving,* above note 2, at 19, 33.

6. McConnell, "Feminist Theory as the Embodiment of Marginalization," above note 2, at 61.

7. This distinction was made by Barbara Stark in "The 'Other' Half of the International Bill of Rights," above note 5, at 23–24. In the same spirit, she distinguishes between the ICCPR's replication of hierarchies and the ICESCR's inversion of them, although the concept of equality embodied in the International Covenant on Economic, Social and Cultural Rights, 993 U.N.T.S. 3 (1966), entered into force Jan. 3, 1976, also seems in many ways to replicate those categories.

8. Analysis is provided in Catharine A. MacKinnon, "Crimes of War, Crimes of Peace," below at No. 14 and Theodor Meron, "Rape as a Crime Under International Humanitarian Law," 87 *American Journal of International Law* 424 (1993).

9. The lives of prostituted women are probably changed the least by the conflagration, because they are compelled to have sex with scores of men on an everyday basis, war or no war.

10. See Application Instituting Proceedings in the I.C.J. filed by Bosnia and Herzegovina, Application of the Convention on the Prevention and Punishment of the Crime of Genocide (Bosnia and Herzegovina v. Yugoslavia Serbia and Montenegro) (Mar. 23, 1993) ¶¶ 45–68 (detailing rapes and sexual torture); Order of Provisional Measures, Application of the Convention on the Prevention and Punishment of the Crime of Genocide (Bosnia and Herzegovina v. Serbia and Montenegro), 1993 I.C.J. 3 (Apr. 8, 1993).

11. David Harvey, *The Condition of Postmodernity: An Enquiry Into the Origins of*

Cultural Change 44 (1989), quoted in Stark, "The 'Other' Half of the International Bill of Rights," above note 5, at 34 (internal quotation marks omitted).

12. Judith Gail Gardam, "The Law of Armed Conflict: A Gendered Regime?" in *Reconceiving,* above note 2, at 171, 175.

13. Robin L. Teske, "Power: An Interdisciplinary Approach," in *Reconceiving,* above note 2, at 231, 246–248.

14. McConnell, "Feminist Theory as the Embodiment of Marginalization," above note 2, at 64.

15. This situation has begun to change, as essays in Parts II and III below progressively reveal.

4. Are Women Human?

1. Universal Declaration of Human Rights, G. A. Res. 217, U.N. GAOR, 3d Sess., at 72–76, U.N. Doc. A/810 (1948). All quotations from the Universal Declaration in this essay can be found here.

2. For data supporting all statements on violence against women in this analysis, see Radhika Coomaraswamy, *Report Submitted by the Special Rapporteur on Violence Against Women, Its Causes and Consequences,* Commission on Human Rights, 50th Sess., Agenda Item 11(a), U.N. Doc. E/CN.4/1995/42 (1995); Radhika Coomaraswamy, *Report of the Special Rapporteur on Violence Against Women, Its Causes and Consequences,* U.N. ESCOR Hum. Rts. Comm'n, 52d Sess., Prov. Agenda Item 9(a), U.N. Doc. E/CN.4/1996/53 (1996); Radhika Coomaraswamy, *Report,* U.N. ESCOR Hum. Rts. Comm'n, 53d Sess., Prov. Agenda Item 9(a), U.N. Doc. E/CN.4/1997/47 (1997).

3. See Traffic in Women and Girls, Sub-Commission on Human Rights Resolution 2002/51 E/CN.4/RES/2002/51 (Apr. 23, 2002). The U.S. Department of State estimates that around 800,000 people are trafficked internationally annually, most of whom are women and children. *Trafficking in Persons Report* 7 (June 2003).

4. The majority of the world's illiterate people are women. See UNESCO, *Statistical Yearbook 1997* 2–6 tbl. 2–2 (estimating 28.8 percent of the world's women and 16.3 percent of the world's men are illiterate).

5. See Interparliamentary Union, *Women in Parliaments, 1945–1995: A World Statistical Study* (1995).

6. See "Women's September 11th: Rethinking the International Law of Conflict," below at No. 25 below for discussion of this concept.

7. Richard Rorty, "Feminism and Pragmatism," 30 *Michigan Quarterly Review* 231, 234 (Spring 1991) ("MacKinnon's central point, as I read her, is that 'a woman' is not yet the name for a way of being human").

5. Postmodernism and Human Rights

1. Sandra M. Gilbert, "Introduction: A Tarantella of Theory," in Hélène Cixous and Catherine Clément, *The Newly Born Woman* ix, x (Betsy Wing, trans., 1986).

2. Mary Joe Frug, "A Postmodern Feminist Legal Manifesto (An Unfinished Draft)," 105 *Harvard Law Review* 1045, 1045 (1992). The parts on method in Catharine A. MacKinnon, *Toward a Feminist Theory of the State* (1989), were written primarily in 1971 and 1972, circulated, and then published in articles in 1982 and 1983 in *Signs*, one part subtitled "An Agenda for Theory." The book as a whole was published seventeen years later.

3. Unknown to me, Foucault may have been writing on similar themes at around the same time or slightly later. Foucault's *Surveiller et punir: Naissance de la prison*, containing some brief abstract passages about knowledge and power in the first chapter, appeared in French in 1975; he spoke on the same ideas in public in 1978. See James Miller, *The Passion of Michel Foucault* 233–234, 301–305 (1993) (discussing the knowledge/power relation as Foucault expressed it during this period); see also Michel Foucault, 1 *Histoire de la sexualité* (1976); Michel Foucault, *Power/Knowledge: Selected Interviews and Other Writings, 1972–1977* (Colin Gordon, ed., and Colin Gordon et al., trans., 1980).

4. See, for example, *Sisterhood Is Global: The International Women's Movement Anthology* (Robin Morgan, ed., 1996) (1984). For analysis of the process in the United States, see Sara Evans, *Personal Politics: The Roots of Women's Liberation in the Civil Rights Movement and the New Left* (1979), Ethel Klein, *Gender Politics: From Consciousness to Mass Politics* (1984), and Ruth Rosen, *The World Split Open: How the Modern Women's Movement Changed America* (2000). For documents, see *In the Company of Women: Voices from the Women's Movement* (Bonnie Watkins and Nina Rothchild, eds., 1996) and *Radical Feminism: A Documentary Reader* (Barbara A. Crow, ed., 2000).

5. See Robert J. Stoller, "A Contribution to the Study of Gender Identity," 45 *International Journal of Psycho-Analysis* 220, 220 (1964).

6. See generally Catharine A. MacKinnon, *Sexual Harassment of Working Women: A Case of Sex Discrimination* (1979).

7. Violence Against Women Act of 1994, Pub. L. No. 103–322, tit. IV, 108 Stat. 1796, 1902–1955.

8. See generally Andrea Dworkin and Catharine A. MacKinnon, *Pornography and Civil Rights: A New Day for Women's Equality* (1988); *In Harm's Way: The Pornography Civil Rights Hearings* (Catharine A. MacKinnon and Andrea Dworkin, eds., 1997).

9. See Kadic v. Karadžić, 70 F.3d 232, 241–242 (2d Cir. 1995) (brought against Radovan Karadžić by Bosnian Croat and Bosnian Muslim women survivors for sexual atrocities in his genocidal "ethnic cleansing" campaign to eliminate all non-Serbs from Bosnia-Herzegovina), *cert. denied,* 518 U.S. 1005 (1996). A New York jury awarded the plaintiffs $745 million in damages on August 10, 2000.

10. Richard Rorty, "Feminism and Pragmatism," 30 *Michigan Quarterly Review* 231, 234 (1991).

11. A splendid illustration is the parody of postmodern writing that was in fact gibberish that was accepted and published in a leading postmodern journal. See generally Alan D. Sokal, "Transgressing the Boundaries: Toward a Transformative Hermeneutics of Quantum Gravity," 46/47 *Social Text* 217 (Spring/Summer 1996). Sokal

said he did this because he was "an unabashed Old Leftist who never quite understood how deconstruction was supposed to help the working class." Alan Sokal and Jean Bricmont, *Fashionable Nonsense: Postmodern Intellectuals' Abuse of Science* 269 (1998). The emptiness at the core of some postmodern writing, deflected by jazzy footwork on the surface, is laid bare by Martha C. Nussbaum, "The Professor of Parody," *New Republic,* 37 (Feb. 22, 1999).

12. Stephen M. Feldman, "The Politics of Postmodern Jurisprudence," 95 *Michigan Law Review* 166, 202 (1996).

13. One aspect of this problem is illustrated by loopy readings that call everything that is critical of the status quo "postmodern." See, for example, Steven G. Gey, "The Case Against Postmodern Censorship Theory," 145 *University* of *Pennsylvania Law Review* 193 (1996) (calling my work postmodern throughout).

14. See Jane Flax, *Thinking Fragments: Psychoanalysis, Feminism, and Postmodernism in the Contemporary West* 32–35 (1990). Flax's analysis is usefully discussed by Seyla Benhabib, *Situating the Self: Gender, Community and Postmodernism in Contemporary Ethics* 211–230 (1992).

15. Jean-François Lyotard, *The Postmodern Condition: A Report on Knowledge* xxiv (Geoff Bennington and Brian Massumi, trans., 1984).

16. Lyotard writes of various "grand narratives" throughout *The Postmodern Condition,* id. Nancy Fraser and Linda J. Nicholson criticize the "quasi-metanarratives" of what they see as nonpostmodern feminism. See Nancy Fraser and Linda J. Nicholson, "Social Criticism Without Philosophy: An Encounter Between Feminism and Postmodernism," in *Feminism/Postmodernism* 19, 26–34 (Linda J. Nicholson, ed., 1990). No "meta" I have ever encountered has also been "quasi."

17. Frug, above note 2, at 1046.

18. An example of sloppy reading combined with the use of this term as epithet to spit on feminist work, without citations, is found in Donna Haraway, "Manifesto for Cyborgs: Science, Technology, and Socialist Feminism in the 1980s," 80 *Socialist Review* 65, 77–78 (Mar.–Apr. 1985). "Fragmentation, indeterminacy, and intense distrust of all universal or 'totalizing' discourses (to use the favoured phrase) are the hallmark of postmodernist thought." David Harvey, *The Condition of Postmodernity: An Enquiry into the Origins of Cultural Change* 9 (1989).

19. This charge is ubiquitous; one example is Celina Romany, "Ain't I a Feminist?" 4 *Yale Journal of Law and Feminism* 23, 23 (1991). A term sometimes used as a synonym is "reductionist." See Martha R. Mahoney, "Whiteness and Women, in Practice and Theory: A Reply to Catharine MacKinnon," 5 *Yale Journal of Law and Feminism* 217, 221 (1993).

20. Fraser and Nicholson falsely assert that social theorists like me assume the universal significance of constructs like sexuality before constructing genealogies of them. See Fraser and Nicholson, above note 16, at 31; see also Judith Butler, *Gender Trouble: Feminism and the Subversion of Identity* 1 (1990) ("For the most part, feminist theory has assumed that there is some existing identity, understood through the category of women.").

21. See generally Catharine A. MacKinnon, "From Practice to Theory, or What Is a White Woman Anyway?" in *Women's Lives, Men's Laws* 22 (2005).

22. See, for example, Jane Flax, "Postmodernism and Gender Relations in Feminist Theory," in *Feminism/Postmodernism,* above note 14, at 39, 45 (accusing feminism of "privileg[ing] the man as unproblematic or exempted from determination by gender relations"); Fraser and Nicholson, above note 16, at 27, 34–35 (advocating the need to replace feminism's "unitary notions of woman and feminine gender identity with plural and complexly constructed conceptions of social identity, treating gender as one relevant strand among others"); see also Susan H. Williams, "Feminist Legal Epistemology," 8 *Berkeley Women's Law Journal* 63 (1993).

23. Tracy E. Higgins, "Anti-Essentialism, Relativism, and Human Rights," 19 *Harvard Women's Law Journal* 89, 91 n.14 (1996).

24. One example is Angela P. Harris, "Race and Essentialism in Feminist Legal Theory," 42 *Stanford Law Review* 581, 591–592 (1990).

25. Higgins, above note 23, at 95 (defining premises of cultural relativists); see Nancy Kim, "Toward a Feminist Theory of Human Rights: Straddling the Fence Between Western Imperialism and Uncritical Absolutism," 25 *Columbia Human Rights Law Review* 49, 56–59 (1993). Ruth Benedict is generally associated with the view that differing views of right and wrong have no validity outside their cultural setting. See Ruth Benedict, *Patterns of Culture* 278 (1989) (1934) (urging acceptance of cultural relativity as "a more realistic social faith, accepting as grounds of hope and as new bases for tolerance the coexisting and equally valid patterns of life which mankind has created for itself from the raw materials of existence"); see also Melville J. Herskovits, "Cultural Relativism and Cultural Values," in *Perspectives in Cultural Pluralism* 11, 14–21 (Frances Herskovits, ed., 1972); Jack Donnelly, "Human Rights and Human Dignity: An Analytic Critique of Non-Western Conceptions of Human Rights," 76 *American Political Science Review* 303 (1982).

26. Feminists beginning with de Beauvoir, together with antiracist analysts of race, largely made "the Other" mean what it now means; so postmodernists did not invent that one either. See Simone de Beauvoir, *The Second Sex* xxviii (H. M. Parshley, ed. and trans., 1989) (1952).

27. A useful discussion of this theme can be found in Elspeth Probyn, "Travels in the Postmodern: Making Sense of the Local," in *Feminism/Postmodernism,* above note 16, at 176.

28. People v. Chen, No. 87–7774 (N.Y. Sup. Ct. Dec. 2, 1988). The *Chen* case is discussed in further detail in Doriane Lambelet Coleman, "Individualizing Justice Through Multiculturalism: The Liberals' Dilemma," 96 *Columbia Law Review* 1093 (1996).

29. People v. Rhines, 182 Cal. Rptr. 478 (Ct. App. 1982).

30. See id. at 483.

31. A recent meta-analysis concluded that, taken together, the body of experimental studies shows that exposure to pornography increases rape-myth acceptance—greater for violent pornography but also holding true for nonviolent pornography. See Mike

Allen et al., "Exposure to Pornography and Acceptance of Rape Myths," 45 *Journal of Communications* 5 (1995). The same consequences of exposure were found in Japan. See Ken-Ichi Ohbuchi et al., "Effects of Violent Pornography upon Viewers' Rape Myth Beliefs: A Study of Japanese Males," 1 *Psychology, Crime and Law* 71, 77–78 (1994).

32. See Butler, above note 20, at 55–60. For conflation of penis with phallus, see Drucilla Cornell, "The Doubly-Prized World: Myth, Allegory and the Feminine," 75 *Cornell Law Review* 644, 661–662 (1990); Ellie Ragland, "Lacan and the Subject of Law: Sexuation and Discourse in the Mapping of Subject Positions That Give the Ur-Form of Law," 54 *Washington and Lee Law Review* 1091 (1997); Adelaide H. Villmoare, "Feminist Jurisprudence and Political Vision," 24 *Law and Social Inquiry* 443, 455–456 (1999). To Lacan, of course, the phallus is not the penis, but the object of desire for that which is lacked. See Jacques Lacan, "The Signification of the Phallus," in *Écrits: A Selection* 281, 285–291 (Alan Sheridan, trans., 1977) (1966). My point is that the penis has a behavioral reality in male dominance—it does actual things—and that theorizing "the phallus" has largely served to distract rather than to focus the project of understanding what it does. The phallus in this discourse is abstract; the penis remains relentlessly concrete, but not on postmodern pages, although even French feminists began concretely initially. See, for example, Benoîte Groult, "Night Porters," in *New French Feminisms: An Anthology* 68 (Elaine Marks and Isabelle de Courtivron, eds., and Elisa Gelfand, trans., 1980); Luce Irigaray, *Ce sexe qui n'en est pas un* (1977); Dominique Poggi, "A Defense of the Master-Slave Relationship," in *New French Feminisms,* above, at 76.

33. Butler, above note 20, at 33.

34. This can be located in postmodern literature virtually at random, but a good example is found in Butler. See id. at 79–141.

35. On "agency," see generally Kathryn Abrams, "From Autonomy to Agency: Feminist Perspectives on Self-Direction," 40 *William and Mary Law Review* 805 (1999); Kathryn Abrams, "Sex Wars Redux: Agency and Coercion in Feminist Legal Theory," 95 *Columbia Law Review* 304 (1995); and James Boyle, "Is Subjectivity Possible? The Postmodern Subject in Legal Theory," 62 *University of Colorado Law Review* 489 (1991). Exemplifying the use of "victim," see Wendy Brown, *States of Injury: Power and Freedom in Late Modernity* 93 (1995). The injury of social subordination is also rendered "the 'injury' of social subordination." Id. at 27; see also Butler, above note 20, at 142–147 (on "agency").

36. Frug, above note 2, at 1052.

37. See, for example, Rosi Braidotti, *Nomadic Subjects: Embodiment and Sexual Difference in Contemporary Feminist Theory* 57–74 (1994); Drucilla Cornell, *The Imaginary Domain: Abortion, Pornography and Sexual Harassment* 95–163 (1995).

38. See Michel Foucault, *Discipline and Punish: The Birth of the Prison* 195–228 (Alan Sheridan, trans., 1978) (discussing panopticism); Irigaray, above note 32, at 25–26 (describing women's entrance into "une economie scopique dominante"); Jacques Lacan, *The Four Fundamental Concepts of Psycho-Analysis* 67–78 (Alan Sheridan, trans., 1978) (1973) (on originating "scopic drive").

39. See Christine Delphy, "The Invention of French Feminism: An Essential Move," 87 *Yale French Studies* 190, 196 (1995).

40. Michel Foucault, "On Power," in *Politics, Philosophy, Culture: Interviews and other Writings, 1977–1984* 96, 106 (Lawrence D. Kritzman, ed., and Alan Sheridan et al., trans., 1988).

41. Judith Butler, "Quandaries of the Incest Taboo," in *Whose Freud? The Place of Psychoanalysis in Contemporary Culture* 39, 40–41 (Peter Brooks and Alex Woloch, eds., 2000). Reports of events of incest form the extensive database analyzed by Diana E. H. Russell, *The Secret Trauma: Incest in the Lives of Girls and Women* (1986). Widely overlooked is the excellent study by Linda Williams that begins with medically documented acts of child abuse and locates survivors seventeen years later to inquire into their memory of the events. Thirty-eight percent did not recall them. See Linda Meyer Williams, "Recall of Childhood Trauma: A Prospective Study of Women's Memories of Child Sexual Abuse," 62 *Journal of Consulting and Clinical Psychology* 1167 (1994).

42. See, for example, Higgins, above note 23, at 119–120. For critique, see Martha C. Nussbaum, *The Fragility of Goodness: Luck and Ethics in Greek Tragedy and Philosophy* 81 (1986).

43. A specific form of this argument is made effectively, on postmodern terrain, in Susan Bordo, "'Material Girl': The Effacements of Postmodern Culture," in *The Female Body: Figures, Styles, Speculations* 106 (Laurence Goldstein, ed., 1991). That postmodernism claims to supersede modernism can be seen, for example, in Christine Di Stefano, "Dilemmas of Difference: Feminism, Modernity, and Postmodernism," in *Feminism/Postmodernism,* above note 16, at 63 ("Postmodernism has taken things one step further" beyond theorists such as Rousseau, Marx, and de Beauvoir). She observes that it may "rerun, in updated garb," what it claims to supersede. Id. at 77. If postmodernism sees itself superseding modernism by discontinuity or rupture, it is not claiming to address modernism's concerns better than it does, just to scratch a different itch, to use Wittgenstein's metaphor for what philosophy does. See Ludwig Wittgenstein, *Vermischte Bemerkungen* 14 (1977), quoted in Richard Rorty, *Philosophy and the Mirror of Nature* vii (1979). Perhaps part of the problem here is that women's concerns are a lot more urgent and life-threatening than itches.

44. A useful discussion of this problem is found in Dennis Patterson, "Postmodernism/Feminism/Law," 77 *Cornell Law Review* 254 (1992).

45. Postmodernists may disagree with this Hegelian sublation as the path from modernism to postmodernism. Maybe they should say what the "post" prefix means in its copula with modernism. If it represents a rupture, why doesn't it have its own name?

46. Gertrude Stein, *Brewsie and Willie* 30 (1946).

47. See Butler, above note 20, at 25 ("A great deal of feminist theory and literature has nevertheless assumed that there is a 'doer' behind the deed"). Nietzsche exposed the fallacy of separating the doer from the deed. See generally Friedrich Nietzsche, *On the Genealogy of Morals: A Polemic* (Douglas Smith, trans., 1996). Or, as Yeats asked, "How can we know the dancer from the dance?" William Butler Yeats, "Among School

Children," in *The Collected Poems of W. B. Yeats* 212, 214 (1956). Behind the point on accountability is a larger one pointing less toward a doer behind the deed—raising whether the self is the cause of one's actions (as in Kant) or the effect of one's actions (as in Sartre)—and more to a doer *beyond* the deed. Neither modernism nor feminism evaporates the subject, as postmodernism seeks to do.

48. Another formulation of this same idea is that feminist postmodernism is "an epistemology that justifies knowledge claims only insofar as they arise from enthusiastic violation of the founding taboos of Western humanism." Sandra Harding, *The Science Question in Feminism* 193 (1986).

49. For a lucid update on the state of this criticism, see Richard Rorty, *Philosophy and Social Hope* 262–277 (1999).

50. The concept comes from Fredric Jameson. See Fredric Jameson, *Postmodernism, or, The Cultural Logic of Late Capitalism* 90 (1991); see also Trina Grillo, "Anti-Essentialism and Intersectionality: Tools to Dismantle the Master's House," 10 *Berkeley Women's Law Journal* 16, 17 (1995); Joan C. Williams, "Dissolving the Sameness/ Difference Debate: A Post-Modern Path Beyond Essentialism in Feminist and Critical Race Theory," 41 *Duke Law Journal* 296, 307 (1991) ("[The] post-modern approach starts from the notion of a fragmented and shifting self").

51. In a sample of one hundred individuals who are multiple in a study conducted for the National Institutes of Mental Health, 97 percent reported experiencing significant trauma in childhood, 83 percent reported sexual abuse, 75 percent reported repeated physical abuse, and 68 percent reported both. See Frank W. Putnam et al., "The Clinical Phenomenology of Multiple Personality Disorder: Review of 100 Recent Cases," 47 *Journal of Clinical Psychiatry* 285, 289–290 (1986). Cumulative, overwhelming, severe, long-lasting abuse was found related to the level of dissociation that results from childhood trauma in a large sample of inpatients. See Nel Draijer and Willie Langeland, "Childhood Trauma and Perceived Parental Dysfunction in the Etiology of Dissociative Symptoms in Psychiatric Inpatients," 156 *American Journal of Psychiatry* 379 (1999); see also Judith Lewis Herman, *Trauma and Recovery* 125–126 (1992).

52. A stark contrast to the conception of multiplicity discussed here is that of Mari J. Matsuda, "When the First Quail Calls: Multiple Consciousness as Jurisprudential Method," in *Where Is Your Body? And Other Essays on Race, Gender, and the Law* 3 (1996).

53. See Braidotti, above note 37, at 13 (referring glancingly to the Bosnian situation in her discussion of language).

54. The printed version is: "[I]t was not until I found some stability and sense of partial belonging, supported by a permanent job and a happy relationship, that I could actually start thinking adequately about nomadism." Id. at 35.

55. Stephen A. Marglin, "Towards the Decolonization of the Mind," in *Dominating Knowledge: Development, Culture, and Resistance* 1, 12–14 (Frédérique Apffel Marglin and Stephen A. Marglin, eds., 1990).

56. Id. at 13.

57. Id.

58. Harvey, above note 18, at 116–117, is particularly cogent.

59. Sokal and Bricmont, above note 11, at 209.

60. A different version of this point is made by Nancy Hartsock, "Rethinking Modernism: Minority vs. Majority Theories," 7 *Cultural Critique* 187, 204–206 (Fall 1997). The postmodernists are to be thanked for drawing a line that makes me feel part of a tradition that I never felt much included in before.

6. The Promise of CEDAW's Optional Protocol

1. U.N. Doc. E/CN.6/1999/WG/L.2 (1999), available at www.un.org/women watch/daw/cedaw/protocol/op.pdf.

2. For further analysis, see Laboni Amena Hoq, "The Women's Convention and Its Optional Protocol: Empowering Women to Claim Their Internationally Protected Rights," 32 *Columbia Human Rights Law Review* 677 (2001).

3. U.N. Doc. A/RES/34/180 (1979).

4. See "Meeting of States Parties to the Convention on the Elimination of All Forms of Discrimination Against Women, Declarations, Reservations, Objections and Notifications of Withdrawal of Reservations Relating to the Convention on the Elimination of All Forms of Discrimination Against Women," CEDAW/SP/2002/2; Hilary Charlesworth and Christine Chinkin, *The Boundaries of International Law: A Feminist Analysis* 102–113 (2000).

5. Article 18 of CEDAW contains reporting requirements. CEDAW's Article 29's interstate procedure is highly reserved and has never been used. For concern over lack of enforcement mechanisms, see Andrew Byrnes and Jane Connors, "Enforcing the Human Rights of Women: A Complaints Procedure for the Women's Convention–Draft Optional Protocol to the Convention on the Elimination of All Forms of Discrimination Against Women," 21 *Brooklyn Journal of International Law* 679 (1996); Anne F. Bayefsky, *The UN Human Rights Treaty System: Universality at the Crossroads* (2001).

6. As recognized, for example, in CEDAW Committee *General Recommendation 19: Violence Against Women* (11th Sess., 1992), U.N. Doc. A/47/38 (1993).

7. See *Words and Deeds: Holding Governments Accountable in the Beijing + 10 Review Process* (Mar. 2004), *at* www.equalitynow.org.

8. Selected examples include Article 2's reference to abolishing "customs and practices which constitute discrimination," Article 4's provisions for temporary special measures to achieve affirmative action, Article 5's mandate to modify culture to equalize women's status and treatment, Article 6's measures against exploitation of trafficking in women, and CEDAW's application to "private life," including marriage and the family as specified in Article 16. These provisions reach further than the sex equality protections of most national and international instruments.

9. Procedures are an exception. For travaux, see "Division for the Advancement of Women, Department of Economic and Social Affairs, The Convention on the Elim-

ination of All Forms of Discrimination Against Women," *The Optional Protocol: Text and Materials* (United Nations, 2000).

10. Concerns expressed, as with other treaty bodies, have included adjudicators who need not be lawyers and possible political influence, both of which can also obtain in domestic courts.

11. Articles 2–7.

12. Article 8.

13. Article 17.

14. See Article 2.

15. Article 2. This was the subject of considerable debate leading to ratification. For analysis, see L. Sucharipa-Behrmann, "The Individual Complaints Procedure Provided For by the Optional Protocol to CEDAW: A First Evaluation," in *Development and Developing International and European Law* 658–659 (1999).

16. Article 2.

17. Article 3.

18. Article 11.

19. Article 4.

20. Article 4(2).

21. Article 7(2).

22. Article 7(3).

23. Articles 8(5) (confidentiality and cooperation), 8(1) and (5) (cooperation invited), and 8(3) (transmission).

24. Article 13; CEDAW Rules of Procedure, Rule 74, *Report of the Committee on the Elimination of Discrimination Against Women*, A/56/38, Annex 1 (2001).

25. Article 7(4).

26. Article 5(1).

27. For a view that this is how most laws work most of the time, see Sally Engle Merry, "Constructing a Global Law—Violence Against Women and the Human Rights System," 28 *Law and Social Inquiry* 941 (2003) ("like state law, [international law's] impact depends on its cultural legitimacy and its embodiment in local cultures and legal consciousness").

28. For some such effects, see *The First CEDAW Impact Study: Final Report* (Toronto: Centre for Feminist Research, York University, and the International Women's Rights Project, 2000); Margaret E. Keck and Kathryn Sikkink, *Activists Beyond Borders: Advocacy Networks in International Politics* (1998).

29. See Articles 12, 13.

30. See Annual Report 28th/29th Sess., Report of the Working Group on Communications, A/58/38 Annex 9 (2003) and A/59/38 (Part I) (2004) and A/60/38 (2005). Since 2004, the Committee on the Elimination of Discrimination against Women has issued two decisions and completed one inquiry under the Optional Protocol. The complaint in B.-J. v. Germany alleging that Germany's divorce laws discriminated against older divorced women was declared inadmissible, with a dissent by two members finding it admissible in part and finding that the woman was not required to

exhaust unreasonably prolonged domestic remedies. U.N. Committee on the Elimination of Discrimination against Women [CEDAW], *Report of the Committee on the Elimination of Discrimination against Women*, 31st Sess., Annex 8, ¶ 8.8 U.N. Doc. A/59/38, available at http://www.un.org/womenwatch/daw/cedaw/31sess.htm#report, then daccessdds.un.org/doc/UNDOC/GEN/NO4/462/77/PDF/NO446277.pdf?Open Element. The Committee's decision in A.T. v. Hungary found that Hungary violated the Convention in failing to protect her effectively from her violent former common law husband. *Report of the Committee on the Elimination of Discrimination against Women*, 32d Sess., Annex III, ¶ 8.8 U.N. Doc. A/60/38, available at http://www.un.org/womenwatch/daw/cedaw/32sess.htm, then daccessdds.un.org/doc/UNDOC/GEN/NO5/275/89/PDF/NO527589.pdf?OpenElement. The Committee recommended Hungary take immediate and effective measures to guarantee the physical and mental integrity of A.T. and her family, ensure that A.T. is given a safe home, receives appropriate child support and legal assistance, and receives reparation proportionate to the physical and mental harm undergone and to the gravity of the violations of her rights. Id. ¶ 9.6. The Committee also issued a report detailing the results of its inquiry into disappearances, rapes, and murders of hundreds of women and girls over the prior decade Ciudad Juárez, Mexico. *Report on Mexico produced by the Committee on the Elimination of Discrimination against Women under article 8 of the Optional Protocol to the Convention, and reply from the Government of Mexico*, U.N. Doc. CEDAW/C/2005/OP.8/MEXICO, available at www.un.org/womenwatch/daw/cedaw/cedaw32/CEDAW-C-2005-OP.8-MEXICO-E.pdf. The Committee concluded that the facts alleged "constitute grave and systematic violations of the provisions of the Convention on the Elimination of All Forms of Discrimination against Women," id. 259, and that the response by Mexico had not been adequate to the Convention's standards, and made recommendations to bring it into compliance. "Along with combating crime, resolving the individual cases of murders and disappearances, finding and punishing those who are guilty, and providing support to the victims' families, the root causes of gender violence in its structural dimension and in all its forms—whether domestic and intra-family violence or sexual violence and abuse, murders, kidnappings, and disappearances must be combated, specific policies on gender equality adopted and a gender perspective integrated into all public policies." Id. ¶ 270. Mexico agreed that "the murders of the Ciudad Juárez women constitute a breach of the women's human rights, the origin of which lies in entrenched cultural patterns of discrimination." Id., Observations by the State Party—Mexico.

7. Making Sex Equality Real

1. Section 15 provides:

"(1) Every individual is equal before and under the law and has the right to the equal protection and equal benefit of the law without discrimination and, in particular, without discrimination based on race, national or ethnic origin, colour, religion, sex, age or mental or physical disability.

(2) Subsection (1) does not preclude any law, program or activity that has as its object the amelioration of conditions of disadvantaged individuals or groups including those that are disadvantaged because of race, national or ethnic origin, colour, religion, sex, age or mental or physical disability."

Can. Const. pt. 1, § 15 (The Canadian Charter of Rights and Freedoms).

2. Section 28 provides: "Notwithstanding anything in this Charter, the rights and freedoms referred to in it are guaranteed equally to male and female persons." Can. Const. pt. 1, § 28.

3. Herbert Wechsler, "Toward Neutral Principles of Constitutional Law," 73 *Harvard Law Review* 1, 33 (1959).

4. Important as it is, discussion of the possible expansion of legislative authority under those provisions of the Charter where litigation may not necessarily be permitted, as well as full discussion of the crucial state action/private action question, will have to await another day.

5. Joseph Tussman and Jacobus tenBroek, "The Equal Protection of the Laws," 37 *California Law Review* 341, 346–351 (1949). The term "fit" was coined by later scholars to refer to the concept these authors clarified.

6. See id., 346. Tussman and tenBroek used this phrase but sought to avoid an inquiry into whether or not legislatures had indeed carved the social world at a natural joint. See also Owen Fiss, "Groups and the Equal Protection Clause," 5 *Philosophy and Public Affairs* 108 (1976), especially at 123, where he discusses the issue.

7. See Bliss v. A. G. of Canada, [1979] 1 S.C.R. 183.

8. Devine v. Devine, 398 So.2d 686 (Ala. Sup. Ct. 1981); Danielson v. Board of Higher Education, 358 F. Supp. 22 (S.D.N.Y. 1972); Orr v. Orr, 440 U.S. 268 (1979).

9. Mississippi University for Women v. Hogan, 458 U.S. 718 (1982).

10. Diaz v. Pan Am. World Airways, Inc., 442 F.2d 385 (5th Cir. 1971), *cert. denied* 404 U.S. 950 (1971); Equal Employment Opportunity Commission v. American Telephone and Telegraph Co., 556 F.2d 167 (3d Cir. 1977).

11. Weinberger v. Weisenfeld, 420 U.S. 636 (1975).

12. See General Electric Co. v. Gilbert, 429 U.S. 125, 135 (1976); Geduldig v. Aiello, 417 U.S. 484, 496–497 (1974); Newport News Shipbuilding and Dry Dock Company v. Equal Employment Opportunity Commission, 462 U.S. 669 (1983).

13. See Canadian Criminal Code §§ 246.6(1), 246.7, 246.1(2), 146(3), 153(2).

14. See Constitution Act, 1982, pt. I, § 2(b).

15. Susan B. Anthony, *The Revolution,* in *A History of Women in America,* 161 (Carol Hymowitz and Michaele Weissman, eds., 1978).

8. Nationbuilding in Canada

1. Canadian Constitution pt. 1, § 15 (the Canadian Charter of Rights and Freedoms). Section 15 provides:

"(1) Every individual is equal before and under the law and has the right to the equal protection and equal benefit of the law without discrimination and, in particular, without discrimination based on race, national or ethnic origin, colour, religion, sex, age or mental or physical disability."

(2) Subsection (1) does not preclude any law, program or activity that has as its object the amelioration of conditions of disadvantaged individuals or groups including those that are disadvantaged because of race, national or ethnic origin, colour, religion, sex, age or mental or physical disability."

2. Can. Const. pt. 1, § 28. Section 28 provides: "Notwithstanding anything in this Charter, the rights and freedoms referred to in it are guaranteed equally to male and female persons."

3. [1989] 1 S.C.R. 143 (Can.).

4. The Meech Lake Accord is in the form of amendments to the Constitution Act, 1867 (British North America Act, 1867, 30–31 Vict., ch. 3). The Accord includes a new Section 2 of the Constitution Act as follows:

"(1) The Constitution of Canada shall be interpreted in a manner consistent with

(a) the recognition that the existence of French-speaking Canadians, centred in Quebec but also present elsewhere in Canada, and English-speaking Canadians, concentrated outside Quebec but also present in Quebec, constitutes a fundamental characteristic of Canada; and

(b) the recognition that Quebec constitutes within Canada a distinct society.

(2) The role of the Parliament of Canada and the provincial legislatures to preserve the fundamental characteristic of Canada referred to in paragraph (1)(a) is affirmed.

(3) The role of the legislature and Government of Quebec to preserve and promote the distinct identity of Quebec referred to in paragraph (1)(b) is affirmed.

(4) Nothing in this section derogates from the powers, rights or privileges of Parliament or the Government of Canada, or of the legislatures or governments of the provinces, including any powers, rights or privileges relating to language."

5. Section 16 of the Meech Lake Accord states: "Nothing in section 2 of the *Constitution Act, 1867* affects section 25 or 27 of the *Canadian Charter of Rights and Freedoms,* section 35 of the *Constitution Act, 1982* or class 24 of section 91 of the *Constitution Act, 1867.*" The provisions referred to in Section 16 protect multicultural rights and the rights of aboriginal peoples.

6. See "Canadian Leader Appeals for Calm on Quebec Dispute," *New York Times,* 1 (June 23, 1990). Last-minute attempts to reach a compromise on the Accord failed and the issues discussed remain unresolved. The Charlottetown Accord, a successor to Meech Lake that contained a distinct society provision, was defeated in a national referendum on October 26, 1992, 54.8 percent against to 44.8 percent for. Anthony Wilson-Smith, "What Happens Next," *Maclean's,* 12 (Nov. 2, 1992); Sandro Contenta, "Bourassa Vows Tough War Against Separatist Wave," *Toronto Star,* B1 (Oct. 27, 1992). A second Quebec referendum on sovereignty, placed on the ballot in November 1995, was defeated by a vote of 50.56 percent against and 49.44 percent for.

After defeat of the second Quebec referendum, the distinct society efforts were criticized as not inclusive of women and aboriginal peoples: "Meech Lake, Charlottetown and the Quebec referendum have all shown the national question will never be resolved unless aboriginal peoples and people of color are part of the resolution. To think that the constitutional question can be settled, white man to white man, 'equal to equal,' is to put blinkers on this changing reality. . . . During Charlottetown, aboriginal women demanded a voice in the negotiations, as did the rest of the women's movement. We fought for the protection of equality rights, and when then-Prime Minister Mulroney and the provincial premiers made a deal behind closed doors, the women's movement organized and helped defeat the accord. . . . Never again, however, will the women's movement accept being silenced in any constitutional process, or in the redesigning of the Canadian federation." Sunera Thobani, "New Deal Impossible Without Women, Aboriginals," *Winnipeg Free Press,* A19 (Nov. 24, 1995).

Contemporaneously with the defeat of the second referendum, Canada's House of Commons passed a parliamentary resolution that affirmed that "'Quebec is a distinct society within Canada' and called on 'all components of the legislative and executive branches' of the federal government 'to be guided in their conduct accordingly.'" Monique Jerome-Forget, "Myths Obscure Debate over 'Distinct Society,'" *The Financial Post,* 77 (Jan. 13, 1996). In 1997, premiers of nine provinces and two territories drafted the Calgary declaration, which affirmed the "unique character" of Quebec based on its French language, culture, and civil law. See "Canada's Long Walk down Troubled Path," *Winnipeg Free Press,* A6 (Aug. 21, 1998). In 2001, the Quebec Liberal Party released a constitutional report that proposed formal constititution recognition of Quebec's "specificity." See Scott Reid, "Unpacking Charest's Proposal," *National Post,* A19 (Jan. 25, 2001). Distinct society status for Quebec remains a live issue in Canadian politics, most recently in the health care arena. See Norman Spector, "More Asymmetry Than Federalism," *The Globe and Mail,* A13 (Sept. 20, 2004).

7. See Spears, "Peterson's Problems as Meech Pact Salesman," *Toronto Star,* D5 (July 2, 1988).

8. U.S. Const. amend. XIV, § 2 (the right to vote in federal elections may not be denied or abridged as "to any of the *male* inhabitants of such State" (emphasis added)).

9. Reed v. Reed, 404 U.S. 71 (1971).

10. "All animals are equal, but some animals are more equal than others," George Orwell, *Animal Farm* 112 (1946).

11. Can. Const. pt. 1, § 1. Section 1 states: "The *Canadian Charter of Rights and Freedoms* guarantees the rights and freedoms set out in it subject only to such reasonable limits prescribed by law as can be demonstrably justified in a free and democratic society."

12. But see Tremblay v. Daigle, 1 S.C.R 489 (1989), in which the Supreme Court of Canada overturned two levels of Quebec courts that had permitted an injunction by a putative father and former boyfriend against Chantal Daigle's abortion. If the constitutional issues were reached, and the Meech Lake Accord were in effect, could opposition to abortion be legally justified as part of the "distinct society" in largely Catholic Quebec?

13. Morgentaler, Smoling & Scott v. Regina, [1988] 1 S.C.R. 30 (Can.).

14. Canadian Constitution pt. 1, § 7 The Canadian Charter of Rights and Freedoms states: "Everyone has the right to life, liberty and security of the person and the right not to be deprived thereof except in accordance with the principles of fundamental justice."

10. On Sex and Violence: Introducing the Antipornography Civil Rights Law in Sweden

1. See Linda Lovelace and Michael McGrady, *Ordeal* 129–134 (1980).

2. See *Ordeal,* id. at 28–30, for Linda's account of this process.

3. See, e.g., William L. Marshall, Canada Department of Justice, "The Use of Pornography by Rapists and Child Molesters" (1985) (unpublished study on file with author); Gene G. Abel et al., "The Components of Rapists' Sexual Arousal," 34 *Archives of General Psychiatry* 895 (1977); Neil M. Malamuth et al., "Testing Hypotheses Regarding Rape: Exposure to Sexual Violence, Sex Differences and the 'Normality' of Rapists," 14 *Journal of Research in Personality* 121 (1980); *In Harm's Way, The Pornography Civil Rights Hearings* 160–165 (Catharine A. MacKinnon and Andrea Dworkin, eds., 1997) (testimony of professionals who work with rapists documenting the role of pornography in rapes they committed).

4. See, e.g., Neil Malamuth, James V. P. Check, and John Briere, "Sexual Arousal in Response to Aggression: Ideological, Aggressive and Sexual Correlates," 50 *Journal of Personality and Social Psychology* 330 (1986); Neil Malamuth and James V. P. Check, "Penile Tumescence and Perceptual Responses to Rape as a Function of the Victim's Perceived Reactions," 10 *Journal of Applied Social Psychology* 528 (1981).

5. Swedish Penal Code ch. 16, § 10b, states: "Any person who in a picture depicts sexual violence or coercion with intent to disseminate the picture or pictures or disseminates such depiction, shall, unless the act in view of the circumstances is justifiable, be sentenced for *unlawful depiction of violence* to a fine or imprisonment for at most two years. This also applies to any person who in moving pictures intrusively or extensively depicts extreme violence towards humans or animals with intent to disseminate such pictures, or disseminates such a depiction.

A person who through negligence disseminates a depiction mentioned in the first paragraph in the course of business or otherwise for the purpose of making money, shall be punished in accordance with the provisions of the first paragraph."

6. The Model Ordinance defines "pornography" as "the graphic sexually explicit subordination of women through pictures and/or words that also includes one or more of the following: a. women are presented dehumanized as sexual objects, things, or commodities; or b. women are presented as sexual objects who enjoy humiliation or pain; or c. women are presented as sexual objects experiencing sexual pleasure in rape, incest, or other sexual assault; or d. women are presented as sexual objects tied up or cut up or mutilated or bruised or physically hurt; or e. women are presented in postures or positions of sexual submission, servility, or display; or f. women's body parts–including but not limited to vaginas, breasts, or buttocks–are exhibited such that women

are reduced to those parts; or g. women are presented being penetrated by objects or animals; or h. women are presented in scenarios of degradation, humiliation, injury, torture, shown as filthy or inferior, bleeding, bruised or hurt in a context that makes these conditions sexual."

The use of "men, children, or transsexuals in the place of women" in this definition is also pornography. Model Ordinance, reprinted in Andrea Dworkin and Catharine A. MacKinnon, *Pornography and Civil Rights: A New Day for Women's Equality* 138–139 (1988).

7. See Andrea Dworkin, "Against the Male Flood: Censorship, Pornography, and Equality," in *Letters from a War Zone* 264–268 (1988).

8. "In the movies known as snuff films, victims sometimes are actually murdered." 130 Cong. Rec. S13192 (daily ed. Oct. 3, 1984) (statement of Senator Specter introducing the Pornography Victims Protection Act). See, e.g., People v. Douglas, Felony Complaint No. NF 8300382 (Municipal Court, Orange County, Cal., Aug. 5, 1983); "List of Possible California Murder Victims Grows," *Boston Globe,* p. 10, col. 3 (June 12, 1985) (discussing case of Ng and Lake); P. Hunt and M. Baird, "Children of Sex Rings," 419:3 *Child Welfare* 195–207, 1990; Carl A. Raschke, *Painted Black: From Drug Killings to Heavy Metal—The Alarming True Story of How Satanism Is Terrorizing Our Communities* 59, 131, 170, 208–209 (1990). For some updates, see Annemie Bulté, Douglas De Coninck, and Marie-Jeanne Van Heeswyck, *Les dossiers X: Ce que la Belgique ne devait pas savoir sur l'affaire Dutroux* (1999); Harvey L. Schwartz, *Dialogues with Forgotten Voices: Relational Perspectives on Child Abuse Trauma and Treatment of Dissociative Disorders* 59–61, 68–74, 457 n.12 (2000).

9. Swedish Penal Code ch. 16, § 11, states: "A person who, on or at a public place, exhibits pornographic pictures by means of displays or other similar procedure in a manner which is apt to result in public annoyance, shall be sentenced for *unlawful exhibition of pornographic pictures* to a fine or imprisonment for at most six months. This also applies to a person who sends through the mail to or otherwise furnishes another with unsolicited pornographic pictures." (Law 1970:225).

10. This experience was reported to Andrea Dworkin by the woman to whom it happened. Andrea reported it in a speech in Toronto, Canada, in February 1984, reprinted in *Healthsharing,* 25 (Summer 1984).

11. This is a paraphrase of the account given in testimony in Minneapolis, Minn., in *In Harm's Way: The Pornography Civil Rights Hearings* 145–147 (Catharine A. MacKinnon and Andrea Dworkin, eds., 1997) (testimony of S. G.).

12. For sexual abuse by doctors connected to pornography, see Minneapolis Hearings Exhibit 11, letter of Marvin Lewis, in *In Harm's Way,* above note 11, at 227.

13. This account was given to the author directly by the survivor.

14. The law of sexual harassment in the United States is full of reports of such events. See, e.g., Robinson v. Jacksonville Shipyards, Inc., 760 F. Supp. 1486 (M. D. Fla. 1991); Iannone v. Frederick R. Harris, Inc., 941 F. Supp. 403 (S.D.N.Y. 1996); Harris v. L & L Wings, Inc., 132 F.3d 978 (4th Cir. 1997); Blakey v. Continental Airlines, Inc., 992 F. Supp. 731 (D.N.J. 1998); Wilson v. Susquehanna Township Police

Dep't, 55 F.3d 126 (3d Cir. 1995); Anjelino v. New York Times Co., 200 F.3d 73 (3d Cir. 1999).

15. Robinson v. Jacksonville Shipyards, Inc., 760 F. Supp. 1486, 1493–1496 (M. D. Fla. 1991).

16. *In Harm's Way*, above note 11, Minneapolis Hearings, at 121–124 (testimony of Ms. B.).

17. Robinson v. Jacksonville Shipyards, Inc., 760 F. Supp. 1486, 1524–1527.

18. Mimi H. Silbert and Ayala M. Pines, "Pornography and Sexual Abuse of Women," 10 *Sex Roles* 857, 861, 865 (1984).

19. The details of this account were provided at a press conference at the Minneapolis Hearings on July 25, 1984, by the young woman whose statement appears in *In Harm's Way*, above note 11, at 265.

20. *In Harm's Way*, above note 11, Minneapolis Hearings, at 108–112 (testimony of R.M.M.).

21. See Dworkin v. Hustler Magazine, Inc., No. CV 86–7768 AWT (C.D. Cal.), 669 F. Supp. 1408 (C. D. Cal. 1987), 867 F.2d 1188 (9th Cir. 1989).

22. See Susan Brownmiller, *Against Our Will: Men, Women, and Rape* (1975).

23. See Dworkin v. Hustler Magazine, Inc., No. CV 86–7768 AWT (C.D. Cal.), "Brief of Amici Curiae in Support of Plaintiff-Appellant," and attached Exhibits; "Hustler Interview: Gloria Steinem's Clit," *Hustler,* 27 (January); "Honey Hooker," *Hustler,* 138–142 (March 1984); "So Many Dykes So Little Time," *Hustler* (March 1984); Norman Jackson Smith, "Susan Brownmiller on Rape: 'Stop and I'll Scream!'" *Hustler,* 31–34, 102 (May 10, 1976).

24. This provision in The Instrument of Government ch. 2, art. 16 (1976:871), was translated into English in this way in *Constitutions of the World* (June 1985) when this talk was given. The Riksdag Web site has subsequently promulgated an official translation as follows: "No act of law or other provision may imply the unfavourable treatment of a citizen on grounds of gender, unless the provision forms part of efforts to promote equality between men and women" (16 § Lag eller annan föreskrift får ej innebära att någon medborgare missgynnas på grund av sitt kön, om ej föreskriften utgör led i strävanden att åstadkomma jämställdhet mellan män och kvinnor eller avser värnplikt eller motsvarande tjänsteplikt. Lag (1976:871)) *at* www.riksdagen.se/english/work/fundamental/government.asp. While this version has the merit of focusing on better and worse treatment, it leaves standing a sense of entitlement to the preferences of inequality by suggesting that efforts to promote equality between men and women, usually efforts that improve women's situation relative to men, amount to "unfavourable treatment" (usually of men) on grounds of gender. Excepting this from the main equality principle, rather than building into the equality principle per se the rectification of an unequal status quo, has the same drawbacks noted in the text.

25. Arne Borg, et al., *Prostitution: Beskrivning, analys, förslag till åtgärder* 42–48, especially 47–48 (1981). Many thanks to Max Waltman for his research and translation assistance on this document.

26. See generally id. at 344–421, especially 360–367, 411–412.

27. Id. at 591. For discussion of Swedish prostitution policy during this period, see id. at 93–102.

28. Sweden passed just such a law effective January 1999: "A person who obtains casual sexual relations in exchange for payment shall be sentenced—unless the act is punishable under the Swedish Penal Code—for the purchase of sexual services to a fine or imprisonment for at most six months." Act Prohibiting the Purchase of Sexual Services, SFS 1998:408. For an update, see National Board of Health and Welfare (Sweden), "Prostitution in Sweden, 2003: Knowledge, Beliefs and Attitudes of Key Informants," Artikelnr 2004-131-28 (Oct. 2004).

29. See "Making Sex Equality Real," above at No. 7.

30. Riksorganisationen för kvinnojourer i Sverigen, now the Riksorganisationen för kvinnojourer och tjejjourer i Sverigen (the National Organization for Women's Shelters and Young Women's Shelters in Sweden).

31. It passed. See the Equal Opportunities Act (Act on Equality Between Men and Women), SFS 1991:433, § 6.

32. Child pornography and defamation can be criminalized in the United States, consistent with free-speech guarantees, see New York v. Ferber, 458 U.S. 747 (1982), and New York Times v. Sullivan, 376 U.S. 254 (1964) respectively, but depictions of sexual violence are not as such illegal.

33. Indeed, the pornography ordinance itself was found to violate the free speech provision of the First Amendment to the U.S. Constitution, see American Booksellers Ass'n v. Hudnut, 771 F.2d 323 (7th Cir. 1985).

34. See Hanna Olsson, *Catrine och rättvisan* (1990), for a full account of Catrine da Costa's murder in 1984 and the trial of the two doctors accused of it. They were convicted of dismembering her body but not of causing her death.

11. Equality Remade: Violence Against Women

1. For a fuller discussion and documentation of this analysis, see Catharine A. MacKinnon, "Toward a New Theory of Equality," in *Women's Lives, Men's Laws* 44 (2005).

2. See, e.g., Dekker v. Stichting Vormingscentrum, [1991] 1 E.C.R. 3941 (noting "Article 2(3) of the Directive leaves to Member States the task of adopting appropriate provisions 'concerning the protection of women, particularly as regards pregnancy and maternity'. That provision appears to mark the limit of the intervention of Community law as it now stands. The directive enjoins strict equality of treatment between male and female workers, which in present circumstances means a prohibition on treating medical conditions attributable to maternity less favourably than conditions due to some other cause. It does not in any way oblige Member States to introduce positive discrimination by giving preferential treatment to the former category, but merely allows them to do so. I consider that the principle of equal treatment for male and female workers must mean a search for remedies to the problems specific to women to which pregnancy always gives rise. However, it is necessary to adjust the rules governing the

labour market only insofar as the risk attaching to maternity remains one of the 'normal' risks of life. It is, surely, in the duality of those two principles that the solution must lie. 'The principle of equal treatment for men and women as regards access to employment, vocational training and promotion, and working conditions must be interpreted as meaning that an employer's refusal to appoint a female worker on the ground that she is pregnant constitutes discrimination directly founded on grounds of sex [but] the dismissal of a female worker outside the periods of maternity leave, on account of periods of absence due to sickness which is attributable to the pregnancy or confinement does not constitute discrimination directly founded on grounds of sex."). See also Sonia Jackson et Patricia Cresswell v. Chief Adjudication Officer, [1992] I E.C.R. 4737 ("A good example of cases in which Community law expressly authorizes . . . positive discrimination on the part of the Member States is afforded by Article 2(3) of Directive 76/207 and Article 4(2) of Directive 79/7. According to those provisions, the directives are without prejudice to provisions concerning the protection of women, particularly as regards pregnancy and maternity (Directive 76/207) and on the grounds of maternity (Directive 79/7)."

3. See, e.g., Herbert Wechsler, "Toward Neutral Principles of Constitutional Law," 73 *Harvard Law Review* 1 (1959).

4. For discussion, see Catharine A. MacKinnon, *Sex Equality,* 35–38 (2001).

5. Plessy v. Ferguson, 163 U.S. 537 (1896).

6. See Georg Weippert, *Das Prinzip der Hierarchie* 29 (1932); Ulrich Scheuner, "Der Gleichheitsgedanke in der völkischen Verfassungsordnung," 99 *Zeitschrift für die gesamte Staatswissenschaft* 245, 260–267 (1939). For embrace of Aristotelian equality, see 3 BVerfGE 58, 135 (1954).

7. See, e.g., Michael M. v. Superior Court, 450 U.S. 464 (1981).

8. Revolutions—national revolutions, revolutions for cultural self-determination—sometimes have the important consequence of removing one layer of men that women are under. Often the promise of such revolutions is betrayed when the women find themselves subordinated to the men they fought to free.

9. See Radhika Coomaraswamy, *Report of the Special Rapporteur on Violence Against Women, Its Causes and Consequences,* U.N. ESCOR Hum. Rts. Comm'n, 52d Sess., Prov. Agenda Item 9(a) ¶¶ 62, U.N. Doc. E/CN.4/1996/53 (1996); Radhika Coomaraswamy, *Report,* U.N. ESCOR Hum. Rts. Comm'n, 53d Sess., Prov. Agenda Item 9(a) ¶¶ 22–23, U.N. Doc. E/CN.4/1997/47 (1997); and Radhika Coomaraswamy, *Preliminary Report of the Special Rapporteur on Violence Against Women, Its Causes and Consequences,* U.N. ESCOR Hum. Rts. Comm'n, 50th Sess., Prov. Agenda Item 11(a) ¶¶ 120–121, U.N. Doc. E/CN.4/1995/42 (1995).

10. Andrews v. Law Society of British Columbia, [1989] 1 S.C.R. 143.

11. Id. at 171 ("The promotion of equality entails the promotion of a society in which all are secure in the knowledge that they are recognized at law as human beings equally deserving of concern, respect and consideration. It has a large remedial component.").

12. Janzen v. Platy Enterprises, [1989] 1 S.C.R. 1252.

13. Cf. Bliss v. Canada, [1979] 1 S.C.R. 183 (pregnancy discrimination is not sex discrimination), with Brooks, Allen and Dixon v. Canada Safeway, [1989] 1 S.C.R. 1219 (pregnancy discrimination is sex discrimination).

14. Butler v. Regina, [1992] 1 S.C.R. 452.

15. Daigle v. Trembley, [1989] 2 S.C.R. 530.

16. Regina v. Sullivan and Lemay, [1991] 1 S.C.R. 489.

17. M. (K.) v. M. (H.), [1992] 3 S.C.R. 6.

18. Regina v. Lavallée, [1990] 1 S.C.R. 852.

19. Regina v. Canadian Newspapers Co., [1988] 2 S.C.R. 122.

20. Moge v. Moge, [1992] 3 S.C.R. 813.

21. Norberg v. Wynrib, [1992] 2 S.C.R. 226 and 2 S.C.R. 318.

22. The ordinances themselves can be found in *In Harm's Way: The Pornography Civil Rights Hearings* 426 (Catharine A. MacKinnon and Andrea Dworkin, eds., 1997).

12. Pornography's Empire

1. Regina v. Hicklin, L.R. 3 Q.B. 360 (1868).

2. This theme is elaborated more fully in Catharine A. MacKinnon, *Toward a Feminist Theory of the State* ch. 11 (1989).

3. The Indian Penal Code (1987) ch. XIV § 292(1) defines obscenity as that which is "lascivious or appeals to the prurient interest or, . . . the effect . . . if taken as a whole . . . tend[s] to deprave and corrupt persons who are likely, having regard to all relevant circumstances," to consume the material. There are exceptions at (2)(a) for materials proven to be "for the public good" on grounds that they are "in the interest of science, literature, art of learning or other objects of general concern," appear on an ancient monument, or are represented in or used on religious objects or for other bona fide religious purposes. Regina v. Hicklin, above note 1, not only formed the basis for § 292 but has also been approvingly cited numerous times by the Indian Supreme Court. See, e.g., Ranjit Udeshi v. State of Maharashtra, A.I.R. 1965 SC 881; Chandrakant Kalyandas Kakodkar v. The State of Maharashtra, A.I.R. 1970 SC 1390; K. A. Abbas v. Union of India, A.I.R. 1971 SC 481; Samresh Bose v. Amal Mitra, A.I.R. 1986 SC 967; Life Insurance Corporation of India v. Prof. Manubhai D. Shah, A.I.R. 1993 SC 171.

4. Each Australian state jurisdiction has statutes prohibiting the publication of obscene or indecent materials. A federal statute prohibits importation of goods that are obscene, indecent, or blasphemous, that unduly emphasize matters of sex, horror, violence, or crime, or that are likely to encourage depravity. See, e.g., Indecent Articles and Publications Act, 1975 (N.S.W.). "Indecency" is not defined, but a Supreme Court adjudication of "indecency" in a South Australia statute ruled that a book "of a sadistic nature" is indecent as an absolute matter, setting the community standard. Devine v. Solomijczuk and Todd, (1983) 9 A. Crim. R. 156. New South Wales also has a Publications Classification Board that rates materials in terms of legal standards, including "child pornography," resulting in restrictions on display or sale. See Police

Offenses Act V (1958) (Vic.) ("obscenity" defined as including "(a) tending to deprave and corrupt persons whose minds are open to immoral influences; and (b) unduly emphasizing matters of sex, crimes of violence, gross cruelty or horror"). Customs (Prohibited Imports) Regulations 4A (federal).

5. Miller v. United States, 413 U.S. 15 (1973), defines obscenity as that which "the average person, applying contemporary community standards," would find, taken as a whole, "appeals to the prurient interest, . . . depicts or describes in a patently offensive way sexual conduct specifically defined by the applicable state law; and . . . whether the work, taken as a whole, lacks serious literary, artistic, political or scientific value."

6. Criminal Code (Canada) §§ 159(1) and 159(2)(a) prohibit the production, distribution, and sale of obscene material. Section 159(8) deems obscene any publication "a dominant characteristic of which is the undue exploitation of sex, or of sex and any one or more of the following subjects, namely, crime, horror, cruelty and violence." They appear in the section of the code headed "Offenses Tending to Corrupt Morals." This language is considerably more conducive to a harms approach; see note 18 below discussing Butler v. Regina, [1992] 1 S.C.R. 452.

7. See Cha. 63, § 181(1)(a) (Kenya, 1985) (criminalizing "(1) Any person who (a) for the purpose of or by way of trade or for the purposes of distribution or public exhibition, makes, produces or has in his possession any one or more obscene" verbal or visual materials "or any other obscene objects or any other object tending to corrupt morals"). It also criminalizes any person who "(e) publicly exhibits any indecent show or performance or any show or performance tending to corrupt morals." As an indication of the problem, Muriithi Mwangi, *Aspects of Criminal Law in Kenya* 77 (1992), says that "[a]n obscene publication is one that displays indecent illustrations or communicates indecent literature" and that a publication will not be obscene "if what is in the publication is generally accepted by members of the society as modest. If most of the magazines on the streets display similar illustrations, the one complained about could not be obscene." For a further update, see "Kenya to Censor Porn," *BBC News* (Aug. 6, 2003) ("A censorship board has been set up in Kenya to deal with what the government says is a 'flood' of pornography in the country's electronic and print media"), *available at* news.bbc.co.uk/1/hi/world/africa/3126851.stm (last viewed Mar. 15, 2005).

8. Zambia Laws, Penal Code cha. 6 (1965), § 156(1), makes it a misdemeanor to make, distribute, or exhibit obscene materials "or any other object tending to corrupt morals." See also the same language in Botswana Penal Code (1968) § 177(1)(a).

9. Reuters reported in 1983 that official censors in Asia from Islamabad to Singapore are "in a quandary as the video craze spreads rapidly through Asia, which zealously attempts to guard its traditional cultural and moral values against creeping Western influence." Nonetheless, "crime syndicates producing pornographic films are cashing in on the video boom." Singapore, it is said, has strict censorship laws. Foreign and Culture Minister Suppiah Dhanabalan said, "If our people are not to be blown hither and thither by every new fad they must have deep convictions of wholesome time-

tested values." Francis Daniel, *Reuters* (Sept. 24, 1983). In Kenya, President Daniel Arap Moi was quoted as saying, in the context of a crackdown on imported pornographic magazines, that Kenyans "should stick to their own cultural values and copy only what is good for us." He reportedly said that "the country's traditional African values were being undermined by such publications." *Reuters* (Feb. 11, 1984). In addition, "in Swaziland, sex on screen is taboo because of cultural taboos. Wellington Sukati, head of programming at the Swaziland TV and Broadcasting Corp., said, 'We don't like nudity at all. We shy away from it. You may breast-feed in public, but the exploitation of nudity on the screen is out.'" "Sex, Nudity and Politics Viewed as Taboo: Africans Gingerly Sift Through U.S. TV Selections," *Los Angeles Times,* 3 (Mar. 1, 1988). Dr. Philista Onyango of the University of Nairobi said, in the context of a discussion of pornography, "The infiltration of Western Culture, with its decadent values, into our society is so great that the best of our traditional values have now been completely submerged," with the result that young people are exposed to sex "far too early." Francis Makokha, "Kenya: Teenage Pregnancies on the Rise," *Inter Press Service* (Sept. 14, 1987).

10. "The puritanical white Afrikaners who rule South Africa are trying to secure their national survival by means of a political system that is heavily dependent on gambling and pornography. . . . A government censorship board scrutinizes every imported or locally produced book, magazine . . . banning all traces of lasciviousness. . . . Yet 150 miles from Johannesburg is one of the world's most extravagant fleshpots: Sun City," which is full of pornographic movies. "Because Sun City is in a 'homeland,' the result of the government's policy of granting nominal independence to tribal groups, it is officially outside South Africa. The policy would ensure the continued dominance of the Afrikaners by eventually making whites the legal majority. For this to work, the 'homelands,' which are 'hopelessly unviable economically,' must survive. The pornography trade helps fill that gap." Allister Sparks, "Las Vegas Aura Thrives in Puritanical S. Africa's Black Homelands," *Washington Post,* 7 (Jan. 4, 1983). This trend continued after the overthrow of the apartheid regime. See Judith Matloff, "As Porn Proliferates, S. Africa Debates Free Speech," *Christian Science Monitor,* 5 (Aug. 8, 1997) ("In the bad old days of apartheid, Calvinist puritanism coupled with political repression spelled strict control in South Africa. Films and books were censored for subversive as well as sexual material. Even a hint of nudity was banned on television. . . . That's all changed in the three years since the end of apartheid. Since Nelson Mandela assumed the presidency in 1994 and vowed to uphold personal freedoms, sex shops have swamped the cities. Today, it is just as easy to buy Penthouse magazine as it is a pack of chewing gum. This new permissiveness has given birth to an uncomfortable debate here. . . . The new government, trying to make everyone happy, is struggling to find a balance between freedom of expression and social control.").

11. Examples include Ghana: "The association of weekly newspapers of Ghana has announced that it will apply sanctions against any weekly newspaper which indulges in the publication of obscenities and pornography." "Obscenity Ban on Ghana's Private Papers," *The Xinhua General Overseas News Service* (Feb. 3, 1989). Kenya: "President Daniel Arap Moi has banned the importation into Kenya of obscene or pornographic

magazines, books and video tapes . . . to protect 'the minds of our youth.'" *Foreign News Briefs* (Feb. 7, 1984). "The Kenyan government has banned nearly 200 porno-graphic films, many of which have been circulating through video libraries in the country." "Kenya Bans Scores of Pornographic Films," *Reuters* (Aug. 6, 1988). India: "Dozens of policemen swept through the capital's movie theaters last week, pulling down movie posters showing semi-nude women and sexually explicit scenes, to show the authorities' determination to enforce a new law on obscenity." Sanjoy Hazarika, "India Is Battling Pornographic Movie Posters," *The New York Times,* 5 (Nov. 1, 1987). This has continued to be the case since this speech was written. "It is worthwhile to note here that the sale, distribution, circulation etc. of 'obscene' materials is banned under Section 292 of the Indian Penal Code, but still they are in the market and selling like hot cakes. Palika Bazaar and Nehru Place market, both situated in the heart of [New Delhi], are hotspots for porn lovers. Though this is a known fact, nothing much has come about from banning the sale of such stuff. One can get the latest and most explicit pieces of pornography here, that too at dirt-cheap rates." "Picking Your Porn, No Great Shakes in Delhi," *Hindustan Times* (Dec. 21, 2004). Moreover, law enforce-ment has not been able to address the emergence of Indian Internet pornography; see Kanika Gahlaut et al., "India porn.com," *India Today,* 60 (Nov. 8, 2004) ("There is very little that the police can do to check this new image of Indian womanhood available for download worldwide for just $3.95 (Rs 180) per month. 'We are very concerned but there are legal and technological limitations,' says Anami Roy, commissioner of police, Mumbai."). Bangladesh: "When the video craze began, the police used to raid places exhibiting pornography, but such raids no longer take place." Tabibul Islam, "Bangladesh: Caught in a Video Whirl," *Inter Press Service* (Dec. 2, 1988).

12. "In several cities and towns, women are marching along the roads with brooms and pails of paint or mud and blacking out posters of semi-nude women selling every-thing from cars to cigarettes . . . It was demonstrations such as these that forced the government last year to pass an act banning 'indecent' advertisements." Sheela Reddy, "India: War on Obscene Posters Is On Again," *Inter Press Service* (Apr. 22, 1987).

13. For example, "'We draw about $250 million a year in retail sales just from our Playmate apparel,' [Christie Hefner] says. Korea, Thailand, India, China, Hong Kong, Japan, Australia, Brazil, and the 'pan-European 1992 market' she describes as growth areas for Playboy video distribution and leisure sales. She is also developing the Playboy Channel for the home market and foreign syndication." Victor Olliver, "Christie Hefner: Her Purpose Is Clear and So Is Her Conscience," *Chicago Tribune,* C1 (Jan. 7, 1990).

14. For example, in Cincinnati, Ohio, pornography is effectively prosecuted and zoned out of town, so men simply go out of the city limits to get it, and all the harms other than those from local public display are still done. This is not an effective ap-proach to the harm.

15. "Although Kenya banned pornographic literature three years ago, a thriving black market for the materials still exists and sex videos are easily available in the country." Makokha, above note 9.

16. New York v. Ferber, 458 U.S. 747 (1982).

17. The Indecent Representation of Women (Prohibition) Act, 1986, Gazette of India Extraordinary, pt. II, § 1, No. 74, 2(c).

18. Regina v. Doug Rankine Co., [1983] 9 C.C.C. (3d) 53 (Ont. Co. Ct.); Regina v. Wagner, [1985] unreported (Alta. Q.B.); Regina v. Ramsingh, [1984] 14 C.C.C. (3d) 230 (Man. Q.B.). This tendency later crystallized in the ruling in Butler v. Regina, [1992] 1 S.C.R. 452, 479 (Can.), where the Court ruled that pornography "results in harm, particularly to women and therefore to society as a whole." In addition to applying to violent materials, the Court's opinion found that "degrading and dehumanizing" materials can be prohibited because they "place women (and sometimes men) in positions of subordination, servile submission or humiliation. They run against the principles of equality and dignity of all human beings." Id.

19. An example is the film *Deep Throat.* See Linda Lovelace and Michael McGrady, *Ordeal* (1980). *Deep Throat* is sold worldwide.

20. For example, a staff report to the Attorney General's Commission on Pornography (1986) asserts that unspecified cable pornography services and their distributors "are heavily involved with or connected to organized crime," since it is the "source of their films." The report also charges that companies including CBS, Time, Inc., RCA, and Coca-Cola are involved in pornography, saying that the last two have a joint agreement "to distribute porn films in Australia" through their subsidiary Columbia Pictures. "Organized Crime Link Claimed," *Television Digest, Inc., Communications Daily* (Mar. 3, 1986).

21. Since the United States adopted more effective controls on child pornography, based on the view that child pornography is child abuse, most child pornography is produced, often with Third World children, in Scandinavia. See Eva Ahlberg, "Sweden, Stung by U.S. Accusations, Attacks Secret Mail Trade in Child Pornography," *Los Angeles Times,* 17 (Dec. 25, 1988) ("'I would rank Sweden among the top source countries,' Donald Grattan, chief of the Child Pornography and Protection Unit of the U.S. Customs Service in Washington, said."). See also "Sweden-Children: Government to Act Against Pornography Racket," *Inter Press Service* (Jan. 19, 1994) ("The Swedish government will ban child pornography following claims by U.S. Customs that Scandinavia is the world's leading exporter of the material."). Although the effectiveness of this law recognizing the abusiveness of production to children is not known, some observers have speculated that because of it, the United States went from the world's largest exporter of child pornography to the world's largest importer.

22. There is voluminous evidence from the UN and other authorities documenting buying and selling of children for sex. Several note the connection with the child pornography trade. See Convention on the Rights of the Child, Nov. 20, 1989, art. 34, G.A. Res. 44/25, Annex, U.N. GAOR, 44th Sess., Supp. No. 49, at 167, U.N. Doc. A/44/49 (1989) ("States Parties undertake to protect the child from all forms of sexual exploitation and sexual abuse. For these purposes, States Parties shall in particular take all appropriate national, bilateral and multilateral measures to prevent: (a) The inducement or coercion of a child to engage in any unlawful sexual activity; (b) The exploitative use of children in prostitution or other unlawful sexual practices; (c) The exploit-

ative use of children in pornographic performances and materials"). See also Optional Protocol to the Convention on the Rights of the Child on the Sale of Children, Child Prostitution, and Child Pornography, May 25, 2000, G.A. Res. 54/263, Annex II, U.N. GAOR, 54th Sess., Supp. No. 49, at 6, U.N. Doc. A/54/49, vol. 3 (2000). Additionally, the United States has entered into some bilateral agreements to facilitate extradition of U.S. citizens committing crimes abroad, including child pornographers. See Agreement for the Surrender of Fugitive Offenders, Dec. 20, 1996, Hong Kong-United States, 36 *International Legal Materials* 842, 849 (1997); Agreement on Cooperation in Criminal Law Matters, with Annex, June 30, 1995, United States-Russia, *available at* 1995 WL 831037 (Treaty); Treaty on Mutual Legal Assistance in Criminal Matters, Nov. 23, 1993, United States-South Korea, *available at* 1993 WL 796842 (Treaty). Although those who work in this area have many reports on the connections between prostitution and pornography of adult women, not even the UN, which has done substantial work on prostitution as an international form of slavery, has noticed that the pornography of adult women is also a form of slavery. See generally Kathleen Barry, *Female Sexual Slavery* (1979); J. Fernand-Laurent, *Report of the Special Rapporteur on the Suppression of the Traffic in Persons and the Exploitation of the Prostitution of Others,* U.N. ESCOR (1st reg. sess.) (Agenda Item 12), U.N. Doc. E/1983/7 (1983), reprinted in *International Feminism: Networking Against Female Sexual Slavery* app. 6 at 131 (Kathleen Barry et al., eds., 1984).

23. This information is from sources familiar with the industry there, which also report that Australian organized crime activity, including pornography, is centered in Hong Kong. Much pornography is reputed to enter Africa through Kuwait.

24. Reported evidence is fragmentary: One French man was charged in Uganda with having pornographic photographs and videotapes showing naked Ugandan women. He was ordered to leave immediately and the material was to have been destroyed by the government. "Uganda Orders Frenchman to Leave Country," *Reuters* (Apr. 25, 1989).

25. See, e.g., Frank Rich, "Naked Capitalists," *New York Times Magazine,* 51 (May 20, 2001) ("[T]he porn business is estimated to total between $10 billion and $14 billion annually in the United States."). For international figures to the date of this volume, see below No. 24n.1.

26. Andrea Dworkin and I discuss these issues, and those in the paragraphs following, in our *Pornography and Civil Rights: A New Day for Women's Equality* (1988).

27. *Public Hearings on Ordinances to Add Pornography as Discrimination Against Women,* Committee on Government Operations, City Council, Dec. 12 and 13, 1983 (Minneapolis, Minn.). The hearings were published in *In Harm's Way: The Pornography Civil Rights Hearings* (Catharine A. MacKinnon and Andrea Dworkin, eds., 1997).

28. This account of the research results is drawn from an agreed statement by major researchers as reported in Michael McManus, Introduction, *Final Report of Attorney General's Commission on Pornography* xviii (1986). Research since then has only extended and strengthened these conclusions.

29. The model definition is as follows: "1. 'Pornography' means the graphic sexually

explicit subordination of women through pictures and/or words that also includes one or more of the following: (a) women are presented dehumanized as sexual objects, things, or commodities; or (b) women are presented as sexual objects who enjoy humiliation or pain; or (c) women are presented as sexual objects experiencing sexual pleasure in rape, incest, or other sexual assault; or (d) women are presented as sexual objects tied up or cut up or mutilated or bruised or physically hurt; or (e) women are presented in postures or positions of sexual submission, servility, or display; or (f) women's body parts–including but not limited to vaginas, breasts, or buttocks–are exhibited such that women are reduced to those parts; or (g) women are presented being penetrated by objects or animals; or (h) women are presented in scenarios of degradation, humiliation, injury, torture, shown as filthy or inferior, bleeding, bruised or hurt in a context that makes these conditions sexual. 2. The use of men, children, or transsexuals in the place of women in (1) (a–h) above is pornography for purposes of this law." For various versions of the ordinance, see *In Harm's Way,* above note 27, at 446 and following.

30. Attorney General's Commission on Pornography, *Final Report* (U.S. Department of Justice, 1986) ("Recommendation 87: Legislatures should conduct hearings and consider legislation recognizing a civil remedy for harm attributable to pornography," at 747. "Pornography, in effect, exemplifies inequality in its violation of human rights," at 748). See generally 747–756.

31. *Pornography and Prostitution in Canada,* Report of the Special Committee on Pornography and Prostitution (vol. 1) (Feb. 1985) (the Fraser Commission), ch. 24, 305–315 ("We recommend that jurisdictions enact by legislation a civil cause of action focusing on the violation of civil rights inherent in pornography," at 313).

32. *Pornography: Report of the Ministerial Committee of Inquiry* (1989) states, "We do not deny that the ordinance is a brilliant strategy for expunging pornography from the face of any society that might adopt it," at 152. The inquiry recommended a modified version of the ordinance centered on the individual harms (at 153), noting concern that the commissions that administer human rights laws might not be equipped to handle trafficking complaints. The answer, of course, is to equip them to do so and to consider offering survivors direct access to court in addition. The inquiry also said that the ordinance "hit too hard at too small a target" (at 152). Its preference for addressing instead "the underlying injustice" was not illuminated by an analysis of what the injustice underlying pornography is, and why it is not addressed by addressing the pornography. One is also left wondering how a law that hits at the entire spectrum of pornography hits too small a target. Does rape law hit too small a target because it does not also hit sexual abuse of children and sexual harassment? Does employment discrimination law hit too small a target because it does not address discrimination in the housing or education? If this law hit materials that were not pornography, one suspects that it would be said to be too broad. Is it perhaps the law's effectiveness that is considered hitting "too hard"? In connection with these evasions by the inquiry, it should be noted that the pressures to protect the traffickers in pornography is substantial and is supported by consumers, for whom access to the materials is the bottom

line. Confining the law to addressing individual harms after they happen, as the inquiry's version would do, concedes and guarantees that they will continue to happen in a world in which the pornography continues to exist with legal impunity.

33. The civil rights ordinance was passed twice in Minneapolis by the city council and vetoed twice by the mayor, once in Indianapolis, where it was signed into law, and once in Bellingham, Washington, by referendum, where it received 62 percent of the vote.

34. American Booksellers Ass'n v. Hudnut, 771 F.2d 323 (7th Cir. 1985), summarily affirmed, 475 U.S. 1001 (1986) (civil rights law against pornography found to violate First Amendment to the U.S. Constitution).

35. Andrea Dworkin, "Against the Male Flood: Censorship, Pornography, and Equality," in *Letters from a War Zone* 274 (1988).

13. Sex Equality Under the Constitution of India: Problems, Prospects, and "Personal Laws"

1. This language is a long-standing interpretation of Aristotle, *Ethica Nicomachea*, v.3 1131a–1131b, 112–117 (J. L. Ackrill and J. O. Urmson, eds., W. Ross, trans., 1980), and Aristotle, *The Politics* 307 (Benjamin Jowett, trans., 1943) ("[e]quality consists in the same treatment of similar persons").

2. See Catharine A. MacKinnon, *Sex Equality* 43–50 (traced in international law), 35–38 (traced in European Union law), 12–17 and passim (traced in United States Equal Protection doctrine) (2001) [hereinafter *Sex Equality*].

3. E. P. Royappa v. State of Tamil Nadu, 1974 A.I.R. S.C. 555; Shri Ram Krishna Dalmia v. Shri Justice S. R. Tendolkar, (1959) S.C.R. 279.

4. For attempts to bridge the sameness-difference divide within the theoretical confines of mainstream equality theory, see generally Michel Rosenfeld, *Affirmative Action and Justice* (1991).

5. See *Sex Equality*, above note 2, at 4–11.

6. For documentation and analysis, see id. at 179–195.

7. For documentation and analysis, see id. at 247–252, 385–428.

8. See Plessy v. Ferguson, 163 U.S. 537 (1896).

9. See Georg Weippert, *Das Prinzip der Hierarchie* 29 (1932); Ulrich Scheuner, "Der Gleichheitsgedanke in der völkischen Verfassungsordnung," 99 *Zeitschrift für die gesamte Staatswissenschaft* 245, 260–267 (1939). For further discussion and documentation, see *Sex Equality*, above note 2, at 8–9.

10. This goes a long way toward explaining the substantial predominance of men among successful sex equality plaintiffs in foundational U.S. sex equality cases under the Constitution.

11. Mahadeb Jiew v. B. B. Sen, 1951 A.I.R. 38 (Cal.) 563, 569.

12. See Andrews v. Law Society of British Columbia, [1989] 1 S.C.R. 143.

13. See, e.g., Prosecutor v. Akayesu, Case No. ICTR 96-4-T (Sept. 2, 1998).

14. See, e.g., Meritor Savings Bank v. Vinson, 477 U.S. 57 (1986).

15. For this history, see Catharine A. MacKinnon, "The Logic of Experience: Reflections on the Development of Sexual Harassment Law," 90 *Georgetown Law Journal* 813 (2002).

16. Other examples include the concept of rape as genocide in Kadic v. Karadžić, 70 F.3d 232 (2d Cir. 1995), and *Akayesu,* above note 13, as well as the critique of pornography developed in the United States through the experiences of women subjected to injury through it, some dimensions of which have been recognized by the Supreme Court of Canada, see Butler v. Regina, [1992] 1 S.C.R. 452, and Little Sisters Book and Art Emporium v. Canada, [2000] 2 S.C.R. 1120.

17. Lakhman Dass v. State of Punjab, 1963 A.I.R., S.C. 222, 240 (Rao, J., dissenting) ("Over-emphasis on the doctrine of classification, or an anxious and sustained attempt to discover some basis for classification, may gradually and imperceptibly deprive the [equality] article of its glorious content. That process would inevitably end in substituting the doctrine of classification for the doctrine of equality: the fundamental right to equality before the law and equal protection of the laws may be replaced by the doctrine of classification."). This was quoted with approval by Justice Krishna Iyer in Col. A. S. Iyer v. Balasubramanyam, (1980) 1 S.C.C. 634, 659.

18. E. P. Royappa v. State of Tamil Nadu, 1974 A.I.R., S.C. 555, 583.

19. See Indra Sawhney v. Union of India, 1992 Supplementary (3) S.C.C. 217; Indra Sawhney v. Union of India, (1995) 5 S.C.C. 429; Indra Sawhney v. Union of India, (1996) 6 S.C.C. 506; Ev Chinnaiah v. State of Andhra Pradesh and Ors, (2004) 4 L.R.I. 705, ¶ 82 ("Our Constitution permits application of equality clause by grant of additional protection to the disadvantaged class so as to bring them on equal platform with other advantaged class of people.")

20. See Dattatraya Motiram More v. State of Bombay, 1953 A.I.R. (Bom.) 311, 55 Bom. L.R. 323 (1953); Government of Andhra Pradesh v. P. B. Vijaykumar, A.I.R. 1995 S.C. 1648. Reservations are what in the United States are termed quotas and affirmative action.

21. Dattatraya Motiram More v. State of Bombay, above note 20. Thamsi Goundan v. Kanni Ammad, A.I.R. 1952 Madras 529, 530 (1952) Madras L.J.R. 68, 69 (order of maintenance to wife by husband only, valid under Article 14 because "women . . . suffer from several disabilities from which men do not suffer."). Despite the sometimes positive outcomes, the language of inferiority is often problematic in these cases, and is not abating. See, e.g., as to caste: "The aim of the Constitution is to equip each member of the weaker sections with the ability to compete with other citizens with dignity on a level playing field. The pitiable condition of scheduled castes is recognized by the Constitution as a national problem." Ev Chinnaiah v. State of Andhra Pradesh and Ors, (2004) 4 L.R.I. 705, ¶ 89; as to sex: "There can be a classification between men and women for certain posts [here a woman as principal of a woman's college, so that] young fallible students may not be subjected to any sort of exploitation." Vijay Lakshmi v. Punjab University & Ors, (2003) 4 L.R.I. 1.

22. Vishaka v. State of Rajasthan, A.I.R. 1997 S.C. 3011.

23. Apparel Export Promotion Council v. A. K. Chopra, (1999) 1 S.C.C. 759.

24. One strong example is the decision by Chinnappa Reddy in Randhir Singh v. Union of India, (1982) 1 S.C.C. 618, granting substantive equal pay for equal work to the drivers for the Delhi police, referring to Article 39(d).

25. See, e.g., MacKinnon MacKenzie & Co. v. Audrey D'Costa, (1987) 2 S.C.C. 469 (requiring equal pay for similar work).

26. Gaurav Jain v. Union of India, (1997) 8 S.C.C. 114, 121, 133. See also Vishal Jeet v. Union of India, (1990) 3 S.C.C. 318.

27. See the examples discussed by Indira Jaising, "Gender Justice and the Supreme Court," in *Supreme but Not Infallible: Essays in Honour of the Supreme Court of India* 288, 306–309 (B. N. Kirpal et al., eds., 2000). At times, the antihierarchical outcomes wrongly lean on biological differences for their rationale.

28. This would address the problem noted by Jaising that "the theoretical problematic of 'equality' enshrined in Article 14 has not been satisfactorily resolved by the Court. In particular, the interrelationship between Article 15 and 15(3) has never been addressed. Article 15(3) has been marginalized and almost relegated to the position of a non-justiciable directive principle." Id. at 315.

29. For a discussion of this point in the caste context, see Indra Sawhney v. Union of India, A.I.R. 1993 S.C. 477.

30. See Nalini Ranjan Singh v. State, A.I.R. 1977 Pat. 171, 179.

31. See Mahadeb Jiew v. B. B. Sen, 1951 A.I.R. 38 (Cal.) 563, 567–569, holding that sex-plus-property discrimination was not sex "alone," hence not prohibited. As noted by Indira Jaising, "[S]ex is intrinsically gendered and socially conditioned. . . . [S]ubstantive equality would sustain discrimination based on the sex plus gendered aspect of sex if the object of such action is to minimize the sex inequality." Jaising, above note 27, at 297. Most discrimination against women is not sex "alone" if sex in the biological sense is distinguished from gender, its social form.

32. Tukaram v. State of Maharashtra, (1979) 2 S.C.C. 143. The same would be true of the Suman Rani rape case, Premchand v. State of Haryana, (1989) Supp. 1 S.C.C. 286, in which the Supreme Court relied on rape myths concerning the alleged easy virtue of a young woman to reduce a mandatory minimum sentence imposed on two policemen found to have raped her. Other cases show a far more progressive approach to rape by the Supreme Court of India. However, none of them grasps that it is, legally, a practice of sex inequality of constitutional dimension. The Court's recent rape jurisprudence, which ranges from abysmal to quite good, would be regularized by such a recognition. Compare, e.g., Mohan Lal v. State of Rajasthan, (2002) 4 L.R.I. 935 (disbelieving woman's account), State of Rajasthan v. Kishanlal, (2002) 2 L.R.I. 547 (disbelieving woman did not consent, terming prosecutrix and defendant perhaps "quite intimate" because he offered to pay her 20 rupees for having sexual intercourse with him) and Bantu and Naresh Giri v. State of Madhya Pradesh, (2001) 4 L.R.I. 822 (commuting death sentence for rape murder of a six-year-old girl because facts are insufficiently rare) with State of Orissa v. Thakara Besra and Anor, (2002) 2 L.R.I. 537 (finding it most unlikely the victim would injure her private parts only to falsely implicate the accused) and Malkhansingh and Ors v. State of Madhya Pradesh, (2003) 3

L.R.I. 229 (upholding conviction where victim identified appellants for the first time in court). The Court's repeated use of rape myths and stereotypes such as the woman of easy virtue said to be habituated to sexual intercourse and the requirement of imminent outcry or proximate reporting (well-criticized in State of Himachal Pradesh v. Gian Chand, (2001) 2 L.R.I. 1416) would be reduced if an understanding of rape as an act of sex inequality was adopted.

33. C. B. Muthamma v. Union of India, A.I.R. 1979 S.C. 1868, 1869.

34. Narashimaha Murthy v. Susheelabai (Smt), (1996) 3 S.C.C. 644 (upholding sex-differential statutory coparcenary division).

35. Githa Hariharan v. Reserve Bank of India, A.I.R. 1999 S.C. 1149, 1150.

36. Indian Divorce Act, 1869 (4 of 1869), § 10. For analysis, see National Alliance of Women (NAWO), *Alternative NGO Report on CEDAW: India* (2000). This provision was changed in Indian Divorce (Amend.) Act, 2001 (51 of 2001), Substitution of new section for section 10, Insertion of new section 10A.

37. See the most recent edition of Mulla's *Principles of Mahomedan Law* (M. Hidayatullah and Arshad Hidayatullah, eds., 1906). For further recent changes, see Alka Singh, *Women in Muslim Personal Law* (1992); Ramala M. Baxamusa, *The Legal Status of Muslim Women: An Appraisal of Muslim Personal Law in India* (Meera Kosambi, ed., 1998).

38. Mohd. Ahmed Khan v. Shah Bano Begum, A.I.R. 1985 S.C. 945.

39. Danial Latifi v. Union of India, (2001) 7 S.C.C. 70.

40. This is also a fault of many Canadian decisions in which women prevail in outcome but the Supreme Court of Canada refuses to predicate their victories on sex equality principles that would solidify and extend rights and raise their legal status. Examples are Regina v. Canadian Newspapers, [1988] 2 S.C.R. 122, and Regina v. Lavallée, [1990] 1 S.C.R. 852. In both cases, women's equality in substance was affirmed and considerably strengthened by the results of the rulings, but the doctrinal recognition of equality rights as the basis for the ruling was not commensurate.

41. Sarla Mugdal v. Union of India, (1995) 3 S.C.C. 635.

42. Madhu Kishwar v. State of Bihar, (1996) 5 S.C.C. 125, 127.

43. See Mary Ann Glendon, *A World Made New: Eleanor Roosevelt and the Universal Declaration of Human Rights* 90, 111 (2001), for an evocative history of this process.

44. For further discussion of this dynamic, see Catharine A. MacKinnon, "Whose Culture? A Case Note on *Martinez v. Santa Clara Pueblo*," in *Feminism Unmodified* 63 (1987).

45. One British piece of advocacy on the question leaves no room for doubt on the outrageous condescension and opportunism involved. See 135 *The Westminster Review,* "Child Marriage in India," 113 (Jan.–June 1891). News reports provide the basic events. *The New York Times* 3 (Feb. 16, 1891); *The New York Times* 5 (Jan. 11, 1891); *The New York Times* 28 (Sept. 26, 1929); *The New York Times* 7 (Aug. 9, 1930) (reporting that "effective in British India June 1, the minimum marriageable age for girls was set at 14 and that for boys at 18.").

46. See, e.g., World Health Organization, *World Report on Violence and Health* (Etienne G. Krug et al., eds., Geneva 2002); Radhika Coomaraswamy, *Report Submitted by the Special Rapporteur on Violence Against Women, Its Causes and Consequences,* Commission on Human Rights, 50th Sess., Agenda Item 11(a), U.N. Doc. E/CN.4/1995/42 (1995).

47. Examples are Orr v. Orr, 440 U.S. 268 (1979); Kirchberg v. Feenstra, 450 U.S. 455 (1981); Palmore v. Sidoti, 466 U.S. 429 (1984). A partial exception is Nevada Department of Human Services v. Hibbs, 123 S.Ct. 1972 (2003), which upholds the Family and Medical Leave Act as a remedy for sex stereotyping in granting family leave by employers.

48. For documentation and analysis, see *Sex Equality,* above note 2, at 684–714.

49. See id. at 684–705 for documentation and analysis.

50. Danial Latifi v. Union of India, (2001) 7 S.C.C. 740, 742–743.

51. Examples are Corne v. Bausch & Lomb Inc., 390 F. Supp. 161, 163 (D. Ariz. 1975) (finding the sexual harassment alleged "nothing more than a personal proclivity, peculiarity, or mannerism"); Barnes v. Train, 13 Fair Empl. Prac. Cas. (BNA) 123, 124 (D.D.C. 1974) (holding regarding allegations of sexual harassment, "[t]his is a controversy underpinned by the subtleties of an inharmonious personal relationship").

52. See Meritor Savings Bank v. Vinson, 477 U.S. 57 (1986).

53. C. Masilamani Mudaliar v. Idol of Sri Swaminathaswami Thirukoli, (1996) 8 S.C.C. 525, 533.

54. State of Bombay v. Narasu Appa Mali, 1952 A.I.R. 39 (Bom.) at 95, 53 Bom. L.R. at 779.

55. Id.

56. Examples include Hicks v. Gates Rubber Co., 833 F.2d 1406 (10th Cir. 1987); Anthony v. County of Sacramento, 898 F. Supp. 1435 (E.D. Cal. 1995); Torres v. Pisano, 116 F.3d 625 (2d Cir. 1997); Watkins v. Bowden, 105 F.3d 1344 (11th Cir. 1997).

57. See Catharine A. MacKinnon, *Sexual Harassment of Working Women: A Case of Sex Discrimination* 57–99 (1979).

58. India Constitution art. 44 (pt. IV, Directive Principles).

59. This approach is consistent with the caution that "[a] uniform law, though is highly desirable, enactment thereof in one go perhaps may be counter-productive to unity and integrity of the nation. . . . It would . . . be inexpedient and incorrect to think that all laws have to be made uniformly applicable to all people in one go. The mischief or defect which is most acute can be remedied by process of law at stages." Pannalal Bansilal Pitti v. State of A. P., (1996) 2 S.C.C. 498, 510.

60. Madhu Kishwar v. State of Bihar, (1996) 5 S.C.C. 125, 134–135. A similar view was reiterated in Ahmedabad Women's Action Group v. Union of India, (1997) 3 S.C.C. 573, 583. It might also be noted that the equality principle is constitutionally enshrined, and judges are called to apply the Constitution, however difficult and mind-boggling.

61. Speaking generally, *iddat* is a waiting period after dissolution of marriage, gen-

erally three menstrual cycles. The purpose is to learn whether the wife is pregnant (a child born during iddat is considered the husband's), to provide for reconciliation if possible, or for widows to mourn. It varies in particulars from country to country. If the woman is pregnant, for example, the iddat may last until the birth of the baby, four months plus ten days or birth whichever is longer, ten months, or one year. In some countries, another marriage ends the iddat. Maintenance is generally available to the wife following a revocable divorce or, if pregnant, after an irrevocable divorce. Revocability turns on the nature of the breakdown. See Jamal J. Nasir, ed., *The Islamic Law of Personal Status*, 137–142 (3d. ed., Kluwen International, 2000).

62. The Canadian case of Moge v. Moge, [1992] 3 S.C.R. 813, provides an example of the principle of equitable sharing after breakdown of marriage in a context of recognized social inequality of the sexes. The case also serves to illustrate the creation of equality-promoting concepts in settings where the sex inequality is traditionally extreme and there are virtually no similarly situated men with whom to compare.

63. Convention on the Elimination of All Forms of Discrimination Against Women, Dec. 18, 1979, 1249 U.N.T.S. 13, 129 ("With regard to articles 5(a) and 16(1) of [CEDAW] declares that it shall abide by and ensure these provisions in conformity with its policy of non-interference in the personal affairs of any Community without its initiative and consent.").

64. For India's report on its compliance with CEDAW to date, see *Consideration of Reports Submitted by States Parties Under Article 18 of the Convention on the Elimination of All Forms of Discrimination Against Women, Initial Reports of States Parties: India,* U.N. Doc. CEDAW/C/IND/1 (1999). For CEDAW's concluding observations, see *Report of the Committee on the Elimination of Discrimination against Women,* 22nd Sess. (17 Jan.–4 Feb. 2000) and 23rd Sess. (12–30 June 2000), Supp. No. 38 (A/55/ 38), 9–12. The Committee, in addition to urgung India to withdraw its declaration to article 16, paragraph 1 of the Convention, also "calls upon the Government to follow the directive pronciples in the Constitution and the Supreme Court decisions and enact a uniform civil code that different ethnic and religious groups may adopt." ¶ 61.

65. An example would be Danial Latifi v. Union of India, (2001) 7 S.C.C. 740 as well as *Shah Bano* itself.

66. In the United States, Califano v. Westcott, 443 U.S. 76 (1979), expressly acknowledged this possibility, as Schachter v. Canada, [1992] 2 S.C.R. 679, did in Canada.

14. Crimes of War, Crimes of Peace

1. Oliver Wendell Holmes, *The Common Law* 1 (1881) ("The life of the law has not been logic, it has been experience.").

2. See Center for Women's Global Leadership, *1991 Women's Leadership Institute Report: Women, Violence, and Human Rights* (1992), Appendix C, "Statistics on Gender Violence Globally," at 77–80.

3. For a discussion of the killing of women as a systematic practice, see *Femicide: The Politics of Woman Killing* (Jill Radford and Diana E. H. Russell, eds., 1992).

4. For the most advanced of Amnesty's efforts to the date of this lecture, see Amnesty International, *Rape and Sexual Abuse: Torture and Ill Treatment of Women in Detention* (1993). The advance is that rape is noticed; the limitation remains that it is noticed only when women are in official custody thus in effect raped by a state.

5. [Name Withheld], Letter to author, Oct. 13, 1992. Most of this information has since been independently corroborated by international reports and published accounts. See *Mass Killing and Genocide in Croatia 1991/92: A Book of Evidence* (1992) (documenting genocide); *Human Rights Watch Report* (Aug. 1992) ("A policy of 'ethnic cleansing' has resulted in the summary execution, disappearance, arbitrary detention, deportation, and forcible displacement of hundreds of thousands of people on the basis of their religion or nationality"); Carl Gustaf Strohm, "Serben vergewaltigen auf obersten Befehl," *Die Welt* (Oct. 1, 1992) (30,000 women pregnant from rape; *Večernji List* (Sept. 11, 1992) (documenting 20 rape/death camps for non-Serb women); Ibrahim Kajan, *Muslimanski Danak U Krvi, Svjedočanstva zločina nad Muslimanima* (1992) (genocide of Muslims and rape camps documented); Women's Group "Treşnjevka," *Report* (Zagreb, Sept. 28, 1992) ("The existence of rape/death camps must be understood as a . . . tactic of genocide, of a 'final solution' . . . a gender-specific onslaught that is systematic. . . . [T]he tortures include rapes, gang-rapes, forced incest, the draining of the blood of captives to provide blood for transfusions for the needs of the criminals, setting children ablaze and drowning babies."). Given these reports, it is inexcusable that Amnesty International's October 1992 report on human rights violations in this war documents only three rapes, and these from an English newspaper rather than firsthand, as other atrocities are documented. See below note 9. Edith Niehuis, head of the German Parliamentary Committee for Women and Youth, called the "systematic mass rapes" in Bosnia an "extermination war against women." "Wir machen euch kleine Tschetniks," *Die Tageszeitung* (Dec. 8, 1992).

6. Universal Declaration of Human Rights, General Assembly Resolution 217 A (III) of Dec. 10, 1948, Preamble ("Whereas disregard and contempt for human rights have resulted in barbarous acts which have outraged the conscience of mankind").

7. An example of formal condonation is the U.S. case in which pornography is recognized as promoting rape, battering, and unequal pay but is protected as free speech. American Booksellers Ass'n v. Hudnut, 771 F.2d 323 (7th Cir. 1985), *aff'd*, 475 U.S. 1001 (1986).

8. For documentation of the use of "reservations" to the major convention prohibiting sex discrimination, see Rebecca Cook, "Reservations to the Convention on the Elimination of All Forms of Discrimination Against Women," 30 *Virginia Journal of International Law* 643 (1990). A lawsuit may be brought to invalidate the ratifications of nations whose exceptions are said to be excessive, voiding their acceptance of the Convention on the Elimination of All Forms of Discrimination Against Women (CEDAW). "Court Ruling Sought on Women's Convention," 1 *Human Rights Tribune* 21 (1992).

9. Amnesty International says that all parties succeed to the international agreements that Yugoslavia ratified. Amnesty International, *Bosnia-Herzegovina: Gross Abuses of Basic Human Rights, International Secretariat* (Oct. 1992). Helsinki Watch

says that Croatia and Yugoslavia (the latter apparently referring to Serbia/Montenegro) are parties to the Geneva Conventions and their Protocols, Croatia by contract on May 11, 1992, and Serbia and Montenegro implicitly, by expressing a wish to be recognized as the successor state to what was Yugoslavia. Ivana Nizich, *War Crimes in Bosnia-Herzegovina* 138–139 (Aug. 1992). Bosnia-Herzegovina ratified the relevant provisions in 1992. Humanitarian law is customary law, with universal jurisdiction, but human rights provisions require affirmative submission to secure jurisdiction.

10. Addressing the Conference on Security and Cooperation in Europe, U.S. Secretary of State Lawrence Eagleburger said that Serbian leaders were guilty of war crimes against humanity and should be prosecuted, "exactly as Hitler's associates were at Nuremberg." "Legal Commission to Start Investigation of Mass Graves in Former Yugoslavia," *Agence France Presse* (Dec. 14, 1992). At the time they were publicly recognized, the atrocities had been going on for approximately a year. There is also some discussion of creating a permanent international war crimes court whose first task would be to try war criminals from this war. "U.S., France Discussing Permanent War Crimes Court," *Reuters* (Dec. 15, 1992).

11. See generally Roy Gutman, "Victims Recount Nights of Terror in Makeshift Bordello," *Newsday* (Aug. 23, 1992) p. 37. A special mission of the European Council concluded, after a preliminary visit, that "the rapes [of Muslim women] are widespread and are part of a recognizable pattern. . . . The general view expressed by interlocutors whom the delegation considered responsible and credible was that a horrifying number of Muslim women had suffered rape and that this was continuing. . . . The most reasoned estimate suggested to the delegation indicated a figure in the region of 20,000 victims. . . . The indications are that at least some of the rapes are being committed in particularly sadistic ways. . . . The delegation also received information strongly suggesting that many women, and more particularly children, may have died during or after rape. . . . [T]he delegation frequently heard . . . that a repeated feature of Serbian attacks on Muslim towns and villages was the use of rape, or the threat of rape, as a weapon of war. . . . [D]ocuments from Serbian sources . . . very clearly put such actions in the context of an expansionist strategy. . . . [R]ape cannot be seen as incidental to the main purposes of the aggression but as serving a strategic purpose in itself." *Investigative Mission into the Treatment of Muslim Women in the Former Yugoslavia* 2–4 (Dec. 24, 1992).

12. Among the scores of examples of this seemingly requisite equalizing of oppressor and oppressed, although it is one of the least egregious, is Amnesty International's *Bosnia-Herzegovina: Rape and Sexual Abuse by Armed Forces* 3 (Jan. 1993): "Reports indicate . . . that all sides have committed these abuses, but that Muslim women have been the chief victims and the main perpetrators have been members of Serbian armed forces." World War II atrocities against Serbs by Croatians and Muslims are often cited by Serbs as historical justification for current Serbian "revenge." Nothing justifies genocide. There is also historical evidence that Serbian war losses have been greatly exaggerated and are being used as a pretext. Phillip J. Cohen, "Holocaust History Misappropriated," *Midstream: A Monthly Jewish Review,* 18–20

(Nov. 1992); Phillip J. Cohen, "Exploitation of the Holocaust as Propaganda: The Falsification of Serbian War Losses" (unpublished manuscript, July 18, 1992). See also War Crimes Investigation Bureau, *Fourth Exodus of the Jews: War in Bosnia-Herzegovina* (Sarajevo, Sept. 1992). Alain Finkielkraut comments on this in his *Comment peut-on être croate?* 50 (1992): "La Serbie falsifie le passé en disant que les Croates étaient tous nazis et les Serbes tous résistants, falsifie le présent en disant que les Croates restent un 'peuple génocidaire,' et mène à l'abri de cette double falsification la première guerre raciale que l'Europe ait connu depuis Hitler. Pour le dire d'un mot: *les nazis de cette histoire ont voulu se faire passer pour les Juifs.*" (Serbia falsifies the past by saying that the Croatians were all Nazis and the Serbs all resisters, falsifies the present in saying that the Croatians remain a 'genocidal people,' and carries out, in the shadow of this double falsification, the first racial war that Europe has known since Hitler. To put it in a word: *the Nazis of this story are trying to pass themselves off as the Jews.*)

13. A. Kaurin, "War Crimes Against Young Girls," *Večernji List* (Sept. 11, 1992) ("They are even conducting orgies on the dead bodies of the torture victims, who are after that thrown [out].").

14. In addition, when the dead are counted, their rapes are not. When raped women are counted, their rapes are not.

15. Asja Armanda, *The Women's Movement, Feminism, and the Definition of War* (Kareta Feminist Group, Oct. 1992).

16. "A Pattern of Rape," *Newsweek,* 34 (Jan. 4, 1992): "In his own defense, one attacker told Rasema, 'I have to do it, otherwise they will kill me.'" According to *Die Welt,* a rapist told his victim: "'We have to do it, because our commanders ordered it, and because you are Muslim—and there are too many of you Muslims. We have to destroy and exterminate you, so that the heroic Serbian people can take over the reins in this area again.'" Strohm, above note 5.

17. Roy Gutman, "Mass Rape: Muslims Recall Serb Attacks," *Newsday* (Aug. 23, 1992) p. 5 (reporting on rape as a tactic of war, where victims were told by Serbian forces they were under orders to rape them); John F. Burns, "A Serbian Fighter's Trail of Brutality," *New York Times* (Nov. 27, 1992) p. A1 (reporting an indicted Serb terrorist says "he and other Serbian fighters were encouraged to rape women and then take them away to kill them").

18. S. Džombic, "Go and Give Birth to Chetniks," *Večernji List* (Nov. 25, 1992).

19. The prior analysis and the facts underlying it are based on my reading of firsthand accounts provided by victims.

20. Many firsthand accounts report this. See also Center for Anti-War Activities, *Save Humanity Report* 6 (Sarajevo, July 7, 1992); Gutman, above note 11. It is unclear whether the brothels simply organize serial rape or whether some men are being paid or receiving other benefits in exchange for access to the women.

21. Džombic, above note 18. My testimonies further support this.

22. Evidence indicates that Jewish babies born in concentration camps were drowned. See *The Trial of German Major War Criminals* pt. 5, 188 (1946). No Jewish

women were documented to have been impregnated, then released, to "bear German babies." However, the Nazis required that special permission be obtained before the fetuses of Eastern European women and German men could be aborted. For discussion of this, see McRae v. Califano, 491 F. Supp. 630, 759 (E.D.N.Y. 1980).

23. [Name Withheld], Letter to author, Oct. 13, 1992. See also "Schwere Vorwürfe gegen UN-Soldaten in Bosnien," *Die Welt* (Oct. 6, 1992).

24. "Investigation Against General MacKenzie," *Večernji List* (Nov. 25, 1992). According to an interview with Ragib Hadzic, head of the Center for Research on Genocide and War Crimes in Zenica, Bosnia, General MacKenzie visited the Sonje restaurant in Dobrinja, which was a brothel and had become a wartime rape/death camp. He reportedly loaded four Muslim women in his UNPROFOR truck, and drove away. The women have never been seen again. "Vergewaltigungen als eine Taktik des Krieges," *Die Welt* (Dec. 2, 1992).

25. Nazis documented many atrocities with photographs, including those shown in *The Trial of German Major War Criminals* pt. 7, 99–101 (1946): "these naked women are being taken to the execution ground. Condemned to death, these women have been forced, by the same Obergruppenführer, to pose before the camera" (photographs presented by Soviet prosecution team). See also Helke Sander and Barbara John, eds., *Befreier und Befreite: Krieg, Vergewaltigungen, Kinder*, 131–134 (1992) (German photographs of dead raped German and Russian women). On the point of media manipulation, my correspondent from Croatia ([Name Withheld], Letter to author, Nov. 28, 1992) notes: "The manipulation of film documentation of atrocities in which Muslim and Croatian victims of Serb aggression have fallaciously been presented as Serb victims of Muslims and Croatians has been a notable strategy of the war against Croatia and Bosnia-Herzegovina." See also A. Kaurin, "War Crimes Against Young Girls," *Večernji List* (Sept. 11, 1992) ("pictures and videotapes of the concentration camps exist"); *Mass Killing,* above note 5, at 234 (dead Croatian boy presented as dead Serbian boy); "Villagers in Croatia Recount Massacre by Serbian Forces," *New York Times* (Dec. 19, 1991); Kajan, above note 5, at 31–34, 51–52.

26. "MacKinnon's central point is that 'a woman' is not yet the name of a way of being human." Richard Rorty, "Feminism and Pragmatism," 30 *Michigan Quarterly Review* 231, 234 (1991).

27. Isaiah Berlin, "Two Concepts of Liberty," in *Four Essays on Liberty* (1969).

28. *Belgian Linguistics Case,* E.C.H.R., 1968, Series A, No. 6, 832.

29. Inter-American Court of Human Rights, Velásquez-Rodriguez v. Honduras, Series C, No. 4 (Judgment of July 29, 1988).

30. Lori Heise, quoted in Center for Women's Global Leadership, *1991 Women's Leadership Institute Report: Women, Violence, and Human Rights* 17 (1992).

31. For illuminating background, see Maxime Tardu, *Human Rights: The International Petition System* 45 (Aug. 1985) ("The potential of [divisive postwar] U.N. debates for conflict escalation was so obvious that all governments became fiercely determined to keep the process under their own control through rejecting individual complaint systems."). See also Louis B. Sohn, "The New International Law: Protection of the

Rights of Individuals Rather Than States," 1 *American University Law Review* 32 (1982).

32. For an example of the inability to see a violation of a woman's human rights to the degree the abuse is deemed "personal," see Lazo-Majaro v. INS, 813 F.2d 1432, 1436–1441 (9th Cir. 1987) (Poole, J., dissenting).

33. See Tardu, above note 31, at Binder 1, Part II, Sec. V, pp. 24 and 25, Sec. VI, p. 44 (German-speaking minorities used as a propaganda base in other countries by insisting on minority rights); Alessandra Luini del Russo, *International Protection of Human Rights* 32 (1971) (nations realized that individual protections cannot be left solely to states).

34. Elizabeth Spelman, *Inessential Woman* (1988); Eva Kuehls, *The Reign of the Phallus* (1985).

35. This is discussed further in my *Toward a Feminist Theory of State* ch. 12 (1989).

36. John Stuart Mill and Harriet Taylor, "On the Subjection of Women," in *Essays on Sex Equality* 123 (Alice Rossi, ed., 1970).

37. Susan Moller Okin, *Women in Western Political Thought* (1980); John Locke, *The Second Treatise of Government* (J. W. Gough, ed., 1966); Thomas Hobbes, *Leviathan* (M. Oakeshott, ed., 1946).

38. This point is made unintentionally by Theodor Meron in his attack on CEDAW for conflicting with existing notions of human rights in various areas. See Theodor Meron, *Human Rights Law-Making in the United Nations* 62–64, 66–67, 72 (1986).

39. See "Court Ruling Sought on Women's Convention," 1 *Human Rights Tribune* 21 (1992).

40. Convention on the Elimination of All Forms of Discrimination Against Women, Dec. 18, 1979, 1249 U.N.T.S. 13 (entered into force Sept. 3, 1981) [hereinafter, CEDAW] art. 6; Convention for the Suppression of Traffic in Persons and the Exploitation of the Prostitution of Others Mar. 21, 1950, 96 U.N.T.S. 271. See also the draft, "U.N. Convention Against Sexual Exploitation," reported in *Ms.,* 13 (Sept./Oct. 1991).

41. In 1966, Thailand enacted the Service Establishments Act, which gives specific legal status to "special service girls." The women had to turn to the establishments for protection from prosecution under prostitution laws, which exempt the customers but not the women. Thanh-Dom Truong, *Sex, Money and Morality: Prostitution and Tourism in Southeast Asia,* 155 (1990). In another sense, wherever prostitution is legalized, the state is trafficking in women.

42. U.S. State Department, *Country Reports on Human Rights Practices for 1991* 818–819 (1992) ("Physical compulsion to submit to abortion or sterilization is not authorized, but continues to occur as officials strive to meet population targets. Reports of forced abortions and sterilizations continue, though well below the levels of the early 1980s. While recognizing that abuses occur, officials maintain that China does not condone forced abortion or sterilization, and that abuses by local officials are punished. They admit, however, that punishment is rare and have yet to provide documentation of any punishments.").

43. An intelligent discussion of these provisions can be found in Karen Engle, "International Human Rights and Feminism: When Discourses Meet," 13 *Michigan Journal of International Law* 517 (1992).

44. E. M. Adams, *The Metaphysics of Self and World: Toward a Humanistic Philosophy* (1991).

45. Simone de Beauvoir, *The Second Sex* (H. M. Parshley, ed. and trans., 1989) (1952).

46. Jacques Maritain, *The Rights of Man and Natural Law* 65 (Doris Anson, trans., 1951; French, 1942): "[The] human person possess[es] rights because of the very fact that it is a person, a whole, a matter of itself and of its acts . . . by virtue of natural law, the human person has to have the right to be respected, is the subject of rights, possesses rights. These are things which are owed to a man because of the very fact that he is a man."

47. Herbert C. Kelman, *Crimes of Obedience* (1989); M. McDougal, H. Lasswell, and L. Chen, *Human Rights and World Public Order* (1980).

48. Mortimer Adler, "Robert Bork: The Lessons to Be Learned" (comments on Robert H. Bork, *The Tempting of America*), 84 *New York University Law Review* 1121 (1990).

49. Max Salomon, *Der Begriff der Gerechtigkeit bei Aristoteles* 26 (1937). (See page 8 regarding Aristotle and page 26 for the Third Reich and the proposition that "equality in the sense of complete equality is identity: one and the same thing.") Illustrating equality thinking during the Nazi period, leading constitutional scholar Ulrich Scheuner, "Der Gleichheitsgedanke in der völkischen Verfassungsordnung," 99 *Zeitschrift für die Gesamte Staatswissenschaft* 245 (1939), states that the substance of the equality right is "Artgleichheit" of Aryans (p. 267). From the "völkisch" tenets of contemporary German law, see page 267, "[daraus] folgt notwendig die Absonderung der artfremden Elmente, insbesondere der Juden, aus dem deutschen Volkskörper, und ihre . . . differentielle Behandlung" (follows necessarily the extraction of elements of alien blood, particularly Jews, from the body of the German people, and their . . . differential treatment). How the Jews were treated is thus rendered "differential treatment." See also the use of the Aristotelian principle at page 260. Scheuner cites the U.S. Supreme Court with approval with regard to racial segregation and miscegenation laws, noting that this leads to "Benachteiligung" (disadvantage) of people of color, which is exactly what is intended, at pp. 265–266. He also notices the Court's beginning to weaken in its defense of segregation.

50. Universal Declaration of Human Rights art. 2, General Assembly Resolution 217 A (III) of Dec. 10, 1948, UNGAORO, 3d Sess., Supp. No. 13, A/810.

51. CEDAW pt. I, art. 1, adopted Dec. 18, 1979.

52. Committee on the Elimination of Discrimination Against Women, General Recommendation No. 19, Violence Against Women, CEDAW/C/1992/L/1/Add.15, Jan. 29, 1992. This document goes very far in recognizing the scope of the problem and in adapting sex equality as a concept to address violence against women. For a useful discussion, see Charlotte Bunch, "Women's Rights as Human Rights: Toward a Revision of Human Rights," 12 *Human Rights Quarterly* 483 (1990).

53. Many other human rights documents, notably Article 3 and Article 26 of the International Covenant on Civil and Political Rights, Dec. 16, 1966, guarantee sex equality. This covenant stands out in allowing, through an Optional Protocol, complaints by individuals as well as state parties, but only applies to those who have accepted it specifically. Yugoslavia did not. Enforcement includes denunciation of violators.

54. These movements are well documented. See *Sisterhood Is Global: The International Women's Movement Anthology* (Robin Morgan, ed., 1996); Center for Women's Global Leadership, *Women, Violence, and Human Rights.* See also Marilyn Waring, *If Women Counted* (1990) (economic discrimination against women, including exclusion of women's work from international accounting systems). The reference to Canada is to the "Montreal Massacre," in which 14 young women were murdered by a man screaming he hated feminists. Jane Caputi and Diana E. H. Russell, "Femicide: Sexist Terrorism Against Women," in Radford and Russell, eds., *Femicide* above note 3, at 13–14.

55. In this sense, equality is derivative in virtually all legal systems. See, e.g., Convention for the Protection of Human Rights and Fundamental Freedoms art. 14, 213 U.N.T.S. 221, E.T.S. 5, U.K.T.S. 71 (1953) (Sept. 3, 1953), which has been held to permit no complaints on its own, but merely refers to equal access to other rights. X and Y v. The Netherlands, E.C.H.R., 1985 Series A, No. 91, para. 32.

56. Andrews v. Law Society of British Columbia, [1989] 1 S.C.R. 143, 171–182.

57. Jane Doe v. Board of Commissioners of Policy for the Municipality of Metropolitan Toronto, [1998] 126 C.C.C. 3d 12.

58. Janzen v. Platy Enterprises, [1989] 1 S.C.R. 1252 (sexual harassment is sex discrimination under the Manitoba human rights code).

59. Brooks, Allen and Dixon v. Canada Safeway, [1989] 1 S.C.R. 1219 (pregnancy discrimination is sex discrimination).

60. Norberg v. Wynrib, [1992] 2 S.C.R. 226.

61. M. (K.) v. M. (H.), [1992] 3 S.C.R. 6.

62. Regina v. Lavallée, [1990] 1 S.C.R. 852.

63. Regina v. Canadian Newspapers Co., [1988] 2 S.C.R. 122.

64. Seaboyer v. Regina, [1991] 2 S.C.R. 577 (litigating "rape shield" provisions of the Canadian Criminal Code, R.S.C., 1985, c. 46, ss. 276 and 277).

65. Rape was redefined in Canada under the new law. Section 276 was amended in 1992 and 2002 and new sections 276.1-276.5 were added in 1992. Section 277 was amended in 2002. See Criminal Code of Canada, R.S. 1985 c. C-46, s. 276 amended by 1992 Statutes of Canada, ch. 38, s. 2 and 2002 Statutes of Canada, ch. 13, s. 13; Criminal Code of Canada ss. 276.1-276.5 added by 1992 Statutes of Canada ch. 38, s. 2; Criminal Code of Canada, R.S. 1985, c. C-46, s. 277 was amended by 2002 Statutes of Canada ch. 13, s. 14, available at http://laws.justice.gc.ca/en/C-46/42801.html. Less positive results occurred in prostitution cases, Regina v. Skinner, [1990] 1 S.C.R. 1235, and in statutory rape, Regina v. Nguyen and Hess, [1990] 2 S.C.R. 906. No serious sex equality argument was made in either one.

66. Daigle v. Trembley, [1989] 2 S.C.R. 530.

67. On women's rights in childbirth, see Regina v. Sullivan and LeMay, [1991] 1 S.C.R. 489.

68. Keegstra v. Regina, [1990] 3 S.C.R. 697; Butler v. Regina, [1992] 1 S.C.R. 452.

69. Women's Help Now and Kareta, "Who Are We? Where Are We?" (leaflet, Zagreb, Oct. 2, 1992); Natalie Nenadic, "How Do You Get Rid of the Guns?" *Every-woman,* 19 (July–Aug. 1991); Katja Gattin for Kareta Feminist Group, "Where Have All the Feminists Gone?" (unpublished paper, Zagreb, Jan. 20, 1992) ("In 1991/1992, Croatia is a woman.")

70. A useful review is Yougindra Khushalani, *Dignity and Honour of Women as Basic and Fundamental Human Rights* (1982).

71. Protocol I, Protocol Additional to the Geneva Conventions of August 12, 1949, art. 76(1) (victims of international armed conflict protected against "rape, forced prostitution and any other form of indecent assault"); Protocol II, Protocol Additional to the Geneva Conventions of August 12, 1949, art. 4(e) (victims of noninternational armed conflicts protected against "outrages upon personal dignity, in particular humiliating and degrading treatment, rape, enforced prostitution and any form of indecent assault"). Murder and torture are prohibited under many international conventions, with additional protections for doing so on ethnic grounds.

72. In re Yamashita, 327 U.S. 1 (1945). Courtney Whitney, Brigadier General, U.S. Army, *The Case of General Yamashita: A Memorandum* 5–16 (1950), contains detailed excerpts from the record of the trial, revealing many rapes. The U.S. Supreme Court upheld the decision of the military tribunal. See also Richard L. Lael, *The Yamashita Precedent: War Crimes and Command Responsibility* 83–84 (1982); L. C. Green, *Essays on the Modern Law of War* 227–228 (1985); Arnold Brackman, *The Other Nuremberg: The Untold Story of the Tokyo War Crimes Trials* 179–180 (1987). Brackman discusses the death sentence of General Iwane Matsui, who was convicted of "failing to take adequate steps to secure the observance and prevent breaches of conventions and laws of war in respect of prisoners of war and civilian internees" in the mass rapes that were called the Rape of Nanking (419; see also 108 and 409).

73. Lael, above note 72, at 83. All that is distinguishable in the Japanese accounts is the pornography and the intention to create pregnancies.

74. Joan Fitzpatrick, "The Use of International Human Rights Norms to Combat Violence Against Women," in *Human Rights and Women: National and International Perspectives* (Rebecca J. Cook, ed., 1994) is a lucid, informed treatment. On the rapes in Bangladesh, see Susan Brownmiller, *Against Our Will: Men, Women, and Rape* 78–87 (1975).

75. *The Trial of German Major War Criminals* pt. 6, 303 (1946) (evidence of Soviet prosecutors); pt. 5, 159, 325–327 (evidence of French prosecutors).

76. Id. at pt. 1, 24: "One hundred and thirty-nine women had their arms painfully bent backward and held by wires. From some their breasts had been cut off, and their ears, fingers and toes had been amputated. The bodies bore the marks of burns." (Russian women's bodies in Stalingrad region after German expulsion.)

77. Opening Statement by Justice Jackson, id. at 53. One exhibit of a Soviet official documenting "revolting acts of rape" by the German invaders observed this: "Unquestionable facts prove that the regime . . . did not consist of certain excesses of individual undisciplined military units, or individual German officers and soldiers. Rather does it point to a definite system, planned far in advance and encouraged by the German Government and the German Army Command, a system which intentionally unleashed within their army the lowest animal instincts among the officers and men." Id. at pt. 7, 26 (notes of V. M. Molotov, National Commissar for Foreign Affairs in USSR, Exhibit USSR 51, dated as early as January 6, 1942). The Nuremberg trial was conducted under the common law of war, even though the violations of the Geneva Conventions under which the Nazi leadership was charged had not been made a specific penal offense. See Howard S. Levie, *The Code of International Armed Conflict* 862 (1986).

78. "Consistent pattern of gross and reliably attested violations of human rights and fundamental freedoms" violates Resolution 1503 (XLVIII) of the Economic and Social Council authorizing the establishment of a subcommission on Prevention of Discrimination and Protection of Minorities. It is empowered to appoint a group to determine violations and bring them to the attention of the subcommission, and it enables the UN to interfere in "domestic" matters. See Felix Ermacora, "Human Rights and Domestic Jurisdiction," 124 *Recueil des Cours* 371, 375, 436 (1968).

79. Bogdan Tirnanić, *Bosanski Bluz* 101 (2000). Michael Moorcock, "Working in the Ministry of Truth: Pornography and Censorship in Contemporary Britain," in *Pornography: Women, Violence, and Civil Liberties* 536 (Catherine Itzen, ed., 1992), quoted this statement, then asked, "Have sex crimes dropped in Serbia?" (550).

80. It should be noted that the Serbs consider the Serbian-occupied areas of Croatia and Bosnia-Herzegovina to be Serbian states, parts of the United States of Serbia. So the Serbian military forces, in addition to being state actors under orders from Belgrade, function under color of official authority of the self-declared Serbian ministates within and against the established governments of Croatia and Bosnia-Herzegovina. Local Serbian irregulars, termed *chetniks,* provide yet another layer of actual and apparent state authority.

15. Turning Rape into Pornography: Postmodern Genocide

1. See Linda Lovelace and Michael McGrady, *Ordeal* (1980).

2. Gloria Steinem, *Outrageous Acts and Everyday Rebellions* 250 (1983).

3. John F. Burns, "A Killer's Tale—A Special Report; A Serbian Fighter's Path of Brutality," *New York Times,* A1 (Nov. 27, 1992) (interview with Herak by Burns); John F. Burns, "2 Serbs to Be Shot for Killings and Rapes," *New York Times,* A6 (Mar. 31, 1993) (testimony by Herak).

4. John F. Burns, "Ending Restraint, U.N. Aides Denounce Serbs for Shellings," *New York Times,* A1 (Apr. 14, 1993).

5. Bogdan Tirnanić, *Bosanski Bluz* 101 (2000). By this, Tirnanić clarified that he

was referring not only to the sexually explicit content of the materials but to the extent of their distribution and public legitimation.

6. Burns, "A Killer's Tale," above note 3.

7. Id. See also Michael Palaich, "Killing, Rape: 'It Was an Order,'" *Seattle Times,* A4 (Mar. 30, 1993); David Crary, "Serb Soldier Recounts Atrocities," *Pittsburgh Post-Gazette,* A4 (Mar. 15, 1993).

8. Burns, "A Killer's Tale," above note 3 ("Mr. Herak identified the women he had attacked—Emina, Sabina, Amela and Fatima among others, the youngest of them teen-agers, the oldest about 35"); "Captors' Court Condemns Serbs to Death," *Vancouver Sun* (Canada), A10 (Mar. 31, 1993) ("In court, he recited the first names of some of his victims: Naila, Zehra, Fatima, Ina, Inesa, Sumbula and two named Sabina"); "Muslim Women Raped Then Killed, Trial Told," *Edmonton Journal* (Canada), A1 (Mar. 15, 1993) (The accused man listed his victims' names—Amela, Mejra, Ina, Enisa, Sumbula, Senada, Alma, Misa and Zehra.").

9. See "Genocide's Sexuality," below at No. 22 nn.15 and 16.

10. Streicher, for publishing, was convicted for incitement to murder and exter-mination, a form of persecution on political and racial grounds, a crime against hu-manity, and executed. *Trial of the Major War Criminals* vol. XXII, 549 (1948) (Nurem-berg, 1947—1949) (finding Streicher guilty on one count); and Vol. I, 365 (sentencing him to death).

11. Id.

12. To the date of this volume, the International Criminal Tribunal for the Former Yugoslavia has not indicted any such figures, but the International Criminal Tribunal for Rwanda has come close and convicted them. See Catharine A. MacKinnon, "Pros-ecutor v. Nahimana, Barayagwiza, and Ngeze," 98 *American Journal of International Law* 325 (2004).

16. Rape as Nationbuilding

1. For an attempted genealogy of this term, see "From Auschwitz to Omarska, from Nuremberg to The Hague," below No. 17; see also Samantha Power, *A Problem from Hell: America and the Age of Genocide* 249–251 (2002).

2. Total Bosnian civilian casualties are estimated at 200,000, in addition to 2 million displaced, see Power, above note 1, at 251, although the exact numbers are unknown. Peter Cary, "Bosnia by the Numbers," *U.S. News & World Report,* 53 (Apr. 10, 1995). Of exhumed genocide victims' bodies in Bosnia, 95 percent have been confirmed to be those of civilians. "Bosnian Muslims Reportedly Account for 90 Percent of Bodies Exhumed So Far," *BBC Monitoring International Reports* (Aug. 2002). These numbers are consistent with those in other modern wars, in which an estimated 90 percent of all casualties are civilians. See Save the Children, *State of the World's Mothers 2002: Mothers and Children in War and Conflict* 9 (May 2, 2002) (citing Graça Machel, *The Impact of War on Children: A Review of Progress Since the 1996 United Nations Report on the Impact of Armed Conflict on Children* 1 (2001)), *available at* www.savethe childrenus.org.

3. Memorably including Secretary of State Warren Christopher, on April 1, 1993, at the International Operations Subcommittee of the House Foreign Affairs Committee hearing: "The killing, the raping, the ethnic cleansing is definitely an atrocious set of acts. Whether it meets the technical definition of genocide is a matter that we'll look into and get back to you." *FY 1994 and 1995 Foreign Relations Budget: Hearing Before the Subcomm. on International Operations of the House Comm. on Foreign Affairs*, 103d Cong. (1993) (statement of Warren Christopher, Secretary of State). Another is on January 19, 1993, under the Bush administration, Patricia Diaz Dennis, assistant secretary of state for human rights and humanitarian affairs: "In Bosnia, our report describes widespread systematic atrocities, including the rapes and killings of civilian victims to the extent that it probably borders on genocide. We haven't yet decided whether or not it's a legal matter. The conduct in Bosnia is genocide, but clearly the abuses that have occurred there over the last year are such that they, as I said, border on that particular legal term." Special State Department Briefing on Report to Congress on Human Rights Practices for 1992 (Jan. 19, 1993), *available at* www.fednews.com/archive.htm.

4. See Richard Boucher, U.S. State Department spokesman, "We've made it clear right from the beginning of this that there were various parties involved in the fighting; that there were people on all sides . . . that were doing bad things." State Department Regular Briefing (Aug. 3, 1992), *available at* www.fednews.com/archive.htm.

5. Theodor W. Adorno, "Cultural Criticisms and Society," in *Prisms* 34 (Samuel Weber and Shierry Weber, trans., 1967) (1955) ("To write poetry after Auschwitz is barbaric.").

17. From Auschwitz to Omarska, Nuremberg to The Hague

1. Calling Croatia and Bosnia-Herzegovina "the former Yugoslavia" is a bit like calling a divorced battered wife "the former Mrs. Whoever."

2. This report was given to me directly by a survivor. Any otherwise unattributed quotations or facts about the conflict in this talk are from survivors who spoke to me.

3. "CCCC" stands for "Само Слога Србина Спашава," which transliterates as "Samo Sloga Srbina Spasava" (the Cyrillic C corresponding to the English letter S), meaning "Only Unity Saves the Serbs."

4. On or about October 14, 1991, Karadžić stated in the Parliament of Bosnia-Herzegovina that Bosnian Muslims "would disappear from the face of the Earth." Norman Cigar, *Genocide in Bosnia* 37 (1995). In the ICTY's trial of Prosecutor v. Krajisnik, the ICTY led evidence that included an intercept of Karadžić and Gojko Dogo, president of the Association of Serbs from Bosnia and Herzegovina, two days prior, stating that should the Muslims persist in their demands, "[t]hey will disappear. That people will disappear from the face of the earth if they start now. Our offer was their only chance." Prosecutor v. Krajisnik, Case No. IT-00-39, Trial Transcript (Feb. 3, 2003), at 322. He continued in the same conversation: "Sarajevo will be a black cauldron where 300,000 Muslims will die. . . . They will be up to their necks in blood and [] the Muslim people will disappear. . . . They simply don't have any way to carry

out a secession. I think this is clear to the army and clear to everyone. It will be a real bloodbath." Id., at 323. He repeated the same words at the tenth session of the Bosnian Serb Assembly. Id., at 359.

5. Himmler said this on October 6, 1943, in Posen. "Speech Delivered at Posen Before the Reichsleiter and Gauleiter on October 6, 1943," in Heinrich Himmler, *Geheimreden 1933 bis 1945 und andere Ansprachen* 169 (J. C. Fest, intro., Bradley F. Smith and Agnes F. Peterson, eds., (Frankfurt, Berlin, and Vienna: Propyläen Verlag, 1974).

6. It is not entirely clear who originated the term "ethnic cleansing," or who first applied it in the Serbian genocidal context. It is said to be a translation of "etnicko cisčenje" in Serbian. According to Drazen Petrovic, "ethnically clean territories" in Kosova were discussed in the mass media after 1981, referring to the behavior of Kosovar Albanians toward the Serbian minority in that province. See Drazen Petrovic, "'Ethnic Cleansing'—An Attempt at Methodology," 5 *European Journal of International Law* 343 (1994). "Slobodan Milosévič, the Serbian leader, used the term 'ethnically clean' in April 1987, in accusing Albanians of trying to force minority Serbs from Kosova, a battle site with a crucial role in Serbian nationalist lore. The phrase has also been traced to the former Soviet Union, where in 1988 Armenians and Azerbaijanis tried to force each other out of the enclave of Nagorno-Karabakh in an operation that Soviet officials described variously as *etnicheskie chistki*—'ethnic purges' and *etnicheskoye chishcheniye*—'ethnic cleansing.' The phrase first appeared in English in a Reuters dispatch on July 31, 1991, quoting Croatia's Supreme Council as accusing the Serbs of expelling Croats from the border areas of Croatia with the aim of 'the ethnic cleansing of the critical areas . . . to be annexed to Serbia.' The phrase was also used by the Bosnian foreign minister in 1993, lamenting that the world had stood aside from both the disintegration of Yugoslavia and the Nazi atrocities of the 1930s." Lawrence Malkin, "Ethnic Cleansing," in *Reader's Companion to Military History* 158 (Robert Cowley and Geoffrey Parker, eds., 1996).

7. Above note 5, at 201.

8. For documentation of this information, see Philip J. Cohen, *Serbia's Secret War: Propaganda and the Deceit of History* 63–85 (1996) (documenting approximately 15,000 Jews, 94 percent of the Jewish population, perished in collaborationist Serbia, making Serbia the first country in Europe declared *Judenfrei*. "[T]he Chetnik movement represented the ideological center of Serbian political culture and enjoyed widespread support among the Serbs. The Ustashas, in contrast, were an aberration in modern Croation history and never attained mass support." at 85).

9. See, e.g., *Trial of the Major War Criminals*, Indictment, Vol. 1, at 29 (1947) (Nuremberg, 1947–1949).

10. Id.

11. See Mladen Loncar, *Sexually Violated Men: A Pilot Study from Bosnia-Herzegovina and Croatia*, WHO Office of the Special Representative for Humanitarian Assistance (Zagreb, n.d.).

12. Article II (1)(c) of Control Council Law No. 10 defines "Crimes Against Humanity" as follows: "Atrocities and offenses, including but not limited to murder, extermination, enslavement, deportation, imprisonment, torture, rape, or other inhumane

acts committed against any civilian population, or persecutions on political, racial or religious grounds whether or not in violation of the domestic laws of the country where perpetrated." Control Council for Germany, *Official Gazette* 50 (Jan. 31, 1946). However, rape "was not prosecuted in any of the 12 subsequent trials, despite the fact that rapes were believed to have taken place systematically and on a massive scale during the Second World War." *ICTY Bulletin* No. 15/16 (Mar. 10, 1997), *available at* www .un.org/icty/BL/15art4e.htm.

13. See "Genocide's Sexuality," below at No. 22, for a fuller investigation of this subject.

14. About a year after this talk was given, this provision was replaced with a rule that provided that "consent shall not be allowed as a defence if the victim (a) has been subjected to or threatened with or has had reason to fear violence, duress, detention or psychological oppression, or (b) reasonably believed that if the victim did not submit, another might be so subjected, threatened or put in fear" and "(iii) before evidence of the victim's consent is admitted, the accused shall satisfy the Trial Chamber in camera that the evidence is relevant and credible." Rule 96, Evidence in Cases of Sexual Assault, ICTY, No. IT/32/Rev. 34 (1994–1995). The original Rule 96 was adopted with the rest of the Rules of Evidence on February 11, 1994; it was revised on January 30, 1995, and May 3, 1995. Seeing this change as a substantial retreat from the original comprehension that consent under the conditions specified in the statute of the tribunal was irrelevant, many survivors lost any trust they had had in the tribunal.

15. In 1992, Telford Taylor was critical of Lieutenant Griffith-Jones's presentation of the case against Julius Streicher, terming it "a compilation of the defendant's speeches and publications" that addressed the legal issues "[o]nly in conclusion, and very summarily." Allowing that this was all "well spoken," he asked, "[W]as the publication of a German newspaper in Germany, no matter how scurrilous, an international crime? And what did it have to do with Counts One and Two, supposedly the business at hand?" Telford Taylor, *The Anatomy of the Nuremberg Trials: A Personal Memoir* 264 (1992). Taylor remained dubious about the evidence against Streicher, opining that while it was "apparently sufficient to convict, might not warrant capital sentences." Id., at 269. In 2004, the International Tribunal for Rwanda found three leading Rwandan media figures guilty of genocide, incitement to genocide, and crimes against humanity. For discussion, see Catharine A. MacKinnon, "International Decision: Prosecutor v. Nahimana, Barayagwiza, and Ngeze," 98 *American Journal of International Law* 325 (2004).

16. See Pierre Vidal-Naquet, "A Paper Eichmann (1980)—Anatomy of a Lie," in *Assassins of Memory: Essays on the Denial of the Holocaust* (Jeffrey Mehlman, trans., 1992).

18. Rape, Genocide, and Women's Human Rights

1. Much excellent documentation became available after this talk was originally published. See Radhika Coomaraswamy, *Report of the Special Rapporteur on Violence Against Women, Its Causes and Consequences*, U.N. ESCOR Hum. Rts. Comm'n, 52d

Sess., Prov. Agenda Item 9(a) ¶ 62, U.N. Doc. E/CN.4/1996/53 (1996); Radhika Coomaraswamy, *Report*, U.N. ESCOR Hum. Rts. Comm'n, 53d Sess., Prov. Agenda Item 9(a) ¶¶ 22–23, U.N. Doc. E/CN.4/1997/47 (1997); and Radhika Coomaraswamy, *Preliminary Report of the Special Rapporteur on Violence Against Women, Its Causes and Consequences*, U.N. ESCOR Hum. Rts. Comm'n, 50th Sess., Prov. Agenda Item 11(a) ¶¶ 120–21, U.N. Doc. E/CN.4/1995/42 (1995). See also Myres S. McDougal et al., "Human Rights for Women and World Public Order: The Outlawing of Sex-Based Discrimination," 69 *American Journal of International Law* 497 (1975) (an account of sex-based discrimination worldwide); United Nations Committee on the Elimination of Racial Discrimination, Commentary and Background Information, CERD General Recommendation on Gender Dimensions of Racial Discrimination, U.N. Doc. CERD/C/54/Misc. 31 (1999) (documenting sterilization abuse on racial, ethnic, and sex-based grounds, n.87, Brazil; n.89, of Black and indigenous women); Phillip G. Stubblefield and David A. Grimes, "Septic Abortion," 331 *New England Journal of Medicine* 310 (1994) (reviewing evidence worldwide of deaths of women from illegal abortions); Ann Tinker et al., *Women's Health and Nutrition: Making a Difference* 14 (World Bank Discussion Paper No. 256, 1994) (estimating that 125,000 to 200,000 women continued to die every year from unsafe and illegal abortions); Center for Reproductive Law and Policy, *Women Behind Bars: Chile's Abortion Laws* (1998) (studying 159 low-income Chilean women jailed for abortion); Madhu Kishwar, "The Continuing Deficit of Women in India and the Impact of Amniocentesis," in *Man-Made Women: How New Reproductive Technologies Affect Women* 30 (Gena Corea et al., eds., 1987); Viola Roggencamp, "Abortion of a Special Kind: Male Sex Selection in India," in *Test Tube Women: What Future for Motherhood?* 266 (Rita Arditti et al., eds., 1984); Xiarong Li, "License to Coerce: Violence Against Women, State Responsibility, and Legal Failures in China's Family Planning Program," 8 *Yale Journal of Law and Feminism* 145 (1996) (examining China's state-mandated family planning policies and their connection to violence against women and female children); Human Rights in China, "Caught Between Tradition and the State: Violations of the Human Rights of Chinese Women," 17 *Women's Rights Law Reporter* 285 (1996); Ellen Keng, Note, "Population Control Through the One-Child Policy in China: Its Effects on Women," 18 *Women's Rights Law Reporter* 205, 209 (1997) (noting sex-selective abortions in China are illegal but remain almost routine because of preference for boys as the single legally permitted child).

2. Letter from Natalie Nenadic to the author from Zagreb, Croatia, Oct. 13, 1992 (on file with the *Harvard Women's Law Journal*).

3. Id.

4. Id.

5. See Theodor Meron, "Rape as a Crime Under International Humanitarian Law," 87 *American Journal of International Law* 424, 424–428 (1993) (rape as a crime against humanity under international law); Letter from Jordan Paust, 88 *American Journal of International Law* 88 (1994) (rape as genocide and other crimes under customary international law).

6. With good documentation, Samantha Power analyzes these excuses illuminatingly in her book *"A Problem from Hell": America and the Age of Genocide* (2002).

7. All otherwise unreferenced information on this genocidal war is taken directly from first-person accounts by survivors with whom I have worked, other than the information on Hungarians in Vojvodina, which comes from observations by other survivors.

8. In fact, after this talk was originally published, the world did see the attempted extermination of the Kosovar Albanians by the Serbs, predicted here, a mass humanitarian emergency responded to by bombing of Serbian attack positions by NATO. See Craig R. Whitney, "NATO's Plan: A Barrage, Not a Pinprick," *New York Times*, A3 (Mar. 24, 1999) ("In Washington, officials speaking on condition of anonymity said air and missile strikes would be aimed at more than just those army and police units waging war against ethnic Albanians in Kosovo Province, but would attack the Yugoslav military more generally, striking at Serbian targets vital to supporting the repression."); Eric Schmitt, "A Wary Senate Gives Support for Air Strikes," *New York Times*, A6 (Mar. 24, 1999); Michael R. Gordon and Eric Schmitt, "Thwarted, NATO Agrees to Bomb Belgrade Sites," *New York Times*, A5 (Mar. 31, 1999); John Kifner, "How Serb Forces Purged One Million Albanians," *New York Times*, A1 (May 29, 1999); Craig R. Whitney, "Bombing Ends as Serbs Begin Pullout," *New York Times*, A1 (June 11, 1999) ("NATO suspended its bombing of Yugoslavia today after Serbian troops began withdrawing from Kosovo, halting an assault that rained 23,000 bombs and missiles on Serbia without losing the life of a single NATO fighter. The halt in the bombing after 78 days set the stage for the United Nations Security Council's swift approval of a resolution that permits 50,000 international peacekeepers to move in to help more than a million Albanian refugees driven out of Kosovo to try to return."); Steven Erlanger, "NATO Troops Roll into Kosovo," *New York Times*, 1 (June 13, 1999); John Kifner and Ian Fisher, "Kosovo Landscape Lays Bare Serbs' Brutal Campaign," *New York Times*, A1 (June 16, 1999) (documenting evidence of Serb atrocities in Kosovo discovered after the end of the NATO bombing campaign). For analysis of the legal implications, see "Women's September 11th: Rethinking the International Law of Conflict," below at No. 25.

9. See, for example, Susan Brownmiller, "Making Female Bodies the Battlefield," in *Mass Rape: The War Against Women in Bosnia-Herzegovina* 180 (Alexandra Stiglmayer, ed., 1994).

10. Similar experiences are reported in Roy Gutman, *A Witness to Genocide* 64–76, 164–167 (1993).

11. See S. Džombic, "Go and Give Birth to Chetniks," *Večernji List* (Nov. 25, 1992).

12. See McRae v. Califano, 491 F.Supp. 630, 759 (E.D.N.Y. 1980), *rev'd on other grounds sub nom.* Harris v. McRae, 448 U.S. 297 (1980).

13. See Džombic, above note 11.

14. Nenadic, above note 2.

15. See "Investigation Against General McKenzie," *Večernji List* (Nov. 25, 1992).

16. See Catharine A. MacKinnon, "Turning Rape into Pornography: Postmodern Genocide," above at No. 15.

17. See generally Louis B. Sohn, "The New International Law: Protection of the Rights of Individuals Rather Than States," 32 *American University Law Review* 1, 9– 17 (1982) (outlining the evolution of human rights law after World War II); M. Tardu, 1 *Human Rights: The International Petition System* 45 (1985) ("The potential of [divisive postwar] U.N. debates for conflict escalation was so obvious that all governments became fiercely determined to keep the process under their own control through rejecting individual complaint systems.").

18. This insight was first expressed to me by Asja Armanda of Kareta Feminist Group.

19. For an analysis that "in 1991/1992, Croatia is a woman," see Katja Gattin for Kareta Feminist Group, "Where Have All the Feminists Gone?" (1992) (unpublished paper, Zagreb) (on file with the *Harvard Women's Law Journal*).

20. On August 30, 1993, His Excellency Muhamed Sacirbey, ambassador and permanent representative of Bosnia and Herzegovina to the United Nations, brilliantly argued before the United Nations Security Council that Bosnia-Herzegovina is being gang-raped, forced into submission through the use of violence and aggression, including rape, deprived of means of self-defense, and then treated as if it had been seduced—forced to embrace the consequences and denied legal relief. His Excellency Muhamed Sacirbey, *Address at the United Nations Security Council* (Aug. 30, 1993) (on file with the *Harvard Women's Law Journal*).

21. Actually, the obligation to act to stop a genocide is less legally clear conventionally than it should be or is often said to be. On Bosnia's case, see Order of Provisional Measures, *Application of the Convention on the Prevention and Punishment of the Crime of Genocide* (Bosnia and Herzegovina v. Serbia and Montenegro), 1993 I.C.J. 3 (April 8), *reprinted in* 32 I.L.M. 888 (1993) (order of provisional measures).

22. Kadic v. Karadžić, 93 Civ. 1163 (S.D.N.Y. 1993). See Doe v. Karadžić, 866 F. Supp. 734 (S.D.N.Y. 1994) (dismissing plaintiffs' claims for lack of subject matter jurisdiction) *judgment reversed by* Kadic v. Karadžić, 70 F.3d 232 (2nd Cir., 1995), *cert. denied*, Karadžić v. Kadic, 518 U.S. 1005 (1996).

23. See S. C. Res. 827, U.N. SCOR, 3217th mtg., U.N. Doc. S/RES/827 (May 25, 1993); S. C. Res. 808, U.N. SCOR, 3175th mtg., U.N. Doc. S/RES/808 (Feb. 22, 1993).

24. Viewed as of 2005, despite the ICTY's accomplishments, this belongs near the top of the list of ways it has fallen short.

19. Gender-Based Crimes in Humanitarian Law

1. See Kelly D. Askin, "Women and International Humanitarian Law," in 1 *Women and International Human Rights Law* 45–47 (Kelly D. Askin and Dorean M. Koenig, eds., 1998) (outlining the non-existent or rare references to sex or gender anywhere in international humanitarian law documents, much less to any crimes that actually include

sex as an element). The Rome Statute of the International Criminal Court changed this by defining persecution on the basis of gender as a crime against humanity at art. 7(1)(h). Persecution is defined as intentional and severe deprivation of fundamental rights contrary to international law by reason of the identity of the group or collectivity at art. 7(2)(h). Gender "refers to the two sexes male and female . . . within the context of society." Art. 7(3). Rome Statute July 17, 1998, U.N. Doc. A/CONF.183/9.

2. See M. Cherif Bassiouni, *Crimes Against Humanity in International Criminal Law* 344–361 (2d rev. ed. 1999) (1992).

3. The Rome Statute also changed this when it included as crimes against humanity "rape, sexual slavery, enforced prostitution, forced pregnancy, enforced sterilization, or any other form of sexual violence of comparable gravity" when these crimes are "committed as part of a widespread or systematic attack directed against any civilian population." Rome Statute art. 17(g), July 17, 1998, U.N. Doc. A/CONF.183/9.

4. For example, Article 6 of the Convention on the Elimination of All Forms of Discrimination Against Women impliedly recognizes that trafficking in women is sex-based discrimination in a way that the 1949 Convention on Trafficking in Women and the 2001 Organized Crime Protocol on Trafficking do not. See Convention on the Elimination of All Forms of Discrimination Against Women, Dec. 18, 1979, G. A. Res. 34/180, U.N. GAOR, 34th Sess., Supp. No. 46, at 193, U.N. Doc. A/34/46, 1249 U.N.T.S. 13 (entered into force Sept. 3, 1981) [hereinafter CEDAW]; but see Convention for the Suppression of the Traffic in Persons and of the Exploitation of the Prostitution of Others, Dec. 2, 1949, U.N. Doc. A/1164, 96 U.N.T.S. 271, and Protocol to Prevent, Suppress and Punish Trafficking in Persons, Especially Women and Children, G. A. Res. 55/25, annex II, U.N. GAOR, 55th Sess., Supp. No. 49, at 60, U.N. Doc. A/45/49 (vol. I) (2001). In the criminal prohibitions, that it is mainly women who are trafficked for sex is recognized; that this practice is integral to discrimination against them as members of a gender-based group is not.

5. Andrea Dworkin, *Woman Hating* 95–154 (1984).

6. Diana E. H. Russell and Nicole Van De Ven, *The Proceedings of the International Tribunal on Crimes Against Women* 144–150 (1976), and *Femicide: The Politics of Woman Killing* (Jill Radford and Diana E. H. Russell, eds., 1992); Natalie Nenadic, "Femicide: A Framework for Understanding Genocide," in *Radically Speaking: Feminism Reclaimed* 456–464 (Diane Bell and Renate Klein, eds., 1996) (including discussion of contribution of Asja Amanda of Kareta Feminist Group).

7. Kadic v. Karadžić, 70 F.3d 232, 250 (2d Cir. 1995).

8. Violence Against Women Act of 1994 (VAWA), Pub. L. No. 103–322, tit. IV, 108 Stat. 1902 (codified as amended at 42 U.S.C. §§ 13931–14042 (2005)).

9. The individual federal cause of action for gender-based violence as sex-based discrimination created by VAWA at 42 U.S.C. § 13981 was invalidated on jurisdictional grounds for purported excess of use of the legislative power; other parts of the law remain in effect. United States v. Morrison, 529 U.S. 598 (2000). For commentary, see Catharine A. MacKinnon, "Disputing Male Sovereignty: On *United States v. Morrison*," in *Women's Lives, Men's Laws* 206 (2005).

10. Kadic v. Karadžić, 70 F.3d 232 (2d. Cir. 1995), *cert. denied*, 518 U.S. 1005 (1996).

11. See Foreign Sovereign Immunities Act of 1976 (FSIA), 90 stat. 2891 (codified as amended at 28 U.S.C. §§ 1330, 1602–1611. (2000) (upheld as constitutional by Verlinden B. V. v. Central Bank of Nigeria, 461 U.S. 480 (1983)). For classic cases on the doctrine generally, see The Schooner Exchange v. McFaddon, 11 U.S. 116 (1812), and Banco Nacional de Cuba v. Sabbatino, 376 U.S. 398 (1964). For discussion of the FSIA in relation to the Alien Tort Claims Act when a foreign state or individual acting in the official capacity of a foreign state is sued, see In re Estate of Marcos Human Rights Litigation, 978 F.2d 493 (9th Cir. 1992).

12. This is most typically achieved through reservations to international treaties. See Rebecca J. Cook, "Reservations to the Convention on the Elimination of All Forms of Discrimination Against Women," 30 *Virginia Journal of International Law* 643, 687–707 (1989–1990) (describing the "preservation of religious or customary laws" as the "sine qua non" of most countries' reservations to CEDAW), and Hilary Charlesworth and Christine Chinkin, *The Boundaries of International Law: A Feminist Analysis* 201–213 (2000)

13. Statute of the International Criminal Tribunal for the Former Yugoslavia (adopted May 25, 1993 by S/RES/827 (1993)) art. 5(g).

14. See Amartya Sen, "More Than 100 Million Women Are Missing," 37 *New York Review of Books* 20 (Dec. 20, 1990).

20. War Crimes Remedies at the National Level

1. See, e.g., Catharine A. MacKinnon, "Crimes of War, Crimes of Peace," above at No. 14 n.4 (describing Amnesty International's minimal documentation of rape as a human rights violation at that time).

2. Application Instituting Proceedings in the I.C.J. filed by the Republic of Bosnia and Herzegovina, Application of the Convention on the Prevention and Publishment of the Crime of Genocide, Bosnia and Herzegovina V. Serbia and Montenegro (filed Mar. 23, 1993) ¶¶ 45–68, *available at* www.icj-cij.org.

3. In the Genocide Convention, "genocide means any of the following acts committed with intent to destroy, in whole or in part, a national, ethnical, racial or religious group, as such: (a) killing members of the group; (b) causing serious bodily or mental harm to members of the group; (c) deliberately inflicting on the group conditions of life calculated to bring about its physical destruction in whole or in part; (d) imposing measures intended to prevent births within the group; (e) forcibly transferring children of the group to another group." Convention on the Prevention and Punishment of Genocide art. II, Dec. 9, 1948, 78 U.N.T.S. 277 (entered into force Jan. 12, 1951).

4. Alien Tort Claims Act, 28 U.S.C. § 1350 (2005).

5. Torture Victim Protection Act of 1991, Pub. L. No. 102–256, 106 Stat. 73 (codified at 28 U.S.C. § 1350 (2005)).

6. Filartiga v. Pena-Irala, 630 F.2d 876, 888–889 (2d Cir. 1980).

7. Id., at 880–882.

8. I originally filed the case together with the National Organization for Women Legal Defense and Education Fund (now known as Legal Momentum) as co-counsel. As it proceeded to trial, Paul, Weiss, Rifkind, Wharton, and Garrison became my co-counsel, in particular, Maria Vullo, Gerry Harper, Fay Rosenfeld, Will Walker, Liza Velazquez, and Eric Block.

9. Kadic v. Karadžić, 866 F.Supp. 734 (S.D.N.Y. 1994).

10. Kadic v. Karadžić, 70 F.3d 232 (2d Cir. 1995), 74 F.3d 377 (2d Cir. 1996). The U.S. government supported our right to proceed with the case.

11. *Cert. denied*, 518 U.S. 1005 (1996).

12. On August 10, 2000, a New York City jury awarded $745 million to our clients in punitive and compensatory damages, as well as an injunction. Christine Haughney and Bill Miller, "Karadzic Told to Pay Victims $745 Million: Civil Trial in N.Y. Ends With Judgment for 12 Women Who Survived Rape, Torture," *Washington Post*, A13 (Aug. 11, 2000); Patricia Hurtado, "A 'Moral' Triumph: Jury Awards $745M for Bosnian Atrocities," *Newsday*, A3 (Aug. 11, 2000); John Sullivan, "American Justice Tackles Rights Abuses Abroad," *New York Times*, D4 (Sept. 3, 2000).

13. As this talk went to press originally, the International Criminal Tribunal for Rwanda (ICTR) in Prosecutor v. Akayesu recognized rape as an instrumentality of genocide, Case No. ICTR-96-4-T, Judgment (Sept. 2, 1998), as well as a crime against humanity. The ICTY subsequently indicted Slobodan Milošević and others for rape as genocide as well. See Prosecutor v. Milošević, Bosnia: Amended Indictment of Slobodan Milošević ¶ 32(c), Case No. IT-02-54-T (Apr. 21, 2004).

14. See, e.g., United States v. Montgomery County Board of Education, 395 U.S. 225, 236–237 (1969); Owen M. Fiss, *Injunctions* 415–476 (1972). See also cases granting civil rights injunctions against prisons: Newman v. State of Alabama, 466 F. Supp. 428, 635–636 (M.D. Ala. 1979); Adams v. Mathis, 458 F. Supp. 302, 308–309 (M.D. Ala. 1978); and mental health systems: Lynch v. Baxley, 386 F.Supp. 378, 396–397 (M.D. Ala. 1974); Wyatt v. Stickney, 344 F. Supp. 373 (M.D. Ala. 1972), *affirmed in part, reversed in part, and remanded*, Wyatt v. Aderholt, 503 F.2d 1305 (5th Cir. 1974). See also Doug Rendleman, "Brown II's 'All Deliberate Speed' at Fifty: A Golden Anniversary or a Mid-Life Crisis for the Constitutional Injunction as a School Desegregation Remedy?" 41 *San Diego Law Review* 1575 (2004); Tracy A. Thomas, "Ubi Jus, Ibi Remedium: The Fundamental Right to a Remedy Under Due Process," 41 *San Diego Law Review* 1633 (2004); Myriam Gilles, "An Autopsy of the Structural Reform Injunction: Oops! . . . It's Still Moving!" 58 *University of Miami Law Review* 143 (2003).

21. Collective Harms Under the Alien Tort Statute: A Cautionary Note on Class Actions

1. "The district courts shall have original jurisdiction of any civil action by an alien for a tort only, committed in violation of the law of nations or a treaty of the United States." 28 U.S.C. § 1350 (1990). This statute was part of the Judiciary Act of 1789. Judiciary Act, ch. 20, § 9, 1 Stat. 73, 77 (1789).

2. Under Federal Rules of Civil Procedure 23.

3. Federal Rules of Civil Procedure 23(b)(1)(B).

4. Federal Rules of Civil Procedure 23(b)(1) and (2).

5. Federal Rules of Civil Procedure 23(c)(2).

6. According to Amchem Products Inc. v. Windsor, 521 U.S. 591, 631 (1997) (Breyer, J. dissenting), citing "Report of The Judicial Conference Ad Hoc Committee on Asbestos Litigation," at 7, 10–11 (March, 1991), asbestos lawsuits were more than 6 percent of all federal civil filings in 1990. See Deborah R. Hensler, "As Time Goes By: Asbestos Litigation After *Amchem* and *Ortiz*," 80 *Texas Law Review* 1899, 1900 (2002), stating that in 1990, one-third of civil cases filed in the Eastern District of Texas were asbestos cases, citing to "Report of The Judicial Conference Ad Hoc Committee on Asbestos Litigation," at 8; Carey C. Jordan, "Medical Monitoring in Toxic Tort Cases: Another Windfall for Texas Plaintiffs?" 33 *Houston Law Review* 473, 478 n.18, stating that as of 1984, 29 percent of pending cases in the Eastern District of Texas were asbestos cases, citing to Deborah R. Hensler et al., *Asbestos in the Courts: The Challenge of Mass Toxic Torts* 25–27 (1985); Jack B. Weinstein and Ellen B. Hershenov, "The Effect of Equity on Mass Tort Law," 1991 *University of Illinois Law Review* 269, 295 n.145 (1991) (stating that "as of the end of June 1990, 7,598 of a total of 10,818 pending civil cases in the Eastern Division of the Northern District of Ohio were asbestos cases"); Stephen Labaton, "Judges Panel, Seeing Court Crisis, Combines 26,000 Asbestos Cases," *New York Times*, A1 (July 30, 1991) ("Asbestos now accounts for the largest number of civil cases in the Federal courts, and asbestos cases are also plaguing many state courts.").

7. Ortiz v. Fibreboard Corp., 527 U.S. 815 (1999).

8. Federal Rules of Civil Procedure 23(b)(1) and (2).

9. Kadic v. Karadžić, 70 F.3d 232 (2d Cir. 1995), *cert. denied*, 518 U.S. 1005 (1996).

10. Doe v. Karadžić, 176 F.R.D. 458, 461 (S.D.N.Y. 1997). *Doe* counsel later clarified the claim as covering persons injured from April 1992 to February 1993.

11. Kadic, above note 9.

12. All the other panelists worked on the *Doe* case at one time or another. The class certification motion was filed when Beth Stephens, original lead counsel, was no longer actively associated with the case, and after Harold Hongju Koh, who contributed at a prior crucial period, had withdrawn as counsel to assume his position with the State Department.

13. Letter from Radovan Karadžić to the court 1 (1997), quoted in Doe v. Karadžić, 176 F.R.D. 458, 463 (S.D.N.Y. 1997).

14. Doe v. Karadžić, 182 F.R.D. 424 (1998).

15. In re Estate of Ferdinand Marcos, 25 F.3d 1467 (9th Cir. 1994).

16. In re Holocaust Victim Assets Litigation, No. 96 Civ. 4849 (E.D.N.Y. 2000).

17. The settlement amount was $1.25 billion to be made in four installments over three years with a first payment of $250 million, according to Joseph P. Fried, "Swiss Banks Reach Holocaust Accord," *New York Times*, A1 (Aug. 13, 1998).

18. See Philippines v. Marcos, Civil Case Nos. 0141 and 0185, slip op. at 17 (Republic of Philippines, Sandiganbayan, July 27, 1999) (Consolidated Resolution, Garchitorena, PJ). That court notes that one lawyer, Robert Swift, who also participated

as counsel in making the limited fund claims in the *Doe* case, was claiming $34,585,000 of the $40 million sought by the lawyers in the *Marcos* settlement.

19. Id., at 20.

20. Id., at 15–16 [emphasis added].

21. Id., at 16.

22. In adjudicating claim preclusion questions in claims brought by individual class members following even unsuccessful class actions, several circuits have found that a vicarious liability or principal/agent relationship provides enough privity to preclude their later claims. See, for example, Pelletier v. Zweifel, 921 F.2d 1465, 1502 (11th Cir. 1991), *cert. denied*, 502 U.S. 855 (1991); Lubrizol Corp. v. Exxon Corp., 871 F.2d 1279, 1288 (5th Cir. 1988); Cahill v. Arthur Andersen & Co., 822 F.2d 14 (2d Cir. 1987); Lambert v. Conrad, 536 F.2d 1183 (7th Cir. 1976). While a subsequent suit by a survivor who was an absent class member against a lower-level perpetrator might not be precluded from seeking relief by a successful resolution of *Doe*, it might—a successful case backed up by the limited-fund theory having a potentially more powerful preclusive effect.

23. The proceedings in the *Holocaust Victim Assets* litigation are multiple and on-going. Robert Swift is also involved in them.

24. See, for example, Exhibit H, Decl. of Haris Silajdzic, Co-Chairman of the Council of Ministers of Bosnia-Herzegovina, Doe v. Karadžić, No. 93 Civ. 878 (S.D.N.Y. 1997); Exhibit E, Declaration of Mediha Filipovic, Parliament Member of Bosnia-Herzegovina, id.

25. Doe v. Karadžić, 192 F.R.D. 133, 144–145 (S.D.N.Y. 2000).

26. John Sullivan, "American Justice Tackles Rights Abuses Abroad," *New York Times*, D4 (Sept. 3, 2000). See also David Rohde, "Jury in New York Orders Bosnian Serb to Pay Billions," *New York Times*, A10 (Sept. 26, 2000) (reporting on the *Doe* case: "The verdict came just weeks after another jury in New York returned a $745 million verdict against Dr. Karadzic in a civil case focusing on women who were raped during the war in the early 1990's.").

22. Genocide's Sexuality

1. Andrea Dworkin, "The Unremembered: Searching for Women at the Holocaust Memorial Museum," *Ms.*, 48, 54 (Nov. 1994).

2. Prosecutor v. Kupreskic et al., No. IT-95-l6-T, Judgment (transcript of oral opinion of Judge Cassese, ICTY, Jan. 14, 2000) (quoting words of Muslim woman from Bosnia-Herzegovina testified to by witness at trial). Judge Cassese uses this quotation to illustrate persecution, not genocide, in that the aim of the acts was expulsion, not destruction. In my view, forced expulsion can be genocidal and the acts described can be genocidal. On this point, see Order of Provisional Measures Application of the Convention on the Prevention and Punishment of the Crime of Genocide (Bosnia and Herzegovina v. Serbia and Montenegro), 1993 I.C.J. 3, ¶ 69 of separate opinion of Judge Lauterpacht (Sept. 13, 1993) (hereinafter Bosnia and Herzegovina v. Yugoslavia).

3. See generally United Nations, Commission of Experts on the Former Yugoslavia,

Final Report of the Commission of Experts Established Pursuant to Security Council Resolution 780 (1992) and Annexes, prepared by Professor M. Cherif Bassiouni and the staff of the DePaul University College of Law and its International Human Rights Law Institute (IHRLI) in Chicago (hereinafter Bassiouni Report).

4. Convention on the Prevention and Punishment of the Crime of Genocide, Dec. 9, 1949, 78 U.N.T.S. 277 (hereinafter Genocide Convention). Article 2 defines genocide as "any of the following acts committed with intent to destroy, in whole or in part, a national, ethnical, racial or religious group, as such: (a) killing members of the group; (b) causing serious bodily or mental harm to members of the group; (c) deliberately inflicting on the group conditions of life calculated to bring about its physical destruction in whole or in part; (d) imposing measures intended to prevent births within the group; (e) forcibly transferring children of the group to another group."

5. As stated by Judge Lauterpacht of the ICJ, acts of "'ethnic cleansing' . . . [are] difficult to regard as other than acts of genocide." Bosnia and Herzegovina v. Yugoslavia, ¶ 69.

6. The sources for the account in the above paragraphs are my clients in Kadic v. Karadžić, 70 F.3d 232 (2d Cir. 1996). Other first-person accounts are provided by Seada Vranic, *Breaking the Wall of Silence: The Voices of Raped Bosnia* (1996); Alexandra Stiglmayer, *Massenvergewaltigung: Krieg gegen die Frauen* (1993). Some of the facts mentioned above were prosecuted successfully by the ICTY, prominently in the Foča case. See generally Prosecutor v. Kunarac, Case No. IT-96-23 and IT-96-23/1T, Judgment (Feb. 22, 2001), finding those rapes as slavery but not genocidal.

7. See Bassiouni Report, above note 3. For statistics on killings, see Annex V, §§ I and V; Annex VI, §§ I C and I D; and Annex X, § II A. For a summary of statistics on sexual assaults, see Annex IX, § I A ("1. There are approximately 1,100 reported cases of rape and sexual assault; 2. About 800 victims are named, or the submitting source appears to know the identity of the victim, but does not disclose it; 3. About 1,800 victims are specifically referred to but are not named or identified sufficiently by the witness reporting the incident; 4. Witness reports also refer to additional numbers of victims through approximations. These reports suggest there may be about 10,000 additional victims the reports could eventually lead to; 5. About 550 of the reported cases refer to victims of rape and sexual assault but are unspecific and do not give any identifying information. . . . This statistical information may not represent the true extent of what has occurred in the former Yugoslavia.").

8. See Mladen Lončar, "Sexual Torture of Men in the War," in *War Violence, Trauma and the Coping Process: Armed Conflict in Europe and the Survivor Response* 212 (Libby Tata Arcel ed., 1998). A man's testicles were bitten off as public torture in the Omarska camp. See Prosecutor v. Tadic, Case No. IT-94-1, Opinion and Judgment, ¶ 206 (ICTY, May 7, 1997).

9. See Catharine A. MacKinnon, "Turning Rape into Pornography: Postmodern Genocide," above at No. 15 (documenting the making of a film of a rape of a Muslim woman by Serbian forces).

10. Id.

11. See Kadic v. Karadžić, above note 6; Prosecutor v. Milošević, Case No. IT-01-51-I, Indictment, ¶ 32 (Nov. 22, 2001). On the larger context of the Bosnian genocide, see Norman Cigar, *Genocide in Bosnia: The Policy of Ethnic Cleansing* (1995); Philip Cohen, *Serbia's Secret War: Propaganda and the Deceit of History* (1996).

12. For a stunning psychoanalytic study of the Freikorps, a private army in Germany between the wars, connecting the rise of fascism with sexual misogyny, see Klaus Theweleit, *Male Fantasies* (1987).

13. Joan Ringelheim perceptively observed that in her interviews with Jewish women Holocaust survivors, "although there are many stories of sexual abuse, they are not easy to come by. Some think it inappropriate to talk about these matters; discussions about sexuality desecrate the memories of the dead, or the living, or the Holocaust itself. For others, it is simply too difficult and painful. Still others think it may be a trivial issue. One survivor told me that she had been sexually abused by a number of Gentile men while she was in hiding, when she was about eleven years old. Her comment about this was that it 'was not important . . . except to me.' She meant that it had no significance within the larger picture of the Holocaust." Joan Ringelheim, "Women and the Holocaust: A Reconsideration of Research," 10 *Signs: Journal of Women in Culture and Society* 741, 745 (Summer 1985). As to the social meaning of the sexual, it is worth pondering that people who can describe thousands of people being killed on a single day in front of them find it a desecration of the memory to talk about brothels, or those who can tell of their families falling on top of them when shot in a pit find it too painful to discuss having been raped. Ringelheim reports that at a conference that presented panels on myriad details of the Holocaust, when she questioned the lack of a single mention of women or gender, the organizers at the Holocaust Memorial Museum said, "We forgot." Joan Ringelheim, "The Split Between Gender and the Holocaust," in *Women in the Holocaust* 340, 346 (Lenore J. Weitzman and Dalia Ofer, eds., 1998).

14. Dagmar Herzog, "Hubris and Hypocrisy, Incitement and Disavowal: Sexuality and German Fascism," 11: 1/2 *Journal of the History of Sexuality* 6, 6 (Jan./Apr. 2002).

15. *Trial of the Major War Criminals*, vol. XXII, at 547 (1948) (Nuremberg, 1947–1949) (reading the conclusions of the court at sentencing).

16. Streicher, for publishing, was convicted for incitement to murder and extermination, a form of persecution on political and racial grounds, a crime against humanity, and executed. *Trial of the Major War Criminals*, above note 15, at vol. XXII, 549 (finding Streicher guilty on one count); and vol. I, 365 (sentencing him to death).

17. George Mosse, *The Image of Man: The Creation of Modern Masculinity* 175 (1996).

18. Gesetz zum Schutze des deutschen Blutes und der deutschen Ehre, 1935 Reichsgesetzblatt, Teil 1, 1146. This provision forbids "marriages between Jews and German nationals of German or related blood" (art. 1) and "sexual intercourse (except in marriage) between Jews and German nationals of German or related blood" (art. 2). For an illuminating historical discussion of the Nazi concept of "blood," see Allyson D. Polsky, "Blood, Race, and National Identity: Scientific and Popular Discourses," 23:

3/4 *Journal of Medical Humanities* 171, 174–178 (Dec. 2002). Only men violating the prohibition on extramarital intergroup sexual intercourse were to be punished with imprisonment or hard labor (art. 5, § 2). Jews were also forbidden to employ German women under forty-five years of age in their households (art. 3).

19. For early documentation, see Hensley Henson, *The Yellow Spot: The Outlawing of Half a Million Human Beings* 216–234 (1936).

20. Photograph in *Voices and Views: A History of the Holocaust* 142 (Deborah Dwork ed., 2002) (photograph of Aug. 15, 1935).

21. See Patricia Szobar, "Telling Sexual Stories in the Nazi Courts of Law: Race Defilement in Germany, 1933 to 1945," 11 *Journal of the History of Sexuality* 131 (Jan./ Apr. 2002). See also Alexandra Przyrembel, "'Race Defilement' in Court" (unpublished paper from Workshop, Yad Vashem, Jerusalem, Nov. 20–23, 2001) (reporting research on over 500 prosecutions for *Rassenschande* in Nazi courts).

22. An overview of the project is provided by the indictment of its operatives under Control Council Law No. 10 in *Trial of the Major War Criminals*, above note 15, vol. IV, at 608, especially indictments of Sollmann, Ebner, Tesch, and Viermetz. The judgments can be found in vol. V at 162–164.

23. See Joshua Hammer, "Hitler's Children," *Newsweek International* (Mar. 20, 2000); Georg Lilienthal, *Der "Lebensborn e. V.": Ein Instrument nationalsozialistischer Rassenpolitik* (1985). The best article in English is Larry V. Thompson, "Lebensborn and the Eugenics Policy of the Reichsführer-SS," 4:1 *Central European History* 54–77 (Mar. 1971).

24. Catrine Clay and Michael Leapman carefully canvass the evidence on the question of whether *Lebensborn* homes were stud farms, including Himmler's reported remark that "I have made it known privately that any unmarried woman who is alone and longs for a child can turn to lebensborn with perfect confidence. . . . [W]e recommend only racially faultless men as 'conception assistants.'" Felix Kersten, *The Kersten Memoirs, 1940–1945* (Hutchinson, 1956), quoted in Catrine Clay and Michael Leapman, *Master Race: The Lebensborn Experiment in Nazi Germany* 71 (1995). German carrots and sticks are reported. Id. at 53–69. It is also noted that the suspicion that *Lebensborn* homes provided for arranged liaisons between suitable potential racial stock and SS men was widespread at the time, id. at 69, but it is asserted that the real disapproval of such arrangements was on grounds that they encouraged conception outside marriage. Marc Hillel and Clarissa Henry, *Lebensborn e. V.: Im Namen der Rasse* (1975), discuss all aspects of the project in detail but never focus on how the women, whether German women or those of occupied countries, became pregnant. One source that purports to provide contemporary evidence that *Lebensborn* included reproductive brothels, *Freiwillige Erzeugen* (voluntary breeding) establishments, is Peter Neumann's account as an officer on leave of his experience with a young German woman. See Peter Neumann, *Other Men's Graves* 74–85 (Constantine Fitz Gibbon, trans., 1958). Dialogue includes: "[Her:] Don't you think it's pretty horrible this business of selling one's body as an instrument of procreation?" [Him:] "You aren't selling your body. You're giving it to Germany, which is a very different matter." Id. at 83.

Many people who have studied the subject in depth seem certain that the homes were maternity homes set up to further racist eugenics, not breeding farms. See also Jacques Delarue, *The Gestapo: A History of Horror* 70–71 (Mervyn Savill, trans., 1964). Evans comments on "the attempts by the Nazis to mobilize women voluntarily by means of a massive propaganda campaign" for reproduction of Germans. Richard J. Evans, "German Women and the Triumph of Hitler," 48:1 *Journal of Modern History*, On-Demand Supplement 123–175 (Mar. 1976), at 149. Manfred Wolfson's "Constraint and Choice in the SS Leadership," 18 *Western Political Quarterly* 551, 557 (Sept. 1965), describes *Lebensborn* as "providing secret confinements in special lying-in homes for the unwed companions of SS men." Annette Timm, "Sex with a Purpose: Prostitution, Venereal Disease, and Militarized Masculinity in the Third Reich," 11:1/2 *Journal of the History of Sexuality* 223, 246–247 (Jan./Apr. 2002), takes the same view, but also references Bluel's account of a "policy of providing soldiers on leave with pleasant female company with a view both to increasing the men's support for the party and to creating social situations that might in the end have positive population political outcomes," id. at 247, which is precisely what Neumann describes. The Nazis destroyed as many of the *Lebensborn* files as they could during the last days of World War II, although some have since been recovered. See "Hitler Race Project Records Revealed," AP Berlin (Nov. 23, 1999).

25. Timm, for example, comments: "Sex in the Third Reich was for too long a virtual terra incognita for historians of Germany. There was an understandable desire to avoid providing titillating details about so murderous a regime." "Sex with a Purpose," above note 24, at 223. Why accounts of sexual atrocities would necessarily be titillating is not explained, as the possible role of sexuality in making the regime murderous is evaded.

26. See Thompson, above note 23, at 71–72, and Lilienthal, above note 23.

27. On the Norwegian *Lebensborn* homes and children generally, see Clay and Leapman, above note 24, at 131–149. Attorney Randi Hagen Spydevold sued the Norwegian government for compensation for *Lebensborn* children in early 2001, alleging Norwegian official cooperation in the maltreatment of an estimated 12,000 children born to Norwegian women by Germans under the *Lebensborn* program. One article on this lawsuit noted that "[a]cross occupied Europe, German soldiers fathered more than 200,000 children." Carl Honore, "Children of Nazis Seeking Peace with Their Past, Norwegian Lawsuit: Many Endured 'Systematic Torture' in Mental Asylums After Germany's Defeat," *National Post* (Sept. 11, 2000). Three hundred thousand *Wehrmacht* soldiers were stationed in Norway, which was governed by the infamous collaborator Viskun Quisling. Can it be that none of these children was conceived through rape?

28. Usually, commentaries use language that presumes that women, whether German women or women of occupied countries, giving birth out of wedlock to children of the Nazi SS had sex with them voluntarily. Larry V. Thompson, above note 23, at 71, speaks of several thousand French women impregnated by occupying soldiers in terms of "the inevitable fraternization between the troops and the natives."

Clay and Leapman, above note 24, at 72 emphasize sexual freedom: "Although the whole concept of selective racial breeding is disgusting, the suggestion of random and wholesale loveless coupling is not wholly appropriate. While some of the pregnancies may well have been motivated by a woman's strong sense of duty to the state, or in some cases have been brought about by coercion, the scant available evidence suggests genuine affection between many of the mothers and their SS lovers. They were, after all, healthy young women with normal emotional needs." Anette Warring, *Tysker-piger—under besoettelse og retsopgr* (1994) states, "During the occupation tens of thousands of Danish women *had affairs* with Wehrmacht soldiers resulting in more than five thousand war children." (emphasis added). Tony Paterson and Allan Hall, "Norwegian Government Sued over Children Nazis Left Behind," *Telegraph* (London), Issue 2102 (Feb. 25, 2001) notes that Himmler's policy "actively promoted sexual relations between German troops and women classed as true Aryans—such as the Norwegians," but also that "an estimated 50,000 Norwegian women were thought to have *had affairs* with Germans during the occupation." As of October 28, 2005, Norway reportedly quietly decided to pay war pensions (for those who adhered to "good national principles" during the occupation) to the few dozen surviving women known to have had sex with German soldiers during World War II, producing an estimated 12,000 children. Eva Simonsen of the University of Oslo described the principle vindicated as no longer punishing these women "for the love stories of their youth." In the same article, the occupying forces are described as "actively encourage[ing] affairs between local women and German soldiers [as] part of an SS plan to enrich the Aryan gene pool." "Norway finally forgives women who slept with Nazi soldiers," news.telegraph.uk (10–28–05). Again, were none of these women raped?

29. Opening statement of the prosecution, the Rusha case, Prosecutor McHaney, 4 *Trials of War Criminals Before the Nuernberg Military Tribunals* 687 (1997).

30. Anna Rosmus, "Involuntary Abortions for Polish Forced Laborers," in *Experience and Expression: Women, the Nazis, and the Holocaust* 76, 78 (Elizabeth R. Baer and Myrna Goldenberg, eds., 2003).

31. *The Black Book of Polish Jewry: An Account of the Martyrdom of Polish Jewry Under the Nazi Occupation* 25 (Jacob Apenslak et al., eds., 1995) (1943).

32. Yaffa Eliach, "Women and the Holocaust: Historical Background," in *Women of Valor: Partisans and Resistance Fighters*, originally published in 6:4 *Journal of the Center for Holocaust Studies* 8, 8 (Spring 1990).

33. *Black Book*, above note 31, at 27. The Jewish community leaders reportedly adamantly refused.

34. See *New York Times* (Jan. 8, 1943) p. 8 (letter, name withheld), reprinted in Zev Garber, *Shoah: The Paradigmatic Genocide* 98 (1994) (discussing authenticity of letter and documenting author as Chaya Feldman).

35. Raul Hilberg, *Perpetrators, Victims, Bystanders: The Jewish Catastrophe, 1933–1945* 213 (1992) (quoting report by the Security Service in Galicia, Kommandeur of Security Police/III-A-4, to Obersturmbannführer Willi Seibert in Berlin and to Standartenführer [Colonel] Heim in Kraków, July 2, 1943, National Archives of the United States, Record Group 242, T175, Roll 575).

36. Birgit Beck, "Vergewaltigung von Frauen als Kriegsstrategie im Zweiten Weltkrieg?" in *Ausübung, Erfahrung und Verweigerung von Gewalt in Kriegen des 20. Jahrhunderts* 34, 43–44 (Andreas Gestrich ed., 1996). See also Doris Bergen, *War and Genocide: A Concise History of the Holocaust* 107, 110 (2003).

37. See above note 13.

38. Judith M. Isaacson, *Seed of Sarah: Memoirs of a Survivor* 144–145 (1990). For an analysis that gives further depth to Anne Frank herself, see Catherine A. Bernard, "Anne Frank: The Cultivation of the Inspirational Victim," in Baer and Goldenberg, above note 30, at 201.

39. Isaacson, above note 38, at 53.

40. Olga Lengyel, *Five Chimneys: The Story of Auschwitz* 185 (1947).

41. Ruth Elias, *Die Hoffnung erhielt mich am Leben: Mein Weg von Theresienstadt und Auschwitz nach Israel* 149 (1988) ("Vergewaltigung der jüdischen Mädchen war erlaubt. Das war doch keine Rassenschande").

42. Survivor quoted by Ringelheim, "The Split Between," above note 13, at 341.

43. See, e.g., the account of Stanley Rustin, "Camps," in *Proceedings of the Conference of Women Surviving the Holocaust* 165 (Esther Katz and Joan M. Ringelheim, eds., 1983) (on Skarzysko).

44. They are legion. See Helen Fein, "Genocide and Gender: The Uses of Women and Group Destiny," 1 *Journal of Genocide Research* 43, 53 (1999) ("What is striking about the Holocaust . . . is the lack of a pattern of gender discrimination and sanctioned rape"); Myrna Goldenberg, "Memoirs of Auschwitz Survivors: The Burden of Gender," in Weitzman and Ofer, above note 13, at 336; Jack G. Morrison, *Ravensbrück: Everyday Life in a Women's Concentration Camp, 1939–45* 177–178 (2000); Melissa Raphael, *The Female Face of God in Auschwitz: A Jewish Feminist Theology of the Holocaust* 183 n.48 (2003).

45. See Julia Roos, "Backlash Against Prostitutes' Rights: Origins and Dynamics of Nazi Prostitution Policies," 11:1/2 *Journal of the History of Sexuality* 67, 69 (Jan./Apr. 2002); Christa Paul, *Zwangsprostitution: Staatlich errichtete Bordelle im Nationalsozialismus* (1994).

46. See Timm, above note 24, at 227.

47. Jewish women were apparently no longer officially permitted to be used in Wehrmacht brothels after March 1942. See *Befreier und Befreite: Krieg, Vergewaltigungen, Kinder* (Helke Sander and Barbara Johr, eds., 1992).

48. Paul, above note 45, 58–75.

49. Morrison collects sources describing these recruitments in detail with no mention of religion, race, or ethnicity. See Morrison, above note 44, at 201–204.

50. See Nanda Herbermann, *The Blessed Abyss: Inmate #6582 in Ravensbrück Concentration Camp for Women* 132 (Hester Baer, trans., 2000) (account by a German Catholic resistance member inmate from 1941 to 1943 who was block elder at Ravensbrück for 400 prostitutes). See also Timm, above note 24, at 224.

51. Heinz Heger, *The Men with the Pink Triangle: The True Life-and-Death Story of Homosexuals in the Nazi Death Camps* 96 (David Fernbach, trans., 1980), and Morrison, above note 44, at 202, both report this.

52. Christa Schulz, "Weibliche Haftlinge aus Ravensbrück in Bordellen der Männerkonzentrationslager," in *Frauen in Konzentrationslagern: Bergen-Belsen, Ravensbrück* 135, 139 (Claus Füllberg-Stolberg, Martina Jung, Renate Reibe, and Martina Scheitenberger, eds., 1994).

53. Heger, above note 51, at 96.

54. See Enno Georg, *Die wirtschlaftlichen Unternehmungen der SS* 116 and n.471 (1963); "Instructions Concerning the Granting of Special Favors to Prisoners," trans. of Document No. NC-400, Office of Chief of Counsel for War Crimes; Reinhild Kassig and Christa Paul, "Haftlings-Bordelle in deutschen KZs," *Emma*, 32–37 (Mar. 1992).

55. Heger, above note 51, at 61. No focused attention appears to have been paid to the ethnicity or nationality of these young men, although Heger's report focuses on Poles. Heger, who was Austrian, was used in this way. The literature, frustratingly, tends to omit racial, ethnic, or religious specifications once a person is sexually defined, for example, as a prostitute or homosexual.

56. As a further factor in nonreporting, it should be noted that through these arrangements, Jewish men had the possible shame of using women in captive settings as rewards from exterminators for forced labor contributing to their own demise, on top of whatever shame might otherwise come from men using captive or prostituted women. There are also reports that Jewish men used Jewish women for sex for survival outside the brothels and raped them; under genocidal conditions, women are under even more pressures not to report intracommunity sexual assaults than they are otherwise. Jewish women also had the possible shame of being used in this way as well as, for those who lived, the shame of having survived possibly for that reason. Perhaps the evocative description of the shaming effects of the *Rassenschande* context also applies in the context of sexual abuse: "They were ashamed of their black hair, their Semitic nose, their defenselessness. . . . They were ashamed of their shame." Joel König, *Den Netzen entronnen* 155 (1967).

57. See Eugen Kogon, *Der SS-Staat: Das System der deutschen Konzentrationslager* 215 (1994) (1947); Ka-Tzetnik 135633, *House of Dolls* (Moshe M. Kohn, trans., 1956). This book was written by Karol Cetynski, also named Yehiel Dinur, based on the diary of Daniella Preleshnik, a fourteen-year-old (in 1939) Polish Jew who was forced into prostitution in Auschwitz's "House of Dolls" brothel. She is identified in some editions as his sister. Christa Paul found that while Ravensbrück was used to supply the brothels in most of the camps, women at Auschwitz were forced into prostitution there for its three brothels and at its satellites. See Paul, above note 45, at 26.

58. *Women in the Holocaust: A Collection of Testimonies* viii (Jehoshua Eibeshitz and Arma Eibeshitz, eds. and trans., 1992); Jehoshua Eibeshitz, in *Remember! A Collection of Testimonies* 12–13 (Anna Eilenberg-Eibeshitz, trans., Esther Sarah Eilenberg, ed., 1992) (story of "Miriam").

59. See Paul, above note 45, at 106 (quoting it).

60. Lengyel, above note 40, at 181.

61. Paul, above note 45, at 104. The literature contains much denial of this fact, concluding to the contrary with varying degrees of insistence and vehemence, based

primarily on lack of evidence and the view that since it was illegal, the Nazis could not have done it. A typical instance is Morrison, above note 44, at 73, 202. For further discussion, see Janet Anschutz, Kerstin Meier, and Sanja Obajdin, "'Dieses leere Gefuhl, und die Blicke der anderen . . . ': Sexuelle Gewalt gegen Frauen," in *Frauen in Konzentrationslagern*, above note 52, at 130–131; Schultz, above note 52, at 135. Until Paul's book, there was not a lot of evidence, but what did exist was firsthand. That the Nazis were law-abiding, particularly in the camps and where forced sex was concerned, seems an odd article of faith.

62. Elizabeth Heineman comments, "Research into Nazi-era brothels challenges our use of the model of 'prostitution' (which forefronts exchange) to describe acts that might better be described as 'rape' (which forefronts violence)." 11:1/2 "Sexuality and Nazism: The Doubly Unspeakable," *Journal of the History of Sexuality* 22, 66 (Jan./Apr. 2002). She understands that brothel sex was rape, but this understanding could illuminate prostitution in general rather than challenge the usage of the term in this setting. Her analysis misses both the exchange of sex for survival in the camps and the forms of coercion involved in that same exchange in most instances of prostitution outside camps. By contrast, Magnus Hirschfeld, Andreas Gaspar, and F. Aquila, eds., in *Sittengeschichte des Zweiten Weltkrieges* 341 (1968), observe: "The term prostitution should not be narrowly defined when speaking of prostitution in war. It not only includes brothels but almost always includes relationships between occupying forces and local women who hope to manage an advantage through love affairs. Often there is also forced prostitution which is equivalent to rape."

63. See Andrea Dworkin, *Scapegoat: The Jews, Israel, and Women's Liberation* 33 (2000).

64. Elie A. Cohen, *Human Behaviour in the Concentration Camp* 135 (1988). See also Edith Bruck, *Who Loves You Like This* 31, 44, 57, 113–115 (2001).

65. Lengyel, above note 40, at 182.

66. Felicia Berland Hyatt, *Close Calls: Memoirs of a Survivor* 76–77 (1991).

67. Cecile Klein, *Sentenced to Live* 73 (1988). For further reports, see Judy Cohen, *Women and the Holocaust* (2001), at www.columbia.edu/acis/.bartleby/jewett; *Auschwitz: True Tales from a Grotesque Land* 14 (Sarah Nomberg-Pryztyk, Eli Pfefferkorn, and David H. Hersch, eds., Roslyn Hirsch, trans., 1985); Raphael, above note 44, at 183 n.48.

68. Leib Langfuss, "The Horrors of Murder," in *The Scrolls of Auschwitz* 209 (Ber Mark, ed., 1985).

69. 2 *Nazism, 1919–1945: A History in Documents and Eyewitness Accounts* 1180 (Jeremy Noakes and Geoffrey Pridham, eds., 1983).

70. Myrna Goldenberg, quoted by Judy Cohen, "Women's Holocaust Narratives: Violence and Sexuality as a Theme in Memoirs by Women Survivors" (2001), at www .interlog.com/~mighty/essays/lessons2.htm. I was originally referred to most of the sources referenced in notes 40 and 64–70 by Judy Cohen's excellent Web site.

71. Heger, above note 51, at 97.

72. This aspect of the freezing experiments is described in *Trial of Major War*

Criminals, above note 15, at vol. II, 525 ("Himmler personally ordered that rewarming by the warmth of human bodies also be attempted," which was done "by placing the chilled victim between two naked [Gypsy] women" from Ravensbrück).

73. They can be seen at Yad Vashem and the Holocaust Memorial Museum.

74. See Prosecutor v. Akayesu, Case No. ICTR-96-4-T, Judgment, 45 (Sept. 2, 1998), ¶¶ 112–129.

75. See generally Binaifer Nowrojee, *Shattered Lives: Sexual Violence During the Rwandan Genocide and Its Aftermath* (1996). The perpetrators were Hutu and all the targets were Tutsi and some moderate and intermarried Hutu. See Human Rights Watch, *Slaughter Among Neighbors: The Political Origins of Communal Violence* 24 (1995).

76. Prosecutor v. Semanza, Case No. ICTR-97-20-T, ¶ 253 (May 15, 2003). The court clarified at idem that the witness explained that "the Accused used the Kinyarwaanda word *kurongora*, which means 'to marry' as well as 'to make love.'"

77. Catherine Bonnet, "Le viol des femmes survivants de genocide du Rwanda," in *Rwanda: Un génocide du XXe siècle* 18 (Raymond Verdier, Emmanuel Ecaux, and Jean-Pierre Chrétien, eds., 1995).

78. United Nations, *Report on the Situation of Human Rights in Rwanda*, Submitted by Mr. Rene Degni-Segui, Special Rapporteur of the Commission on Human Rights, under paragraph 20 of the Resolution S-3/1 of May 25, 1994, E/CN.4/1996/68, Jan. 29, 1996, at 7 (estimating from at least 250,000 pregnancies to at most 500,000 cases of rape in the Rwandan genocide). One typical account: "The soldiers told the Interahamwe to go to work, and they killed people and also singled out some girls and put them aside. According to the witness they 'had their way' with these girls and then killed them. Most of the women killed were stripped of their clothing, 'so that Tutsi women could be seen naked.' The Interahamwe continued to 'have their way' until they left satisfied at around 11 P.M." Prosecutor v. Rutuganda, Case No. ICTR-96-3-T, Judgment and Sentence, ¶ 271 (Dec. 6, 1999).

79. See Nowrojee, above note 75, at 15–19; Prosecutor v. Nahimana, Case No. ICTR-99-52-T, Judgment and Sentence, ¶¶ 114, 139, 117–180, 182, 188, 210, 245, 935, 964, 1079 (Dec. 3, 2003).

80. See, e.g., Prosecutor v. Akayesu, above note 74, at ¶ 449.

81. See, e.g., Prosecutor v. Musema, Case No. ICTR-96-5-D, Judgment and Sentence, ¶ 932 (Jan. 27, 2000).

82. Id. at ¶ 933.

83. See, e.g., Rhonda Copelon, "Surfacing Gender: Reconceptualizing Crimes Against Women in Time of War," in *Women's Rights, Human Rights: International Feminist Perspectives* 199 (Rebecca Cook, ed., 1996); contrast Nowrojee, above note 75, at 34–36.

84. Genocide Convention, above note 4.

85. "Contrary to popular belief, the crime of genocide does not imply the actual extermination of [a] group in its entirety, but is understood as such once any one of the acts mentioned in Article 2(2) through 2(2)(e) is committed with the specific intent

to destroy 'in whole or in part' a national, ethnical, racial or religious group." *Akayesu*, above note 74, ¶ 497.

86. See, e.g., Comisión para el Esclarecimiento Histórico (CEH), *Guatemala: Memoria del Silencio* ¶ 2249 (CEH, 1999) ("when sexual violence [rape], that form of violence directed specifically against women, is utilized in a massive and public manner it is an indication of the intention to exterminate a group."). See also United States Commission on International Religious Freedom, *Hearing on Communal Violence in Gujarat, India, and the U.S. Response*, Washington, D.C., June 10, 2002; Ruth Baldwin, "Gujarat's Gendered Violence," in *Nothing Sacred: Women Respond to Religious Fundamentalism and Terror* 185 (Betsy Reed, ed., 2002).

87. The Supreme Court of Canada instructively so found in Regina v. McGraw, [1991] 3 S.C.R. 72, 83–84.

88. Kadic v. Karadžić, above note 6, established this conceptualization under international law in the United States under the Alien Tort Claims Act in the Second Circuit.

89. *Akayesu*, above note 74, at ¶¶ 731–734. Why the Yugoslav Tribunal hesitated to prosecute genocidal rape until its Milošević indictment (see *Milošević*, above note 11, at ¶ 32), tending to charge rape as anything but genocide and as genocide all violent acts but rape, remains difficult to explain.

90. See, e.g., James Yin and Shi Young, *The Rape of Nanking: An Undeniable History in Photographs* (1996).

91. That the Nazi genocide killed and transported Jews *to* Germany for liquidation and the Bosnian genocide killed and deported or ejected all non-Serbs *from* Bosnia-Herzegovina only defines the perpetrators' respective territorial ambitions and levels of organization; it does not make one a genocide, the other not.

92. This is at least reported in Joanne Csete, *The War Within the War: Sexual Violence Against Women and Girls in Eastern Congo* 25 (2002). Such reports may reflect the complex many-sidedness of the conflict or the lack of information of outsiders on its ethnic dimensions.

93. Helpful work on this topic is Roger Smith, "Genocide and the Politics of Rape," paper presented at the conference of the Association of Genocide Scholars, College of William and Mary, Williamsburg, Va. (June 14–16, 1995); Hsu-Ming Teo, "The Continuum of Sexual Violence in Occupied Germany, 1945–49," 5:2 *Women's History Review* 191 (1996).

94. I did not say that genocidal rape is worse, here or anywhere, and I do not think it is. It apparently bears repeating that nothing here implies, suggests, or presupposes any hierarchy of harm, value, or seriousness between rape in war, rape in genocide, rape in slavery, and rape in other settings. For example, to say that genocide goes beyond war is simply an empirical observation that genocide is not confined to wartime settings. Nor is the purpose here to create a typology or to produce criteria on the basis of which rapes can be classified one way or another. Nor is this analysis a moral discussion.

95. Prosecutor v. Jelisic, Case No. IT-95-10-T, Judgment, ¶¶ 78–83 (Dec. 14,

1999); Case Concerning Legality of Use of Force (Yugoslavia v. Belgium), 1999 I.C.J., *available at* 1999 WL 1693067, ¶ 35 (June 2, 1999); see also Prosecutor v. Bagilishema, Case No. ICTR-95-1A-T, ¶ 64 (opinion of Judge Gunawardana, June 7, 2001); Prosecutor v. Kayishema and Ruzindana, Case No. ICTR-95-1-T, Judgment, ¶¶ 95–97 (May 21, 1999) ("'in part' requires the intention to destroy a considerable number of individuals who are part of the group. Individuals must be targeted due to their membership in the group to satisfy this definition."). Of interest also is the ICJ's opinion in the Kosova bombing case, finding that the NATO bombings, although intensive and sustained, including of populated areas of Yugoslavia, were not genocidal in part because they did not entail destructive intent "towards a group as such." Case Concerning Legality of Use of Force (Yugoslavia v. Belgium), above, at ¶ 40.

96. Attorney General of Israel v. Eichmann, (1968) 36 *Israel Law Review* 18 (District Court, Jerusalem), ¶ 190.

97. Ad Hoc Committee on Genocide, 3 GAOR, Part I, Sixth Committee Summary Records (1948), 124–125 (76th mtg.), as cited in Hurst Hannum, "International Law and Cambodian Genocide: The Sounds of Silence," 11 *Human Rights Quarterly* 82 110 n.101 (XXXX); *Kayishema and Ruzindana*, above note 95, at ¶ 99: "'Destroying' has to be directed at the group *as such*, that is, *qua group.*"

98. Prosecutor v. Sikirica et al., Case No. IT-95-8-T, Judgment on Defence Motion to Acquit, ¶ 89 (ICTY, Sept. 3, 2001).

99. *Report of the International Law Commission on the Work of Its Forty-eighth Session, May 6–July 30, 1996*, U.N. Doc. A/51/10, 88.

100. Bassiouni Report, above note 3, II H I 3.

101. *Akayesu*, above note 74, ¶ 521; also *Rutuganda:* "because they belonged to the Tutsi group and for the very fact that they belonged to the said group," above note 78, ¶ 399.

102. *Rutuganda*, above note 78, ¶ 60.

103. See Catharine A. MacKinnon, "A Sex Equality Approach to Sexual Assault," *Sexual Coercion: Understanding and Management* 265 (Robert Prentky, Eric Janus, and Michael Seto, eds., 2003), for further elaboration.

104. The history of the addition of "as such" to the language of the convention is no guide. Venezuela, offering a compromise between those who wanted to delete motive and those who wanted to retain or even strengthen it, proposed adding "as such"; the idea was that motives would be included but not enumerated. See Nehemiah Robinson, *The Genocide Convention: A Commentary* 60–61 (1960); William A. Schabas, *Genocide in International Law: The Crime of Crimes* 245–253 (2000). Whether the term added a motive element that was otherwise not there or removed one that might have been stronger remains cloudy.

105. This analysis is presented in Catharine A. MacKinnon, *Toward a Feminist Theory of the State* (1989).

106. See *Femicide: The Politics of Woman Killing* 10–11 (Jill Radford and Diana E. H. Russell, eds., 1992).

107. This is argued in MacKinnon, above note 105.

108. For a stunning study in the latter, see Lisa Cardyn, "Sexualized Racism/Gen-

dered Violence: Trauma and the Body Politic in the Reconstruction South" (May 2003) (Ph.D. dissertation, Yale University).

109. Sometimes resistance succeeds. In the case of African Americans, for example, rape had a shattering effect without entirely destroying community cohesion. The long-term effects of systematic rape by white men in particular on that community could doubtless use further study. The fact that rape is racist does not alone make it genocidal, which is not to say that it is not destructive. The distinctions lie in other aspects of the genocide definition, specifically with intent.

110. Indeed, from slavery forward, the perpetrators of the rapes have been arguably obsessed with preserving African Americans as a distinct group while destroying their family structure and serving to obliterate the distinctiveness of each culture from which they came. The point was to exploit them for labor and keep the new group, African Americans, socially distinct to maintain white supremacy. If this group was destroyed qua group, against whom would whites define themselves as superior by distinction? Who would do the hard and unpleasant and low-paid work? However murderous, racism against African Americans has had a stake in preserving rather than destroying the group as such. That American racism, including the rape under slavery, included crimes against humanity is incontestable. The ICTY's opinion in the Foča case, in conceiving some rapes in the Bosnian situation as "slavery" (see Prosecutor v. Kunarac, above note 6), was thus able to bring out many functions of sexual subordination through this parallel; but putting them in the slavery framework at the same time failed to contextualize the acts within the genocide of which they were a part.

111. See *Musema*, above note 81, at ¶ 933 ("Accordingly, the Chamber notes that on the basis of the evidence presented, it emerges that acts of serious bodily and mental harm, including rape and other forms of sexual violence were often accompanied by humiliating utterances, which clearly indicated that the intention underlying each specific act was to destroy the Tutsi group as a whole. The Chamber notes, for example, that during the rape of Nyiramusugi, Musema declared: 'The pride of the Tutsis will end today.' In this context, the acts of rape and sexual violence were an integral part of the plan conceived to destroy the Tutsi group. Such acts targeted Tutsi women, in particular, and specifically contributed to their destruction and therefore that of the Tutsi group as such. Witness N testified before the Chamber that Nyiramusugi, who was left for dead by those who raped her, had indeed been killed in a way. Indeed, the Witness specified that 'what they did to her is worse than death.'").

112. Id.

113. Group itself, for purposes of genocidal intent, includes being "identified as such by others, including perpetrators of the crimes." *Kayeshima*, above note 95, at ¶ 98. See also *Bagilishema*, above note 95, at ¶ 65; *Rutuganda*, above note 78, at ¶ 56; *Musema*, above note 81, at ¶ 161. Given that identity is a social fact, in substantial part comprised of identification by others, this is appropriate.

114. For general information, see *Traumatic Stress: The Effects of Overwhelming Experience on Mind, Body, and Society* (Bessel A. van der Kolk, Alexander C. Mc-Farlane, and Lars Weisaeth, eds., 1996).

115. See Diana E. H. Russell and Rebecca M. Bolen, *The Epidemic of Rape and*

Child Sexual Abuse in the United States (2000). For summaries of and references to data, see Catharine A. MacKinnon, *Sex Equality* 776–778 (2001).

116. A powerful example of being tortured as a Jew (in Argentina) is provided by Jacobo Timerman, *Prisoner Without a Name, Cell Without a Number* (Toby Talbot, trans., 1981).

117. Quoted in Nowrojee, above note 75, at 25. There was much talk during the Bosnian conflagration about Muslim men rejecting raped Bosnian Muslim women. Our experience was that the rejection was no greater and in many cases less than what is standard for men in the United States relative to women in their families who are raped.

118. Quoted in *Kupreskic*, above note 2, ¶ 752.

119. See Andrea Dworkin, "Remembering the Witches," in *Our Blood: Prophesies and Discourses on Sexual Politics* 16 (1976) ("Gynocide is the word that designates the relentless violence perpetrated by the gender class men against the gender class women."). See also Mary Daly with Jane Caputi, *Webster's First New Intergalactic Wickedary of the English Language* 77 (1987). For a discussion of femicide, see *Femicide in Global Perspective* 20–23 (Diana E. H. Russell and Roberta A. Harmes, eds., 2001).

120. Dworkin, above note 63, at 48.

121. Prosecutor v. Krstic, Case No. IT-98-33-T, Judgment, ¶ 596 (Aug. 2, 2001).

122. Prosecutor v. Niyitegeka, Case No. ICTR-96-14-T, Judgment and Sentence, ¶ 463 (May 16, 2003) (finding accused guilty of sexual violence to the body of a dead woman as an inhumane act, a crime against humanity) ("The Accused ordered Interahamwe to undress the body of a Tutsi woman who had just been shot dead, and to sharpen a piece of wood, which he then instructed them to insert into her genitalia. The body of the woman with the piece of wood protruding from it was left on the roadside for some three days thereafter."). Although the defendant was also found guilty of genocide, this particular act was not included in those findings.

123. Shabnam Hashmi, quoted in Baldwin, above note 86, at 185. See also Concerned Citizens Tribunal, *Crime Against Humanity: An Inquiry into the Carnage in Gujarat* (2002); Citizens Committee for Extraordinary Report on Gujarat, India, *Submissions to the CEDAW Committee for Seeking Intervention on Gender Based Crimes and the Gendered Impact of the Gujarat Carnage* (May 2003).

124. In addition to being genocidal when they occur in genocides as conventionally defined, sexual atrocities in some circumstances outside genocides may well be "crimes against humanity" under existing international humanitarian law, which does not require a showing of intent and now prohibits widespread and systematic attacks on the basis of sex as well as other grounds. See Rome Statute of the International Criminal Court, 1998, U.N. Doc. A/CONF.183/9 (1998), reprinted in 37 *International Legal Materials* 999 (Art. 7.1 defines "crime against humanity" as any of the following acts when committed as part of a widespread or systematic attack directed against any civilian population, with knowledge of the attack: . . . (g) Rape, sexual slavery, enforced prostitution, or any other form of sexual violence of comparable gravity. (h) Persecution against any identifiable group or collectivity on political, racial, national, ethnic, cultural, religious, gender as defined in paragraph 3, or other grounds that are universally rec-

ognized as impermissible under international law, in connection with any act referred to in this paragraph or any crime within the jurisdiction of the Court. 'Gender' refers to "the two sexes, male and female, within the context of society").

125. Heineman, above note 62, at 55.

23. Defining Rape Internationally: A Commentary on *Akayesu*

1. For a useful review, see Prosecutor v. Kunarac, Case No. IT-96-23-T and IT-96-23/1-T, Judgment, ¶ 442 (Feb. 22, 2001) (grouping factors constitutive of rape into three broad categories: "(i) the sexual activity is accompanied by force or threat of force to the victim or a third party; (ii) the sexual activity is accompanied by force or a variety of other specified circumstances which made the victim particularly vulnerable or negated her ability to make an informed refusal; or (iii) the sexual activity occurs without the consent of the victim").

2. Compare, e.g., the language of France, which prohibits rape as any act of sexual penetration committed against another person by "violence, contrainte, menace, ou surpris," C.Pén art. 222, with that of the United Kingdom, which provides that "[a] person (A) commits an offence [of rape] if he intentionally penetrates the vagina, anus, or mouth of another person (B) with his penis, B does not consent to the penetration, and A does not reasonably believe that B consents." Sexual Offences Act, 2003, ch. 42 (Eng.).

3. For a critique of the redundancy of requiring both coercion and nonconsent, as most states in the United States do, see Catharine A. MacKinnon, *Toward a Feminist Theory of the State* 172 (1989).

4. For a superb analysis of rape as a deprivation of autonomy, see Stephan J. Schulhofer, *Unwanted Sex: The Culture of Intimidation and the Failure of Law* (1998).

5. See Catharine A. MacKinnon, "Unequal Sex: A Sex Equality Approach to Sexual Assault, *Women's Lives, Men's Laws* (2005).

6. Statute of the International Criminal Tribunal for the Former Yugoslavia, S.C. Res. 827, U.N. Doc. S/RES/827 (1993), *available at* http://www.un.org/icty/basic/statut/statute.htm [hereinafter ICTY Statute]; Statute of the International Criminal Tribunal for Rwanda, S.C. Res. 955, U.N. Doc. S/RES/955 (1994), *available at* http://www.un.org/ictr/statute.html [hereinafter ICTR Statute].

7. For an excellent analysis of the reality of the sexual atrocities in the Rwandan genocide, see Binaifer Nowrojee, *Shattered Lives: Sexual Violence During the Rwandan Genocide and its Aftermath, available at* http://www.hrw.org/reports/1996/Rwanda.htm. For documentation of the sexual assaults in Croatia and Bosnia–Herzegovina in the conflict there, see *Final Report of the Commission of Experts Established Pursuant to Security Council Resolution* 780 (1992), U.N. Doc. S/1994/674 (1994).

8. Article 4 of the ICTR Statute grants power to prosecute as war crimes the following relevant violations of Common Article 3 of the Geneva Conventions and Additional Protocol II: "violence to life, health and physical or mental well-being of persons, in particular murder as well as cruel treatment such as . . . outrages upon personal

dignity, in particular humiliating and degrading treatment, rape, enforced prostitution and any form of indecent assault . . . [and] threats to commit any of the foregoing acts." ICTR Statute art. 3. The statutes of both the Rwandan and Yugoslav tribunals prohibit genocide as conventionally defined: "Genocide means any of the following acts committed with intent to destroy, in whole or in part, a national, ethnical, racial, or religious group, as such: killing members of the group; causing serious bodily or mental harm to members of the group; deliberately inflicting on the group conditions of life calculated to bring about its physical destruction in whole or in part; imposing measures intended to prevent births within the group; forcibly transferring children of the group to another group." ICTY Statute art. 4; ICTR statute art. 2. The same list of crimes against humanity is included in the statute of each tribunal: "murder; extermination; enslavement; deportation; imprisonment; torture; rape; persecutions on political, racial, and religious grounds; other inhumane acts, . . . when committed as part of a widespread or systematic attack" against a civilian population. ICTY Statute art. 5; ICTR statute art. 3. However, the ICTR statute distinctively specifies that crimes against humanity must be based on grounds: "on national, political, ethnic, racial or religious grounds," ICTR Statute art. 3, while the ICTY statute specifies that crimes against humanity must be "committed in armed conflict, whether international or internal in character," ICTY Statute art. 5, effectively retaining the original legal connection of crimes against humanity to a wartime setting, as at Nuremberg.

9. Prosecutor v. Akayesu, Case No. ICTR-96-4-T, Judgment, para. 688 (Sept. 2, 1998).

10. Convention Against Torture and Other Cruel, Inhuman, or Degrading Treatment or Punishment art. 1(1), adopted Dec. 10, 1984, S. Treaty Doc. No. 100-20 (1988), 1465 U.N.T.S. 85 ("For the purposes of this Convention, the term 'torture' means any act by which severe pain or suffering, whether physical or mental, is intentionally inflicted on a person for such purposes as obtaining from him or a third person information or a confession, punishing him for an act he or a third person has committed or is suspected of having committed, or intimidating or coercing him or a third person, or for any reason based on discrimination of any kind, when such pain or suffering is inflicted by or at the instigation of or with the consent or acquiescence of a public official or other person acting in an official capacity. It does not include pain or suffering arising only from, inherent in or incidental to lawful sanctions.") [hereinafter Convention Against Torture].

11. *Akayesu*, above at note 9, ¶ 687 ("The United Nations Convention Against Torture and Other Cruel, Inhuman and Degrading Treatment or Punishment does not catalogue specific acts in its definition of torture, focusing rather on the conceptual framework of state-sanctioned violence. The Tribunal finds this approach more useful in the context of international law. Like torture, rape is used for such purposes as intimidation, degradation, humiliation, discrimination, punishment, control or destruction of a person. Like torture, rape is a violation of personal dignity, and rape in fact constitutes torture when it is inflicted by or at the instigation of or with the consent or acquiescence of a public official or other person acting in an official capacity.").

12. Id. at ¶ 597.

13. Id. at ¶ 688.

14. ICTR Statute art. 3, S.C. Res. 955, U.N. Doc. S/RES/955 (1994).

15. *Akayesu*, above at note 9, ¶¶ 692–697.

16. ICTR Statute art. 2(b); Prosecutor v. Akayesu, Case No. ICTR-96-4-I, Amended Indictment, (June 17, 1997) (the first count was genocide; the charge for sexual violence is included in paragraphs 12(A)–(B) of the amended indictment).

17. See Kadic v. Karadžić, 70 F.3d 232, 236–237 (2d Cir. 1995) (describing the "various atrocities, including brutal acts of rape, forced prostitution, forced impregnation, torture, and summary execution, carried out by Bosnian–Serb military forces as part of a genocidal campaign conducted in the course of the Bosnian civil war").

18. *Akayesu*, above at note 9, ¶ 731 ("These rapes resulted in physical and psychological destruction of Tutsi women, their families and their communities. Sexual violence was an integral part of the process of destruction, specifically targeting Tutsi women and specifically contributing to their destruction and to the destruction of the Tutsi group as a whole.").

19. Id. Many of the raped women were killed. For a vivid eyewitness description, see Roméo Dallaire, *Shake Hands with the Devil* 430 (2004).

20. *Akayesu*, above at note 9, ¶¶ 707, 731–733.

21. Prosecutor v. Delalic, Case No. IT-96-21-T, Judgment, ¶¶ 478–479 (Nov. 16, 1998) *available at* http://www.un.org/icty/celebici/trialc2/judgement/cel-tj981116e.pdf (noting that "The Trial Chamber draws guidance on this question from the discussion in the recent judgment if the ICTR, in the case of [*Akayesu*]," and agreeing with the definition of rape in *Akayesu*). The *Delalic* tribunal also notably held that rape could be a form of torture, concluding that "the violence suffered by [the witness] in the form of rape, was inflicted upon her by [the defendant] because she is a woman. . . . This represents a form of discrimination which constitutes a prohibited purpose for the offence of torture." Id. at ¶ 941.

22. A letter of April 27, 1994, to Judge Antonio Cassese, President, and Judge Elisabeth Odio Benito, Vice-President of the ICTY, from the International Women's Human Rights Clinic at the City University of New York and the Center for Constitutional Rights, among others, argued for the elimination of the ban on the defense of consent and suggested *in camera* adversarial hearings where the likelihood of a voluntary sexual relationship, should the accused seek to put it into evidence, could be assessed.

23. Prosecutor v. Furundžija, Case No. IT-95-17/1-T, Judgment, ¶ 271 (Dec. 10, 1998). In its ruling on war crimes, specifically outrages upon personal dignity, including rape, the trial chamber noted that, as to Witness A, "Consent was not raised by the Defence, and in any case, Witness A was in captivity. Further, it is the position of the Trial Chamber that any form of captivity vitiates consent." Id.

24. Id. at ¶ 174 ("The Trial Chamber notes the unchallenged submission of the Prosecution in its Pre-trial Brief that rape is a forcible act: this means that the act is accomplished by force or threats of force against the victim or a third person, such

threats being express or implied and must place the victim in reasonable fear that he, she, or a third person will be subjected to violence, detention, duress or psychological oppression" [citations omitted]).

25. *Akayesu*, above at note 9, ¶ 596 ("The Chamber considers that rape is a form of aggression and that the central elements of the crime of rape cannot be captured in a mechanical description of objects and body parts.").

26. *Furundžija*, above at note 23, ¶ 185 (". . . the Trial Chamber finds that the following may be accepted as the objective elements of rape: (i) the sexual penetration, however slight: (a) of the vagina or anus of the victim by the penis of the perpetrator or any other object used by the perpetrator; or (b) of the mouth of the victim by the penis of the perpetrator . . . ").

27. Id. at ¶ 180("all jurisdictions surveyed by the Trial Chamber require an element of force, coercion, threat, or acting without the consent of the victim"). See also the trial chamber's discussion of *Furundžija* in Prosecutor v. Kunarac et al., Case Nos. IT-96-23-T & IT-96-23/1-T, Judgement, ¶ 440 (Feb. 22, 2001), *available at* http://www .un.org/icty/kunarac/trialc2/judgement/kun-tj010222e.pdf ("In the view of the present Trial Chamber, the legal systems there surveyed, looked at as a whole, indicated that the basic underlying *principle* common to them was that sexual penetration will constitute rape if it is not truly voluntary or consensual on the part of the victim. The matters identified in the *Furundžija* definition—force, threat of force or coercion—are certainly the relevant considerations in many legal systems but the full range of provisions referred to in that judgement suggest that the true common denominator which unifies that various systems may be a wider or more basic principle of penalising violations of sexual *autonomy*.").

28. Prosecutor v. Semanza, Case No. ICTR-97-20-T, Judgment (May 15, 2003).

29. Prosecutor v. Kajelijeli, Case No. ICTR-98-44A-T, Judgment (Dec. 1, 2003).

30. *Furundžija*, above at note 23, ¶ 177.

31. Id. ("The Trial Chamber therefore considers that, to arrive at an accurate definition of rape based on the criminal law principle of specificity (*Bestimmtheitgrundsatz*, also referred to by the maxim "*nullum crimen sine lege stricta*"), it is necessary to look for principles of criminal law common to the major legal systems of the world.").

32. Id. at ¶ 178. Prosecutor v. Tadic, Case No. IT-94-1-A, Judgement (July 15, 1999), *available at* http://www.un.org/icty/tadic/appeal/judgement/tad-aj990715e.pdf.

33. See, e.g., *Calling the Ghosts* (Mandy Jacobson, dir., released Oct. 7, 1996) (a documentary film portraying the suffering of two women, Jadranka Cigelj and Nusreta Sivac, who were held captive in Omarska).

34. See Prosecutor v. Tadic, Case No. IT-94-1, Decision on the Prosecution Motion to Withdraw Counts 2 Through 4 of the Indictment Without Prejudice, Trial Chamber II (June 25, 1996). According to press reports, "the rape charges were withdrawn when the victim said she was too afraid of reprisals to testify." Marlise Simons, "An Ex–Bosnian Serb Commander Admits Rape of Muslims in War," *New York Times*, A10 (Mar. 10, 1998).

35. ICTY Statute Rules of Procedure and Evidence, Rule 96(ii), U.N. Doc IT/32 (March 14, 1994), reprinted in 33 *International Legal Materials* 484, 536.

36. See ICTY Statute Rules of Procedure and Evidence, Amended Rule 96(ii), U.N. Doc IT/32/Rev.2 (May 5, 1994) ("In cases of sexual assault . . . (ii) consent shall not be allowed as a defence if the victim (a) has been subjected to or threatened with or has had reason to fear violence, duress, detention or psychological oppression, or (b) reasonably believed that if the victim did not submit, another might be so subjected, threatened or put in fear").

37. Given that "consent" in national laws typically includes, for example, having sex under threat or without active resistance, survivors were not convinced that they would be believed or considered raped when they said that they were told that their children would be treated better, or their communications would be passed to them, if they complied sexually. Further, given the genocidal circumstances and, typically, the conditions of incarceration under which the rapes took place, they did not think that they should have to go through such proof.

38. As of July 21, 2005, twenty-eight indictments by the ICTY charged rape or other sexual assault as something other than genocide in the ex-Yugoslav region. Twelve additional cases, most of them for the atrocities at Srebrenica, charged genocide on facts that did not mention sexual assault.

39. The ten cases involving thirteen individuals are: Prosecutor v. Stakic, Case No. IT-97-24-T, Judgement (July 31, 2003), *available at* http://www.un.org/icty/stakic/trialc/judgement/stak-tj030731e.pdf (Prijedor); Prosecutor v. Plavsic, Case No. IT-00-39&40-PT, Sentencing Judgement (Feb. 27, 2003), *available at* http://www.un.org/icty/plavsic/trialc/judgement/index.htm (Bosnia and Herzegovina); Prosecutor v. Milošvić, Case No. IT-02-54-T, ¶ 32(c) (Nov. 22, 2002), *available at* http://www.un.org/icty/indictment/english/mil.ai040421-e.htm ("The causing of serious bodily and mental harm to thousands of Bosnian Muslims during their confinement in detention facilities within Bosnia and Herzegovina, including those situated within the territories listed above, as specified in Schedule C to this indictment. Members of these groups, during their confinement in detention facilities and during their interrogation at these locations, police stations and military barracks, were continuously subjected to, or forced to witness, inhumane acts, including murder, sexual violence, torture and beatings."); Prosecuter v. Brdanin & Talic, Case No. IT-99-36-PT, Decision on Form of Further Amended Indictment and Prosecution Application to Amend (June 26, 2001), *available at* http://www.un.org/icty/brdjanin/trialc/decision-e/10626FI215879.htm (Krajina); Prosecutor v. Sikirica, Case No. IT-95-8, Sentencing Judgment (Nov. 13, 2001), *available at* http://www.un.org/icty/sikirica/judgement/sik-tsj011113e.htm (Keraterm); Prosecutor v. Krajisnik, Amended Indictment, No. IT-00-39 (Mar. 21, 2000), *available at* http://www.un.org/icty/indictment/english/kra-lai000321e.htm (Bosnia and Herzegovina); Prosecutor v. Jelisic, Case No. IT-95-10-T, Judgement (Dec. 14, 1999), *available at* http://www.un.org/icty/jelisic/trialc1/judgement/jel-tj991214e.pdf (Brcko); Prosecutor v. Kovacevic, IT-97-24-I, Am. Indictment (June 23, 1998), *available at* http://www.un.org/icty/indictment/english/kov-1ai980623e.htm (Prijedor); Prosecutor v. Zeljko & Meakic, Case No. IT-95-4-I, Indictment (June 2, 1998), *available at* http://www.un.org/icty/indictment/english/mea-i980602e.pdf (Omarska); and Prosecutor v. Karadžić & Mlalic, Case No. IT-95-18-I, Indictment (Nov. 16, 1995), *available at* http://

www.un.org/icty/indictment/english/kar-ii951116e.htm (Bosnia-Herzegovina). Notable omissions involving persons or locations as to which sexual violance was reported include *Sikirica*, supra, ¶ 1 n.1 ("On 5 May 1998, Judge Vohrah approved the withdrawal of charges against five of the co-accused."); and *Jelisic*, supra. All these cases involve Serbian perpetrators and Bosnian Muslim or Bosnian Croat victims. No charges of genocide appear to have been brought for sexual assaults in Croatia. Neither Karadžić nor Mladic was originally charged with rape as persecution, a crime against humanity, Prosecutor v. Karadžić & Mladic, IT-95-5-I, Initial Indictment, ¶ 19 (July 24, 1995), *available at* http://www.un.org/icty/indictment/english/kar-ii950724e.htm ("As set forth below, they are criminally responsible for the unlawful confinement, murder, rape, sexual assault, torture, beating, robbery and inhumane treatment of civilians . . . ."), and with rape in detention with intent to destroy Bosnian Muslim and Bosnian Croat people as such through subjection, inter alia, to rape and sexual assault. *Id.* ¶ 22 (noting the conditions of detention and rape but not specifically charging it as criminal). When their indictments were amended, Mladic was charged with rape as complicity in genocide going to the elements of serious bodily and mental harm and conditions of life calculated to bring about their physical destruction. See Prosecutor v. Mladic, Case No. IT-95-5/18-I, Amended Indictment, ¶¶ 33, 34(b)–(c) (Oct. 11, 2002), *available at* http://www.un.org/icty/indictment/english/mla-ai021010e.htm. Karadžić was charged with sexual violence in a paragraph that could go to genocide or complicity in genocide. *See* Prosecutor v. Karadžić, Case No. IT-95-5/18, Amended Indictment, ¶ 17(b) (May 31, 2000), *available at* http://www.un.org/icty/indictment/english/kar-ai000428e.htm (charging him with the "causing of serious bodily or mental harm to Bosnian Muslims and Bosnian Croats during their confinement in camps and detention facilities, and during their interrogations at these locations, police stations and military barracks, where detainees were continuously subjected to, or forced to witness, inhumane acts including murder, sexual violence, torture, beatings and robbery"). The Mladic amended indictment noted that the campaign of persecutions "escalated to or include" genocidal conduct. *Mladic*, supra. ¶ 33.

40. Despite the express *Akayesu* recognition of rape as genocide in 1998, as of November 2003, rape still had not been charged as genocide in a single additional ICTR case. By January 2004, almost all ICTR cases with facts alleging sexual assault had been amended to charge them as genocide, as well as other crimes, under the prosecutorial leadership of Hassan Bubacar Jallow. Prominent exceptions, not so amended, are Prosecutor v. Semanza, Case No. ICTR 97-20-T, Judgment (May 15, 2003), and Prosecutor v. Kajelijeli, Case No. ICTR 98-44A-T, Judgment (Dec. 1, 2003). Another is Prosecutor v. Rugambarara, Case No. 2000–59–I "Case No. 2000-59-I, ¶¶ 3.19(i)" etc., ¶¶ 3.19(i), 3.29 (July 1, 2000) (alleging for example, that Rugambarara was alleged, with Laurent Semanza, to have ordered Interahamwe "to rape and kill all the Tutsis with no exceptions," and the torture of Tutsi women "included the slicing off of their breasts and the penetration of their private parts with spears and other objects," ¶ 3.29)

41. See Catharine A. MacKinnon, "Genocide's Sexuality," above No. 22, at 313, for further analysis.

42. This is a mythic name. The crimes occurred in those parts of what had been Yugoslavia that the Serbian fascist factions wished to annex and render Serb-only, not in civilian Serbia or Montenegro.

43. Prosecutor v. Furundžija, Case No. IT-95-17/1-T, Judgement, Introduction (Dec. 10, 1998), *available at* http://www.un.org/icty/furundzija/trialc2/judgement/fur -tj981210e.pdf.

44. Id. at ¶ 46.

45. The ICTR's full official title—Statute of the International Criminal Tribunal for the Prosecution of Persons Responsible for Genocide and Other Serious Violations of International Humanitarian Law Committed in the Territory of Rwanda and Rwandan Citizens Responsible for Genocide and Other Such Violations Committed in the Territory of Neighboring States—mentions genocide, reflecting the international community's awareness of this reality as well.

46. For further exploration of the parameters of the definition, compare Prosecutor v. Niyitegeka, Case No. ICTR-96-14-T, Judgement, paras. 463–67 (May 16, 2003) (vaginally penetrating a dead woman with a stick was found not rape but an "other inhumane act," based upon the reasoning that a corpse cannot be coerced), with Prosecutor v. Akayesu, Case No. ICTR 96-4-T, Judgment, para. 686 (Sept. 2, 1998) ("thrusting a piece of wood into the sexual organs of a woman as she lay dying constitutes rape in the Tribunal's view"), and Prosecutor v. Muhimana, Case No. ICTR 95-1B-T, Judgment, para. 557 (April 25, 2005) (finding that slicing a pregnant woman open vertically while she and her fetus were alive is not rape). In my view, the act in *Muhimana* was not rape but sexual violence (as well as torture), certainly gendered violence.

47. Prosecutor v. Kunarac et al., Case Nos. It-96-23-T & IT-96-23/1-T, Judgement, para. 440 (Feb. 22, 2001), *available at* http://www.un.org/icty/kunarac/trialc2/ judgement/kun-tj010222e.pdf.

48. Id. at ¶ 458. ("In practice, the absence of genuine and freely given consent or voluntary participation may be *evidenced* by the presence of the various factors specified in other jurisdictions—such as force, threats of force, or taking advantage of a person who is unable to resist.").

49. Prosecutor v. Kunarac, Case No. IT–96–23 and IT–96–23/1–A, Appeals Judgment, ¶ 129 (June 12, 2002).

50. Id. at ¶ 131.

51. Id. at ¶ 132.

52. Id.

53. Id. at ¶ 133.

54. Prosecutor v. Musema, Case No. ICTR–96–13–T, Judgment, ¶ 220 (Jan. 27, 2000) (endorsing the definition of rape in *Akayesu*).

55. Prosecutor v. Niyitegeka, Case No. ICTR–96–14–T, Judgment, ¶ 456 (May 16, 2003).

56. Prosecutor v. Semanza, Case No. ICTR–97–20–T, Judgment, ¶ 344 (May 15, 2003).

57. Id. ¶ 346.

58. Id. at ¶ 344.

59. Id. at ¶ 253. The witness explained that Semanza used the Kinyarwanda word *kurongora*, which means "to marry" and also "to make love." Id. This term is discussed in greater depth in *Akayesu*, above note 9 ¶¶ 152–154.

60. Prosecutor v. Kajelijeli, Case No. ICTR–98–44A–T, Judgment, ¶ 914 (Dec. 1, 2003).

61. Id. at ¶ 911.

62. Id. at ¶ 915 ("Given the evolution of the law in this area, culminating in the endorsement of the *Furundzija/Kunarac* approach by the ICTY Appeals Chamber, the Chamber finds the latter approach of persuasive authority and hereby adopts the definition as given in *Kunarac* and quoted above.").

63. Pursuant to the ICTR's Statute, "A person who planned, instigated, ordered, committed or otherwise aided and abetted in the planning, preparation or execution of a crime in articles 2 to 4 of the present Statute shall be individually responsible for the crime." ICTR Statute art. 6(1) The Statute also provides that "the fact that any of the acts . . . was committed by a subordinate does not relieve his or her superior of criminal responsibility if he or she knew or had reason to know that the subordinate was about to commit such acts or had done so and the superior failed to take the necessary and reasonable measures to prevent such acts or to punish the perpetrators thereof." Id. art. 6(3).

64. *Semanza*, above note 56, ¶¶ 937–938.

65. *Semanza*, above note 56, e.g., ¶¶ 63–64, 73 (Ramaroson, J., dissenting).

66. Prosecutor v. Muhimana, Case No. ICTR–95–1B–T, Judgment, ¶ 546 (Apr. 25, 2005).

67. Id. at ¶ 546.

68. Id. at ¶ 550.

69. For further analysis, see Catharine A. MacKinnon, *Genocide's Sexuality*, supra note.

70. See Catharine A. MacKinnon, *Sex Equality* 772–776 (2001), for documentation in the United States.

71. See generally Radhika Coomaraswamy, Report of the Special Rapporteur on Violence Against Women, Its Causes and Consequences, U.N. ESCOR, Comm. Hum. Rts., 52d Sess., Prov. Agenda Item 9(a), U.N. Doc. E/CN.4/1996/53 (1996); Radhika Coomaraswamy, Report of the Special Rapporteur on Violence Against Women, Its Causes and Consequences, U.N. Comm. Hum. Rts., 53d Sess., Agenda Item 9, U.N. Doc. E/CN.4/47 (1997).

72. Incorporating *Akayesu*'s insight, both California and Illinois define gender violence for civil purposes in part to include "[a] physical intrusion or physical invasion of a sexual nature under coercive conditions." Cal. Civ. Code Ann. § 52.4(c)(2) (West 2003); 740 Ill. Comp. Stat. Ann. 82/5(2) (West 2004).

73. Article 7(1)(g) of the Statute of the International Criminal Court specifies that rape is a crime against humanity when committed as part of a widespread or systematic attack directed against any civilian population with knowledge of the attack. Rome Statute of the International Criminal Court, July 17, 1998, art. 7(1)(g), U.N. Doc. A/

CONF.183/9, *available at* http://www.ohchr.org/english/law/criminalcourt.htm [hereinafter Rome Statute].

74. Interpol reports that South Africa has the highest per capita rate of rape in the world. *SA Holds Guinness Rapes Record* (Oct. 17, 2003), http://www.news24.com/News24/South_Africa/News. see also www.undc.org/unoda/crime_clcp_surveys.html (documenting the same 1995–2002) The highest provincial rate was recorded in the Northern Cape at roughly 190 incidents per 100,000 people. South Africa: Amnesty International's Human Rights Concern, at www.amnestyusa.org/countries/south _africa (2005). These figures are based on police statistics for the year 2003–2004, which only reflect the number of rapes *reported*. At the twenty-fifth anniversary conference of the Child Accident Prevention Foundation of Southern Africa in 2003, the organization Resources Aimed at the Prevention of Child Abuse and Neglect estimated that 500,000 rapes actually occurred in South Africa when about 50,000 rapes had been reported. *SA Holds Guinness Rapes Record* (Oct. 17, 2003), www.news24.com/News24/South _Africa/News.

75. See Rome Statute arts. 6, 7(1)(g) The conventional meaning of genocide was adopted, which is considered a definition. Rape was not defined under the Rome Statute itself. For elements of rape under the various crimes in the Rome Statute, International Criminal Court, Elements of Crimes Adopted by the Assembly of States Parties, First session, New York, Sept. 3–10, 2002, ICC-ASP/1/3, *available at* http://daccessdds.un .org/doc/UNDOC/GEN/N02/603/35/PDF/N0260335.pdf?OpenElement, with the *Akayesu* definitional elements italicized, see id. art. 7(1)(g)-1 ("Crime against humanity of rape: (1) The perpetrator *invaded* the body of a person by conduct resulting in penetration, however slight, of any part of the body of the victim or of the perpetrator with a sexual organ, or of the anal or genital opening of the victim with any object or any other part of the body; (2) The *invasion* was committed by force, or by threat of force or coercion, such as that caused by fear of violence, duress, detention, psychological oppression or abuse of power, against such person or other person, or by taking advantage of a *coercive environment*, or the *invasion* was committed against a person incapable of giving genuine consent; (3) The conduct was committed as part of a widespread or systematic attack directed against a civilian population; (4) The perpetrator knew that the conduct was part of or intended the conduct to be part of a widespread or systematic attack directed against a civilian population."); id. art. 7(1)(g)-6 ("Crime against humanity of sexual violence: (1) The perpetrator committed an *act of a sexual nature* against one or more persons or caused such person or persons to engage in an *act of a sexual nature* by force, or by threat of force or coercion, such as that caused by fear of violence, duress, detention, psychological oppression or abuse of power, against such person or persons or another person, or by taking advantage of *a coercive environment* or such person's or persons' incapacity to give genuine consent; (2) Such conduct was of a gravity comparable to the other offences in article 7, paragraph 1(g) of the Statute; (3) The perpetrator was aware of the factual circumstances that established the gravity of the conduct"); id. art. 8(2)(b)(xxii)-1 ("War crime of rape: [Elements 1 and 2 are identical to the crimes against humanity elements] (3) The

conduct took place in the context of and was associated with an international armed conflict; (4) The perpetrator was aware of factual circumstances that established the existence of an armed conflict"); id. art. 8(2)(b)(xxii)-6 ("War crime of sexual violence: [Element 1] is identical to (1) in the foregoing; (2) The conduct was of a gravity comparable to that of a grave breach of the Geneva Conventions; (3) The perpetrator was aware of the factual circumstances that established the gravity of the conduct; (4) The conduct took place in the context of and was associated with an international armed conflict; (5) The perpetrator was aware of factual circumstances that established the existence of an armed conflict").

76. International Criminal Court, Rules of Procedure and Evidence Adopted by the Assembly of States Parties, First session, New York, Sept. 3–10, 2002, ICC–ASP/1/3. For example, see id. Rule 70 (prohibiting inference of consent to sexual violence by words or conduct of a victim among others where a coercive environment undermined voluntary and genuine consent, or from silence or lack of resistance); id. Rule 71 (prohibiting admission of evidence of prior or subsequent sexual conduct of victim or witness); and id. Rule 72 (providing in camera procedure to consider relevance or admissibility of evidence of consent in cases of sexual violence to balance probative value against prejudice). No definitions, elements, or procedures go to genocide, the conventional definition apparently being regarded as sufficient.

77. Examples include Sierra Leone, Congo, and Sudan. See Statute of the Special Court for Sierra Leone Aug. 14, 2000, U.N. Doc. No. 5/2002/246, *available at* http://www.sc-sl.org/scsl-statute.html; Thekla Hansen–Young, "Comment, Defining Rape: A Means to Achieve Justice in the Special Court for Sierra Leone," 6 *Chicago Journal of International Law* 479 (2005). The ICC opened an investigation in the Democratic Republic of Congo after reports by states, international organizations, and nongovernmental organizations of thousands of deaths by mass murder and summary execution and a pattern of rape and torture in the DRC since 2002. See Press Release, the Hague, *The Office of the Prosecutor of the International Criminal Court Opens Its First Investigation* (June 23, 2004), http://www.icc-cpi.int/pressrelease_details&id=26&1=en .html. The ICC also is investigating alleged crimes against humanity and war crimes in Darfur, Sudan. See Press Release, The Hague, *The Prosecutor of the ICC Opens Investigation in Darfur* (press release, The Hague, June 6, 2005), http://www.icc-cpi.int/press/pressreleases/107.html.

24. Pornography as Trafficking

1. Paul Fishbein, founding president of Adult Video News, estimated to CBS News that some 800 million so-called adult videos are rented each year in the United States alone, earning an estimated $20 billion annually in a global industry estimated to earn $57 billion annually. See Richard Corliss, "That Old Feeling: When Porno Was Chic," *Time,* 1 (Mar. 29, 2005). Much of the pornography industry remains organized crime, making it unlikely that all earnings are reported anywhere. See U.S. Department of Justice, Attorney General's Commission on Pornography, *Final Report* 277–298 (July,

1986) available at www.communitydefense.org/lawlibrary/agreport.html [hereinafter, *Final Report*].

2. As to pornography, these injuries are documented in testimony in *In Harm's Way: The Pornography Civil Rights Hearings* (Catharine A. MacKinnon and Andrea Dworkin, eds., 1997) [hereinafter *In Harm's Way*]. As to prostitution, they are documented in Melissa Farley et al., "Prostitution and Trafficking in Nine Countries: An Update on Violence and Posttraumatic Stress Disorder," in *Prostitution, Trafficking, and Traumatic Stress* 33 (Melissa Farley, ed., 2003) [hereinafter Farley I]. See also *Not for Sale: Feminists Resisting Prostitution and Pornography* (Christine Stark and Rebecca Whisnant, eds., 2004) [hereinafter *Not For Sale*].

3. This analysis is argued in Catharine A. MacKinnon, "Not a Moral Issue," in *Feminism Unmodified* 146 (1987). Canadian obscenity law provides a partial exception, criminalizing the "undue exploitation of sex, or of sex and any one or more of the following subjects, namely, crime, horror, cruelty and violence." Criminal Code, R.S.C. 1985, ch. C-46, § 163(8) (Can.). This provision has been interpreted on a gendered harm theory. See Butler v. Regina, [1992] 1 S.C.R. 452.

4. In addition to the other citations in this analysis, one example is the 2005 trafficking resolution adopted by the United Nations Commission on the Status of Women, *Eliminating Demand for Trafficked Women and Girls for All Forms of Exploitation,* E.S.C. Res. 49/2, U.N. ESCOR Commission on the Status of Women, 49th Sess., Supp. No. 7, at 13, U.N. Doc.E/CN. 6/2005/11 (2005).

5. "The Minneapolis Hearings," in *In Harm's Way,* above note 2, at 65 (testimony of Linda Marchiano).

6. For an early analysis of the largely unsuccessful attempts of women in sexual materials to protect their privacy rights, see Ruth Colker, "Pornography and Privacy: Towards the Development of a Group-Based Theory for Sex-Based Intrusions of Privacy," 1 *Law and Inequality* 191 (1983). See also Dworkin v. Hustler Magazine, Inc., 867 F.2d 1188 (9th Cir. 1989) (dismissing all libel and privacy violation claims made against a pornographic magazine that had used Dworkin's name in sexually explicit cartoons and finding that she had no proprietary interest she could protect). For a discussion of a history of similar U.S. cases, such as one in which a judicial remedy was denied an actress in a Wasa Bread ad for its unauthorized modification in pornography, see Lisa R. Pruitt, "Her Own Good Name: Two Centuries of Talk About Chastity," 63 *Maryland Law Review* 401, 475 (2004) (describing Geary v. Goldstein, 831 F. Supp. 269 (S.D.N.Y. 1993)).

7. That pornography has carved out for itself a de facto legal exemption from the law of libel, which in the United States is not that robust to begin with, is clear from the rulings in Dworkin v. Hustler Magazine, Inc., 867 F.2d 1188 (9th Cir. 1989), Leidholdt v. L. F. P., Inc., 860 F.2d 890 (9th Cir. 1988), and many other cases.

8. Preliminary results of a study of 854 prostituted women in nine countries reveal that women in prostitution who had pornography made of them in prostitution had significantly more severe symptoms of post-traumatic stress disorder than did women in prostitution who did not report that pornography was made of them. Melissa Farley,

"'Renting an Organ for 10 Minutes': What Tricks Tell Us About Prostitution, Pornography, and Trafficking," delivered at "Pornography: Driving the Demand in International Sex Trafficking," cosponsored by Captive Daughters and the International Human Rights Law Institute of DePaul University, Chicago, Illinois, March 14, 2005 [hereinafter Farley II] (presenting new analysis of data from the sample reported at Farley I above, note 2.

9. *Final Report* supra note 1, 291–297. Since that time, legitimate corporations have increasingly gone into trafficking pornography on the distribution end, prominently General Motors (through its subsidiary DirecTV), AT&T (through its broadband cable company), and EchoStar Communications Corporation (backed by media mogul Rupert Murdoch), along with Comcast, TimeWarner, and Cox Communications. Gail Dines, "From Fantasy to Reality: Unmasking the Pornography Industry," in *Sisterhood Is Forever* 312 (Robin Morgan, ed., 2003) (citing Timothy Egan, "Erotica, Inc.—A Special Report; Technology Sent Wall Street into Market for Pornography," *New York Times*, A1 (Oct. 23, 2000), and Frank Rich, "Naked Capitalists," *New York Times Magazine*, 51 (May 20, 2001). Dines has continued to track major mainstream corporations' involvement in the pornography industry. See Gail Dines, "The Big Business of Pornography and Sex Trafficking," delivered at Captive Daughters and International Human Rights Law Institute of DePaul University College of Law Conference, "Pornography: Driving the Demand for International Sex Trafficking," Chicago, Ill. (Mar. 14, 2005).

10. "The Minneapolis Hearings," in *In Harm's Way*, supra note 2, at 114 (testimony of T. S).

11. John Miller is the current head of the Office to Monitor and Combat Trafficking in Persons in the U.S. Department of State. www.state.gov/g/tip.

12. Just one articulate example is Linda Boreman, who had this to say in response to a question about her so-called sexual past in the porn industry: "It wasn't sexual. I never experienced any sexual pleasure, not one orgasm, nothing. I learned how to fake pleasure so I wouldn't get punished for doing a bad job." Quoted in Gloria Steinem, "The Real Linda Lovelace," in *Outrageous Acts and Everyday Rebellions* 275 (1983); see also Linda Lovelace and Michael McGrady, *Ordeal* (1980) (Linda Boreman's autobiography).

13. For inside documentation of the force involved in making *Playboy*, see the testimony of Miki Garcia to the Attorney General's Commission on Pornography. *Public Hearing, U.S. Dep't of Justice, Attorney General's Commission on Pornography* (Los Angeles, CA, Oct. 17, 1985) (interview with Ms. Garcia), reprinted in Catharine A. MacKinnon, *Sex Equality*, 1539–1543 (2001).

14. See United States v. Extreme Assocs., Inc., 352 F. Supp. 2d 578 (W.D. Pa. 2005). For a description of Zicari's film content, see Shannon McCaffrey, "Prosecutors Mount Attack Against Adult-Porn Market," *Miami Herald* (Apr. 4, 2004) (describing a video titled *Forced Entry* that "shows simulations of women being spat on, raped and murdered"). One suspects that at least the spitting and probably the rape, and who knows what else, are not simulated.

15. The ideas capsulized here are argued fully in Catharine A. MacKinnon, "Pros-

titution and Civil Rights," in *Women's Lives, Men's Laws* 151–161 (2005), and Catharine A. MacKinnon, "Pornography Left and Right," id. at 327–344.

16. After I said this, I found this in the mouth of a trick: "Guys get off on controlling women, they use physical power to control women, really. If you look at it, it's paid rape. You're making them subservient during that time so you're the dominant person. She has to do what you want." Farley II, above note 8, at 9.

17. See People v. Freeman, 758 P.2d 1128, 1134 (Cal. 1988) (affirming conviction of a pornographer for paying women for sex acts, but finding that the film of their acts was not "obscene," the California Supreme Court explained, "When considered aside from the payment of the acting fees, itself fully lawful otherwise, the sexual acts depicted in the motion picture here were completely lawful"); People v. Fixler, 128 Cal. Rptr. 363, 366 (Cal. Ct. App. 2d 1976) (upholding a pornographer's conviction for "pandering" by paying a fourteen-year-old girl to commit sex acts, the court also noted, "While First Amendment considerations may protect the dissemination of printed or photographic material regardless of the manner in which the material was originally obtained, where a crime is committed in obtaining the material, the protection afforded its dissemination would not be a shield against prosecution for the crime committed in obtaining it").

18. Farley II, supra note 8, at 5.

19. See Donna M. Hughes, "Prostitution Online," in *Prostitution, Trafficking, and Traumatic Stress* 115 (Melissa Farley, ed., 2003).

20. *The Secretary-General, on the Question of South Africa, delivered to the Seventh United Nations Congress on the Prevention of Crime and the Treatment of Offenders, Report of the Secretary-General, Victims of Crime: The Situation of Women As Victims of Crime*, U.N. Doc. A/CONF.121/16 ¶ 51 (May 17, 1985).

21. One illustrative discussion can be found in Ann D. Jordan, "Human Rights, Violence Against Women, and Economic Development (The People's Republic of China Experience)," 5 *Columbia Journal of Gender and Law* 216, 228 (1996).

22. On my reading, the first time the relatively redundant term "enforced prostitution" entered the deliberations of the Committee on the Convention of the Elimination of All Forces of Discrimination Against Women (CEDAW) was in 1991, in a discussion of Burkina Faso. the CEDAW, U.N. Committee on the Elimination of Discrimination Against Women, Report of ¶ 109 UN.Doc. A/46/38 (April 3, 1991). The first time the relatively oxymoronic "voluntary prostitution" appeared there was in a 1993 discussion of Kenya's compliance with article 5. CEDAW Committee Report, UN GAOR 48th Sess., Supp. No. 38, ¶ 109, U.N. Doc. A/48/38 (Feb. 25, 1994).

23. For documentation, see Mary Lucille Sullivan, "Can Prostitution Be Safe? Applying Occupational Health and Safety Codes to Australia's Legalised Brothel Prostitution," in *Not For Sale*, supra note 2, at 252.

24. Further discussion of this convergence can be found in "Sex and Violence: On Introducing the Antipornography Civil Rights Law in Sweden," above at No. 10.

25. United States v. X-Citement Video, Inc., 513 U.S. 64 (1994) (interpreting in a scienter requirement to uphold federal child pornography legislation).

26. See, e.g., Neil Malamuth, "Rape Fantasies as a Function of Exposure to Violent

Sexual Stimuli," 10 *Archives of Sexual Behavior* 33 (1981); Neil Malamuth and James Check, "The Effects of Mass Media Exposure on Acceptance of Violence Against Women: A Field Experiment," 15 *Journal of Research in Personality* 436 (1981); Neil Malamuth, "Factors Associated with Rape as Predictors of Laboratory Aggression Against Women," 45 *Journal of Personality and Social Psychology* 432 (1983); Dolf Zillmann and Jennings Bryant, "Effects of Massive Exposure to Pornography," in *Pornography and Sexual Aggression* 115 (Neil Malamuth and Edward Donnerstein, eds., 1984); Larry Baron and Murray A. Straus, "Sexual Stratification, Pornography, and Rape in the United States," in *Pornography and Sexual Aggression* 186 (Neil Malamuth and Edward Donnerstein, eds., 1984); Neil Malamuth and James Check, "The Effects of Aggressive Pornography on Beliefs in Rape Myths: Individual Differences," 19 *Journal of Research in Personality* 299 (1985); Neil Malamuth, James Check, and John Briere, "Sexual Arousal in Response to Aggression: Ideological, Aggressive and Sexual Correlates," 50 *Journal of Personality and Social Psychology* 330 (1986); Diana E. H. Russell, "Pornography and Rape: A Causal Model," 9 *Political Psychology* 41 (1988); D. Demare, Hilary M. Lips, and John Briere, "Sexually Violent Pornography, Anti-Woman Attitudes, and Sexual Aggression: A Structural Equation Model," 27 *Journal of Research in Personality* 285 (1993); Neil Malamuth, T. Addison, and Mary Koss, "Pornography and Sexual Aggression: Are There Reliable Effects and Can We Understand Them?" 11 *Annual Review of Sex Research* 26 (2000).

27. "The Minneapolis Hearings," in *In Harm's Way,* above note 2, at 116 (testimony of T. S.).

28. Id.

29. Mimi H. Silbert and Ayala M. Pines, "Pornography and Sexual Abuse of Women," 10 *Sex Roles: A Journal of Research* 857, 864 (1984).

30. Farley I, above note 8, at 46.

31. Id.

32. See Mary Lucille Sullivan, "Making Sex Work: The Experience of Legalised Prostitution in Victoria, Australia" 279 (Nov. 2004) (unpublished Ph.D. dissertation, University of Melbourne) (on file with author) (quoting an article written by a woman working in one of Melbourne's legal brothels, "STD Potential Videos," in the Prostitutes' Collective of Victoria's magazine, *Working Girl* 1991, at 6, saying that the brothel where she worked ran "porno videos . . . continually" and that she believed the videos "give clients a false impression of what services are provided" and made safe sex difficult to enforce).

33. Comparing pornography use of men who said they were tricks with men who said they were not, pornography use was found to be statistically significantly higher among the tricks. Farley II, above note 8.

34. For an analysis focused on gay male pornography, see Christopher N. Kendall and Rus Ervin Funk, "Gay Male Pornography's 'Actors': When 'Fantasy' Isn't," in *Prostitution, Trafficking, and Traumatic Stress,* above note 2, at 93.

35. Neil Malamuth, J. Heim, and Seymour Feshbach, "Sexual Responsiveness of College Students to Rape Depictions: Inhibitory and Disinhibitory Effects," 38 *Social*

Psychology 399 (1980); John Briere and Neil M. Malamuth, "Self-Reported Likelihood of Sexually Aggressive Behavior: Attitudinal versus Sexual Explanations," 17 *Journal of Research in Personality* 315 (1983); Testimony of Edward Donnerstein, in *In Harm's Way*, above note 2, at 44–60.

36. The United States did, however, ratify the International Agreement for the Suppression of the White Slave Traffic, May 18, 1904, 35 Stat. 1979, 1 L.N.T.S. 83.

37. Convention for the Suppression of the Traffic in Persons and of the Exploitation of the Prostitution of Others, Mar. 21, 1950, art. 1, 96 U.N.T.S. 271, 272.

38. As one trick explained, "Prostitution is an act of force, not of love. She gives up the right to say no." Another said, "I paid for this. You have no rights. You're with me now." Farley II, above note 8. These express the reality, well understood by the men who use the women, of what is euphemized as consent for women in prostitution.

39. U.N. Econ & Soc. Council [ECOSOC], *Note by the Secretary General, Draft Convention for the Suppression of the Traffic in Persons and of the Exploitation of the Prostitution of Others*, U.N. ESCOR, U.N. Doc. E/1072 (1949) at 17 (Jan. 19, 1949).

40. United Nations Economic and Social Council [ECOSOC], U.N. Doc. E/CN.5/115/Add.5, (1949) at 4 (commenting on art. 17, which addresses "measures [for] . . . the prevention of prostitution").

41. Id. at 5.

42. This was beautifully expressed by Edward M. Morgan, Convention on the Suppression of the Traffic in Persons and of the Exploitation of the Prostitution of Others, prepared on behalf of the Legal Division, Commonwealth Secretariat, U.K., at 8 (1989) ("[E]ven when both prostitute and client are legally culpable, enforcement of penal provisions is typically directed solely against the prostitute, thus leaving the demand for the prostitute's services unquenched and ensuring the continued existence of the sex trade. Prohibition can therefore be not only ineffective, but may also be considered to be discriminatory and inequitable").

43. Commenting on the elimination of "for gain" from the definition of the offenses, compared with the 1937 Draft Convention, the Secretary-General remarked: "[A]lthough this convention is mainly directed against those who engage in the offences mentioned for the purpose of gain, its eventual aim is to protect the victims of such persons, regardless of the purpose of the offenders. The purpose of gain is therefore irrelevant. Moreover, the gainful intents may be difficult to prove, and its inclusion in the definition of the offence may therefore prevent effective prosecution of offenders." See Draft Convention for the Suppression of the Traffic in Persons and of the Exploitation of the Prostitution of others, Note by the Secretary-General, above note 39, at 17. The participants in the drafting discussions were also worried about proof problems.

44. The Convention on the Rights of the Child and the Convention to Eliminate the Worst Forms of Child Labor both expressly recognize that children are sexually exploited when they are used in pornography. Articles 34 and 35 of the 1989 Convention on the Rights of the Child require state parties to take appropriate measures to prevent "the abduction of, sale of, or traffic in children for any purpose or in any

form," "the inducement or coercion of a child to engage in any unlawful sexual activity," "the exploitative use of children in prostitution or other unlawful sexual practices," and "the exploitative use of children in pornographic performances and materials." Convention on the Rights of the Child, Nov. 20, 1989, arts. 34–35, 1577 U.N.T.S. 3, 55 (entered into force Sept. 2, 1990). The 1999 Convention Concerning the Prohibition and Immediate Action for Elimination of the Worst Forms of Child Labor, art. 3, prohibits "the use, procuring or offering of a child for prostitution, for the production of pornography or for pornographic performances," "all forms of slavery or practices similar to slavery, such as the sale and trafficking of children, debt bondage and serfdom and forced compulsory labor, including forced or compulsory recruitment of children for use in armed conflict." *Concerning the Prohibition and Immediate Elimination of the Worst Forms of Child Labor*, June 1, 1999, art. 3, 38 *International Legal Materials*, 1207, 1208.

45. Protocol to Prevent, Suppress and Punish Trafficking in Persons, Especially Women and Children, Supplementing the United Nations Convention Against Transnational Organised Crime, G. A. Res. 55/25, U.N. GAOR, Nov. 15, 2000, U.N. Doc. A/55/383, Appendix II.

46. Victims of Trafficking and Violence Protection Act of 2000, H. R. 3244, 106th Cong., § 103(9), Pub. L. No. 106–386 (codified as amended at 22 U.S.C. §§ 7101–7110 (2000)).

47. Id. § 7102.

48. Model Law to Combat Trafficking in Persons, art. I, § 100, U.S. State Department News Release (Mar. 12, 2003).

49. Id. § 102.

50. Press Release, White House Office of the Press Secretary, Trafficking in Persons National Security Presidential Directive (Feb. 25, 2003), www.whitehouse.gov/news/releases/2003/02/20020225.html. Actually, slavery often refers to the difficulty of leaving as much as or more than the means of entry. "Female sexual slavery is present in ALL situations where women or girls cannot change the immediate conditions of their existence; where regardless of how they got into those conditions they cannot get out; and where they are subject to sexual violence and exploitation." Kathleen Barry, *Female Sexual Slavery* 40 (1979). Taken together, United States v. Kozminski, 487 U.S. 931 (1988), and United States v. Mussry, 726 F.2d 1448 (9th Cir. 1984), support the view that a person's belief because of physical or legal threat that they have no alternative but to perform the work demanded is partially constitutive of a Thirteenth Amendment slavery claim. For additional discussion, see MacKinnon, "Prostitution and Civil Rights," above note 15, at 151–161. Moreover, Congress specifically repudiated a narrow reading of *Kozminski* that would confine it to violent coercion in the Victims of Trafficking and Violence Protection Act of 2000, 114 Stat. 1464, § 102(b)(13). Tellingly, the Appeals Chamber for the International Criminal Tribunal for the Former Yugoslavia has recognized that when rights of ownership are proven exercised over a person, such that they are enslaved, their lack of consent, for example, to rape, does not need to be proven. See Prosecutor v. Kunarac, Case No. IT-96–23 and IT-96–23/1-A, Judgment, ¶ 120 (June 12, 2002).

51. Council Framework Decision 2002/629/JHA of July 19, 2002, on Combating Trafficking in Human Beings, art. 1.1(c), 2002 O. J. (L 203/4) 2.

52. Id. art. 1.1(d) (emphasis added).

53. U.N. Economic and social Council [ECOSOC], *Recommended Principles and Guidelines on Human Rights and Human Trafficking, Addendum to the Report of the United Nations High Commissioner for Human Rights,* U.N. Doc. E/2002/68/Add.1, Substantive Sess. 2002, Agenda Item 14(g) at 3, UNESCOR (May 20, 2002).

54. U.N. High Commissioner for Human Rights, Sub-Commission on Human Rights, *Traffic in Women and Girls,* Res. 2002/51 at 5, U.N. Doc. E/2002/23 (Apr. 23, 2002).

55. Convention on the Elimination of All Forms of Discrimination Against Women, June 17, 1980, G. A. Res. 34/180, 34 U.N. GAOR Supp. (No. 46) at 193, Dec. 18, 1979, U.N. Doc. A/34/46, 1249 U.N.T.S. 13 (entered into force Sept. 3, 1981).

56. See Sweden's Fifth Periodic Report to CEDAW, *Report of the Committee on the Elimination of Discrimination Against Women,* 25th Sess. at 23, U.N. Doc. CEDAW/C/SWE/5 (Dec. 18, 2000).

57. The CEDAW Committee members in its early sessions often asked specifically not only whether prostitution was outlawed in a given state but, if it was, whether its sanctions also applied against the "client." For example, The Philippines was asked about the "client . . . who benefited from the trade in white slavery" and whether he "walked away with impunity while the real victims were severely penalized." *Report of the Committee on the Elimination of Discrimination Against Women,* 3d Sess., ¶ 95 (1984); see also *Report of the Committee on the Elimination of Discrimination Against Women,* 4th Sess., ¶ 139 (1985) (several experts asked Panama "whether prostitution related only to the prostitute or also to clients and procurer"; *Report of the Committee on the Elimination of Discrimination Against Women,* 6th Sess., ¶ 61 (1987) (asking the Republic of Korea under Article 6 "whether not only the client but also the prostitute were punishable"); see id. ¶¶ 144, 220 (regarding Sri Lanka); *Report of the Committee on the Elimination of Discrimination Against Women,* 7th Sess., ¶¶ 254 (1988) (regarding Japan, asking "whether the law against prostitution contained punitive measures against men"); id. ¶ 277; see also id. ¶ 681 (noting that in Hungary, prostitution was a crime regardless of sex, but "the other party was not liable to prosecution"); *Reports of the Committee on the Elimination of Discrimination Against Women,* vol. 4, 8th Sess., ¶¶ 82 (1989) (asking Ireland for details of legal treatment under law of clients in prostitution); *Report of the Committee on the Elimination of Discrimination Against Women,* 10th Sess., ¶ 206 (1991) (mimeo), reprinted in *Official Records of the General Assembly,* Forty-sixth Session, Supp. No. 38 (A/46/38) (The Philippines reporting under article 6 concerning "sanctions imposed on customers of prostitutes, such as sex-tourists"); *Report of the Committee on the Elimination of Discrimination Against Women,* 11th sess., ¶ 173 (1992) (mimeo), reprinted in *Official Records of the General Assembly,* 47th Sess. Supp. No. 38 (A/47/38) (China reporting that prostitutes' "customers might be rounded up and provided with legal and moral education" or "required to engage in productive labour"); *Report of the Committee on*

the Elimination of Discrimination Against Women, G.A. 48th Sess., Supp. No. 38 (A/48/38) (Feb. 25, 1994), 12th CEDAW Sess., 1993 ¶ 554 (United Kingdom replying to a question under article 6 of "how many men had been convicted for accosting women on the street and what their sentences were"). Since that time, inquiry into pornography has often been added. See below note 58. Thanks to Ali Fawaz for his research assistance.

58. E.g., Of the United Kingdom, CEDAW Committee members asked whether the government considered its current law adequate with regard to rape and pornography. The government conceded that the legislation was inadequate but said that the continued exploitation of women in the media by means of sexually explicit pictures was a grave concern and needed to be remedied. The UK government stated that it was committed to enforcing laws in a manner that excluded improper publications, controlled proper standards, and upheld decency. *Report of the Committee on the Elimination of Discrimination Against Women,* 12th Sess., ¶ 553, U.N. Doc. A/48/38 (Supp.) (1993). In 1993, Committee members also asked the government of France for its position on pornography. France said that pornography was punished by imprisonment or monetary fines. Id. ¶ 336. The Netherlands, asked in 1994 to explain an increase in sexual violence, said that it was not influenced by the fact that pornography was not prohibited. It conjectured that the availability of pornography for adults had had a restraining influence on the incidence of violence against women. *Report of the Committee on the Elimination of Discrimination Against Women,* 13th Sess., ¶ 274, U.N. Doc. A/49/38 (1994). In 1995, the representative of Norway explained that sex business has been considered to be comparatively limited there, but a recent tendency toward more hard-core pornography was observed. It was assumed that prostitution may be increasing because of the internationalization of the sex trade, a matter regarded as serious by the government. Norway's focus on combating child pornography and persons that profit from prostitution resulted in sharpening the provisions in its penal dode prohibitions of pornography and pimping. *Report of the Committee on the Elimination of Discrimination Against Women,* 14th sess., ¶ 470, U.N. Doc. A/50/38 (1995). In 1996, the Committee noted the adoption of a landmark law against trafficking in persons, prostitution, and pornography with extraterritorial applications in Belgium as a decisive step to address the issue of sexual exploitation of women. *Report of the Committee on the Elimination of Discrimination Against Women,* 15th sess., ¶ 178, U.N. Doc. A/51/38 (1996). In Singapore, pornography was reportedly banned and advertising codes enacted prohibiting the portrayal of women as sex objects. Report of the Committee on the Elimination of Discrimination against Women, 24th session (15 January–2 February 2001) and 25th session (2–20 July 2001). ¶ 58, U.N. Doc. A/56/38 (2001). Thanks to Kirsten Erickson for her research on this point.

59. Committee on the Elimination of Discrimination Against Women, 11th sess., General Recommendation No. 19, ¶ 12, U.N. Doc. A/47/38 (Jan. 30, 1992) (discussing articles 2(f), 5, and 10(c) of CEDAW).

60. Protocol to the African Charter on Human and Peoples' Rights on the Rights

of Women in Africa, art. 13(m) July 11, 2003, O.A.U. Doc. CAB/LEG/66.6 (entered into force Nov. 26, 2005).

61. Fourth World Conference on Women, Sept. 4–15, 1995, *Beijing Declaration and Platform for Action,* at ¶ 118, U.N. Doc. A/CONF.177/20/Rev. 1.

62. Id. ¶ 119.

63. Id. ¶ 130.

64. Id. ¶ 225.

65. Id. ¶ 244(b).

66. For a sampling of expressly sex discriminatory laws that have remained in force since Beijing, see Equality Now, *Words and Deeds: Holding Governments Accountable in the Beijing + 10 Review Process* (2005), available at www.equalitynow.org. On pornography, American Booksellers Association v. Hudnut, 771 F.2d 323 (7th Cir. 1985), *aff'd,* 475 U.S. 1001 (1986), stands for precisely the opposite of this commitment and has remained in effect, ratified by the highest court of the nation.

67. The U.S. Senate ratified the ICCPR on February 23, 1978. See S. Res. 95–20, 95th Cong., S. Exec. Report 102–23 (1978).

68. Human Rights Committee, 68th Sess., 1834th mtg., *General Comment No. 28,* ¶ 22, U.N. Doc. CCPR/C/21/Rev.1/Add.10 (2000).

69. ICCPR, Dec. 16, 1966, 993 U.N.T.S. 3, art. 20; U.S. Reservation (1), S. Res. 95–20, 95th Cong., S. Exec. Report 102–23 (1978) ("That article 20 does not authorize or require legislation or other action by the United States that would restrict the right of free speech and association protected by the Constitution and laws of the United States").

70. For fuller discussion of this theme, see Andrea Dworkin, *Pornography: Men Possessing Women* 9 (1980) ("The question . . . is not whether the First Amendment protects pornography or should, but whether pornography keeps women from exercising the rights protected by the First Amendment."); Andrea Dworkin, "Against the Male Flood: Censorship, Pornography, and Equality," in *Letters from a War Zone* 253, 268–270 (1988); Catharine A. MacKinnon, "Francis Biddle's Sister," in *Feminism Unmodified* 192–197 (1987).

71. The ordinance defines pornography as "the graphic sexually explicit subordination of women, whether in pictures or in words, that also includes one or more of the following: (1) Women are presented as sexual objects who enjoy pain or humiliation; or (2) Women are presented as sexual objects who experience sexual pleasure in being raped; or (3) Women are presented as sexual objects tied up or cut up or mutilated or bruised or physically hurt, or as dismembered or truncated or fragmented or severed into body parts; or (4) Women are presented being penetrated by objects or animals; or (5) Women are presented in scenarios of degradation, injury, abasement, torture, shown as filthy or inferior, bleeding, bruised, or hurt in a context that makes these conditions sexual; or (6) Women are presented as sexual objects for domination, conquest, violation, exploitation, possession, or use, or through postures or positions of servility or submission or display. The use of men, children, or transsexuals in the place of women in paragraphs (1) through (6) above shall also constitute pornography

under this section." Indianapolis and Marion County, Indiana, Code ch. 16, § 16–3(q), in *In Harm's Way,* above note 2, at 444. With limitations, "the production, sale, exhibition, or distribution of pornography" is a cause of action for discrimination against women. Id. at 442.

72. *Hudnut,* 771 F.2d at 329 (holding that "we accept the premises of this legislation. Depictions of subordination tend to perpetuate subordination. The subordinate status of women in turn leads to affront and lower pay at work, insult and injury at home, and battery and rape on the streets. In the language of the legislature, [p]ornography is central in creating and maintaining sex as a basis of discrimination. Pornography is a systematic practice of exploitation and subordination based on sex which differentially harms women. The bigotry and contempt it produces, with the acts of aggression it fosters, harm women's opportunities for equality and rights [of all kinds].' Indianapolis Code sec. 16-1(a)(2). Yet this simply demonstrates the power of pornography as speech").

73. *Hudnut,* 475 U.S. 1001 (1986).

25. Women's September 11th: Rethinking the International Law of Conflict

1. This obvious observation about international law since at least the Treaty of Westphalia, Peace Treaty Between the Holy Roman Emperor and the King of France and Their Respective Allies, Oct. 24, 1648, 1 Consol. T.S. 198, is illuminated in the present setting by, among others, Antonio Cassese, "Terrorism Is Also Disrupting Some Crucial Legal Categories of International Law," 12 *European Journal of International Law* 993, 993–98 (2001); Robert K. Goldman, "Certain Legal Questions and Issues Raised by the September 11th Attacks," 9 *Human Rights Brief* 2 (2001); and Noah Feldman, "Choices of Law, Choices of War," 25 *Harvard Journal of Law and Public Policy* 457 (2002).

2. Of this list, international humanitarian law has the best facial history, long prohibiting some violence against women in wartime in very clear terms. See, e.g., Francis Lieber, Instructions for the Government of Armies of the United States in the Field (The Lieber Code), U.S. War Department, General Orders No. 100, § 2, art. 37 (Apr. 24, 1863) ("The United States acknowledge and protect, in hostile countries occupied by them . . . the persons of the inhabitants, especially those of women; and the sacredness of domestic relations"); and the Geneva Convention Relative to the Protection of Civilian Persons in Time of War, art. III, Aug. 12, 1949, 75 U.N.T.S. 287.

3. Attempts to get the drafters of the Universal Declaration of Human Rights to consider women's humanity are analyzed in Mary Ann Glendon, *A World Made New: Eleanor Roosevelt and the Universal Declaration of Human Rights* 111–12, 164 (2001). A particularly telling example is the absence of express mention of violence against women or sexual aggression in the Convention on the Elimination of All Forms of Discrimination against Women, G.A. Res. 180, at 193 U.N. GAOR, 34th Sess., Supp.

No. 45, at 193, U.N. Doc. A/34/46 (December 18, 1979) [hereinafter CEDAW]. The Committee on the Elimination of Discrimination Against Women remedied this in General Recommendation No. 19 by interpreting the definition of discrimination in CEDAW Article 1 to "include [ ] gender-based violence—That is violence which is directed against a woman because she is a woman or which affects women disproportionately." CEDAW, General Recommendation No. 19, ¶ 7, U.N. Doc. A/47/38 (February 1, 1992). The area of trafficking in women provides an example on another level. Although trafficking in women has long been criminal under the law of nations, not until the Palermo Protocol were some of its real power dynamics directly addressed. See *Protocol to Prevent, Suppress and Punish Trafficking in Persons, Especially Women and Children, Supplementing the United Nations Convention Against Transnational Organized Crime*, G.A. Res. 25 (II), at 54, U.N. Doc. A/55/383 (November 2, 2000) (including "the abuse of power or of a position of vulnerability . . . for the purpose of exploitation" as one element in the definition of trafficking).

4. See below note 9, 12, and 13 and discussion in Parts II and III.

5. This international mobilization has been read by some as simply marching to the tune of the United States. See, e.g., Slavoj Žižek, "The Smell of Love," in *Welcome to the Desert of the Real* 135 (2002). This U.S.-centric reading of post-September 11th events, the rest of the world its lackeys, does not explain changes on the international level that the United States does not entirely control, nor does it address the question of why the rest of the world does next to nothing about violence against women, nationally or internationally, with or without U. S. involvement.

6. See, e.g., In-depth Study on All Forms of Violence Against Women, (A/58/508/Add.2), G.A. Res. 185, U.N. GAOR, 58th Sess., U.N. Doc. A/RES/58/185 (March 18, 2004); The Secretary-General *Advancement of Women—Violence Against Women, Report of the U.N. Secretary-General*, U.N. Doc. A/59/281 (August 20, 2004); CEDAW, General Recommendation 19, above note 3; Organization of American States, Inter-American Convention on the Prevention, Punishment and Eradication of Violence Against Women (Convention of Belém do Pará), OEA/Ser.L/V/I.4 rev. 8, 22 May 2001, 33 *International Legal Materials* 1534 [hereinafter Convention of Belém do Pará]; Protocol to the African Charter on Human and Peoples' Rights on the Rights of Women in Africa, July 11, 2003, arts. 1(j), 3(4), 4(2), 5(d), 11(3), 22(b), 23(b), *available at* http://www.africa-union.org (last visited Nov. 5, 2005) (into force November 26, 2005) [hereinafter African Protocol]; M.C. v. Bulgaria, 646 European Court of Human Rights ¶¶ 166, 185 (2004) (concluding that the European Convention for the Protection of Human Rights and Fundamental Freedoms requires Member States effectively prosecute nonconsensual sex acts, including in the absence of physical resistance by the victim, and holding that Bulgaria did not fulfill its positive obligation to effectively criminalize rape). The U.N. Human Rights Committee's concluding observations are also at times critical of states parties for inadequate measures against key abuses of women. *See. e.g.*, Human Rights Committee, *Concluding Observations of the Human Rights Committee: Yemen*, ¶ 11, U.N. Doc. CCPR/CO/84/YEM (Aug. 9, 2005); Human Rights Committee, *Concluding Observations of the Human Rights Committee:*

Kenya, ¶¶ 10, 11, U.N. Doc. CCPR/CO/83/KEN (Apr. 29, 2005); Human Rights Committee, *Concluding Observations of the Human Rights Committee: Uzbekistan*, ¶¶ 23, 24, U.N. Doc. CCPR/CO/83/UZB (Apr. 26, 2005).

7. "Violence against women" has operational meaning in international investigations. See, e.g., Coomaraswamy, below note 14; the *Report of the U.N. Secretary-General*, above note 6. International definitions can be found in the Convention of Belém do Pará ("Violence against women shall be understood to include physical, sexual and psychological violence: a. that occurs within the family or domestic unit or within any other interpersonal relationship, whether or not the perpetrator shares or has shared the same residence with the woman, including, among others, rape, battery and sexual abuse; b. that occurs in the community and is perpetrated by any person, including, among others, rape, sexual abuse, torture, trafficking in persons, forced prostitution, kidnapping and sexual harassment in the workplace, as well as in educational institutions, health facilities or any other place; and c. that is perpetrated or condoned by the state or its agents regardless of where it occurs." above note 6 at 1535) and the African Protocol ("'Violence against women' means all acts perpetrated against women which cause or could cause them physical, sexual, psychological, and economic harm, including the threat to take such acts; or to undertake the imposition of arbitrary restrictions on or deprivation of fundamental freedoms in private or public life in peace time and during situations of armed conflicts or of war." above note 6, at article 1(j)) This term has the virtue of being concrete but the vice of not addressing violence against comparatively powerless groups who, socially rather than biologically female, are feminized as targets for male violence, including sexual violence. Boys and gay men are the largest of such groups. The term "gender–based violence" solves this problem. See, e.g., CEDAW General Recommendation 19, above note 3. (However, this recommendation, being an interpretation of CEDAW, applies only to women.)

8. See Kofi Annan's speech to the UN General Assembly on 20 September 1999, "Two Concepts of Sovereignty," UN Press Release SG/SM/7136 GA/9596, 20 September 1999, reprinted in Kofi Annan, *The Question of Intervention: Statements by the Secretary-General* 37, 39 (1999).

9. The FBI reports 648 women and 2,175 men were killed at the World Trade Center on September 11, 2001. Federal Bureau of Investigation, *Crime in the United States Special Report: The Terrorist Attacks of September 11, 2001: A Compilation of Data* 302 (2001), *available at* http://www.fbi.gov/ucr/cius_01/01crime5.pdf (last visited Nov. 11, 2005) [hereinafter *Uniform Crime Reports*]. At all locations together, 739 women and 2,303 men died of the atrocities that day. Id.

10. See *New York Times*, Portraits: 9/11/01 The Collected Portraits of Grief (2d ed. 2003), available at www.nytimes.com/pages/national/portraits/index.html (last visited January 15, 2005).

11. A five-page letter found in the luggage of Mohammed Atta, one of the September 11th hijackers, left at Logan International Airport in Boston, stated in part: "You will be entering paradise. You will be entering the happiest life, everlasting life. . . ." "Excerpts from Letter Thought to Be Instructions," *New York Times*, Sept.

28, 2001, B4. Another document used by the hijackers the night before the attacks stated: "When the confrontation begins, strike like champions who do not want to go back to this world. . . . Know that . . . the women of paradise are waiting. . . ." "Notes Found After the Hijackings," *New York Times*, Sept. 29, 2001, B3. See also Joseph Lelyveld, "All Suicide Bombers are not Alike," *New York Times Magazine*, Oct. 20, 2001, 49. Atta's will specified that only "good Muslims" should prepare his body and that his funeral should exclude women: "I don't want any women to go to my grave at all during my funeral or any occasion thereafter." Philip Shenon and David Johnson, "Suspect's Will Suggests a Longtime Plan to Die," *New York Times*, Oct. 4, 2001, B5 (quoting Atta).

12. In recent years, the number of women murdered in the United States was 3215 in 2003, 3251 in 2002, 3214 in 2001, 2076 in 2000, and 3085 in 1999. Federal Bureau of Investigation, *Crime in the United States*, available at www.fbi.gov/ucr/ucr.htm (follow "2003" hyperlink; then follow "Table 2.3" hyperlink; and follow "2002;" then follow "Table 2.4;" and follow "2001;" then follow "Table 2.4;" and follow "2000;" then follow "Table 2.4;" and follow "1999;" then follow "Table 2.4.") (last visited Nov. 5, 2005). For some years, the sex murder victims was not known to the data authorities, so the numbers could be larger. See id. (follow "2004" hyperlink; then follow "Report Summary" hyperlink). The number of women known to be murdered by men varies each year, but men tend to outnumber women as women's killers by about 10 to 1. Federal Bureau of Investigation, Federal Bureau of Investigation, *Crime in the United States*, http://www.fbi.gov/ucr/ucr.htm (follow "2003" hyperlink; then follow "Table 2.7" hyperlink; and follow "2002;" then follow "Table 2.8;" and follow "2001;" then follow "Table 2.8.") (last visited Nov. 5, 2005).

13. One-thousand two-hundred forty-seven women were killed by male intimates in 2000. Bureau of Justice Statistics, Inmate Partner Violence, 1993–2001, www.ojp .usdoj.gov/bjs/abstract/ipv01.pdf-/ (last visited October 15, 2005). For some years, the sex of murder victims was not known to the data authorities, so the numbers could be larger. See id. At least one-third of murdered women are estimated to have been killed by intimate male partners, with the victim-offender relationship unknown in an additional third. Bureau of Justice Statistics, Homicide Trends in the U.S.: Intimate Homicide, www.ojp.usdoj.gov/bjs/homicide/intimates.htm (last visited October 15, 2005). Studies that look more closely at the incidence of men murdering intimate women partners in the United States find that the correct number is closer to fifty percent. See, e.g., The New Mexico Intimate Partner Violence Death Review Team "Getting Away with Murder III: Intimate Partner Violence Deaths 1999–2000," 39; Linda Langford, Nancy E. Issac, Stacie Kabat, *Homicides Related to Intimate Partner Violence in Massachusetts, 1991–1995*, (Peace at Home, 1999) (finding that forty-three percent of all female homicide victims in the state were killed by current or former intimate partners, and that the "current U.S. system of data collection, the Supplementary Homicide Reports (SHR) compiled by the FBI, does not . . . fully document all of the Partner Victims;" and that in Massachusetts from 1991 to 1995, the SHR was found to have missed twenty-nine percent of the partner victims and to have failed to document

"Other Victims" as homicides related to intimate partner violence). In addition, the SHR has no categories for victim-offender relationships such as ex-boyfriend or ex-girlfriend. See id. at 6. Thus, intimate male-on-female violence tends to be under-counted even when death results.

14. Lori Heise, Mary Ellsberg, and Megan Gottemoeller, *Population Reports Ending Violence Against Women*, 5 (1999) (finding by World Health Organization multicountry study that approximately ten to fifty percent of women are physically assaulted by their male partners at some point in their lives); Radhika Coomaraswamy, *Report of the Special Rapporteur on Violence Against Women, its Causes and Consequences*, esp. ¶¶ 120–21, U.N. Doc. E/CN.4/1995/42 (Nov. 22, 1995) [hereinafter *Preliminary VAW Report*]; esp. ¶ 62, U.N. Doc. E/CN.4/1996/53 (February 7, 1996) [hereinafter *Second VAW Report*]; Radhika Coomaraswamy, *Report of the Special Rapporteur on Violence Against Women, Its Causes and Consequences*, esp. ¶¶ 22–23, U.N. Doc. E/CN.4/1997/47 (June 17, 1997) [hereinafter *Third VAW Report*].

15. See 1 *The Charter of the United Nations: A Commentary* 668–670 (Bruno Simma et al., eds., Oxford 2002) (discussing scope of "armed attack"). However, in-ternational law has increasingly incorporated nonstate acts and actors into its frame-work, for example, under Protocol II to the Geneva Conventions. Protocol Addi-tional to the Geneva Conventions of 12 August 1949, and Relating to the Protection of Victims of Non-International Armed Conflicts, June 8, 1977, 1125 U.N.T.S. 609, [hereinafter Protocol II]. Certain jus cogens norms, such as against genocide, have al-ways applied to private as well as public actors. But as the Report of the High-level Panel on Threats, Challenges and Change conceded, "The norms governing the use of force by nonstate actors have not kept pace with those pertaining to States." High-level Panel on Threats, Challenges and Change, *A More Secure World: Our Shared Responsibility*, ¶ 159, U.N. Doc. A/59/565 (December 2, 2004) [hereinafter *High-level Report*].

16. International standards regarding the resort to force have invasion of one state by another principally in mind. For example, "use or threat of force" within Article 2(4) of the UN Charter is generally understood to be broader than "armed attack," meaning it encompasses mere frontier incidents or skirmishes including ones by irreg-ulars at the borders of states. See Military and Paramilitary Activities (Nicaragua v. United States), 1986 I.C.J. 14, at ¶ 195 (June 27) [hereianafter *Nicaragua*]. The Rome Statute of the International Criminal Court (ICC) is still broader, recognizing that armed conflict can take place between two nonstate actors but, if no governmental authorities are involved, it wants to see "protracted armed conflict" between "organized armed groups." The Rome Statute, art. 8, ¶ 2(f).

17. See Catharine A. MacKinnon, *Sex Equality* 715–745, 772–787 (2001) (providing extensive sources discussing and documenting the inefficacy of states in the United States in addressing violence against women, including domestic violence and sexual attacks). With cultural variation, similar patterns hold around the world. See *Second VAW Report*, above note 14, ¶¶ 54–114, 117–123, 130.

18. But note that the UN Charter begins, "We the Peoples," not "We the States." U.N. Charter preamble.

19. Article 51 of the UN Charter provides that "[n]othing shall impair the inherent right of individual and collective self-defense." This provision might be read to extend to private actors in a genocidal civil war but, in the classic formulation, the right to self-defense applies to states, largely because it is the exception to the UN Charter's Article 2(4) ban, which (at least until after September 11th) has been read to apply only to states. For the International Court of Justice's (ICJ) interpretation of collective self-defense generally, including under this regime, see *Nicaragua*, above note 16, at ¶¶ 195–200. For states, the right of self-defense is often seen as customary as well, rather than being entirely supplanted by the Charter. See id. ¶ 193.

20. See, e.g., B. Sharon Byrd, "Till Death Do Us Part: A Comparative Law Approach to Justifying Lethal Self-Defense by Battered Women," 1 *Duke Journal of Comparative and International Law* 169, 172–176 (1991); Sandra K. Lyons and David McCord, "Moral Reasoning and the Criminal Law: The Example of Self-Defence," 30 *American Criminal Law Review* 97, 107–110 (1992); *Second VAW Report*, above note 14, ¶¶ 8–10, 130 (criticizing the United Arab Emirates for failing to accept self-defense claims such as that of "a 16-year-old Filipina migrant worker, Sarah Balabagan, who was reported to have stabbed her employer to death in self-defense after having been raped at knife-point by him") (describing the frequent mitigation of men's crimes for killing women, not extended to women who kill their abusers in self-defence). Perhaps legal standards that preclude women from using force in self-defense might be found to violate the International Covenant on Civil and Political Rights, arts. 6, 26, G.A. Res. 220A (XXI), at 52, U.N. Doc. A/6316 (Dec. 19, 1996), 999 U.N.T.S. 171 [hereinafter ICCPR].

21. An International Criminal Tribunal for the former Yugoslavia (ICTY) Trial Chamber has held that paragraph (1) (c) of Article 31 of the Statute of the ICC, providing that self-defense excludes criminal responsibility if the act is in response to "an imminent and unlawful use of force in a manner proportionate to the degree of danger" to the person "protected," codifies customary international law. Prosecutor v. Kordic, Case No. IT-95-14/2-T ¶ 451 (Feb 26, 2001). The Appeals Chamber appeared to approve this view. See Prosecutor v. Kordic, Case No. IT-95-14/2-A ¶ 837, (December 17, 2004).

22. For one judicial recognition of this criticism in the U.S. setting, see State v. Wanrow, 588 P.2d 1320 (Wash. 1978) where the so-called Battered Women's Syndrome is an attempt to address this problem. See Phyllis L. Crocker, "The Meaning of Equality for Battered Women Who Kill Men in Self-Defense," 8 *Harvard Women's Law Journal* 121, 123, 126 (1985) ("The traditional doctrine of self-defense is based on the experiences of men; it neither contemplates nor acknowledges those acts of self-defense by women that are reasonable, but different from men's. . . . The male experience permeates both the elements of the defense and the standards of reasonableness.")

23. See Lyons and McCord, above note 20, at 108. See also Byrd, above note 20, at 172.

24. See *Nicaragua,* above note 16, at ¶¶ 194, 237. An excellent review is provided by Christine Gray, *International Law and the Use of Force* 105–108, 111 (2000). See also Jost Delbruck, "Proportionality," in 3 *Encyclopedia of Public International Law* 1140, (Rudolph Bernhardt, ed., 1997).

25. "In one country, for example, women throughout the country are serving lengthy prison sentences for killing their abusers in self-defense. Conversely, men who kill their intimate partners are often excused or their sentences mitigated after the provocation defence or the defence of honor has been raised and accepted by the court." *Second VAW Report,* above note 14, at ¶ 130.

26. A good overview on this subject, as well as of the dichotomy between war and peace, can be found in Nathaniel Berman, "Privileging Combat? Contemporary Conflict and the Legal Construction of War," 43 *Columbia Journal of Transnational Law* 1 (2004). Note that protections for civilians in armed conflict are not unlimited. Civilians can lose their protections if they take part in hostilities or, under the doctrine of reasonable collateral damage, if their unintended losses are proportional to a military advantage thereby gained. Note that protections for civilians in armed conflict are not unlimited. Civilians can lose their protections if they take part in hostilities or, under the doctrine of reasonable collateral damage, if their unintended losses are proportional to a mililtary advantage thereby gained. These doctrines have echoes between the sexes, for example then women are punished if they fight back or are effectively treated as roadkill in men's conflicts among each other, as in unprosecuted war rapes.

27. See Theodor Meron, "Rape as a Crime Under International Humanitarian Law," 87 *American Journal of International Law* 424 (1993); Christine M. Chinkin, "Rape and Sexual Abuse in International Law," 5 *European Journal of International Law* 326 (1994).

28. See Prosecutor v. Akayesu, Case No. ICTR-96-4-T, ¶¶ 686–688 (Sept. 2, 1998) [hereinafter *Akayesu*]; Catharine A. MacKinnon, "Defining Rape Internationally: A Commentary on *Akayesu*" 44 *Columbia Journal of Transnational Law* (forthcoming, 2006).

29. All the relevant features of this problem are displayed in the debate over the legality of the military commissions that the United States is advancing to try individuals accused of activities associated with and following September 11th. See, e.g., Joan Fitzpatrick, "Jurisdiction of Military Commissions and the Ambiguous War on Terrorism," 96 *American Journal International Law* 345, 345–348 (2002) (discussing the contradictions produced by simultaneous application of war and crime models); Harold Hongju Koh, "The Case Against Military Tribunals," 96 *American Journal of International Law* 337 (2002); Ruth Wedgwood, "Al Qaeda, Terrorism, and Military Commissions," 96 *American Journal of International Law* 328 (2002). The larger legal issues raised in this context are being adjudicated in criminal cases involving the detainees. See, e.g., Richard A. Serrano, "Detainee Challenges 'Combatant' Status; Lawyers for a Man Held at a Military Jail in South Carolina Plan to Test the President's Authority

to Decide the Legal Standing of Terrorism Suspects," *L.A. Times*, Sept. 18, 2005, at A22; Mitch Frank, "Terror Goes on Trial," *Time Magazine*, Mar. 7, 2005, at 34; Jerry Markson, "U.S. Can Confine Citizens Without Charges, Court Rules," *Washington Post*, Sept. 10, 2005, A01.

30. Common Artcile III of the Geneva Convention Relative to the Protection of Civilian Persons in Time of War provides "In the case of armed conflict not of an international character occurring in the territory of one of the High Contracting Parties, each Party to the conflict shall be bound to apply, as a minimum, the following provisions: 1. Persons taking no active part in the hostilities, including members of armed forces who have laid down their arms and those placed hors de combat by sickness, wounds, detention, or any other cause, shall in all circumstances be treated humanely, without any adverse distinction founded on race, colour, religion or faith, sex, birth or wealth, or any other similar criteria. To this end, the following acts are and shall remain prohibited at any time and in any place whatsoever with respect to the above-mentioned persons: (a) violence to life and person, in particular murder of all kinds, mutilation, cruel treatment and torture; (b) taking of hostages; (c) outrages upon personal dignity, in particular humiliating and degrading treatment; (d) the passing of sentences and the carrying out of executions without previous judgment pronounced by a regularly constituted court, affording all the judicial guarantees which are recognized as indispensable by civilized peoples." above note 2.

31. Id.

32. This appears quite well-established, but all the sources are press. See *Saturday Early Show: New Videotape from Osama bin Laden* (CBS television broadcast, October 30, 2004) ("On the tape, bin Laden admitted for the first time that he ordered the September 11 attacks."). See also *Weekend Edition: New Osama bin Laden Tape Rears Its Ugly Head*, (NPR radio broadcast, Oct. 30, 2004); Transcript of Interview by Tayseer Alouni of Al-Jazeera Television with Osama bin Laden (Oct. 2001), available at http://archives.cnn.com/2002/WORLD/asiapcf/south/02/05/binladen.transcript/index .html.

33. See Walter Pincus and Dana Milbank, "The Iraq Connection: Al Qaeda-Hussein Link Is Dismissed," *Washington Post*, June 17, 2004, at A1 (reporting that Vice President Dick Cheney termed evidence of ties "overwhelming," and an April 2004 Harris poll showed as many as forty-nine percent of Americans believed that "clear evidence" of a connection had been found). The September 11 Commission concluded that, although Iraqi officials may have met bin Laden or his aides at some point, "To date, we have seen no evidence that [any contacts between bin Laden and Iraq] ever developed into a collaborative operational relationship. Nor have we seen evidence indicating that Iraq cooperated with al Qaeda in developing or carrying out any attacks against the United States." National Commission on Terrorist Attacks upon the United States, The 9–11 Commission Report 66 (2004).

34. See Lassa Oppenheim, *International Law: A Treatise* 550 (8th ed. 1955) (explaining that the ultimate issue is one of fact: "whether the individuals concerned were sufficiently closely associated with the state for their acts to be regarded as acts of the

state rather than acts of private individuals"); Emmerich de Vattel, *The Law of Nations* 162 (Gaunt 2001) (1834) (stating that acts of private citizens can be attributed to the state if it "approve[d]" or "ratifie[d]" the act, thus becoming "the real author of the injury"). A similar rule pertains in attribution of civil damages. See Cotesworth and Powell (Great Britain v. Colombia) (1875), reprinted in John Bassett Moore, 2 *History and Digest of the International Arbitrations to Which the United States Had Been a Party* 2050 (1898) (citing de Vattel for the proposition that "[O]ne nation is not responsible to another for the acts of its individual citizens, except when it approves or ratifies them. It then becomes a public concern, and the injured party may consider the nation itself the real author of the injury.").

Views vary on standards for attribution of nonstate actor behavior to states. See Nicaragua, above note 16, at ¶¶ 114–116. Expounding a test of "effective control" by states, the ICJ there found that acts by the Contras taken with U.S. support (finance, training, equipment) were not imputable to the United States, while the United States was held responsible for acts that were a direct result of the U.S. military or its paid agents. Id. at ¶ 115. The core concept is developed in United States Diplomatic and Consular Staff in Tehran (United States v. Iran), 1980 I.C.J. 3, 27–35, 42 (May 24), in which the takeover of the U.S. embassy by armed students, subsequently embraced by the government, was attributed to Iran. In Prosecutor v. Tadic, Case No. IT-94-1-T, Judgment, ¶¶ 116–144 (July 15, 1999), the ICTY Appeals Chamber, weighing the responsibility of Yugoslavia for acts of Bosnian Serb forces, relaxed the requirement for attributing their unlawful acts to the state to "overall control" over the organized paramilitary groups. That court held that the extent of requisite state control varies such that the question "is whether a *single* private individual or a *group that is not militarily organized* has acted as a *de facto* state organ when performing a specific act." Id. ¶ 137. See also Prosecutor v. Tadic, Case No. IT-94-1-T, Separate and Dissenting Opinion of Judge McDonald Regarding the Applicability of Article 2 of the Statute, ¶¶ 18–34 (May 7, 1997). The international community appears to be moving toward accepting the Tadic majority's understanding of attribution post-Afghanistan: "The control required by international law may be deemed to exist when a State (or, in the context of an armed conflict, the party to the conflict) *has a role in organising, coordinating or planning the military actions* of the military group, in addition to financing, training and equipping or providing operational support to that group." Tadic, Judgment, ¶137. See also *Responsibility of States for Internationally Wrongful Acts*, G.A. Res. 83, art. 8, U.N. Doc. A/RES/56/83 (Dec. 12, 2001) (attribution to state appropriate if nonstate actor "in fact [is] acting on the instructions of, or under the direction or control of, that State in carrying out [the wrongful] conduct."). In one national court, some progress was made toward international accountability for the actions of a rogue entity leader. See Kadic v. Karadžić, 70 F.3d 232 (2d Cir. 1996), *cert. denied*, 518 U.S. 1005 (1996) [hereinafter *Karadžic*].

35. See Treaty of Westphalia, above note 1. The 1945 UN Charter regime significantly furthered this development. Before the Charter, states responded to nonstate violence through the use of force, for example in raiding the Emir of Tripoli after the

Barbary pirates interfered with Mediterranean shipping, and in pursuing Pancho Villa into Mexico.

36. President Bush reportedly told his aides, "We're at war," when he heard of the second plane hitting the second tower. Dan Balz, "A Bond Cemented by Chemistry: Crisis Highlights Links and Differences Between Bush Administrations," *Washington Post*, Sept. 15, 2001, A3. On September 11th, President Bush stated, "we stand together to win the war against terrorism." "Address to the Nation on the Terrorist Attacks," 2 *Public Papers* 1100 (Sept. 11, 2001). On September 16th, he said, "It is time for us to win the first war of the 21st century decisively, so that our children and our grandchildren can live peacefully into the 21st century." "Remarks on Arrival at the White House and an Exchange with Reporters," 2 *Public Papers* 1116 (Sept. 16, 2001). On September 20th, he stated, "On September 11th, enemies of freedom committed an act of war against our country." "Address Before a Joint Session of the Congress on the United States Response to the Terrorist Attacks of September 11," 2 *Public Papers* 1140 (Sept. 20, 2001). And on September 25th, President Bush stated that, "Two weeks ago there was an act of war declared on America. . . . [W]e're at war, a war we're going to win." "Remarks to Federal Bureau of Investigation Employees," 2 *Public Papers* 1160–1162 (Sept. 25, 2001). Bush noted of the Patriot Act that "[t]his Government will enforce this law with all the urgency of a nation at war." "Remarks on Signing the USA PATRIOT ACT of 2001," 2 *Public Papers* 1307 (Oct. 26, 2001). See Donald Rumsfeld, Editorial, "A New Kind of War," *The New York Times*, Sept. 27, 2001, A21 (referring *passim* to U.S. effort against terrorism as "this war"). In his 2004 State of the Union Address, President Bush appeared to acknowledge the legal issue when he said: "I know that some people question if America is really in a war at all. They view terrorism more as a crime, a problem to be solved mainly with law enforcement and indictments. . . . After the chaos and carnage of September the 11th, it is not enough to serve our enemies with legal papers. The terrorists and their supporters declared war on the United States, and war is what they got." "President's State of the Union Message to Congress and the Nation," reprinted in *The New York Times*, Jan. 21, 2004, A18. Although a declaration of war is not essential—creating a state of armed conflict is the issue—bin Laden's fatwa of 1998, below note 53, could be read as a declaration of war.

37. Actually, S.C. Res. 1368, Preamble, U.N. Doc. S/RES/1368 (Sept. 12, 2001), does more than this. It notes that the Security Council is "[r]ecognizing the inherent right of individual or collective self-defence in accordance with the Charter." See also S.C. Res. 1373, Preamble, U.N. Doc. S/RES/1373 (Sept. 28, 2001). Varying views on the scope and contours of the right of self-defense under the U.N. Charter are ventilated in articles on the legality of the U.S. war against Iraq. See, e.g., William H. Taft IV and Todd F. Buchwald, "Preemption, Iraq, and International Law, in Future Implications of the Iraq Conflict," 97 *American Journal of International Law* 553, 557 (2003) (viewing the attack as lawful as collective self-defense, especially in light of 1990 and 2003 Security Council resolutions); Richard N. Gardner, "Neither Bush Nor the 'Jurisprudes,' in Future Implications of the Iraq Conflict," id. at 553, 585 (2003) (discussing

the risks of an enlarged self-defense scope in light of the Cuban Missile Crisis); Jane E. Stromseth, "Law and Force After Iraq: A Transitional Moment, in Future Implications of the Iraq Conflict," id. at 553, 628 (2003) (cautioning against a broad preemption doctrine); Jürgen Habermas, "Interpreting the Fall of a Monument," 4 *Georgetown Law Journal* 701 (2003) (arguing that although the war in Iraq is incompatible with the U.N. Charter, the war represents not the defeat of international law but the passing of the normative authority of the United States).

38. See Lord Robertson, "North American Treaty Organization (NATO): Statement by NATO Secretary General, Lord Robertson," 40 *International Legal Materials* 1268 (2001).

39. This is not to take any position on the "unlawful combatant" debate, but it should be noted that armed forces of states are not always automatically entitled to prisoner of war status if the state systematically violates the law of armed conflict.

40. For useful reviews, see Rosalyn Higgins, "The General International Law of Terrorism," in *Terrorism and International Law* 13 (Rosalyn Higgins and Maurice Flory eds., 1997); 1 *International Criminal Law*, 776–80 (M. Cherif Bassiouni ed., 2d ed. 1987); W. Michael Reisman, "International Legal Responses to Terrorism," 22 *Houston Journal of International Law* 3 (1999). The U.N. General Assembly has not yet concluded a comprehensive convention to fill any gaps between the existing twelve counterterrorism agreements. See Gerhard Hafner, "Certain Issues of the Work of the Sixth Committee at the Fifty-Sixth General Assembly," 97 *American Journal of International Law* 147 (2003).

41. See, e.g., S.C. Res. 1368 and S.C. Res. 1373, above note 37.

42. For discussions of definitional issues, see Jordan J. Paust, "A Definitional Focus," in *Terrorism: Interdisciplinary Perspectives* 18, 18–25 (Yonah Alexander and Seymour Maxwell Finger eds., 1977); Elizabeth Chadwick, *Self-Determination, Terrorism, and the International Humanitarian Law of Armed Conflict* 2–3 (1996); Susan Tiefenbrun, "A Semiotic Approach to a Legal Definition of Terrorism," 9 ILSA *Journal of International and Comparative Law* 357 (2003). The latter element mentioned in the text would exclude state terrorism, which many people (including me) think should be covered. For an illuminating discussion, see U.N. Economic and Social Council [ECOSOC], Sub-Committee on Promotion and Protection of Human Rights, *Terrorism and Human Rights*, ¶¶ 37–67, U.N. Doc. E/CN.4/Sub.2/2001/31 (June 27, 2001) (prepared by Kalliopi K. Koufa). The *High-level Report* takes an integrative approach to this question. Referring to existing definitions, the report describes terrorism as, in addition to acts covered by existing conventions on the subject, "any action . . . that is intended to cause death or serious bodily harm to civilians or non-combatants, when the purpose of such an act, by its nature or context, is to intimidate a population, or to compel a Government or an international organization to do or to abstain from doing any act." *High-level Report*, above note 15, ¶ 164(d).

43. Catharine A. MacKinnon, *Toward a Feminist Theory of the State* (1989); Kate Millett, *Sexual Politics* (1970).

44. Compare "International Convention for the Suppression of the Financing of

Terrorism, G.A. Res. 54/109, Annex, U.N. Doc.A/RES/54/109 (Feb. 25, 2000) (requiring that the threat be directed against a civilian or noncombatant), with 8 U.S.C. § 1182(a)(3)(B)(iii)(II) (2005) (lacking this element). Under the Convention, an act is terrorism only if it is intended to coerce action by a government or international organization; under U.S. law, intent to compel action by any third party is enough. The International Convention Against the Taking of Hostages views "all acts of taking of hostages as manifestations of international terrorism." G.A. Res. 34/146, Preamble/U.N. Doc.A/C.6/34/L.23 (Dec. 17, 1979). It identifies the political objective of a hostage-taker by defining such an offender as a person "who seizes or detains and threatens to kill, to injure or to continue to detain a hostage . . . in order to compel a third party, namely, a State . . . to do or abstain from doing any act as . . . a condition for the release of the hostage." Id. at art. 1, ¶ 1. See Christopher L. Blakesley, *Terrorism, Drugs, International Law, and the Protection of Human Liberty* 17–20 (1992) (defining terrorism as violence aimed at innocents or non-combatants to gain an edge over or to coerce a third party); *High-level Report*, above note 15, ¶ 164(d).

45. Perhaps it was for the United States to leave the three holy places. See Walter Pincus, "Bin Laden Fatalistic, Gaunt in New Tape," *Washington Post*, Dec. 28, 2001, A1. Or that Americans should feel the fear the Palestinians feel. On both points, see, e.g., Cam Simpson, "U.S. Fears More Attacks," *Chicago Tribune*, May 14, 2003, A6 "I swear to God that America will never dream of security or see it before we live it and see it in Palestine, and not before the infidel's armies leave the land of Muhammad." (quoting Osama bin Laden).

46. Although, assuming an armed conflict, it could be. See Geneva Convention relative to the Protection of Civilian Persons in Time of War, above note 2, at art. 33; Protocol II, above note 15, at art. 4; Protocol Additional to the Geneva Conventions of 12 August 1949, and Relating to the Protection of Victims of International Armed Conflicts, art. 51, June 8, 1977, 1125 U.N.T.S. 3, 16 *International Legal Materials* 1391 [hereinafter Protocol I]. For prescient discussion of this interface, see Gregory M. Travalio, "Terrorism, International Law, and the Use of Military Force,"18 *Wisconsin International Law Journal* 145 (2000).

47. See United Nations Diplomatic Conference of Plenipotentiaries on the Establishment of an International Criminal Court, June 15 to July 17, 1998, *Final Act of the United Nations Diplomatic Conference of Plenipotentiaries on the Establishment of an International Criminal Court*, Annex 1(E), U.N. Doc. A/CONF.183/10 (July 17, 1998) (recommending "that a Review Conference Pursuant to article 123 of the Statute of the International Criminal Court consider the crimes of terrorism and drug crimes with a view to arriving at an acceptable definition and their inclusion in the list of crimes within the jurisdiction of the Court"). See also *Commentary on the Rome Statute of the International Criminal Court: Observers' Notes, Article by Article* 98–99 (Otto Triffterer ed., 1999).

48. For an updated list, see U.N. Treaty Collection, http://untreaty.un.org/English/Terrorism.asp.

49. That this would have been ex-U.S. President Clinton's legacy remains an un-

realized fantasy. For a narrower but consonant recommendation that post-conflict Truth and Reconciliation Commissions as presently structured investigate crimes against women, see Elizabeth Rehn and Ellen Johnson Sirleaf, United Nations Development Fund for Women (UNIFEM), *Women, War and Peace: The Independent Experts' Assessment on the Impact of Armed Conflict on Women and Women's Role in Peacebuilding* 106–107, 140 (2002), available at www.reliefweb.int/rw/lib.nsf/AllDocs ByUNID/3f71081ff391653dc1256c69003170e9.

50. In the Rome Statute, crimes against humanity lost their formerly required nexus to a state of war, although an act, to qualify, still must have been committed as "part of a widespread or systematic attack directed against any civilian population, with knowledge of the attack." See The Rome Statute, art. 12, ¶ 3. Note in this conncetion that in the two ad hoc tribunals, the ICTY and the International Criminal Tribunal for Rwanda (ICTR) have addressed violence against women as crimes against humanity were in the reality context of armed conflict and genocide.

51. Most thinking about the status of non-party states under the Rome Statute has revolved around whether their nationals could be prosecuted, not whether nonparty states could have access to remedies. For one discussion of the "third party" treaty debate in the ICC context, see Madeline Morris, "High Crimes and Misconceptions: The ICC and Non-Party States," 64 *Law and Contemporary Problems* 13 (2001).

52. The Rome Statute, art. 7 ¶ 1(g), defines acts of sexual violence as crimes against humanity when committed as part of a widespread or systematic attack directed against a civilian population with knowledge of the attack.

53. Convention on the Prevention and Punishment of the Crime of Genocide, Dec. 9, 1949, 78 U.N.T.S. 277, art. 2. Although considering September 11th as genocide minimizes the multinational identities of the victim group, a similar mix is often present in genocides, which are defined by intent. See id. Potential examples of genocidal intent reported in connection with the September 11th attacks include: On February 23, 1998, Shaykh Osama Bin-Muhammad Bin-Laden issued his Jihad Against Jews and Crusaders charging that: "[T]he ruling to kill the Americans and their allies—civilian and military—is an individual duty for every Muslim who can do it in any country in which it is possible to do it. . . . We—with God's help—call on every Muslim who believes in God and wishes to be rewarded to comply with God's order to kill the Americans and plunder their money wherever and whenever they find it." "A Wealthy, Shadowy Mastermind," *Atlanta Journal Constitution*, Aug. 21, 1998, C2. A text of a videotaped statement by bin Laden broadcast on Al-Jazeera television stated, "God has blessed a group of vanguard Muslims, the forefront of Islam, to destroy America." "Bin Laden's Statement: 'The Sword Fell,' " *The New York Times*, Oct. 8, 2001, B7. Al-Jazeera also aired a videotape featuring September 11th hijacker Ahmed Alhaznawi stating: "It is time to kill the Americans in their own homeland, among their sons, and near their forces and intelligence." Tim Golden, "Videotape Links Al Qaeda with Sept. 11 Hijackers," *The New York Times*, Apr. 16, 2002, A5. On May 21, 2003, Al-Jazeera aired an audio tape from Ayman Al-Zawahari, senior aide to Osama bin Laden, exhorting Muslims to "[c]arry out attacks against the embassies, companies, interests and officials

of the U.S., Britain, Australia and Norway. Burn the ground under their feet. . . . The crusaders and the Jews only understand the language of murder, bloodshed . . . and of the burning towers." "New Al-Qaeda Tape Calling for Attacks," Al JaZeera, May 21, 2003, available at http://english.aljazeera.net/NR/exeres/293D19D4-CBB9-4296-B158 -D54246F6259E.htm (last visited Oct. 15, 2005).

54. Joseph J. Lador Lederer, "A Legal Approach to International Terrorism," 9 *Israel Law Review* 194, 211 (1974).

55. This analysis is discussed in Catharine A. MacKinnon, "Genocide's Sexuality," in *Political Exclusion and Domination* (Stephen Macedo and Melissa S. Williams eds. 2005) [hereinafter, "Genocide's Sexuality"]. The trial decision in the *Akayesu* case does face the role of sexual atrocities in genocide defined on existing grounds. See *Akayesu*, above note 28, ¶ 731.

56. See, e.g., Catharine A. MacKinnon, "On Torture: A Feminist Perspective on Human Rights," *Human Rights in the Twenty-First Century: A Global Challenge* 21 (Kathleen Mahoney and Paul Mahoney, eds., 1992); Catharine A. MacKinnon, "Rape, Genocide, and Women's Human Rights," *Mass Rape: The War Against Women in Bosnia-Herzegovina* (Alexandra Stiglmayer, ed., 1993); Hilary Charlesworth and Christine Chinkin, *The Boundaries of International Law: A Feminist Analysis* 234–235 (2000).

57. See United Nations War Crimes Commission, 4 *Law Reports of Trials of War Criminals* 1–2 (1948) (successfully prosecuting Japanese General Tomoyuki Yamashita for rape, murder, and mass executions carried out in The Philippines during World War II).

58. See, e.g., Prosecutor v. Kunarac, Kovac, & Vukovic (Foča), Case Nos. IT-96-23-T and IT-96-23/1-T, ¶¶ 515–43, 651 (Feb. 22, 2001) (holding that serial rape in a brothel-like setting constitutes slavery); Prosecutor v. Milošević, Case No. IT-99-37-I, Indictment, ¶ 36 (November 22, 2001) (indicting for rape as act of genocide).

59. See, e.g., Akayesu, above note 28. The U.N. Special Court for Sierra Leone is also addressing issues of sexual abuse, including forced marriage, in the context of that conflict. For an example, see the case of Augustine Gbao (or Gao), whose indictments can be found at www.sc-sl.org/Documents/SCSL-04-15-PT-122-6181-6191.pdf and www.sc-sl.org/Documents/SCSL-04-15-PT-12-6192-6202.pdf, together with a summary of the case at www.sc-sl.org/RUFcasesummary.html.

60. See Rome Statute, art. 7(g) (in or out of war), 8(b)(xxii), 8(e)(vi).

61. See Virginia Woolf, *Three Guineas* 13 (1st Harbinger ed. 1963) (1938).

62. This thought leads one to wonder if women as a group are already so destroyed that our destruction as such is unimaginable, an analysis explored in Genocide's Sexuality, above note 55. When women are assaulted as women members of their ethnic communities, they are covered at least technically in some jurisdictions. See *Karadžić*, above note 34.

63. Charles Black observed that the U.S. constitutional concept of state action in the law of race is Protean: "[I]f and where it works, it immunizes racist practices from constitutional control. Those who desire to practice racism are therefore motivated, even driven, to test it through total possibility . . . and its potential variety is simply the

variety of all possible action by that complex entity that is called the state. [Commitment] to a single and exclusive theory of state action . . . would be altogether unprincipled, in terms of the most vital principle of all—the reality principle." Charles L. Black, Jr., "Foreword: State Action, Equal Protection, and California's Proposition 14," 81 *Harvard Law Review* 69, 90 (1967). The same could be said of issues of sex raised by sexual violence under constitutional and international law.

64. For discussion in the context of the United States, where making, sale, and use of pornography attracts rights of constitutional dimension, see Catharine A. MacKinnon, *Only Words* (1993). Although the dynamics are distinct in significant respects, it is instructive (and sustains the parallel) to observe that, since September 11th, proposals in England, the Netherlands, and Italy would forbid propaganda that "glorifies" terrorism. See www.statewatch.org/news/2005/aug/italy-new-terror-laws.pdf and www.edri.org/edrigram/number3.16/terrorism.

65. George W. Bush, "Address to the Nation on the Terrorist Attacks (September 11, 2001)," 37 *Weekly Compiled Presidential Documents* 1301, 1301 (September 17, 2001).

66. Among international instruments that prohibit failures to act are: ICCPR, above note 20, at art. 15, ¶ 2 (arts. 1(3), 2, and 3 impose affirmative duties to act, and art. 41 discusses the competence of the Committee to receive complaints regarding the failure of a country to fulfill its obligations); CEDAW above note 3, at 194; International Convention on the Protection of All Migrant Workers and Members of Their Families, G.A. Res. 45/148, at 261, U.N. GAOR, 45th Sess., U.N. Doc. A/45/49 May 2, 1991.

67. This principle has been developed in the Inter-American regional system in cases involving violence against women by irregular forces putatively linked to states. See Velásquez-Rodriguez Case, 4 *Inter-American Court of Human Rights (ser. C)* at 31 (1988). "Harbouring" is not unique to the war context. It is used in the context of trafficking in women in the Protocol to Prevent, Suppress and Punish Trafficking in Persons, Especially Women and Children, Supplementing the United Nations Convention Against Transnational Organized Crime, above note 3, Annex II, art. 3. See also Island of Palmas (United States v. Netherlands), 2 *Review of International Arbitration Awards* 829, 839 (Perm. Ct. Arb. 1928), and Declaration on Principles of International Law Concerning Friendly Relations and Cooperation Among States in Accordance with the Charter of the United Nations, G.A. Res. 2625, at 121 U.N. GAOR, 25th Sess., Supp. No. 28, U.N. Doc. A/5217 (Oct. 24, 1970).

68. See José Alvarez, "The U.N.'s 'War' on Terrorism," 31 *International Journal of Legal Information* 238, 243 (2003).

69. See S.C. Res. 1540, ¶ 2, U.N. Doc. S/RES/1540 (Apr. 28, 2004).

70. Those who have used this number include U.S. Secretary of Defense Donald Rumsfeld (CNN Transcript # 091903CN.V54 Sept. 19, 2001); White House Press Secretary Ari Fleischer, "Ari Fleischer Holds White House Briefing," *FDCH Political Transcripts* (Sept 21, 2001) ("I just remind you that the Al Qaeda organization is present in some sixty countries, and those who harbor and support terrorists are the targets of the president's action to protect our country."); William Walker, "Windening His

Sights,", *Toronto Star*, Mar. 10, 2002, B1, ("Bush says terrorists are being harboured by sixty countries and trained at camps in several of them, including Somalia, Sudan, Syria and Lebanon"); Richard Norton-Taylor, "This Marks the Death of Deterrence," *Guardian*, Oct. 9, 2002, 18 ("Vice President Dick Cheney has suggested this includes no fewer than 60 states. . . .").

71. See U.N. Development Programme, *Human Development Report 2002 : Deepening Democracy in a Fragmented World*, at 11 (2002), *available at* http://hdr.undp .org/reports/global/2002/en/pdf/complete.pdf; Mary Robinson, "Making Human Rights Matter: Eleanor Roosevelt's Time Has Come," 16 *Harvard Human Rights Journal* 1, 8 (2003).

72. See Uniform Crime Reports, above note 9.

73. On the operation of this process, see *Restatement (Third) of the Foreign Relations Law of the United States* §102 (1986). For analysis, see Michael Byers, *Custom, Power and the Power of Rules: International Relations and Customary International Law* (1999); Anthony A. d'Amato, *The Concept of Custom in International Law* (1971); Oscar Schachter, *International Law in Theory and Practice* 1–15 (1991); "Statement of Principles Applicable to the Formation of General Customary International Law," (International Law Association, Committee on the Formation of Customary (General) International Law, London Conference, 2000), available at http://www.ila-hq.org.pdf/ CustomaryLaw.pdf The United States might also consider whether ratifying the 1966 Optional Protocol to the ICCPR, Dec. 19, 1966, 999 U.N.T.S. 302, would help victims such as those of September 11th.

74. For some of the well-known information on Afghan women's situation prior to the invasion, see S.C. Res. 1076, ¶ 11, U.N. Doc. S/RES/1076 (Oct. 22, 1996); S.C. Res. 1193, U.N. Doc. S/RES/1193 (Aug. 28, 1998); S.C. Res. 1214, ¶ 12, U.N. Doc. S/RES/1214 (Dec. 8, 1998); S.C. Res. 1267, U.N. Doc. S/RES/1267 (Oct. 15, 1999); U.N. Economic and Social Council [ECOSOC], Sub-Committee on Promotion and Protection of Human Rights, The Secretary-General, *Report of the Secretary-General on the situation of women and girls in Afghanistan, submitted in accordance with Sub-Commission resolution 1999/14,* U.N. Doc. E/CN.4/Sub.2/2000/18 (July 21, 2000).

75. Article 41 of the ICCPR recognizes the jurisdictional compentence of the Human Rights Committee to receive communications for noncompliance. ICCPR, above note 20, art. 41, ¶ 1. The declaration of the United States on this article can be found at 138 Cong. Rec. 8068 Decl. III(3) (1992). The United States might also consider whether ratifying the 1966 Optional Protocol to the ICCPR, Dec 19, 1966, 999 U.N.T.S. 302, would help victims such as those of September 11th.

76. For documentation of the examples cited in this paragraph, and more, see *Preliminary VAW Report*, above note 14, and *Second VAW Report*, above note 14.

77. See Amartya Sen, "More Than 100 Million Women Are Missing," 37 *New York Review of Books* 20, Dec. 20, 1990, 61, 66.

78. An instructive thought experiment is to ask how the world would have responded if all 648 women in the World Trade Center had been raped by foreign men, and whether that response would change if, say, the same number of mostly American women were raped there by mostly American men on a single day.

79. See, e.g., sources above note 6.

80. These facts, although many readers remain inexplicably startled by them, have been robustly established with solid empirical methodology for over twenty years. Myriad such empirical documentation is collected in Catharine A. MacKinnon, *Sex Equality* 715–897 (2001). See also Diana E. H. Russell and Rebecca M. Bolen, *The Epidemic of Rape and Child Sexual Abuse in the United States* (2000); Staff of Senate Committee on the Judiciary, 102d Cong., 1st Sess., *Violence Against Women: A Week in the Life of America* (Comm. Print 1992); Mary P. Koss et al., *No Safe Haven: Male Violence Against Women at Home, at Work, and in the Community* (1994).

81. See, e.g., Andrea Dworkin, "A Battered Wife Survives," in *Letters from a War Zone: Writings 1976–1989* 100, 100–106 (1988); Margaret T. Gordon and Stephanie Riger, *The Female Fear* (1989). See also *Domestic Violence: Terrorism in the Home: Hearing Before the Subcommittee on Children, Family, Drugs, and Alcoholism of the Senate Committee on Labor and Human Resources*, 101st Cong. (1990).

82. See *Second VAW Report*, above note 14, ¶ 57 ("The mere existence of violence against women in general and domestic violence in particular spreads fear among women, often restricting the way in which they lead their lives."). See also id., ¶ 27 ("[A]cts or threats of violence, whether occurring in private or in public life, instill fear and insecurity in women's lives and are obstacles to the achievement of equality, development and peace, resulting in high social, health and economic costs to the individual[.]").

83. For some literature ignored, see Susan Brownmiller, *Against Our Will: Men, Women, and Rape* 229 (1975) (observing that "men who commit rape have served in effect as front-line masculine shock troops, terrorist guerillas in the longest sustained battle the world has ever known"); Robin Morgan, *The Demon Lover: On the Sexuality of Terrorism* (1990) (analyzing terrorism in feminist terms). Andrea Dworkin in 1977 titled her first speech exclusively on pornography, "Pornography: The New Terrorism." Dworkin, above note 81, at 197–202. For some legally focused analysis in similar vein, see Amy E. Ray, "The Shame of It: Gender-Based Terrorism in the Former Yugoslavia and the Failure of International Human Rights Law to Comprehend the Injuries," 46 *American University Law Review* 793 (1997).

84. See, e.g., Kofi Annan, address to the General Assembly on September 23, 2003, http://www.un.org/apps/sg/sgstats.asp?nid=517) (referring to September 11th as having brought the international system to a "fork in the road").

85. The *High-level Report*, above note 15, ¶ 148(b), which mentions gender in passing as an ideological rather than a material factor, is no exception. Causes and facilitators of terrorism are said to include poverty (although more women than men are poor without resorting to terrorism), lack of social and political rights (although women are more deprived of them than men are), and political grievances, organized crime, and collapse of states (all of which affect both sexes without making women violent to the degree men are).

86. This analysis pushes one step further the logic of Meron on the national/international distinction in the war context: "Why protect civilians from belligerent violence, or ban rape . . . and yet refrain from enacting the same bans or providing the same

protection when armed violence has erupted 'only' within the territory of a sovereign state? If international law . . . must gradually turn to the protection of human beings, it is only natural that the aforementioned dichotomy should gradually lose its weight." Theodor Meron, "The Humanization of Humanitarian Law," 94 *American Journal of International Law* 239, 261 (2000).

87. On this point and other gendered dimensions of September 11th and its aftermath, see Hilary Charlesworth and Christine Chinkin, "Sex, Gender, and September 11th," 96 *American Journal of International Law* 600 (2002).

88. Enforcement of Resolutions 687 and 1441, S.C. Res. 687, U.N. Doc. S/RES/687 (Apr. 3, 1991); S.C. Res. 1441, U.N. Doc. S/RES/1441 (Nov. 8, 2002), was the primary rationale offered in formal settings, although Zelikow's white paper offered a general theory of pre-emptive self-defense. Philip Zelikow, "The Transformation of National Security: Five Redefinitions," *The National Interest*, Spring 2003, 17. For discussion from a perspective supportive of the invasion of Iraq, see Ruth Wedgwood, "The Fall of Saddam Hussein: Security Council Mandates and Preemptive Self-Defense," 97 *American Journal of International Law* 576 (2003).

89. This is not to say that preemptive self-defense is unknown internationally. Classical writers such as Brierly argued against a narrow reading of Article 51. See J. L. Brierly, *The Law of Nations* 416–421 (6th ed. 1963). Elihu Root, "The Real Monroe Doctrine," 8 *American Journal of International Law* 427, 432 (1914), argued: "[t]he exercise of the right of self-protection may and frequently does extend in its effect beyond the limits of the territorial jurisdiction of the state exercising it . . . [and a sovereign state may] protect itself by preventing a condition of affairs in which it will be too late to protect itself." See also Wedgwood, above note 88. But pre-Charter legal views should be weighed cautiously here. And since states often use self-defense to justify aggressing, Article 51 of the UN Charter has conventionally been read to require an actual armed attack before force can be used in self-defense. See Gardner, above note 37, at 585–587; Harold Hongju Koh, "On American Exceptionalism," 55 *Stanford Law Review* 1479, 1523 (2003); Patrick McLain, "Note, Settling the Score with Saddam: Resolution 1441 and Parallel Justifications for the Use of Force Against Iraq," 13 *Duke Journal of Comparative and International Law* 233, 278 (2003).

90. See S.C. Res. 678, U.N. Doc. S/RES/678 (Nov. 29, 1990); S.C. Res. 686, U.N. Doc. S/RES/686 (Mar. 2, 1991); S.C. Res. 687, U.N. Doc. S/RES/687 (Apr. 3, 1991); S.C. Res. 688, U.N. Doc. S/RES/688 (Apr. 5, 1991). The question whether the Security Council resolutions constitute authorization for the no-fly zones they did not repudiate is debated. See Scott L. Silliman, "The Iraqi Quagmire: Enforcing the No-Fly Zones," 36 *New England Law Review* 767 (2002) (arguing that the resolutions do not constitute authorization).

91. That Iraqi women have yet to be liberated through this incursion, as is typical when some men replace other men through war, remains apparent. For two indications, see Kathryn Westcott, "Where Are Iraq's Women?" BBC News, May 8, 2003, available at http://news.bbc.co.uk/2/hi/middle_east/3007381.stm (last visited Nov. 8, 2005) and "Climate of Fear: Sexual Violence and Abduction of Women and Girls in Baghdad," 15 Human Rights Watch Report at 8e, July, 2003, http://hrw.org/reports/2003/

iraq0703/iraq0703.pdf (last visited Jan. 20, 2005). This information also serves to underline the point that war often has sex-specific negative consequences for women, both during and after.

92. "[N]othing in the Charter shall impair the inherent right of self-defense if an armed attack occurs." U.N. Charter art. 51.

93. "War is no proper *Employment*, nay, it is so monstrous and horrid, that nothing but mere *Necessity*, or perfect *Charity*, can make it *lawful. . . . To bear Arms is*, in St. *Austin's* Judgment, *no Crime, but to bear Arms on the account of Booty is Wickedness with a Witness*." Hugo Grotius, 2 *Of the Rights of War and Peace in Three Volumes*, 635 (Gaunt 2001) (1715). Collective security has grown broader in practice under Chapter VII's rationale of defense of peace, as illustrated by the response to the Kosova bombing. See, e.g., Independent International Commission on Kosovo, *The Kosovo Report: Conflict, International Response, Lessons Learned* (2001), www.reliefweb.int/library/documents/thekosovoreport.htm (last visited January 20, 2005) (concluding that the intervention was not compatible with Charter norms but was still "legitimate."). By this, the Commission seemingly meant that the precedent was too narrow to undermine the U.N. Charter, but international action to prevent gross and sustained violations of human rights as there justified international action. See Tom J. Farer, "The Prospect for International Law and Order in the Wake of Iraq," 97 *American Journal of International Law* 621, 625 n.13 (2003).

94. See, e.g., Nicholas J. Wheeler, *Saving Strangers: Humanitarian Intervention in International Society* (2000); Jonathan I. Charney, "Anticipatory Humanitarian Intervention in Kosovo," 93 *American Journal of International Law* 834, 837 (1999) (arguing humanitarian intervention may be justified if limited to genocide, crimes against humanity, and war crimes); Christopher C. Joyner and Anthony Clark Arend, "Anticipatory Humanitarian Intervention: An Emerging Legal Norm," 10 *USAFA Journal of Legal Studies* 27, 32 (2000) (defending anticipatory humanitarian intervention with limits); International Commission on Intervention and State Sovereignty, *The Responsibility to Protect: Report of the International Commission on Intervention and State Sovereignty* 32 (2001), www.iciss.ca/pdf/Commission-Report.pdf (last visited Oct. 17, 2005) [hereinafter Responsibility to Protect Report] (justifying military intervention for human protection purposes in order "to halt or avert: large scale loss of life, actual or apprehended, with genocidal intent or not, which is the product either of deliberate state action, or state neglect or inability to act, or a failed state situation; or large scale 'ethnic cleansing,' actual or apprehended, whether carried out by killing, forced expulsion, acts of terror or rape."); Danish Institute of International Affairs, *Humanitarian Intervention: Legal and Political Aspects*, 106–107 (1999), www.dupi.dk/www.dupi.dk/htdocs/en11240.ssi (last visited Jan. 14, 2005); Ken Roth, *Human Rights Watch 2004 World Report*, 17 (2004), www.hrw.org/wr2k4/index.htm (last visited Jan. 14, 2005) ("War often carries enormous human costs, but we recognize that the imperative of stopping or preventing genocide or other systematic slaughter can sometimes justify the use of military force.") Antonio Cassese, "Ex iniuria ius oritur: Are We Moving Towards International Legitimation of Forcible Humanitarian Countermeasures in the

World Community?" 10 *European Journal of International Law* 23, 27 (1999) (submitting "under certain strict conditions resort to armed force may gradually become justified, even absent any authorization by the Security Council"). But see Simon Chesterman, *Just War or Just Peace?* (2002) (concluding that humanitarian intervention without Security Council authorization is unlawful). Note that the Responsibility to Protect Report recognizes rape as potentially justifying resort to forcible intervention, but only when part of an "ethnic cleansing," that is, not when women only are the victims of the onslaught. *Responsibility to Protect Report* xii, 32, 33. The *High-level Report* endorsed the "responsibility to protect" approach, "authorizing military intervention as a last resort, in the event of genocide and other large-scale killing, ethnic cleansing or serious violations of international humanitarian law which sovereign Governments have proved powerless or unwilling to prevent," although not without Security Council authorization. *High-level Report*, above note 15, ¶ 203.

95. Article 1 of the Genocide Convention obligates the signatories to act against genocide: "The Contracting Parties confirm that genocide, whether committed in time of peace or in time of war, is a crime under international law which they undertake to prevent and to punish." Convention on the Prevention and Punishment of the Crime of Genocide, art. 1, Dec. 11, 1948, 78 U.N.T.S. 277, available at www.unhchr.ch/html/menu3/b/p_genoci.htm. This provision—which focuses on acts before (when they can be prevented) and after (when they are punished) genocide takes place—is generally thought to refer to actions short of force. It does not precisely specify what is to happen *during* a genocide. It does not say that the parties undertake to *stop* genocide, which signally may require resort to force, although perhaps that is what prevention has to mean.

96. See U.S. Department of the Army, Article 15-6 Investigation of the 800th Military Police Brigade (prepared by Major Gen. Antonio M. Taguba) (released October 19, 2004), http://news.findlaw.com/hdocs/docs/iraq/tagubarpt.html (last visited Jan. 16, 2005) [hereinafter *Taguba Report*].

97. See, e.g., Frank Rich, "Saving Private England," *The New York Times*, May 16, 2004, B1 (quoting Rush Limbaugh "The photos of the abuses at Abu Ghraib 'look like standard good old American pornography,' [Limbaugh] said as the story spread, as if he might grandfather wartime atrocities into an entertainment industry that, however deplorable to Islam, has more fans in our Christian country than Major League Baseball.").

98. Scheherezade Faramarzi, "Former Iraqi Prisoner Turns Against His American Jailers for Humiliating Him as Allegations of U.S. Torture Are Investigated," *Associated Press*, May 2, 2004 (quoting Dhia al-Shweiri).

99. See, e.g., *The Torture Papers: The Road to Abu Ghraib* (Karen J. Greenberg and Joshua L. Dratel eds., 2005); Mark Danner, *Torture and Truth: America, Abu Ghraib, and the War on Terror* (2004). See also, Seymour Hersh, "Torture at Abu Ghraib," *The New Yorker*, May 10, 2004, 42; ABC News World Tonight with Peter Jennings, "Pattern of Abuse, Who Knew?" May 10, 2004 (discussing the pictures of detainees being tortured and other evidence of torture provided in the International

Red Cross Report); "All Things Considered: American Torture of Iraqi Detainees" (NPR radio broadcast, May 3, 2004). While the *Taguba Report* included only a single explicit finding using the word "torture," it came to the general conclusion that "[s]everal U.S. Army Soldiers have committed egregious acts and grave breaches of international law at Abu Ghraib/BCCF and Camp Bucca, Iraq." *Taguba Report,* above note 96, at 15, 50.

100. See "Globe Caught with Pants Down: Paper Duped into Running Porn Photos," *Boston Herald*, May 13, 2004, A6.

101. "[A]t no time did the photograph meet Globe standards. Images contained in the photograph were overly graphic, and the purported abuse portrayed had not been authenticated. The Globe apologizes for publishing the photo." "For the Record," *Boston Globe*, May 13, 2004, A2. The *Herald* described the pictures as "graphic photos of alleged sexual abuse of Iraqi women by U.S. soldiers [that] turned out to be staged shots from a hardcore porn Web site." Above note 100. The photos in Abu Ghraib were obviously "staged," as well, but were nonetheless seen as documenting real abuse.

102. Some perceptive observers have seen a connection. See, e.g., Susan J. Brison, "Torture, or 'Good Old American Pornography,'" 50/23 *Chronicle of Higher Education*," (June 4, 2004) B10, ("As commercial porn was being mistaken for photos of real torture, the photos of actual torture at Abu Ghraib were being equated with porn."). This could happen because there is commonly little or no significant difference between the two. The presumed distinction that conventional pornography, unlike torture, is made under conditions of consent or freedom or desire is just that: presumed.

103. See September 11th Victim Compensation Fund of 2001, 67 Fed. Reg. 11,233, 11,238 (Mar. 13, 2002) (Statement by the Special Master).

104. Mahfoud Bennoune notes another ignored crisis of normality: "In Algeria, every year since 1993, we had the equivalent of the victims of September 11 . . . that is, victims of the fundamentalists." interview by Karima Bennoune with Mahfoud Bennoune, "'A Disease Masquerading as a Cure': Women and Fundamentalism in Algeria," in *Nothing Sacred: Women Respond to Religious Fundamentalism and Terror* 75, 86 (Betsy Reed ed., 2002).

105. Walter Benjamin, "Theses on the Philosophy of History," in *Illuminations* 255, 259 (Hannah Arendt, ed., Harry Zohn, trans., Harcourt, Brace & World, 1968) (1955).

106. United States v. Morrison, 529 U.S. 598 (2000), held the civil remedies provision of the federal Violence Against Women Act, which provided a federal cause of action for sex discrimination in instances of gender-motivated violence, unconstitutional for exceeding Congressional power in an area traditionally regulated by states, rather than being a remedy permitted under Section 5 of the Equal Protection Clause or the Commerce Clause.

107. Bush v. Gore, 531 U.S. 98 (2000), found an Equal Protection Clause violation in the standards used for recounting votes in the U.S. presidential election of 2000 in the state of Florida.

108. For a range of views, see Vera Gowlland-Debbas, "The Limits of Unilateral Enforcement of Community Objectives in the Framework of U.N. Peace Maintenance,"

11 *European Journal of International Law* 361 (2000) (criticizing the view that member states have implied authority to unilaterally defend collective goals that Security Council resolutions affirm when the veto paralyzes the Council itself); Anne-Marie Slaughter, "Good Reasons for Going Around the U.N.," *The New York Times*, Mar. 18, 2003, A33 (observing that most international lawyers probably find use of force against Iraq illegal under U.N. Charter, but contending rules may need "to evolve, so that what is legitimate is also legal"); W. Michael Reisman, "Assessing Claims to Revise the Laws of War," 97 *American Journal of International Law* 82 (2003) (arguing that preemptive self-defense is not novel because it can contribute to order). Peacekeepers preventively deployed, depending on their mandate, can converge with preemptive defense. See Richard A. Falk, "What Future for the U.N. Charter System of War Prevention?" 97 *American Journal of International Law* 590 (2003) (discussing the tension between the invasion of Iraq and the U.N. Charter rules). One could also argue that September 11th was one act in the middle of a war that began with the attack on the Khobar Towers, continued with the bombings of the U.S. African embassies, the U.S.S. Cole, and the Bali nightclub, and proceeded to the bombings in Morocco, Saudi Arabia, Spain, and forward. This possible chronology does not purport to address the roots of the conflict. Of course, there is a tension between seeing September 11th as a unique one-off event and seeing it as part of a war.

109. Linda Boreman often described that call this way. One published account is: "I learned that Chuck was searching for me with both his pistol and his automatic rifle by his side. . . . I called the police. They knew who I was and they listened to my story about my husband coming after me with a gun. I gave up forever on police help when I was told, 'Lady, we can't get involved in domestic affairs.'" Linda Lovelace and Mike McGrady, *Ordeal* 225–226 (1980). Domestic indeed. The German Constitutional Court's well-developed concept of "mittelbare Drittwirkung" of basic substantive rights—literally meaning indirect third-party effect—such that the highest values of the Constitution have a "radiating effect" throughout all areas of law, including in private law governing horizontal relationships between individuals—converges instructively here with the emerging international notions on nonstate actors. See Lüth Case (1958) 7 BverfGE 198; Basil S. Markesinis, 2 *Always on the Same Path: Essays on Foreign Law and Comparative Methodology* 26–73, 132–218 (2001); Ralf Brinktrine, *The Horizontal Effect of Human Rights in German Constitutional Law: the British Debate on Horizontality and the Possible Rolemodel of the German Doctrine of "Mittelbare Drittwirkung der Grundrechte,"* 4 *European Human Rights Law Review* 421 (2001).

110. See Noelle Quenivet, "The World After September 11: Has it Really Changed?" 16 *European Journal of International Law* 561 (2005) (arguing that less has changed than some think).

111. See Attorney General of Israel v. Eichmann (Isr. Sup. Ct. 1962) 36 *Israel Law Review* 277; Agreement Between the Government of the Kingdom of the Netherlands and the Government of the United Kingdom of Great Britain and Northern Ireland Concerning a Scottish Trial in the Netherlands, Sept. 18, 1998, 38 *International Legal Materials* 926 (treaty under which Lockerbie bombing was adjudicated). See also Leila

Nadya Sadat, "Terrorism and the Rule of Law," 3 *Washington University Global Studies Law Review* 135 (2004) (arguing that the United States should have addressed the Taliban and Al Qaeda as a police matter, rather than going to war).

112. See, e.g., President George W. Bush, "Address to the Nation (Sept. 7, 2003)" reprinted in "In The Struggle for Iraq: In Bush's Words: 'We Will Do What Is Necessary' in the Fight Against Terror," *The New York Times*, Sept. 8, 2003, A10.

113. See *High-level Report*, above note 15. Whether any approach is succeeding is another question. In many respects, the approach to September 11th by the United States in particular can be observed to be inapt, even counterproductive.

114. Meantime, intensified conventional efforts that require little if any change should not be neglected. Efforts of the CEDAW Committee and the Human Rights Committee should continue, joined by the Torture Committee and others pushing for national enforcement of existing obligations and legislative reform where needed, including implementing the many proposals from the Beijing Platform for Action that address violence against women to which nations are already committed. *See* World Conference on Women, Beijing, Sept. 4–15, 1995, *Report of the Fourth World Conference on Women*, U.N. Doc. A/CONF.177/23/Add.1 (Oct. 27, 1995). Violence against women with impunity might be expressly recognized in some circumstances as "a consistent pattern of gross and reliably attested violations of human rights and fundamental freedoms" under ECOSOC Resolution 1503, giving rise to complaints to the Human Rights Committee's communications procedure. U.N. Econ. & Soc. Council [ECOSOC], *Procedure for Dealing with Communications Relating to Violations of Human Rights and Fundamental Freedoms*, U.N. Doc. E/CN.4/RES/7(XXVI) (May 27, 1970). The Secretary-General could exert further leadership, and the restructuring ideas could be injected into Head-of-State Summit reform proposals. The mandate of Security Resolution 1325, U.N. Doc. S/RES/1325 (Oct. 31, 2001), could be strengthened and extended. Going forward, the Genocide Convention and the definition of genocide in the Rome Statute could be amended to add "sex" as a ground, and sexual atrocities expressly as acts, or otherwise reconsidered in light of acts that aim at the destruction of women as such and of information on the place of sexual atrocities in genocide as currently defined. A new special rapporteur on violence against women could be given a mandate to investigate and recommend comprehensive overhaul and consolidating and restructuring of international efforts against violence against women in the post-September 11th era.

115. For an argument that women are an international group, and states a masculine entity, see Introduction, "Women's Status, Men's States," above in this volume at 1.

116. For a fine collection of these strategies, see *Post-Conflict Justice* (Cherif Bassiouni ed., 2002).

117. See Mary Ellen O'Connell, "Lawful Self-Defense to Terrorism," 63 *University of Pittsburgh Law Review* 889 (2002) (arguing that the United States used disproportionate force in Afghanistan, otherwise arguably a lawful exercise of self-defense, killing far too many civilians).

118. See Rehn and Sirleaf, above note 49, at 3 (stating that while civilian fatalities accounted for five percent of all war deaths at the start of the twentieth century, they now account for over seventy-five percent of all fatalities). See also The Secretary-General, *Report of the Secretary-General to the Security Council on the protection of civilians in armed conflicts*, ¶ 3, U.N. Doc. S/2001/331 (Mar. 30, 2001) ("[A]s internal armed conflicts proliferate, civilians have become the principal victims. It is now conventional to say that, in recent decades, the proportion of war victims who are civilians has leaped dramatically, to an estimated 75 percent, and in some cases even more.").

Index

abortion: denial of right to, 161, 181; forced, 150, 214–15, 225, 333n42; opposition to in Quebec, 310n12; restrictions on, 27, 188, 211, 331n22; unconstitutionality of in Ireland, 25

Abu Ghraib, abuses at, compared to pornography, 273, 401nn97, 99

abuse. *See* sexual abuse

academy, place in women's movement of, 62

Ad Hoc Committee on Genocide, 224

Adler, Mortimer, 151

affirmative action, requirement of, 75, 121–24

Afghanistan: condition of women in, 270; relation of to Al Qaeda, 268

African American women: enslavement of, 54, 134, 188, 226–27; as victims of racism, 361n110

African Union Protocol on the Rights of Women, 8, 9, 256–57, 285n44, 286n51

Akayesu decision (ICTR), 221, 224–25, 237–46, 347n13; definition of rape in, 238, 245, 246; focus on realities in, 246; rape as genocide in, 239

Algeria, victims of fundamentalists in, 401n104

Alien Tort Claims Act (U.S.), 198, 202, 205, 206, 281n1, 359n88

American Booksellers v. Hudnut, 258, 292n22, 323n34, 329n7

Amnesty International, reports of torture in Bosnia-Herzegovina by, 21, 143

Andrews v. Law Society of British Columbia (Canada) 27; interpretation of equality rights provision in, 77

annihilation, as final solution under Third Reich, 156

Anthony, Susan B., 76

antiarbitrariness standard, 126

antiessentalism, 50, 51–52

antipornography ordinance, 48, 87, 94, 111, 118, 251, 258, 322–23n32; actionable practices in, 118; as civil rights law, 118–19; functional definition of pornography in, 99; injury located in equality law in, 99; legislative history of, 323n33; opponents of, 87; pornography as sex discrimination in, 118

antitrafficking laws, criminal, and pornography, 252–55

apartheid, end of, 318n10

Argentine Republic v. Amerada Hess Shipping Corp. (U.S.), 283n24

Aristotle, equality principle of, 105–107, 108, 120, 121, 149

Armanda, Asja, 161, 163

"armed conflict," in international law, 261. *See also* war

asbestos litigation, 203, 204; volume of, 348n6

Attorney General's Commission on Pornography (U.S.), 90

A.T. v. Hungary, 306–307n30

Auschwitz, 142, 172, 179–80, 216, 219; brothels in, 356n57; industrial murder in, 176

Australia, legalized prostitution in, 251

Austria, sex equality in, 105

Bai, Phulmani, 130

Balkin, Jack, 49

Barbary pirates, 389n35

battering, 17, 31–32, 45, 109, 275; and "battered women's syndrome," 24; cycles of, 32; as feature of sex difference, 122; legal approaches to, 26, 27, 32, 118; psychology of victims of, 156, 157; as sex discrimination, 48; and thrill of dominance, 31–32. *See also* sexual assault; Violence Against Women Act